Guide to Psychoanalytic Developmental Theories

Joseph Palombo • Harold K. Bendicsen
Barry J. Koch

Guide to Psychoanalytic Developmental Theories

Springer

Joseph Palombo
626 Homewood Ave, Suite 307
Highland Park IL 60035
USA

Harold K. Bendicsen
640 E. Belmont Ave.
Addison IL 60101
USA

Barry J. Koch
1117 Rosedate St.
Castle Rock CO 80104
USA

ISBN 978-0-387-88454-7 e-ISBN 978-0-387-88455-4
DOI 10.1007/978-0-387-88455-4
Springer Dordrecht Heidelberg London New York

Library of Congress Control Number: 2009926237

Printed on acid-free paper

Springer is part of Springer Science+Business Media (www.springer.com)

To the students, graduates, and faculty of the Chicago Institute for Clinical Social Work

JP

To the memory of
Paul Stein & Morris Sklansky
my teachers and mentors
whose influence endures

HB

To Jennifer, Kelsey, and Carly

BK

Preface

This work was an outgrowth of our frustration as teachers. With the receding interest in psychoanalysis during the past two decades, we found ourselves having to provide remedial materials to students to fill in the gaps in their knowledge of psychoanalytic theory. In addition, we felt that their unfamiliarity with the history of the psychoanalytic movement limited their ability to appreciate the context in which the creative ferment of the first half of the twentieth century occurred.

It seemed to us, as clinicians, that a good place to start would be to introduce readers to developmental theories, given that a foundational concept of psychoanalysis is that an understanding of psychopathology requires a developmental framework. Providing students with this background, we felt, would enhance their development as clinicians.

The authors we have chosen to include in this book represent those whose contributions have gained wide recognition in psychoanalytic circles and whose works encompass aspects of the life cycle. Not every author provides a description either of the same phenomena or of the same life stages. Some are more inclusive whereas others are more selective. In one instance, that of Heinz Hartmann, we found it necessary to include his work not because he proposed a theory of development, but because of the influence of his reformulation of metapsychology on those who subsequently proposed their own developmental theories. We sought to cover the broad trends through which psychoanalysis evolved and selected those authors whose work seemed representative of that trend. The sections into which we divided the book represent our view of those major trends.

The sections on Drive Theory, Ego Psychological Theories, Object Relations Theories, and Interpersonal Theory seemed to us uncontroversial, although some may disagree with the inclusion of a specific author under one or the other of those headings. The theories of Erikson, Stern, and Kohut present challenges in that they do not fit comfortably under any of the preceding headings. Interestingly, in their work, Greenberg and Mitchell (1983) make no mention of Erikson or Stern, and consider Kohut to subscribe to a mixed drive and object relations model. Since Erikson extended ego psychology far beyond its original boundaries and was the first to present a model that encompassed the entire life cycle, we decided to devote an entire section to his work. The commonalities between Stern and Kohut are more superficial than profound. At the superficial level, each moved away from the concept of the ego and replaced it with their own versions of the concept of self. At a deeper level, their innovations had profound theoretical implications for these authors.

Finally, we introduce Attachment Theory under its own section for a variety of reasons. The initial rejection of Bowlby's theory by psychoanalysis set his theory apart from the mainstream. By the time psychoanalytic circles began to take notice of his contributions, attachment theory had undergone a significant transformation. Developmental psychologists had accumulated a large body of evidence in support of its categories of attachment and had made linkages between Bowlby's concept of Internal Working Models and the traditional psychoanalytic concepts of mental representations. In addition, a bridge to psychoanalysis was being built on the foundations of the emerging discoveries in the neurosciences.

The theoretical background of each developmental theory seemed insufficient to us to provide a full picture of the context in which the theories emerged, as few of our students were aware of the spirit of discovery that excited the early contributors under Freud's tutelage. We decided, therefore, to introduce each chapter with a biographical note on the author of the theory.

As we undertook that task, we faced the dilemmas of how to balance the amount of historical information we provide with the theoretical summaries that needed to be included. The richness of the early history of psychoanalysis could hardly be condensed in a few paragraphs. We consequently decided that where possible we would err on the side of length over that of brevity in the biographical materials. Readers will note the uneven amount of space devoted to each author's biographical information. The section on Sigmund Freud is the longest for obvious reasons, since he is the fountainhead from whom all subsequent theories sprang. A considerable amount of information exists in the case of some authors, such as Anna Freud, Margaret Mahler, Melanie Klein, Erik Erikson, and Heinz Kohut, each of whom has at least one biographical volume dedicated to a description of their life and work. The challenge we faced was that of summarizing and extracting the relevant material from what was available. In contrast, we had great difficulty in obtaining biographical information on Otto Kernberg, Daniel Stern, and Peter Fonagy. For these, we could only give what was publicly available, which sheds little light on the life history of the contributor.

A second dilemma we faced had to do with the necessity to include broader aspects of an author's theoretical framework. Our fear was that without this background, students would not fully appreciate the implications for developmental theory and therefore major issues would remain obscure. We decided that where applicable we would include a section on the author's broader theoretical contribution. In our efforts to accomplish this goal, we ran into the secondary problem that some major contributors, such as Hartmann and Kohut, did not formulate developmental theories. Yet it seemed imperative to include their work as without that information students' understanding of such major paradigms such as ego psychology, object relations theory, and self psychology would be incomplete. We resolved this dilemma by offering summaries of the theoretical frameworks of such authors and, where possible, we inferred from their theories the structure of a possible developmental theory that would be consistent with their work.

As for the theories of development themselves, we discovered that there is no consensus among psychoanalysts as to what constitutes a comprehensive developmental theory. There is no consensus as to the methodology to employ in data collection or of the components necessary for such a theory to explain adequately those data. Most authors have followed Freud's example, often modeling their theories on his methodology and addressing the issues he considered essential.

In the Preface of the first volume to their comprehensive seven-volume edited work on *The Course of Life* (Greenspan & Pollock, 1989), Greenspan and Pollock state:

> Psychoanalytic developmental psychology is one of the basic foundations for our understanding of how the mind works, how it is organized in its adaptive and pathologic configurations, and how psychological treatment can be used to foster adaptive development. As an in-depth psychology, it provides special insights into man's emotional life, including subtleties of wishes, feelings, thought, and experiences that influence behavior and are ordinarily outside of awareness (the dynamic unconscious). Psychoanalytic developmental psychology also can be viewed as being the basis for a general developmental psychology, embodying a comprehensive approach to understanding the multiple lines of human development from infancy through the stages of adulthood (Vol. 1; p. vii.).

In this work, we made no attempt to propose a definition of what should constitute a developmental theory, although in our Introduction we identify some of the methodological perspectives that theorists have used historically and some of the questions that these authors have posed in their efforts to construct their theories.

We had a concern that our descriptions of the authors' theories were too theoretical and abstract. We thought that it would probably have been helpful to readers to have clinical illustrations of each of the major constructs contained within the theories. However, on further consideration, we decided that to include such examples would nearly double the length of the book. The idea was unworkable. Instead, we tried assiduously to translate into plain English each major concept and rely on the reader to pursue the literature for further illustrations of the clinical applicability of those constructs.

Furthermore, we thought it would enhance students' understanding of the developmental frameworks if we were to provide a clinical example taken from the author's own work. When available, we provide such a clinical example at the end of each chapter. However, to our surprise, we were unable to find published case materials by several major authors, as in the case with Heinz Hartmann, Eric Erikson, Daniel Stern, and John Bowlby. Our extensive searches of the literature failed to turn up such illustrations. Since we did not want to take examples from followers of those authors, we decided to include a relevant excerpt from their work that typified their thoughts on an aspect of their developmental theory. In those cases, we have titled the section *In His/Her Own Words.*

In the course of reading our chapters, readers will encounter words or phrases that are typed in bold. We highlight these words or phrases to draw attention to them as keywords that are central to an understanding of an aspect of the theory. These words are listed at the end of each chapter and may serve students as guides for further exploration of the theory's content.

The structure of each chapter is as follows: Biographical Information, Conceptual Framework (where applicable), Theory of Developmental, Case Illustration or In His/Her Own Words (an excerpt from the author's work), Summary and Conclusion, Keywords, References, Major Works, and Supplementary Readings.

We realize that some of our readers would not be reading the entire work sequentially. Therefore, we attempted to make each chapter as self-sufficient and comprehensible on its own as possible. This meant that in some instances materials had to be repeated; however, we have attempted to keep these repetitions to a minimum.

Readers may be struck by the mismatch between some of the normal or pathological behaviors that some authors attribute to children and adolescents during particular phases or stages of development. These are in contrast to the behavior we conventionally expect nowadays of children and adolescents. What was once considered normative and typical has changed considerably over time. In our descriptions, we made no efforts to modify the authors' original examples, but attempted to render their own work as accurately as we could. We leave it to our readers to evaluate each developmental theory.

Highland Park, IL — Joseph Palombo
Addison, IL — Harold K. Bendicsen
Castle Rock, CO — Barry J. Koch

Reference

Greenspan, S. I., & Pollock, G. H. (1989). *The course of life, Vol. 1: Infancy*. Madison, CT: International Universities Press.

Acknowledgments

We would first like to express our gratitude to our colleagues who have reviewed our work and provided invaluable suggestions and comments. We remain responsible for the final product.

Our first thanks goes to Susan Moss who provided guidance on the structure of our chapters during the early days of the project. She also sifted through our first draft making editorial and substantive suggestions. We are immensely grateful for the time and effort she put into her contribution.

Our colleagues Samuel Weiss, Craigan Usher, Erika Schmidt, Rita Sussman, and June Aimen read the entire first draft and provided comments and suggestions that shed light on our work from their differing perspective. Their contributions have served to improve substantially our work, although we take responsibility for the final product.

We are indebted to Scot Ausborn, Librarian at the Chicago Institute for Psychoanalysis for his assistance in researching references for Abraham (Chap. 1, on Sigmund Freud), Mahler (Chap. 9), and Kernberg (Chap. 10).

We want to express our deep appreciate to Stanley Greenspan and Allan Schore for taking the time to provide biographical details that we include in their chapters. Our deep appreciate also goes to Peter Blos Jr. for giving generously of his time and providing his assistance in uncovering details of his father's, Peter Blos', life. We thank Robert Emde for shedding light on aspects of Rene Spitz's involvement at the University of Colorado School of Medicine and in starting the Denver Psychoanalytic Society.

I would also like to express my gratitude to my long time friend, James Monaco, who read the first draft and offered a perspective that was of value in the modification of the Introduction to the work.

Were it not for my wife's unwavering acceptance of my preoccupation with this project, I would never have found the inner resources to devote to it – JP.

I want to thank my wife, Kathleen, my patient proofreader, who contributed significantly to the clarity of my contribution.

I also want to credit my classmates and the faculty for the remarkable psychoanalytic training I received from the Child and Adolescent Psychoanalytic Psychotherapy Training Program at the Chicago Institute for Psychoanalysis – HB.

I am deeply grateful to my wife, Jennifer, whose patience with my need for time to devote to this project left her to tending the household tasks and taking care of our children. She also contributed valuable thought and constructive critiques that helped improve the quality of our manuscript – BK.

Grateful acknowledgment is made to the following publishers for permission to use previously published materials included in:

Chapter 2

Hartmann, H. (Ed.). (1964). Problems of infantile neurosis. *Essays on ego psychology: Selected problems in psychoanalytic theory* (pp. 207–214). New York: International Universities Press.

Chapter 3

Freud, A. (1966). *The ego and the mechanisms of defense* (Revised Edition, pp. 35–37), New York: International Universities Press.

Chapter 4

Spitz, R. A. (1965). *The first year of life: A psychoanalytic study of normal and deviant development of object relations* (pp. 86–88). New York: International Universities Press.

Chapter 5

Blos, P. (1962). "Two illustrations of deviate adolescent development." *On Adolescence: A psychoanalytic interpretation* (pp. 237–241). New York: Free Press.

Chapter 6

Greenspan, S. I. (2003). *The clinical interview with the child* (3rd ed., pp. 116–118). Washington, DC: American Psychiatric Publishing.

Chapter 7

Klein, M. (1984). *Narrative of a child analysis: The conduct of the psycho-analysis of children as seen in the treatment of a ten-year-old boy* (pp. 457–461). New York: Simon & Schuster.

Chapter 8

Winnicott, D. W. (1980). *The Piggle: An account of the psychoanalytic treatment of a little girl. The thirteenth consultation* (pp. 165–178). New York: International Universities Press.

Chapter 10

Kernberg, O. F. (1976). Transference and countertransference in the treatment of borderline patients. *Object-relations theory and clinical psychoanalysis* (excerpted case material from pp. 168–173). New York: Jason Aronson, Inc – an imprint of Rowman & Littlefield Publishers, Inc.

Chapter 11

Erikson, E. H. (1980). Elements of a psychoanalytic theory of psychosocial development. In S. I. Greenspan & G. H. Pollock, (Eds.), *The course of life: Psychoanalytic contributions toward understanding personality development. Vol. 1: Infancy and early Childhood* (chart appearing on p. 21). New York: International Universities Press (originally published by the Mental Health Study Center, US Department of Health and Human Services, DHHD Publication No. (ADM) 80–886).

Chapter 12

Kvarnes, R. G., & Parloff, G. H. (Eds.) (1976). *A Harry stack Sullivan case seminar: Treatment of a male schizophrenic* (pp. 12–13). New York: W. W. Norton & Company.

Chapter 13

Stern, D. N. (1977). *The first relationship: Infant and mother* (pp. 44–46). Cambridge: Harvard University Press.

Chapter 14

Adapted portions of pages 170–183 from Palombo, J. (2008). Self psychology theory. In B. A. Thyer (Ed.), *Comprehensive handbook of social work and social welfare: Human behavior in the social environment* (Vol. 2, pp. 163–205). New Jersey: Wiley.

Kohut, H. (1971). *The analysis of the self* (pp. 283–284). New York: International Universities Press.

Chapter 15

Bowlby, J. (1958). Excerpt from "The Nature of the Child's Tie to his Mother." *International Journal of Psycho-Analysis*, 39, 350–374.

Chapter 16

Ainsworth, M. D. S., Blehar, M., Waters, E., & Wall, S. (1978). *Patterns of attachment: A psychological study of the strange situation* (pp. 299–301). New Jersey: Lawrence Erlbaum – an imprint of Taylor & Francis Group, LLC.

Ainsworth, M. D. S., Blehar, M., Waters, E., & Wall, S. (1978). *Patterns of attachment: A psychological study of the strange situation.* New Jersey: Lawrence Erlbaum – an imprint of Taylor & Francis Group, LLC (table titled "Summary of Episodes of the Strange Situation" p. 37).

Hesse, E. (1999). The adult attachment interview. In J. Cassidy & P. R. Shaver (Eds.), *Handbook of attachment: Theory, research, and clinical applications*. New York: Guilford Press (table 2 titled "AAI Classifications and Corresponding Patterns of Infant Strange Situation Behavior" p. 399).

Chapter 17

Schore, A. N. (2005). Attachment, affect regulation, and the developing right brain: linking developmental neuroscience to pediatric (pp. 206–207). *Pediatrics in Review 26*(6), 204–217.

Chapter 18

Fonagy, P., Gergely, G., & et al. (2002). *Affect regulation, mentalization, and the development of the self* (pp. 301–306). New York: Other Press.

About the Authors

Joseph Palombo, M.A., is a Clinical Social Worker who is the Founding Dean and Faculty Member of the Institute for Clinical Social Work; a Faculty Member of the Child and Adolescent Psychoanalytic Therapy Program, Chicago Institute for Psychoanalysis, a Staff Member of the Rush Neurobehavioral Center, Rush-Presbyterian-St. Luke's Medical Center; and in Private Practice. He was the cochair of the Child and Adolescent Mental Disorders section of the task force of the *Psychodynamic Diagnostic Manual*. His publications include numerous papers and two books titled *Learning disorders and disorders of the self in children and adolescents*, and *Nonverbal Learning Disabilities: A clinical perspective,* published by W. W. Norton.

Harold Bendicsen, LCSW, BCD, is a Clinical Social Worker who maintains a private practice in Elmhurst, Illinois. He holds a certificate in Child and Adolescent Psychoanalytic Psychotherapy from the Chicago Institute for Psychoanalysis. He has held clinical, supervisory and administrative positions in child welfare agencies, residential treatment centers, and social service agencies. He is an Adjunct Professor at Loyola University Chicago School of Social Work and a member of the faculty of the Child and Adolescent Psychoanalytic Psychotherapy Training Program at the Chicago Institute for Psychoanalysis.

Barry J. Koch, Ph.D., LCSW is an Assistant Professor and Field Coordinator for Newman University's Master of Social Work program in Colorado Springs, where he teaches courses in advanced clinical practice, HBSE, social policy, and psychopathology. He received his BSW from the University of Cincinnati in 1982, his MSW from the University of Kentucky in 1987, and his Ph.D. in Chicago from the Institute for Clinical Social Work in 2004. Dr. Koch draws 23 years of clinical practice experience, treating a wide variety of mental health issues from a psychodynamic perspective, including 15 years as the director of a clinical training facility near the campus of Miami University in Oxford, Ohio. He left his clinical practice for full time academic pursuits in 2005.

Contents

Introduction

In this work, we summarize the major psychoanalytic developmental theories that have evolved since Freud's early formulations. We decided to set each theory within the historical context in which its author created it by providing a biographical glimpse of the author's own life. Much as Freud's self-analysis was pivotal to his "discovery" of the oedipal conflict, each author's personal history contributed to the theory he or she originated. We also emphasize that the historical continuity of each successive edition of a theory reflects an evolutionary process in which each author took cognizance of the modifications of psychoanalytic metapsychology and the intellectual trends that existed at the time of the formulation of his or her developmental theory.

In this introduction, we provide our readers with some reflections and a set of perspectives through which to evaluate each of these theories without unduly biasing these evaluations. We present our thoughts in the following three sections: the first section is titled Freud as Fountainhead; the second section is Models of Development, and the third section is Paradigms and Developmental Theories.

In the first section, *Freud as Fountainhead*, we begin with a brief overview of the principles that guided Freud in the articulation of his developmental theory. We review the issues of his methodology and the legacy he bequeathed to those of his followers who attempted to produce developmental theories. In the second section on *Models of Development*, we take a broader perspective to the assessment of developmental theories. We begin with a consideration of the methodological issues that the authors of such theories encounter and some of the questions that require answers in the formulation of a theory. We then offer the criterion of narrative coherence and completeness as a standard by which to compare the different theories.

The last section, on *Paradigms and Developmental Theories*, deals with a set of more abstract issues, one that many authors do not address directly but that is of critical importance in enunciating the philosophical presuppositions that undergird each theory. The central concern these issues address is the question: Are developmental theories *paradigms* formulated in accordance with scientific principles or are they socially constructed *stories* that reflect the social and cultural milieu in which the author formulated the theory? A discussion of this issue is of critical importance given that currently a serious controversy exists among psychoanalytic theorists.

Freud as Fountainhead

Freud represents the fountainhead from which most subsequent psychoanalytic developmental theories have flowed, many of which we include in this work. Every theory we consider begins either by agreeing or by disagreeing with Freud's metapsychological assumptions and his methodology. Psychoanalytic practitioners generally agree with the principle established by Freud that developmental theories play a central role in understanding typical and pathological human conduct. These theories provide a conceptual framework for the relationship between past occurrences, present personality structure, and psychopathology. In addition, they are integral to the conduct of clinical practice because psychoanalytic clinical theories subscribe to the *principle of developmental psychopathology*, that is, that all psychopathology can be understood either as reflective of what occurred during development or as a return to an earlier developmental phase. These theories embrace the notion that a *tight linkage* should exist between a developmental theory, its theory of psychopathology, and its clinical theory (see Palombo, 1991a, 1991b).

Freud's Methodology

From a methodological perspective, there is no evidence that Freud conducted systematic observations on his or other children to collect data upon which to construct his theory of development. Three assumptions guided his thinking. The *first assumption* is that **ontogeny** recapitulates **phylogeny**, an assumption to which he referred as the existence of "archaic heritages." In psychoanalytic metapsychology, the concept of ontogeny states that following birth organisms undergo a set of invariant stages or phases that are unique and occur in a given sequence. The concept also states that each member of the species recapitulates phylogenetically the major events of the history of the species. Freud states regarding the ego and the libido, "... both of them are at bottom heritages, abbreviated recapitulations of the development which all mankind has passed through from its primeval days over long periods of time" (Freud, 1917a, p. 354). Therefore, what biologists call a **phenotype**, a particular subject, ontogenetically incorporates aspects of his or her phylogeny. The *second assumption* is that regressive states in symptomatic adults were replicas of earlier childhood states (Freud, 1917b). The *third assumption* is that during psychoanalysis, it was possible to lift the **repression** around a forgotten memory and recover the actual events that occurred in childhood (Freud, 1895). Based on these assumptions, Freud felt that he could reconstruct the entire developmental sequence from the analyses of his adult patients. Thus, he established a direct relationship between his theory of psychopathology, his clinical theory, and developmental events, maintaining the *tight linkage* between the three.

Ontogeny Recapitulates Phylogeny

With respect to the first assumption, that is, ontogeny repeats phylogeny, Freud borrowed that principle from the biological theories current during his day. Freud used a mixture of Lamarckian and Darwinian principles to articulate his views of how we evolved in our social relationships (Freud, 1913). He believed that what occurs during development reflected the actual history through which our early ancestors lived. For example, the Oedipus complex reflected the internalization of what occurred when human beings still lived in small tribes and tribal chieftains were the object of their children's jealousy. The children would plot the overthrow of their fathers in order to ascend to power. Human beings incorporated these patterns into their sexual and aggressive instincts, which then find expression in the oedipal phase at around age 4. Present day biologists consider the principle that ontogeny recapitulates phylogeny in Freud's sense of the use of the term to be false; however, they consider that, during fetal development, ontogeny does recapitulate the *embryonic stages* of our evolutionary ancestors. This latter interpretation has little applicability to psychological development.

Development Reconstructed

For decades after Freud enunciated it, psychoanalysts accepted the second assumption that regressive states observed in symptomatic adults who were undergoing psychoanalysis were replicas of earlier childhood states. Freud had constructed his developmental theory from these data. Through circular reasoning and lacking any data from the direct observations of children, Freud maintained that it was possible to find confirmation for his developmental theory in the symptoms that his patients manifested in the clinical setting. As we will see, this assumption remained unchallenged until Stern's contribution appeared in 1985.

Repressed Memories of Sexual Abuse Led to Neurosis

The basis for Freud's third assumption was his early conviction that a direct relationship existed between the sexual abuse that he believed his patients had suffered and their neurotic symptoms. For him, psychoanalysis provided a method through which to uncover the historical events that led to the patient's illness. Later on, when the data did not support this contention for all patients, he corrected his view that a causal relationship exists between what patients remembered and what had actually occurred. He concluded that in some cases, the recollections that occurred during psychoanalysis were *fantasies* that represented distortions of the actual events that had occurred. The patient's instinctual drives and wishes were responsible for those distortions (Freud, 1905, pp. 190–191).

Controversy surrounds the issue of whether he rejected the notion that the abuse had actually occurred because he feared alienating his colleagues and the influential relatives of his patients or whether he did so out of pure theoretical necessity (Masson, 1985). However, he retained his conviction that a tight linkage existed between his developmental theory and his theory of psychopathology. The causal linkage was not between an actual event and a symptom, but rather between an unacceptable wish and the guilt that it produced that led to the symptoms. Internal conflict became the central organizing feature of the human condition. Each phase of development, the oral, the anal, and the phallic/oedipal, had its own set of conflicts. If unresolved these conflicts manifested themselves in patients' neurotic symptoms and it was possible, therefore, to reconstruct the patients' developmental histories from their recollections.

As we will see, in spite of its problematic nature, a fact that did not gain wide recognition until much later, these assumptions, which were embedded in Freud's methodology for the construction of a theory of development, were carried forward into the work of Abraham (1924/1927), Blos (1967), Erikson (1980), Anna Freud (1936/1966), Hartmann (1964), Kernberg (1975), Klein (1923), Mahler (1968), Mahler, Pine, & Bergman (1975), and Winnicott (1965). Each sought to find confirmation for their developmental theories in their patients' symptoms. Mahler in particular, in spite of her direct observation of young children, formulated some of her key concepts, such as the phases of primary autism and the symbiotic phase, not as a result of infant observation, but rather because the concepts had to be postulated as theoretically necessary in order to explain some childhood disorders. Mahler's theory not only maintained the tight linkage between clinical and developmental theories, but the theory also circularly confirmed itself. Stern (1985) challenged these assumptions by bringing to our attention the voluminous work on infant observations that had accumulated during the 1950s through the 1980s, but that psychoanalysts had virtually ignored with the notable exception of Spitz.

Freud's Legacy

We can infer three principles from these assumptions that Freud bequeathed to us with respect to developmental theories that present us with further conceptual challenges. The *first principle* is that a developmental theory is a critical adjunct to understanding psychopathology because of the light that it sheds on the genesis of disorders. Few psychoanalysts question the proposition that such a tight linkage exists between childhood events and the psychopathology that ensues. The construct of **developmental psychopathology** remains one of the enduring contributions of psychoanalytic theory (Freud, 1918).

The *second principle* is that developmental theory provides the foundation for a clinical theory because it articulates the interventions that therapists use in work with their patients. The patients' transferences that evolve during the therapeutic process reflect the events and attitudes that patients experienced in earlier years. Understanding the nature of those transferences makes possible an understanding of the origins of the problem and supplies a guide to the interventions to use to alleviate a patient's distress (Freud, 1912). Differing psychoanalytic or **psychodynamic** schools have arisen around different interpretations of this principle. Some schools view childhood conflicts as central to the human condition. The advocates of this position, such as those who subscribe to drive theory and ego psychology, agree with the concept of a tight linkage between development, psychopathology, and clinical interventions (Kernberg, 1976). Others consider psychological deficits or flaws in human character to be cardinal features of the human condition. The advocates of this position, such as the adherents to relational theory (Hoffman, 1992; Mitchell, 1988), reject the concept that a tight linkage exists between the past and the present difficulties of patients. Each school prescribes its own techniques for clinical interventions.

The *third principle* is that observations of patients' **regressed states** provide the data on which to construct a developmental theory; that is, the symptoms a patient currently manifests are replicas of an actual earlier developmental stage through which the person traveled (Freud, 1925). This means that some aspect of the person's personality failed to progress because the person faced issues that were too problematic to be resolved. The failure to resolve the conflicts of that stage laid down a vulnerability that became reactivated later in life. This principle endures to this day, although some theorists, such as Kohut, reformulate it by substituting the defense of disavowal for that of repression. Kohut maintained that it is not the repressed events that reemerge, but rather the developmental failure caused by those events that manifests as symptomatic behaviors.

The legacy left by these principles extends beyond the purely methodological issues of what constitutes valid data for the construction of a developmental theory. Embedded in the principles are fundamental philosophical assumptions as to whether we can access reality directly through observation or can only arrive at it through indirect means. Philosophers couch this issue in terms of whether positivism or social constructivism (Hoffman, 1992) and hermeneutics can lead to the truth about our universe. We return to this issue in the last section of this introduction.

Models of Development

In contrast to the early decades of the history of psychoanalysis when successions of development theories reached their apex and were dominant, no such theory has achieved a similar hegemony nowadays. Libidinal drive theory came first. It was followed by ego psychology's and object relations' modifications to that theory. Erikson and his life cycle theory appeared next followed by Mahler's separation-individual theory. Sullivan's interpersonal theory represents an interlude between these historical developments. Stern's theory succeeded Mahler's theory and was the last to gain broad acceptance. Stern's theory has now receded into the background and is being progressively replaced by efforts to formulate a theory based on neurodevelopmental principles (Fonagy & Target, 2003; Greenspan, 1989, 1997; Schore, 1994). These last efforts are controversial and their completion remains a work in progress.

Moving beyond individual theories, each developmental theory confronts a set of concerns that it must address. In what follows, we outline some of these concerns. We consider the *methodological issues*, some *questions* that developmental theories should answer, and the *narrative structure* of developmental theories. Each of these contributes to the ultimate structure of the model of development that ensues.

Methodological Considerations

Historically, from a methodological perspective, theorists have taken three different perspectives in their descriptions of development. They are the ***descriptive perspective***, the ***interpersonal perspective***, and the ***intrapersonal or intrapsychic perspective***. Each of these describes psychological phenomena by giving the observer a spatial location in relation to the subject that is the object of their observations (see Palombo, 2006, pp. 7–11).

The descriptive perspective involves taking an "objective" position in relation to the subject, much as scientists view physical phenomena. The location of the observer is a "cosmic" position. From this perspective, the observer conceives of psychological phenomena as emanating from structures that include a set of functions that have enduring existence and that can be described from a neutral position. These structures represent mechanisms that are subject to "laws of nature" that are universally applicable. This perspective is a positivist perspective, borrowed from the natural sciences, and is central to Freud's metapsychology. Freud conceived of himself as a scientist whose insights came from such a perspective. In comparing himself to Copernicus, he felt he was able to view the human psyche from a transcendental position. Therefore, he could explain symptomatic behavior through the underlying, unseen, unconscious motivations that directed those behaviors while simultaneously describing psychological mechanisms in universal terms. This position is also evident when he discusses development. Here, he takes both an external perspective through which he can describe the interactions between parent and child, and simultaneously takes an internal perspective through which he can infer the unconscious psychological processes that he presumed to be taking place within the child, that is, the drives cathect an object. Most ego psychologists subscribe to this perspective, as do attachment theorists.

The interpersonal perspective always involves more than one person and locates the observer in the space between the interacting subjects. It retains aspects of the positivism of the descriptive perspective by simultaneously proposing conjectures as to people's interactions with others and their internal psychological states. Some have called this perspective the view of a "two-person psychology." The observer is an invisible investigator, who has the ability to describe the processes in which the subjects engage. The phenomena occur in the intersection of the fields created by the interacting subjects. Whereas the invisible observer takes a position that is equidistant from the interacting subjects and can report on the processes that guide the relationships, at times, the observer jumps to a different view reporting on the intrapsychic processes that the subjects have internalized. At that point, the observer takes a descriptive perspective of the subjects' psychic processes, describing those as identifications, projections, and projective identifications. The observer feels privileged to give an account of those processes. In spite of that, theorists who take this perspective generally claim that people construct reality from their subjective experiences, making no claim of an independent external reality. Most object relations theorists and Sullivan's interpersonal theory falls squarely within this perspective. These theorists believe that no underlying general principle guides everyone's conduct, rather understanding a person involves uncovering the *patterns* that characterize that particular person's personality.

In *the intrapersonal or intrapsychic perspective*, the location of the observer is an imaginary point within the subject's mind. The observer is intent on understanding the subject's experiences, motives, and the meanings the subject ascribes to those experiences. Empathy permits the observer to understand and apprehend the contents of another person's mind, leading to an understanding of how a person feels, thinks, and perceives reality (Kohut, 1959). This perspective allows the observer to resonate affectively with the internal state of the subject. It assumes that because of the common human bond that exists between all human beings, the observer can decipher the psychic reality of others and the special meanings they attribute to their experiences. Self-psychology, which adheres to a hermeneutic point of view, in particular, Kohut's concept of empathy as vicarious introspection, is paradigmatic of this perspective.

In summary, each perspective has strengths and weaknesses when applied to the creation of developmental theories. The strength of the descriptive perspective is that it can provide generalizations about mental phenomena that act as guides to an understanding of all subjects; that is, they can provide universal rules for human thought and conduct. Their weakness is that they have difficulty in explaining subjectivity and the uniqueness of each person's experiences. The interpersonal perspective is subject to its own set of difficulties. On the one hand, it provides insights into the interactional aspects of human relations, in particular, the social and cultural dimensions, but on the other hand, it too must justify how it is possible for an external observer to enter into the mental lives of subjects to explain their internal dynamics. For the intrapersonal perspective, meanings are singular and often idiosyncratic to each person. People construe meanings from their experiences based on their particular cognitive maturity, exposure to the social context, and the psychodynamics operating at the time of their exposure to events. However, a major problem for this perspective, which we encounter with Freud's developmental theory, is that we cannot universalize the meanings that people ascribe to experiences. Freud wished to universalize the meanings that children construed from their encounters with their caregivers, efforts that led to the application of the myth of Oedipus to a particular phase of development for all persons. Developmental theories that operate from this perspective are constrained in their ability to generalize on their descriptions of phases or stages.

We arrive at the unsettling conclusion that each of these methodologies presents an irresolvable dilemma. If we wish our theory to be applicable universally and capable of being obtained through objective observations, we either end up with a behaviorist theory or one that has difficulty accounting for how people ascribe meanings to their experience. On the other hand, if our theory focuses too narrowly on how people construe meanings from their experiences, we will have difficulties in generalizing as to how people arrive at those meanings and run the risk of being left without a theory of development.[1]

Questions for Developmental Theories

Regardless of which of these three perspectives theorists take, they confront a series of questions that they should answer. Providing answers to each of these questions challenges the theorist to take positions on thorny issues. These among many others are some of the questions:

- What is the balance between the contributions of nature and nurture in influencing the direction that development takes?
- What role does the social context in which a child is raised play in development?
- Most theories emphasize the significance of the caregiver in children's development. Does the theory describe how the quality of the caregiving affects development?
- Does progression through the course of development occur in stages or phases that are normatively sequential or do the dominant themes extend through the person's lifespan, or, to put it differently, is the developmental progression continuous or discontinuous? (see Appendix A for a discussion of this issue.)
- What forces drive the developmental process? Are there ontogenetic, epigenetic, or evolutionary forces that determine the path through which development travels?
- What are the processes that lead to the formation of mental structures, such as mental representations or defenses?
- Does the theory take into consideration the integration of affects in moving forward or retarding the course of development?
- Are conflicts, deficits, or both central to the derailment of development?
- How much carryover is there of early influences into adult personality, whether positive or negative?

[1] See Chap. 19. Conclusion for an elaboration of the issues associated with the philosophical underpinnings of these perspectives.

- Does the theory account for self-righting tendencies, that is, the capacity for resilience and for protective factors to undo the effects of adverse events?

Hardly any psychoanalytic developmental theory undertakes to provide answers to all these questions. Most theorists follow an agenda set by historical factors or predetermined theoretical preferences. Consequently, it is difficult to propose a set of criteria by which to evaluate a given theory. We are left with the criteria of *coherence* and *completeness*, that is, that a theory must be internally consistent and be sufficiently inclusive so as not neglect to address any major set of concerns or data. For an approximation of a criterion by which to judge the coherence and completeness of developmental theories, we turn to a discussion of their narrative structure.

Narrative Structure of Developmental Theories[2]

There is general agreement that clinicians construct case histories, or **narratives**, out of patients' data. As narratives, these case histories have a protagonist, a plot, a beginning, middle, end, and a dramatic core that is critical to the psychodynamics that motivates the patient. We suggest that a useful heuristic device for comparing and contrasting different developmental theories is to view them as narratives with a structure, whose central metaphor provides the organizing theme that lends coherence to the narrative (Palombo, 1992).

Literary circles use the term narrative to characterize a form of written expression. They applied the term to such works as epics, sagas, romances, novels, and other genres (Polkinghorne, 1988; Scholes & Kellogg, 1966). Among the questions that philosophers and psychoanalysts ask is, what do historians and clinicians add to a simple chronicle of events that transforms the text into a narrative? (Mitchell, 1980). White (1980) noted that the difference between a chronicle and a historical account, that is, a narrative, is that the chronicle provides a simple list of events, whereas a historical account adds to that list of events *a theme that unifies and gives coherence* to the events in the list. The historian is the agent who interprets the chronicle and adds the theme that makes the story intelligible.

In a different context, Scholes and Kellogg, in their work *The Nature of Narrative* (1966), gave two distinguishing characteristics of a narrative: (a) the presence of a story and a storyteller (p. 4), and (b) its fictional rather than factual or historical character. Sarbin, a psychologist, extends the application of the concept of narrative beyond the fictional. He argues that the case histories that clinicians write are narrative in character. In contrast to the literary definition of the term, he gives the following definition:

> ... *Narrative* is coterminous with *story* as used by ordinary speakers of English. A story is a symbolized account of actions of human beings that has a temporal dimension. The story has a beginning, a middle, and an ending. The story is held together by recognizable

[2] What follows in this chapter represents a modified version of Palombo (1996).

> patterns of events called plots. Central to the plot structure are human predicaments and attempted resolutions.
>
> Sarbin (1986, p. 3)

When we apply this definition to the structure of developmental theories, the position states that developmental theorists do not simply chronicle the events of childhood, but rather, as historians of childhood, the creators of the theories, add their own interpretations and thematic organization to those observations. The resulting theory resembles a narrative (Howard, 1991; Schafer, 1980, 1981, 1983; Spence, 1982, 1987; White, 1980).

Root Metaphors

We can enhance our understanding of the narrative structure of developmental theories by conceptualizing the central organizing feature of the theory as subscribing to a root metaphor. Pepper (1942) describes the concept of **root metaphor** as follows:

> "A man desiring to understand the world looks about for a clue to its comprehension. He pitches upon some area of common sense fact and tries to understand other areas in terms of this one. This original idea becomes his basic analogy or root metaphor. He describes as best he can the characteristics of this area, or… discriminates its structure. He undertakes to interpret all fact in terms of these categories" (p. 91).

Theories attempt to redescribe parts of the universe through a metaphor (see Lakoff & Johnson, 1980). This metaphor explains the phenomena more meaningfully because, at first, it translates them into a language that is more familiar and understandable. As the theory grows in complexity, the theorist introduces a technical language that makes the phenomena more experience distant, and more abstract. We may say that scientists retranslate their observations into a metaphorical language that permits the formulation of hypotheses that are verifiable or falsifiable. For example, for physics, mathematics is its preferred language; for chemistry, it is that of the elements that constitute all matter; for biology, it is that of the cellular structure of living organisms (Palombo, 1996).

Pepper suggests that an examination of intellectual history reveals that six root metaphors were used to model the universe (Pepper, 1942; Sarbin, 1986). They are (a) *animism*, the notion that all nature is imbued with life; (b) *formism*, the Aristotelian concept that each organism has within it the seed of its structure, which will guide its development; (c) *mysticism*, the belief that a person may merge with nature or the universe to attain a higher level of being; (d) *mechanism*, the concept that all processes including those of human development may be understood as analogous to a machine; (e) *organicism*, the theory that all living matter, as organisms, may grow through the ingestion of nutriments and follow a developmental sequence; and finally, (f) *contextualism*, which is the view that the best approach to understand all human phenomena is to view them in their historical contextual environment and understanding their meaning. Of these six, the ones with which we are most familiar in the psychological domain, and which we address in this work, are the **mechanistic**, the **organismic**, and the **contextual metaphor**.

Most current psychoanalytic developmental theories rely on two particular types of root metaphors to organize their data, the *mechanistic* and the *organismic*. The mechanistic metaphor draws an analogy between minds and machines; that is, minds operate like mechanical devices that have component parts and that require energy to function, much as computers function. It uses a descriptive perspective in giving accounts of mental phenomena. The organismic metaphor draws an analogy between minds and living organisms, that is, minds operate like living organisms that require adequate nourishment to survive. It uses both descriptive and interpersonal perspectives in theory construction. Some theories adhere to the *contextual* metaphor that focuses on the meaning of experience rather than on mechanical or organismic analogues. These theories use an intrapersonal perspective in their explanations of psychological phenomena.

Root metaphors lead observers to frame the questions they pose of developmental theories within the language of the metaphor. Consequently, the answers to those questions follow from the analogies made to the metaphor. For example, if a theory uses the metaphor that the mind is like a computer, the answer to the question of what constitutes pathology is that a breakdown of some component of the computer has occurred. The conceptual categories applied to the phenomena come from the model the metaphor uses. Since phenomena do not fall into "natural categories," that is, categories are creations of our minds rather than found naked in nature, the metaphor dictates the categories that divide the field of observation and hence shapes those observations. Adherence to a root metaphor compels the theorist to maintain the perspective of that metaphor or risk incoherence. If the theorist steps outside the metaphor to account for phenomena, the result is a mixed metaphor. As we know, mixing metaphors is a cardinal sin in literary expression. Similarly, in the construction of theories it ensures conceptual confusion.

We can compare and contrast the root metaphors that theories use. We can also direct criticisms at a theory for its use of a particular root metaphor. Alternatively, we can maintain that one root metaphor is superior to another if it presents fewer conceptual problems than do others. However, it is not possible to argue that one root metaphor gives a more accurate description of the universe than does another. Such a statement presumes that the metaphor is not a metaphor but a presentation of reality. In what follows, we discuss the uses made by some psychoanalytic developmental theories of these root metaphors. Each theory provides a model of what constitutes normative development. In what follows, we will refer to each theory as offering a model of development.

Because of the methodological problems this analysis presents, this section of our introduction may itself be regarded as a story, or a narrative, that deals playfully with the issues surrounding the formulation of psychoanalytic models of development. Our discussion of developmental theories may appear reductionistic, or may seem to caricature the positions we are describing. While this may in part be true, we do not believe that we significantly distort the positions we present. The heuristic point we wish to make is that one means of comparing and contrasting developmental theories is by examining the root metaphors of those theories as central organizers of the narrative the theory presents.

Root Metaphors in Developmental Theories

Oddly enough, psychoanalytic developmental theories rarely conform to a single root metaphor. Most violate the simple principle of not mixing metaphors, which our teacher of *English* drilled into us. We note the confusion that results when a developmental theory employs more than one root metaphor. On first appearance, the narratives these theories present seem to make sense and do not reveal the deeper incoherences and inconsistencies to which they succumb. Among those who violate this principle are all who adhere to a drive or energy model while simultaneously utilizing a different metaphor, such as an organismic or contextual metaphor. Freud is a prime example of someone who during his lifetime layered his metapsychology with metaphors that reflected the scientific interests of his times, utilizing first a mechanistic metaphor, then shifting to an organismic metaphor, all the while making use of a contextual metaphor in his clinical work and interpretation of dreams.

Models Based on Mechanistic Metaphor. The mechanistic metaphor is the dominant metaphor in the physical sciences. Phenomena are analogous to the components of a machine. The universe is like a perfect automaton whose laws scientists wish to discover. The modern variants of the mechanistic metaphor compare the mind to a computer that processes information (Holt, 1972).

Freud's **dynamic point of view** is perhaps the best example of a mechanistic/hydraulic model of the functioning of mind (Freud, 1894, pp. 60–61; 1917b, 1924). It is a point of view in which libidinal and aggressive energies drive all human feelings, thoughts, and behaviors. Freud's model likens the mind to a steam engine that deals with the pressures produced by sexual or aggressive drives (Freud, 1923). The ego is an energy processing apparatus that transforms primitive, unneutralized, primary process energy into more refined, usable, and sublimated secondary process energy. The filtering system that effects this transformation is the ego that moves the energy from the id to the object that it cathects and back to the ego. With no channel through which the energy can flow outwardly, it becomes trapped within the system itself and interferes with its functioning. The result is psychopathology in the form of regressions or arrests that lead to neuroses or other disorders.

Ego psychological theories and object relationship theories [with the possible exception of Kernberg's (1975) object relations theory] utilize some variant of this metaphor in their dynamic metapsychological points of view. The dynamic point of view in ego psychology describes the interplay between the drives, the ego, the superego, and the reality that people confront. Imbalances between the drives and the ego lead to trauma due to the flooding of the ego by drive energies. A punitive superego will respond to the unacceptable expression of drive energies with guilt as the hallmark of neurotic disorders. Finally, if the ego cannot mediate between the pressure of the drives that seek discharge and the constraints of the reality it confronts, it may collapse, leading to severe regressions or it may erect defensive barriers that severely constrain its ability to function and adapt.

Models Based on Organismic Metaphor. The organismic root metaphor is the most popular metaphor in psychoanalytic circles. Developmental theorists who favor this metaphor conceive of the human mind as an organism that becomes progressively differentiated from less developed (i.e., immature) to more developed (i.e., mature) states. Some of the theorists we consider, such as Spitz (1965) and Erikson (1964), espouse a related metaphor, the epigenetic model of development. **Epigenesis**, in contrast to ontogenesis, is a term derived from embryology that describes the process through which an organism develops through a set of hierarchical stages while preserving traits from prior stages. These traits have their origin in the heritable components that organisms carry within them genetically. The developmental model emphasizes the unfolding of preprogrammed stages or phases that emanate from within the organism over against the environmental forces that impinge on the organism.

Within the organismic metaphor, the mind requires nourishment to develop and grow. The nutriment comes in the form of an exchange between the partners in a relationship. The child forms a relationship to a caregiver and takes nourishment in the form of love, care, affection, devotion, or attunement. Children ingest the nutriments through such processes as imitation, and various forms of **internalization**, such as **incorporation** (drive theory), **introjection** (object relations theory), and **identification** (ego psychology) (see Schafer, 1968, for clarification of the confusion surrounding these terms). The nutritional value of the relationship becomes protein for growing children. They metabolize what they ingest which turns it into psychic structure. This metaphor emphasizes the adequacy, or inadequacy, of the child's relationship to the object. It places a value on the object's responsiveness to the needs of the child as determining whether the child will progress satisfactorily through subsequent phases. If the nourishment the object offers is toxic, that is, contaminated by anger or depression, then the child develops a case of psychic indigestion and cannot metabolize the incorporated object.

Other psychobiological processes include the principles of homeostasis, of flight/fight response to danger, or of adaptation. Typical development is measurable either by the extent to which the person approximates an ideal state of growth during each stage, or by the extent to which the person adapts to his or her environment. On the other hand, since the person's psychic unfolding is dependent on nutriment provided by caregivers, failure to receive appropriate nourishment or exposure to toxins, that is, to trauma, leads to psychopathology.

In the chapter sections that introduce each set of theories, we elaborate on the variant of the root metaphor each theory uses to illustrate this perspective. We will note that (a) Freud used an ingestion model (1912, 1917; Schafer, 1968), (b) Mahler used an embryological model (1968, 1975), (c) Kohut used a translocation model (1971, 1977, 1984), (d) Stern referred to the Domains of the Self at the caregiver's attunement (1985), and (e) attachment theories used an evolutionary perspective (Bowlby, 1969). Other theories, included in this work, which are consistent with this model, are those of Abraham, Anna Freud, Hartmann, Spitz, Blos, Greenspan, Klein, Winnicott, and Kernberg.

Models based on the contextual metaphor. The contextual metaphor avoids some of the objectionable aspects of the mechanistic and ingestion models of growth. Pepper (1942) states:

> When we come to contextualism, we pass from an analytical into a synthetic type of theory. It is characteristic of the synthetic theories that their root metaphors cannot satisfactorily be denoted even to first approximation by well-known common-sense concepts... The best term out of common sense to suggest the point of origin of contextualism is probably the historic event" (p. 232).

The contextual metaphor proposes that each system is composed of a set of interrelated elements whose sum is greater than the individual parts. Furthermore, any part is not understandable independently of other parts, though not every part is necessarily related to every other part. Such are theories whose central conceptual organization centers on understanding how individuals ascribe meanings to their experiences. Those meanings are woven together into a historical narrative that, like a tapestry, depicts the person's life.

Whereas it is possible to construct a developmental theory using this metaphor by focusing on the domain of meaning, such a theory would be very different from the traditional developmental theories discussed earlier. Its aim would be to give an account of the genesis and organization of the meanings of experience. Its task would be to examine human experience and its encoding into a set of signs. It would explain how a person construes meanings from self-experience, and would give an account of the elements that shape the meanings of those experiences. In addition, it would clarify the way in which each person develops a unique interpretation of the particular life episodes to which he or she is exposed, and would describe the progression through which each person moves to gather the components of self-experience into meaningful themes that integrate the parts into a whole. This whole will then constitute the person's self-narrative. It is not an accident that since most relational psychoanalytic theories subscribe to this metaphor they have had difficulty in articulating a developmental theory consistent with their view. The developmental model that Palombo provides of Kohut's self-psychology is an example of a developmental theory that conforms to the contextual metaphor. Its central organizing narrative theme is patients' search of self-cohesion.

In sum, the use of this analysis of each developmental theory provides a criterion by which to assess the coherence and completeness of the theory. By coherence, we refer to the consistency with which a theorist applies the metaphor and avoids the use of more than one metaphor, since mixed metaphors result in confusion rather than clarity. Completeness requires that the theory cover as many of the phenomena that infants and children manifest as possible.

Paradigms and Developmental Theories

We now turn to the question of whether developmental theories are paradigms or culture-bound creations that reflect the child rearing mores of the social/cultural group of the author. That is, are developmental theories paradigms with a set of hypotheses that articulate universal propositions about the course of development, or do they constitute "ideal types" or prototypes, based on a social/cultural group's view of a healthy individual? This controversy echoes the broader debate that is still taking place among philosophers and psychoanalysts.

Kuhn popularized the term ***paradigm*** in his classic work *The Structure of Scientific Revolutions* (1970a). In that work, Kuhn sought to establish the thesis that in the history of the natural sciences a succession of different theories gained ascendancy. Each theory had a period of hegemony only to find itself overthrown and displaced by a different theory. These theories, which Kuhn called paradigms, consist of sets of propositions or hypotheses that order investigators' observations. The hypotheses are law-like statements that presume to describe causal relationships between events. The laws embodied in these hypotheses are universally applicable irrespective of the context. When a paradigm is overthrown, a new one replaces it.

Some infer from Kuhn's thesis that theories are no more than culture-bound editions of explanations scientists give of their surroundings at the time of their creation. Each edition reflects the bias of a particular period in history. Others, including some philosophers of science, disagree with this interpretation of Kuhn's work and find the notion that knowledge is culture bound as unacceptable because it means that there are no ultimate truths, each culture's set of truths are as valid as those of any other culture (Kuhn, 1970b). These differing interpretations of Kuhn reflect the tension between those who adhere to a **positivistic** perspective and those who subscribe to **hermeneutic** or **social constructivist** approaches. These philosophical debates have their reverberations in psychoanalytic circles (Stern, 2002).

Positivists contend that science is a systematic public enterprise controlled by logic and empirical fact, whose purpose it is to formulate the truth about the natural world (see Bernstein, 1983). Sensory observation is the source of external or experience distant data. Self-reports from patients of their introspections, which Freud believed to be obtained through evenly hovering attention and association, have their source in the internal near psychological events. Both of these sources yielded equally valid data. Natural laws emerge from these observations and reflect an order inherent in nature. These laws or general hypotheses may be ordered into a hierarchy of increasing generality and complexity. Testing these hypotheses involves an appeal to facts disclosed in common observation of data. Predictions are possible based on tested hypotheses. The vision is of a universe of objects with independent existence (see Scheffler, 1982).

Critics of positivism, broadly identified as the postmodern movement, such as the **intersubjectivists** and **relational theorists**, offer alternate views. They hold that realities are multiple rather than singular and fixed. All data are theory bound and contextual rather than objective and decontextualized; the observer and the observed cannot be separated. Since it is not possible to establish causal relationships between events, only the recognition of patterns in sequences of events is possible, and finally, inquiry is never entirely value free (Guba, 1990). These principles lead to the conclusion that theories are ideographic, that is, they provide descriptive accounts of the patterns to which the phenomena they describe conform. Each discipline bases itself on different belief systems, different methodologies, and each aspires to different goals. Some radical critics of positivism go so far as to claim that even the natural sciences offer no more than sophisticated culture-bound theories of the segment of the universe they explain. Others insist that there are irreconcilable differences between the natural and the social sciences. They claim that while positivist approaches are successful for the natural sciences, constructivist or hermeneutic approaches are more appropriate to the social sciences (Saleeby, 1994).

Freud, trained as a neurologist, saw himself as a scientist who was simply describing the world, as it existed. This positivistic stance led psychoanalysts to insist for decades that psychoanalysis should take its place among the domain of sciences, such as the physical and biological sciences. During the first half of the twentieth century through the 1960s1958, psychoanalysts such as Hartmann (1958, 1964) and Rapaport (1951, 1960) hoped to emulate the model of the natural sciences and move psychoanalytic theory to the status of a scientific paradigm. They wished to discover the general laws that guided human development and the functioning of the mind. According to their view, a developmental theory formulated the universal phases or stages through which children mature. Theories of psychopathology similarly expressed the universality of neurotic conflict, or modeled themselves after the medical view that toxins, such as trauma, cause patients' illnesses. As positivists, these psychoanalysts insisted that psychoanalytic theories, as paradigms, utilized the scientific method to arrive at their metapsychological formulations. Their descriptions of the functioning of the human mind reflect the objective reality that exists independently of our explanations.

With the decline of the hegemony of positivism, these hopes faded for psychoanalysts. Hermeneutic and social constructivist approaches, with their relativistic biases, displaced the certainty that the positivists wished to attain (Berger & Luckmann, 1966; Gergen & Gergen, 1983, 1986; Hoffman, 1992; McGuire, 1990; Ricoeur, 1980). The hegemony of ego psychology was displaced by a proliferation of psychoanalytic theories such as object relations, attachment, self-psychology, intersubjectivity, interpersonal, relational, and other theories. Each of these attempted to respond to particular criticisms of Freud's classical model.

In response to these criticisms, the positivists, such a Basch (1976, 1988) and Lichtenberg (1983), attachment theorists (Schore, 1994, 2000), and others rejected the contention that those concepts derive from the social-cultural context within which they are created and that the social-cultural context imbues every member of its community with a worldview, which they cannot transcend. Often, these theorists do not always state explicitly the philosophical ground on which they founded their theories, which leads to confusion about their position. More recently, with the effort to integrate the findings of the neurosciences with psychoanalytic metapsychology (Solms & Turnbull, 2002), some are proposing the use of complexity or chaos theory as a systems approach that resolves many of the problems these critics of the positivist positions raise (Miller, 2004).

So far, we have simplified the issues by presenting polarized positions. In reality, the controversy is much more complex with numerous participants presenting differing views in the debate. Some schools neglect to propose their own developmental theories, whereas others see no need for such a theory. Psychoanalysts continue to evolve in their position to respond to criticism leveled at them.

Summary and Conclusion

Psychoanalytic practitioners generally agree with the principle established by Freud that developmental theories play a central role in understanding human conduct. These theories provide a conceptual framework for understanding the relationship between past occurrences, present personality structure, and psychopathology. In addition, they are integral to the conduct of clinical practice because psychoanalytic clinical theories subscribe to the principles of developmental psychopathology, that is, that all psychopathology can be understood either as reflective of what occurred during development or a return to an earlier developmental phase.

Historically, Freud adhered to three assumptions in the construction of his developmental theory. These assumptions were that ontogeny repeated phylogeny, that is, that each member of the species reenacted developmentally the major events of the history of the species; that regressive states were replicas of earlier childhood states; and that during psychoanalysis, lifting the repression around a forgotten memory helped recover the actual events that occurred in childhood. The basic principle that undergirds these assumptions is that a direct relationship exists between his theory of pathology, his clinical theory, and developmental events. We characterized this relationship as tightly linked. The differing schools of psychoanalysis that evolved subsequently retained some of these assumptions while rejecting one or more of the three principles.

To facilitate the task of comparing and contrasting different theories we discussed the different methodologies available for the formulation of developmental theories, methodologies that use a descriptive, interpersonal, or intrapersonal perspective. Each methodology has its strengths and limitations, but combining methodologies in the construction of a developmental theory may lead to contradictory perspectives from which data are collected. Furthermore, for a developmental theory to propose a comprehensive model it must provide answers to several questions, including questions such as how much nature and nurture contribute to the developmental progression; does development proceed if stages or phases, or are each set of issues that children encounter continuous during the life cycle; how are psychological structures formed; and other questions.

We suggested a possible criterion for the assessment of the coherence and completeness of these theories to be not only the inclusiveness of the answers given to these questions, but also in the type of narrative that organizes the data within a theory. Each narrative incorporates a root metaphor. This metaphor provides a central theme around which the content of the narrative is organized. By applying this criterion, it becomes possible to evaluate whether a developmental theory is coherent or incoherent, that is, whether the theory uses a mixed metaphor whether it organizes its data consistently within its metaphor, and whether it is complete in the explanations that it gives.

Finally, we addressed the issue of whether developmental theories are paradigms or culture-bound creations that reflect the child-**rearing mores of the social/cultural group. We suggested that some theorists are committed to the position that psychoanalysis must take its place among the sciences, using its methodology to affirm or falsify hypotheses. Others take a *social-constructivist* or *hermeneutic* stance, believing that psychoanalysis as a human science cannot appropriately comply with the requirements of the physical sciences. Some contributors to psychoanalytic theory, who challenge the view that psychoanalysis is a science, interpret Freud's clinical work as resembling that of hermeneutic scholars who approached the study of texts. They cite his analysis of patients' dreams as an example of the use of such an interpretive methodology. However, hermeneutic and social-constructivist approaches face the problem that their methodologies do not lend themselves to the collection and organization of empirical data on which to construct a developmental theory.

Keywords Contextual metaphor • Developmental psychopathology • Descriptive perspective • Dynamic point of view • Epigenesis • Hermeneutic • Incorporation • Identification • Internalization • Interpersonal perspective • Intrapersonal perspective • Introjection • Narratives • Mechanistic metaphor • Ontogeny • Organismic metaphor • Paradigm • Phenotype • Phylogeny • Positivistic • Psychodynamic • Regressed states • Repression • Root metaphor • Social constructivist

References

Abraham, K. (1924/1927). A short study of the development of the libido, viewed in the light of mental disorders. In *Selected papers of Karl Abraham*. New York: Basic Books.

Basch, M. F. (1976). Psychoanalysis and communication science. *The Annual of Psychoanalysis* (Vol. 4, pp. 385–421). New York: Universities Press.

Basch, M. F. (1988). *Understanding psychotherapy: The science behind the art*. New York: Basic Books.

Berger, P. L., & Luckmann, T. (1966). *The social construction of reality: A treatise in the sociology of knowledge*. New York: Doubleday, Anchor Books.

Bernstein, R. J. (1983). *Beyond objectivism and relativism: Science hermeneutics and praxis*. Philadelphia: University of Pennsylvania Press.

Blos, P. (1967). The second individuation process of adolescence. *Psychoanalytic Study of the Child, 22*, 162–186.

Bowlby, J. (1969). *Attachment and loss, Vol. I: Attachment*. New York: Basic Books.

Erikson, E. H. (1964). *Childhood and society*. New York: W.W. Norton.

Erikson, E. H. (1980). Elements of a psychoanalytic theory of psychosexual development. In S. I. Greenspan & G. H. Pollack (Eds.), *The course of life: Psychoanalytic contributions toward understanding personality development. I. Infancy and early childhood*. Washington, DC: US Government Printing Office, National Institute of Mental Health.

Fonagy, P., & Target, M. (2003). *Psychoanalytic theories: Perspectives from developmental psychopathology*. Philadelphia: Whurr Publishers.

Freud, A. (1936/1966). *The ego and the mechanisms of defense*. New York: International Universities Press.

Freud, S. (1894). The neuro-psychoses of defence. In J. Strachey (Ed.), *The standard edition* (Vol. 3, pp. 43–69). London: The Hogarth Press.

Freud, S. (1895). Studies on hysteria. In J. Strachey (Ed.), *Standard edition* (Vol. 2). London: The Hogarth Press.

Freud, S. (1905). Three essays on the theory of sexuality. In J. Strachey (Ed.), *The standard edition* (Vol. 7, pp. 125–247). London: The Hogarth Press.

Freud, S. (1912). The dynamics of the transference. In J. Strachey (Ed.), *Standard edition* (Vol. 12). London: The Hogarth Press.

Freud, S. (1913). *Totem and taboo*. In J. Strachey (Ed.), *Standard edition* (Vol. 13, pp. 1–163). London: The Hogarth Press.

Freud, S. (1917a). *Introductory lectures on psycho-analysis, Part III* (Standard edition, Vol. 16). London: The Hogarth Press.

Freud, S. (1917b). Lecture XXII. Some thoughts on development and regression – Aetiology. In J. Strachey (Ed.), *The standard edition* (Vol. 16, pp. 339–357). London: The Hogarth Press.

Freud, S. (1918). From the history of an infantile neurosis. In J. Strachey (Ed.), *The standard edition* (Vol. 17, pp. 3–124). London: The Hogarth Press.

Freud, S. (1923). The Ego and the Id. In J. Strachey (Ed.), *The standard edition* (Vol. 19, pp. 3–66). London: The Hogarth Press.

Freud, S. (1924). The dissolution of the Oedipus complex. In J. Strachey (Ed.), *The standard edition* (Vol. 19pp. 173–182). London: The Hogarth Press.

Freud, S. (1925). *Inhibitions, symptom and anxiety*. In J. Strachey (Ed.), *The standard edition* (Vol. 20). London: The Hogarth Press.

Gergen, K. J., & Gergen, M. M. (1983). Narratives of the self. In T. Sarbin & K. Scheibe (Eds.), *Studies in social identify* (pp. 254–273). New York: Praeger.

Gergen, K. J., & Gergen, M. M. (1986). Narrative form and the construction of psychological science. In T. Sarbin (Ed.), *Narrative psychology* (pp. 254–273). New York: Praeger.

Greenspan, S. I. (1989). *The development of the ego: Implications for personality theory, psychopathology, and the psychotherapeutic process*. Madison, CT: International Universities Press.

Greenspan, S. I. (1997). *The growth of mind and the endangered origins of intelligence*. Reading, MA: Addison-Wesley.

Guba, E.G. (1990). The alternative paradigm dialogue. In E. G. Guba (Ed.), *The paradigm dialogue* (pp. 17–30). Newbury Park: Sage.

Hartmann, H. (1958). *Ego psychology and the problem of adaptation*. New York: International Universities Press.

Hartmann, H. (1964). The development of the ego concept in Freud's work. In H. Hartmann (Ed.), *Essays in ego psychology* (Ch. 14). New York: International universities Press.

Hoffman, I. Z. (1992). Some practical implications of a social-constructivist view of the psychoanalytic situation. *Psychoanalytic Dialogues*, *2*(3), 287–304.

Holt, R. R. (1972). Freud's mechanistic and humanistic images of man. *Psychoanalysis and Contemporary Science*, *1*, 3–24.

Howard, G. S. (1991). Culture tales: A narrative approach to thinking, cross-cultural psychology, and psychotherapy. *American Psychologist, 46*(3), 187–197.

Kernberg, O. F. (1975). *Borderline conditions and pathological narcissism*. New York: Jason Aronson.

Kernberg, O. F. (1976). *Object relations theory and clinical psychoanalysis*. New York: Jason Aronson.

Klein, M. (1923). The development of a child. *International Journal of Psychoanaylsis, 4,* 419–473.

Kohut, H. (1959). Introspection, empathy, and psychoanalysis. *Journal of the American Psychoanalytic Association, 7*, 459–483.

Kohut, H. (1971). *The analysis of the self.* New York: International Universities Press.

Kohut, H. (1977). *The restoration* of *the self.* New York: International Universities Press.

Kohut, H. (1984). In A. Goldberg (Ed.), *How does analysis cure?* Chicago: The University of Chicago Press.

Kuhn, T. S. (1970a). *The structure of scientific revolutions* (2nd ed., Foundations of the Unity of Science, No. 2). Chicago: University of Chicago Press.

Kuhn, T. S. (1970b). Reflections on my critics. In I. Lakatos & A. Musgrave (Eds.), *Criticism and the growth of knowledge*: Proceedings of the International Colloquium in the Philosophy of Science, 1965, London (Vol. 4p. 2). Cambridge: Cambridge University Press.

Lakoff, G. & Johnson, M. (1980). *Metaphors we live by* (pp. 31–278). Chicago: University of Chicago Press.

Lichtenberg, J. D. (1983). *Psychoanalysis and infant research*. New Jersey: The Analytic Press.

Mahler, M. S. (1968). *On human symbiosis and the vicissitudes of individuation* (Chaps. 1 & 2). New York: International Universities Press.

Mahler, M. S., Pine, F., & Bergman, A. (1975). *The psychological birth of the human infant* (Part 11, pp. 39–122). New York: Basic Books.

Masson, J. M. (1985). *The assault on truth: Freud's suppression of the seduction theory*. New York: Penguin Press.

McGuire, M. (1990). The rhetoric of narrative: A hermeneutic critical theory. In B. K. Britton & A. D. Pellegrini (Eds.), *Narrative thought and narrative language* (pp. 219–236). Hillsdale, NJ: Lawrence Erlbaum.

Miller, M. L. (2004). Dynamic systems and the therapeutic action of the analyst. In J. Reppen, J. Tucker, & M. A. Schulman (Eds.), *Way beyond Freud: Postmodern psychoanalysis observed.* London: Open Gate Press.

Mitchell, S. A. (1988). *Relational concepts in psychoanalysis: An interation*. Cambridge, MA: Harvard University Press.

Mitchell, W. J. T. (Ed.). (1980). *On narrative*. Chicago: The University of Chicago Press.

Palombo, J. (1991a). Bridging the chasm between developmental theory and clinical theory, Part 1: The chasm. In A. Goldberg (Ed.), *The annual of psychoanalysis* (Vol. 19, pp. 151–174). Hillsdale, NJ: The Analytic Press.

Palombo, J. (1991b). Bridging the chasm between developmental theory and clinical theory, Part 2: The bridge . In A. Goldberg (Ed.), *The annual of psychoanalysis* (Vol. 19, pp. 175–193). Hillsdale, NJ: The Analytic Press.

Palombo, J. (1992). Narratives, self-cohesion, and the patient's search for meaning. *Clinical Social Work Journal, 20*(3), 249–270.

Palombo, J. (1996). Paradigms, metaphors, and narratives: Stories we tell about development. *Journal of Analytic Social Work, 4*(3), 31–59.

Palombo, J. (2006). *Nonverbal learning disabilities: A clinical perspective*. New York: W. W. Norton.

Pepper, S. (1942). *World hypotheses*. Berkeley, CA: University of California Press.

Polkinghorne, D. E. (1988). *Narrative knowing and the human sciences*. New York: State University of New York Press.

Rapaport, D. (1951). The conceptual model of psychoanalysis. In M. Gill (Ed.), *The collected papers of David Rapaport* (pp. 405–431). New York: Basic Books.

Rapaport, D. (1960). The structure of psychoanalytic theory: A systematizing attempt. *Psychological Issue, 2(2), Monograph* 6.

Ricoeur, P. (1980). Narrative time. In W. J. T. Mitchell (Ed.), *On narrative* (pp. 165–186). Chicago: The University of Chicago Press.

Saleeby, D. (1994). Culture, theory, and narrative: The intersection of meanings in practice. *Social Work, 39*(4), 351–359.

Sarbin, T. R. (1986). The narrative as a root metaphor for psychology. In T. R. Sarbin (Ed.), *Narrative psychology: The storied nature of human conduct* (pp. 3–21). New York: Praeger.

Schafer, R., (1968). *Aspects of internalization*. New York: International Universities Press.

Schafer, R. (1980). Narration in the psychoanalytic dialogue. In W. J. T. Mitchell (Ed.), *On narrative* (pp. 25–50). Chicago: The University of Chicago Press.

Schafer, R. (1981). *Narrative actions in psychoanalysis*. Worchester, MA: Clark University Press.

Schafer, R. (1983). *The analytic attitude*. New York: Basic Books.

Scheffler, I. (1982). *Science and subjectivity*. Indianapolis: Hackett.

Scholes, R., & Kellogg, R. (1966). *The nature of narrative*. London: Oxford University Press.

Schore, A. N. (1994). *Affect regulation and the origin of the self: The neurobiology of emotional development*. Hillsdale, NJ: Lawrence Earlbaum.

Schore, A. N. (2000). Attachment and the regulation of the right brain. *Attachment and Human Development, 2*(1), 23–47.

Solms, M., & Turnbull, O. (2002). *The brain and the inner world: An introduction to the neuroscience of subjective experience*. New York: Other Press.

Spence, D. P. (1982). *Narrative truth and historical truth*. New York: W.W. Norton.

Spence, D. P. (1987). *The Freudian metaphor: Toward paradigm change in psychoanalysis*. New York: W.W. Norton.

Spitz, R. A. (1965). *The first year of life: A psychoanalytic study of normal and deviant development of object relations*. New York: International Universities Press.

Stern, D. B. (2002). What you know first: Construction and deconstruction in relational psychoanalysis. In S. Fairfield, L. Layton, & C. Stack (Eds.), *Bringing the plague: Toward a postmodern psychoanalysis* (pp. 167–194). New York: Other Press.

Stern, D. N. (1985). *The interpersonal world of the infant*. New York: Basic Books.

White, H. (1980). The value of narrativity in the representation of reality. In W. J. T. Mitchell (Ed.), *On narrative* (pp. 1–24). Chicago: The University of Chicago Press.

Winnicott, D. W. (1965). *Maturational processes and the facilitating environment: Studies in the theory of emotional development*. London: Hogarth Press.

Section I
Drive Theory

We begin our journey through the descriptions of psychoanalytic developmental theories with a biographical sketch summarizing Freud's life followed by an abstract of his seminal work and a description of his developmental theory. As the founder of psychoanalysis, Freud created a set of theories that left their imprint on all psychodynamic theories that followed. Following a positivist path, Freud viewed himself as a scientist, using the observational tools available to him to describe the phenomena that drew his interest. As a scientist, he proposed hypotheses to explain his observations and felt that he found confirmation for them in his work with patients.

Yet, his was not a monolithic, systematic, unitary set of ideas. Over the years, through his exposure to different clinical phenomena and to events around him, he modified and reworked old ideas even as he proposed new ones. The complexity of his thinking did not lead him to amend his early discoveries; he simply grafted new ones on to the old. What resulted was a set of theories identified as Freud's metapsychology. The metapsychology is composed of five different points of view that incorporate most of the positions taken by Freud during his lifetime. They are (a) the *economic*, the point of view that takes into account the manner in which energy is built up and discharged by the person's psyche; (b) the *topographic*, the point of view that describes the psychological regions of the conscious, preconscious, and unconscious; (c) the *dynamic*, the point of view that discusses the balance of forces and counter forces acting on the drives; (d) the *genetic*, the developmental point of view; and (e) the *structural*, the point of view that became the dominant perspective in ego psychology and that regards the ego, the id, and the superego as the major agencies of the mind. There is much overlap between the points of view and little agreement as to their boundaries. Some of Freud's followers took earlier formulations as foundational for their views, whereas others insisted on retaining his later formulation as representing orthodox psychoanalysis. We characterize Freud's theory as a "drive theory" because of the primacy he gave to the libidinal and aggressive drives. However, he identified the unconscious as his greatest discovery and whereas nowadays there is a general rejection of the drives as central to human motivation, every psychoanalytic theory retains the concept of the unconscious in one form or another.

The fundamental premise of Freud's theory was that early infantile sexuality, as an instinctual drive, propels all development. Although he constructed his developmental scheme from his experiences with adult patients and never systematically observed or treated children or adolescents, he proposed that development describes the trajectory that the drives follow. Using a hybrid mechanistic/hydraulic and organismic model, he proposed that drive energies were initially directed at the infant's core self (ego) and then proceeded "ontogenetically," that is in a sequential manner with one stage building on the prior one, to invest in the oral, anal, and phallic zones of the child's body. Eventually, the drive energies, during the oedipal phase, were directed at the caregivers (primary libidinal objects). Mature development, the phase of "object love," is the ability to invest an "object" (a person) of the opposite sex with libidinal energies. As stated earlier, methodologically two principles informed his views of development: (1) that ontogeny recapitulates phylogeny, that is, that in the case of human development a child's developmental phases (ontogeny) recapitulated human evolutionary history (phylogeny), and (2), that the course of development could be reconstructed from the regressed states of symptomatic adults in psychoanalysis and from the fixation they manifested to earlier phases of their development. In effect, he considered all psychopathology as "developmental psychopathology," a tenet that is fundamental to all psychodynamic perspectives and that maintains that all pathology is rooted in childhood.

We reintroduce the contributions that Karl Abraham made to Freud's early developmental model because of the significant dimension that he added. Abraham's contribution consisted in elaborating the psychosexual stages of development and incorporating the functions that the aggressive drive serves during those stages. Followers of Freud have neglected to acknowledge and credit Abraham for these contributions. By including them in this section, we hope to restore these contributions to their rightful place.

Chapter 1
Sigmund Freud (1856–1939)

Publishing Era (1888–1950)

Biographical Information

Sigismund Schlomo Freud was born in Freiberg, Moravia (now Pribor, Czechoslovakia) on May 5, 1856. He began using the shortened "Sigmund" after entering the University of Vienna in 1873 at age 17. Freud's Hasidic Jewish family history was complicated by early deaths and frequent remarriages, common at the time. Freud's father, Jacob, a poor wool merchant, married Amalia Nathanson, when he was 40 and she was 20. This was his third marriage, which produced seven children of which Sigmund was the oldest. When Sigmund Freud was four, the aspiring middle-class family moved from Leipzig to Vienna, where the Freud's family life centered on helping the brilliant Sigmund actualize his academic potential. In 1873, he graduated Gymnasium with distinction at age 17 and then entered the University of Vienna. The University's liberal atmosphere was remarkably free of anti-Semitism and he flourished in its stimulating environment.

Laboratory Research, Military Service and Medicine

While still living at his parent's home, Freud studied in the physiology laboratory of Ernst Wilhelm von Brucke from 1876 to 1882, where he cultivated his keen curiosity as an investigator. Freud was influenced especially by two professors who were known as Darwinians (Ritvo, 1965), Carl Claus, who taught zoology, and Brucke, whom Freud considered a fatherly figure, and whose commitment to medical positivism had the single greatest impact on his intellectual life. Freud served 1 year of compulsory service in the Austrian military from 1879 to 1880 where he tended sick soldiers. To counter the boredom during that period, he translated John Stuart Mills' essays into German. Freud earned his medical degree at the age of 25 in 1881. In 1882, he secured a junior post at Vienna's General Hospital, which he held until 1886 when he resigned to open his private practice in psychiatry. With this move, he shifted his professional interests to psychiatry from research in neuroanatomy (Gay, 1988, pp. 30–37; Sulloway, 1979, pp. 13–21).

J. Palombo et al., *Guide to Psychoanalytic Developmental Theories*,
DOI: 10.1007/978-0-387-88455-4_1, © Springer Science+Business Media, LLC 2009

Jean Martin Charcot and Josef Breuer

To satisfy his insatiable curiosity about developments in related fields, from 1885 to 1886, Freud studied hypnosis in Paris at the Salpetriere with Jean Martin Charcot, whose lectures on the *Diseases of the Nervous System* (1881) he translated into German. Charcot believed hypnosis was an organic pathological condition seen only in hysterics and neurotics. Freud began using hypnosis in 1887 in his collaboration with Josef Breuer (1842–1925), whom he met in 1887 through Ernst Brucke's circle of highly respected colleagues. Eventually, Freud gave up hypnosis altogether in 1897, considering it ineffective and preferring to use Breuer's **cathartic method**, which consisted in letting patients freely associate by reporting whatever crossed their minds. Breuer became Freud's fatherly mentor, close professional collaborator, coauthor of *Studies on Hysteria* (1895c), and financial supporter. By 1898, the collaboration with Breuer was all but over as Breuer expressed persistent doubts about Freud's conclusions on hysteria and the theory of neuroses that Freud was promoting. He could not accept Freud's conjectures that these disorders stemmed from infantile sexuality.

Martha Bernays

Freud met Martha Bernays (1861–1951) in 1882 when she was visiting one of his sisters at his house. Freud quickly fell in love and was engaged 2 months later. They married in 1886. Martha gave birth to three sons and three daughters in an 8-year period. The first child born to the Freuds was Mathilde in 1887, followed by Jean Martin, named after Charcot, in 1889, Oliver in 1891, Ernst in 1892, and Sopherl (Sophie) in 1893. Annerl or Anna, the youngest was born in December 3, 1895 in Vienna (see the biographical statement in the Anna Freud section for additional family details). In 1896, Freud had turned 40 and the need to earn a living to support his family inexorably shaped his career decisions.

Wilhelm Fliess: The Project, Freud's Self-Analysis, and The Cocaine Episode

In 1887, Freud met Wilhelm Fliess (1858–1928), a visiting Berlin physician, who was part of Josef Breuer's circle. In some ways, Fliess started out as Freud's unrestrained creative muse or, as Freud put it in a letter to Fliess, his "Publicum," i.e., his audience (Nunberg, 1969/1970, p. 103). Their close friendship grew stronger as the friendship with Breuer faded. Fliess is credited with the concepts of latency, the sexual significance of olfaction, and bisexuality, which Freud used selectively.

Freud never published the *Project for a Scientific Psychology* (1895a). Its significance lies in the ambitious effort it represents to uncover the neurobiological mechanisms that undergird our mental lives. It was an ambitious excursion, which he communicated to Fliess through an exchange of letters during 1895–1896. Freud had encountered three problems he could not solve: (1) What factors entered into the choice of a specific set of neurotic symptoms? (2) Why does sexuality always seem to be the ubiquitous cause of neurotic disorders? In addition, (3) what physiological mechanisms does the ego employ to activate repression? Freud found the solutions to these problems, in particular the last one, to be elusive and refractory. Eventually, he was forced to abandon his *Project* and the quest for a neurophysiological explanation for the functioning of the mental apparatus. Freud asked Fliess to destroy the copy of the *Project* he had sent for review, but Fliess never did so. However, the ideas contained in the *Project* continued to exert a heuristic influence on Freud. He translated many of its constructs into his psychoanalytic framework, including such ideas as reality testing, the formal distinction between primary and secondary processes, and the wish-fulfillment theory of dreams.

During 1897–1898 Freud, using **free association** to access personal dream material, wrote frequently to Fliess about his self-analysis. Free association is the technique of letting patients state whatever comes to mind, unrestrained by any effort to inhibit thoughts and feelings. In these communications, he credited this "heroic" experiment with a number of seminal discoveries that became central to psychoanalytic theory. These included (a) his abandonment of the seduction theory of the etiology of the neuroses, (b) the Oedipus complex, that is, the family romance, (c) unconscious guilt, (d) the phases of sexual development, later characterized as the psychosexual synthesis (Makari, pp. 85–125), (e) the revelatory nature of parapraxes or slips of the tongue, (f) the power of repressed aggressive feelings, (g) dream mechanisms, and (h) a psychological explanation for addiction as a form of displaced masturbation (Gay, 1988, pp. 96–102).

Between 1884 and1885, what has became known as the Cocaine Episode took place. A German army physician had prescribed cocaine on a limited basis to bolster the endurance of the troops. Freud encountered the then little known substance called cocaine while working in Theodor Meynert's Psychiatry Department of the General Hospital in Vienna and became impressed with its simultaneously painkilling, soothing, and stimulating properties. Freud conducted research on this remarkable substance and published his findings in 1884 in a paper entitled "On Coca." He grew to lament that he had not published first the fact of its anesthetizing qualities, about which he had told colleagues, and lost out to Carl Koller, who is credited as the discoverer of the use of cocaine as an important local anesthetic in minor surgery. He wrote of "the cocaine business" in a letter to Martha on October 29, 1884, lamenting that he had missed out on the lion's share of recognition for its use in surgery and implying that his love struck interests distracted him and caused him to do sloppy research. Freud, however, was still an enthusiastic proponent of its use for relief of depression, exhaustion, and enhancing overall well-being. He continued to use it in ever-decreasing amounts until he discontinued it all together in the mid 1890s, appreciating more fully its addictive features (Gay, 1988, pp. 42–45).

Although the collaboration with Fliess initially was intense, leading Freud to believe that a homosexual dimension colored the relationship, after 1900, the reliance on Fliess diminished substantially and ended unhappily in 1904, in a dispute primarily over ownership and originality of ideas (Gay, 1988, pp. 274–277). The publication of *The Interpretation of Dreams* in 1900 had marked a turning point in Freud's effort to establish a new path for himself.

Professorship and Relocation

Since 1885, Freud had been stuck in the lowly rank of Privatdozent in the department of psychiatry, which was a position as an unsalaried university lecturer remunerated directly by students' fees. Only political connections could guarantee promotions. In 1902, after a long wait, Emperor Franz Josef awarded Freud the prestigious rank of Professor Extraordinarius, which meant that he would use the title "Herr Professor." This was the ticket to social prestige and higher fees (Gay, 1988, pp. 136–137). Freud felt that psychoanalysis became legitimized with his acceptance into the academic community. In 1891, Freud moved his office and family into Berggasse 19 where he worked and lived until 1938.

Study Groups

As the relationship with Fliess faded, Freud confronted the need for a new audience and sounding board. In the fall of 1902, at the suggestion of Wilhelm Stekel (1886–1940), a former psychoanalytic patient of Freud's, Freud initiated the Wednesday Psychological Society. Freud invited four physicians, including Alfred Adler and Stekel, to the meeting. Later, interested lay people were invited. It convened in Freud's apartment and was later renamed the Wednesday Evening Meetings. Early in1908, the Wednesday Psychological Society became the more formal, collegial, and professional Vienna Psychoanalytic Society. In 1910, the meetings were moved to the Doktoren Collegium (the College of Physicians). Freud attended the meetings regularly, hardly ever missing a meeting until his illness in 1923 (Gay, 1988, 1988, pp. 173–179; Nunberg, 1965, pp. 153–156).

Visit to America

Having been invited to lecture by Granville Stanley Hall, President of Clark University in Worchester, Massachusetts, Freud in September 1909 paid his only visit to America. Hall, with J. J. Rousseau, was one of the coinventors of the concept of adolescence (Esman, 1993; Kaplan, 1984; Ross, 1972; Sulloway, 1979, p. 263).

Freud sailed from Bremen, Germany on August 20, 1909 with Sandor Ferenczi and Carl Jung. Once in New York, Ernest Jones and A. A. Brill met him. On September 10, Hall presented Freud with an honorary degree of Doctor of Laws. Freud delivered five improvised lectures on psychoanalysis, which were well received ("Five Lectures on Psychoanalysis," 1910a, *SE* Vol. 11). During his stay, Freud met William James, the celebrated American psychologist. Freud considered the American trip as the most successful celebration of psychoanalysis growing appeal and acceptance. It was an enthusiasm soon to be tempered by growing ambivalence toward the unruly Jung, Freud's heir apparent (Gay, 1988, pp. 206–213).

The Committee

In the summer of 1912, due to the painful theoretical disagreements with Wilhelm Stekel, Alfred Adler, and Carl Jung, Freud accepted an idea from Ernest Jones, an orthodox psychoanalytic loyalist, to form a secret committee that would guard psychoanalytic orthodoxy. Members included Freud, Jones, Sandor Ferenczi, Otto Rank, Karl Abraham and Hanns Sachs. A wealthy Budapest beer baron, Anton von Freund, who had been Freud's patient, funded the Committee's activities, along with the psychoanalytic publishing enterprise. Max Eitingon and Anna Freud joined the group in 1919. The members swore their unswerving loyalty to Freud and to three fundamental tenets of psychoanalysis, the unconscious, repression, and infantile sexuality. To seal the membership, Freud gave a signet ring to each of the participants. Freud wrote later, "The idea of a united small body, designed, like the Paladins of Charlemagne, to guard the kingdom and policy of their master, was a product of my own romanticism" (Gay, 1988, pp. 229–230). Bitter rivalries broke out usually with Ferenczi and Rank on one side, Jones and Abraham and the rest on the other side as group cooperation became impossible. By 1925, the Committee ceased to exist, its watchdog functions absorbed into the international training commission established at the Eighth International Psychoanalytic Congress in Bad Homburg (Grosskurth, 1992, pp. 341–355).

Karl Abraham (1877–1925)[1]

Karl Abraham was born on May 3, 1887 in Bremen, Germany, into a small insular Orthodox Jewish community. Abraham decided at about age 18 to become a dental student. After a semester, he changed to medicine and in 1896 transferred to the

---

[1] Abraham's biographical information and theoretical contribution are included in this section because he, along with Freud, created the mature psychosexual model that is critical to drive theory's developmental framework. Using Freud's 1905 foundation, Abraham further researched the organization of the libidinal stages and made significant contributions in validating Freud's model.

University of Freiburg where he graduated in 1901 at age 24. At the University of Freiburg, Abraham came under the influence of Dr. Keibel, then a young lecturer in histology and embryology. Abraham developed a lifelong interest in embryology and later combined this curiosity with Freud's theory of libido and infantile psychosexual development; **libido** being the psychological representation of the sexual drive.

After a brief period as an assistant brain pathologist at the Berlin Municipal Asylum at Dalldorf, in 1904, Abraham accepted a position at the Burgholzli, the Mental Hospital of Zurich University. Eugene Bleuler, who extended Emile Kraepelin's work on schizophrenia, held the chair in psychiatry at that institution. At the time, Carl G. Jung was Bleuler's first assistant and the chief resident physician. This event represents a turning point in Abraham's life. Bleuler was one of the first to demonstrate an interest in Freud's work, an interest that bucked the dominant trend in academic psychiatry.

Freud was 50 and Abraham was 30 when they met. Abraham and Freud rapidly established a cordial, trusting relationship, which with Freud's encouragement in December 1907, led Abraham to settle in Berlin and begin a private psychiatric practice. Abraham founded the Berlin Psychoanalytic Society in August 1908 and the Berlin Psychoanalytic Institute in 1920. The first graduate was Franz Alexander in 1921, who later became the first Director of the Chicago Institute for Psychoanalysis. At the 1918 Congress in Budapest, Hermann Nunberg had advanced the position that all future psychoanalysts should undergo a personal analysis (Nunberg, 1965, p. 157). Significantly, there is no evidence that Abraham himself ever underwent either a personal or a training analysis. Abraham became a sought after training analyst with notable patients such as Alix Strachey, Edward and James Glover, Helene Deutsch, Karen Horney, and Melanie Klein. She, in turn, credited him with influencing her ideas on the significance of the destructive impulse and tracing its roots and its relationship to mental development. However, she rejected his developmental theory of the vicissitudes of libido.

While all the members of the psychoanalytic community were enthusiastic about their participation in psychoanalytic activities, Abraham had an abundance of vitality that he brought to his involvement. The energy Abraham poured into spreading psychoanalysis became legendary. In addition to attending to his considerable practice, Abraham wrote papers, presided over meetings, and enlisted recruits to the cause. Of particular consequence for psychoanalysis was his series of papers on manic-depression, now known as bipolar affective disorder (BPAD), written during his Zurich period, and later the development of libido. In addition, he kept a wary eye on the political storm centers in Zurich and Vienna for deviation from orthodoxy. His wise counsel to Freud during these turbulent and formative years was substantial and, after the storms subsided, fully appreciated.

In the summer of 1925, Abraham was writing to Freud from bed due to apparent symptoms of bronchitis. In actuality, he seems to have been suffering from undiagnosed lung cancer and was to die within 6 months. He steadily weakened and on Christmas Day Abraham died at the age 48. Abraham has the distinction of being one of Freud's most loyal followers beginning with their first meeting in 1907 at the December meeting of the Wednesday Psychological Society through to his death.

Freud took Abraham's death very hard; and the loss was a profound shock to the entire psychoanalytic community. Freud applied to Abraham's obituary notice the famous phrase that Horace lavished on a man of integrity: *integer vitae scelerisque puru,* Blameless of life and free of vice (Abraham, 1974; Gay, 1988, pp. 178–483).

Makari states, "...Karl Abraham offered a newly nuanced, unified psychosexual theory. Abraham connected libido, childhood experience, character structure, love relations and social adaptation, all of which made possible a richer description of a human life. Rado remembered: 'Abraham invented a use of Freudian language, combined with the ordinary clinical terms of psychiatry, to be able to tell the essential story of a patient" (2008, p. 378).

The First World War and The Emergence of The Death Instinct

Partly in response to the atrocities and misery of the Great War (1914–1918), Freud began to lay additional emphasis on Thanatos, the death wish. Freud reluctantly acknowledged Wilhelm Stekel as the first to use the term in 1910 through an examination of the death wish (later in 1920 Freud referred to the death instinct) and death symbolism in dreams (Roazen, 1974, pp. 211–222). Freud, however, in his early formulation, understood aggression as a dimension inherent in the ego (life preservative) and not an independent drive. Freud was reluctant to accord aggression, specifically the death instinct, a status equal to that of libido until the formulation of the dual instinct theory in 1920 (Freud, 1905b, 1920b). He was well aware of the complexities of this antithesis and even questioned the theoretical usefulness of such a dichotomy because of their mixed and uneven developmental trajectories (Fenichel, 1945, pp. 58-61). Originally, Freud posited that Eros, the life instinct, was the primary life force whose energy or libido is directed toward the enhancement or reproduction of life. "In this framework, aggression was viewed simply as a reaction to the blocking or thwarting of libidinal impulses and was neither an automatic nor an inevitable part of life" (*Kaplan and Sadock*, 2003a, p. 151). In 1915, with the publication of *Instincts and Their Vicissitudes* aggression began to play a more significant role in instinctual life (Nunberg, 1965, pp. 157–161).

In *Beyond the Pleasure Principle* (1920b) Freud put forth the final stage of his views on the hypothesis of the death instinct, a self-destructive force, and, with that, a truly independent aggressive drive came into existence. He posited the existence of **Eros** and **Thanatos**, the **life instinct** and the **death instinct**. This formulation became known as the dual instinct theory. Both instincts undergo repression as a general form of social control necessary now to save people from themselves.

The World War I left a deep imprint on Freud, having seen three of his sons serve in the military and been exposed to the "appalling daily display of human beastliness" (Gay, 1988, p. 197). In addition, Freud was impressed with a presentation he heard Sabina Spielrein make to the Vienna Psychoanalytic Society in 1911 entitled "Destruction as the Cause of Becoming." Subsequent personal experiences may well have contributed to his belief in the existence of a death instinct. Freud was deeply affected by the loss in 1920 of his first and much beloved daughter, Sophie, to influenza. In 1923, Freud was diagnosed with cancer of the palate. Furthermore, in 1923, Freud lost his beloved grandson, Heinele, Sophie's younger son, to tuberculosis, a death that left him deeply depressed. The horror of World War I, the Spielrein presentation along with Freud's three personal confrontations with the frailty of life probably contributed to his laying additional emphasis to his conviction of the existence of Thanatos and destructive aggression (Gay, 1988, pp. 396–408; Mitchell & Black, 1995, pp. 18–19).

Psychoanalysis of Anna Freud (1895–1982)

As we discuss later in the chapter on Anna Freud, Freud took on the analysis of his youngest daughter between the years 1918 and 1922, when Freud was 62 and Anna was 23. This analysis, along with that of the Wolf Man, was among Freud's longest analyses to have occurred at the time. It took place six times per week. Both he and Anna considered it successful from the standpoint of deepening her capacity for sublimation. Specifically, Anna's "masculinity complex," in which girls turn away from their incestuous love for their fathers and easily abandon their sexual feminine role, was understood not as a move toward homosexuality, but rather as an escape from sexuality. The vestal Anna transformed her sexuality and her oedipal interest in masturbation, into the desire to communicate, to be understood, and to seek not sexual pleasure but the social pleasure of praise. Her father rejected eligible male suitors as she developed female companionships with Dorothy Burlingham and Eva Rosenfeld, whose trust and lifelong devotion filled her with great joy (Peters, 1985, p. 47). In 1921, Freud invited Lou Andreas-Salome, who had been practicing psychoanalysis for a decade, to mentor Anna. A second analysis with Freud took place during 1924–1925. This analysis was interrupted due to Freud's spreading cancer. With Freud less available, Max Eitingon in Berlin was the second mentor to whom Anna turned to help her with the decisive next step career decisions (Young-Bruehl, 1988, pp. 103–139).

Cancer

In September 1922, Freud was diagnosed with a tumor of his palate. The first operation in April 1923 confirmed the suspicion of cancer, leaving him in considerable pain and with an uncomfortable prosthesis. Freud could not give up smoking his strong cigars, which greatly aggravated his mouth cancer and led directly to his death 17 years later (Gay, 1988, pp. 417–446). Incredibly, Freud had delayed getting the swelling treated for months. Freud's surgeon, Dr. Hajek, and Felix Deutsch, an internist and Freud's personal physician, trivialized the first operation and conspired to conceal the true diagnosis from Freud. Deutsch was concerned that the diagnosis of a malignancy and the radical nature of the second surgery might prompt Freud to prefer a Stoic suicide. Accordingly, he consulted the members of the Committee, who concurred in keeping the cancer diagnosis secret from both Freud and Anna. Both Freud and Anna then went off to their eagerly anticipated trip to Rome. Upon their return Freud was told of the cancer and its concealment, he was furious at the concealment and dismissed Deutsch as his physician but kept him as Anna's doctor (Young-Bruehl, 1988, p. 119). When Jones told Freud about the Committee's deception 15 years later, he was incensed and said "Mit welchem Recht?" (Freely translated as, "By what right did you make that decision?" (Schur, 1972, p. 361).

The Goethe Prize and The Final Years

Frustrated at not having won a Nobel Prize, Freud found some consolation in 1930, with the award of the coveted Goethe Prize for literature by the city of Frankfurt. As he was too ill to attend, Anna Freud accepted for him on August 30 (Gay, 1988, pp. 571–572). Germany, under Adolf Hitler, declared a union (Anschluss) with Austria through annexation on March 13, 1938. Direct and indirect attacks on Austrian Jews started immediately. One year later, by March 1939, all of Czechoslovakia was under German control. In September of that year, Germany declared war on Poland. In Vienna, the eminent surgeon Hans Pichler exerted his considerable influence to protect the Freud family. However, on March 22, 1939, the Nazis Gestapo took Anna Freud in for questioning on the nature of the Vienna Psychoanalytic Society. She was released later that evening after reassuring the Gestapo that the Society as a scientific organization was nonpolitical. This event overcame all of Freud's resistance to leaving Vienna. On June 4, with the considerable assistance of Princess Marie Bonaparte, Freud finally received his passport to leave Austria. Freud arrived in London on June 6 with his family and possessions. In his final year, he saw a few patients and worked principally on the manuscript of *Moses and Monotheism*. When the pain, fatigue, and gangrene became unbearable, at Freud's direction and with notification to Anna, he instructed his personal physician to proceed with their "contract." After three morphine injections over 2 days, Freud died under the care of Dr. Max Schur, on September 23, 1939 at 20 Maresfield Garden, in Hampstead (Gay, 1988, p. 651; Schur, 1972, pp. 504–529).

Conceptual Framework

Albert Einstein (1879–1955), Charles Darwin (1809–1882), and Sigmund Freud (1856–1939) are arguably three of the most profound, creative, and influential intellectual minds of the past 150 years. Each is responsible for a revolution in thinking that allowed for enormous leaps in explanatory power, having created separate and monumental paradigm shifts in their respective fields (Kuhn, 1962; Mayr, 1991, pp. 1–3). Each was concerned with discovering the laws of nature: Einstein (Albert

Einstein Archives, http://www.albert-einstein.org/head2.html), with the laws of the physical world from the cosmos to subatomic particles, Darwin, with the laws of evolutionary biology, and Freud, with the laws of the unconscious mind.

The underpinnings to Freud's paradigm were complex in that Freud relied on a mix of evolutionary ideas that included three components. First, it drew on Jean Lamarck's (1744–1829) principle of the inheritance of acquired characteristics in reaction to special environmental conditions. Lamarck advocated that a supreme being guided the ever more complex changes that occur in organisms leading them toward a state of perfection (Mayr, 1982. p. 353). For example, giraffes grew longer necks because leaves were harder and harder to reach. Second, Freud's paradigm relied on Ernst Haeckel's (1834–1919) extension of the embryological hypothesis that ontogeny recapitulates phylogeny; that is, in individual development the stages of the history of the species are repeated. Third, it acknowledged Charles Darwin's (1809–1882) principle of common descent through natural selection and survival of the fittest. Whereas Freud originally was a committed Darwinian, later in life he relied more on the discredited Lamarckian notions (Mayr, 1991, p. 134) as evidenced in these works: *Totem and Taboo* (1912b–1913), *Group Psychology and the Analysis of the Ego* (1921), *The Future of an Illusion* (1927a), *Civilization and Its Discontents* (1930) and *Moses and Monotheism* (1939).

For Freud, the sexual and aggressive drives were the fundamental driving forces for all human behavior. Human beings are born with untamed instinctual forces that push for discharge. Each child is born in a state of **primary narcissism** with a fixed and immutable quantity of libidinal and aggressive energy. This energy is at first directed toward the erogenous zones, the oral, anal, and genital areas. As caregivers provide gratification in the form of nurturance, infants transfer libidinal energy to their caregivers, and a cathexis of those objects follows. The investment of the caregivers results from the satisfaction of the instinctual drives. When the object does not provide the necessary satisfaction, which can occur with the loss of or disappointment in the object, the drive energies are withdrawn from the object and are reinvested in the ego. This produces the state of **secondary narcissism**, which may be accompanied by a variety of symptoms. Society's role is to tame those drives, and to transform them into energies that are usable for constructive purposes.

From a developmental perspective, Freud considered children to be "energy processing" organisms, whose urges to discharge are subject to the pleasure principle. Children are incapable of delaying the discharge of their urges. The primary aim of the organism is to reduce the buildup of tension that results from the constant pressure of the drives. The libidinal drives follow a prescribed form of expression, and unfold in a predictable sequence, the sequence being the familiar one of the oral, anal, and phallic/oedipal phases. The issues that each child faces during these phases are set by the history of the species. The psychic contents of each phase are also ontogenetically determined.

An outcome of the pressures that drives exert on the ego is that conflict is inherent in all development. The forces that lead the child to wish to discharge drive energies are antithetical to the reality the child faces. The demands of society are contrary to the demands of the instincts. Consequently, for a child to move on developmentally, that child must learn to postpone the pleasures of discharge, and to find less direct and more realistic ways of attaining gratification. Since postponement and delay entail frustration, conflict must ensue. Every developmental phase, therefore, presents children with a set of conflicts that they must resolve before it becomes possible for them to move ahead developmentally.

The ego activates defenses to protect itself against the onslaught of the drives. The defenses serve not only as shields against the more intense drives but also as regulators of discharge of drive energies. The other component of the ego's structure is derived from the neutralized drive energies that result from conflict resolution. These energies are transformed into identifications the child makes with parental figures and which eventually constitute the ego's executive functions.

In turn, the superego, or the conscience, emerges out of the resolution of the child's oedipal strivings at around the ages of four to six. The superego results from the internalization of the parental prohibitions, especially those of the father. What begins as the introjection of aspects of parent relationships becomes consolidated into the superego with the postponement of the hope for gratification of oedipal desires.

Freud believed that the myth of Oedipus best characterized the issues confronting the child in this phase of development. The onset of this phase is ontogenetically determined. He saw in that myth the key with which to explain not only neurotic phenomena manifested by troubled people, but also the normal expression of the psychological conflicts that children face. Conflict, which is central to all development and psychopathology, reflects the struggle between the person's primitive drive needs and the demands of society. The corollary issues that emerge in that phase are indicative of the vicissitudes of the instinctual drives. The issue of activity and passivity, of masculinity and femininity, of phallic intrusiveness or castrated receptivity are all part of the achievement of dominance in this phase. Anatomy plays a central role in the evolution of the phase.

Freud's Metapsychological Framework

With the publication of *The Interpretation of Dreams* in 1900, Freud produced the first of two monumental syntheses of the intellectual trends in European scientific circles, the first, described as the "model of the mind" synthesis (Makari, 2008, p. 83), is his descriptions of the operations of the human psyche as articulated in his metapsychology. The second is the **psychosexual** synthesis, which culminated with the publication of the *Three Essays on Sexuality* (1905a). This theory was absorbed into the first synthesis, creating a commanding explanatory framework that includes mental health, mental illness and human sexuality.

Between 1885 and 1905, Freud constructed his psychoanalytic psychology from a kaleidoscopic blend of three dominant intellectual currents (1875–1900): the speculations of French psychiatrists regarding the *origins of mental illness*, the theories of German scientists regarding *biological and physical phenomena*, and existing theories regarding *sexuality*. Each field attempted to clarify the bewildering array of forces that were the cause of mental illness. French psychiatrists conjectured that intergenerational hereditary degeneracy was the cause of mental illness and hysteria in particular. They believed that trauma not brain lesions precipitate hysteria and that through hypnosis they could access the mechanisms responsible for the formation of the symptoms. With Josef Breuer's help Freud, in the *Studies on Hysteria*, modified and synthesized these ideas into "his notions of defense neurosis, mental conflict, psychical analysis, and transference" (Makari, 2008, p. 48).

German biophysics–psychophysics was an intellectual scientific movement that put forward the hypothesis that human physiology could be understood as consisting of the transformations of energy that obeys the laws of hydraulics and mechanics. Freud first attempted to apply these notions in the *Project* (1895a). However, when his efforts were unsuccessful, he turned to psychological explanations to clarify psychological causation and mental conflict. In the *Interpretation of Dreams* Freud formulated a revolutionary model of the mind in which his economic, topographical, and dynamic metapsychological hypotheses were put forward to work to explain the laws of the unconscious (Makari, 2008, pp. 53–84).

The discipline devoted to the study of sexuality, or sexology as it was then called, was a hotly divided field. Investigators were convinced that sexuality did not emerge until puberty and focused on studying adult deviations or perversions. They considered the norm for the expression of adult sexuality to be sexual intercourse between a man and a woman. Some believed the cause of perversions to be degenerative heredity or natural variation. An important finding suggested that psychological factors could also be the cause of perversions, as would encounters in childhood with abusers or with premature sexual stimulation of immature children.

Into this complex, rapidly changing state of affairs, Freud formulated his second grand synthesis in 1905 using the additional explanatory power of the developmental theory he had evolved. The proposal that Freud made in the *Three Essays on Sexuality* provided commanding internal coherence, in spite of the fact that the model lacked empirical verifiability. By proposing a universal biological life force he called **libido**, Freud bridged the biological and psychological worlds with a theory of the interaction of drives linked to mental processes. He declared that perversions were a normal part of development beginning with childhood sexuality. Perversions resulted from repression and underwent transformations through sublimation or through symptom formation in neuroses (Makari, 2008, pp. 85–125).

As we approach Freud's five foundational metapsychological hypotheses, it is helpful to keep in mind two propositions that are fundamental to psychoanalytic theory. These propositions firmly anchor psychoanalysis in the positivist philosophical tradition (see the Introduction). The first is the principle of **psychic determinism** or the law of causality. This principle maintains that in the mind, as in physical nature, every event has antecedent causes; that is, nothing happens by chance or accident. Each psychical event, each thought, and each associated feeling, is influenced or determined by the ones that preceded it (Brenner, 1973). The second proposition is that the overwhelming majority of psychic processes, both normal and abnormal, are **unconscious**. Consciousness is an exceptional rather than a regular attribute of psychic processes. Furthermore, we cannot have direct access to the unconscious. We are aware of the unconscious only indirectly; i.e., through derivatives such as dreams and slips of the tongue (Brenner, pp. 1–14). These two propositions reflect Freud's conviction that he anchored his contributions to psychology in the methodology of the scientific research current in his day.

Before describing his developmental theory, we discuss his five metapsychological hypotheses in the approximate chronological order in which they appeared. We begin with the *economic*, followed by the *topographic*, the *dynamic*, the *genetic*, and the *structural hypothes***is**. The first four hypotheses constitute what is now known as **Drive Theory**. The structural hypothesis, which enlarged the ego's executive role, became the foundation on which Anna Freud and Heinz Hartmann built ego psychology (Arlow & Brenner, 1964; Brenner, 1955/1973; Rapaport, 1960, 1967). The outline that follows sketches Freud's most significant theoretical contributions recognizing that he never undertook a systematic reformulation of his conceptualizations. As stated earlier, he added to his theoretical edifice as he and his followers elaborated on the existing framework and generated new ideas.

The Economic Hypothesis or the Entropy Model (From 1895)

The **economic hypothesis**, Freud's first model of the mind, was the one he and Breuer used to describe the psychological pressures or forces that either were in conflict with one another or pressed for expression. They indirectly drew an analogy between the Newtonian mechanistic view of the workings of physical objects and the **law of entropy**, on the one hand, and the workings of the mind, on the other. This mechanistic view held that the concept of energy is central to understanding the workings of the psyche. The drives constituted the motive forces that activate the human psyche. According to mechanistic principles, energy that accumulates within a system leads to a buildup of pressure, which unless relieved would lead to the destruction of the system. The law of entropy stated that, in nature, systems tend to move from a higher to a lower level of organization, the death instinct being an example of the forces that lead to the disintegration of organisms. These processes are foundational to an understanding of Freud's metapsychology as he applied these principles to the workings of the mind. He conceived of the mind as an energy processing apparatus that obeys the law of entropy (see Standard Edition, 17, p. 116). The accumulation of energy within the psyche is converted into anxiety; unless the energy is discharged or transformed symptom formation ensues. Energy transformation leads to higher levels of organization whereas symptom formation leads to lower levels.

The **constancy principle** and the **pleasure principle** are the cornerstones of the economic hypothesis. The constancy principle states that the psychic apparatus tends to reduce any accumulated energy either through its graduated discharge or through the repression of the resulting excitation by ego defenses. Referring to the cases in *Studies in Hysteria* (1895c), Freud and Breuer explained that the goal of cathartic therapy was to assist the patient to discharge the built up tensions by talking about them and abreacting the feelings, that is, discharging the feelings, associated with them (see Laplanche & Pontalis, 1973, pp. 341–347).

Closely related to the constancy principle is the pleasure principle. The **Pleasure–Unpleasure Principle**, as it came to be known, posited that the goal of psychical activity is to avoid unpleasure. Increases in excitation resulting from the accumulation of undischarged energies produce unpleasure. Whereas the discharge of the accumulated tension associated with those energies produces pleasure (Laplanch & Pontalis, 1973, pp. 322–325 and 341–347; Schur & Ritvo, 1970; Sulloway, 1979, pp. 62–63).

Before we leave the economic model, it is helpful to point out the distinction that psychoanalysis makes between the terms *instinct* and *drive*, which often are used interchangeably though incorrectly. Controversy surrounds the translation of the word *Trieb* into *instinct*. The term *Trieb* does not refer to an innate, inherited, biological capacity, but rather connotes a powerful force that persistently strives for expression, which has somatic roots such as hunger or sexuality. An **instinct**, on the other hand, refers to an innate or genetically inherited species-specific goal directed set of behaviors (Waelder, 1960, pp. 97–99). Since the literature has followed the tradition of translating *Trieb* into instinct, we will follow that usage. A **drive** is the psychological manifestation of an instinct. For example, Freud speaks of a sexual instinct, but its psychological representation is the libidinal drive (Hartmann, 1948 in Brenner, p. 16).

The Topographical Hypothesis (From 1895)

Freud's **topographic hypothesis** provides a geographic and an archaeological metaphor for various psychological processes. The topographic hypothesis encompasses the view that divides the mind into three separate regions: the **conscious**, the **preconscious**, and the **unconscious**. For Freud, consciousness was a form of inner perception; it is as though the mind's eye shines a light onto the areas of awareness. Preconsciousness includes those areas that are outside of our direct awareness but may be brought to our awareness by turning our attention to them. The unconscious is the area that is hidden from us because it is actively repressed. Its content is the id, which is a repository of the unacceptable sexual and aggressive impulses.

The Dynamic Hypothesis (From 1895)

The **dynamic hypothesis** takes into account the notion of intrapsychic forces acting in opposition to one another. *Dynamic*, as different from *static*, refers to a feature of the unconscious which presses for recognition, but which is prevented from reaching consciousness by an opposing force. In this interplay, a conflict arises due to the resistances the ego encounters in the process of attempting to bring into consciousness thoughts or feeling. The dynamic hypothesis, therefore, consists of the entire panorama of the interplay of opposing mental forces, such as the ego vs. the drives, the ego vs. reality, the ego vs. the superego (Laplanche & Pontalis, 1973, p. 126).

The Genetic Hypothesis (From 1905)

The **genetic hypothesis** is central to an understanding of Freud's developmental theory. This asserts that the course of ontogeny, or individual development, follows inborn laws that represent a sequential series of invariant phases or stages. As we saw in the Introduction, this strongly held belief in ontogeny became the frame of reference for systematizing the data of his patients' case histories. It became the foundation for the theory of psychosexual or libidinal development, which includes the concepts of **regression** and **fixation**. Regression is a mechanism through which a child returns to an earlier phase of libidinal development when confronted with a conflict that is difficult to resolve. Fixation is an arrest at a phase of development become of difficulties the child cannot overcome. As Freud expanded his theoretical purview, he generated several fertile constructs about the developmental process. These include the concepts of identification, which is the process through which a child acquires characteristics of an adult to whom the child becomes attached; object choice that is the person that the child cathects with libidinal or aggressive energy; and the significance of early experiences for adult behavior (Rapaport, 1960, pp. 22–23; Ritvo, 1974; Sulloway, 1979, pp. 135–415).

The Structural Hypothesis (1923-1926)

The **structural hypothesis** differentiates the three agencies of the mind, the id, the ego, and the superego/ego ideal. Freud proposed this clear differentiation between the three agencies in *The Ego and the Id* (1923b). The id represented the instincts/drives, whereas the ego was a more coherent organization that regulates or opposes the id instincts, mediating between them and the external world. A division exists within the ego separating moral functions from the rest, called the superego. Mental conflict is the struggle between the id and the ego, between the ego and the superego, or between the demands of the id and those of reality.

The **id** (German "Das es" for "it") stands for that which is irrational, uncontrolled. It consists of the mental representations of the instinctual drives. Id energies press for gratification and impel the ego to act. Consistent with the dual-instinct theory, the energy for the id comes from two sources, aggressive energy deriving from the aggressive instinct and libido deriving from the erotic instinct. The ego is formed from energies that come from the id, energies that have been neutralized and transformed into psychological structures.

The **ego** (German "Das Ich" for "I" refers to the self, the idea of "me") is a "coherent organization of mental processes" (Freud, 1923b). In the beginning, as the ego differentiates from the id, the ego gradually emerges as that transformed part of the id, which is in contact with the outside world, making the ego the perceptual agent and executive for the id. In other words, infants achieve instinctual gratification by perceiving the opportunity for gratification in the environment and exploiting those opportunities by bringing their mouths into contact with the breast. After a few years, a marked change takes place. The ego begins to exercise a modest level of control over the id and may even oppose instinctual wishes in situations of conflict by employing such measures as repression. **Repression** is a counterforce, a defense that the ego initiates to keep the unacceptable id wishes from emerging in consciousness because of the threat they represent to the ego. As various ego functions emerge, the development of thought in the form of trial action assumes special importance. It represents a delay in the discharge of all but a small amount of available mental energy, thus providing an efficient way of energy utilization.

The **superego** (German "uber Ich" for superego) is a specialized part of the ego. It resembles the ego in that some of its elements are readily accessible to consciousness while others are not. Contained within the superego are moral injunctions and prohibitions, as well as, ideal aspirations, usually referred to as the **ego-ideal** (see Freud, 1914b). As an organized division of the mind, the super ego owes its origin in particular to identification with parental morality and ethics.

Defense Mechanisms Employed Throughout Development

The concept of **anxiety** is central to understanding the nature of the conflict between the agencies of the mind and the ego's use of defenses. When the ego is threatened by an id impulse, it responds with anxiety, which necessitates the mobilization of defenses to protect it. In the companion work to *The Ego and the Id* (1923b), *Inhibitions, Symptoms and Anxiety* (1926), Freud reformulated his thoughts about anxiety. In the first formulation of the concept of anxiety, a libidinal force presses for expression. The ego sensing danger evokes the defense of repression preventing the discharge of the drive. The result is the damming up of libido, which produces anxiety (Freud, 1895b). Later Freud reversed himself and reconceptualized anxiety. Instead of the buildup of libido causing anxiety, anxiety now arose simply from the ego's perception of the danger. When conflicts occur between the ego and the id neurotic symptoms may emerge. In this same work, Freud introduced the concept of signal or anticipatory anxiety and posited the notion that, as development unfolds, a normal sequence of unconscious danger situations emerges in which distinct levels of anxiety appear, loosely corresponding to the psychosexual phases.

Freud introduced the term defense early in his work as a set of unconscious mechanisms the ego uses to fend off anxiety producing affects. The prototypical defense was repression. Early writings laid the groundwork for the original nine **defense mechanisms**, which include the following: Repression, turning against the self, reversal, projection, introjection, or identification, regression, reaction formation, isolation, and undoing (see Table 1.1).

Table 1.1 S. Freud defense mechanisms, major work in which he refers to the defense, description of the defense, and a clinical example

Defense mechanism	Referenced in	Description	Clinical example
Repression	The Neuro-Psychoses of Defence (1894)	The ego keeps unacceptable thoughts and feelings out of conscious awareness to neutralize the accompanying anxiety through the mechanism of repression. In Freud's original topographic model of the mind, the repression barrier separates the preconscious from the unconscious.	An adult, who witnessed recurrent domestic violence as a child and felt considerable anxiety at the time, finds herself feeling anxious. The current anxiety is reawakened by the memory of those events, which had been repressed. The anxiety, however, is associated with hateful feelings she has toward her father, whom she perceives as the abuser. These hateful feelings conflict with her desire to be her father's favorite and with her libidinal wishes toward him, creating an intrapsychic conflict. The ego directs the defense of repression at both the libidinal and aggressive feelings, which the ego tries unsuccessfully to repress.
Turning against the self	Instincts and their Vicissitudes (1915b)	This is one of the earliest defenses employed by the ego. It affects the instinctual process itself. It involves turning unacceptable impulses directed toward others against the self. The anxiety that children experience in anticipation of the retaliation that can come from the outside world, which is frequently combined with anxiety originating in fantasy, leads the ego to turn the instinctual impulses against the self.	A child who is being abused by a parent sees herself as bad. She reasons that she must have done bad things or else the abuse would not occur. The child sees the parent as hateful for not providing the love and psychological nourishment she needs. At the same time, she fears that her hateful feelings will destroy the object toward whom her libidinal drives find discharge. In order to deal with the anxiety these feelings generate and to preserve the object, the child turns the hateful feelings toward herself, and believes those feelings generate the parent's response.

(continued)

Table 1.1 (continued)

Defense mechanism	Referenced in	Description	Clinical example
Reversal	Instincts and their Vicissitudes (1915b)	This defense involves the ego's attempt to deal with external dangers by actively intervening to change the conditions encountered in the world. The ego alters feelings, attitudes, traits, etc. into their opposite in order to preserve its own existence. This is one of the earliest defense mechanisms the ego employs.	A variant of the case mentioned above would include the use of this mechanism of defense. The child who hates her parent because she is abused, finds the hatred intolerable and turns it into loving feelings toward that parent. The ego reverses the aggressive drives and turns them into libidinal feelings.
Projection	Some Neurotic Mechanisms in Jealousy, Paranoia, and Homosexuality (1922b)	Use of this defense is common among children during the earliest phases of development and is considered a primitive defense. It involves attributing to others unacceptable thoughts and feelings that arise from id impulses. It requires the capacity to differentiate between the ego and the external world. This mechanism works through a process that separates the connection between thoughts associated with dangerous instincts and the ego.	A child feels considerable anxiety about his anger at a younger sibling, who has displaced him and deprived him of his caregivers' attention. Knowing that his caregivers would disapprove of these feelings, he claims that his sibling is responsible for their constant bickering because the sibling hates him. The child represses his rage and attributes it to the sibling.

Incorporation, Introjection, or identification	Some Neurotic Mechanisms in Jealousy, Paranoia, and Homosexuality (1922b)	The process through which the superego develops is through the use of this defense mechanism. The defense involves internalizing those aspects of the object that involve approval and disapproval of the child. Approval is associated with libidinal energies and disapproval is associated with aggressive energies. Anxiety arises when the child experiences the object of approval or disapproval as coming from within rather than from outside, since the standards and expectations are now part of the child's internal world. The child has taken in the parents' values.	A person who has lost a parent experiences guilt because of past conduct that led to that parent's disapproval. The child deals with the anxiety generated by that guilt by attempting to "act grown up," taking on the characteristics of the dead parent and behaving as the child believes the parent would have wished.
Regression	Appendix to Inhibitions, Symptoms, and Anxiety (1926)	This is also one of the earliest defense mechanisms employed by the ego. The essential feature of this defense is the return to an earlier libidinal phase in order to avoid the anxieties of the present. Patients with obsessional neurosis often employ this defensive technique.	A boy who has entered the phallic/oedipal phase is struggling with the aggressive feelings he feels towards his father and at the same time is made anxious by his libidinal feelings directed at his mother. In the face of the intolerable anxiety these impulses evoke, the child regresses to the oral phase, wishing to be fed instead of feeding himself, which he is perfectly capable of doing. He becomes clingy and overly dependent, speaking and acting like a baby.

(continued)

Table 1.1 (continued)

Defense mechanism	Referenced in	Description	Clinical example
Reaction formation	Appendix to Inhibitions, Symptoms, and Anxiety (1926)	This defense secures the ego against the return of repressed impulses. In order to avoid the breakthrough into consciousness of an impulse, the ego uses the instinct's capacity for reversal by replacing an unwanted impulse in consciousness with its opposite. It is different from reversal in that the ego does not only convert the impulse into its opposite, but also the person protests too much that it is the opposite of what in actuality the person feels.	A child in the midst of being toilet trained experiences the impulse of playing with his feces. Knowing that such play is unacceptable, in order to deal with the anxiety generated he insists on having his diapers changed repeatedly, even when they are barely soiled. He continually expresses pride in how clean he is and how compliant he is to being toilet trained.
Isolation	Appendix to Inhibitions, Symptoms, and Anxiety (1926)	This defense involves the process of sequestering the unacceptable impulses through the repression of feelings associated with a particular content. Through this process, instinctual impulses are detached from their context, while being retained in consciousness. The person isolates ideas from affect so that associations seem meaningless, and therefore less charged. This defense is also associated with obsessional neurosis in particular.	A child who feels enraged at his caregivers because he feels that thay have treated him unfairly begins coolly to torment his cat, ignoring the poor creature's distress. His cruelty represents the sequestration and displacement of his rage at his caregivers.

Undoing	Appendix to Inhibitions, Symptoms, and Anxiety (1926)	This defense involves erasing the effects of unacceptable thoughts or feelings by engaging in conduct that eradicates the effects of the underlying impulse. Patients who use ritualistic behaviors may be silently "atoning" for the guilt produced by the repressed unacceptable wishes.	A girl, in the midst of the oedipal phase, has developed a bedtime ritual of arranging all her dolls in a row on the shelf next to her bed, spending an inordinate amount of time in the activity. She insists that the order in which this has to be done be the same every night or else she has to start over from the beginning. The girl is defending against aggression she directs during her play with the dolls, mistreating them and punishing them. Unconsciously, her anger is at her mother, whom she perceives as the rival for her father's attention.

Theory of Development

Freud's developmental model describes the psychosexual phases that progress ontogenetically and epigenetically. It provides an account of the biologically determined process that gives form to the systematic unfolding of a set of potentials adaptively interacting with the environment.

The Psychosexual Framework

In *Three Essays on the Theory of Sexuality* (1905a), Freud established the first psychological developmental model, the psychosexual framework, an expression of the genetic hypothesis. This framework traces instinctual development, the vicissitudes of the libido, or pleasurable energy, through the maturation of various erotogenic zones, which are specific areas of the body charged with psychosexual energy; these are the mouth, the anus, and the phallus (Freud, 1905a, pp. 183–184). It remained for Abraham fully to work aggression into the psychosexual model. Abraham elaborated these **psychosexual phases** (Freud, 1905a), dividing the oral and the anal phases into two phases each, the libidinal and the aggressive. He maintained the developmental sequence, in harmony with Freud's positions that a shift occurs from one erotogenic zone to another (Makari, 2008, pp. 374–379).

The *Three Essays on the Theory of Sexuality* (1905a) is considered Freud's most significant contribution to the theory of development (1905a, p. 126). It is divided into three parts. In part one, "The Sexual Aberrations," Freud considers the nature of sexual aberrations including homosexuality, bisexuality, the perversions, and others. These aberrations of component instincts result from deviations and fixations in libidinal development. Libido was broken down into three parts: the impulse, the aim, and the object. Homosexuality, like heterosexuality, emerged from a common biological sexual impulse. For homosexuals, the impulse was the same as for typically developing individuals, the aim was the sexual act itself, and the object was of the same gender of the individual. Because there is one sexual instinct from which all manifestations of sexual behavior derive, the perversions are part of abnormal sexual development as are the psychoneuroses. Using the metaphor from photography, Freud states that "the neuroses are … the *negative* of perversions" (1905a, p. 165, our italics), by which he means that whereas in the neuroses the underlying motivating impulses are repressed and remain unseen, in the perversions those impulses find expression as images in fantasy or enactment in symptoms (see Quinodoz, 2005, p. 59). Freud turned to Fleiss and his promotion of the concept that perhaps inborn bisexuality is a normal constituent of biological functioning. Bisexuality could be used to account for perversions in women and hysteria in men. Freud believed that "perverse actions were exactly the same in content as the repressed fantasies of hysterics." (Makari, 2008, p. 99) Therefore, neuroses (viz., hysteria) and perversions are opposite sides, positive and negative, of the same human sexuality coin.

Gay (1988) reports that in response to a letter he received from an American woman, Freud answered:

> I gather from your letter that your son is a homosexual. I am most impressed by the fact that you do not mention this term yourself in your information about him. May I question you why you avoid it? … Homosexuality is assuredly no advantage, but it is nothing to be ashamed of, no vice, no degradation, it cannot be classified as an illness; we consider it to be a variation of the sexual function, produced by a certain arrest of sexual development (p. 610).

In part two, "Infantile Sexuality," Freud sets forth the framework for the psychosexual model. This section includes a broad range of propositions from the concept of erotogenetic zone, which are bodily orifices whose stimulation produces pleasure, to the concept of a latency phase that precedes adolescence, to an outright challenge to the prevailing opinion that sexuality begins at puberty, to children's notions about reproduction. Of significance to us is the section on the phases of development of sexual organization. The infant's sexuality begins with the pleasure associated with the stimulation of the erotogenic zones. During the pregenital phase, the infant's investment is autoerotic, that is, the flow of libido is directed at the pleasurable zones. This is the oral phase where the mouth is the source of greatest pleasure. Organized around sadistic impulses, the anal phase follows because the child responds to the demands for toilet training by wishing to hold on to his bowels in reaction to his parents' expectations that he give up their contents. The problem of what to do with masturbation was solved, for now, by marginalizing it as an after effect of trauma, and making it a normal aspect of infantile sexuality through the expression of erotic daydreams, while keeping it as the 'primary addiction' in hysteria. In the third edition of *Three Essays* (1914), Freud inserted Ernst Haeckle's Darwinian notion that ontogeny recapitulates phylogeny. Freud joined Haeckle's concept that the development of the individual repeats the development of the species with the notion of the **polymorphous perverse** disposition of the infant. By polymorphous perversion, Freud is referring to the infant's indiscriminate search for pleasure from whatever erogenous source is available, acting upon the impulse rather than repressing it. This disposition in the unrepressed baby was a vestige of our primitive ancestors. Here evolution made its bold appearance through the genetic metapsychological explanation for the psychosexual developmental model.

In part three, "The Transformations of Puberty," Freud provides an equally rich set of concepts that have entered the vocabulary of classical psychoanalytic theories of adolescent development. He discussed the differentiation between sexuality in men and women and arrived at the conclusion that "the sexuality of little girls is of a wholly masculine character" (*SE*, 1905a, p. 219). The leading zone in females is the clitoris, an anatomical part "homologous to the masculine genital zone of the glans penis" (*SE*, 1905a, p. 221). In puberty, for girls, the centrality of the masculine clitoris undergoes repression and, after a period of sexual anesthesia, sexual excitation is transmitted "to the adjacent female sexual parts, just as -to use a simile – pine shavings can be kindled in order to set a log of harder wood on fire" (*SE*, 1905a, p. 221). At this point the leading zone is transferred to the vaginal orifice. This is different in boys who retain their leading zone unchanged from childhood. Freud proposed that finding a sexual love object is similar to the prototype of infants sucking at their mother's breast. A satisfactory resolution to the Oedipus complex depends on a functional incest barrier and on experiencing a positive latency period. The incest barrier is laid down with the internalizations of the parental prohibitions and the formation of a superego. Finally, neuroses emerge when "a young man falls in love seriously for the first time with a mature woman or a girl with an elderly man in a position of authority." Then the incomplete resolution of the issues of this phase becomes manifest.

During Freud's lifetime many contributors expanded the original three-phase framework (each with two subphases) into six, recognizing that adolescence was essentially a reworking and recapitulation of Freud/Abraham's first three (Freud, 1905a, p. 22; Jones, 1922). Here, we include the original three-phase model (Abraham, 1924b, p. 496). With the addition of aggression as the second instinct, he clarified that all of sexuality consisted of fusions, to one degree or the other, of both instincts (Freud, 1905a, 1912a, 1920b). Abraham did not include ages to the phases, so we must infer them. Abraham referred to the table as provisional and compared it to attempting to set a time table to the movement of express trains in that the end points can be known, but the in between, halting-places, vary with each individual (Abraham, 1924b, pp. 495–496) (see Table 1.2).

In what follows, we present Freud's mature formulation on psychosexual development from 1898 through 1940 (1905d, pp. 244-245) as modified by Abraham in his publications on the subject between 1921 and 2 years after his death in 1925 (Abraham, 1917, 1921, 1924a, 1924b, 1925; Freud, 1898, 1905d, 1906, 1908a, 1908b, 1910a, 1910b, 1912a, 1912c, 1913a, 1913b, 1914b, 1916-1917, 1917a, 1918, 1919, 1920a, 1922b, 1923a, 1923b, 1924c, 1925, 1927b, 1931a, 1931b, 1933, 1940a [1938], 1940b [1938]. This final formulation is modified from *Kaplan and Sadock* (2003b), *Synopsis of Psychiatry.* pp. 201–203) and from Fenichel (1945), *The Psychoanalytic Theory of the Neuroses*, pp. 54–101)

There are six developmental phases:

1. The oral, which lasts from birth through 1 to 1½ years of age
2. The anal, which lasts from 1½ to 3 years of age
3. The phallic/urethral/narcissistic, which lasts from the ages of 3–4
4. The genital/Oedipus, which lasts from the ages of 3 to 5–6 years of age

Table 1.2 The three stages and substages of model of development with stages of object sexual investment

Stages of libidinal organization	Stages of object love
I. A. Earlier oral stage (sucking)	Auto-erotism (without object) (preambivalent)
I. B. Later oral stage (cannibalistic, biting)	Narcissism (total incorporation of the object) (Ambivalent)
II. A. Earlier anal-sadistic stage	Partial love with incorporation (Ambivalent)
II. B. Later anal-sadistic stage	Partial love (Ambivalent)
III. A. Earlier genital stage (phallic)	Object-love with exclusion of genitals (Ambivalent)
III. B. Final genital stage	Object love (Postambivalent)

Modified version of Abraham (1927, p. 496)

5. Latency, which lasts for 5 or 6 to 11 or 13 years of age
6. Late genital or the adolescent phase, which lasts from puberty through young adulthood

Six sets of processes are associated with each phase: (a) *the significance of the erogenous zones*; (b) *the dynamics and behavioral characteristics of the phase*; (c) *specific core defenses associated with the phase*; (d) *the central issues and tasks that organize* **the** *phase*; and (e) *the character traits that result from the successful resolution of the issues associated with the phase.*

Oral Phase (from birth to 1/1.5 years) (Abraham, 1924a; Freud, 1905a, pp. 150–151, 179–185)

Erogenous zone: The mouth, tongue, lips, and skin are the primary sense organs or erogenous zones that organize the processes that take place during this phase.

Dynamics/behavioral characteristics: The oral erogenous zone dominates the organization of the infant's psyche through the first 18 months. Oral sensations include thirst, hunger, pleasurable tactile sensations and those related to swallowing and satiation (Freud, 1905a, pp. 179–180). There are two drive components: libidinal and aggressive. The libidinal components manifest early, with the infant seeking gratification and experiencing the quiescence that occurs at the end of nursing. Oral aggressive manifestations including biting, chewing, spitting and/or crying accompany wishes and fantasies of biting, devouring and destroying. Abraham divided the original oral phase into the infant's preambivalent sucking phase and an ambivalent biting phase. Ambivalence refers to the coexistence of love, that is, libidinal investment, and hate, that is, aggression directed towards an object. The biting phase that marks the beginning of ambivalent feelings towards the object is concurrent with teething; it involves the cannibalistic destruction of the object (Abraham, 1924b, pp. 450–451). When an infant experiences an increase in tension in the absence of the object, the infant hallucinates the gratifying experience with the object, thus recreating it in her absence.

Phase specific core defenses are projection, introjection, reversal, repression, and turning against the self.

Central issues/tasks: The task during this phase is for the infant to get basic needs met and for the ego to deal successfully with the oral components of both libidinal and aggressive drives.

Phase specific anxiety level is automatic anxiety as distinct from the more developmentally advanced signal anxiety. Freud associated this with the reaction to birth, the human's first experience with the affect anxiety. Infants fear that their very existence is threatened due to unbearable frustration over hunger, excessive stimulation (loud noises, toxic smells), fever, unusual temperatures and so on. Automatic anxiety was later renamed annihilation anxiety by ego psychologists (Freud, 1926; Berzoff, Flanagan, & Hertz, 1996, p. 75). Annihilation anxiety is also the experience associated with the fear of the loss of the object during which infants fear that their very existence is threatened. When infants feel abandoned or the object becomes unavailable, anxiety overwhelms the ego.

Character traits that result from the successful resolution of oral phase themes/issues include the development of curiosity, a capacity to give and to receive from others without excessive dependency or envy. In addition, a capacity to rely on others with a sense of trust accompanied by a sense of self-confidence and the capacity for self-reliance become evident (Abraham, 1924a, 1925).

Anal Phase (1/1.5 to 3 years) (Freud, 1905a, pp. 185–187, 239; Abraham, 1921; Jones, 1913, 1918)

Erogenous zone: The anus is the toddler's primary erogenous zone in this phase.

Dynamics/behavioral characteristics: Anal-erotism and anal-sadism are the central dynamics of this phase, with the anal-erogenous zone as the chief organizer for all excitation that is discharged through defecation. Anal-erotism manifests as the toddler's sexual pleasure in anal functioning, specifically in retaining the precious feces and in releasing/presenting them as a valuable gift to the parent. Anal-sadism manifests as expressions of the toddler's aggressive wishes connected to discharging feces, which for infants represent powerful and destructive weapons. In children, these wishes manifest in scatological behaviors such as fantasies of bombings and explosions. Both oral and anal experiences generate sadistic impulses, which interact with each other and undergo sublimation to produce the power necessary for the toddler to carry on the struggle for existence. Abraham suggested the anal phase be divided into two phases due to the child's ambivalent attitude that includes both tender and contemptuous feelings. In the anal sadistic process two positions, those of elimination and retention, become possible fixation points. In the first, the toddler derives hostile excretory pleasure from defecation and is invested in destroying and losing the object. In the second, pleasure in retention occurs, which the toddler equates with the preservation of the object. Eventually, the toddler becomes invested in controlling the object and displays its love with the willingness to sacrifice the feces for the object's sake (Abraham, 1924b, pp. 432, 501).

Phase specific core defenses include all the defenses of the previous phase and, in addition, identification, undoing, reaction formation, isolation, and regression.

Central issues/tasks: The primary aim of anal erotism is the toddler's capacity to enjoy the pleasurable sensations associated with excretion that become possible with the maturation of voluntary anal sphincter control. Later experience teaches the child that holding back the fecal mass may increase stimulation of the rectal mucosa. Those anal-retentive tendencies can provide security against anxiety. While the connection between orality and sadism is analogous to that between anality and sadism, two factors must be added to these as emerging during the anal phase. First, the toddler imagines the act of elimination to be as destructive as that of incorporation. Second, the toddler considers the factor of social power to be involved in sphincter mastery. In training for cleanliness, the child finds opportunities to express opposition against adults over the dependency/independence issue. The fact that the toddler experiences pleasure at a time when feelings of omnipotence predominate enhances the magical narcissistic overvaluation of toddler's own feces.

Coprophilia, i.e., obsession with feces, and smearing are pathological behaviors traced to this phase. The anal period is essentially a period during which the toddler strives for independence. The toddler wishes to separate and become individuated from parents. The toddler struggles against parental control and dependence on parental functions. The toddler attains autonomy and more mature/higher levels of interdependence at the risk of excessive shame and self-doubt.

Phase specific anxiety level is the toddler's fear of the loss of the love object or separation anxiety.

Character traits resulting from successful resolution of anal phase themes/issues: The resolution of toddlers' conflicts of this phase provides the basis for successful autonomy. This resolution also results in a capacity for independence and personal initiative without guilt, a capacity for autonomous behavior without a sense of shame or self-doubt, without ambivalence, and a capacity for willing cooperation without either excessive willfulness, self-diminution or a sense of defeat.

The anal triadic configuration that emerges during this phase includes obstinacy, pedantic orderliness, and parsimony, which can constitute, either in whole or in part, adult personality features and/or styles. Freud theorized that the permanent character traits are either unchanged prolongations of the original instincts, sublimations of those instincts, or reaction formations against them (Freud, 1908b, 1917c; Rothgeb, 1973, p. 196).

Phallic/Urethral/Narcissistic Phase (3–4 years) (Freud, 1905a, p. 205, 239; Abraham, 1917)[2]

Erogenous zone: The genitals, the penis, and the vagina are the primary erogenous zones of this phase.

Dynamics/behavioral characteristics: Urethral erotism refers to the youngsters' pleasure in urination, as well as, the pleasure in urethral retention analogous to anal retention. Young children invest aspects of urethral function with sadism reflecting anal sadistic urges. The loss of urethral control, as in enuresis, may have regressive significance that reactivates anal phase conflicts. Urethral erotism is frequently linked with ambition and the fantasy that the young boy can put out a fire with his urinary stream (*Civilization and Its Discontents, 1930*).

Phase specific core defenses include all defenses of the prior phases.

Central issues/tasks: For the young boy, the central task of this phase is to sublimate the narcissistic grandiosity associated with guiding and controlling his urine stream and to gain mastery over performance issues and overcome the vulnerability to loss of control.

Phase specific anxiety level: The young child's phase specific anxiety is related to the loss of the love of the love object and to **castration anxiety**. The boy is in the throes of the oedipal struggle and fears his father's retaliation by the removal of his precious penis.

Character traits resulting from successful resolution of urethral phase themes/issues: Urethral competence provides the young child with a sense of pride and pleasure. A sense of competence emerges from the successful performance and accomplishment of tasks (Freud, 1908c; Abraham, 1924b). Urethral performance can be an opportunity for the mastery of body functions as the small

[2] Note that Freud and Abraham remained silent as to the parallel processes in girls during this stage and during the next stage. This silence is consistent with Freud's overall phallocentric view of development in which he regarded girls as castrated boys.

boy seeks to imitate and match the father's adult performance. The resolution of urethral conflicts sets the phase for budding gender differentiation and subsequent identifications.

Genital/Oedipal Phase (3–5/6 years) (Abraham, 1925; Freud, 1905a, pp. 162–163, 187–190, 226)

Erogenous zone: The genitals, the penis and the vagina are the erogenous zones of this phase.

Dynamics/behavioral characteristics: Romantic feelings towards the parent of opposite sex and fears of the same sex parent become recurrent themes for the child during the paradigmatic **oedipal phase**. The child discovers genital differences and derives distinctive meanings as to their significance.

In the case of the boy, he identifies with the father whom he fears as a harmful and dangerous competitor for the mother. The boy wants to displace and castrate his father. By internalizing the father's threat and making it a part of his own psychology, the boy becomes more able to institute defenses against this level of anxiety. At the same time, the boy struggles to control his frightening, incestuous and parricidal wishes. His gratification in sharing with the father's sexual omnipotence, via a fantasy of oral incorporation, helps him master the anxiety.

The consolidation of the superego occurs as the boy identifies with his father and internalizes the father's prohibitions against incestuous wishes. The superego can then exist in harmony with the ego; it can also exist in disharmony and give rise to guilt feelings or if oedipal resolution is incomplete it can motivate a boy to punish himself with no overt, i.e., conscious, reason (Arlow & Brenner, 1964, pp. 39–41).

As for the girl, Freud postulated that because of her existing castrated condition, since she does not have a penis, she becomes angry with mother for placing her in such a state and envies the boy, his equipment and his position. Her loving, longing feelings for mother conflict with her fears of engulfment by the mother. The girl then turns to her father as a heterosexual object choice, wishing for a baby from him as compensation for the anger and disappointment at mother. However, because these wishes confront her in a dilemma that is impossible to resolve, she develops **penis envy** as a substitute for her desire for a child. What ensues is a *spongy* superego, which is a superego that is not as rigid and controlling as that of boys.[3]

Phase specific core defenses include all of the defenses of the prior phases.

Central issues/tasks: The central issues of this phase for boys and girls are the resolution of the oedipal conflict. The resolution lays the foundation for gender identity and serves to integrate the residues of previous phases of psychosexual development into a predominantly genital-sexual orientation. The establishment of the oedipal situation is essential for subsequent identifications that will serve as the basis for enduring dimensions of character organization.

[3] For a balanced discussion of Freud's phallocentrism in the oedipal formulation of women's psychology, see Berzoff et al., 1996, Chap. 10.

Phase specific anxiety level: At the phallic level, the specific anxiety is castration anxiety and the beginning of superego anxiety, that is, fear of one's conscience or guilt.

Character traits resulting from successful resolution of phallic/oedipal phase themes/ issues: This phase provides the foundation for an emerging sense of sexual identity, a sense of curiosity without embarrassment, initiative without guilt, as well as, a sense of mastery over objects and persons in the environment, and over internal processes and impulses. An appetite for intellectuality, generosity, sociability, optimism (Abraham, 1924a, pp. 399–404), an interest in community affairs and concern with acquisition and loss of possessions are capacities credited to this phase (Abraham, 1925). Considerable internal resources are devoted to the regulation of drive impulses and to their direction to constructive ends, a process called sublimation (Freud, 1924d). Whereas Freud attributes the traits described above to boys, the outcome for girls is the character traits of passivity, receptivity, narcissism, masochism and, as a result of the sublimation of masturbatory activity, the capacity for plaiting and weaving (S. Freud, 1933, p. 132); all of which stem from the girls' perceptions of themselves as lacking a penis.

Latency Phase (5/6–11/13, puberty) (Freud, 1905a, pp. 176–179)

Erogenous zone: The zone is nonspecific in this phase.

Dynamics/behavioral characteristics: Latency is a phase of relative quiescence or inactivity of the sexual drive. Far from being a period devoid of sexual interest and activity, Freud believed that latency was a time of partial muffling of sexual impulses, with energy diverted into other channels. Infantile amnesia or forgetting of earlier life events turns everyone's childhood into something like a prehistoric glacial epoch in which no importance is attached to the beginnings of sexual life (Freud, 1905a, p. 178; Freud, 1939, p. 66; Sulloway, 1979, p. 176).

Behavioral characteristics of this phase include the instinctual impulses coming under greater control due to the establishment of the superego and further ego development. Sexual interests become latent with homosexual interests and friendships being a substitute for both boys and girls. A sublimation of libidinal and aggressive energies into industrious learning and purposeful play activities occurs. Curiosity opens up the desire to explore the environment. Children become more proficient in dealing with the world and with people around them. Their skills expand and, with the relative strength of regulatory elements, behaviors arise that tend to be obsessive and hyper-controlling.

Phase specific core defenses include all the defenses of the previous levels and in addition sublimation, reaction formation, reversal, obsessive-compulsive defenses (Freud, 1905a, p. 178)

Central issues/tasks: The primary task of this phase is the further integration of oedipal identifications and a consolidation of sex-role identity and sex roles. The relative quiescence and control of instinctual impulses allows for the development of ego and mastery skills. Further identificatory components may be added to the oedipal ones based on broadening contacts with other significant figures outside the family, such as teachers and coaches.

Phase specific anxiety level: During this phase, children experience all the anxieties characteristic of previous levels as the consolidation of the superego occurs. Shame, disgust and morality are central axes of anxiety (Freud, 1905a, p. 178).

Character traits resulting from successful resolution of latency phase themes/issues: During this period, the integration and consolidation of previous attainments in psychosexual development and the establishment of decisive patterns of adaptive functioning takes place. The child can develop a sense of industry and a capacity for mastery of objects and concepts that allows autonomous function with a sense of initiative without running the risk of failure, defeat, or a sense of inferiority. These important attainments need to be integrated further and ultimately form the essential basis for a mature adult life of satisfaction in work and love.

Late Genital or Adolescence Phase (from puberty to young adulthood) (Freud, 1905a, pp. 207–230; Jones, 1922)

Erogenous zone: The erogenous zones of this phase are the genitals, the penis and vagina.

Dynamics/behavioral characteristics: Puberty heralds this phase, which sees the reemergence of infantile masturbation. This phase recapitulates the phallic/oedipal phase (Jones, 1922). The physiological maturation of the systems of genital functioning and the attendant hormonal systems leads to an intensification of drives, particularly libidinal drives. This produces a regression in personality organization, which reopens conflicts of previous phases of psychosexual development and provides the opportunity for a resolution of those conflicts in the context of achieving a mature sexual and adult identity (Fenichel, 1945, p. 111, Freud, 1936, pp. 137–138).

Phase specific core defenses: All of the defenses associated with prior phases are evident in this phase.

Central issues/tasks: The primary tasks of this phase are the ultimate separation from dependence on and attachment to the parents and the establishment of mature, nonincestuous object relations. In addition, the resolution of the issues of this phase leads to the establishment of a mature sense of personal identity and the acceptance and integration of a set of adult roles and functions that permit new adaptive integrations with social expectations and cultural values.

Phase specific anxiety level: Phase specific levels of anxiety may include some or all the manifestation of anxiety that occur in previous levels, but these anxieties are organized primarily under superego anxiety. In addition, at this phase of development the ego ideal evolves as a structural component of the super-ego. The super-ego emerges as a comprehensive psychic structure that embodies the three functions of "self-observation, of conscience and of [maintaining] the ideal." (Freud, 1933, p. 66 and pp. 64–65) In making the distinction between the super-ego and the ego ideal, Freud is establishing the difference between a sense of guilt and a sense of inferiority (Laplanch & Pontalis, 1973, p. 145). "The final transformation which the fear of the super-ego undergoes is, it seems to me, the fear of death (or the fear for life) which is a fear of the super-ego projected on to the powers of destiny" (Freud, 1926, p. 140).

Character traits resulting from successful resolution of adolescent phase themes/ issues: The successful resolution and reintegration of previous psychosexual phases in the full adolescent genital phase sets the phase for a mature personality with a capacity for satisfying genital functioning and a self-integrated and consistent sense of identity. Such a person has reached a gratifying capacity for self-realization and meaningful participation in the areas of work and love and in the creative and productive application to fulfilling and meaningful goals and values.

Case Illustration: Little Hans

In 1903, Max Graf (1873-1958), a musicologist, joined the Wednesday Psychological Society and in 1906, Graf began supplying Freud with written reports on the sexual development of his 3–year–old son, Herbert. Some years earlier Freud had treated Mrs. Graf and so had direct knowledge about the family. On Herbert's third birthday (1907), Freud had carried a rocking horse up four flights of stairs to the family apartment as a birthday gift. Max Graf began to consult with Freud about Herbert, who was 4 years and 9 months and had developed a phobia about horses. Freud gave Herbert the pseudonym of *Little Hans* and referred to him as "our hero" because this case of a typical childhood neurosis corroborated the infantile origin of adult neuroses. Freud believed that this case illustrated inferences drawn in *Three Essays on the Theory of Sexuality* (1905a). This celebrated case is considered the founding case of child psychoanalysis, even though Freud did not personally treat Herbert. Freud saw Herbert in his office only once; however, he consulted irregularly with his father and gave advice to guide the family in parenting the child. The consultations lasted 5 months and concluded, in the early summer of 1908, when Little Hans firmly identified with his loving father and became symptom free. With the permission of Mr. and Mrs. Graf, Freud published the account of Little Hans in 1909. In writing up the case, Freud quotes extensively from the notes that Hans' father gave him while interspersing comments and interpretations as he finds confirmation for his theories in the young boy's illness.

In a note in the postscript to the case, Freud indicated that, in 1922, he accidentally ran into a strapping, well-adjusted youth of 19, who was the grown up *Little Hans.* By that time his parents had divorced, each had remarried, and he remained on good terms with them. He had forgotten everything related to his encounter with psychoanalysis, which Freud attributed to childhood amnesia. Herbert Graf (1904–1973) eventually went on to become a noted stage director for the Metropolitan Opera in New York, wrote a number of books and articles on the subject, lived a productive life and died in Geneva (Gay, 1988; pp. 255–261 and Schoenewolf, pp.43–62).

What follows is a summary of Freud's *Analysis of a Phobia in a Five-Year Old Boy* (1909).

Introduction

Hans was almost 3-years old when his father noticed that Hans had developed an interest in who had and who did not have a penis. Hans was a "…cheerful, good natured, and lively little boy…" (Freud, 1909, p. 6) who, like all children during this stage, developed a preoccupation with his "widdler." He asked his mother if she had a wee-wee maker and she said she did. He asked his father and others the same question as well. At the zoo in front of the lion's cage, he noticed the lion's wee-wee maker. Observing a cow being milked, he said to his father that there was milk coming out of the cow's wee-wee maker. Seeing water come out of a steam engine, he wondered where its wee-wee maker was. He was able to understand that animate objects had wee-wee makers whereas inanimate ones did not. He then became fascinated with touching his penis.

At 3 years and 6 months-of-age, his mother caught Hans playing with his penis and threatened him with castration if he persisted. She said she would ask Dr. A to cut it off and asked Hans how he would wee-wee without one. Hans replied "With my bottom" (Freud, 1909, p. 8). Freud marks this event as the beginning of Hans' castration complex. At around this time, his sister Hanna was born, an event that required that Hans be moved out of the parent's bedroom to make room for Hanna's crib. He watched Hanna being given a bath and began to be curious about his sister's tiny wee-wee maker. Soon after, he developed an intense interest in storks and activities associated with birth. Hans, having lost his position as the only child, began to question the story of the stork being responsible for Hanna's arrival. If the stork brought children, then, he reasoned, Hanna could be returned to where she came from.

Next, Hans' father reported that the boy displayed an attraction towards both boys and girls. He hugged both boys and girls enthusiastically. Freud interpreted this interest as evidence of bisexuality. At four and a quarter years-of-age Hans, while being given his usual morning bath, noticed that his mother powdered him around his penis taking care not to touch it. Hans said, "Why don't you put your finger there?" Mother responded, "Because that'd be piggish." "What's that? Piggish? Why?" he asked. "Because it's not proper." Hans laughingly said, "But it's great fun." (p. 19). On walks with his father, Hans considered it pleasurable to have his father unbutton his knickers and assist Hans in urinating. Hans enjoyed this activity, which Freud interpreted as an opportunity for the development of homosexual inclinations. Freud also understood the entire set of events as ample confirmation of infantile sexuality (p. 20).

The Analysis of Hans' Phobia

When Hans was 4 years, 9 months-of-age, Hans' father wrote to Freud that Hans had developed a fear that "*a horse will bite him in the street*" (p. 22). His father speculated that the grounds for the fear no doubt "was prepared by sexual over-excitation due to his mother's tenderness," since she would give in to Hans' insistence that she take him to bed with her, if he pestered her enough. When Hans had an anxiety dream that he would lose his mother, she tried to reassure him by taking him to bed with her. At this point, Freud attributes Hans' intensified anxiety to his repressed affection for his mother. Father also thought that the fear was connected to Hans' earlier interest in the large penises that horses have and he inferred that as his mother was "so large she must have a widdler like a horse" (p. 22, reference p. 10). Father further reported that Hans became afraid to go out into the street and his spirits were a bit low in the evening, otherwise he was progressing well on all other fronts.

His parents observed Hans engaging frequently in masturbatory activity at night in bed. However, Freud discounted that activity as the source of the anxiety and the emerging phobia. About a month later, Hans was able to go out for a walk in the park with his father, at which point his fear of horses was transformed into a wish to look at them. After a bout of influenza, his fears of venturing outdoors returned. At this point, his fears took the form that, if he went out, white horses would bite him, especially if he were to touch them. Father interpreted that to mean that Hans was not talking about being afraid of what would happen if he touched a horse, but rather the consequences of touching his penis.

To label the symptoms for Hans and make him aware of their irrationality, his Father began referring to Hans' fears as *nonsense.* He suggested that they take more walks to get over the fears. Hans insisted on attributing his worsening fear to putting his hand on his penis every night (p. 30). He seemed to associate his conflict over masturbatory activities with the fact that girls might not have a penis, consequently he could lose his. He seemed worried about the large penises that horses have and complained that his was smaller. His father tried to assure him it would grow, as he grew up. As a way to reassure himself against his mother's earlier threat that he would lose it if he played with it, Hans told his father, "It's fixed in, of course" (p. 35). Freud notes that the possibility that some people did not have penises was "bound to have a shattering effect on his self-confidence and to have aroused his castration anxiety" (p. 36). A dream soon followed in which a big giraffe and a crumpled one appeared in his room. The big giraffe called out as Hans took away the crumpled one. Then it stopped calling out and Hans sat down on the crumpled one. His father interpreted the dream to mean that he – father–represented the big giraffe who often calls out to mother not to taken Hans into bed with her. Hans wishes to defy his father and sit on top of his mother; an expression of his wish to seduce mother.

Soon after, Father and son visited the zoo and Hans complained that a police officer would arrest them for smashing a window. Since no window had been smashed, Father interpreted this complaint as related to Hans' guilt feelings for anger at father who was Hans' rival for mother's affection. This represented the other side of Hans' oedipal conflict. In Father's eyes, this confirmed the establishment of the incest taboo. Later that day, Father took Hans to visit the Professor [Freud] with the intent of helping him confront the undiminished fear of horses. In response to a question from Freud, Hans commented that he was bothered by what horses wear in front of their mouths and by the black surrounding their mouths. Freud invited Hans to look at his father and suggested that the father's eyeglasses and moustache matched the description he gave of the horses' harness. The fear of horses was a displacement of his fear of his father. Freud, referring to the confirmation of the Oedipus, told Hans that long ago "… I had known that a little Hans would come who would be so fond of his mother that he would be bound to feel afraid of his father because of it" (p. 42). Father asked Hans why he was afraid of him, to which Hans said that father hit him. Father was astonished, but remembered that this was a reflexive reaction on father's part after Hans head butted him in the stomach. Freud interpreted this as Hans' hostility towards his father and possibly as punishment for such a feeling. The interpretation hit the mark as Hans asked Freud "Does the Professor talk with God?" (p. 42). Hans had identified with the horses that could bite and that were a threat to him. Now he was the one who could be like the horses and could threaten his father. This identification coincided with Han's defiant behavior.

In another context, Hans associated the horses' different colors with "Doing lumpf" – defecating; brown horses resembling fecal products. These associations further reminded him of women's black and yellow underwear or drawers, which he had noticed when he observed his mother on the toilet. Looking at underwear, a sight that afforded him much pleasure, had now turned to disgust (pp. 54-56). When Father confronted Hans about his mixed feelings toward his mother, Hans responded with a complex fantasy. The fantasy was associated with an incident of a plumber who had come to fix a fixture at the public bath that the family frequented during vacation. Hans said, "I was in the bath, and then the plumber came and unscrewed it. Then he took a big borer and stuck it into my stomach" (p. 65). His father interpreted that fantasy as related to Hans' annoyance at his father for pushing him out of mother's bed with his big penis.

Hans, in an effort to make sense out of where babies come from, next revisited old memories and fantasies about his sister's birth, the roles of the stork and the midwife, the red stork box into which Hanna was placed, the mother's bleeding and birthing screams. Hans next entertained sadistic fantasies about whipping horses and beating mother and recalled seeing mother beat carpets. Further fantasies/wishes of naked boys in the street and Hans laying down in the grass squeezing an egg out between his legs and playing with a rubber doll with a pen knife being squeezed out between its legs, all attested to the continuing effort to explain the birth process.

Freud felt that Hans' parents had delayed much too long explaining to him the facts of life, to which he was arriving through the understanding he was gaining from the analysis. To help him understand they drew the analogy between giving birth to producing lumpf. This explanation led to considerable symptomatic improvement. Hans later admitted he gets jealous when he sees mother giving father a kiss. Father then interpreted a wish Hans' had that his father die and be driven away in a funeral cart enabling Hans to take the place of father with mother. Hans imagined himself being his father producing babies, but not giving birth. In his play with puppets, Hans made it clear that he had figured out his future role. "Instead of putting his father out of the way, he granted him the same happiness that he desired himself; he made him a grandfather and married *him* to his own mother too" (p. 97). In Hans' concluding fantasy the plumber returned and removed his behind and widdler and gave him a bigger behind and widdler like those of his father. Han's was more enlightened about sexual matters and now having gotten over his phobia of horses, had resumed his happy disposition.

Discussion

In the summarizing section, Freud makes three points. First, Hans was normal little boy who was experiencing the unfolding psychosexual drama intensified at three and one half years of age by the birth of his sister. The nature of the drama followed and confirmed the outline put forward in *Three Essays on the Theory of Sexuality* (1905d). Hans' behavior and symptoms, and fantasies illustrated the dynamics of the oedipal phase.

Second, Freud examined the onset, course and resolution of the anxiety attacks and the ensuing horse phobia. The horses falling down represented both mother's childbirth and father's dying. The arrival of Hans' sister raised the question of his father's role in her birth. The anxiety was due to the repression of Han's aggressive tendencies.

Third, Hans recovered from his neurotic affliction due to the benefits of the analysis. The excessive effects of repression, which was driven by the parents' punitive condemnation of his masturbation, were replaced in the analysis by a "temperate and purposeful control on the part of the highest agencies of the mind" (p. 145). In addition, Freud states that he would have given Hans additional sexual enlightenment by discussing the vagina and copulation, thereby ending his stream of questions. Freud ends this case by suggesting that it represents a model of childhood neuroses that derive from similar childhood complexes (Freud, 1909, pp. 3–147; Gay, 1988, pp. 255–261; Rothgeb, 1973, pp. 202–207; Schoenewolf, 1990, pp. 43–62).

Summary and Conclusion

Freud's far-reaching and multifaceted contributions provided the foundations for the developmental theories that followed. After a brief span of time working as a neuroanatomist, his attention was drawn to psychological phenomena, in particular to the neuroses that some of his patients displayed. Working with Breuer, he stumbled upon what he conjectured to be the origins of these disorders in the early sexual abuse that he thought his patients had suffered. Simultaneously, he along with Breuer, uncovered the method of free association as a technique for the cure of these disorders.

Freud felt challenged to elaborate on these discoveries by grounding them in a theoretical framework that was consistent with the scientific ethos in which he had been trained. Having failed, in the 1895 *Project*, in the effort to provide a neurological explanation for mental phenomena, he turned to strictly psychological explanations for these phenomena. With this step, he founded the new discipline of psychoanalysis.

With the publication of the *Three Essays on Sexuality (1905a)*, he synthesized three of the dominant intellectual currents that were prevalent at the time, those of French psychiatry, German biophysics-psychophysics, and the theories of sexuality. This synthesis provided a framework for understanding the causes of mental illness and laid the foundations for a theory of development.

Freud then spent the rest of his life fashioning and refashioning a set of explanatory theories to account for the clinical phenomena he observed. He gave expression to these efforts through his five metapsychological hypotheses, *the economic*, *the topographic*, *the genetic*, *the dynamic*, and *the structural*. In this chapter, we focused on the genetic or developmental hypothesis or point of view, a point of view to which Karl Abraham made significant contributions.

In the *Three Essays on Sexuality* (1905a), Freud's most creative excursion into developmental theory, he laid out the elements that are constitutive of the ontogenesis of the libidinal drive. Here, he accounts not only for typical development from birth through adolescence, but also for the departures from that trajectory and the various forms of psychopathology that can ensue. In the absence of data derived from the direct observation of children, the descriptions he provides of the paths taken were reconstructed from the clinical data of his adult patients in analysis.

The six phases into which Freud's developmental theory has traditionally been divided is a composite derived from his collected works as well as the refinements and elaborations contributed by Karl Abraham. During the oral phase (birth to 1½ years), the oral cavity is the primary erogenous zone the child invests with libidinal and aggressive energy. The central task of this phase is for infants' emerging egos to deal with libidinal and aggressive impulses and to defend against the fear of annihilation. A successful resolution of this phase leads to the capacity to deal with dependency needs and develop trust in others and confidence in one's self.

During the anal phase (1½–3 years of age), the anus is the primary erogenous zone that is invested in libidinal an aggressive energy. The central task in this phase is for the toddlers' egos to cope with the issues of control over excretion and retention of body products; activities which are accompanied by fantasies of power and destruction. They must also attend to the anxiety over the fear of losing the love of the object. The successful resolution of this phase results in a capacity for independence unaccompanied by feelings of shame or self-doubt.

During the phallic phase (ages 3–4 years of age), the genitals are the primary erogenous zones. The central task of this phase is that of the boy's ego must come to terms with the threat of castration that comes from the boy's competitiveness with his father as he enters into the Oedipal phase proper. A successful resolution of this issue is the development of a sense of pride and pleasure in accomplishments. Freud had little to say about the parallel developments in the girl during this phase.

During the genital/oedipal phase (3-5 and 6 years of age), the genitals continue to be primary erogenous zones. The central task differs for the boys and girls. The boy's ego must negotiate the reaction evoked by his libidinal impulses towards his mother and the aggressive impulses directed at father, as well as deal with the anticipated responses from caregivers to those impulses. A successful resolution for boys comes with the internalization of the father's prohibitions resulting in the formation of the super ego. For the girl, the obverse of this configuration occurs. The girl's ego must cope with the libidinal impulses directed at her father and the aggressive/competitive impulses directed a mother. A successful resolution comes about when the girl can give up her resentment at her mother for not giving her a penis in exchange for the postponement of the wish that father would give her a baby.

During the latency phase (5 and 6 to 11 and 12 years of age, puberty), the erogenous zone is nonspecific. The central task is the consolidation of the gains made by the ego during the prior phases. The ego must also come to terms with anxieties aroused by feelings of shame and guilt. The final phase that Freud describes is the late genital or adolescent phase (from puberty to young adulthood). Once more, the primary erogenous zones involved in this phase are the genitals. The central task is the completion of the separation from and dependence upon the caregivers as well as the establishment of personal and gender identity. A successful resolution occurs with the attainment of mature genital functioning as reflected in the capacity to love and engage in a productive career.

We end the chapter with a summary of the story of Freud's analysis of Little Hans as paradigmatic of the oedipal phase struggles in a boy that illustrated the principles set forth in the *Three Essays*. In Little Hans Freud became convinced he found confirmation not only for developmental theory, but also for the means through which to resolve the issues of that phase.

Keywords Anal phase • Anxiety • Castration anxiety • Cathartic method • Cathexes • Conscious • Constancy principle • Defense mechanisms • Drive • Drive theory • Dynamic hypothesis • Economic hypothesis • Fixation • Free association • Hypothesis • Ego • Ego-ideal • Eros - the life instinct • Genetic hypothesis • Genital/oedipal phase • id • Identification • Introjection • Isolation • Latency phase • Late genital or adolescent phase • Law of entropy • Libido • Oedipus phase • Oral phase • Penis envy • Phallic/urethral/narcissistic phase • Pleasure-unpleasure principle • Polymorphous perverse sexuality • Preconscious • Primary narcissism • Psychic determinism • Projection • Reaction formation • Regression • Repression • Reversal • Secondary narcissism • Structural hypothesis • Superego • Thanatos – the death instinct • Topographic hypothesis • Turning against the self • Unconscious • Undoing • Unpleasure

References

Abraham, H. A. (1974). Karl Abraham: An unfinished biography. *The International Review of Psycho-Analysis, 1*, 17–72.

Abraham, K. (1902a). On a case of hernianapsia with color blindness (for red-green) with intact field vision. *Psychiatrischer Verein*, XXVII.

Abraham, K. (1902b). A contribution to the understanding of Delirum Tremens of morphine addicts. *Zentralblatt fur Nervenheilkunde und Psychiatrie, 25*, 369–380.

Abraham, K. (March, 1904). On experiments with veronal in states of agitation in general paralysis. *Zentralblatt fur Nervenheilkunde und Psychiatrie, 27*, 176–180.

Abraham, K., & Ziegenhagen (1904). Cytodiagnostic investigations in dementia paralytica. *Psychiatrischer Verein*, XXVII.

Abraham, K. (1917). Ejaculation praecox. In Ernest Jones (Ed.). *Selected papers of Karl Abraham*. 1927. New York: Basic Books.

Abraham, K. (1921). Contributions to the theory of the anal character. In Ernest Jones (Ed.). *Selected papers of Karl Abraham*. New York: Basic Books.

Abraham, K. (1924a/1927). The influence of oral erotism on character formation. In Ernest Jones (Ed.). *Selected papers of Karl Abraham*. New York: Basic Books.

Abraham, K. (1924b/1927). A short study of the development of the libido, viewed in the light of mental disorders. In Ernest Jones (Ed.). *Selected papers of Karl Abraham*. New York: Basic Books.

Abraham, K. (1925/1927). Character formation on the genital level of the libido. In Ernest Jones (Ed.). *Selected papers of Karl Abraham*. New York: Basic Books.

Arlow, J. A., & Brenner, C. (1964). *Psychoanalytic concepts and the structural theory*. New York: International Universities Press.

Berzoff, J., Flanagan, M. L., & Hertz, P. (1996). *Inside out and outside in: Psychodynamic clinical theory and practice in contemporary multicultural contexts*. New York: Jason Aronson.

Brenner, C. (1973). *An elementary textbook of psychoanalysis*. New York: International Universities Press.

Charcot, J. M. (1881). *Lectures on the diseases of the nervous system*. London: New Sydenham Society.

Esman, A. (1993). G. Stanley Hall and the invention of adolescence. *Adolescent Psychiatry, 19*, 6–20.

Fenichel, O. (1945). *The psychoanalytic theory of the neuroses*. New York: W. W. Norton & Company, Inc.

Ferenczi, S., & Rank, O. (1924/1925). *The development of psychoanalysis*. New York: N. M. D. Publishing Co.

Freud, A. (1936/1966). *The ego and the mechanisms of defense*. New York: International Universities Press, Inc.

Freud, S. (1895a/1950). *Project for a scientific psychology* (Standard Edition, Vol. 1, pp. 281–391). London: Hogarth Press.

Freud, S. (1895b). On the grounds for detaching a particular syndrome from neurasthenia under the description anxiety neuroses (Standard Edition, Vol. 2, pp. 87–117). London: Hogarth Press.

Freud, S., & Breuer, J. (1895c). *Studies on hysteria* (Standard Edition, Vol. 2). London: Hogarth Press.

Freud, S. (1898). Sexuality and the aetiology of the neuroses. (Standard Edition, Vol. 3. pp. 261–289). London: Hogarth Press.

Freud, S. (1900). *The interpretation of dreams* (Standard Edition, Vols. 4-5). London: Hogarth Press.

Freud, S. (1905a). *Three essays on the theory of sexuality* (Standard Edition, Vol. 7, pp. 125–245). London: Hogarth Press.

Freud, S. (1905b). *Fragment of an analysis of a case of hysteria* (Dora) (Standard Edition, Vol. 7, pp. 1–122). London: Hogarth Press.

Freud, S. (1906). My views on the part played by sexuality in the aetiology of the neuroses. (Standard Edition, Vol. 7. pp. 271–282). London: Hogarth Press.

Freud, S. (1907). The sexual enlightenment of children. (Standard Edition, Vol. 9, pp. 129–140). London Hogarth Press.

Freud, S. (1908a). 'Civilized' sexual morality and modern nervous illness. (Standard Edition, Vol. 9, pp. 177–204). London: Hogarth Press.

Freud, S. (1908b). *Character and anal erotism* (Standard Edition, Vol. 9, pp. 167–176). London: Hogarth Press.

Freud, S. (1908c). *On the sexual theories of children* (Standard Edition, Vol. 9, pp. 205–226). London: Hogarth Press.

Freud, S. (1909). *Analysis of a phobia in a five-year old boy* (Standard Edition, Vol. 20, pp. 3–149). London: Hogarth Press.

Freud, S. (1910a). *Five lectures on psycho-analysis* (Standard Edition, Vol. 11, pp. 1–56). London: Hogarth Press.

Freud, S. (1910b). A special type of object choice made by men. (Standard Edition, Vol. 11, pp. 163–176). London: Hogarth Press.

Freud, S. (1910c). Leonardo da Vinci and a dream from his childhood. (Standard Edition, Vol. 11, pp. 59–138). London: Hogarth Press.

Freud, S. (1912a). *Dynamics of transference* (Standard Edition, Vol. 12, pp. 97–108). London: Hogarth Press.

Freud, S. (1912b–1913). *Totem and taboo: Some points of agreement between the mental lives of savages and neurotics* (Standard Edition, Vol. 13, pp. vii–162). London: Hogarth Press.

Freud, S. (1912c). Contributions to a discussion of maturbation. (Standard Edition, Vol. 12, pp. 239–254). London: Hogarth Press.

Freud, S. (1912d). On the universal tendency to debasement in the sphere of love. (Standard Edition, Vol. 11, pp. 177–190). London: Hogarth Press.

Freud, S. (1913a). The disposition to obsessional neurosis. (Standard Edition, Vol. 12, pp. 311–326). London: Hogarth Press.

Freud, S. (1913b). The claims of psycho-analysis to scientific interest. (Standard Edition, Vol. 13, pp. 165–192). London: Hogarth Press.

Freud, S. (1914a). *On the history of the psychoanalytic movement* (Standard Edition, Vol. 14, pp. 1–66). London: Hogarth Press.

Freud, S. (1914c). On narcissism: An introduction (Standard Edition, Vol. 14, pp. 67–102). London: Hogarth Press.

Freud, S. (1915a). *Papers on metapsychology and other works* (Standard Edition, Vol. 14, pp. 261–272). London: Hogarth Press.

Freud, S. (1915b). *Instincts and their vicissitudes* (Standard Edition, Vol. 14, pp. 109–140). London: Hogarth Press.

Freud, S. (1916–1917). Introductory lectures on psychoanalysis. (Standard Edition, Vol. 15–16, pp. 3–483). London: Hogarth Press.

Freud, S. (1917a). *On transformation of instinct as exemplified in anal erotism* (Standard Edition, Vol. 17, pp. 125–134). London: Hogarth Press.

Freud, S. (1918). The taboo of virginity. (Standard Edition, Vol. 11, pp. 191–207). London: Hogarth Press.

Freud, S. (1919). *A child is being beaten: A contribution to the study of the origins of sexual perversions* (Standard Edition, Vol. 17, pp. 175–204). London: Hogarth Press.

Freud, S. (1920a). The psychogenesis of a case of homosexuality in a woman. (Standard Edition, Vol. 19, pp.145–174). London: Hogarth Press.

Freud, S. (1920b). *Beyond the pleasure principle* (Standard Edition, Vol. 18, pp. 1–64). London: Hogarth Press.

Freud, S. (1921). *Group psychology and the analysis of the ego* (Standard Edition, Vol. 18, pp. 65–144). London: Hogarth Press.

Freud, A. (1922a). Beating fantasies and daydreams. *International Journal of Psychoanalysis*, 4, 89–102.

Freud, S. (1922b). Some neurotic mechanisms in jealousy, paranoia and homosexuality. (Standard Edition, Vol. 18, pp. 221–234). London: Hogarth Press.

Freud, S. (1923a). The infantile genital organization (an interpolation into the theory of sexuality) (Standard Edition, Vol. 19, pp. 139–146). London: Hogarth Press.

Freud, S. (1923b). *The ego and the id* (Standard Edition, Vol. 19, pp. 1–66). London: Hogarth Press.

Freud, S. (1924). *The dissolution of the oedipus complex* (Standard Edition, Vol. 19, pp. 171–180). London: Hogarth Press.

Freud, S. (1925). Some psychical consequences of the anatomical distiction between the sexes. (Standard Edition, Vol. 19, pp. 243–260). London: Hogarth Press.
Freud, S. (1926). *Inhibitions, symptoms and anxiety* (Standard Edition, Vol. 20, pp. 75–176). London: Hogarth Press.
Freud, S. (1927a). *The future of an illusion* (Standard Edition, Vol. 21, pp. 1–56). London: Hogarth Press.
Freud, S. (1927b). Fetishism. (Standard Edition, Vol. 21, pp. 149–158). London: Hogarth Press.
Freud, S. (1930). *Civilization and its discontents* (Standard Edition, Vol. 21, pp. 57–146). London: Hogarth Press.
Freud, S. (1931a). Libidinal types. (Standard Edition, Vol. 21, pp. 215–222). London: Hogarth Press.
Freud, S. (1931b). Female sexualitys. (Standard Edition, Vol. 21, pp. 223–246). London: Hogarth Press.
Freud, S. (1933). New Introductory Lectures on Psycho-Analysis (Standard Edition, Vol. 22, pp. 3–184). London: Hogarth Press.
Freud, S. (1939). *Moses and monotheism* (Standard Edition, Vol. 23, pp. 3–137). London: Hogarth Press.
Freud, S. (1940a). An outline of psychoanalysis. (Standard Edition, Vol. 23, pp.141–208). London: Hogarth Press.
Freud, S. (1940b). Splitting of the ego in the process of defense. (Standard Edition, Vol. 23, pp. 271–278). London: Hogarth Press.
Gardiner, (1971). *The wolf-man*. New York: Basic Books, Inc.
Gay, P. (1988). *Freud: A life for our time*. New York: W. W. Norton & Company.
Grosskurth, P. (1992). Idyll in the Hartz mountains. In T. Gelfand & J. Kerr (Eds.), *Freud and the history of psychoanalysis*. Hillsdale, NJ: The Analytic Press.
Jones, E. (1913/1923). Hate and anal erotism in the obsessional neurotic. In *Papers on psychoanalysis*. London: Baillire.
Jones, E. (1918). Anal-erotic character traits. In *Papers on psychoanalysis*. London: Baillire. *Journal of Abnormal Psychology*, 13
Jones, E. (1922). Some problems of adolescence. In *Papers on psychoanalysis*. London: Bailliere, Tindall and Cox.
Jones, E. (1926, April). Karl Abraham: An introductory memoir. *International Journal of Psycho-Analysis* pp. 155–181.
Kaplan, L. J. (1984). *Adolescence: The farewell to childhood*. New York: Simon and Schuster.
Kuhn, T. S. (1962). *The structure of scientific revolutions*. Chicago: University of Chicago Press.
Lamarck, J. B. (1786/1914). *Zoological philosophy* (H. Elliot, Trans. & Ed.). London: Macmillan.
Laplanch, J., & Pontalis, J.-B. (1973). *The language of psychoanalysis*. New York: W. W. Norton & Company.
Laughlin, H. P. (1967). *The neuroses*. Washington: Butterworths.
Laughlin, H. P. (1979). *The ego and its defenses*. New York: Jason Aronson.
Laycock, T. (1860). *Mind and brain: Or the correlations of consciousness and organization*. Edinburg: Southerland and Knox.
Makari, G. (2008). *Revolution in mind: The creation of psychoanalysis*. New York: HarperCollins Publishers.
Mayr, E. (1982). *The growth of biological thought: Diversity, evolution, and inheritance*. Cambridge, MA: Harvard University Press.
Mayr, E. (1991). *One long argument: Charles Darwin and the genesis of modern evolutionary thought*. Cambridge, MA: Harvard University Press.
Mitchell, S. A., & Black, M. (1995). *Freud and beyond: A history of modern psychoanalytic thought*. New York: Basic Books.
Nagera, H. (1966). *Early childhood disturbances, the infantile neurosis, and the adult disturbances: Problems of a developmental psychology*. New York: International Universities Press.
Noshpitz, J., & King, R. J. (1991). Pathways of growth. In *Essentials of child psychiatry: Normal development*. New York: Wiley.

Nunberg, H. (1932 German/1955). *Principles of psychoanalysis: Their application to the neuroses* (Foreword by Sigmund Freud, M. Karr & S. Karr, Trans.). New York: International Universities Press.

Nunberg, H. (1965). Introduction to the minutes of the vienna psychoanalytic society. In *Practice and theory of psychoanalysis* (Vol. 2). New York: International Universities Press.

Nunberg, H. (1969/1970). *Memoirs, reflections and ideas*. New York: Psychoanalytic Research Press.

Perry, B. D. (1995). Incubated in terror: Neurodevelopmental factors in the 'cycle of violence'. In J. D. Osofsky (Ed.), *Children, youth and violence*. New York: Guilford.

Peters, U. W. (1985). *Anna Freud: A life dedicated to children*. New York: Schocken Books.

Quinodoz, J. (2005). *Reading Freud: A chronological exploration of Freud's writings*. London: Routledge.

Rank, O. (1924/1945). *The trauma of birth*. New York: Alfred A. Knopf.

Rank, O. (1924/1952). *The Trauma of the birth*. New York: Robert Brunner.

Rapaport, D. (1960). The structure of psychoanalytic theory: A systematizing attempt. In *Psychological issues* 6 (Vol. 2, No. 2). New York: International Universities Press.

Rapaport, D. (1967). The conceptual model of psychoanalysis. In M. Gill (Ed.), *The collected papers of David Rapaport*. New York: Basic Books.

Ritvo, L. B. (1974). The impact of Darwin on Freud. *Psychoanalytic quarterly*, *43*, 177–192.

Ritvo, L. D. (1965). Darwin as the source of Freud's Neo-Lamarckianism. *Journal of the American Psychoanalytic Association*, *13*, 499–517.

Roazen, P. (1984). *Freud and his followers*. New York: New York University Press.

Romaes, G. J. (1888). *Mental evolution in man: Origin of human faculty*. London: Kegan Paul Trench & Co.

Ross, D. (1972). *G. Stanley Hall: The psychologist as prophet*. Chicago: The University of Chicago Press.

Rothgeb, C. (Ed.) (1973). *Abstracts of the standard edition of the complete psychological works of Sigmund Freud*. New York: International Universities Press.

Sadock, B. J., & Sadock, V. A. (2003a). *Kaplan and Sadock's synopsis of psychiatry*. Philadelphia: Lippincott, Williams & Wilkins.

Sadock, B. J., & Sadock, V. A. (2003b). *Kaplan and Sadock's Synopsis of Psychiatry*. Philadelphia: Lippincott Williams & Wilkins. pp pp. 201–203

Schoenewolf, G. (1990). *Turning points in analytic therapy: The classic cases*. Northvale, NJ: Jason Aronson.

Schur, M. (1972). *Freud: Living and dying*. New York: International Universities Press.

Schur, M., & Ritvo, L. B. (1970). A principle of evolutionary biology for psychoanalysis Schneirla's evolutionary and developmental theory of biphasic processes underlying approach and withdrawl and Freud's unpleasure and pleasure principle. *Journal of the American Psychoanalytic Association*, *18*, 422–439.

Strenger, C. (2006). Freud's forgotten evolutionary project. *Psychoanalytic Psychology*, *23*(2), 420–429.

Sulloway, F. J. (1979) *Freud: Biologist of the mind-beyond the psychoanalytic legend*. New York: Basic Books

Tabor, C. W. (1997). *Tabor's cyclopedic medical dictionary* (18th edition). Philadelphia: F. A. Davis Company.

Waelder, R. (1930/1936). The principle of multiple function. *Psychoanalytic Quarterly,* 5.

G. & C. Merriam Company. (1981). *Webster's new collegiate dictionary*. Springfield, MA: Author.

Waelder, R. (1960). *Basic theory of psychoanalysis*. New York: International Universities Press.

Wolff, P. H. (1963). Developmental & motivational concepts in Piaget's sensori-motor theory of intelligence. *Journal of the American Academy of Child & Adolescent Psychiatry*, *2*(2), 225–243.

Young-Bruehl, E. (1988). *Anna Freud: A biography*. New York: Summit Books.

Major Works (S. Freud and K. Abraham)

Abraham, K. (1921/1927). Contributions to the theory of the anal character. In *Selected papers of Karl Abraham*. New York: Basic Books.

Abraham, K. (1924/1927). The influence of oral erotism on character formation. In *Selected Papers of Karl Abraham*. New York: Basic Books.

Abraham, K. (1924/1927). A short study of the development of the libido, viewed in the light of mental disorders. In *Selected papers of Karl Abraham*. New York: Basic Books.

Abraham, K. (1925/1927). Character formation on the genital level of the libido. In *Selected papers of Karl Abraham*. New York: Basic Books.

Abraham, K. (1927). A short study of the development of the libido, viewed in the light of mental disorders. In *Selected Papers*. London: Hogarth Press.

Freud, S. (1891/1953) *On aphasia*. New York: International Universities Press.

Freud, S. (1895a/1950). *Project for a scientific psychology* (Standard Edition, Vol. 1, pp. 281–391). London: Hogarth Press.

Freud, S. (1895b). *On the grounds for detaching a particular syndrome from neurasthenia under the description anxiety neuroses* (Standard Edition, Vol. 2, pp. 87–117). London: Hogarth Press.

Freud, S., & Breuer, J. (1895c). *Studies on hysteria* (Standard Edition,Vol. 2). London: Hogarth Press.

Freud, S. (1900). *The interpretation of dreams* (Standard Edition, Vols. 4–5). London: Hogarth Press.

Freud, S. (1901). *The psychopathology of everyday life* (Standard Edition, Vol. 6). London: Hogarth Press.

Freud, S. (1905a). *Three essays on the theory of sexuality* (Standard Edition, Vol. 7, pp. 125–245). London: Hogarth Press.

Freud, S. (1905b). *Fragment of an analysis of a case of hysteria* (Dora) (Standard Edition, Vol. 7, pp. 1–122). London: Hogarth Press.

Freud, S. (1908a). *Character and anal erotism* (Standard Edition, Vol. 9, pp. 167-176). London: Hogarth Press.

Freud, S. (1908b). *On the sexual theories of children* (Standard Edition, Vol. 9, pp. 205–226). London: Hogarth Press.

Freud, S. (1909). *Analysis of a phobia in a five-year old boy* (Standard Edition, Vol. 20, pp. 3–149). London: Hogarth Press.

Freud, S. (1910). *Five lectures on psycho-analysis* (Standard Edition, Vol. 11, pp. 1–56). London: Hogarth Press.

Freud, S. (1912a). *Dynamics of transference* (Standard Edition, Vol. 12, pp. 97–108). London: Hogarth Press.

Freud, S. (1912b–1913). *Totem and taboo: Some points of agreement between the mental lives of savages and neurotics* (Standard Edition, Vol. 13, pp. vii–162). London: Hogarth Press.

Freud, S. (1914a). *On the history of the psychoanalytic movement.* (Standard Edition, Vol. 14, pp. 1–66). London: Hogarth Press.

Freud, S. (1914b). *On narcissism: An introduction* (Standard Edition, Vol. 14, pp. 67–102). London: Hogarth Press.

Freud, S. (1915a). *Papers on metapsychology and other works* (Standard Edition, Vol. 14, pp. 261–272). London: Hogarth Press.

Freud, S. (1915b). *Instincts and their vicissitudes* (Standard Edition, Vol. 14, pp. 109–140). London: Hogarth Press.

Freud, S. (1917a). *On transformation of instinct as exemplified in anal erotism* (Standard Edition, Vol. 17, pp. 125–134). London: Hogarth Press.

Freud, S. (1917b). *Mourning and melanclolia* (Standard Edition, pp. 237–260). London: Hogarth Press.

Freud, S. (1919). *A child is being beaten: A contribution to the study of the origins of sexual perversions* (Standard Edition, Vol. 17, pp. 175–204). London: Hogarth Press.

Freud, S. (1920b). *Beyond the pleasure principle* (Standard Edition, Vol. 18, pp. 1–64). London: Hogarth Press.

Freud, S. (1921). *Group psychology and the analysis of the ego* (Standard Edition, Vol. 18, pp. 65–144). London: Hogarth Press.

Freud, A. (1922a). Beating fantasies and daydreams. *International Journal of Psychoanalysis, 4*, 89–102.

Freud, S. (1923a). *The infantile genital organization (an interpolation into the theory of sexuality)* (Standard Edition, Vol. 19, pp. 139–146). London: Hogarth Press.

Freud, S. (1923b) *The ego and the id* (Standard Edition, Vol. 19, pp. 1–66). London: Hogarth Press.

Freud, S. (1924). *The dissolution of the oedipus complex* (Standard Edition, Vol. 19, pp. 171–180). London: Hogarth Press.

Freud, S. (1926). *Inhibitions, symptoms and anxiety* (Standard Edition, Vol. 20, pp. 75–176). London: Hogarth Press.

Freud, S. (1927a). *The future of an illusion* (Standard Edition, Vol. 21, pp. 1–56). London: Hogarth Press.

Freud, S. (1930). *Civilization and its discontents* (Standard Edition, Vol. 21, pp. 57–146). London: Hogarth Press.

Freud, S. (1939). *Moses and monotheism* (Standard Edition, Vol. 23, pp. 3–137). London: Hogarth Press.

Supplementary Readings

Binion, R. (1968). *Frau Lou: Nietzsche's wayward disciple*. Princeton, NJ: Princeton University Press.

Blum, H. (2007). Little Hans: A contemporary overview. In *Psychoanalytic study of the child* (Vol. 62, pp. 44–60). New Haven: Yale University Press.

Ellenberger, H. F. (1970). *The discovery of the unconscious: The history and evolution of dynamic psychiatry*. New York: Basic Books, Inc.

Ruitenbeck, H. M. (Ed.) (1973). *Freud as we knew him*. Detroit: Wayne State University Press.

Gilman, S. L., King, H., Porter, R., Rousseau, G. S., & Showalter, E. (1993). *Hysteria beyond Freud*. Berkely: University of California Press.

Goldberg, A. (2004). *Misunderstanding Freud*. New York: Other Press.

Roazen, P. (1985). *Helene Deutsch: A psychoanalyst's life*. Garden City, NY: Anchor Press.

Schorske, C. E. (1981). *Fin-De-siecle Vienna: Politics and culture*: Chicago: University of Chicago Press.

Wakefield, J. C. (2007). Little Hans and attachment theory: Bowlby's hypothesis reconsidered in the light of new evidence from the Freud archives. In *Psychoanalytic study of the child* (Vol. 62, pp. 61–91). New Haven: Yale University Press.

Zaretsky, E. (2004). *Secrets of the soul: A social and cultural history of psychoanalysis*. New York: Alfred A. Knopf.

Section II
Ego Psychological Theories

The shift from drive theory to ego psychology represents a change of emphasis rather than a fundamental departure from the premises of drive theory. When Freud (1923) proposed the tripartite model of the mind as constituted of the ego, the id, and the superego – to which Freud refers at times as the ego-ideal – what later came to be known as the structural model of metapsychology came into being. Hartmann and Anna Freud are both credited with the shift to this model. Both they and later ego psychologists embraced it as the *standard model* for all psychoanalytic theories. The ego became the central mediator between the demands of the drives, the superego, and the environment. The delineations of the functions of the ego and its defenses became a central focus for developmental theories. Conflict between id impulses and the ego, the superego, or the environment is fundamental to the human condition. The anxiety created by conflict mobilizes ego defenses. If these defenses are only partly successful, the symptoms that emerge give rise to a neurosis, such as hysteria, phobia, obsessive-compulsive disorder, or anxiety disorder. If the defenses fail, the ego is overwhelmed and psychosis ensues.

Even though he never proposed a developmental theory, we begin with **Hartmann** because of his enormous contribution to this version of psychoanalytic theory. He unquestioningly viewed psychoanalysis as a science that belonged among the medical sciences (Hartmann, 1959). He strongly advocated for this position even as the entire paradigm came under criticism from those outside of psychoanalytic circles (Nagel, 1959). Those critics not only questioned its status as a science but accused its followers of espousing a theory that was untestable, much as astrology was untestable. Hartmann elaborated the structural model by extending evolutionary theory to psychoanalysis, adding the adaptive point of view to the genetic, topographic, economic, structural, and dynamic perspectives.

Anna Freud, in her classic work *The Ego and the Mechanisms of Defense*, elaborated on Freud's concept of ego defenses and added a set of her own. She contributed the concept of developmental lines that trace a variety of functions from infancy to adolescence. **Spitz**'s work was instrumental in bringing to our attention the devastating effects of severe maternal deprivation on institutionalized infants. He suggested that caregivers provide infants with auxiliary ego functions that enhance their capacity to survive. **Blos** provided the classic statement on adolescent development. He extended his predecessors' contributions, incorporating their major concepts into what he considered constitutive of adolescence as a developmental phase.

The model of development that all these theorists espoused is the organismic model. They believed that, like all organisms, human beings require nourishment to survive. In the case of human beings, the nourishment takes the form of psychological investment in the form of caring, affection, or love from caregivers. Caregivers' failure to provide such nourishment leads to developmental fixations, arrests, or conflicts that interfere with the normal developmental trajectory and produce psychopathology. Whereas the drives remain central as motivators of human thoughts, feelings, and conduct, ego psychologists emphasize their adaptive function. The environment begins to assume greater importance in shaping drive expression than Freud had considered.

Finally, **Greenspan** began his career as an ego psychologist, writing a text describing the development of the ego (1989). However, he later substituted the term *self* for *ego*, although he does not provide a formal definition of the concept but refers to its stages by describing the levels of its development through six stages. Greenspan remained true to his positivist roots, grounding his finding into science-based research methodologies.

Greenspan has been a strong advocate for the position that affects and cognition are inextricably linked together from birth on. Through his work on the treatment of children within the autistic spectrum, he arrived at a six-stage developmental schema that describes the emotional, intellectual, and social growth of the child. His premise was that emotions serve to create and organize many of the mind's most important functions. The developmental process begins with the emergence of the capacity to invest a freestanding image with emotional meaning to make it into a meaningful multisensory, affective image (i.e., an idea). His early recognition of the impact of neuropsychological differences on children and the contribution of those differences to some forms of psychopathology placed him in a unique position among ego psychologists.

References

Greenspan, S. I. (1989). *The development of the ego: Implications for personality theory, psychopathology, and the psychotherapeutic process*. Madison, CT: International Universities Press.

Hartmann, H. (1959). Psychoanalysis as a scientific theory. In S. Hook (Ed.), *Psychoanalysis, scientific method and philosophy* (pp. 3–37). New York: New York University Press.

Nagel, E. (1959). Methodological issues in psychoanalytic theory. In S. Hook (Ed.), Psychoanalysis, scientific method and philosophy (pp. 38–56). New York: New York University Press.

Chapter 2
Heinz Hartmann (1894–1970)

Publishing Era (1917–1966)

Biographical Information

Heinz Hartmann was born on November 4, 1894 in an upper class gentile Viennese family of distinguished historians and academics. His parents, Ludwig Hartmann and Grete Chrobak, married in 1892. The marriage was remarkable in that the Chrobak family was devoutly Roman Catholic while Ludwig, originally from a Protestant family, became an atheist and adamantly opposed religious practices. Because all schools, public and private, were operated under the auspices of the Church, Heinz and his 1-year-older sister, Else, were home schooled at the family estate at Gerasdorf. Heinz received individual instruction until he was 14 years of age and from then on attended public schools. The home atmosphere was that of an international salon in character, emphasizing musical performances (the composer Johannes Brahms, 1833–1897, was a frequent visitor) and debates by intellectuals on political issues. With such extraordinary stimulation, Heinz thrived and was able to cultivate his talents. He played the violin, taught himself piano, wrote poetry, painted watercolors, and kept a pet fox.

Prior to graduating from the University of Vienna medical school in 1920, Heinz spent a year in the Army. Twice he was nearly killed not by enemy bullets, but by avalanches, each time dug out by his comrades. His years at the University were not confined to a rigid course of medical studies. He audited lectures on philosophy, psychology, and sociology taught by distinguished professors of his day. He also studied pharmacology and published two papers in 1917 and 1918 on the metabolism of quinine that serve as a testament to his expertise in the experimental method.

After graduation, he pursued several careers before turning to psychoanalysis. He remained as the staff of the University of Vienna Psychiatric and Neurological Institute clinics from 1920 to 1934, with the exception of one year, 1926, in which he undertook psychoanalytic training in Berlin to continue the training he had started in Vienna. In 1924, he published a paper that validated Freud's theory of symbolization and demonstrated that mechanisms analogous to repression operate in putatively organic amnesias. This paper thrust Hartmann into psychoanalytic prominence.

Hartmann had arranged for a training (didactic) analysis in Berlin with Karl Abraham, however, because of Abraham's premature death in 1925, the analysis

J. Palombo et al., *Guide to Psychoanalytic Developmental Theories*,
DOI: 10.1007/978-0-387-88455-4_2,

never got started. In Berlin, Hartmann underwent his first psychoanalysis with Sandor Rado. In 1927, Hartmann published his textbook, Fundamentals of Psychoanalysis, the first such textbook, which eventually became a classic. He wrote it while in analysis with Rado. By the late 1920s, having moved back to Vienna, Hartmann had become a trusted member of the Vienna Psychoanalytic Institute and grew to be the leading theoretician in orthodox psychoanalytic circles. As a theoretician, Hartmann developed an approach of first gaining theoretical distance from the clinical material, then defining its implications with exactness, striving to place it in the perspective of a scientific general psychology (Gitelson, 1965).

Hartmann married Dora Karplus in 1928; she was a pediatrician, who later become an analyst. Dora, the youngest of four children, came from a distinguished family of lawyers and professionals; her maternal great-uncle was Josef Breuer. Dora met Heinz while she was a medical school student at the University of Vienna, and he was a member of the medical faculty.

Although trained as an academic psychiatrist and as the staff of the University of Vienna Psychiatric Clinics, Hartmann grew to be deeply respectful of Freud's contributions. However, Freud originally distrusted Hartmann, due to the psychiatric establishment's ambivalence toward psychoanalysis. In 1934, Hartmann chose to resign his post at the University Clinic because of disagreements with the newly appointed head of the Clinic and political decisions made by a reactionary government. These would have forced him to compromise his personal and scientific principles in order to gain a professorship.

Anna Freud also was initially dubious of Hartmann's concepts, but with her approval and under her auspices, Hartmann began to win converts to his enlargement of the ego's role in adaptation. Although Hartmann was too academic for Freud's taste, she recognized the need to innovate and cultivate creativity. When Hartmann left the University Clinic in Vienna, Adolph Meyer, the father of American psychiatry, offered him a position as full professor at Johns Hopkins Institute. To counter this possible move, Freud invited him to continue his training analysis, free of charge, if he would stay in Vienna. Hartmann accepted and entered his second analysis in 1934, which continued into 1936.

In 1937, Hartmann presented a paper before the Vienna Psychoanalytic Society entitled "Me." This paper was later translated into English in 1958, as *The Ego and the Problem of Adaptation*. This paper marks the beginning of Ego Psychology. With the Nazi annexation of Austria, Hartmann and his family moved first to Paris in 1938, where he joined the Paris Psychoanalytic Institute, and then to Geneva and later Lausanne, Switzerland, before settling in New York in January 1941. In Paris and Switzerland, the multilingual Heinz could work as a psychoanalyst. In New York, both Dora and Heinz passed the necessary foreign medical graduate licensure examinations. Dora, over Heinz' objections, was analyzed by Ludwig Jekels, supervised by a long list of celebrated psychoanalysts, and became a psychoanalyst. Hartmann became a member of the New York Psychoanalytic Institute and became a teacher and training analyst as he had been at the Vienna and Paris Institutes. As Freud's heir apparent, he brought enormous prestige to the New York Institute and helped to heal its severe political infighting and nasty polarizing splits, but never became a public voice for popularizing psychoanalysis.

He collaborated with Rado in the editorship of the *Internationale Zeitschrift fur Psychanalyse* from 1932 to 1941. In addition, he, along with Anna Freud and Ernst Kris, founded *The Psychoanalytic Study of the Child* in 1945 and was one of its managing editors. Later, Hartmann invited his Viennese colleagues Ruth S. Eissler and Rudolph M. Loewenstein to accept a coeditorship position for *The Psychoanalytic Study of the Child.* Hartmann's work on ego psychology having just been published in the *Internationale Zeitschrift fur Psychoanalyse*, they found much common ground in the innovative material. In 1942, when the Loewensteins settled in New York, they found a gracious, hospitable Hartmann. Hartmann soon invited Loewenstein to teach at the Institute and even audited his course to give him pointers and feedback on teaching methods. Afterwards, Hartmann invited Lowenstein to join what was to be a 15-year collaboration with Ernst Kris (with the exception of 3 years after Kris' death) in a variety of writing projects that extended the ego psychology themes Hartmann first laid out in 1937.

From 1948 to 1951 he was the Medical Director of the Treatment Center at the New York Psychoanalytic Institute, from 1952 to 1954 as the President of the New York Psychoanalytic Society, and from 1953 to 1959 as the President of the International Psycho-Analytic Association and, succeeded Ernest Jones, as Honorary President until his death. The marriage with Dora lasted 42 years. He died suddenly in Stony Point, New York on May 17, 1970 at the age of 75 of coronary thrombosis, a disease that first afflicted him in 1944. Dora who never smoked, but who had a family history of lung cancer, died of the disease in 1974. Both were cremated and their remains buried in Fextal valley in Switzerland (Hartmann, 1994, pp. 3–11).

Hartmann, who was fluent in German, French, and English, was devoted to music and was equally at home at the Louvre and the ancient ruins of Sicily. He lived a life of liberal humanism. His qualities as a human being were extraordinary. He was known and remembered for his theoretical ability, his brilliance as a teacher, intellectual acumen, his uncompromising integrity, his devotion to his family, and for his loyalty to orthodox psychoanalysis. He welcomed contributions from all fields as a way to encourage biopsychosocial thinking, awareness of cultural influence, and the propagation of developmental theory. He saw psychoanalysis as central to a general psychology (Eissler & Eissler, 1964; Eissler & Loewenstein, 1970).

Remarkably, while Hartmann was the first and foremost formalistic theoretician, his writings from 1937 onward contain only meager illustrations of clinical application of his concepts and virtually no case examples. Apparently, as he associated increasingly with the ageing and dying Freud, Hartmann may have firmly identified with his withdrawn master's increasing removal from clinical matters, turning to, and aligning himself with Freud's theoretical abstractions, metapsychology, and the application of psychoanalysis to cultural and religious speculations (Roazen, 1984, p. 518).

Conceptual Framework

To appreciate the magnitude of the changes brought about by Hartmann's contribution, we review briefly the impact of Freud's publication of *The Ego and the Id* in 1923. In that work, Freud introduced a massive revision of his psychology. Prior to 1923, as we have seen, Freud's positivist framework included nonsystematic statements about intrapsychic functioning subsequently gathered into five overlapping hypotheses: the economic, the topographic, the dynamic, the genetic, and the structural. Each of these hypotheses included statements about psychological elements in a functional relationship to each other. In *The Ego and the Id* (1923b), Freud formulated the three-part structure of the mental apparatus: the id, ego, and superego (and the ego ideal). The progression in Freud's thinking about the expanded roles of the ego and superego (and ego ideal) can be found in *On Narcissism: An Introduction* (1914) and in *Group Psychology and the Analysis of the Ego* (1921). This conceptualization that later came to be known as the **structural theory** permitted greater understanding of the individual's negotiations with the external world and with interpersonal relationships in that world. The structural theory, however, was still closely linked with drive theory in that the ego was seen as drawing its energy from the id and developing as a result of frustration and conflict.

Hartmann's legacy is that he drew attention to the **adaptive point of view** and its role in development. The adaptive hypothesis stated that infants are preadapted to cope with the demands of the environment in which they are born. Both Freud and Hartman drew different inspirations from Darwin's account of evolution. Freud emphasized the dark, archaic, instinctual relationship to other species, whereas Hartmann stressed the notion that animals were designed to adapt to the environment. Through the process of evolution, organisms interacted in a "continual reciprocal relationship" with their surroundings (Mitchell & Black, 1995, p. 36). As the father of ego psychology, Hartmann was the psychological architect who moved the psychoanalytic enterprise beyond the intrapsychic focus of drive/defense and psychopathology to a general theory of human development. He moved psychoanalysis "from an isolated, self-contained treatment method to a sweeping intellectual discipline;" a discipline that indirectly encouraged contributions from nonpsychoanalytic sources (1995, p. 35).

Even though the adaptive hypothesis can be considered a post-Freudian advance, it is very much an expansion and modification of ideas that Freud and his colleagues worked with in the aftermath of the horrors of the World War I. Following that war, Freud and his followers developed a deeply pessimistic perspective of human nature and emphasized the struggle to transform amoral primitive childhood urges into civilized adult behaviors and norms. In contrast, ego psychology took a different direction, as it began to take shape in the late 1930s both in Vienna and in England and was elaborated after the World War II mostly by expatriates who immigrated to the United States to escape Nazi persecution. Consistent with American optimism and the notion of unlimited opportunity, a sense of hopefulness about human nature took hold among psychoanalysts and a shift in attention from the chaotic id to the resilient possibilities of the ego received increasing attention. Berzoff and her colleagues (1996) state

> "ego psychology encourages practitioners to think about the developmental processes across the life cycle, the unfolding of human capacities in response to the interaction between environmental influences and inborn developmental potentials, about the inborn forces that propel individuals toward ever more complex and goal-directed patterns of

organization, and about the ways individuals either adapt to their social and physical environments or modify those environments to make them more compatible with personal needs and wishes."

Berzoff, Flanagan, and Hertz, 1996, p. 68

Ego psychology provides a theoretical framework for repairing abnormal psychosocial functioning and facilitating a better fit between an individual's psychological needs and the normative expectations of society.

The Ego Reconceptualized

Hartmann believed that because "the ego is man's special organ of adaptation," infants are born and immediately get equipped to fit into their physical and psychological environment (Hartmann, 1950, pp. 78–79). This equipment consists of a set of intrinsic potentials or **conflict-free ego** capacities. The potential embedded in these functions can flourish in an "**average expectable environment**," that is, in an environment that is responsive to the child's psychological needs (Hartmann, 1939).

Unlike the Freuds, Hartmann "believed that the id and the ego develop simultaneously and function independently, yet in synchrony. They evolve from an undifferentiated matrix with reciprocal influences on each other, emerging as 'products of differentiation' (Hartmann, 1950, p. 79). Each had its own biological roots and energy source" (Austrian, 2002, p. 26). Consequently, the ego's central role in development was to facilitate not only conflict among various agencies of the mind that is the id, ego, and superego, but also adaptation to the environment. Hartmann argued that the ego development comes about "as a result of three sets of factors: inherited ego characteristics (and their interaction), influences of the instinctual drives, and influences of outer reality" (Hartmann, 1950, p. 79).

Primary and Secondary Autonomous Ego Functions

Hartmann divided ego functions into primary autonomous functions and secondary autonomous functions (Hartmann, 1939). **Primary autonomous ego functions**, such as the cognitive functions of perception, intelligence, thinking, comprehension, language, learning, and the synthetic function of the ego are innate, inherited ego characteristics, and conflict-free. **Secondary autonomous ego functions** are those functions that were once involved in developmental conflicts, such as oral, anal, or phallic/oedipal and were freed as a result of the resolution of those conflicts through the process of neutralization (Hartmann, 1950, p. 81). For example, a child's ability to think clearly may be contaminated by conflicts around sexuality or aggression. Secondary autonomy of that function results in clear, unambiguous thinking following the resolution of those conflicts (Hartmann, 1939). When the transformation, from energies embroiled in conflict to neutralized energies, occurs a **change in function** results (1939, pp. 25–26).

Freud had maintained that in **sublimation**, the ego harnesses instinctual energy and channels it into socially acceptable pursuits. For example, the voyeur became a photographer. Hartmann's concept of **neutralization** was different. Neutralization actually strips the drives of their sexual and aggressive qualities. Those energies then become conflict free or autonomous and available for use by the ego; they become secondary autonomous functions. Such ego functions become independent from the id and the ego can use the available energies in the service of adaptation and mastery. In the case of secondary autonomous functions, the energy was neutralized, the conflict removed, and the ego function then contributes to adaptation (Hartmann, 1939).

The **synthetic function of the ego** was a term that Hartmann borrowed from Nunberg (1930). It is one of the autonomous ego functions deemed by Hartmann to occupy a place of organizational significance as "the centralization of functional control" or personality integration. It involves the ability to synthesize (or to integrate and organize) experiences and thus adapt to reality. He predicted that the synthetic function may one day extend the sphere by which psychoanalytic and physiological, especially brain, processes and concepts can become integrated (Hartmann, 1959/1964, p. 117; Summers, 1994, p. 7).

Finally, Hartmann ended his 1950 paper, *Comments on the psychoanalytic theory of the ego*, with the question, what constitutes ego strength? "Any definition will have to include as an essential element the consideration of the autonomous functions of the ego, their interdependence, and their structural hierarchy, and especially of whether or how far they are able to withstand impairment through the process of defense" (Hartmann, 1950, p. 94).

Ego Defenses

Hartmann devoted considerable time to the study of the ego's defenses and their functions from the perspective of adaptation. However, he seems not to have expanded on the defenses elaborated by Freud (1926) or on those of Freud (1936). He devoted virtually no publications to this topic. He believed that both defensive and adaptive functions were organized as part of the ego's synthetic function (see Nunberg, 1930; Summers, 1994, p. 7). The ego mobilizes defenses to protect itself from four types of dangers including conflict among the id, ego, and superego, conflict in interpersonal relationships, conflict in relation to social norms, and the disruption that occurs in response to trauma.

Consistent with his interest in the origin of the defenses, Hartmann speculated on the relationship between defenses and ego functions. During development, what started in a situation of conflict may secondarily become, through a change of function, part of the nonconflictual sphere. "What developed as an outcome of defense against an instinctual drive (and against reality, or against the superego) may grow into a more or less structured function. It may come to serve different functions, like adjustment, organization, and so on." In other words, it may come to serve adaptation. For example, every reactive character formation, originating in defense against the drives, will gradually take over a wealth of other functions in the framework of the ego." Such functions may indeed become stable, even irreversible and are considered secondary autonomous functions (Hartmann, 1950, pp. 81–82).

Adaptation and Accommodation

Hartmann saw adaptation as reciprocal and evolving, not as a static process. He used two technical terms to describe a person whose ego is modified in the service of adaptation. **Alloplastic change** occurs when the person alters the environment to cope with challenges that he or she may encounter. In the opposite situation, **autoplastic change** occurs when the person shifts to accommodating to the environment by modifying aspects of him or herself to deal with reality. For the individual to successfully adapt, Hartmann hypothesized four ego tasks involving the reconciliation of inter and intra-systemic conflicts: (a) maintaining a balance between individual and external realities; (b) establishing harmony within the id among its competing instinctual drives; (c) maintaining a balance among the three competing mental agencies: id, ego, and superego; and (d) maintaining a balance between its role in helping the id and its own independent role that goes beyond instinctual gratification (Hartmann, 1939, p. 39). Also, in discussing the ego's adaptive nature to the reality principle, Hartmann suggested that the ego can make modest compromises in its adjustment to the demands of reality and still function adequately. These compromises called defensive maneuvers, as opposed to unconscious defense mechanisms, are often preconscious, situationally specific, can become routine patterns, and tend to be more mobile (Hartmann, 1956b. p. 41).

Ego-Syntonic and Ego-Dystonic Responses

While the terms **ego-syntonic** and **ego-dystonic** do not originate with Hartmann, he refers to them frequently in his publications after 1939 (Hartmann, 1939, pp. 86–99). The term "ego-syntonic" was first used by Freud in "*On Narcissism: An Introduction*" (1914) and later in "*Two Encyclopedia Articles*" (1923a) to describe instincts or ideas that are acceptable to the ego, i.e., compatible with the ego's integrity and its demands. He used the expression to describe the view of the ego as total, integrated, ideal. The term "ego-dystonic," was used to describe those instincts or ideas, which are antagonistic to the ego and are, consequently, repressed.

In His Own Words

We were unable to find any published case material by Hartmann. The following excerpt is intended to illustrate how he may have approached a clinical situation. (Excerpted from Hartmann (1964). Problems of infantile neurosis. In H. Hartmann

(Ed.), *Essays on Ego Psychology: Selected problems in psychoanalytic theory* (pp. 207–214). New York: International Universities Press. Reprinted with permission from International Universities Press.)

As to our topic of infantile neurosis, at present we have more questions than answers. Still, it is pleasant to think that most of the discomfort many of us feel in approaching this problem today is due to the fact that we know actually much more; that is, we know much more about developmental psychology in general, which makes us more ambitious in specifying our hypotheses. We know more about normal development, and we all agree that an understanding of neurotic development is not possible if it is not based on a very detailed analysis and on precise knowledge of what normal development is. Consequently, we have to deal with a greater number of hypotheses on this subject today.

It is actually not so easy to say what we call an infantile neurosis. You remember that when Freud first approached this problem, he found that what he actually considered a neurosis was frequently considered naughtiness or bad upbringing by the parents and the teachers. Today we are confronted with the reverse situation; i.e., in rather broad circles, every naughtiness, actually every behavior of the child that does not conform to the textbook model, and every developmental step that is not according to plan are considered as "neurotic." What does this mean? It means that the broad range of normal variations of behavior is not recognized, and that the specific features of what analysts call a neurosis get lost sight of. Apart from this, however, many of the very early neuroses are really different from what we are used to calling neurosis in the adult. Many problems in children which we call neurotic are actually limited to a single functional disturbance; and the way from conflict to symptom is often shorter than in adult neurosis.

What Anna Freud said long ago (1945) is, of course, true, namely that the apparently strong ego of a neurotic child is actually weak, and also that infantile neurosis may mean "calcification." This danger is inherent in rigid fixations on certain instinctual aims, or on certain defenses. The consequence then is that parts of the growing personality are, at least temporarily, excluded from further development. But there are several points to be considered here. First, there are also very recalcitrant and durable fixations that do not lead to neurosis or psychosis and still interfere with some aspects of later development. I remind you, for instance, of those "distortions" of the ego (Freud, 1937b) with whose help the development of a neurosis may be avoided. Such phenomena, though still little considered in analysis, are probably very frequent. Also the fixations on early specific frustrations, described by Anna Freud, do not necessarily lead to neurosis, though they may determine symptom formation if neurosis develops. Early traumatization may have similar effects.

Thus, in childhood, there are a variety of factors that may, in a sense, be called "pathogenic," but do not by themselves lead to neurosis or psychosis. There are also neurotic phenomena in childhood that are amenable to correction and modification in the course of growth and development, which I have to mention here in order not to make the picture too one-sided. The theoretical basis on which we can build here is a thought that Freud expressed in some of his later papers (e.g., 1926), namely, that the repressed instinctual demand is not necessarily rigidly preserved in the id. That is, it may be elaborated by the ego, or used by the ego, as is commonly the case in the more normal passing of the oedipus complex when repressed instinctual drives are sublimated and used in the resulting identifications. This gives us an explanation for the fact that the calcification we often find after childhood neuroses may be only a transient phenomenon; and this will make us less inclined to dispute, on theoretical grounds, the possibility of a spontaneous cure of these neuroses. It will appear even more plausible if we keep in mind the modifying power of maturation, also mentioned by Anna Freud, on the side of the id, but also of the ego, through which some anxiety conditions may lose their importance.

There is no yardstick for the pathogenic potential of infantile neurosis except for the long-run developmental consideration. We have to bear in mind that every new phase of maturation creates new potential conflict situations and new ways of dealing with these conflicts; but, on principle, it also carries with it, to a certain degree, the possibility of modifying the impact of earlier conflict solutions. The new aspect of the subsequent phases is the changed dominance of certain instinctual and certain ego functions; this includes also phase-specific capacities to deal with conflict situations and, in some degree, to revise old conflict solutions. The main thing in approaching these problems is that the genetic, the historical, aspect of later conflicts must be clearly distinguished from their phase-specific possibilities.

I want to make just one more point about the capacity of modifying, reversing, or compensating for developments which, if unchecked, may lead to pathology. An essential aspect of this is the capacity of the child to neutralize instinctual energy, libidinal, and aggressive. This faculty for neutralization may be different in regard to libido and aggression. And this faculty for substituting neutralized for instinctual energy must be viewed in connection with the substitution of ego aims for instinctual aims – the two processes varying partly independently, as seen in the cases of sexualization or aggressivization of ego functions. This is particularly relevant for the understanding of fixations and their consequences – which shows a continuum from the rigid fixation on an instinctual demand to those, on the other end of the line, that finally survive predominantly as an individual form, or direction, or intensity of an ego function.

All these show that the impact of development on infantile neurosis cannot be judged without using, in each individual case, all the tools that child psychology has developed as well as a knowledge of the relative relevance of these many factors mentioned, and of many others not mentioned here. The question of the extent to which infantile neurosis will determine later neurosis, or psychosis, or character development, or positive achievement is basically an empirical question. But developmental theory can give us models, it can tell us what factors have to be considered, in such a study, and what their most likely interaction is. Thus, theory can direct clinical studies on childhood neurosis, but it could not possibly replace them. And that is why we hope that in the following discussion, we will hear many clinical examples to enrich and also to test our developmental hypotheses.

Summary and Conclusion

One of the many Viennese who became drawn to the psychoanalytic enterprise and the captivating presence of the aging Freud, Hartmann was among the flood of intellectual Jewish refugees who fled the Nazi holocaust and eventually came to New York. Building on Freud's *The Ego and the Id* (1923b1980), he has been called the "enthusiastic father" (Monte, , p. 181) of ego psychology. Shortly before leaving Vienna, he presented a paper in 1937 to the Vienna Psychoanalytic Society entitled "Me," which later was published as *Ego Psychology and the Problem of Adaptation* (1939/1958). This profoundly influential essay established Hartmann's place in the history of psychoanalysis as Freud's heir. Along with Anna Freud's *The Ego and the Mechanisms of Defense* (1936), it marked the beginning of ego psychology.

Hartmann undertook an approach to developmental theory that involved first gaining distance from the clinical material, then defining its implications with academic and scientific precision. This academic approach at first was distasteful to Freud. Anna Freud was also initially cool to Hartmann's concepts, but later came to accept his ideas regarding the ego's role in adaptation. Referred to as the adaptive hypothesis, it complemented Freud's five metapsychological points of view, and assured that psychoanalysis would become an all-encompassing multidisciplinary intellectual enterprise.

The adaptive point of view maintains that infants are born with the equipment they need to adapt to their environment. In contrast to Freud, who emphasized the dark and instinctual aspects of human nature, Hartmann emphasized the idea that infants were designed to adapt to their environment. He shifted the emphasis of psychoanalysis from the view that a chaotic id motivated all thoughts and action to a position that endorsed the existence of a resilient ego capable of coping with the drives, the superego, and the environment. The effect of these proposals was to move psychoanalysis beyond the less hopeful focus on intrapsychic processes of drive/defense and psychopathology to a more optimistic general psychology of human development.

Hartmann emphasized the primacy of the ego in development, not only in its role as manager of conflicts that occur between id, ego, and superego, but also in adapting to the environment. The equipment with which infants are born enables them to adapt to their environment. It includes a set of potentials that Hartmann referred to as conflict-free ego capacities, or primary autonomous ego functions. He believed the potentials that exist within these functions could flourish if the child is provided an environment that is reasonably responsive to his or her needs, which he referred to as an average expectable environment. One of the primary autonomous ego functions is the synthetic function of the ego, which involves the ability to integrate or synthesize experiences and thus adapt to reality. Both defensive and adaptive functions were part of the ego's synthetic function.

Hartmann also proposed that during development, drives are freed from conflict and undergo a transformation through which their sexual and aggressive qualities are neutralized. They accrue to the ego secondary autonomous ego functions, which are independent from the id and are available to the ego to be used in the service of adaptation.

Hartmann described two ways through which modifications in the ego occurs in the service of adaptation. Alloplastic change takes place when people attempt to change their environment to cope with challenges they face. Autoplastic change occurs when people attempt to accommodate to the environment by modifying themselves to deal with reality.

Keywords Adaptive point of view • Alloplastic change • Autoplastic change • Average expectable environment • Change in function • Conflict-free ego • Ego-dystonic • Ego-syntonic • Neutralization • Primary autonomous ego functions • Secondary autonomous functions • Structural theory • Sublimation • Synthetic function of the ego

References

American Psychiatric Association. (2000). *Diagnostic and statistical manual of mental disorders* (4th ed., text revision). Washington, D. C.: Author.

Austrian, S. G. (Ed.). (2002). *Developmental theories through the life cycle*. New York: Columbia University Press.

Berzoff, J., Flanagan, L. M., & Hertz, P. (1996). *Inside out and outside in: Psychodynamic clinical theory and practice in contemporary multicultural contexts*. New York: Jason Aronson.

Eissler, R. S., & Eissler, K. R. (1964). Heinz Hartmann: A biographical sketch. *Bulletin of the Menninger Clinic, XXVIII*, 289–301.

Eissler, R. S., & Loewenstein, R. M. (1970). In memoriam. *Psychoanalytic Study of the Child, 25*.

Freud, A. (1945). *The writings of Anna Freud, Vol. IV: Indications for child analysis* (pp. 3–38). New York: International Universities Press.

Freud, S. (1914). On Narcissism: An introduction. *SE, XIV*, 67–102.

Freud, S. (1921). Group psychology and the analysis of the ego. *SE, XVIII*, 67–143.

Freud, S. (1923a). Two encyclopedia articles. *SE, XVIII*, 233–259.

Freud, S. (1923b). The Ego and the Id. *SE, XIX*, 1–66.

Freud, S. (1926). Inhibition, symptoms and anxiety. *SE, XX*, 75–175.

Freud, S. (1937a). Analysis terminable and interminable. *SE, XXIII*, 209–253.

Freud, S. (1937b). Constructions in analysis. *SE, XXIII*, 255–269.

Gitelson, M. (1965). Heinz Hartmann. *International Journal of Psychoanalysis, 46*, 2–4.

Hartmann, H. (1939). *Ego psychology and the problem of adaptation*. New York: International Universities Press.

Hartmann, H. (1950). Comments on the psychoanalytic theory of the ego. *Psychoanalytic Study of the Child, 5*, 74–96.

Hartmann, H. (1956b). The development of the ego concept in Freud's work. *International Journal of Psychoanalysis, 37*, 425–438.

Hartmann, H. (1959/1964). Essays on Ego Psychology. New York: International Universities Press.

Hartmann, L. (1994). Heinz Hartmann: A memorial tribute and filial memoir. *Psychoanalytic Study of the Child, 49*, 3–11.

Mitchell, S. A., & Black, M. (1995). *Freud and beyond: A history of modern psychoanalytic thought*. New York: Basic Books.

Monte, C. F. (1980). *Beneath the mask* (2nd ed.). New York: Holt Reinhold and Winston.

Nunberg, H. (1930/1931). The synthetic function of the ego. *International Journal of Psychoanalysis, 12*, 123–140.

Roazen, P. (1984). *Freud and his followers*. New York: New York University Press.

Summers, F. (1994). *Object relations theory and psychopathology: A comprehensive text*. New Jersey: The Analytic Press.

Major Works

Hartmann, H. (1927). *The fundamentals of psychoanalysis*. Leipzig: G. Thieme.
Hartmann, H. (1934). Experimental contribution to the psychology of obsessive-compulsive psychoses. *Journal of Psychiatry and Neurology, 50.*
Hartmann, H. (1939). Psycho-Analysis and the concept of mental health. *International Journal of Psycho-Analysis, 20*, 308–321.
Hartmann, H. (1944). The psychiatric works of Paul Schilder. *Psychoanalytic Review, 31*(1), 296.
Hartmann, H. (1948). Comments on the psychoanalytic theory of instinctual drives. *Psychoanalytic Quarterly, 17*, 368–388.
Hartmann, H., & Kris, E. (1945). The genetic approach in psychoanalysis. *Psychoanalytic Study of the Child, 1*, 11–29.
Hartmann, H., Kris, E., & Loewenstein, R. (1946). Comments on the formation of psychic structure. *Psychoanalytic Study of the Child, 2*, 11–38.
Hartmann, H., Kris, E., & Loewenstein, R. (1949). Notes on the theory of aggression. *Psychoanalytic Study of the Child, 3/4*, 9–36.
Hartmann, H. (1950a). Psychoanalysis and developmental psychology. *Psychoanalytic Study of the Child, 5*, 7–17.
Hartmann, H., Kris, E., & Loewenstein, R. (1951). Some psychoanalytic comments on culture and personality. In G. Wilbur & W. Muensterberger (Eds.), *Psychoanalysis and Culture*. New York: International Universities Press.
Hartmann, H. (1952). The mutual influences in the development of the ego and the id. *Psychoanalytic Study of the Child, 7*, 9–30.
Hartmann, H. (1953). Contributions to the metapsychology of schizophrenia. *Psychoanalytic Study of the Child, 8*, 177–198.
Hartmann, H. (1955). Notes on the theory of sublimation. *Psychoanalytic Study of the Child, 10*, 9–29.
Hartmann, H. (1956a). Notes on the reality principle. *Psychoanalytic Study of the Child, 11*, 31–53.
Hartmann, H. (1957). Ernst Kris (1900-1957). *Psychoanalytic Study of the Child, 12*, 9–15.
Hartmann, H. (1958). Comments on the scientific aspects of psychoanalysis. *Psychoanalytic Study of the Child, 13*, 127–146.
Hartmann, H. (1960). *Psychoanalysis and moral values*. New York: International Universities Press.
Hartmann, H., & Loewenstein, R. (1962). Notes on the superego. *Psychoanalytic Study of the Child, 17*, 42–81.
Hartmann, H. (1964). Concept formation in psychoanalysis. *Psychoanalytic Study of the Child, 19*, 11–38.
Hartmann, H. (1964). *Essays on ego psychology*. New York: International Universities Press.
Hartmann, H., & Loewenstein R. M. (1964). *Papers on psychoanalytic psychology. Psychological Issues Monograph*. New York: International Universities Press.
Hartmann, H. (1966). In R. Eissler & R. Loewenstein (Eds.), *Psychoanalysis: A general psychology*. New York: International Universities Press.

Supplementary Readings

Cooper, M. G., & Lesser, J. G. (2005). *Clinical social work practice: An integrated approach* (2nd ed.). Boston: Pearson Education, Inc.
Goldstein, E. (1995). *Ego psychology and social work practice* (2nd ed.). New York: Free Press.
Schamess, G. (2002). Ego psychology. In J. Berzoff (Ed.), *Inside out and outside in: Psychodynamic clinical theory and practice in contemporary multicultural contexts* (pp. 67–101). New York: Jason Arronson.

Chapter 3
Anna Freud (1895–1982)

Publishing Era (1922–1982)

Biographical Information

As we have seen, Sigmund and Martha Freud had 6 children in an 8-year period. Anna was born in 1895 in Vienna. For reasons that are unclear, Martha decided not to breast feed Anna as she had done with her other children. In fact, she took a vacation lasting several months shortly after Anna's birth. Although we can only speculate the reasons behind her mother's actions, it is clear that Anna and her mother were never to have a close relationship. When Anna was 1-year old, Martha's sister, Minna Bernays, came to live in the Freud home and served as an additional caregiver to the Freud household. A third person, Josefine Cihlarz, a nursemaid was hired after Anna's birth, and stayed with the family until Anna completed her first year of schooling. Anna believed that she was Josefine's favorite. Later in life, she reminisced that she considered Josephine as her "primary caretaker" and "psychological mother."

The year following Anna's birth, Freud's father Jakob died, an event that preoccupied him considerably. In addition, for the following 3 years, Freud was deeply absorbed in working on his book on dreams. As a result, it appeared that Freud was unable to attend sufficiently to Anna during her infant and toddler years. For her part, Anna developed the conviction that she was in competition with psychoanalysis for her father's attention. Furthermore, Anna was quite jealous of, and had a competitive and difficult relationship with her 2-year-older sister Sophie, who was her mother's favorite. During those years, she felt abandoned by her father and neglected by her mother.

Anna started school in 1901, when she was 6-years old. She suffered from a lisp, as had Freud when he was a child. A speech therapist successfully treated the problem and it never recurred (Young-Bruehl, 1988). She frequently found school boring, complaining that it was not challenging enough and dealt with her boredom by reading and writing. Her intellectual inspiration came not from her teachers, but rather from the people who came to visit her father, whom she sought to emulate.

J. Palombo et al., *Guide to Psychoanalytic Developmental Theories*,
DOI: 10.1007/978-0-387-88455-4_3, © Springer Science+Business Media, LLC 2009

Teacher and Psychoanalyst

In 1909, when Anna was 14, Freud introduced her to psychoanalysis by allowing her to sit in on meetings of the Vienna Psychoanalytic Society. She had earlier become fascinated with the subject, having begun to read her father's works on her own (Young-Bruehl, 1988). In 1912, she received her Matura diploma, the final degree at her Lyceum. As an 18-year-old a much older Ernest Jones, who was 35-years old and who was forming the London Psychoanalytic Society, courted her. Freud saw this courtship as inappropriate. Anna was suspicious of Jones' motives, suspecting that his interest was to gain access to her father. She eventually broke off the relationship with him.

It also appears that Anna suffered from episodes of depression during her early years. Among those was the episode that coincided with Sophie's planned wedding. Anna, who was 16-years old at the time, was sent to stay with her grandmother in Italy and her father decided that she should not come home to attend the wedding until she had fully recuperated from her condition. The correspondence between her and her father surrounding these events reveals that he interpreted Anna's depression as associated with her rivalry with her sister. She vehemently denied any such connection.

In 1914, she started a teaching apprenticeship in an elementary school where she spent 6 years as a teacher. Four years later, Freud took the highly unusual step of taking Anna into analysis, which was to have two stages, the first lasting for 4 years (1918–1922) and the second lasting from 1924 to 1925. In 1923 (Young-Breuhl, 1988, p. 120), when Freud became quite ill with cancer of the mouth, Anna decided to stay at home to nurse him, which she did until his death in 1938. Between 1923 and 1924, Hans Lampl was courting Anna who was discouraged by her father from responding positively because he considered Hans unsuitable for reasons that are not altogether clear (Young-Breuhl, 1988, p. 121). During Freud's long illness, Anna became the conduit through which communication between Freud and his colleagues occurred, keeping them informed of his medical condition. In addition, Anna's involvement with her father created severe tension between her and her mother, who felt displaced by her daughter. In 1920, her sister Sophie died suddenly from influenza, but due to rail strikes, she was unable to attend the funeral. There are indications that she dealt with her reactions to her sister's death in her analytic work with her father. In spite of the rivalry with her sister, Anna took on Sophie's son into treatment and considered him her first patient.

In the 1920s, she began to pursue earnestly her interest in psychoanalysis by joining an informal study circle that included August Aichhorn, whose work with delinquent children further inspired her interest in the treatment of children. Also in the early 1920s, a young group of University of Vienna medical students, which included Wilhelm Reich and Otto Fenichel, began to attend the Vienna Society's meetings. The members of this group joined Anna Freud and Heinz Hartmann in another study group that Rene Spitz attended (Young-Bruehl, 1988). In 1924 members of the secret Committee, which guarded the orthodoxy of psychoanalysis, asked Sigmund Freud if Anna, who was about to turn 29, could join their deliberations to replace Otto Rank who was being slowly ostracized for holding contrary positions. Freud agreed and gave Anna the customary ring signifying memberships (Young-Breuhl, 1988, pp. 148–150). By 1925, her position of leadership in the psychoanalytic movement was consolidated when she joined the executive board of the Vienna Psychoanalytic Institute and started working as a training analyst.

Anna had started practicing child analysis in 1923, following the completion of the first phase of her analysis with her father. She, along with Melanie Klein, Berta Bornstein, and Hermine Hug-Hellmuth, were among the first to practice psychoanalysis with children (Young-Bruel, 1988, p. 176). In 1926, Anna Freud published a series of lectures titled Introduction to the Technique of Child Analysis, which served to catalyze the debate with Melanie Klein (Young-Breuhl, 1988, p. 166). In 1935, at the conclusion of the second stage of Anna's analysis, Dorothy Burlingham sought her help regarding her oldest son. Anna took the child into analysis. Dorothy, who had come to Vienna from America, entered analysis with Sigmund Freud. She and Anna Freud formed a relationship that grew in intensity and complexity through the years, which they eventually saw as an "ideal friendship" that lasted for a lifetime. Anna not only treated Burlingham's children, but also struggled with the desire to become part of the family, and eventually played the role of both stepparent and psychoanalyst to the children.

Eva Rosenfeld, the friend of a patient in analysis with Sigmund Freud, had turned to Anna Freud for help in mourning the loss of three of her children in a brief period. In 1927 and with Burlingham's help, Rosenfeld and Anna opened, in the Hietzing district of Vienna, a special school operated on Dewey's progressive educational principles and on psychoanalytic principles. The first teacher hired was Peter Blos and the second was his friend Erik Erikson; both of whom were influenced by Anna Freud. Most of the children in this school were in analysis, often with Anna Freud, in conjunction with their attendance at the school. The school, which remained opened until 1931, gave Anna an opportunity to apply psychoanalytic principles to the education of children (Heller, 1992). She and Burlingham were to use the knowledge acquired in that school in the war nurseries they later established in Hampstead.

Child Analysis

Anna Freud believed that psychoanalysis of children differed markedly from that of adults. The differences were partly due to the timing of the occurrence of the Oedipal Stage and partly due to developmental considerations, which she believed required technical modifications of analytic practice. Among the technical modifications were the fact that first, children did not seek help on their own, but rather were brought by their caregivers who were concerned about them. A long tangential dispute with other child analysts occurred around the related issue of whether children suffered psychologically from their conflicts or whether they simply manifested that suffering through their symptoms. Second, Freud insisted that children could not give an account of their histories; instead, the analyst had to rely on the caregivers' reports for that information. This meant that the analyst had to obtain information about the patient from someone other than the patient, a technical innovation not permitted in the analysis of adults. Third, children required a "preparatory stage" during which they could be encouraged to be introspective and could recognize the conflicts from which they suffered; a stage during which educational instruction had to be given to the caregivers and to the child to help in the transition to analytic work. Finally, children could not freely associate in the same manner as adults, rather the information about their unconscious conflicts was obtained through play, also an innovation not used with adult patients.

For Anna Freud, much more important than these technical concerns was her conviction that children could not develop the type of transference neurosis that adults do. For such a transference to occur, the child has to have traversed the Oedipal stage and internalized a superego. She dismissed Klein's notion that this stage could occur during the first or second year of life and maintained with her father that it only came to fruition between the ages of three and four when the child was sufficiently aware of the differential role that his or her parents played within the family. Young children, she believed, were still too dependent on the caregivers, needing them as external enforcers of prohibitions because they had not internalized a superego. Consequently, they could not develop a transference that could be the subject of analysis. Later on, she softened her stance regarding the analyzability of children. She minimized the importance of the technical differences, but maintained that children are analyzable if they had entered the Oedipal stage.

The Emergence of Ego Psychology and Sigmund Freud's Death

Anna Freud's second book, *The Ego and the Mechanisms of Defense*, appeared in 1936. She gave the first edition of the book to her father, a gift that pleased him greatly. In it, she enlarges the purview of the structural point of view that her father articulated in his later work on the *Ego and the Id* (1923). In tandem with the contributions of Hartmann, this work defines the ego psychological perspective. We discuss the various ego defenses that she identified in the section on development later.

Anna continued to nurse her father through the years as he fought a long battle with cancer. The Freuds left Vienna for England in 1938 following the Nazis invasion of Austria. In 1939, Freud's cancer was so advanced that it became intolerable to him. Finally, he asked his physician to assist in ending his life and died on September 23, 1939. Once again, Anna dealt with her grief by throwing herself into the work with children affected by the war.

The War Nurseries

The American Organization Foster Parents' Plan for War Children, based in New York, had a long history of funding projects that dealt with the effects of war on children. Following the fall of France, that organization asked Anna Freud and Dorothy Burlingham to take charge of three nurseries that would provide services to children in the greater London area, which they led from 1941 to 1945. These became residential nurseries for children who had lost a parent or whose parents, primarily their mothers, could not care for them because of their contribution to the war effort. In two volumes, the first *War and Children* (1943) and the second *Infants without Families: Reports on the Hampstead Nurseries* (1944), Freud and Burlingham describe their pioneering work in the advocacy of attending to the psychological needs of children separated from their caregivers. They provided extensive data on the effects of separation and loss in early childhood. All the nursery workers wrote hundreds of detailed observations. These observations contributed to the development of Anna Freud's overall theoretical framework. In particular, the papers offered more insight into the development of attachment to parents and their impact on ego and superego development.

Infants without Families (1944) was the first major summary from the war nurseries reports. Later, in 1973, *Infants without Families* was published again as The Writings of Anna Freud, Volume 3: *Infants without Families: Reports on the Hampstead Nurseries* (1939–1945). This later work included not only the initial summaries, but also observations on various themes as well as examples. Many of the 56 monthly reports that span the period from February 1941 to December 1945 were published in this volume. It details both the child's immediate state of distress and the long-term disruption to development. The primary conclusion of this volume is the identification of three major needs of the developing child: (1) the need for intimate interchange of affection with a maternal figure; (2) the need for ample and constant external stimulation of innate potentialities; and (3) the need for unbroken continuity of care (Freud, 1973, p. xx)

Also contained in these reports is one of the earliest summaries of the development of relationships during the first year of life; describing how a baby develops an attachment to the mother that serves as the pattern for later relationships. The reports also describe how most of the children in the nursery were better off physically than those from poor homes had been before the war. Psychologically, those children felt more secure with their own mother than with strangers (Edgcumbe, 2000).

Overall, these reports contributed to a greater understanding of what a child needs to develop normally. They also served as a building block for Anna Freud's detailed theory of development regarding the child's cathexis to objects and the role investment in the object plays in cognitive, emotional, and personality development. The reports presage Bowlby's later work on attachment.

The Controversial Discussions

The debate with Melanie Klein first broke into the open in 1926 when Anna Freud gave a series of five lectures on child analysis, later included in *The Psychoanalytic Treatment of Children*, first published in English in 1946. As we will see later in this work, Klein was encouraged by Abraham, with whom she was in analysis, to propose an alternative developmental path than that of Sigmund Freud's. Children, she believed, have an active fantasy life as infants (Klein uses the term *phantasy*). They progress from a paranoid position to a depressive positive before entering the Oedipal Stage. Klein asserted that the superego does not develop with the dissolution of the Oedipus complex, but rather it develops *with* the Oedipus complex at the end of the first year and beginning of the second year of life. In addition, Klein believed that psychoanalysis with children was no different from that of adults, except for the modification in techniques required because of their age. In Klein's view, the only difference was that children do not freely associate verbally as adults do, although their play in sessions is equivalent to adult's verbal free associations.

The period between 1941 and 1945 saw the reemergence of the controversy between Anna Freud and Melanie Klein (King & Steiner, 1990). Anna Freud agreed to participate from 1942 to 1944 in what came to be known as "The Controversial Discussions" in an effort to resolve the issues. The feud between the two had grown to such proportions that it threatened to undermine the entire psychoanalytic enterprise in England. The ultimate resolution saw the British society divided into three groups: Klein's group, Anna Freud's group, and an Independent Group. By then, Berta Bornstein had persuaded Anna Freud to give up the idea of an introductory or preparatory phase as necessary in the analysis of children.

Following this exhausting period, in 1948, Anna Freud organized a training program in child psychoanalysis for former workers in the war nurseries. She accepted nonmedical people into this program, which was a deviation from the practice of psychoanalytic institutes in the United States. More than two decades earlier, a controversy regarding the acceptance of nonmedical people for psychoanalytic training resulted in writing a paper to address this issue by her father. The controversy began when Theodor Reik, a nonmedical member of the Vienna Psychoanalytic Society, was charged with violating an old Austrian law against "quackery," a law that made it illegal to treat patients without having a medical degree. Freud wrote his paper, entitled *The Question of Lay Analysis* (1926b), in response to this charge. He held strongly to the belief that psychoanalysis was not to be regarded as purely a concern of the medical profession. He did believe, however, that it was necessary for a psychoanalyst to receive specialized training. The charge against Theodor Reik was eventually dropped.

The Productive Years

Following the war years, Anna Freud increasingly gained international recognition for her contributions to psychoanalysis and to the cause of children's psychological needs. In 1952, the year following her mother's death, the Hampstead Clinic opened, which she directed until her retirement. The patients at the Hampstead Clinic inspired her to new ideas about developmental pathology. She created a diagnostic profile, which was an innovation for psychoanalysts. In 1965, she published her book *Normality and Pathology in Childhood: Assessment of Development*. This book comprehensively outlined her developmental point of view, including her idea of multiple developmental lines and her distinction between normal and pathological development. In 1982, Anna Freud suffered a stroke. She lived quietly through her last few months until she died on October 9, 1982, at the age of 87. The Hampstead Clinic would eventually be renamed as the Anna Freud Centre.

Her Legacy

Anna Freud is widely regarded as the originator of child psychoanalysis, although Melanie Klein may claim equal credit. Having grown up in the household of the creator of psychoanalysis and been instructed by him, Anna Freud absorbed her father's theories, in particular, the structural point of view, much as the air she breathed. The belief prevalent at the time was that Freud's discoveries were as sound as were the discoveries of the structure of the atom. She never questioned the view of the human psyche that Sigmund Freud promulgated in his later work; she sought only to extend and enlarge upon his work. In that respect, her emphasis on the structural model of the mind placed her, along with Hartmann, as leaders in the emerging ego psychological psychoanalytic movement. As we will see in the section that follows, Anna Freud embraced Sigmund Freud's theory of development as fact. Her experience as a schoolteacher and as a child analyst led her to find confirmation of those theories for both children's normal and pathological development.

Theory of Development

Anna Freud focused her attention on the ego, which she saw as the "seat of observation." Her work on the ego and its defenses (1936), along with Hartmann's contributions, defines the ego psychology perspective. She was the analyst and teacher of Erik Erikson, and set the stage for his work when she called for a more comprehensive look at what engages the world of the child's ego, not just libido. Her emphasis on a child's real relationships is in conflict with Melanie Klein's emphasis on the *phantasy* life of the child.

Anna Freud accepted her father's theory that children traverse a series of developmental stages, the oral, anal, and phallic/oedipal stages. She proposed the delineation of children maturation through the description of events in their development, organizing them along **developmental lines.** These development lines tracked the unfolding of a specific maturational theme at different period of the children's lives and indicated what was typical or atypical. This proposal represented a major departure from the methodology that relied on the reconstruction of development. Instead, it depended upon data derived from the day-to-day observation of children. In spite of the novelty of this approach, the underlying dynamics at play were formulated to fit into Freud's original metapsychology. The gains made by the innovative strips of this advance were incorporated into a revised version of the established psychodynamics.

Anna Freud also believed that development moved back and forth along multiple lines of development. Progress along these lines at times necessitates regressions. Consequently, the descriptions provided by the developmental lines can be used to determine a child's readiness for a variety of life experiences, or assist in identifying deficits in capacities the child requires to function adequately. She proposed that the level a child reaches on a developmental line is the result of a combination of drive and ego development and its relationship with the nurturing environment. Because of the wide variations in normal development, she did not date the stages in a developmental line according to age. In our discussion, we have therefore inferred the age ranges in these descriptions. She proposed a prototypical developmental line that may be used as a pattern for other lines of development (see Table 3.1).

In addition to this prototype of a developmental line, Anna Freud proposed the following three developmental lines, which she calls "toward body independence":

The developmental line "from suckling to rational eating"

- The infant is nursed at the breast or bottle-fed (approximately 0–2 months)
- The infant is weaned from the breast or bottle (approximately 2–7 months)
- The child is in transition from being fed to self-feeding and is eventually able to self-feed using a spoon, fork, etc. (approximately 7–15 months)
- The child is able to self-feed using a spoon, fork, etc. (approximately 15–30 months)
- During the 30–48 months age-range, the child experiences a gradual fading out of the equation between food and mother.

The developmental line "from wetting and soiling to bladder and bowel control"

- The infant has complete freedom to wet and soil.
- The dominant role in drive activity passes from the oral to the anal zone (at around 24 months). The toddler's attitude toward the object world is ambivalent, fluctuating from love to hate. If the mother can sympathetically mediate between the environment's demand for cleanliness and the child's oppositional anal tendencies, toilet training will proceed without upheavals. If the mother demands anal and urethral control in a harsh and uncompromising manner, a major battle will ensue.
- During the period from 30 to 48 months, the child accepts the mother's and the environment's attitudes about cleanliness. Bowel and bladder control is established.

The developmental line "from irresponsibility to responsibility in body management"

- During the first few months of life, children change from modes of discharging aggression diffusely through their bodies to directing it toward the external world.
- Following the first few months of life, advances occur in ego functioning. Children begin to orient themselves to the external world and understand their participation in events in the world and the cause and effect relationships associated with those activities.

Table 3.1 The prototype of a developmental line: *from dependency to emotional self-reliance and adult object relationships*

Stage 1	0–7 months	This is a period during which a biological unity between the mother and infant couple exists, which means that infants experience their mothers as part of themselves, and the mothers, conversely, experience the child psychologically to be part of themselves.
Stage 2	7–15 months	In the **anaclitic stage**, the relationship between children and their caregivers is one of dependence. This relationship is naturally fluctuating. When drives are aroused the need for the object increases, when they are satisfied it is reduced. The extent to which children's needs are satisfied determines the images of a good or bad mother they internalize. Failure of the mother to be reliable, need-fulfilling, and comforting in this stage leads to problems in individuation.
Stage 3	15–30 months	This stage heralds the beginning of **object constancy** (see Mahler, 1975). In this stage, children achieve a consistent internal representation of the object, one that is more stable and one that children can maintain regardless of whether the objects satisfy or do not satisfy their needs. Children are now able to form relationships that can survive disappointments and frustrations.
Stage 4	30–48 months	Toddlers' positive and negative feelings focus on the same person and that capacity becomes noticeable to others. People refer to this stage as the "terrible twos." Children are in conflict. They wish both to be independent and to retain the tie to their mother. If the relationship to the object is unstable during this stage, children will have difficulty maintaining a balance between their positive and negative feelings and integrating libidinal and aggressive impulses. This imbalance can lead to aggressive behavior. A consolidation of object constancy, which began during the 15–30 months age range, occurs during this stage.
Stage 5	4–7 years	This stage includes the **phallic-oedipal stage** and is characterized by possessiveness of the parent of the opposite sex and jealousy of and rivalry toward the parent of the same sex.
Stage 6	7–11 years	The latency period is the stage during which a reduction of children's drives and a transfer of libido from parents to peers and others in their environment occurs. A full integration of the child into the community of school peers cannot happen before the child has transferred his or her libido from the parents to the community. The later part of this stage is one in which reactions to adoption would be particularly severe.
Stage 7	11–13 years	Anna Freud refers to this period as "the preadolescent prelude to the adolescent revolt" (1963, p. 248). A regression occurs from the reasonableness of the latency period to a demanding and rebellious attitude, which is characteristic of earlier stages. This regression strengthens oral, anal, and phallic drive components, reviving infantile fantasies and intensifying intrapsychic conflicts.
Stage 8	13–18 years	During the **adolescent stage**, which begins at this age, the struggle to master the surge of sexuality and aggression is on the ascendance. Two new defense mechanisms emerge to deal with the instinctual demands of the body, intellectualization, and asceticism. The adolescent struggles to transfer emotional investment from parents to new objects.

- During the 30–48 months age range, the child voluntarily endorses the rules of hygiene and medical necessities.

Other developmental lines include: The developmental line "from egocentricity to companionship"

- Infants have a self-centered outlook to the object world and are completely asocial. They have no perception of the world as external and existing separately from them (approximately 0–7 months).
- Children relate to other children as to lifeless objects or toys that they handle and discard as their mood demands. Children remain essentially asocial (approximately 7–15 months).
- The child relates to other children as helpmates in carrying out a desired task. As soon as the task is completed, the other child is no longer needed. The child has a narcissistic orientation to others. He or she sees other children as rivals for the mother. The child notices differences among rivals, which leads to envy. The presence of others loosens the magnetic love affair with the mother (approximately 15–30 months).
- Other children are seen as partners and objects in their own right (approximately 30–48 months).
- The child is able to see other children as objects in their own right. The child is capable of friendships and companionship (approximately 4–7 years).

The developmental line "from body to the toy and from play to work"

- Children play with their own bodies or their mothers' bodies, with no clear differentiation between the two (approximately 0–7 months).
- The properties of the mother's and the child's bodies are transferred on to some soft substance, such as a pillow (approximately 7–15 months).
- A child who was previously clinging to one specific transitional object develops a more indiscriminate liking for soft toys of various kinds (approximately 15–30 months).
- Soft cuddly toys fade out of use gradually. During this time, direct satisfaction from the play activity itself gives way to the pleasure in the completion of tasks (approximately 30–48 months).
- The ability to play is transformed into the ability to work. The child acquires several additional capacities during this period, including the ability to control and modify impulses so that materials can be used constructively instead of destructively, and the ability to carry out plans becomes established (approximately 4–7 years).

Defense Mechanisms

As we have seen, Sigmund Freud introduced the term defense early in his work as unconscious mechanisms the ego uses to fend off anxiety-producing affects (Freud, 1894). The prototypical defense was repression. For Anna Freud, the motivation for the employment of defenses by the ego lies in what she identified as three types of anxieties: (1) **instinctual anxiety**, (2) **superego anxiety** or anxiety produced by one's conscience, and (3) **objective anxiety**.

In the case of *instinctual anxiety*, the ego sets out to defend against instinctual impulses; defenses reflect the conflict between the id and ego. In analysis, the ego's defenses pit themselves directly against the analyst, since the analyst is trying to unearth repressed material. The ego defends not only against the instinctual impulses, but also against affects, such as hatred, anger, and rage, associated with those instincts. In the case of *superego anxiety*, the conflict is between the ego and the superego. The ego registers the emergence of an instinctual libidinal or aggressive impulse in consciousness. Since such impulses are unacceptable to the superego, which prohibits their gratification, the threat to the ego leads it to institute a set of defenses. *Objective anxiety* refers to ego defenses motivated by the dread of forces outside the self. The conflict is between the ego and the external world.

Sigmund Freud's early writings laid the groundwork for the original nine defense mechanisms discussed earlier in the chapter on Sigmund Freud, which include the following: Repression, turning against the self, reversal, projection, introjection or identification, regression, reaction formation, isolation, and undoing (Freud, 1894, 1915, 1922, 1926a). To these Anna Freud added the following defense mechanisms: Altruism, asceticism, avoidance, denial, displacement, identification with the aggressor, and intellectualization. In the chart that follows, we describe each of these defenses and provide a clinical example (see Table 3.2).

On Adolescence

Anna Freud's 1936 publication of the *The Ego and the Mechanisms of Defense* (1936) established her credentials as an authority on the postlatency or adolescent phase. Although in that work she based her views on material on the treatment of only a few pubescent children and her autobiographical data (Young-Bruehl, 1988, p. 210), her insight into teenagers and their defenses broke new ground (Appignanesi & Forrester, 2000, p. 294). She contributed two original defenses, identification with the aggressor and altruistic surrender, adding to the existing set of defenses and defensive modes.

In 1958, Anna Freud returned to the topic and summarized her views on the subject of adolescence. Her contributions included the ideas that some male adolescents seek to prolong the phase far beyond that normally expected and that adolescence is as a recapitulation of an earlier phase. The first proposal is credited to Bernfeld (1923), but the concept was actually was put forward earlier (1904) by Hall (Easman, 1993, pp. 15, 19). The second idea is found in Freud (1905) and later clarified by Jones (1922) in his statement, "the individual recapitulates and expands in the second decennium of life the development he passed through during the first 5 years…" (Jones, 1922, p. 399).

Table 3.2 Anna Freud's defense mechanisms, their definitions, and illustrative examples

Defense Mechanism	Description	Clinical example
Altruism ("Altruistic Surrender")	This defense involves the attainment of satisfaction through service to others. Use of this defense enables a person to take an interest in the gratification of other people's instincts. In so doing, it indirectly allows the person to gratify his or her own instincts, despite the superego's objections. In involves a surrender of instinctual wishes to an object seen as better qualified to fulfill them. It has its origin in infantile conflict with parental authority concerning some form of instinctual gratification.	A man whose child has been abducted is overwhelmed by his anger and aggressive impulses. He channels the resultant energies into organizing a public campaign designed to increase awareness and strengthen or reform existing laws in an effort to see that this same experience does not happen to someone else. Through this effort, he contributes positively to society at the same time keeping his instinctual aggressive wishes from gaining full expression through vengeful or murderous activity.
Asceticism	Young people sometimes pass through a stage in which they mistrust enjoyment in general, so they deal with these desires for enjoyment by imposing stronger prohibitions on their instincts. This defense involves moral renunciation of pleasures to avoid anxiety associated with impulse gratification.	A young girl feels uncomfortable with her emerging sexual desires. To protect herself from the libidinal impulses that feel like a threat, she becomes a vegetarian and attempts to deny her desires by turning to an ascetic lifestyle. She states that she has no interest in worldly pleasures, and attributes this stance to her aspiration to some form of higher consciousness.
Avoidance	This is a primitive defense, which involves the avoidance of important aspects of reality that are perceived to be sources of unpleasure.	A young boy experiences humiliation at the hands of a classmate. As a result, he feels angry and engages in aggressive fantasies directed at his classmate. To keep these impulses at bay, he goes far out of his way to avoid encounters with this classmate.
Denial	This defense is employed in situations in which it appears impossible to escape pain. It involves negating important aspects of external reality that are perceived to be potential sources of unpleasure. Unpleasant external stimuli are removed from consciousness through the mechanism.	A child receives news that her father is going to have to leave for a long period due to military deployment. She feels helpless and angry, as a result she experiences a great deal of anxiety. She attempts to handle this anxiety by refusing to believe that it is true. Even after her father has departed, she continues to insist that he will be home soon.

Displacement	This defense involves shifting of feelings or conflicts about one person on to another person or object that is perceived to be less of a threat. This defense works with other defenses. For example, in the defense of projection, unacceptable ideas or impulses are displaced into the outside world. The defense of sublimation involves the displacement of instinctual aims to conform to higher social values.	A boy who is admonished by his father becomes angry feeling the criticism is unfair. Since he does not feel it acceptable to direct his anger at his father, he deals with this anger by directing it at his younger sibling.
Identification with the aggressor	This defense is employed when an external object, such as a threatening or disapproving authority figure, arouses anxiety. The defense involves managing the anxiety by identifying with the source of the threat. This is accomplished by introjecting a characteristic of the threatening figure, or by imitating the aggression of the threatening figure. Anxiety is reduced by transforming oneself from the one who is threatened to the one who makes the threat. Identification plays a role in the development of the superego, and contributes to mastery of instinctual impulses.	A boy is consistently criticized by his father and is often physically punished. He feels he has no way to please his father and cannot safely direct his anger at him. The boy manages the resulting anxiety by taking a critical and punitive stance toward his peers. This makes him feel like he is now the one who is in charge. He acts in an overly critical way toward them, and frequently gets into physical altercations.
Intellectualization	With the arrival of puberty, adolescents experience an increase in libido and aggression as well as an enlargement of their intellectual capabilities. This defense involves using the newly acquired intellectual capabilities to *think* about instinctual conflicts rather than experiencing them directly. The intensified use of intellectual defenses during adolescence is part of the ego's attempt to master instincts through thought. The goal is to link instinctual processes with thoughts so that they can become accessible to consciousness and under control.	A girl raised by a single mother, who treats her repeatedly in a punitive and abusive manner, feels there is no safe outlet for the built up anger and aggression she feels towards her mother. She also feels that she has no power to change her circumstances. When she speaks of her mother, she deals with these impulses by being argumentative, oppositional, and using her intellect to give derogatory descriptions of her mother, which she delivers in a calculated and unemotional manner.

She also articulated clinical positions about adolescence that became widely accepted. These include the concept of adolescence is a normal developmental *disturbance*. The upheaval associated with this disturbance is necessary and inevitable, even though some adolescents defend themselves well against it, giving the appearance of a relatively smooth transition into adulthood. The upheaval is a manifestation of the internal adjustments that take place during latency, at which time a reconfiguration of the ego's defenses occurs to cope with the upsurge in drive activity. The upheaval reflects an interruption in the peaceful growth period of latency.

Furthermore, she maintained that it is normal for adolescents to behave in an inconsistent and unpredictable manner. Conflicting forms of behavior and attitudes coexist. Regarding these alternating emotional state, Richmond and Sklansky (1984) state that, "She described the adolescent as being altruistic and egocentric; devoted and unfaithful; gregarious and solitary; blindly submissive to a leader and defiant of authority; idealistic and cynical; sensitive and callous; ascetic and libertine; optimistic and pessimistic; enthusiastic and indifferent" (p. 98). Easman (1993) noted that she was unaware of the influence of Hall's contribution (1993, pp. 15, 19) in proposing these paired opposites and the *sturm un drang* nature of this phase.

Diagnostic Profile

Anna Freud created a diagnostic profile for child analysts based on her understandings of the developmental needs of children. Because of her belief that developing children confront a "shifting internal scene" (Freud, 1962, p. 149), which is not characteristic of adults, she created this profile to address children's age-appropriate tasks that adults do not face. She believed that the most important thing a diagnostician can do is to determine the child's capacity to develop progressively, or to determine to what extent damage has been done to that capacity. To accomplish this task, it was necessary to arrive at a clear understanding of where a child currently stands in terms of his or her mastery of developmental tasks. If a diagnostician can acquire this information, it will lead to a determination of the permanence or transitory nature of the pathology, which will in turn influence what treatment methods will be employed.

The outline in Table 3.3 was presented by Anna Freud in her work *Assessment of Childhood Disturbances* (1962). It provides instructions to diagnosticians for the formulation of their assessment of a child. We reproduce it here in the form of requests for information or questions that the diagnostician should answer. Items I to IV require the diagnostician to provide a statement of the data collected, whereas Items V to VIII require the diagnostician to draw inferences from those data organized along the lines of classical ego psychological categories. In section V.B.2, we provided an expanded list and definition of specific ego functions. Item IX requires a diagnostic statement that conforms to Anna Freud's conceptualization of normality and pathology in her 1965 work (see Table 3.3)

Table 3.3 Anna Freud's diagnostic profile

Diagnostic profile
I. *Reason for referral:* Describe arrests in development, behavior problems, anxieties, inhibitions, symptoms, etc.
II. *Description of child:* Describe the child's appearance, moods, manner, etc.
III. *Family background and personal history:* Provide a summary of the family's background, the personal histories of the caregivers and the child's developmental history.
IV. *Possibly significant environmental influences:* Supply any other information that is relevant to the assessment of the child's presentation.
V. *Assessments of development*
A. Drive development
1. Libido
a). Stage of development: Has the child proceeded forward through to an age-adequate stage of development (oral, anal, phallic, latency, preadolescence, adolescence)?
b). Libido distribution: Has the child's self as well as the object world been adequately cathected and is the child's narcissism sufficient to ensure self-esteem?
c). Object libido: Has the child achieved an age-appropriate quality of object relationships, such as object constancy, oedipal, or adolescent stages?
2. Aggression
a). Quantitatively, how intense or modulated is the child's expression of aggression?
b). Qualitatively, does the quality of aggression correspond to the level of libido development? Does the child use specific defenses against individual drives, and if so are these adequate and effective to deal with the anxiety involved? Is the child dependent on external support to maintain those defenses?
c). Does the child direct his or her aggression at the object world or the self? Are defenses employed against individual drives, or against drive activity in a more general sense? Are those defenses age adequate, too primitive, or balanced? Are they effective in dealing with anxiety?
B. Ego development
1. Is the ego apparatus intact or defective?
2. Are ego functions, such as memory, reality testing, speech, intact or defective? (As A. Freud appears not to have left a definitive listing of ego functions, the following is a list extrapolated from her publications)
a). **Change of function** refers to the ability of the ego to loosen or free up capacities from their connection to conflict with the drives. (a) There are the innate capacities referred to as **primary autonomous functions,** which are inborn and conflict free. These may become embroiled in conflict and regain autonomous status once the conflict is resolved. An example is that of a child who begins to stutter because he believes that speech represents a form of aggression. Once the conflict is resolved, the child's speech regains it primary autonomous status. (b) **Secondary autonomous functions** are functions that were formerly embroiled in conflict around developmental issues, such as oral, anal, or phallic oedipal concerns. Once the conflicts are resolved secondary autonomy is achieved and energies accrue to the ego. An example would be that of a person whose conflicts around orality are transformed into a career as a chef.
b). **Synthetic-integrative functions** refer to the ego's capacity to reconcile intrapsychic incongruities and to actively relate internal and external events together in a stable, consistent presentation.
c). **Reality testing** is the capacity to distinguish between inner and outer stimuli, to assess the accuracy of perception, and the ability for reflective awareness and to match subjective perceptions with outer reality. Included under this function is the **sense of reality**, which consists of the ability to distinguish the boundaries between self and world.

(continued)

Table 3.3 (continued)

Diagnostic profile
d). **Judgment** refers to the understanding of cause and effect and is the ability to anticipate the consequences of one's actions, as well as, the appropriateness of this anticipation in behavioral and emotional expressions.
e). **Impulse control** refers to the capacity to regulate and delay drive or impulse expression.
f). **Object relations** refer to the capacity to invest others with libidinal and/or aggressive energy. It is possible to distinguish different types of object relationships by the degree and kind of relatedness, their primitiveness (narcissistic attachment or symbiotic-object choices), and the degree to which others are perceived independently of oneself and the capacity to use interpersonal interaction to manage self-esteem.
g). **Thought processes** refers to cognitive capacities such as memory, concentration, attention, the ability to conceptualize, transpose primary into secondary process, and to use trial action in thought.
h). **Defensive functions** are mechanisms the ego uses to manage drives, superego injunctions, and reality. Defenses may be successful in their aims or weak and ineffectual.
i). **Regression** involves the adaptive capacity to temporarily retreat to earlier levels of functioning to consolidate developmental gains, the capacity to move back and force from higher to lower libidinal and aggressive stages without remaining caught in a less progressive level than is age-adequate, and to relax cognitive acuity in order to promote creativity and mastery.
3. Does the ego deploy its defenses in an organized manner against individual drives, or against drive activity, such as instinctual pleasure, in general?
4. To what extent do the defenses the child employs interfere with ego functioning?
C. Superego Development
1. What is the extent and organization of the child's superego?
2. How supportive, severe, unpredictable, demanding, uneven, or indulgent is it?
3. How well does it regulate the child's well-being?
D. Development of the total personality: How well has the child progressed along the various *lines of development*, and what level has the child reached in each line?
VI. *Genetic assessments (regression and fixation points):* What events in the child's history have led to developmental fixation and regressions, if any? Do fixations and regressions exist and are these temporary or permanent? If temporary, are they part of normal development, and do they represent attempts at adaptation?
VII. *Dynamic and structural assessments:* In attempting to ascertain the child's level of maturity, the severity of the disturbance, and the intensity needed in therapeutic intervention, do the conflicts represent:
1. External conflicts between the id-ego and the outside world?
2. Internal conflicts between ego-superego and id?
3. Internal conflicts between incompatible drives?
VIII. *Assessment of some general characteristics:* In assessing the child for personality characteristics that can predict reactions to treatment and potential for recovery, how would you characterize the child's:
1. Frustration tolerance?
2. Sublimation potential?
3. Over-all attitude to anxiety?
4. Does the child's development demonstrate that progressive developmental forces versus regressive tendencies are dominant?
IX. *Diagnosis:* Putting together all of the above data in order to arrive at a complete and meaningful assessment:

(continued)

Table 3.3 (continued)

Diagnostic profile
1. Does the child falls within the range of "variations of normality"?
2. Are the child's symptoms transitory?
3. Are the child's regressions permanent?
4. Are organic deficiencies distorting development?
5. Are destructive processes disrupting development?

Case Illustration

The following case is taken from Freud (1966), *The ego and the mechanisms of defense, revised edition* (originally written in 1936) pp. 35–37. It serves as an illustration of the employment of defenses against instinctual impulses and affects. (Reprinted with permission from International Universities Press.)

A young girl came to me to be analyzed on account of states of acute anxiety, which were interfering with her daily life and preventing her regular attendance at school. Although she came because her mother urged her to do so, she showed no unwillingness to tell me about her life both in the past and in the present. Her attitude toward me was friendly and frank, but I noticed that in all her communications she carefully avoided making any allusion to her symptom. She never mentioned anxiety attacks which took place between the analytic sessions. If I myself insisted on bringing her symptom into the analysis or gave interpretations of her anxiety, which were based on unmistakable indications in her associations, her friendly attitude changed. On every such occasion, the result was a volley of contemptuous and mocking remarks. The attempt to find a connection between the patient's attitude and her relation to her mother was completely unsuccessful. Both in the consciousness and in the unconscious that relation was entirely different. In these repeated outbursts of contempt and ridicule, the analyst found herself at a loss and the patient was, for the time being, inaccessible to further analysis. As the analysis went deeper, however, we found that these affects did not represent a transference reaction in the true sense of the term and were not connected with the analytic situation at all. They indicated the patient's customary attitude toward herself whenever emotions of tenderness, longing, or anxiety were about to emerge in her affective life. The more powerfully the affect forced itself upon her, the more vehemently and scathingly did she ridicule herself. The analyst became the recipient of these defensive reactions only secondarily, because she was encouraging the demands of the patient's anxiety to be worked over in consciousness. The interpretation of the content of the anxiety, even when this could be correctly inferred from other communications, could have no result so long as every approach to the affect only intensified her defensive reaction. It was impossible to make that content conscious until we had brought into consciousness and so rendered inoperative the patient's method of defending herself against her affects by contemptuous disparagement – a process that had become automatic in every department of her life. Historically, this mode of defense by means of ridicule and scorn was explained by her identification of herself with her dead father, who used to try to train the little girl in self-control by making mocking remarks when she gave way to some emotional outburst. The method had become stereotyped through her memory of her father, whom she had loved dearly. The technique necessary to understand this case was to begin with the analysis of the patient's defense against her affects and to go on to the elucidation of her resistance in the transference. Then, and then only, was it possible to proceed to the analysis of her anxiety itself and of its antecedents (Freud, 1966, pp. 35–37).

Summary and Conclusions

Anna Freud was among the first to practice child psychoanalysis, along with Melanie Klein and Hermine Hug-Hellmuth. Anna Freud disagreed with Klein about the nature of psychoanalysis of children. She believed that psychoanalysis of children differed markedly from that of adults in several important ways: children do not seek help on their own, they cannot give an account of their histories, they require a preparatory stage, they cannot freely associate in the same way as adults, and they cannot develop the type of transference neurosis that adults do.

In *The Ego and the Mechanisms of Defense* (1936), Anna Freud enlarged the structural point of view. This work, along with the contributions of Hartmann, defines the ego psychological perspective. She added to her father's original nine defense mechanisms eight more: altruism, asceticism, avoidance, denial, displacement, identification with the aggressor, intellectualization, and sublimation.

At the Hampstead War Nurseries from 1941 to 1945, she along with Dorothy Burlingham pioneered the advocacy of attending to the psychological needs of children separated from their caregivers. This work served as a building block for her theory of development.

Anna Freud believed that development moves back and forth along multiple lines of development, and that a child can develop in one area, but not in another. Her developmental lines concept proposed that the level a child reaches on a developmental line is the result of the interaction of drives, ego development, and its relation to the nurturing environment. She proposed the existence of multiple developmental lines, and made a distinction between normal and pathological development. She was the first to trace a single dimension of development from infancy to adolescence. Lastly, her diagnostic profile encapsulates the major constructs of the ego psychological perspective into what might constitute as an inventory of a child's psychological status.

Keywords Adolescent stage • Altruism • Altruistic surrender • Anaclitic stage • Asceticism • Avoidance • Denial • Displacement • Instinctual anxiety • Intellectualization • Developmental lines • Egocentricity • Identification with the aggressor • Latency stage • Object constancy • Objective anxiety • Phallic-oedipal stage • Superego anxiety

References

Appignanesi, L., & Forrester, J. (2000). *Freud's women*. New York: Other Press.

Bernfeld, S. (1923). Uber eine typische Form der mannlichen Pubertat. Imago IX. (Can we get an English translation of this title?)

Easman, A. (1993). G. Stanley Hall and the invention of adolescence. *Adolescent Psychiatry*, 19, 6–20.

Edgcumbe, R. (2000) *Anna Freud: A view of development, disturbance, and therapeutic techniques*. London: Routledge.

Freud, A. (1936). *The writings of Anna Freud, Vol. 2: The ego and the mechanisms of defense*. New York: International Universities Press.

Freud, A., & Burlingham, D. (1943). *War and children*. New York: Medical War Books.

Freud, A., & Burlingham, D. (1944). *Infants without families*. New York: International Universities Press.

Freud, A. (1958). Adolescence. In R. S. Eissler (Ed.), *Psychoanalytic study of the child* (Vol. 13, pp. 255–278). New York: International Universities Press, Inc.

Freud, A. (1962). Assessment of childhood disturbances. *The Psychoanalytic Study of the Child*, 17, 149–158.

Freud, A. (1963). The concept of developmental lines. *The Psychoanalytic Study of the Child*, 18, 245–265.

Freud, A. (1965). *Normality and pathology in childhood: Assessments of development*. New York: International Universities Press.

Freud, A. (1966). *The ego and the mechanisms of defense* (revised edition). Connecticut: International Universities Press.

Freud, A. (1936/1966). *The writings of Anna Freud, Vol. 2: The Ego and the Mechanisms of Defense* (revised edition). Connecticut: International Universities Press.

Freud, A. (1973). *The writings of Anna Freud, Vol. 3: Infants without families: Reports on the Hampstead Nurseries (1939–1945)*. New York: International Universities Press.

Freud, S. (1894). *The neuro-psychoses of defence* (Standard Edition, Vol. 3, pp. 162–185). London: Hogarth Press.

Freud, S. (1915). *Instincts and their vicissitudes* (Standard Edition, Vol. 14, pp. 109–140). London: Hogarth Press.

Freud, S. (1922). *Some neurotic mechanisms in jealousy, paranoia, and homosexuality* (Standard Edition, Vol. 18, pp. 221–232). London: Hogarth Press.

Freud, S. (1923). *The Ego and the Id* (Standard Edition, Vol. 19, pp. 3–66). London: Hogarth Press.

Freud, S. (1926a). *Inhibitions, symptoms, and anxiety* (Standard Edition, Vol. 20, pp. 77–175). London: Hogarth Press.

Freud, S. (1926b). *The question of lay analysis* (Standard Edition, Vol. 20, pp. 177–259). London: Hogarth Press.

Hall, G. S. (1904). *Adolescence: Its psychology and its relations to physiology, anthropology, sociology, sex, crime, religion and education*. New York: Appleton.

Heller, P. (1992). *Anna Freud's letters to Eva Rosenfeld*. Connecticut: International Universities Press.

Jones, E. (1922). Some Problems of Adolescence. In *Papers on Psycho-Analysis* (5th ed., pp. 389–412). London: Bailliere, Tindall & Cox.

King, P., & Steiner, R. (1990). *The Freud-Klein controversies 1941–1945*. London: Routledge.

Mahler, M. S. (1975). *The psychological birth of the human infant*. New York: Basic Books.

Richmond, M. B., & Sklansky, M. (1984). Structural change in adolescence. In D. D. Brockman (Ed.), *Late adolescence: Psychoanalytic studies*. New York: International Universities Press.

Young-Breuhl, E. (1988). *Anna Freud: A biography*. New York: Summit Books. Major Works *The Writings of Anna Freud,* published in 8 volumes by International Universities Press:

Volume 1: Introduction to psychoanalysis: Lectures for child analysts and teachers (1922–1935)
Volume 2: The ego and the mechanisms of defense (1936)
Volume 3: Infants without families: Reports on the Hampstead Nurseries (1939–1945)
Volume 4: Indications for child analysis and other papers (1945)
Volume 5: Research at the Hampstead Child-Therapy Clinic and other papers (1956–1965)
Volume 6: Normality and pathology in childhood: Assessment of development (1965)
Volume 7: Problems of psychoanalytic training, diagnosis, and the technique of therapy (1966–1970)
Volume 8: Psychoanalytic psychology of normal development

Freud, A. (1962). Assessment of childhood disturbances. *The Psychoanaytic Study of the Child*, 17, 149–158.

Freud, A. (1963). The concept of developmental lines. *The Psychoanalytic Study of the Child*, 18, 245–265.

Supplementary Readings

Coles, R. (1992). *Anna Freud: The dream of psychoanalysis*. Reading, MA: Addison-Wesley.

Edgcumbe, R. (2000) *Anna Freud: A view of development, disturbance, and therapeutic techniques*. London: Routledge.

Heller, P. (1992). *Anna Freud's letters to Eva Rosenfeld*. Madison, CT: International Universities Press.

King, P., & Steiner, R. (1990). *The Freud-Klein controversies 1941–1945*. London: Routledge.

Chapter 4
Rene Spitz (1887–1974)

Publishing Era (1945–1974)

Biographical Information

Rene Arpad Spitz was born in Vienna, to a wealthy Jewish family on January 29, 1887, in the very same building in which Sigmund Freud had opened his first office for the practice of medicine (Steele, 1975). He spent most of his childhood in Hungary. He declined the opportunity to enter the family business, choosing instead to become a physician, graduating from the University of Budapest in 1910 at the age of 23. While studying medicine, he came upon the works of Sigmund Freud, which he read avidly. Sandor Ferenczi, who was one of his teachers, stimulated further his interest in psychoanalysis, which led him to consult Freud in Vienna in 1911 and to begin a "didactic analysis" with Freud (Emde, 1992), an analysis undertaken primarily for training rather than therapeutic purposes. This was the first such analysis that Freud conducted. From then on, Spitz considered Freud as his mentor.

During World War I, he served in the medical corps of the Austrian Army on the Eastern front. Between 1924 and 1928, he was a member of the Vienna Psychoanalytic Society and later became a member of the German Psychoanalytic Society in Berlin. Between 1932 and 1938 Spitz moved to Paris where he taught psychoanalysis and child development at the *Ecole Normale Superieure*. There he frequently attended conferences of the Paris Psychoanalytic Society. During the rise of the Nazi regime in the 1930s, Spitz, who had a Hungarian passport, often carried valuables and money across borders for various analysts, at great risk to himself. He eventually fled the advance of the Nazis and came to the United States in 1938. From 1938 to 1957, he was a training and supervising analyst and a member of the faculty of the New York Psychoanalytic Institute.

The Importance of Infant Observation

During the 1940s, psychoanalysts considered Spitz' published work peripheral and controversial. The controversial aspects of Spitz's work were his views regarding the effects of environmental deprivation on children's development, which were in

J. Palombo et al., *Guide to Psychoanalytic Developmental Theories*,
DOI: 10.1007/978-0-387-88455-4_4, © Springer Science+Business Media, LLC 2009

conflict with the prevailing view that the drives determined the direction of a child's development. The rejection of his position came in the face of the evidence he had gathered and in spite of the fact that, at the time, he was one of the few researchers interested in collecting data from the direct observation of infants through films. For 29 years, beginning in 1945, Spitz published research findings on ego functions and defenses that took into account the influences of the environment and the neurobiological underpinnings of development. He drew his conclusions from the findings of the many disciplines he had consulted, including ethology, embryology, and pediatrics. His work influenced many of the leading investigators of his day, including Bowlby, Brazelton, Campos, and Fraiberg (Emde,1992).

Spitz did not begin his research and observations of infants and their mothers until he was in his late forties (Steele, 1975). His first publication in 1945 (at the age of 58) discussed the concepts of diacritic and coenesthetic organization (see Theory of Development section for a description of these concepts). One of Spitz' greatest contributions was the importance he placed on infant observation and assessment. In contrast to Freud, he based most of his thinking on empirical investigations of infants rather than inferring their development from the analysis of adults (Emde, 1992). Because of this, he gained recognition for the innovative investigative strategies he employed. He was also one of the first investigators to film his observations. His studies of infants deprived of adequate mothering are his best-known works.

"Hospitalism" and Anaclitic Depression

Until his classic studies revealed the detrimental effects of this practice, babies awaiting adoption were kept in institutions for prolonged periods prior to placement in homes. The rationale for the practice appears to have been that this period provided an opportunity for the development of the baby's personality to take place. His published and filmed observations of infants separated from their caregivers and placed in two different institutions provided dramatic evidence of the contrasting practices in the care of children (Cartwright, 2004; Gemelli, 1996; Spitz, 1945b).

The first institution, a prison for delinquent girls in Argentina, had an attached nursery that housed the girls' infants. The second was an orphanage in Mexico, called the "Foundling Home," where the infants were breast fed by their mothers until 3 months of age, at which point the birth mothers gave up their infants, placing them in this institution. Spitz noted that both institutions provided adequate physical care, hygiene, and nourishment to the infants. In the first institution, the infants had been separated from their mothers because their mothers were incarcerated. However, the prison allowed the mothers to visit their infants frequently to care for them. The infants seemed to thrive and were unaffected by the separation. In contrast, in the Foundling Home, the infants had multiple caregivers, they were left to lie in their cribs all day with sheets draped around the cribs, cutting off visual contact from their surroundings. They were fed on strict hourly schedule and received little stimulation. Most of these infants exhibited signs of severe emotional withdrawal, developmental delays, and susceptibility to infections. Spitz discovered that the deprivation of adequate mothering led to severe developmental disorders, often in the form of **hospitalism** or **anaclitic depression** (anaclitic being the Greek term for "to lean upon") (1945b, 1946a, 1946b). These terms refer to specific conditions to which children who suffer severe emotional deprivation succumb and form part of the **failure to thrive syndrome**. Many of these children developed **marasmus** (Greek for "to waste away"), attributed to the severe depression from which they suffered and subsequently died because of their vulnerability to infections. By the age of 18 months, 32 of the 91 infants died from a variety of causes. Of the rest, who ranged in age from 2½ to 4½ months, few could walk unassisted and only one had acquired a vocabulary of a few words.

An indication of the bias against appreciating the effects of the environment on children's development, at the time, was the response from psychoanalysts when Spitz showed them his films. They were outraged at him for exposing them to such horrors. They accused him of cruelty because of the reactions he had elicited from them. Only much later were his contributions appreciated and his work credited for the impact it had on child placement practices.

In 1956, at age 70, Spitz moved to Denver, Colorado and became the Visiting Professor at the University of Colorado School of Medicine. He helped organize the Denver Psychoanalytic Society and was its first president. He also assisted in the development of the Denver Psychoanalytic Institute and became its first training analyst (Steele, 1975). Together with Robert Emde and Charles Kaufman, he created a seminar on developmental psychobiology, which attracted many scholars to the University of Denver (Gaskill, 1976).

A major contribution to developmental theory appeared in his work *A Genetic Field Theory of Ego Formation* (1959), which proposed a series of psychic organizers in infancy. This work made note of the fact that development is uneven, with periods of stability followed by periods of transformation. Spitz later proposed a theory of the emergence of self during the first 2 years, seeing the acquisition of the "semantic *no*" as a developmental milestone that marked a shift from passive obedience to a more active stance (Emde, 1992). Finally, he proposed that basic communication exists in infancy, even before the development of speech. This work was followed by *The First Year of Life: A Psychoanalytic Study of Normal and Deviant Development of Object Relations* (1965), in which he elaborated the ideas condensed in the prior book. In this work, he describes in detail some of the experimental work he carried out with infants to provide an empirical foundation for his hypotheses.

Spitz lived and worked in Denver until his death on September 14, 1974 at the age of 87.

Theory of Development

Spitz was a pioneer in applying positivist, experimental, research methods to Sigmund Freud's psychoanalytic concepts of child development. In general, he focused on the unfolding object relations between infants and primary caregivers and, in particular, on the nature of the libidinal object. In *A Genetic Field Theory of Ego Formation* (1959), Spitz provided an outline of the manner in which development unfolds. He stated, "Freud's early work in the field of embryology and of neural development greatly influenced his genetic approach to psychic development" (p. 10).

Spitz based his theory on Freud's concept of psychic energy, on his sequence of libidinal stages, and on his formation of psychic structure. In contrast to the other ego psychologists, Spitz emphasized the importance of innate factors through his distinction between ***maturation*** and ***development***. Maturation is the process through which change and growth occur both physically and psychologically. Human psychological development unfolds through a set of interactions among the constraints that innate givens and environmental factors impose on maturation or through the facilitation of benign factors, such as responsive caregivers. This view takes into account not only the factors that may restrict development, but also those that may enhance it.

Spitz proposed that there are ***critical nodal points*** or ***critical periods*** during development (1965, p. 118). During such periods, if infants do not acquire the age-appropriate psychological functions, then it will be difficult if not impossible for them to acquire those functions later. However, maturational forces may take over permitting other factors to serve similar functions and to replace the missing function. The integration that results will then deviate from the norm.

Fixation points: "The point of fixation marks that point at which either the drive (the partial drive) or the object relations, or both, have reached the maximum of gratification which is made available to them" (1959, p. 87). When infants either cannot or do not invest the object during the maturational process, a fixation point occurs leaving behind undeveloped ego nuclei that become part of a "fragmented ego" (1959, pp. 86–87). Spitz proposed the law of dependent development, the construct that the progression of stages was sequential and that each stage requires the establishment of the prior stage before achieving dominance. When a developmental imbalance is firmly established at one level, then it will modify the pattern of the next major organizer.

Three stages denote infants' earliest psychological development. Spitz argued that each stage is marked by the appearance of specific affective behaviors that herald the beginning of a new stage. He calls the phenomena associated with these stages **ego organizers,** a construct he borrowed from embryology. "The organizer is a theoretical construct. It designates a state of coordination and integration of a number of functions both somatic and psychological. The result of this integration is a new level of organization which actually changes the properties of the elements from which it originates" (1959, p. 83). Three organizers characterize these stages: *the smiling response, the eight-month anxiety, and negation* (1959). These organizers manifest as behaviors that provide evidence for the infant's level of object relatedness. The first stage, the objectless stage, culminates with the emergence of the smiling response. The second stage, the establishment of the libidinal object, reaches its apex with the manifestation of the eight-month anxiety. Finally, the third stage, the beginning of human communication, is marked by the emergence of the capacity for negation.

The Objectless Stage (Birth to 10–12 Weeks)

For Spitz, during the **objectless stage**, the infant exists in a state of nondifferentiation. No demarcation between ego and id is evident. The infant functions according to the Nirvana principle during which the goal is the reduction of all tension through discharge. Toward the end of this stage, the smiling response emerges. The infant has little awareness of the object, which only represents a stimulus to which it responds. The stimulus, i.e., the caregivers represents a "preobject," hence the stage is a "preobject relations" stage (Spitz, 1959, pp. 15–20). Toward the end of this stage, a shift occurs from visceral perception to sensory perception. Reality testing begins to develop; memory traces of experiences are laid down and object relations have their inception (Spitz, pp. 23–24).

The Precursors of the Object

*The first organizer of the psyche is the **smiling response*** (1965, pp. 117–120). At the beginning of the second month, infants will smile when presented with a stimulus that represents the configuration of the human face. Infants will follow a moving human face with their eyes, and will gaze at their mother's eyes while nursing. The significance of the smiling response is that it represents the opening signs of the dialogue between infant and caregiver. It puts into motion the action–reaction cycle that is essential for the establishment of the stage of libidinal object relations. This response occurs around the second to the fourth month of life during a state of nondifferentiation, suggesting that in early infancy there is no differentiation between ego and id. The affective response to the "precursor of the object," that is, the primary caregiver, is indicative of the new stage and it marks the beginning of the establishment of the "reality ego," the point at which the infant can give up functioning in accord with the pleasure principle (1965, p. 39). It is also indicative of the establishment of a rudimentary ego, a **body ego** that will begin to regulate id discharges (1965, p. 106). It also marks the beginning of the division into conscious, preconscious, and unconscious components of the psyche.

Spitz proposed that investment in a libidinal object was not an instinctual given but, rather, it was an acquired ego capacity reflecting a developmental achievement that was necessary for essential human connectedness. The complex interactional patterns that develop between mother and infant constitute a "**dialogue**" that is a "sequential action-reaction-action cycle within the framework of mother–child relations. … It is this action-reaction-action cycle that enables the baby to transform step by step meaningless stimuli into meaningful signals" (1965, pp. 42–43). Through this construct, he brought to life Hartmann's concept of "adaptation" by specifying criteria for the "good mother" and the "average acceptable environment" and, in so doing, allowed them to be identified. The dialogue constitutes a communication system between infants and their caregivers.

Coenesthetic and Diacritic Functioning

Spitz proposed two concepts to theorize about the ways in which this early form of human communication occurs. He terms these the coenesthetic and diacritic modes of functioning (1945a, 1965). These two modes of functioning bear a relationship to Freud's primary and secondary process. Spitz followed in the tradition of many psychoanalytic investigators before him and coined new words to illustrate new or different directions in theorizing and hypotheses formulation. Spitz created these terms coenesthetic (from the Greek "koinos" for "coene" or "cene" meaning common or general plus "eisthesis" meaning sensibility) and diacritic (from "diacrinein," meaning to separate, distinguish; "dia" meaning through, plus "krinein" meaning to separate) (modified from Spitz, 1945a, p. 149).

During the **coenesthetic mode of functioning**, which is present at birth and evident during the first 4–6 months, "perception takes place on the level of deep sensibility and in terms of totalities, in an all-or-none fashion" (1965, p. 134). This mode of communication includes the emotions and affective interchanges that occur between mother and infant. Infants operate at both an expressive and a receptive level. Expressively they communicate through nonverbal signals, which adults perceive without conscious awareness. Receptively, infants at first operate at the level of conditioned reflexes, which evoke the vegetative system. Somatic manifestations are visceral and postural. The nature of perception "is better qualified by the adjective 'sensitive' than 'sensory,' since its manifestations are perceived as vague, extended, diffuse sensations such as gastro-intestinal, sexual, precordial (writers note: epigastrium or stomach region) or dizziness sensation" (Spitz, 1945a, p. 149). The capacity for this form of communication undergoes repression during latency.

The **diacritic mode of functioning** evolves from the coenesthetic mode and becomes an integrated sensory organization by the second year. This mode of functioning is centered in the cortex and involves cognition, specifically conscious thought processing, and intentional and volitional acts. Its mode of perception is through the sensory organs and these perceptions enable the infant to distinguish intensity in an approximate quantifiable manner. In addition, these perceptions are localized and circumscribed. These higher-level sensory perceptions are essential for the organism's survival. This form of processing information is considered equivalent to secondary process thinking (1965, p. 44).

The Establishment of the Libidinal Object (3 Months to 12–15 Months)

During the second stage, that of the establishment of the **libidinal object**, *the second organizer of the psyche is the* ***eight-month anxiety*** that appears (1965, pp. 160–164). At around 8 months, in the presence of a stranger, infants will turn away, they will cover their faces, they may cry, or express distress. Indications are that the infants experience intense anxiety. This ego organizer is indicative of the fact that infants can now distinguish between familiar and unfamiliar persons. They can compare the memories of the people with whom they are familiar with the stimulus of an unfamiliar person. The unfamiliar stranger evokes the memories of the discomfort the infants experiences when separated from a caregiver. In other words, the eight-month anxiety is a reactivation of the infants' unpleasure when they felt abandoned by the caregivers. The eight-month anxiety is a critical period that provides evidence of the development of "a libidinal object" (Spitz, 1965, pp. 150–156). A reorganization of the ego has taken place.

The anxiety the infant experiences is also an affective sign that signals a major change in the infant's psychic economy. The infant's ego becomes more structured, as more functions such as defense mechanisms and identification accrue to it, and as a greater consolidation of the boundary between the ego and the id emerges. Furthermore, a differentiation between the two drives, the libidinal and the aggressive drives, comes into play. At around this time, infants are able to fuse together the good and a bad object, from the preambivalent stage, into a single libidinal object.

The Beginning of Human Communication (from 15 Months on)

The third organizer of the psyche, the capacity for ***negation*** (1965, pp. 188–195), heralds the beginning of **human communication**. This organizer appears between the 15th and 18th month and marks the inception of mental operations in the use of symbolic forms of communication. An exception to the verbal content of this communication is the use of the nonverbal gesture to indicate "no" by shaking one's head.

The Origin of No and Yes

Spitz generated a developmental line of elementary communication beginning with the archaic differentiation of "no" and "yes." He located the origin of "no" in twin streams of influence, the infant's phylogenetic rooting behavior in the nursing experience and the ontogenetic component, which transforms oral instinctual behavior into symbolic expression. Left to right negative head shaking is the visible indicator of the fact that the semantic abstraction of a refusal or denial has been achieved. Spitz inferred that negative head shaking means: "I do not want this" (1965, p. 100). The "no" represents the growing separateness between "not-I" and "I" leading to the eventual establishment of the self by 15–18 months. During the anal phase, there is a reactivation of the original rooting behavior and the head shaking becomes consolidated as the unmistakable expression of the negative (Spitz, 1945a, pp. 99–102).

With respect to the opposite position, Spitz also traces a developmental line of "yes." It is more complicated than that of its counterpart, "no." From a semantic level, affirmation is the antonym of negation and from a philosophical standpoint negation can only logically exist if it is predicated on the prior existence of an affirmation or an assent. Spitz points out that from the psychoanalytic point of view the situation is different. "Affirmation is the essential attribute of an instinct. No conscious counterpart, no ideational content is required to elicit the appetitive properties" (Spitz, 1957, p. 104). So while "no" does not exist in the unconscious, the essential quality of the drive, when unopposed, is "yes." To summarize, at an archaic level of psychological nondifferentiation, the directional quality of drive and discharge is "reception" and "taking in," at the level of object relations it is the "striving toward," on the ideational level it symbolizes affirmation and assent and on a semantic level affirmation is manifested by "yes" (Spitz, pp. 105–106).

With respect to motor discharge, up and down head nodding signifies affirmation and assent. From an anatomical standpoint it has been assumed that head shaking preceded head nodding due to immature neck musculature. Upon careful examination of filmed nursing experiences, it was discovered that when the nipple was withdrawn before the infant was sated, the infant's head by 3 months will nod in a clear approach movement to try to regain the nipple. Preconditions for head nodding behavior are sufficient maturation of neck musculature and the infant needs to be able to both see and reach the nipple, bottle, rattle, etc. Spitz leaves this discovery wondering if the capacity for head nodding is also an essential feature of the differentiation of "non-I" from "I" process (Spitz, 1957, pp. 103–116).

The "I," the "Ego," and the "Self"

Spitz appears to be among the earliest investigators to differentiate among these three concepts. The push to clarify the confusion surrounding these concepts comes from ego psychology and its emphasis on adaptation together with the expansion in infant observation. The ontogenesis of semantic (the study of the relationships among meanings) communication and of self-awareness is the contextual framework for the differentiation.

The "I" is a product of the emerging awareness of the ego and is preceded by the infant's awareness of the "non-I" by the 3-month mark. "Non-I" refers to the infant's existence in a state where primary narcissism is dominant, a state in which the sense of separateness and the capacity for ideation are nonexistent. Between the next 3–6 months, the infant through its actions develops an awareness of the "I." The "I" is conceived as a cognitive precipitate of experience. By contrast, the "ego" as a psychic system is a construct of psychoanalytic theory making.

By 15 months the self, also a cognitive precipitate of experience, emerges as a higher level of integration than the "I." The "self" is understood to be a continuation of the "I," which takes place as a result of the vicissitudes of object relations. In the precursor stage of object relations, the object was a constituent part of the "non-I" at the pre object level. The awareness of the "I" from the "non-I" signals the elevation of the object to part object status. True object relations evolve as the result of progressive emotional interchanges arriving at the whole object state, the achievement of the dignity of the love object. Spitz credits the ego as the mediator of the cyclical, back and forth object relations experience which results in ever more complex psychic structuralization. These relations are actuated through the instrumentality of the "I." During this process the "I" accumulates cathectic charges, which compels the ego to become more aware of the "I"s function in the unfolding drama of object relations. As the cathectic investment increases the ego is compelled to differentiate the "I" which evolves into and achieves identity as the self.

Spitz then ties the evolution of the self to developmental nodal points to the ego organizers. At 3 months the "non-I" begins to differentiate into the "I," heralded by the smiling response due in part to oral frustration. At this point, the separateness of the subject from the surround takes place. Then at 8 months the origin of object relations proper begins, marked by stranger anxiety and with this milestone, the incipient awareness of the self occurs. Over the next 6 months, the child's growing need for autonomy makes him more aware of his separateness. By 15 months, this culminates in the establishment of the defense known as identification with the aggressor, which manifests by the use of "No" in word and gesture. This development is mobilized by volitional frustration and the limits placed on the child's agency. With this capacity for negation, the self is consolidated. (Spitz, 1957, pp. 119–121) (see Table 4.1)

Table 4.1 The ego organizers

First ego organizer The smiling response Appears between 2 and 4 months	• The organizers are the original indicators of increasing internal psychological complexity. • The infant will smile not only at the face of the primary libidinal object, but also at the gestalt of any reasonably configured human face. • In the dyadic nursing experience, the smiling response represents the reciprocal totality of kinesthetic, tactile and visual interaction. • The smiling response occurs during the early oral psychosexual stage of development; its libidinal dynamics include: a. The **preobjectal** stage is a primitive stage in object relations that combines **autoerotism** and **primary narcissism**. Autoerotism is the earliest stage in which the drives are present from the beginning of life. At first, they are amorphous energy potentials in the undifferentiated psyche. All energies are directed toward the undeveloped/undifferentiated ego where there is no distinction between self and nonself. Primary narcissism is distinguishable from autoerotism in that the latter is objectless while in the former the "I" is distinguishable (Freud, 1914). b. The oral or primal cavity is the cradle of perception, both inside (coenesthetic sensations, usually unconscious) and outside (diacritic perceptions, usually conscious) of the body, and is the bridge to differentiation of perception. Probably the sector of the body ego that seems the most highly cathected is the representation of the mouth.
Second ego organizer Eight-month anxiety Appears at around 8 months	• This organizer provides a sign that the infant can now differentiate mother from other people and, consequently, understands the presence of different people as an indication that mother has left him. • It represents a cognitive leap in that the infant now is aware that the schema of mother is at variance with the schema of nonmother.

(continued)

Table 4.1 (continued)

Third ego organizer	• This organizer heralds the appearance of defiance in the form of "no" • It is closely associated with the anal stage of development.
Negation	• This organizer encouraged a consideration of the developmental aspects of superego formation, in particular, the oedipal outcome leading to a defensively motivated process, identification with the aggressor (Freud, 1936). • With increasing locomotion, the mother now disapproves of and curbs the child's unacceptable behaviors.
Appears at about 15th–18th month	• Negation is an enriching aspect to the preoedipal drama shaped by ego functions such as mastery, impulse regulation and modulation of affects and the enhanced cognitive ability for abstract conceptualizations. • The child's sense of assertiveness and intentionality, his self-image as an agent of change (effectance) are imprinted now in powerful ways.

Case Illustration

Though Spitz was active as a psychoanalytic practitioner, he published less in clinical psychoanalysis than he did in infant research (Emde, 1983). The following, taken from *The First Year of Life* (Spitz, 1965, pp. 86–88), therefore serves as an illustration of his style of infant observation gleaned from a detailed experimental study of the smiling response (Spitz & Wolf, 1946). It details some of his observations and conclusions that led to one of his key contributions to developmental theory. This study involved 145 children from birth to 12 months (reprinted with permission from International Universities Press).

Beginning with the second month of life, the human face becomes a privileged visual percept, preferred to all other "things" of the infant's environment. Now the infant is able to segregate and distinguish it from the background. He invests it with his complete and prolonged attention. In the third month, this "turning toward" in response to the stimulus of the human face culminates in a new, clearly defined, species-specific response. By this time the progress of the infant's physical maturation and psychological development permits him to coordinate at least one part of his somatic equipment and to use it for the expression of a psychological experience: he will now respond to the adult's face with a smile. Except for the infant's following the human face with his eyes in the second month, this smile is the first active, directed, and intentional behavioral manifestation, the first indicator of the infant's transition from complete passivity to the inception of active behavior, which henceforth will play an increasingly important role.

In the third month of life, the baby responds to the adult's face by smiling if certain conditions are fulfilled: the face must be presented straight on, so that the infant can see both eyes; and the face must move. It is immaterial what part of the face or of the head moves, whether the movement is head nodding, mouth movement, etc. At this age level, nothing else, not even the baby's food, provokes this response. To be sure, if you present to a bottle-raised child the selfsame bottle full of milk, nipple and all, a marked change will frequently occur in his behavior. Infants advanced beyond their chronological age will stop their activity, and at times they will perform sucking movements with their mouths. At times they will try to extend their arms in the direction of the bottle; but they will not smile at a bottle. Developmentally less advanced babies may not even change their behavior; yet to the face of the adult they will respond with a smile.

This population was diversified according to ethnic, social, and national background. The infants were exposed to a number of stimuli and experimental situations at regular intervals.

It was established that the smiling response appears as an age-specific behavioral manifestation of the infant's development from the age of 2 months to the age of 6 months. Under the conditions specified above, 98% of the infants smiled during this period in response to the face of any individual, friend or stranger, regardless of sex or color (significant above the 0.1 percentile level of confidence).

Chronologically this response is strictly limited. Before 2 months of age, that is, between birth and the end of the second month, only 2% of our infant population smiled in *response* to the presentation of *any* stimulus (significant above the 0.1 percentile level of confidence).

At the opposite end, after the age of 6 months, the vast majority of our infant population did not smile any more when the stimulus that had elicited their smile between two and 6 months was presented to them by a *stranger.* Thus in the second half of the first year indiscriminate smiling responses at the grownup's face ceased in more than 95 per cent of our population. In less than 5 per cent of the infants observed by us this smiling response continued. In other terms, children before the age of 2 months will not smile *reliably* at anybody, or anything; the same children, after reaching the age of 6 months, reserved their smiling response for their mothers, for their friends, in one word, for their love objects, and would not smile at strangers. (Spitz, 1965, pp. 86–88)

Summary and Conclusion

Spitz went against the prevailing view that drives determine the direction of a child's development by documenting the effects of environmental deprivation on a child's development. He placed great importance on direct observation of infants as the source of his ideas. He was one of the first to use direct infant observation and film in his investigations.

Spitz believed that an infant deprived of adequate mothering is prone to developmental deficits. He used the term *hospitalism* to describe maternal deficits that were due to long-term institutionalization, and *anaclitic depression* to refer to children who became depressed after separation from their mothers and thus had no one to "lean on" for the nurturance they required. He discovered the full implications of severe maternal deprivation in the **failure to thrive syndrome**.

He outlined an alternative developmental model, noting that there are predictable shifts in the infant's behavioral attitude toward others. He concluded that these external manifestations were indicators or signposts of increasing internal psychological complexity marking critical developmental turning points by the "organizers of the psyche" (Mitchell & Black, 1995, pp. 38–43). Finally, his observations on mother/ infant interaction preceded and anticipated the work of the attachment theorists.

Spitz proposed that an infant's earliest psychological development takes place within three stages, and that the beginning of each stage is accompanied by the appearance of specific affective behaviors, phenomena that he referred to as *ego organizers*. The first stage is the objectless stage. During this stage, the ego organizer is the *smiling response,* which occurs around the second to fourth month of life. This signals the beginning of object relations. During the second stage, which occurs at around 8 months of life, the libidinal object is established and the second ego organizer is the *eight-month anxiety* emerges. At this time, an infant can now distinguish between familiar and unfamiliar persons, which may lead to anxiety when in the presence of a stranger. The third stage, which occurs between the 15th and 18th month of life, heralds the beginning of human communication, which manifest through the third ego organizer, the capacity for *negation*. This milestone includes the acquisition of the "semantic no," a shift from passive to active, which serves to facilitate the development of self.

Spitz also proposed that development occurs unevenly with periods of stability followed by periods of transformation, and that certain times represent *critical periods* of development. At these times, if infants do not acquired essential psychological functions, they will find it difficult to acquire them later on. He also believed that development was sequential, with each stage requiring the establishment of the prior stage before achieving dominance.

Keywords Anaclitic depression • Autoerotism • Body ego • Coenesthetic mode of functioning • Critical nodal points • Critical periods • Development • Dialogue • Diacritic mode of functioning • Eight-month anxiety • Failure to thrive syndrome • Fixation points • Hospitalism • Human communication • Libidinal object • Marasmus • Maturation • Negation • Objectless stage • Organizers • Preobjectal • Primary narcissism • Smiling response

References

Cartwright, L. (2004). Emergencies of survival: Moral spectatorship and the 'new vision of the child' in postwar child psychoanalysis. *Journal of Visual Culture*, *3*(1), 35–49.

Emde, R. N. (1983). *Rene A. Spitz: Dialogues from infancy*. New York: International Universities Press.

Emde, R. N. (1992). Individual meaning and increasing complexity: Contributions of Sigmund Freud and Rene Spitz to developmental psychology. *Developmental Psychology*, *28*(3), 347–359.

Freud, A. (1936). *The writings of Anna Freud, Vol. 2: The ego and the mechanisms of defense*. New York: International Universities Press.

Freud, S. (1914). *On narcissism: An introduction* (Standard Edition, Vol. 14). London: Hogarth.
Gaskill, H. S. (1976). Rene A. Spitz – 1887–1974. *Psychoanalytic Study of the Child, 31*, 1–3.
Gemelli, R. (1996). *Normal child and adolescent development*. Washington, D.C.: American Psychiatric Press.
Mitchell, S. A., & Black, M. (1995). *Freud and beyond: A history of modern psychoanalytic thought*. New York: Basic Books.
Spitz, R. A. (1945a). Diacritic and coenesthetic organization. *The Psychoanalytic Review, 32*, 146–160.
Spitz, R. A. (1945b). Hospitalism: An inquiry into the genesis of psychiatric conditions in early childhood. *Psychoanalytic Study of the Child, 1*, 53–74.
Spitz, R. A. (1946a). Hospitalism: A follow-up report. In *The Psychoanalytic Study of the Child* (Vol. 2, pp. 113–117). London: Hogarth.
Spitz, R. A. (1946b). Anaclitic depression. *Psychoanalytic Study of the Child, 2*, 313–342.
Spitz, R. A. (1959). *A genetic field theory of ego formation: Its implication for pathology*. New York: International Universities Press.
Spitz, R. A. (1965). *The first year of life: A psychoanalytic study of normal and deviant development of object relations*. Madison, CT: IUP, Inc.
Spitz, R. A., & Wolf, K. M. (1946). The smiling response: A contribution to the ontogenesis of social relations. *Genetic Psychology Monographs, 34*, 57–125.
Steele, B. F. (1975). Rene A. Spitz, M.D. – 1887–1974. *Psychoanalytic Quarterly 44*, 3–4.

Major Works

Spitz, R. A. (1945a). Diacritic and coenesthetic organization: The psychiatric significance of a functional division of the nervous system into a sensory and emotive part. *The Psychoanalytic Review, 32*, 146–160.
Spitz, R. A. (1945b). Hospitalism: An inquiry into the genesis of psychiatric conditions in early childhood. *Psychoanalytic Study of the Child, 1*, 53–74.
Spitz, R. A. (1946a). Anaclitic depression. *Psychoanalytic Study of the Child, 2*, 313–342.
Spitz, R. A., & Wolf, K. M. (1946). The smiling response: A contribution to the ontogenesis of social relations. *Genetic Psychology Monographs, 34*, 57–125.
Spitz, R. A. (1951). The psychogenetic diseases in infancy. *Psychoanalytic Study of the Child, 6*, 255–275.
Spitz, R. A. (1955). The primal cavity: A contribution to the genesis of perception and its role for psychoanalytic theory. *Psychoanalytic Study of the Child, 10*, 215–240.
Spitz, R. (1957). *No and yes: On the genesis of human communication*. New York: International Universities Press.
Spitz, R. A. (1958). On the genesis of superego components. *Psychoanalytic Study of the Child, 13*, 375–404.
Spitz, R. A. (1959). *A genetic field theory of ego formation: Its implication for pathology*. New York: International Universities Press.
Spitz, R. A. (1961). Early prototypes of ego defenses. *Journal of the American Psychoanalytic Association, 9*, 626–651.
Spitz, R. A. (1965). *The first year of life: A psychoanalytic study of normal and deviant development of object relations*. Madison, CT: IUP, Inc.
Spitz, R. A. (1962). Autoerotism re-examined. *The Psychoanalytic Study of the Child, 17*, 283–315.
Spitz, R. A. (1964). The derailment of dialogue. *American Psychoanalytic Association, 12*, 752–775.
Spitz, R. (1972). "Bridges: On anticipation, duration, and meaning." *Journal of the American Psychoanalytic Association, 20*, 721–735.

Supplementary Readings

Emde, R. N. (1983). *Rene A. Spitz: Dialogues from infancy*. New York: International Universities Press.

Emde, R. N. (1992). Individual meaning and increasing complexity: Contributions of Sigmund Freud and Rene Spitz to developmental psychology. *Developmental Psychology, 28*(3), 347–359.

Gaskill, H. S. (1976). Rene A. Spitz – 1887–1974. *Psychoanalytic Study of the Child, 31*, 1–3.

Mitchell, S. A., & Black, M. (1995). *Freud and beyond: A history of modern psychoanalytic thought*. New York: Basic Books.

Steele, B. F. (1975). Rene A. Spitz, M.D. – 1887–1974. *Psychoanalytic Quarterly (44)*, 3–4.

Chapter 5
Peter Blos (1904–1997)

Publishing Era (1941–1998)

Biographical Information

Peter Blos was born on February 2, 1904 in Karlsruhe, Germany, to Edwin Blos and Eva Lewinstein-Blos. His father was a doctor who inspired Peter by speaking often about the spiritual teachings of Gandhi and Luther. Eva had a large circle of friends, and particularly liked dancing and acting. Blos himself later developed interests in artistic pursuits such as music, craftsmanship, and poetry. Blos flourished in this highly stimulating intellectual environment. His uncle, Georg Friedrich Nicolai (Eva's brother) was Edwin's best friend. Nicolai achieved fame as an ardent protester of World War I. His book *The Biology of War*, written in 1915, was one of the most powerful antiwar documents of its time. The book was unique in its intellectual prowess and audacity, having been written by a German living in Germany who attacked the illusion of German moral and cultural superiority. It was thus considered highly subversive by the German government (Zuelzer, 1982).

Blos became close friend with Erik Homberger (who later changed his last name to Erikson) at age 16, when they met in high school. Wishing to become a science teacher, Blos enrolled in the University of Heidelberg's department of education. After earning his teaching certificate in 1925, Eva Rosenfeld, a friend of the Blos family, introduced Blos to Anna Freud. Anna Freud recommended him as a tutor to Bob Burlingham (the eldest child of Dorothy Burlingham), who was in psychoanalysis with Anna Freud. He also tutored the other Burlingham children. Anna Freud offered Blos the position of director of the Hietzing Schule, which he accepted (Houssier, 2002). She also offered him a free "didactic analysis" (training analysis), which he declined. In part, this reticence may have been due to his discomfort with the fact that Anna Freud was analyzing one of her best friend's children. Blos invited his friend Erik Erikson to assist him as a teacher at the school (Motto, 1972); there the psychoanalyst August Aichhorn, who had a particular interest in treating delinquent children, became his mentor (Houssier, 2002). During this period, he also met and married his wife, Marta Grone, a Swedish woman whose father was a physician.

J. Palombo et al., *Guide to Psychoanalytic Developmental Theories*,
DOI: 10.1007/978-0-387-88455-4_5,

Between 1931 and 1934, Blos was in analysis with Salomea Isakower. Shortly after he started the analysis, Eva Rosenfeld decided to close the Hietzing Schule, leaving Blos with no job or income. He moved to Sweden, where his wife's parents lived, to find employment. Sometime during that period, he completed his dissertation, receiving his Ph.D. in Biology in 1934. Shortly after, he answered an ad for a science teacher in a private high school in New Orleans in the United States. He accepted the position, left Sweden for the United States, and went on to teach in New Orleans before eventually moving to New York. Blos' immigration was not directly connected to his concerns about the rise of Nazism; rather, it was the closing of the Hietzing Schule that required that he leave Vienna. Erik Erikson left Europe for the United States very soon after Blos, and was welcomed by Blos when he arrived in New York. Both Blos and Erikson went on to teach at the Harvard School of Medicine. Their relationship was marked by periods of intimacy and periods of distance. There appeared to be elements of unresolved competitiveness between them that kept them apart.

In 1938, Blos started his research on adolescents, after which he published his first work, *The adolescent personality: A study of individual behavior*, in 1941. The work led to professional acclaim and recognition as someone who had a deep understanding of adolescent development, an area that had not been previously well researched. Subsequent to that publication, he started a psychotherapy practice in which he saw adolescents.

At this point in his life, Blos had not yet decided to become a psychoanalyst. His attraction to psychoeducational principles dominated the period of time he had spent in Vienna. With the move to the United States, he had little contact with the members of the Hietzing Schule, with the exception of August Aichhorn, with whom he continued to correspond. However, once in New York, Blos resumed his personal analysis with Salomea Isakower, who had also moved to New York. This second round of analysis lasted from 1947 to 1951, and subsequently led to his becoming a member of the New York Psychoanalytic Institute. During the 1950s and 1960s, Blos taught and supervised clinicians at the Jewish Board of Guardians, an agency in New York City that provided a broad range of services to children and adolescents. This work stimulated much of his conceptualization of the problems of adolescents, and significantly broadened his exposure to clinical material. His extensive clinical experience with adolescents in the 1950s led to the completion of the book *On Adolescence* in 1961. This work, in which he delineated the phases of adolescent development from latency to postadolescence, brought him international recognition and became a classic in psychoanalytic literature.

In 1965, he became a special member of the New York Psychoanalytic Society, in recognition of the stature of his contributions. He was not invited to full membership because at the time only medical doctors could have that status in the society. He was given an appointment as Supervisor and Instructor in the Child Analysis Program at the New York Psychoanalytic Institute the following year (Esman, 1997).

In *The second individuation process of adolescence* (1967), Blos referred to the entire phase of adolescence as a "**second individuation process**." In this work, he emphasized the developmental necessity of shedding family dependencies, and the similarity of this period to the completion of the first individuation, which occurred at the end of the third year with the achievement of object constancy. This work solidified his reputation as an expert in the area of adolescence and earned him further recognition as a major contributor to psychoanalytic thought.

The origin of the term "individuation" can be traced to Jung's *Psychological Types* (1926), in which he referred to the process of differentiation of the individual from the collective psychology. There is no indication that Blos borrowed this construct from Jung. Mahler (1963) later referred to individuation in infancy as a "hatching from the symbiotic membrane to become an individuated toddler" (p. 323), a quote that Blos does cite in his 1967 article (Blos, 1967). Blos at first differentiates his concept of second individuation from the earlier edition of Mahler's separation-individuation, but later clarifies that the mental and emotional events that are characteristic of this phase in adolescence should not be thought of as a replica of the first separation-individuation. Kaplan (1984) further addresses this confusion when she states that Blos was the first psychoanalyst to speak of adolescence as a "second individuation," but he, like Mahler,

> ...was precise in maintaining the distinction between the word 'separation' and the word 'individuation.' Individuation, an ongoing growth process from birth to adulthood, undergoes two major spurts, one during the first three years of life, and another during adolescence. Adolescent individuation, which involves the reconciliation of genitality with morality is altogether different from the separation-individuation of infancy. Separation-individuation occurs once and only once, during the first three years of life; it refers only to an infant's gradual recognition and acceptance of the boundaries between his own self and those of his mother" (pp.94–95).

Blos reconnected with Erik Erikson in the 1970s, when Erikson was suffering from prostate cancer. They became close for a time, only to part ways again after that reunion. Blos retired from active teaching in 1977. His wife Marta died of lung cancer in 1978, after which he married Betsy Thomas Blos. He continued to publish works about adolescence through the remainder of his life, including *Psychoanalytic perspectives on the 'more disturbed' adolescent* (1981), *Son and father: Before and beyond the Oedipus complex* (1985), *The borderline and severely neurotic child* (1987b), *The place of the adolescent process in the analysis of the adult* (1989), and *The development of the ego: Implications for personality theory, psychopathology, and the psychotherapeutic process* (1993).

Blos died on June 12, 1997, at the age of 94, in Holderness, New Hampshire.

Theory of Development

Blos chose as the focus of his developmental theory what he referred to as the "intermediate steps," a reference to a quote from Sigmund Freud in which he said "The starting points and the final aim of the process... are clearly visible.

The intermediate steps are still in many ways obscure to us" (Freud, 1905b, p. 208). Blos considered the phases of adolescent development to be examples of these intermediate steps. Although he agreed with the significance of the pregenital and preoedipal phases of drive and ego development, he thought it also important to consider personality development from a broader perspective, rather than seeing it as solely the result of libidinal progression. Blos did not address development before latency. His developmental theory of adolescence begins with the latency period and follows Hartmann's organismic model with its ontogenetic sequences.

The emergence of ego psychology led him to look at latency in a way he had not previously considered, eventually seeing it as "the essential preparatory transformation without which adolescence as a developmental phase cannot establish itself" (Blos, 1962, p. viii). Blos' formulations of adolescent development drew significantly from those of the ego psychologists, particularly Heinz Hartmann and Anna Freud. For example, Blos' study of the potentials inherent in the emotional upheavals associated with adolescence was influenced by Hartmann's statement, "The potentialities for formation of personality during latency and adolescence have been underrated in psychoanalytic writing" (Hartmann, Kris, & Loewenstein, 1946, p. 11). Blos drew from Hartmann's adaptive point of view in his delineation of the phase of adolescence proper. He described how the withdrawal of libido from infantile love objects in this phase threatens the ego's integrity; as a result the ego employs defenses to counteract its weakening hold on reality. He concluded that these defenses eventually open the road to adaptive processes, as previously described by Hartmann (1956, p. 41). He also pointed out that integrative and adaptive ego activity characterizes the closing phase of adolescence. He considered these functional changes to be the outstanding achievement of this phase that arrive with the establishment of a "rank order" of ego functions.

Blos studied the many tensions that confront the ego of the adolescent and how the adolescent manages them. Drawing from Hartmann's (1939b/1964) distinction of "defensive maneuvers" (located in the preconscious) and "defense mechanisms" (located in the unconscious), he proposed that defenses are not the only mechanisms that adolescents use to remain stable. Blos believed that adolescents more often draw from their preconscious rather than their unconscious and concluded that, in the treatment of adolescents, it is not necessary to fear that weakened defenses will mobilize primary processes.

Regarding the social challenges that adolescents face, Blos drew ideas from Hartmann's notion of an "average expectable environment" (1939a). Blos saw the process of "fitting in" to the social environment as an interaction between the adolescents' physical and mental equipment, on the one hand, and the average expectable environment, on the other hand.

Anna Freud's work also significantly influenced Blos. For example, he viewed adolescence as a second edition of childhood. In acknowledging the three sources of pressures in adolescence (id, outer world, superego), he came to the conclusion that both periods have in common a phenomenon that Anna Freud (1936) captured with the statement "a relatively strong id confronts a relatively weak ego" (p. 140).

Anna Freud's work on defense mechanisms (1936) was also influential to Blos' conceptualizations of adolescence. For example, she considered intellectualization, which links drives with ideational contents in order to make them more manageable, to be a common defense among adolescents. Hartmann (1939a) agreed and added that this defense mechanism may serve not only to defend against instinctual drives, but also serves as an adaptive process. He also believed that the defenses of denial and avoidance have adaptive sides. Anna Freud described other defense mechanisms of adolescence, including asceticism, which prohibits the drive expression. Blos carried over into his conceptual framework many of these formulations.

Anna Freud's ideas also contributed to Blos' views of latency and preadolescence. She believed that an increase in drive characterized preadolescence, leading to an extended resurgence of pregenitality (A. Freud, 1936). In Blos' theory of development, the achievements of latency give way to the increase in drive energy that occurs in puberty. Blos also noted that in the phase of early adolescence, efforts to mediate between drives and the outer world are fumbling and inefficient. Anna Freud (1936) stated this in terms of the superego becoming a more open adversary, leaving the ego in a state of weakness, isolation, and inadequacy. Also in the phase of early adolescence, Blos noted a strong proclivity toward action. He believed that a full and exciting outer life helps the adolescent counteract his unbearable feelings of emptiness, isolation, and loneliness. In explaining this developmental phenomenon, he drew from Anna Freud's (1958) work, in which she demonstrated this restitutive function through her study of orphaned children.

In Blos' phase of adolescence proper, he addressed the challenges adolescents face in the search for new love objects. He drew from Anna Freud's (1936) description of the role that identification plays in the love life of the adolescent. She conceived of identification as the defense children use to hold onto objects at a time when they retreat to narcissism. Before new love objects can replace those the ego has relinquished, the ego is impoverished because of the withdrawal of investment in the actual parents and the estrangement of the superego from the ego. In Anna Freud's words, "The ego alienates itself from the superego" (Freud, 1936, p. 166). The phase concludes with the entry into young adulthood.

In what follows, we review systematically Blos' development model, which he divided into five phases: (a) Latency, which lasts from ages 7 to 11; (b) Preadolescence, which lasts from ages 11 to 13; (c) Adolescence, which lasts from ages 13 to 18 and is divided into two subphases, Early Adolescence lasts from ages 13 to 15 and Adolescence Proper last from the ages of 15 to 18; (d) Late Adolescence, which lasts from ages 18 to 20; and (e) Postadolescence, which covers the years of young adulthood. The child confronts three sets of major issues during each phase, the processes that organize children's *ego functions and drive activities*, their shifting relationships with *parental objects*, and the means with which they cope with their *social environment.*[1]

Latency: 7–11 Years

The **latency** period sets the groundwork for the successful approach, entrance into, and passage through adolescence. Its completion is a prerequisite for entering the adolescent phase of **drive organization**. During this phase, adolescents must deal with sexual and aggressive drives associated with puberty as well as the psychological derivatives of these drives that are necessary for the ego to develop. Latency children have to integrate the following psychological, cognitive, social, and biological challenges in order to make a successful transition into adolescence:

Ego functions and drives. In this phase, latency children's egos and superegos begin to achieve a growing control over the drives. The children manifest greater stability in affect and mood. Their egos must be strong enough to resist regression when stressed by internal, psychological, or physical demands or by social expectations. Latency children's defenses have to protect their egos from the threats that the drives, the superego, or the environment may present. With the emergence of operational thought, latency children must be able to use judgment and logic in dealing with life tasks.

Parental objects. Latency children replace their dependence on parents for feelings of worth with a sense of self-esteem attained from earlier social achievements. Latency children are able to tap their own resources to regulate self-esteem. They achieve more stable identifications with significant others, which promotes their independence.

Social environment. Latency children's social awareness increases. They are able to separate rational thinking and fantasy; their awareness of the appropriateness of public vs. private behavior continues to grow. Latency children have to have a dependable understanding of and empathy for others. They adequately handle their independence and mastery of the environment without as much assistance from the outside world as they formerly had to have.

Preadolescence: 11–13 Years

The phase of **preadolescence** (early puberty, Blos, 1962, p. 72) signals the end of the latency period. In this phase it is necessary to consolidate the gains made in the latency period before a child can enter the subsequent adolescent phase of development. If this consolidation does not occur, the child may experience

[1] In our description of these phases, we retain Blos' examples of the adolescents' behaviors, even though these are dated and, at times, far removed from the behaviors of adolescents today.

intensified prelatency needs. The primary characteristic of this phase is the upsurge of pregenitality, described later. The primary task of this phase, therefore, is to handle this upsurge in a way that permits the advance to the adolescent phase of development (Blos, 1958). In this phase, both boys and girls can find any stimulus sexually exciting. For boys in particular an erection can occur due to non-specific stimuli including anger, fear, shock, general excitement, as well as of course, frankly erotic stimuli (Blos, 1962, p. 57).

Ego functions and drives. Preadolescents experience a quantitative increase in libidinal and aggressive drives, and experience an upsurge of **pregenitality**; that is, of the drives associated with pregenital phases, oral, anal, and phallic impulses. The urge to gratify these drives meets a disapproving superego that leads to internal conflict. To deal with this conflict, the preadolescents' ego uses defenses like repression, reaction formation, and displacement.

Boys and girls psychological development follow different paths. For boys, the increase in drive intensity leads to a resurgence of pregenitality, which heralds the end of latency. An increase in oral greediness and anal activity, that manifests in restlessness, "dirty" language, disregard for cleanliness, etc. becomes evident. Castration anxiety is a universal occurrence and the central theme of male preadolescence. Girls, by contrast, must repress their infantile sexuality before being able to move into the oedipal period. They often turn away from their mothers because of their disappointment in her, perceiving her as a castrated woman. This repressed sexuality leads girls in preadolescence often to exaggerate their heterosexual desires by attaching themselves to boys (Blos, 1958).

Parental objects. Boys turn away from the opposite sex to protect against castration anxiety, whereas girls turn toward the opposite sex to defend against the pull to the **preoedipal mother** to whom they remain attached. Preadolescents take in a person of the same sex as an ego ideal, leading to "the gang stage;" this ego ideal is used as a defense against castration anxiety (**the homosexual defense**). Boys must renounce the wish for a baby in order to complete the task of the Oedipal period. Girls struggle with relationships more than boys do in this period; the prolonged and psychologically painful detachment from the mother is the major task of this period. Many conflicts occur between mothers and daughters during this period

Social environment. The preadolescent develops skills and interests that are typical of this age based on the need for peer approval, such as collecting stamps, coins, matchbook covers, etc.[2] In this phase, boys and girls behave differently. Boys behave in a hostile, belittling, and avoidant manner toward girls. They deny anxiety rather than attempt to establish a relationship. Typically, their conflicts are related to the fear and envy of the female. Girls experience a "thrust of activity" as they engage in play acting and tomboyish behaviors. They deny their femininity. Their unresolved conflict over penis envy is the central conflict for them.

[2] These examples, drawn from Blos, are obviously dated, reflecting preadolescents' interests of those days. To make them applicable to present day adolescents they require updating to the activities of youth as we know them.

Adolescence: The Second Individuation Process: 13–18 Years

Blos conceptualized the entire phase of **adolescence** as the second individuation **process**. As a child, the adolescent completed the first individuation phase by the end of the third year with the attainment of object constancy (Blos, 1965). Both periods, early adolescence and late adolescence, have in common four attributes, (a) a heightened vulnerability of the personality's organization because of the urgency for changes in psychic structure to meet challenges posed by the upsurge of drives; (b) structural changes that come with disengagement from internalized infantile objects; (c) a "hatching" process during which infantile object ties are loosened and a shedding of family dependencies takes place; and (d) the emergence of psychopathology when failures of individuation occur.

Early Adolescence: Roughly Ages 13–15

Ego functions and drives. During **early adolescence** the adolescents' values and moral precepts become independent from authority. Feelings of loneliness, isolation, and depressed moods come along with cathectic shifts, which threaten the early adolescents' sense of self-control. Blos recognized a defense unique to American adolescents that he labeled **uniformism**, which he believed was rooted in the American family structure. He describes this defense as the tendency of adolescents to accept an external code of behavior as a way of dealing with their ego's struggle against the drives, which represents the expectation for conformity with conventional conduct. When under the influence of group pressure, adolescents no longer experience drives as dangerous; drives are pushed aside and replaced with a uniform performance of behavior. "The greatest source of security, therefore, lies in the shared code of what constitutes adequate behavior" (Blos, 1962, p. 118). The community usually considers the boy or girl who does not fit into this uniformism to be a threat.

Parental objects. The process of separation from early object ties begins. Early adolescents' superego weakens, leaving the ego with little direction from the conscience; the gap between ego and superego widens; the ego becomes impoverished; and, adolescents feel a sense of void or inner turmoil.

Social environment. During early adolescence, a search occurs for new love objects to replace early familial love objects. Early adolescent boys form friendships that involve the idealization of a friend; friends are chosen based on the possession of something the boy would like to have, something that he feels is missing. They are in conflict about tender feelings for their fathers and opposition to their fathers, and need to come to terms with the father as the oedipal love object. The early adolescent girl will feel despair or depression if she lacks or loses a girlfriend; she will idealize and have "crushes" toward both boys and girls; this "bisexual tendency" is less repressed in girls than in boys. Girls can express their masculinity whereas boys are ashamed of their femininity; the decline of the bisexual tendency marks the beginning of "Adolescence Proper."

Adolescence Proper: Roughly Ages 15–18

Ego functions and drives. Appropriate sexual drives emerge during **adolescence proper** (Advanced Puberty. Blos, 1962, p. 72), bringing along with them new anxieties for adolescents. Common defenses include **asceticism**, in the form of self-denial of pleasurable activities. This self-denial represents the prohibited expression of instinctual desires. Another defense is the use of intellectualization, in the form of argumentation and debate, which represents the turning of instinctual desires into more acceptable ideas.

Adolescents' extraordinarily rich fantasy life becomes manifest in this phase. As the cathectic shifts occur from one object to another, these fantasies represent a form of rehearsal or "trial actions." Keeping a diary or journal is common to help fill emotional voids between old objects that adolescents attempt to discard and new objects that are not yet found. With the maturation of adolescents' ability to analyze their own thinking and construct theories, higher order levels of thought emerge. The creativity that was so prevalent in earlier adolescence declines toward the end of adolescence proper.

Parental objects. Two themes are dominant during this phase. First are the Oedipal wishes and conflicts that reemerge. Identification with same sex parent has to be achieved before heterosexual love can occur. Previously the parent was overvalued (idolized), now he or she becomes undervalued and becomes a fallen idol. The second theme is the final disengagement from infantile love objects, until the process of mourning the loss brings about a resolution. This phase is about the search for new objects or the active avoidance of them.

Social environment. Adolescents' abandon narcissistic and **bisexual** positions, permitting heterosexual object seeking. Gratification of drives is now sought from the object rather than the self. Object hunger, that is the desire for intimacy with another, can be experienced as overwhelming. The first choice of a heterosexual love object is often similar to or strikingly unlike the same-sex parent. Sexual identity formation is the ultimate achievement of this phase. Codes of behavior are common, which contribute to a shared sense of security through the recognition of sameness.

Late Adolescence & Postadolescence: Roughly Ages 18–20

There are four developmental preconditions for adolescent character formation during **late adolescence**: 1) Late adolescents must complete the second individuation process (see section above). 2) Since character originates in conflict, the way late adolescents deal with the residual trauma from prior phases determines the outcome. 3) To demonstrate the continuity of their egos' development, late adolescents must resist external distortions that call into question the validity of their own perceptions. 4) The emergence of sexual identity, acting as a catalyst to character formation, begins to bring closure to this phase (Blos, 1968).

Ego functions and drives. The developmental task of this phase is the coming together of a unified ego, which finds expression through stability in work, love, and ideology. Adolescents' ego integrity is restored in this phase, after experiencing impoverishment in early adolescence. Late adolescents' psychic structure solidifies, that is they become more stable and less susceptible to regressive trends. This is the phase of character consolidation. Blos uses the term "**character**" to describe an adolescent's "distinctive traits or qualities" and their "typical or idiosyncratic ways of conducting oneself" (Blos, 1968, p. 20). He believed that character originates in conflict; that is, it results from adapting to exposure to danger situations. The late adolescent's character formation is a sign of the completion of the passage through adolescence (1968). Character becomes consolidated as infantile ties are severed. Character formation may be the cardinal achievement of adolescence.

Parental objects. Infantile conflicts, such as Oedipal residues, do not disappear in this phase, but rather are integrated into the ego and when resolved become self-representations. Late adolescents face several key turning points during this phase. An "identity crisis" (Erikson, 1956) can occur if the adolescent fails to establish "ego identity". A shift must occur in which aggressive and libidinal cathexes are directed to love and hate objects in the outer world. It is not uncommon to see a reluctance to finish this last phase of childhood in some late adolescents. Finally, late adolescents have to deal with the residues left over from previous phases of childhood that survived adolescent transformations and are carried forward and become activated.

Social environment. Late adolescents make gains in the capacity for purposeful action, for social integration, predictability, emotional stability, and self-esteem. Two common types of failures to master conflicts with inner and outer reality result in **miscarried adolescence**, which is due to defective egos, impaired capacity for learning, or trauma; and **incomplete adolescence**, which is due to systemic disturbances, inhibitions that block the path to learning, or the avoidance of anxiety.

Postadolescence: Young Adulthood

Once an adolescent resolves conflicts related to the phases of early adolescence and adolescence proper (such as disengagement from early object ties), and he or she has managed to achieve consolidation of social roles and identifications in the phase of late adolescence, the task of harmonizing these component parts of the personality remains. The major task of the phase of **postadolescence** is to bring together the achievements of the earlier phases into the complete personality (Blos, 1962).

Ego functions and drives. The process of harmonizing drive and ego organization is at its greatest intensity. The postadolescent relies on dignity and self-esteem rather than superego injunctions and instinct gratification. The postadolescent's ego ideal takes over the regulatory function of the superego.

Parental objects. Postadolescents have to come to terms with their parents' ego interests and attitudes. Their previous reliance on the parents has to be transformed into self-reliance.

Social environment. This phase represents the transition from adolescence to adulthood. The task of this phase is to create specific ways to implement life tasks in the external world, which are represented by the choice of an occupation and courtship, marriage, and parenthood. Adolescence is completed when the personality has been organized sufficiently to permit parenthood. The moral personality emerges, having internalized and integrated the social values of his or her community.

Case Illustration

The following case is taken from the chapter titled "Two Illustrations of Deviate Adolescent Development" in Blos' *On Adolescence* (1962, pp. 237–241). This case illustrates several aspects of his developmental theory, including how male and female delinquency is structured differently, and how potential points of fixation can lead to different crises. The case highlights how early identification with the mother leads a girl into an initial negative oedipal position, how the girl eventually abandons the first love object (the mother) and seeks completeness by turning toward the father, how a girl defends against the regressive pull toward the preoedipal mother, and ways in which the phase of preadolescence is very different for a boy and a girl (reprinted with permission from Simon & Schuster).

When Nancy was 13-years old she presented the family, the school authorities, and the court with a problem of sexual delinquency; her stealing was known only to her mother. At home Nancy was uncontrollable and loudmouthed; she used obscene language, cursed her parents, and had her own way disregarding any adult interference. "The names Nancy calls me are so sexy," were the mother's repeated complaints. Despite this seeming independence Nancy never failed to report her sexual exploits to her mother, or at least to hint at them sufficiently so they would rouse her mother's curiosity, anger, guilt, and solicitude. With glee she showed her mother stories she had written consisting mostly of obscene language. Nancy was an avid reader of "dirty sex books"; she stole money from her mother for their purchase. Nancy's mother was willing to give her the money, but Nancy explained to the social worker that this was not what she wanted; "I wanted to *take* the money and not have it *given* to me."

Nancy blamed her mother angrily for not having been firm with her when she was a little girl: "Mother should have known that I acted up in order to get her attention and to have adults fuss over me." She would never marry a husband who says only "Dearie, dearie," but a man who slapped her when she was wrong. The criticism implied in this remark was obviously directed against her weak father. She did not blame him for being a man of no education, who earned a modest income as a butcher, but for his indifference and his ineffectual role in the family. Nancy grew up in a small apartment in a crowded city neighborhood. Nancy's family wanted for her the "finer things in life" and found ways and means to pay for them; thus Nancy had lessons in dancing, acrobatics, and elocution; with puberty all these activities came to an end.

Nancy was preoccupied with sex to the exclusion of almost everything else. This interest reached abnormal proportions soon after menarche at age 11. She boasted of her many boyfriends, of having sexual relations, and of asking her peers at school to join her "sex club." Nancy only liked "bad boys" who stole, lied, and had a criminal record, boys who "know how to get around a girl." She herself wanted to steal and smoke, but she did not accompany the boys on their delinquent excursions because she "might get caught." Nancy puzzled over why she could always get a fellow if another girl was after him but not otherwise. She had established a position of respect among the girls because she would challenge them quickly to a fist fight; "I have to show them that I am not afraid of them."

Nancy admitted to the social worker that she desired sexual relations but denied having ever given in to her desire; she said that she used her body only to attract boys and get their attention. She was, however, observed being intimate with several boys on a rooftop and was found there "dazed, disheveled, and wet." It was at this time that the case was taken to court; Nancy was put on probation under the condition that she receives treatment. In the light of the evidence, Nancy did not deny any longer to the social worker that she had sexual relations, but she now expressed her hope to have a baby. She explained that she engaged in sexual relations to take revenge on her mother. She, Nancy, would keep the baby and marry the boy. Her mother, she was convinced, did not want her and, in fact, had never wanted her. At this time Nancy had a dream in which she had sexual relations with teenage boys; in the dream she had 365 babies, one a day for a year from one boy whom she shot after this was accomplished.

Nancy daydreamed a great deal; her fantasies concerned marriage and she was consumed by the wish for a baby. She was afraid of not being attractive to boys and never getting married. Physically, Nancy was well-developed for her age, but she was dissatisfied with her own body, especially her skin, hair, height, eyes (glasses), and ears (the lobes were attached to the sides of her face). At home she was extremely modest and never allowed her mother to see her naked. Nancy could think of only one reason for all her troubles, disappointments, and anxieties – her mother; she was to be "blamed." She accused the mother of taking her friends – boys and girls – away from her, of begrudging her the happiness she found in having friends, of putting a lock on the phone to cut her off from the world. Nancy said she needed girl friends, close friends who would become her blood sisters; she and Sally scratched their initials into each other's arms with a razor blade as proof of their eternal friendship. The mother scolded Nancy when she showed her the scars; to the daughter this was another demonstration of her mother's not wanting her to have any close girlfriends. In disappointment, she tried to run away from home, but the tie to her mother always proved to be too strong; before long she returned.

Despite her vehement rejection of her mother, Nancy, nevertheless, needed her presence at every turn. She would, for instance, insist that her mother accompany her on her visits to the social worker. Being at a loss about a summer job, Nancy thought that her mother should take a job as a camp counselor and she would assist her as junior counselor. Nancy was totally unaware of her mother's unfitness for such a job, or was she able to assess reasonably her own abilities.

If mother, Nancy continued her accusations, had only had more babies, not just one child and a girl at that, Nancy was sure that her life would have taken a different turn. During the first interview with the social worker, who inquired sympathetically about Nancy's purpose for seeing her, she preserved a long sullen silence; then suddenly began to cry. In her first words she expressed her overwhelming need to be loved; she said: "As an only child I have always been so lonesome." She had always wanted a baby brother or sister and begged her mother to have one. She had a dream in which she was taking care of babies; they were really her girlfriend's babies. Nancy's mother remarked in the dream. "It's a shame that such cute children have no proper mother to take care of them; let's adopt them." In the dream Nancy was overjoyed and ran to her social worker to tell her that they were adopting babies. The worker replied that it would cost a lot of money, and Nancy answered: "But don't you know we are loaded?" After waking from this dream Nancy asked her mother to take in a foster child. "The child," Nancy said, "will have to be a boy as I only know how to diaper boys." She fancied herself having a summer job taking care of children, in a family, way out in the country. When she was a little older, at 14, she actually took a summer job with children as a helper in the nursery school of a community center. There she was a child among children, an older sister who helped the little ones with their play. Nancy always liked to babysit; she loved to hold a baby in her arms, especially if it was very young. When her cousin became pregnant Nancy looked forward to taking care of the baby, but added: "I will babysit free for three months, that's fun, but later I shall get paid."

Nancy attached herself during these years of sexual preoccupation to a young pregnant woman of twenty who had married at the age of sixteen, had had three children, and lived an erratic and promiscuous life. Nancy vicariously shared this woman's sex life and motherhood; she took care of the children during their mother's absence from her home. This necessitated staying overnight when this young woman did not return for a day or two; consequently, Nancy became a truant. Once she brought the three children to her own home to take care of them while her woman friend was off on a sexual escapade and had not been heard from for three days. Nancy emphatically sided with her girlfriend against the husband with whom Nancy said, she was once in love. She also protested violently her mother's accusations against her friend, commenting to the social worker: "My mother has a mind like a sewer." Nancy knew that she understood her girl friend; she knew that she was unhappy because her father had died early in her life and she never loved her mother. "It's no use," Nancy said, "arguing with mother," and summed it up by saying: "My mother and I just don't understand each other." After these fights, Nancy suddenly became afraid that the aggravation she had caused might kill her mother who suffered from high blood pressure.

Nancy found a temporary haven, albeit a dangerous one, in the home of this married girlfriend. She felt safe in the close friendship with this pregnant mother who knew how to attract men and get many babies. Nancy also relished the jealous anger of her own mother who disapproved of this friendship. Nancy felt she possessed a girlfriend-mother with whom she could share everything. During this time Nancy withdrew from the girls of her own age, feeling that they had nothing in common any longer. An embarrassing testimony of the fact that she had outgrown her peers was her response to a group of girls discussing clothes; to the question, "What kind of clothes do you like best?" Nancy blurted, "Maternity clothes." Such incidents drew Nancy more deeply into the make-believe family life with her girlfriend. Nancy loved this woman, and said to the worker, "I can't get her out of my mind."

In her relationship to the social worker Nancy fluctuated between closeness and distance; this instability is well expressed by her own words: "When I think of coming to the office, I don't want to come; but when I am here, I am glad, and I feel like talking." She finally admitted that she would like to be confidential with the social worker, but gave her a warning by confessing that she really was a "compulsive liar." She suggested to the worker that they both should reveal to each other the secrets of their lives; then they could learn from each other. The need for intimacy, which exerted its emotional pull toward the social worker, was conversely responsible for her repeated running away from her.

Nancy finally came to repudiate the "crude, rough stuff of teenagers" and her fancy moved into the direction of acting. Here she drew on the interests and playful activities of her latency years. Wild and childish daydreams of meeting movie actors, fainting in front of them, and being discovered as the new star eventually gave way to a sober approach to the study of acting. From acting Nancy expected to "become a lady"; by this she meant to be gentle, to speak gently, to act gently; then, she was sure people would like her.

Nancy clung to her acting all through her adolescence; in fact, at 16 she achieved a modest degree of recognition in summer stock productions. The stage had become the legitimate territory where her impulsiveness was allowed expression in many directions and where her exhibitionistic needs were slowly tamed by the aesthetic code of acting itself. By this time Nancy had become somewhat of a prude; she was a good mixer with her peers but only to promote her self-interest in dramatic productions. As good a manipulator as her mother always had been, Nancy now became narcissistically related to her environment and learned how to exploit others. The interest in acting became Nancy's identity, around which her personality integration took shape. The core of this identity hails back to the "finer things in life" which Nancy's mother had always wanted for her daughter. In adolescence Nancy reverted to these imposed aspirations which were instilled in the child by lessons in the performing arts during the latency years. It was precisely this artistic endeavor which served in adolescence as an avenue for sublimation of the unresolved fixation to the mother. The vocational identity rescued Nancy from regression and delinquency, but it also prevented a progression to mature object finding; after all, it was still the mother whose desire she continued to gratify by her artistic activity. When reminded once at the age of 16 of her wish for babies, she snapped back in disgust, "Babies is kid stuff" (pp. 237–241).

Summary and Conclusions

Blos did not address development before latency. He focused his developmental theory entirely on the phases of adolescence. Blos' formulations of adolescent development drew significantly from those of the ego psychologists. In his conceptualizations of adolescent development, he drew from Hartmann's adaptive point of view the delineation of the phase of adolescence proper, and from Anna Freud's work on the defense mechanisms.

Blos follows Mahler's organismic model with its ontogenetic sequences. He saw *latency* (roughly ages 7–11) as setting the foundation for passage into adolescence. The *preadolescent* phase (roughly ages 11–13) signals the end of the latency period and leads to an increase in libidinal and aggressive drives. Boys and girls psychological development take different paths during this phase. Blos conceptualized the entire phase of *adolescence* (roughly ages 13–18) as "the second individuation process." He emphasized the developmental necessity of shedding family dependencies and the similarity of this period to the completion of the first individuation phase. He separates the phase of *adolescence* into two parts: *early adolescence* (roughly ages 13–15), during which the adolescent is heavily influenced by peer pressure and faces the challenge of separation from early object ties, and *adolescence proper* (roughly ages 15–18), during which appropriate sexual drives and higher order levels of thought emerge. During the phase of *late adolescence* (roughly ages 18–20) that follows, psychic structure solidifies and stability finds expression in the areas of work, love, and ideology. Finally, the phase of *postadolescence* sees the harmonizing of the component parts of the personality. This phase represents the transition from adolescence to adulthood.

Keywords Adolescence • Adolescence proper • Asceticism • Bisexual • Character • Drive organization • Early adolescence • Homosexual defense • Incomplete adolescence • Late adolescence • Latency • Miscarried adolescence • Postadolescence • Preadolescence • Pregenitality • Preoedipal mother • Second individuation process • Uniformism

References

Blos, P. (1941). The adolescent personality: A study of individual behavior. *The American Journal of Sociology*, 47(2), 234–235.

Blos, P. (1962). *On adolescence: A psychoanalytic interpretation*. New York: Free Press.

Blos, P. (1965). The initial stage of male adolescence. *Psychoanalytic Study of the Child*, 20, 145–164.

Blos, P. (1967). The second individuation process of adolescence. *Psychoanalytic Study of the Child*, 22, 162–186.

Blos, P. (1968). Character formation in adolescence. *Psychoanalytic Study of the Child*, 23, 245–263.

Blos, P. (1979). *The adolescent passage: Developmental issues*. New York: International Universities Press.

Blos, P. (1981). Psychoanalytic perspectives on the 'more disturbed' adolescent. *Journal of the American Psychoanalytic Association*, 29, 161–175.
Blos, P. (1985). *Son and father: Before and beyond the Oedipus complex*. New York: Free Press.
Blos, P. (1987). The borderline and severely neurotic child. *Journal of the American Psychoanalytic Association*, 35, 189–201
Blos, P. (1989). The place of the adolescent process in the analysis of the adult. *Psychoanalytic Study of the Child*, 44, 3–18.
Blos, P. (1993). The development of the ego: Implications for personality theory, psychopathology, and the psychotherapeutic process. *Journal of the American Psychoanalytic Association*, 41, 858–862.
Erikson, E. H. (1956). Ego identity and the psychosocial moratorium. In H. L. Witmer & R. Kosinsky (Eds.), *New perspectives for research in juvenile delinquency* (pp. 1–23). Washington, DC: U.S. Children's Bureau Publication no. 356.
Esman, A. H. (1997). Obituary: Peter Blos. *International Journal of Psycho-Analysais*, 78, 813–814.
Freud, A. (1936). The Writings of Anna Freud, Vol. II: The ego and the mechanisms of defense. New York: International Universities Press.
Freud, S. (1905). Three essays on the theory of sexuality. (Standard Edition, Vol. 7. pp. 125–245).
Freud, A. (1958). Child observation and prediction. In *Psychoanalytic Study of the Child* (Vol. 13). New York: International Universities Press.
Hartmann, H.(1939a). *Ego psychology and the problem of adaptation*. New York: International Universities Press.
Hartmann, H. (1939b/1964). Psychoanalysis and the concept of mental health. In *Essays on ego psychology*. New York: International Universities Press.
Hartmann, H. (1950a). Psychoanalysis and developmental psychology. *Psychoanalytic Study of the Child*, 5, 7–17.
Hartmann, H. (1956). "Notes on the Reality Principle." *Psychoanalytic Study of the Child*. Vol. XI. New York: International Universities Press.
Hartmann, H., Kris, E., & Loewenstein, R. (1946). Comments on the formation of psychic structure. *Psychoanalytic Study of the Child*, 2, 11–38.
Houssier, F. (2002). Le rôle de l' immigration dans le parcours d' E.H. Erikson et de P. Blos (Erik Erikson and Peter Blos: The role of immigration in their travels.) *Topique*, 80, 51–61.
Jung, C. G. (1926). *Psychological types*. London: Routledge and Kegan Paul.
Kaplan, L. J. (1984). *Adolescence: The farewell to childhood*. New York: Simon & Schuster.
Mahler, M. S. (1963). Thoughts about development and individuation. *Psychoanalytic Study of the Child*, 8, 307–324.
Motto, L. R. (1972). An appreciation: Peter Blos. *The Reiss-Davis Clinic Bulletin*, 9, 66–68.
Zuelzer, W. (1982). *The Nicolai case*. Detroit: Wayne State University Press.

Major Works

Blos, P. (1941). The adolescent personality: A study of individual behavior. *The American Journal of Sociology*, 47(2), 234–235.
Blos, P. (1954). Prolonged male adolescence: The formulation of a syndrome and its therapeutic implications. *American Journal of Orthopsychiatry*, 24, 733–742.
Blos, P. (1958). Preadolescent drive organization. *Journal of the American Psychoanalytic Association*, 6, 47–56.
Blos, P. (1962). *On adolescence: A psychoanalytic interpretation*. New York: Free Press.
Blos, P. (1965). The initial stage of male adolescence. *Psychoanalytic Study of the Child*, 20, 145–164.

Blos, P. (1967). The second individuation process of adolescence. *Psychoanalytic Study of the Child*, 22, 162–186.
Blos, P. (1968). Character formation in adolescence. *Psychoanalytic Study of the Child*, 23, 245–263.
Blos, P. (1970). *The young adolescent: Clinical studies*. New York: Free Press.
Blos, P. (1971). The child analyst looks at the young adolescent. *Daedalus* 100, 961–978.
Blos, P. (1972a). The function of the ego ideal in adolescence. *Psychoanalytic Study of the Child*, 27, 93–97.
Blos, P. (1972b). The epigenesis of the adult neurosis. *Psychoanalytic Study of the Child*, 27, 106–135.
Blos, P. (1972c). Silence: A clinical exploration. *Psychoanalytic Quarterly*, 41, 348–363.
Blos, P. (1974a). Twelve to sixteen: Early adolescence. *Psychoanalytic Quarterly*, 43, 331–333.
Blos, P. (1974b). The geneology of the ego ideal. *Psychoanalytic Study of the Child*, 29, 43–88.
Blos, P. (1976a). The split parental imago in adolescent social relations-an inquiry into group psychology. *Psychoanalytic Study of the Child*, 31, 7–33.
Blos, P. (1976b). When and how does adolescence end? *Adolescent Psychiatry*, 5, 5–17.
Blos, P. (1979). *The adolescent passage: Developmental issues*. New York: International Universities Press.
Blos, P. (1980). Modifications in the traditional psychoanalytic theory of female adolescent development. *Adolescent Psychiatry*, 8, 8–24.
Blos, P. (1981). Psychoanalytic perspectives on the "more disturbed" adolescent. *Journal of the American Psychoanalytic Association*, 29, 161–175.
Blos, P. (1983). The contribution of psychoanalysis to the psychotherapy of adolescents. *Psychoanalytic Study of the Child*, 38, 577–600.
Blos, P. (1984). Son and father. *Journal of the American Psychoanalytic Association*, 32, 301–324.
Blos, P. (1985a). *Son and father: Before and beyond the Oedipus complex*. New York: Free Press.
Blos, P. (1985b). Intergenerational separation-individuation-treating the mother-infant pair. *Psychoanalytic Study of the Child*, 40, 41–56.
Blos, P. (1987a). Freud and the father complex. *Psychoanalytic Study of the Child*, 42, 425–441.
Blos, P. (1987b). The borderline and severely neurotic child. *Journal of the American Psychoanalytic Association*, 35, 189–201.

Supplementary Readings

Esman, A. H. (1997). Obituary: Peter Blos. *International Journal of Psychoanalysis*, 78, 813–814.
Houssier, F. (2002). Le rôle de l' immigration dans le parcours d' E.H. Erikson et de P. Blos (Erik Erikson and Peter Blos: The role of immigration in their voyages.) *Topique*, 80, 51–61.
Jung, C. G. (1926). *Psychological types*. London: Routledge and Kegan Paul.
Kaplan, L. J. (1984). *Adolescence: The farewell to childhood*. New York: Simon & Schuster.
Mahler, M. S. (1963). Thoughts about development and individuation. *Psychoanalytic Study of the Child*, 8, 307–324.
Motto, L. R. (1972). An appreciation: Peter Blos. *The Reiss-Davis Clinic Bulletin*, 9, 66–68.
Zuelzer, W. (1982). *The Nicolai case*. Detroit: Wayne State University Press.

Chapter 6
Greenspan (1941–)

Publishing Era: 1972 to the Present

Biographical Information

Stanley I. Greenspan[1] was born in Brooklyn, NY on June 1, 1941. Both his parents were immigrants. His mother came from Poland at the age of 16, fleeing from the anticipated Nazi invasion of that country; whereas his father immigrated at age 9 from Western Poland. A 3-year older brother completed the family unit.

In high school, Stanley developed an interest in math with the prospect of getting a degree in engineering. He went to Harvard for his undergraduate education, where he majored in Economics and graduated *cum laude* in 1962. While at Harvard, he was exposed to, and influenced by the work of Henry A. Murray. Murray was a psychologist who wrote on the influence of social, psychological, and cultural factors on personality development; he was also the founder of the Boston Psychoanalytic Institute.

Following his graduation, he was accepted at the Yale Medical School, from which he graduated in 1966. At the time, Yale had an outstanding department of psychiatry dominated by many of the luminaries in psychoanalysis. He received his training in adult psychiatry at Columbia-Presbyterian Medical Center's Psychiatric Institute in New York City and his training in child psychiatry at the Hillcrest Children's Center, Children's Hospital Center, in Washington, DC. There, he came under the influence of Reginald Lourie, a prominent child psychiatrist, who was the head of the Department of Psychiatry at Washington's Children's Hospital and consultant to NIMH. He met his wife Nancy Thorndike Greenspan, who had been associated with the US Department of Health and Human Services and the World Health Organization. Greenspan coauthored with her two books, *The Clinical Interview with the Child* (1983) and *First Feelings: Milestones in the Emotional Development of Your Baby and Child: From Birth to Age 4* (1985).

During his tenure at NIMH, which spanned the years between 1971 and 1987, he held several positions and rose to the position of Chief of Mental Health Study

[1] In a phone interview, on April 27, 2008, Stanley Greenspan, giving generously of his time, provided Joseph Palombo with some of the information contained in the biographical section.

J. Palombo et al., *Guide to Psychoanalytic Developmental Theories*,
DOI: 10.1007/978-0-387-88455-4_6,

Center and Director of the Clinical and Infant Development Program. During this period, he completed his training in child and adult psychoanalysis at the Washington Psychoanalytic Institute. He subsequently became Supervising Child Psychoanalyst at that Institute and in 1975 was appointed Clinical Professor of Psychiatry, Behavior Sciences and Pediatrics at the George Washington University Medical Center.

At NIMH, Greenspan was responsible for numerous studies, which led to the collection of data on children with neurological challenges. The charge of his department was to develop strategies for intervention in the lives of the affected children and to undertake programs for the prevention of those conditions. His experiences during those years were formative in the direction he later took in his work with and his advocacy on behalf of children with special needs.

Between 1980 and 1998, Greenspan, along with George H. Pollock, the former Director of the Chicago Institute for Psychoanalysis, coedited a seven-volume series titled *The Course of Life: Psychoanalytic Contributions Toward Understanding Personality Development*. First published by NIMH and currently published by the International Universities Press, this series of volumes brought together the outstanding psychoanalytic thinkers of the day, who contributed papers (see Greenspan & Pollock, 1989a, 1989b, 1991a, 1991b; Pollock & Greenspan, 1993a, 1993b, 1998).

During the years that followed his departure from NIMH, Greenspan has undertaken numerous projects that have had a broad impact on the lives of children through his clinical practice, the training he has provided to professionals, his research endeavors, and the dissemination of information about those conditions. Many of the projects he has undertaken have research components attached to them. A major organizing feature of these projects is **DIR/Floortime® approach** to the treatment of children with special needs, in particular to children with diagnoses within the autistic spectrum. Floortime refers to the technique that practitioners use, which includes sitting on the floor when working with a child attempting to make eye contact and connecting affectively with the child (for an application of this approach see Greenspan & Wierder, 2006)

> DIR® stands for the Developmental, Individual Differences, Relationship-based approach. It is a comprehensive, interdisciplinary approach that focuses on the emotional development of the child. It takes into account the child's feelings, relationships with caregivers, developmental level and individual differences in a child's ability to process and respond to sensory information. It focuses on the child's skills in all developmental areas, including social-emotional functioning, communication, thinking and learning, motor skills, body awareness, and attention. The goal of treatment is to help the child master the healthy emotional milestones that were missed in his early development and that are critical to learning. Building these foundations helps children overcome their symptoms more effectively than simply trying to change the symptoms alone." (from the DIR/Floortime® foundation Web site; http://www.floortime.org).

In 1996, Greenspan founded the Interdisciplinary Council on Developmental and Learning Disorders (ICDL) and now holds the Chair of its Advisory Board. This organization sponsors educational programs, whose goal is to improve the prevention, assessment, diagnosis, and treatment of children with developmental and learning disorders. In 2007, ICDL opened a graduate school that offers a PhD in

Infant and Early Childhood Mental Health and Developmental Disorders; it also publishes a new journal titled *Journal of Developmental Processes*.

In 2003, a consortium of psychoanalytic organizations[2] asked Greenspan to Chair a taskforce to produce a psychodynamic diagnostic manual that would complement the current Diagnostic and Statistical Manual (DSM IV) of the American Psychiatric Association. The charge to the taskforce was to develop a diagnostic framework that embodied the in-depth understanding of psychodynamics that psychoanalytic theory provides. Greenspan brought this project to fruition with the publication of the **Psychodynamic Diagnostic Manual (PDM)** in 2006. Included in this manual under the section "The Classification of Mental Health and Developmental Disorders in Infancy and Early Childhood" is the diagnostic classification manual that ICDL developed earlier in collaboration with the Zero to Three Project, of which Greenspan was the founding chair.

In addition to his contributions to the cause of children with special needs, Greenspan's accomplishments include the publication of over 40 books and 100 articles. He has been awarded numerous prizes and honors, among these are the prestigious Edward A. Strecker Award for outstanding contributions to American Psychiatry and the American Psychiatric Association's Ittleson Prize for outstanding contributions to Child Psychiatry Research.

Theory of Development

From the earliest days of his career, Greenspan demonstrated an interest in developing a conceptual framework that broadly combined diverse psychological perspectives with psychoanalytic metapsychology. This interest was complemented by a desire to find clinical applications for the framework, particularly in work with children. His work was buttressed by robust empirical data obtained through the many research projects into which he was involved at NIMH. During the days when ego psychology was near its zenith, he took up the challenge of enlarging its perspective by adding that of operant learning theory, **Piaget's genetic epistemology** (Piaget, 1972), and by taking into account the neurobiological factors that impact development. His vision appears to have been to synthesize these varied theories into a coherent view of human development (Greenspan, 1974, 1976, 1979).

In *Intelligence and Adaptation* (1979), Greenspan attempted to bring together Piaget's psychology, which deals with children's cognitive development, and psychoanalytic metapsychology, which focuses on people's emotional lives. In this groundbreaking monograph, he laid the foundation for what evolved into his

---

[2] The Consortium comprised the following organizations: the American Psychoanalytic Association, the International Psychoanalytic Association, the American Psychological Association – Division of Psychoanalysis (39), the American Academy of Psychoanalysis, and the National Membership Committee on Psychoanalysis in Clinical Social Work.

own developmental perspective. One pillar of that foundation became his **developmental - structuralist approach** to the classification of adaptive and pathological personality organization, which focused on the manner in which children organize and differentiate their experiences of the world at each level of development. He regarded this approach as describing the **architecture of the mind**.

Piaget, through his structuralist perspective (see Piaget, 1972) had proposed that each organism inherits a genetic program that gradually provides the biological equipment necessary for constructing a stable internal structure of its experiences with the environment. The structures represented the interrelationship between invariant functions that emerge during development (Piaget, pp. 85-93). Greenspan proposed that the characteristics attributed to those structures by Piaget are compatible with the internal representations conceptualized within psychoanalytic theory. He concluded that the structures have three characteristics those of wholeness, of performing transformations from one state to another, and of providing the organism with a capacity for self-regulation.

The second foundational pillar, to which Greenspan arrived through the data he collected from the observation of children, was that infants progress during their development through six levels of organization, called stages. Each level represents a reorganization of previous levels. As new structures become dominant, their functions are hierarchically integrated; that is to say, the children's organizational capacity progresses to higher levels as they mature. Maturation is the result of the interaction between endowment and the environment. Furthermore, children must complete the tasks of any given stage before they can proceed to the next one.

In *Psychopathology and Adaptation in Infancy and Early Childhood* (1981), Greenspan describes the six levels as follows (1) **homeostasis**; (2) **attachment**; (3) **somatic/psychological differentiation**; (4) **behavioral organization, initiative, and internalization**; (5) **capacity for organizing internal representations**; and (6) **representational differentiation and consolidation**. In this work, Greenspan specified that each stage includes three dimensions, which are (a) the child's **functional – the emotional developmental level**; (b) the individual differences in sensory activity, processing, and motor planning; and (c) the relationships and interactions with caregivers family members and others (see Greenspan, 1981, p. 29). These stages are elaborated further in *The Development of the Ego: Implications for Personality Theory, Psychopathology, and the Therapeutic Process* (1989).

Greenspan conceived of psychopathology as resulting from the interferences that neurological, emotional, or environmental factors interposed between the stages as the child progresses from one level to the next. For example, neurobiological deficits provide a filter as to how the child perceives and processes events in his or her life. Consequently, these factors will either facilitate or impede the child's development (Greenspan & Porges, 1984).

Greenspan began his intellectual career as a traditional ego psychologist and used its language and concepts freely in the development of his early framework. As he moved away from this drive-based point of view, he reframed his position. By 1997, he displaced the term "ego" by the concept of "self" or "sense of self."

Emotions as Architects of the Mind

Greenspan has been a strong advocate of the position that affects and cognition are inextricably linked from birth on. His six stage developmental schema, which describes the emotional, intellectual, and social growth of the child, led him to focus in particular on the functional–emotional dimension of development. His premise is that emotions serve to create and organize many of the mind's most important functions. The developmental process begins with "the emergence of the capacity to invest a freestanding image with emotional meaning to make it into a meaningful multisensory, affective image (i.e., an idea or image)" (2004, p. 37). In 2001, he along with his colleagues Georia DeGangi and Serena Wieder published the *Functional Emotional Assessment Scale (FEAS) for infancy and early childhood.* This work offered tools through which clinicians and researchers could assess a child's level of development along the six stages, and the progress a child may make as an outcome of interventions through such techniques as the application of the DIR/Floortime® approach.

Initially, Greenspan's developmental scheme included only the first six stages that described developmental through 2½ years of age. With the publication of the book coauthored with Shanker (Greenspan & Shanker, 2004), the developmental scheme was extended to include the entire lifespan divided in 17 stages. Since the data for those stages are speculative and not founded on as robust data as those of the first six stages, we merely list them here. They are:

Stage 7, Multicause, Comparative, and Triangular Thinking
Stage 8, Emotionally differentiated gray-area thinking
Stage 9, Intermittent reflective thinking in relation to a sense of self, and an internal standard
Stage 10, Reflective thinking with an expanded self; the adolescent themes
Stage 11, Reflective thinking with an expanded self; considering the future
Stage 12, Reflective thinking with an expanded self; the adult years
Stage 13, Reflective thinking and the separation, internalization, and stabilization of the self
Stage 14, Reflective thinking and commitment, intimacy, and choice
Stage 15, Extending the self to incorporate family and children
Stage 16, Middle age
Stage 17, The aging process

Greenspan has charted the critical stages in the development of the mind. He proposed that emotions and not cognitive stimulation serve as the mind's primary architect. By this, he means that, from a developmental perspective, emotions play a critical role in creating, organizing, and orchestrating many of the mind's most important functions. Most of these processes occur before the first thoughts are registered in the infant's mind. What the infant experiences is not the cognitive aspects of communication, but subtle emotional exchanges. By learning to discriminate and generalize, the infant's affects organize experience and ultimately thinking. Cognition emerges from the infant's affective exchanges with caregivers and the establishment of connections between feelings and actions or their symbolic representation. Feelings give rise to gestural language that then acquires symbolic significance.

Greenspan derived these hypotheses primarily from his work with children who have disorders within the autistic spectrum. With regard to the emotional architecture of the mind, inborn differences in sensory makeup lead children to respond differently to sensations. Some children have developmental problems that hamper their ability to make connections between thought and affect. They cannot generalize among situations because of their inability to evoke the affects appropriate to the situations they confront. Interventions that facilitate the child's ability to cue emotional responses to a caregiver's communications provide strategies that can reverse the effects of a child's disconnection from its caregiver. In short, emotions organize experience and behavior and facilitate cognitive development.

Once children have firmly established the foundation on which to make connections between emotions and actions, they are in a position to make the transition from emotion to abstraction. They have acquired a set of memories and intuitions that organize its experience into categories. The earliest sense of causality, reality, and logic is emotional. We categorize ideas and information according to their physical features as recorded by our senses but we also categorize them by their affective content. This capacity to form abstract concepts occurs prior to the acquisition of verbal language. Concepts have emotional foundations that integrate the essence of disparate and even competing experiences into a body of principles that will stand up to logical analysis. The principle then is that the second aspect of thinking is logical analysis of emotionally derived ideas and concepts; the first aspect being the emotional processing of experiences. Capacities that we generally consider innate, such as the ability to learn language, require an emotional base in order to acquire purpose and function.

The Six Stages of Functional/Emotional Development

The six functional/emotional stages of development are the earliest self, the related self, the willful self, the preverbal self, the symbolic self, and the thinking self.

Stage One, The Earliest Self, Occurs from Birth on. Interest in the World and the Capacity for Regulation Emerge

The major developmental issues at the stage of the **earliest self** include the development of the capacity for regulation and interest in the world. At this early stage of development, children cannot differentiate themselves from the rest of the environment. Consciousness consists only of an experience of alertness and aliveness. The first level involves making sense of sensation and dealing with shared attention and regulation. During this stage, infants take pleasure in the stimuli that reach their senses. They vocalize a great deal and spend time looking at their caregivers' faces and staring into their eyes. Their experiences lay the foundation for the development of structures of the mind that provide the functions of security and for the acquisition of the capacity to regulate their states of mind. Whereas each infant reaches different levels of achievement at each stage as compared to other infants, deficits in either neurological or emotional areas may exist that divert some from a normative path.

At the neurobiological level: "Neuronal connections occur in the area of the brain that processes sensory information and helps the baby to initiate movements.... and in the areas that support emotional interest in the world" (p. 273).

Stage Two, The Related Self, Occurs from 2 to 4 Months on. Early Evidence of Attachment Emerges

The major issues at the stage of the **related self** include engaging and relating to others. Infants focus on the primary caregiver and begin to differentiate human from inanimate objects. They find pleasure in the engagement with the caregiver. A sense of shared humanity becomes manifest as the child's sense of self emerges in relationship to the caregivers. Pleasurable feelings characterize relationships with others as feelings of intimacy gain ascendancy. Synchronic interchanges occur between infant and caregiver, which indicate that the caregiver is actively signaling the infant, whereas the infant cannot yet fully decode these signals.

At the neurobiological level: "Further activity in the areas supporting emotion, integration of visual, sensory, and motor areas, and right-sided neuronal connections supports the recognition of patterns (sights, movements) and promotes emotional relating, expressiveness, and signaling" (2004, p. 274).

Stage Three, The Willful Self, Occurs from 4 to 8 Months on. Evidence of Intentionality Emerges

In the stage of the **willful self**, the preverbal dialog and nonverbal means of communication are dominant as infants use gesture, vocal, and facial expressions to convey feelings. Infants begin to understand that caregivers receive and respond to their messages. A sense of separateness and differentiations from others begins to take hold as a boundary between "me" and "you" develops. Infants begin to use a range of feelings to express their intentions. In the dialog, caregivers become active participants in responding to their infants. At the cognitive level, infants begin to understand cause and effect relationships.

At the neurobiological level: "As the baby processes and initiates more selective responses to environmental clues, growth in the areas that support sequencing and reading and expressing gestures and emotion (two-way communication) are more active" (2004, p. 274).

Stage Four, The Preverbal Self, Occurs from Nine to 18 Months on. The Capacities for Problem-Solving and Mood Regulation Become Ascendant

The **preverbal self** unfolds within the caregivers' context. It becomes more complex, more organized, and more coherent. By the age of 15 months, children can deal with ambivalent feelings toward their caregivers, such that loving feelings can coexist with angry ones. The emerging capacity to communicate verbally permits children to widen the domain of their exploratory activities. While imitation is motivated by feelings, brain development in cognitive areas permits the child to learn social behaviors, to use verbal language, and to process information through thought. As the abilities for pattern recognition and imitation grow in complexity, so do the capacities to experience deep emotions that acquire their own set of personal meanings. These form the foundations of the sense of self (Greenspan, 1997, pp. 68-73).

The emotional dialog with the caregiver leads to coregulated interchanges that serve as models for problem solving and indicate the attainment of a higher level of integration than existed previously. At this stage, the level of communication becomes increasingly complex, although it remains at the presymbolic level. The toddler is now able to discriminate among the basic emotions. This begins the process of acquiring beliefs and values that are funneled from the culture through the caregivers to the toddler.

At the neurological level: The cerebral cortex becomes more active. "Left-sided neuronal branching surges as toddler sequences sounds and occasional word(s) to problem-solve. Right-sided growth continues together with the ability to figure out larger patterns in the world and interact with a wider range of emotions." (p. 274)

Stage Five, The Symbolic Self, Occurs from 18 Months on. This Fifth Level of Development Is Characterized by the Creation of Symbols and the Use of Words and Ideas

During the stage of the **symbolic self,** children develop the capacity to put into words their experiences, feelings, intentions, and wishes. They use other symbolic forms for pretend play and drawings, such as fantasy and play acting. They use words and actions together; somatic or physical words are used to convey feeling states; action words are used instead of actions to convey intentions; feelings are conveyed as real rather than as signals.

The child is now able to create an internal world by using images, ideas, and symbols. Symbolic expression becomes a shorthand through which the child can express desires and goals and organize experiences. "*The child makes the transition from an action mode of being, in which satisfaction lies in behavior, to the symbolic mode of being, through the maturing possibilities of her neurology combined with the richness of her affective experiences.*" (Greenspan, 1997, p. 76; our italics) We may refer to a symbolic sense of self "as the child has learned to use symbols to create an internal sense of security as well as to think about the world inside and around him" (Greenspan, p. 82).

At the neurobiological level: "Left-sided neuronal branching becomes denser as the child comprehends, uses, and sequences more words and masters some of the basic grammar. The visual-imaging parts of the brain grow as the child begins to engage more and more in pretend play. Both sides of the brain are becoming more specialized as language is rapidly being acquired" (2004, p. 274).

Stage Six, The Thinking Self, Occurs from Two and Half Years on. During the Sixth Level, Emotional Thinking, Logic, and a Sense of "Reality" Develop

During the stage of the **thinking self,** children become capable of building bridges between ideas as the ability to think logically develops. Symbolized or represented experiences are connected together logically to enable thinking. This includes the ability to differentiate between feelings, to create connections between differentiated feeling states and logical thinking. A child's first ideas emerge as discrete islands of thought with little relation between them. As caregivers respond to symbolic expressions in pretend play, in the third and fourth years children begin to form bridges among their ideas and between their own thoughts and those of others. The connection that they make depends on the caregiver's ability to read and respond to ideas, allowing the children to respond without stress or anxiety to a variety of emotional themes. Once children learn to build bridges among symbols, they can begin to construct a cohesive internal world of their own (Greenspan, 1997, p. 85).

Children's sense of self emerges in the context of a secure stable emotional relationship that provides an opportunity for interchanges of emotional communications that they represent symbolically. These emotional interchanges form the core of a unified sense of self, as the children translate their intentions and desires into images and symbols that include the meanings of their experiences. "This integrated image, what is sometimes called 'a personal narrative,' does not suddenly appear from nowhere. It is merely the surface representation of deep behavioral, emotional, and symbolic patterns that have been forming for sometime. Nor is it fixed. It continues to evolve through subsequent life experiences" (Greenspan, 1997, p. 93). The personal narrative incorporates past preverbal and presymbolic patterns and serves as a template for children to interpret past as well new experiences. It therefore does not necessarily represent what actually occurred in the past, but is a construction that serves to give meaning to feelings, thoughts, and behaviors.

At the neurobiological level: "The brain undergoes a growth spurt, metabolizing glucose (sugar) at twice the adult rate. Increased activity occurs in the areas of the brain that deal with the creation and comprehension of words, and connects among words. Increased activity continues throughout childhood and then gradually shifts to adult rate" (2004, p. 274).

Case Illustration

From Greenspan, S. I. and Greenspan N. T. (2003) The Clinical Interview of the Child. Third Edition. The American Psychiatric Publishing, Inc. Washington; D.C. pp. 116–118. (Published with permission from The American Psychiatric Publishing, Inc.)

Interview

When I entered the waiting room to greet Steve, a 6½-year-old boy, he was crawling under the couch, making high-pitched gleeful sounds. His mother looked worried. All the magazines were strewn over the floor. When his mother tried to comfort him, rubbing his back, he squirmed away, and mother said, "He doesn't like to be touched." He came along easily, if not a bit overenthusiastically, into my office. He tripped over his own feet, walking with a wide, somewhat unstable gait. He looked rigid and tight in his motor tone as he thumped around the room. His words were indistinct as he talked in a slightly hoarse voice, ran words together quickly, and mispronounced many sounds. Yet he was understandable. His fine motor coordination was quite clumsy as he quickly went searching through the toy closet, dropping small items and having difficulty manipulating the smaller, finer toys. Later, he had difficulty in drawing circles and squares, and so forth.

He made fleeting, mildly impersonal contact with me through a quick glance and immediately thereafter went to the toys. A frantic quality quickly emerged as he tossed all the toys on the floor in a disorganized manner. He then kept asking me to name each toy and other objects in the room. When I commented on his "interest in knowing names of things," he again made fleeting eye contact and kept asking me to name items.

Often, he did not respond to my gestures or words with gestures or words of his own. Only about 40% of the time did he seem tuned in and responsive. He kept moving, at times running, around the room, looking excited, occasionally tripping, momentarily looking confused, and then would become excited again.

This pattern went on for about 10 min. He then came across a stick and, with a gleeful look, repetitively banged it against a chair. He then jumped on some crayons that I had spilled on the floor, and, taking a policeman doll, he began banging it on the floor, saying "Bad boy, bad boy." He momentarily looked "blank" and began rocking back and forth while sitting on the floor. He then looked at me and asked, "Do you have any candy?" I commented that he wanted me to give him some candy, and he said "yes" and then started to throw a sponge ball at me, not stopping until I physically restrained him. He then said, "I want that horse" (a rubber play horse).

Nearing the end of the interview, I asked him about his parents, school, dreams, etc., and he only answered with regard to school, talking about "hitting kids" and "being bad." He named some children but would not elaborate.

He left the interview still quite active, with a fleeting glance.

Comments [Greenspan Continues]

There were indications of uneven maturation as evidenced by a possible overreactivity to touch, difficulties with gross and fine motor coordination, difficulty comprehending or focusing on my gestures and words, hoarse and indistinct speech, and difficulty with modulating his activity level and impulses. There was also a perseverative quality to his questions such as "What's this?" and a ritualistic quality to some activities such as banging. In addition, there was a brief episode of rocking. All these observations raise questions about physical–neurological compromises.

His mood vacillated between undifferentiated excitement and an indifferent quality. He related to me but only fleetingly and with little depth. Relatedness was therefore also below age expectations. There was little of the age-appropriate range of affects of modulation (e.g., only undifferentiated excitement). Anxiety may be inferred in relation to the loss of relatedness (i.e., blank look), rocking, and the impulsiveness (e.g., throwing a ball at me) that occurred after the "bad boy" theme and request for candy.

The interview suggested that anxiety is disruptive to an already vulnerable integrative capacity and may be experienced at the most primitive level of somatic disorganization.

Developmentally, he evidenced compromises of a marked nature at all levels. Attention and engagement were intermittent and unstable. Two-way gestural communication and the overall ability to be intentional also were only partially established. There were some representational capacities, but they were only fleetingly present and not used as a predominant mode of communicating. He did show a few islands of differentiated representational capacity when he was logical in asking me for candy.

Thematic concerns were communicated in the following sequence: aggressiveness, loss of control, being a "bad boy," disorganization, hunger, and anger. They reflected islands of cohesive thematic interests. Organization, range, and depth were all significantly below age expectations. By age 6½, cohesive, rich themes would be expected. There were no highly "bizarre" themes, however.

My subjective reactions vacillated between apprehension about his impulsiveness, lack of involvement, and some relief at the fleeting eye contact, indicating a potential for involvement.

Summary and Conclusions

Greenspan has had a longstanding interest in integrating cognitive and neurobiological theories into a psychoanalytic developmental theory. He proposed a *developmental-structuralist* approach, in part derived from Piaget, to organize the data he had collected about children's typical and atypical development. This approach assumed that organisms acquire internal psychological structures from the interaction between their innate potential and the environment to which they must adapt.

A second assumption made by Greenspan is that affects and cognition are bound together. Affects serve as organizers of the human mind. Cognition and ideation emerges from the emotional communicative exchanges that occur between infants and their caregivers. By linking their emotions and their actions, infants develop the capacity for abstraction. The capacities for understanding causality, appraising reality, and thinking logically all have emotional roots.

Based on these premises, Greenspan arrived at a developmental scheme constituted of six levels that unfold ontogenetically. During *Stage One, the Earliest Self*, infants struggle to make sense of the stimuli to which they are exposed. They are challenged to develop the capacity for self-regulation and to begin connecting with others in their world. The major issue that confronts infants in *Stage Two, the Related Self*, is engagement with the caregiver through mutual interactions. During *Stage Three, the Willful Self*, infants engage in a nonverbal dialog with their caregivers. They begin to express their intentions and emotions through willful activities. Communication becomes more organized and coherent during *Stage Four, the Preverbal Self*. Infants begin to deal with and resolve their ambivalent feelings toward their caregivers. *Stage Five, the Symbolic Self*, heralds the acquisition of language and the capacity to put feelings into words. Children can now create a world of internal images through symbols and to benefit from the sense of security they derive from their newly found understanding of the world. Finally, *Stage Six, the Thinking Self*, permit children to develop the capacity for logical thought and form bridges between feelings and ideas. The child's sense of self is sufficiently stable to permit an emotional engagement with others and the integration of a personal narrative.

Interferences in the movement through each level or from one level to the next may be due to neurological, emotional, or environmental causes. The result of these interferences manifests as psychopathology. The DIR/Floortime® approach provides people with the appropriate training techniques of intervention that may permit an affected child to overcome the interferences that stand in the way of movement to the next level.

Keywords Architecture of the mind • Attachment • Behavioral organization, initiative, and internalization • Capacity for organizing internal representations • Developmental - structuralist approach • DIR/Floortime® approach • Earliest self; Functional - the emotional developmental level • Homeostasis; Metapsychological differentiation • Piaget's genetic epistemology • Preverbal self • Psychodynamic Diagnostic Manual (PDM) • Related self • Representational differentiation and consolidation • Somatic/psychological differentiation • Symbolic self • Thinking self • Willful self

References

Greenspan, S. I. (1974). The clinical uses of operant learning approaches: Some complex issues. *American Journal of Psychiatry*, *131*(8), 852–857.

Greenspan, S. I. (1976). The identification and treatment of adult brain dysfunction. *American Journal of Psychiatry, 133*(9), 1013–1017.
Greenspan, S. I. (1979). *Intelligence and adaptation: An integration of psychoanalytic and Piagetian developmental psychology*. New York, NY: International Universities Press.
Greenspan, S. I. (1981). *Psychopathology and adaptation in infancy and early childhood.* Madison, CT: International Universities Press.
Greenspan, S. I. (1989). *The development of the ego: Implications for personality theory, psychopathology, and the psychotherapeutic process*. Madison, CT: International Universities Press.
Greenspan, S. I. (1997). *The growth of mind: And the endangered origins of intelligence*. Reading, MA: Addison-Wesley.
Greenspan, S. I., DeGangi, G. A., & Wieder, S. (2001). *The Functional Emotional Assessment Scale (FEAS) for infancy and early childhood: Clinical and research applications*. Bethesda, MD: Interdisciplinary Council on Developmental and Learning Disorders.
Greenspan, S. I., & Greenspan, N. T. (1985). *First feelings: Milestones in the emotional development of your baby and child*. New York, NY: Viking.
Greenspan, S. I., & Greenspan, N. T. (2003). *The clinical interview with the child* (3rd ed.). Washington, DC: American Psychiatric Publishing.
Greenspan, S. I., & Pollock, G. H. (1989a). *The course of life, Vol. 2: Early childhood*. Madison, CT: International Universities Press.
Greenspan, S. I., & Pollock, G. H. (1989b). *The course of life, Vol. 1: Infancy*. Madison, CT: International Universities Press.
Greenspan, S. I., & Pollock, G. H. (1991a). *The course of life, Vol. 3: Middle and late childhood.* Madison, CT: International Universities Press.
Greenspan, S. I., & Pollock, G. H. (1991b). *The course of life, Vol.4: Adolescence*. Madison, CT: International Universities Press.
Greenspan, S. I., & Porges, S. W. (1984). Psychopathology in infancy and early childhood: Clinical perspectives on the organization of sensory and affective-thematic experience. *Child Development*, 55(1), 49–70.
Greenspan, S. I., & Shanker, S. G. (2004). *The first idea: How symbols, language, and intelligence evolved from our primate ancestors to modern humans*. Cambridge, MA: Da Capo Press.
Greenspan, S. I., & Wieder, S. (2006). *Engaging autism: Using the floortime approach to help children relate, communicate, and think*. Cambridge, MA: Da Capo Lifelong Books.
PDM. (2006). *Psychodynamic Diagnostic Manual (PDM). A collaborative effort of the American Psychoanalytic Association, International Psychoanalytic Association, Division of Psychoanalysis (39) of the American Psychological Association, American Academy of Psychoanalysis and Dynamic Psychiatry, and National Membership Committee on Psychoanalysis in Clinical Social Work*. Silver Springs, MD: Alliance of Psychoanalytic Organizations.
Piaget, J. (1972). *The principles of genetic epistemology*. New York, NY: Basic Books.
Pollock, G. H., & Greenspan, S. I. (1993a). *The course of life, Vol. 5: Early adulthood.* Madison, CT: International Universities Press.
Pollock, G. H., & Greenspan, S. I. (1993b). *The course of life, Vol. 6: Late adulthood.* Madison, CT: International Universities Press.
Pollock, G. H., & Greenspan, S. I. (1998). *The course of life, Vol. 7: Completing the journey.* Madison, CT: International Universities Press.

Major Works

Brazelton, T. B. and Greenspan, S. I. (2000). The Irreducable needs of Children: What Every Child Must Have in Order to Grow, Learn and Flourish. New York; Perseus Publishing.
Greenspan, S. I. (1979). *Intelligence and Adaptation: An integration of psychoanalytic and Piagetian developmental psychology*. New York, NY: International Universities Press.

Greenspan, S. I. (1981). *Psychopathology and adaptation in infancy and early childhood.* Madison, CT: International Universities Press.

Greenspan, S. I. (1989). *The development of the ego: Implications for personality theory, psychopathology, and the psychotherapeutic process*. Madison, CT: International Universities Press.

Greenspan, S. I. (1997). *The growth of mind: and the endangered origins of intelligence*. Reading, MA: Addison-Wesley.

Greenspan, S. I. (2003). *The clinical interview with the child* (3rd ed.). Washington, DC: American Psychiatric Publishing.

Greenspan, S. I., & Shanker, S. G. (2004). *The first idea: How symbols, language, and intelligence evolved from our primate ancestors to modern humans*. Cambridge, MA: Da Capo Press.

Section III
Object Relations Theories

Object relations theory proposes to explain the way in which inner representations are formed and how they manifest in human conduct. The origins of this theory lay in Freud's view that drive discharge occurred through the investment of the object, i.e., the caregiver, the "object" being the target of the drive. Object relations theories diverged from this by postulating that human beings are primarily motivated to *seek object contact*, not to *discharge drives*. These theories tried to address issues that drive theory and ego psychological theories had neglected. For example, although object relations theorists acknowledge that there is an ego, they consider it to be object seeking and even say that it exists only in so far as it is connected to an object. One outgrowth of object relations theories is the emphasis on the concepts of self-representation and object-representation, concepts that were introduced by Hartmann (1964, p. xii) (see also Jacobson, 1964), which develop through experiences with objects. Self-structure is formed as a result of the internalization of early experiences in relationships with objects and the formation of stable self-representations and object-representations.

Object relations theories suggest that if relationships with early caregivers are satisfying, the representation of the object that the child internalizes will be of a *good object* and imbued with love. However, if the experiences are not satisfying, the representation will be of a *bad object* imbued with hate. Since self-representations develop in parallel with those of object representations, the developmental task consists in reconciling the good and bad primitive object representations. If this occurs, the child can experience ambivalence toward the object and achieve object constancy, that is, a stable object-representation that is distinct from the self-representation. Furthermore, the child internalizes the patterns of the early interactions between it and the caregiver; these relational patterns prescribe how the person will relate to others in the world and in therapy.

Klein, influenced and encouraged by Abraham, interpreted Freud's drives to be central to the organization of infants' fantasies, or *phantasies*, as she preferred to designate them because they were unconscious. Her emphasis, however, was on infants' *relationships* to their objects and the internalization of their experiences with those objects. Their inner worlds became populated by the phantasies they had of their caregivers. **Winnicott** became embroiled in the controversy between Anna

Freud and Klein's views of children's development and the implication of those views for treatment. Being an original thinker who cut his own path into the thicket of psychoanalytic theory, he declared himself as belonging to the group of independent psychoanalysts who chose a middle road in the dispute. **Mahler** steered her own course by deemphasizing the prominence of the drives and formulating her unique view that children's development is analogous to what occurs to an embryo. Children progress from a symbiotic phase during which they are undifferentiated from their caregivers and progress to a phase during which they achieve separation and individuation. Finally, **Kernberg** synthesized the ego psychological and developmental models of Freud, Klein, Jacobson and Mahler to build a framework that is verifiable through research strategies. He proposed that his framework had broad application to the explication of the dynamics of some types of psychopathology, in particular the narcissistic and borderline personality disorders.

The developmental theories that emerged from object relations theories remain within the positivist, science-based perspective of the drive theorists. They subscribed to an organismic model that conceives of the child as in need of positive psychological nourishment to thrive. However, the children's fantasies may contaminate what they take in irrespective of the responses the external world provides. In brief, this organismic model emphasized the adequacy, or inadequacy, of the child's relationship to the object. It valued the object's responsiveness to the needs of the child, seeing it as determining whether the child will progress successfully through the subsequent developmental phases. If the nutriment that the object offers was toxic, i.e., enveloped by anger or detachment, then the child developed a case of psychic indigestion, and could not metabolize the incorporated object. In its extreme form, some developmental models played many variations on the theme of this metaphor. In particular, Klein's descriptions of the vicissitudes of children's psychic indigestion are an example. Children may throw up what they take in, as in the defense of projection that is dominant in the paranoid position; or, they may re-ingest what they have thrown up, as in the defense of projective identification; or, children may refuse further nourishment and collapse into an anorectic, depressed state and fail to thrive, as in the depressive position.

References

Hartmann, H. (1964). *Essays on ego psychology: Selected problems in psychoanalytic theory.* New York, NY: International Universities Press.

Jacobson, E. (1964). *The self and the object world.* New York, NY: International Universities Press.

Chapter 7
Melanie Klein (1882–1960)

Publishing Era (1923–1960)

Biographical Information

Melanie Klein was born Melanie Reizes in 1882. Her father, Moriz Reizes, was a medical doctor in Deutsch-Kreutz, a small town about 70 miles from Vienna. He was married twice, the first marriage lasting a short time and ending when he was 37 years old. His second marriage in 1875, at age 47, was to Libussa Deutsch, Melanie's mother, who was 24 years younger than him. The couple had three children very quickly, Emilie in 1876, Emanuel in 1877, and Sidonie in 1878. The family moved to Vienna shortly before Melanie's birth on March 30, 1882 (Segal, 1992).

Later in life, Klein reflected on some of the causes for early discontent. Her mother told her that she was an unexpected child. Unlike her three siblings, she was not breast fed by her mother, but had a wet nurse. Furthermore, she often felt as though her three siblings were a unit and that she was not a part of that unit. Yet, as the youngest of the four siblings, she was inspired with a strong sense of competitiveness. Her father, whose approval she longed for, and who was in his fifties when Melanie was born, was not available to spend time with her and openly stated his preference for her sister Emilie. Her parents' marriage was not an amiable one, Libussa often expressed to her family her contempt for her husband (Grosskurth, 1986).

Her sister Sidonie died of complications of tuberculosis at age 8, when Klein was 4 years old (Segal, 1992). This was the first of many deaths she had to endure during her lifetime. Her father died of pneumonia in 1900 at age 72, when she was 18 years old. Her brother Emanuel, with whom she had a strong attachment and who suffered from a bipolar disorder, was addicted to cocaine and morphine, died at age 25, when she was 20 years old.

Shortly after her father's death, she met Arthur Klein, a chemical engineering student, and married him in 1903, at age 21. Melanie had doubts about the marriage from the beginning, but did not express them to her mother or brother, whom she sensed realized that Arthur was a difficult person. Her marriage was not a loving one; she experienced Arthur as rigid and inflexible. Despite her stated disgust for sex, Melanie became pregnant within two months of the wedding. Her first child, Melitta, was born in 1904. Her second child, Hans, was born in 1907. During this

J. Palombo et al., *Guide to Psychoanalytic Developmental Theories*,
DOI: 10.1007/978-0-387-88455-4_7,

pregnancy, she went into a deep depression. Hans died at age 27 from an accidental fall while walking in the mountains when Melanie was 52 (Grosskurth, 1986).

After the birth of Hans, with Melanie in a state of exhaustion and depression, her mother moved in with her and took command of the household. Melitta disliked Libussa, Libussa made it known to Melitta that her mother was emotionally troubled. Melanie's depression was so severe that she went to a sanitarium in Switzerland for 2½ months in 1909. In 1911, Melanie and Arthur moved to Budapest and Libussa, who believed that the Klein household could not function without her, moved with them. Melanie became pregnant again in 1913, a realization that did not make her happy. Her third and final child, Erich, was born in 1914. Four months after Erich's birth, Libussa died of cancer (Grosskurth, 1986).

In 1914, while seeking a channel for her creative and intellectual energies, Melanie read Sigmund Freud's (1901) paper on dreams. This work so inspired her that she decided to enter into analysis with Sandor Ferenczi (Segal, 1992). After meeting Freud for the first time in 1918, she committed herself to the study of psychoanalysis as her life's work. During her analysis with Ferenczi, she became aware of her professional interest in children, and as a result focused her attention on child analysis.

Two incidents reflect Karl Abraham's influence on Klein and her career. First, with the opening of the children's clinic, Abraham appealed to Ferenczi to encourage Klein to come to Berlin to conduct child analyses, as she had been doing in Budapest. She evidently, unhesitatingly, accepted the offer and arrived in Berlin on February 11, 1922. Second, the encouragement that he provided enhanced Klein's confidence. Soon after her arrival, she delivered two papers, "The Technique of Early Analysis" and "An Obsessional Neurosis in a Six-Year-Old Girl." These papers immediately generated controversy. It became evident that she was beginning to depart from some of Freud's most fundamental principles. Abraham's approval of her work, despite the fact that she was challenging some of the core ideas of psychoanalysis, not only served as encouragement to Klein to further pursue her ideas, but also led to a strain in Abraham's relationship with Freud (Grosskurth, 1986). In 1923, Abraham told Freud that he was impressed with her "amazing insights into infantile instinctual life" (Makari, 2008, p. 426). Abraham, who advocated for a greater role for aggression in human development, encouraged her to incorporate these ideas into her formulations. When she was attacked for her radical statements, he publicly supported her position. Finally, when Klein participated in a congress in Wurzburg in 1924, he expressed his opinion that child analysis was the future of psychoanalysis; an opinion that led Klein to an early appreciation of the importance of the contribution she was making to psychoanalysis and provided a boost to the energies she was putting into her work.

Melanie separated from Arthur in 1919, their divorce becoming effective in 1925 or 1926. The separation produced a burst of creative energy. She had her first paper, "The Development of the Child" published in the *International Journal of Psycho-Analysis* in 1923. In 1924, she began an analysis with Karl Abraham. This analysis lasted 15 months, coming to a precipitous end due to Abraham's sudden death in December 1925. In the same year, she presented a paper in which she first raised the highly controversial idea of an earlier date for the Oedipus Complex than that proposed by Freud.

Klein moved to England in 1926 and established herself with the British Psychoanalytic Society (Segal, 1992). The period from 1926 through the 1930s was the most productive of her life. Important works of this time period included "Early Stages of the Oedipus Complex" (1928), "The Importance of Symbol Formation in the Development of the Ego" (1930), "The Psychoanalysis of Children" (1932), and "A Contribution to the Psychogenesis of Manic Depressive States" (1935), among others. The book *The Psychoanalysis of Children*, in its radical departures from classical psychoanalytic thinking, served as a marker of the height she had reached in the British Psychoanalytic Society. In addition, it inspired her adversaries, who were committed to Anna Freud's views, to further conflicts. At this time, some believed the "British School" to be the "Kleinian School."

In 1924, Klein's daughter Melitta married Walter Schmideberg in Vienna. Three years later, she graduated with distinction from Friedrich-Wilhelms-Universitat in Berlin. She then followed her mother to England in 1928 to write her thesis. Melitta had a Swedish passport, which permitted her to enter England with no trouble, but her husband Walter was unable to secure entry to England until 1932. Melitta thus left her husband behind and moved in with her mother, with whom she lived for 4 years. In 1932, when Walter finally arrived in England, Melitta moved out of Klein's home and into her own home with her husband. This event seemed to be a turning point in Melitta's relationship to her mother, after which much conflict ensued. Melitta had entered analysis with Edward Glover, the second most powerful person in the British Psychoanalytic Society (second only to Ernest Jones). During this analysis, she came to realize that she had an unhealthy dependence on her mother. She concluded that it was necessary for her mother to accept her as a colleague and equal. She wrote a letter to her mother that essentially declared her independence from her, a letter that Glover may have helped her write. Many in the British Society believed at this time that Glover and Melitta had joined forces to discredit Klein, as they began to attack her openly. Speculation continues as to why these attacks took place, but since they occurred during the period of the analysis, they may have been related to material that emerged during the analysis (Grosskurth, 1986).

From 1935 to 1941 Klein served as D.W. Winnicott's clinical supervisor. As the Nazis came to power in Austria, many Jewish analysts were forced to leave Vienna. The arrival of the Freuds in London in 1938 brought considerable conflict and an open split between Anna Freud and Klein, and several losses. Her ex-husband Arthur Klein died in 1939, the same year as Sigmund Freud. Her sister Emilie died in 1940, adding more losses with which she had to deal.

The period following Freud's death was contentious. Some of his followers struggled over whose ideas were to take their place as the rightful heir to those of Freud and for control of the future direction of psychoanalysis. Klein emphasized that her theories were not a deviation from those of Freud, whereas Anna Freud contended that Klein's theories could not coexist with her father's theories. As we have seen, these disagreements led to what became known as the "Controversial

Discussions," which took place from 1942 to 1944 (see the section "Controversial Discussions" in Chap. 3).

Central points of disagreement included the timing of the Oedipus Complex and its relationship to superego development. Klein believed that the superego develops *with* the Oedipus Complex at the end of the first year and beginning of the second year of life. In addition, she insisted that psychoanalysis with children was possible provided their play during sessions was considered equivalent to verbal free associations. Anna Freud, on the other hand, believed that psychoanalysis of children could not be conducted in the same manner as with adults, stressing instead a continued connection to the family environment and a period of preparation for analysis. Anna Freud and Melanie Klein also differed in their ideas about transference, Klein believing that child patients establish transference immediately, while Anna Freud believed that children do not form transferences that recapitulate early parental experiences until after their adolescence (King & Steiner, 1990). Ultimately, the British society divided into three groups: Klein's group, Anna Freud's group, an Independent Group that included Winnicott, a fact that upset Klein considerably.

Klein continued to publish numerous works from 1945 through the 1950s, including "Notes on Some Schizoid Mechanisms" (1946), "The Origins of Transference" (1952), and "Envy and Gratitude" (1957). In the spring of 1960, Klein was found to be anemic. She struggled for several months feeling constantly tired until a definitive diagnosis of cancer of the colon was declared. A successful operation was performed in September 1960. However, she fell out of bed a few days later, broke her hip, and died from complications of that fall on September 22, 1960, at the age of 78.

Theory of Development

Melanie Klein's conceptual framework occupies a middle place between classical Freudian psychoanalytic thinking and the object relations movement, although she is credited with being the originator of this movement. For her, the term **object relations** refers to more than the actual relationships with whom the person is involved; it also encompassed the **internal representations** of others, of the self, and of the unique position of that person in the world. Unlike Freud, she believed that object relations are present from the beginning of life and that transferences develop through the same processes as those through which object relations develop. She viewed development as organized around the phantasies infants have of relationships to the object.

Klein made a distinction that is conceptually important in object relations between "**fantasies**" and "**phantasies**." Fantasies are conscious thoughts that are the product of the imagination. Phantasies,[1] in Klein's view, are the unconscious

[1] In our discussion, we will follow her usage.

thoughts that are associated with instincts. Klein most often applied the term *phantasy* in her discussion of a developing infant's phantasies about the mother's breast. Phantasies serve to help the infant deal with anxiety. They also help the infant make sense of what constitutes "inside world" and "outside world" - *phantasy* is the realm of inside world, and reality is the realm of outside world. *Fantasy*, on the other hand, refers to a person's conscious creation of an imagined reality of what may be possible. A person may fantasize how they might be able to fulfill not only their most basic needs, but also their dreams and aspirations. Fantasies may also contain within them some aspects of unconscious *phantasies*. The distinction between these concepts is central to Klein's theory because in her view "unconscious phantasies underlie not only dreams but also all thought and activity, both creative and destructive, including the expression of internal object relations in the analytic situation" (Spillius, 2001, p. 371).

Historically, what is particularly interesting, is that Klein did not write the paper or present the idea of *phantasy*. Regarding the origin of this important concept in the literature, Likierman (2001) states:

> Considering that ideas about unconscious phantasies were so central to Klein's developing theory, it is all the more surprising to discover that she was not the presenter of this single paper, entitled "The nature and function of phantasy" (Isaacs, 1948). The paper was written and presented instead by Klein's articulate, scientifically-minded adherent, Susan Isaacs" (p. 136).

Whereas her theory retains the drives as giving shape to the infant's experience of the world and of the others, she emphasized the importance of those drives in shaping how infants experience their relations to caregivers. Ego and superego development resulted from the internalization of object relations. She believed that psychoanalytic theory had focused too much on the libidinal component of the drives and not enough on the aggressive drives. Consequently, she parted from the classical view that guilt comes from sexual longing toward the object rather than from destructive wishes. These ideas manifest Karl Abraham's influence on Klein's work. In her work *Envy and Gratitude* (1957), she credits him for being a pioneer in exploring the roots of destructive impulses and of their relation to mental disturbances, but she later rejected his structural theory of development. Her ideas about the projective and introjective cycles and her concept of projective identification, concepts that we define below, are major contributions to psychoanalytic thought that endure to this day in most object relations theories. All forms of psychopathology are related to object relationship conflicts.

Klein built her theories largely from the observations and analysis of her own children. Later, she added to and refined her theories because of her interactions with her patients. She believed Freud's concept of sequential stages of development was too limiting and proposed instead the idea of "**positions**" that may endure for the person's lifetime. As a result, her variant of the organismic model of development does not subscribe to the epigenetic unfolding of a pre-existing program. Rather, the model proposes that the establishment of a set of enduring patterns results from the phantasies children have of their early relationship.

Paranoid-Schizoid Position: 0 to 3–4 Months

Early Object Relations

The earliest object relationships involve infants phantasizing danger or attack coming from the outside, which creates annihilation anxiety. The term "paranoid" as in paranoid–schizoid position, refers to the infants' fear of annihilation. Infants' first experience of feeding and of mother's presence initiates an object relationship. This relationship is at first to a **part-object** directed specifically toward the mother's breast, since infants have no awareness of the whole object. The breast is gratifying and thus loved, becoming the "**good breast**," but it is also frustrating and thus hated, becoming the "**bad breast**." Infants have no mental ability to distinguish between the two. Consequently, infants use the defense of **splitting**, which leads to a position that is termed "**schizoid**." Splitting involves the representation of the good breast as being separate from that of the bad breast. The good breast becomes the prototype for all gratifying objects; the bad breast becomes the prototype for all external and internal persecutory, that is, bad objects. Infants' emotions are extremely powerful, making them perceive bad objects as terrifying and good objects as ideal in their capacity to provide gratification.

Infants are born with both growth impulses, that is **life instincts**, and aggressive impulses, that is **death instincts**. Infants are born with an aggressive drive and with sadistic desires that are easily activated by frustrations. Sadistic impulses are directed not only at the mother's breast, but also against the inside of her body. The resolution of the conflicting drives is crucial in personality development. The death instinct arouses anxiety, which originates in the fear of annihilation. Infants experience anxiety from both internal and external sources. Feelings of love and destructive impulses toward the same object create anxiety and guilt. Destructive impulses are most powerful in the earliest stages of development.

Ego Development

In this position, infants' emerging egos strive to protect the good object from the bad object. The ego is a structure that, at first, is in fragments that functions from birth. Infants' anxiety is related to the processes involved in putting the pieces together, picking out the good pieces, and doing away with the bad ones. Defenses the infant uses during this stage include *splitting*, which involves keeping good and bad objects separate from one another; ***omnipotence***, which involves the phantasy of having the power to control all that happens; ***idealization***, which involves clinging to the belief that the good object is perfect; and ***denial***, which involves not facing any reality that does not conform to the infant's phantasy.

One of the ego's first activities is to defend against anxiety through the use of the processes of projection and introjection. **Projection** involves externalizing good or bad impulses or qualities and attributing their origin to an object, whereas

introjection involves the internalization of impulses or qualities that are attributed to the object. The interaction between the processes of introjection and projection determine ego development. Strategies infants use to reduce their anxiety include (a) projecting onto the bad object in phantasy the rage evoked by their frustration, (b) internalizing the bad object in order to control the danger through the use of the defense of introjection, and (c) identifying with the object in an effort to control their own aggressiveness onto whom they have projected their own aggressive impulses through **projective identification**. This defense involves identifying with or internalizing impulses or characteristics that were projected onto the object. The balance between good and bad objects moves infants toward integration of ego and object. In projective identification, the child attributes to another, usually the mother or her breast, unsatisfying experiences because the nourishment the child received was contaminated with hateful feelings. Having projected those feelings onto the object, the child is now in need of the relationship in order to survive. The only option left is identification with the very object onto whom the child had projected the unsatisfying feelings. The same process can occur around satisfying experience. The ensuing conflict between the good and bad objects becomes central to the child's development.

Psychopathology

If infants are forced to endure too many bad experiences with the object, they will use more primitive defenses, which will inhibit their psychological growth. Fixation in the Paranoid–Schizoid Position results in severe character pathology. Paranoid disturbances in adults result from persecutory anxiety experienced in the first months of life.

Depressive Position: 3–4 to 6 Months

Object Relations

A new developmental phase starts when infants no longer need to use splitting as a defense and begin the process of integrating good and bad object representations (Summers, 1994). This phase begins at 3–4 months and lasts until around 6 months. In this phase, infants realize that they have the power to do harm to the object, and feel remorse. Klein calls this phase the **depressive position**. The concept of the mother as a whole, unique, and separate person, who is a complete object rather than a part-object, develops. As a result, the infant moves from seeing objects as partial i.e., good or bad, and begins to experience objects as whole. Fear of "loss of the loved object" occurs during this phase when the ego transitions from incorporating partial objects to incorporating the whole object.

The capacity to emerge from depressive states and regain feelings of inner security is the criterion for a well-developed personality. The foundations for normal development are laid in this phase as relations to people as whole objects develop. Persecutory anxiety relating to internal and external objects diminishes; the good internal objects become more firmly established, and feelings of greater security follow.

The movement from the paranoid–schizoid position to the depressive position occurs as a result of the child's gradual separation from the mother, resulting in the child emerging as a separate person. Regarding this movement between positions, Klein states:

> With the introjection of the complete object in about the second quarter of the first year marked steps in integration are made. This implies important changes in the relation to objects. The loved and hated aspects of the mother are no longer felt to be so widely separated, and the result is an increased fear of loss. States akin to mourning and a feeling of guilt emerge, because the aggressive impulses are felt to be directed against the loved object (Klein, 1946, p. 149).

In other words, during the first year of life, the infant comes to perceive his or her mother as a whole object, and eventually realizes that the "good" and "bad" breast are both within the mother. The infant then feels bad that he or she has been attacking not only the "bad," but also the "good" within the mother, and feels guilt and sadness. As a result, the psychological birth of the child is accompanied by guilt and sadness, as the child must introject the whole mother in order to become a whole and separate self.

Ego Development

As relations between the child and both the internal and external world improve, the ego gains strength. Infants are more able to express emotions and communicate with people. Oral impulses and desires continue to predominate, and infants' sexual organization progresses.

Infants focus feelings of anxiety and guilt onto their mother as a person. In their effort to deal with their aggressive impulses toward mother, infants suppress these feelings through the defense of repression. **Depressive anxiety**, the second form of anxiety, results from the fear of doing harm to the object. Depression is the result of this unresolved depressive anxiety.

In addition, the ego uses **manic defenses** to ward off depressive anxiety. These manic defenses involve feelings of elation and excitement directed at avoiding the pain associated with the depressive feelings. As infants recognize that the object is a whole person, and thus the source of both pleasurable and painful experience, feelings of vulnerability and dependency emerge, and the infant develops a concern that any negative impulses felt toward the object could destroy it. Manic denial of these impulses is the primary defense used against the anxieties that are generated by these impulses and the potential impact they could have on the object and its responses. The superego forms a few months before the beginning of the Oedipus Complex and is initiated by the introjection of the object (Klein, 1958).

Psychopathology

If the manic defenses endure over time, they will inhibit a person's capacity to experience feelings at all. Since feelings form the basis of intimate relationships, denial of these feelings may lead to isolation. Problems in intimate relationships later in life can be traced to difficulties in this phase. The underlying dynamics are of unresolved fears of injuring the love object. If the infant had been able to take in successfully and establish his or her good object while in the Paranoid–Schizoid Position, he or she will be able to manage the conflicts and anxieties of the Depressive Position successfully. If not, regression to the Paranoid–Schizoid Position may occur.

Depressive Position: 6 Months to 12 Months

Object Relations

The fundamental steps in working through the challenges of the Depressive Position take place when the infant is internalizing the complete object during the second half of the first year. The infant transfers loving feelings and desires from the first and unique object, the mother, to other objects. The first relationship the child has to the outside world and to reality is of sadistic phantasies aimed at the mother's body.

Ego Development

The ego is still quite undeveloped at this point. The function of **symbol formation** and phantasy activity is significant. Symbolism is the foundation of all phantasy and sublimation. The child's relationship to the outside world and reality is built upon symbolism.

The task of this phase is to master the most severe anxiety. It begins during a period dominated by sadistic impulses. **Envy** is an expression of these impulses, and it is one of the most potent factors in undermining feelings of love and gratitude since it affects the earliest relation to the mother by supplying inspiration to rob from, spoil, and destroy her. The sadistic impulses create danger because they not only offer relief from anxiety, but also threaten the child who may be targeted for attack through the very same means employed to fend off anxieties, others' sadism.

The child expects to find within the mother the father's penis, excrement, and children. The boy's earliest phantasy of parental coitus is that it results in the father's penis becoming incorporated in the mother. The Oedipal phase, therefore, begins with the child searching for a new object, i.e., the father's penis. For the girl, identification with the mother results directly from Oedipal impulses. The struggle that causes boys' castration-anxiety is absent in girls.

Girls also struggle at this point, but the challenge they face is of a different type. When a girl discovers her lack of a penis, she interprets this to be the result of her hatred of the mother. Feeling guilty, she regards it as punishment. Freud thought that the girl's discovery of the lack of a penis caused her to turn away from the mother and direct her feeling to her father. Klein sees the deprivation of the breast as the cause of turning to the *father*.

Depressive Position: 12–24 Months

Klein disagrees with classical psychoanalytic thinking regarding the onset of the Oedipus Complex. In her view, it starts at the end of the first year or the beginning of the second year. The frustration the child experiences at weaning launches Oedipal tendencies. The classical view that the Oedipal dilemma emerges in the fourth or fifth year is actually better understood as not beginning at, but rather ending at this phase of development.

Klein proposed a "**femininity-phase**" or "**femininity complex**" for boys similar to the castration-complex of girls. In this phase, there is a frustrated desire for a special organ. The boy fears punishment for his wishes to destroy the mother's body, which is analogous to the girl's anxiety and castration fears. The fear of the mother is overwhelming because it is combined with the fear of castration by the father. This phase is characterized by anxiety related to both the womb and the father's penis. It subjects the boy to a tyrannical superego formed from the image of both mother and father.

Klein sees the development of girls as handicapped by the fact that boys in reality do possess a penis, which has put them in rivalry with their fathers, whereas girls have only the unsatisfied desire for motherhood. Since the girl once directed her destructive wishes against the mother, she anticipates the mother to destroy her capacity for motherhood. Therefore, penis envy is a product of Oedipal conflicts, not its cause, as Anna Freud maintained.

Further ego development takes place during this period. Toddlers make use of their growing ability to adapt to external reality. They have an increasing capacity to control bodily functions. They are better able to distinguish internal dangers from those instigated by external reality. Obsessional mechanisms form an important part of ego development at this time. These mechanisms, which can be observed in bedtime rituals, rituals related to cleanliness, food, and a general need for repetition, enable the ego to keep anxiety temporarily at bay so that it can achieve greater strength and integration.

Case Illustration

The following case illustration is taken from *Narrative of a Child Analysis: The Conduct of the Psycho-analysis of Children as Seen in the Treatment of a Ten-Year-Old Boy* (Klein, 1984, pp. 457–461). This treatment lasted a total of 93 sessions. The session reprinted here is the second next to the last session. Klein believed this treatment served to illustrate the use of her technique in greater detail than any case she had presented previously. She includes her interpretive comments to the patient's material throughout the illustration, and concludes with her notes about the session (reprinted with permission from Simon & Schuster).

Ninety-Second Session

Richard was again more depressed and absent-minded to begin with. He said that he had been playing with John Wilson and John's friends. He at once got out the goods train and the electric train and made a station large enough to accommodate both. The electric train went to 'Z' and Richard said that he and Mrs K. were on it. The goods train went out as well, but Richard did not give details of its destination. He made angry sounds representing the trains whenever they came near to each other. The play centered on avoiding collisions between the trains. They were often quite near to colliding, but Richard always prevented the disaster at the last moment, this conflict visibly giving rise to great mental strain in him. During this play Richard had repeatedly made suggestions about changes of times, choosing particularly times at which he knew quite well that Mrs K. saw other patients.

Mrs K. said she could not arrange the times he asked for but offered alternatives.

Richard, at one moment when both trains were standing in the station, suddenly said he felt unwell and had a pain in his tummy. He looked pale.

Mrs K. interpreted the station as Richard's inside. He expected all the time a collision inside him between the electric train, containing Mrs K. and the good Mummy, and the hostile goods train, standing for all the angry patients and children from whom Richard wanted to take Mrs K. away and run with her to his home town (Note I). Therefore he also wanted to change the time of his sessions, which meant taking Mrs K. away from everybody else. While Richard was striving to avoid a collision between the trains, because he did not wish to hurt Mrs K. and Mummy and their children and wanted to finish the analysis peacefully, he did not seem to believe that he could avoid the collision internally. This meant that he and Mrs K. would be hurt or damaged by his rivals. Therefore he had seemed so tense during this play and had a tummy ache (Note II).

Richard said, looking at Mrs K. in surprise, 'The pain has now quite gone—why?' The colour had come back into his face.

Mrs K. interpreted that the pain, like his throat in the earlier sessions, was connected with anxieties about his inside, and that when he understood these anxieties and consciously experienced them, the pain went.

Richard now made the goods train run after the electric train and again at the last moment stopped both of them in order to prevent disaster, moving the goods train to the other end of the table. A little later the engine from the goods train, leaving the carriages behind, ran into the station; although Richard tried to believe that now no disaster could occur, he obviously felt uncertain because he very soon pushed the engine behind Mrs K.'s bag, saying angrily, 'Silly thing'.

Mrs K. interpreted that the electric train was now standing for her. Richard took her away from her patients and children, as was shown when the electric train was running away from the goods train but in danger of being damaged by it. Then he expressed the same anxiety in a different way: the goods train engine—now standing for Mrs K. (the 'silly thing' which he had pushed behind Mrs K.'s bag)—ran into the station by itself, which meant that Mrs K. and he were no longer together. The carriages stood for Daddy and the patients and children, now all Richard's rivals (Note III). The engine also represented the external Mrs K., the good Mummy who was his main help and support.

Richard emphatically said that Mrs K. was with him on the electric train, and he showed her that he was one of the carriages, Mrs K. the other. He unhooked the two and joined them together again and then added that she and he were together and had their genitals together as well.

Mrs K. interpreted that Richard had felt that he could not prevent the disaster to him and Mrs K. He had suddenly realized that she would not stay with him any more but would join her other patients and her family. Hence he had unhooked the carriages and then joined them together again.

Richard said that if Mrs K. wanted to leave her other patients it had nothing to do with him.

Mrs K. interpreted that this was just why Richard had become so angry with her, the engine, the 'silly thing', because he felt that it was not Mrs K. who wanted to leave her children and patients (the carriages) and stay with him, but Richard who wished to separate them.

Richard very soon joined the goods train engine and its carriages together again, and now a collision between the trains occurred. But he did it very carefully.... At one moment, while playing with the trains, he had shown distrust of Mrs K., asking her whether she could keep a secret. He said a very important person (whose name he mentioned) had travelled through 'X' that morning. He again asked Mrs K. not to talk about it.

Mrs K. interpreted that his distrust of her had increased because she was leaving him and therefore became more the 'wicked brute' mother.

Richard asked whether Mrs K. was a doctor for the mind as others are doctors for the body.

Mrs K. said yes, one could say so.

Richard said that the mind was even more important than the body, though he thought that the nose was very important too.

Mrs K. interpreted that the nose also stood for Richard's genital, and that he was afraid that something was wrong with it, that it was damaged and would not develop properly, and this was the reason why he was afraid of becoming a 'dunce'. He doubted whether Mrs K. could actually cure the genital as well as the mind.

Richard, soon after the train disaster, put away the toys.

Mrs K., referring back to one of the drawings of the previous session, inquired again about the fish at the bottom, which was in the claws of what Richard called a crab and which was very similar to the octopus of earlier drawings.

Richard again said the fish got away, and then he added that the two claws were the two breasts.

Mrs K. interpreted that Richard's anger was represented by the two claws of the crab. At the same time he wished that the breast should be able to save itself and cut off the claws. But having attacked the breast, he felt that now the breast would change into claws and attack him; and then he, in order to save himself—now having turned into the fish—would have to cut off the breast (Note IV).

Richard said that he did not want any more to look under the surface of the drawing (which meant beneath the line). He suggested that they should look instead at what was going on above the water (referring to the ship which he had drawn with pleasure)....Then he spoke about having played recently with John Wilson and his friends and said that he, Richard, had bombed the Burma Road in their play.

Mrs K. interpreted that if he had bombed the Burma Road, he was Japanese.

Richard, looking puzzled, said that then he must be the Japanese ship.

Mrs K. again interpreted the various sides of his personality which were represented by the British Salmon and by the Japanese ship; he had expressed this formerly when he was sometimes German and sometimes British. The ship being himself also contained people—the little men—standing for Daddy who, he was afraid, would harm the good Mummy inside him. This was the same as the fear of Hitler's genital being the 'secret weapon' inside him, which would drive him to harm Mrs K. or Mummy. The British submarine stood for his good self containing the good Mrs K. and Mummy.

Richard's mood during this session was on the whole much like that of the Ninetieth Session, with much unhappiness and tension. His increased desire to be cuddled showed repeatedly in his touching Mrs K., and he dropped things so as to be able to touch her legs when picking them up. He was obviously all the time trying to restrain his aggressiveness because of the fear of injuring his loved objects.

Notes to Ninety-Second Session

I. The collision between the good objects and what he felt to be the bad ones (because he had attacked them and wanted to deprive them) was also a conflict between one part of himself felt to be good and allied with the good object and the hostile part of himself allied with the objects felt to be bad.

II. It is important to consider the discrepancy between internal and external situations and the fact that while Richard externally tried to put things right, in order to prevent disaster, he could not get rid of the feeling of internal disaster which expressed itself in physical pain and in very noticeable mental strain. Psycho-analytic experience shows that efforts to deal with external situations and relations have several aims: not only is the relation to the external world to be improved—which implies making reparation to the first external objects—but anxieties relating to the internal world are to be assuaged. External relations thus become also the means of testing out internal ones. If a relatively good balance between external and internal is not established, these attempts will be unsuccessful.

III. There is an interpretation from a different angle which my work on the ego would now suggest. I had already interpreted that one part of his self, felt to be good and allied with the good object, was fighting his destructive part combined with the bad objects. But his ego was not strong enough to deal with the impending disaster. I would conclude that the engine which he put behind my bag (which had in his analysis often represented myself) stood for his destructive impulses which he could not himself control and which were to be controlled by the analyst—ultimately by his good object. This good object was also felt to be the restraining and therefore helpful superego.

IV. This is an instance which illustrates the fact that attempts at reparation and at control of destructive impulses cannot prevent the projection of the individual's destructive impulses on to the object. Since he had torn my breasts, the breast remained an object he distrusted and which would bite and claw him. This is an instance of the complexity of processes which are simultaneously operative. We see here the expression of destructive impulses and the wish to control them—even to annihilate them, which may mean annihilating a very important part of the self (cf. 'Notes on Some Schizoid Mechanisms'). In this way the good object is to be saved; yet at the same time there is distrust of it because it might retaliate and thus become dangerous (Klein, 1961/1984, pp. 457–461).

Summary and Conclusions

Klein first became a force in psychoanalysis with the publication of "The Development of the Child" in 1923. She challenged some of the central tenets of psychoanalysis, most notably the timing of the Oedipus Complex, proposing that it took place at the end of the first year, rather than the fourth or fifth year. She vied with Anna Freud, in the period following Sigmund Freud's death, for the future direction of psychoanalysis. She disagreed with Anna Freud about the nature of psychoanalysis of children, believing that children could be analyzed using essentially the same techniques as those used with adults, and that children are capable of establishing transferences.

Klein disagreed with Freud's idea of development as occurring in stages, proposing instead the idea of "positions" that may endure for the person's lifetime. She conjectured that the early object relations is first a *part-object relationship*, specifically to the mother's breast. Infants can experience the breast as either gratifying (*good breast*) or ungratifying (*bad breast*). The *good breast* becomes the prototype for all gratifying objects, while the *bad breast* becomes the prototype for all persecutory objects. During the initial *paranoid–schizoid position*, infants phantasize danger as coming from the outside. The *depressive position* begins when infants begin the process of integrating good and bad object representations, moving from experiencing objects as part-objects to whole objects. She proposed that the accompanying anxiety related to fear of "loss of the loved object" occurs during this phase, which is considerably earlier in age than what Freud proposed in the scheme he presented in 1926.

Klein viewed development as organized around the phantasies infants have of relationships to the object. She believed that ego and superego development results from the internalization of object relations. In this sense, her ideas represent a middle place between classical psychoanalysis and the object relations movement. Her ideas about the projective and introjective cycle and specifically her concept of "projective identification" represent major contributions to psychoanalytic metapsychology.

Keywords Bad breast • Death instincts • Denial • Depressive position • Depressive anxiety • Envy • Fantasies • Femininity complex • Femininity-phase • Good breast • Idealization • Internal representations • Introjection • Life instincts • Manic defense • Object relations • Omnipotence • Paranoid–schizoid position • Part-object • Phantasies • Positions • Projection • Projective identification • Projective identification • Schizoid • Splitting • Symbol formation

References

Freud, S. (1901). *On dreams* (Standard Edition, Vol. 5, pp. 631–685). London: Hogarth Press.

Freud, S. (1926). *Inhibitions, symptoms and anxiety* (Standard Edition, Vol. 20, pp. 77–174). London: Hogarth Press.

Grosskurth, P. (1986). *Melanie Klein: Her world and her work*. New York, NY: Alfred A. Knopf.

Isaacs, S. (1948). The nature and the function of phantasy. *International Journal of Psycho-Analysis*, *29*, 73–98.

King, P., & Steiner, R. (1990). *The Freud-Klein Controversies 1941–1945*. London: Routledge.

Klein, M. (1930). The importance of symbol-formation in the development of the ego. *International Journal of Psycho-Analysis*, 11, 24–39.

Klein, M. (1932). *The psycho-analysis of children*. London: Hogarth.

Klein, M. (1935). A contribution to the psychogenesis of manic depressive states. *International Journal of Psycho-analysis*, 1(16), 145–174.

Klein, M. (1946). Notes on some schizoid mechanisms. In *Envy and gratitude and other works* (pp. 1–24). New York, NY: Delacorte.

Klein, M. (1952). The origins of transference. *International Journal of Psycho-Analysis*, 33, 433–438.

Klein, M. (1957). *Envy and gratitude: A study of unconscious forces*. New York, NY: Basic Books.

Klein, M. (1958). On the development of mental functioning. *International Journal of Psycho-Analysis*, 39, 84–90.

Klein, M. (1984). Narrative of a child analysis. R. Money-Kyrle (Ed.), *The Writings of Melanie Klein* (Vol. 4). New York: Free Press. (Original work published in 1961).

Likierman, M. (2001). *Melanie Klein: Her work in context*. London: Continuum.

Makari, G. (2008). *Revolution in mind: The creation of psychoanalysis*. New York, NY: HarperCollins.

Segal, J. (1992). *Melanie Klein*. London: Sage.

Spillius, E. B. (2001). Freud and Klein on the concept of phantasy. *International Journal of Psychoanalysis*, 82(2), 361–373.

Summers, F. (1994). *Object relations theories and psychopathology: A comprehensive text* Hillsdale, NJ: The Analytic Press.

Major Works

Klein, M. (1923). The development of a child. *International Journal of Psychoanaylsis*, 4, 419–473.

Klein, M. (1924). The role of school in the libidinal development of the child. *International Journal of Psychoanalysis*, 5, 312–331.

Klein, M. (1926). Infant analysis. *International Journal of Psychoanalysis*, 7, 31–63.

Klein, M. (1927a). Symposium on child-analysis. *International Journal of Psychoanalysis*, 8, 339–370.

Klein, M. (1927b). The psychological principles of infant analysis. *International Journal of Psychoanalysis*, 8, 25–37.

Klein, M. (1928). Early stages of the Oedipus conflict. *International Journal of Psychoanalysis*, 9, 167–180.

Klein, M. (1929a). Infantile anxiety-situations reflected in art, creative impulse. *International Journal of Psychoanalysis*, 10, 436–443.

Klein, M. (1929b). Personification in the play of children. *International Journal of Psychoanalysis*, 10, 193–204.

Klein, M. (1930). The importance of symbol-formation in the development of the ego. *International Journal of Psycho-Analysis*, 11, 24–39.

Klein, M. (1931). A contribution to the theory of intellectual inhibition. *International Journal of Psychoanalysis*, 12, 206–218.

Klein, M. (1932). *The psycho-analysis of children*. London: Hogarth.

Klein, M. (1935). A contribution to the psychogenesis of manic depressive states. *International Journal of Psycho-analysis*, 1(16), 145–174.

Klein, M. (1940). Mourning and its relation to manic-depressive states. *International Journal of Psychoanalysis*, 21, 125–153.

Klein, M. (1945). The Oedipus complex in the light of early anxieties. *International Journal of Psychoanalysis*, 26, 11–33.

Klein, M. (1946). Notes on some schizoid mechanisms. In *Envy and gratitude and other works* (pp. 1–24). New York, NY: Delacorte.

Klein, M. (1948). A contribution to the theory of anxiety and guilt. *International Journal of Psycho-Analysis*, 29: 114–123.

Klein, M. (1952a). Some theoretical conclusions regarding the emotional life of the infant. In J. Riviere (Ed.), *Developments in psycho-analysis* (198–236). London: Hogarth Press.

Klein, M. (1952b). The mutual influences in the development of ego and id. *Psychoanalytic Study of the Child*, 7, 51–53.

Klein, M. (1952c). The origins of transference. *International Journal of Psycho-Analysis*, 33, 433–438.

Klein, M. (1955). On identification. In: *The writings of Melanie Klein 1946–1963*. New York, NY: Free Press.

Klein, M. (1957). *Envy and gratitude: A study of unconscious forces*. New York, NY: Basic Books.

Klein, M. (1958). On the development of mental functioning. *International Journal of Psycho- Analysis*, 39, 84–90.

Klein, M. (1960). A note on depression in the schizophrenic. *International Journal of Psychoanalysis*, 41, 509–511.

Klein, M. (1961). *Narrative of a child analysis*. London: Hogarth Press.

Supplementary Readings

Grosskurth, P. (1986). *Melanie Klein: Her world and her work.* New York, NY: Alfred A. Knopf.

Isaacs, S. (1948). The nature and the function of phantasy. *International Journal of Psycho-Analysis, 29*, 73–98.

King, P., & Steiner, R. (1990). *The Freud–Klein Controversies 1941–1945*. London: Routledge.

Likierman, M. (2001). *Melanie Klein: Her work in context.* London: Continuum.

Segal, J. (1992). *Melanie Klein.* London: Sage.

Spillius, E. B. (2001). Freud and Klein on the concept of phantasy. *International Journal of Psychoanalysis*, 82(2), 361–373.

Summers, F. (1994). *Object relations theories and psychopathology: A comprehensive text* Hillsdale, NJ: The Analytic Press.

Winnicott, D. W. (Ed.). (1935). The manic defense. In *Through paediatrics to psycho-analysis* (pp. 129–144). New York, NY: Basic Books.

Chapter 8
Donald Winnicott (1896–1971)

Publishing Era (1931–1971)

Biographical Information

Donald Woods Winnicott was born on April 7, 1896 in Plymouth, Devon, England. He was the youngest of three children, having two older sisters. His father Frederick was a merchant who devoted much time to his business dealings, his religion (Methodist), local politics, and later to community involvements, eventually earning a Knighthood in 1924. His father spent little time at home. Donald's mother Elizabeth suffered from depression, often putting Donald in the position of trying to cheer her up. Overall, Donald lived an enjoyable and consistent childhood. The well-to-do Winnicott household included an aunt, a nanny, a governess, a cook, and several household helpers. As a result, women surrounded young Donald throughout his childhood. This constant exposure to women likely stimulated his interest in the inner life of females. In addition, having to cope with the needs of his depressed mother, who died in 1925 of heart problems, may have led him to devote his life to the care of others, particularly women who were suffering. Winnicott grew to be only 5ft. 7in. tall and spoke with a high-pitched voice, leading some who listened to his radio broadcasts to think that a woman was speaking (Jacobs, 1995).

When Winnicott was 14 years old, his father sent him to boarding school after he used the unacceptable word "drat" in front of him. This banishment from the family home may have contributed in part to his later interest in the effects of the environment on children's development (Jacobs, 1995). Winnicott spent the years 1910–1914 at The Leys boarding school. Here, he developed an interest in the natural sciences, and particularly enjoyed Charles Darwin's *On the Origin of Species*.

An early example of Winnicott's independent thinking was his assertion that he had no interest in entering his father's business; instead, he expressed an interest in becoming a physician. He entered the Cambridge University in 1914, and eventually earned both a BA and an MA. In 1917, he joined the Royal Navy and served as a medical officer on a destroyer. He left the Royal Navy shortly before the end of World War I to resume his medical training at the Hospital Medical College from which he graduated in 1920, specializing in pediatrics. At St. Bartholomew's, he

J. Palombo et al., *Guide to Psychoanalytic Developmental Theories*,
DOI: 10.1007/978-0-387-88455-4_8,

studied under Dr. Thomas Horder, who taught the importance of the relationship between patient and doctor. Having read Freud's *The Interpretation of Dreams* in medical school, Winnicott became interested in psychotherapy, which influenced him to pursue psychoanalytic training at the Institute of Psycho-Analysis in London (Rodman, 2003).

In 1923, Winnicott married Alice Taylor, who suffered from severe psychiatric problems that included hallucinations and delusions. This relationship, which consumed much of his time and energies, may have been a manifestation of rescue fantasies related to his depressed mother. He arranged for a student of Melanie Klein to psychoanalyze Alice. The marriage lasted a total of 25 years, with Winnicott initiating a divorce in 1949 (Jacobs, 1995).

Also in 1923, Winnicott began his own psychoanalytic treatment with James Strachey, having been referred to him by Ernest Jones. This analysis lasted for 10 years. Strachey later broke the sanctity of the confidentiality of the analyst/patient relationship to reveal to his wife, Alix, that Winnicott suffered from erectile difficulties (Kahr, 1996). This information, along with the fact that Winnicott did not father children in either of his two marriages, led some to assume that he was sexually impotent. Strachey eventually advised Winnicott to seek contact with Melanie Klein to further his interests in psychoanalysis.

For almost three decades, Winnicott had a stormy relationship with Klein. The relationship started in 1932 when he read Klein's *The Psycho-Analysis of Children*, which helped him understand his child cases. Klein became his clinical supervisor for 6 years from 1935 to 1941. This supervision stimulated Winnicott to explore how mothers shape the mental lives of their babies. Winnicott had wanted Klein to be his analyst, but she refused because she wanted him to analyze her own son. Winnicott instead continued his analysis with one of Klein's associates, Joan Riviere. This treatment lasted 5 years (Rodman, 2003). Over time, Winnicott struggled with the rift between Klein and her adversary, Anna Freud, which manifested in "The Controversial Discussions" that took place from 1942 to 1944 (see Chaps. 3 and 6). Winnicott sided with the Independent Group, which especially riled Klein.

In 1941, after Great Britain became involved in World War II, Winnicott met Clare Britton, a social worker and a patient of Melanie Klein's, who was working with evacuated children in a hostel in Oxfordshire. He began a secret affair with her in 1944 and eventually married her in 1951 (Rodman, 2003). Winnicott's highest level of productivity occurred in the years following his marriage to Clare. During the 1950s and 1960s Winnicott's reputation grew as he lectured, wrote, and was involved in radio broadcasts.

A series of heart attacks that started in 1948 led him to retire in 1963 from his job at Paddington Green Children's Hospital, after 40 years of service. He devoted much of his energy in the 1960s to raising money for a statue of Sigmund Freud to be placed in a prominent public place in London. On October 2, 1970, the statue was unveiled. Donald Winnicott died on January 25, 1971 from heart failure at the age of 75 (Rodman, 2003).

Theory of Development

D.W. Winnicott emerged as a force in psychoanalytic theory and practice at a contentious time in the politics of psychoanalytic thought, when followers of Anna Freud and of Klein were in conflict over whose ideas were the rightful heir to Freud's legacy. Winnicott avoided allegiance to either camp, choosing instead to stay out of the dispute and concentrate on his own ideas. He had a unique talent for communicating his ideas in words that were easy to understand. The originality of his thoughts found expression in many concepts that achieved great popularity. Among those concepts are *transitional objects*, *good enough mother*, *holding environment*, *true and false self*, etc. (upon which we elaborate later in this chapter).

Whereas Winnicott never formulated a systematic developmental theory, Summers (1994) states that it is possible to infer "a system of thought...that organizes all his ideas on development and psychopathology into a coherent whole" (p. 137). He came upon his ideas through his clinical observations and experiences, in particular with children. Reports indicate that he had taken over 20,000 case histories during his first 25 years as a physician and psychiatrist in a hospital setting (Davis & Wallbridge, 1981). The editor of *The Piggle*, Winnicott's book that provides an account of the treatment of a little girl, estimated that he had seen as many as 60,000 mothers and children over a period of 40 years. Winnicott described his own contributions as "testing out my own ideas as they came to me in the course of my clinical work" (Winnicott, 1975, p. ix). His theoretical position shifted away from Freud's classical drive theory to his own version of object relations theory, which included the contribution of the environment to development and mental health. He also emphasized the mother–child relationship over the father–child relationship. Finally, he de-emphasized the importance of oedipal issues in the formation of the self. Although heavily influenced by the work of Freud, his developmental theory has no links to Freud's psychosexual phases, for which he substituted his own framework.

Winnicott saw development in terms of phases of dependence between mother and child. The environment plays a critical role in the development of the child. The individual and the environment are interdependent. Every human being is involved in a **maturational process** that propels the person to develop in a given direction. About this process, he stated that "any stage in development is reached and lost and reached and lost over and over again; the attainment of a stage in development only gradually becomes fact, and then only under certain conditions" (Winnicott, 1988, p. 37). A **facilitating environment** is necessary for the maturational process to succeed. Shortcomings in the facilitating environment inhibit the maturational process.

His developmental model is divided roughly into three phases. The earliest phase is the Phase of Absolute Dependence, which has two subphases, followed by the Phase of Relative Dependence, and lastly comes the Phase Toward Independence.

Phase of Absolute Dependence

Winnicott used the statement "There is no such thing as an infant" (Winnicott, 1960a, p. 39) to capture the idea that mother and infant form an inseparable unit. Whenever we encounter an infant, we also encounter **maternal care**, without which there would be no infant. He believed that maternal care was what allowed the infant's ego to become powerful and stable (Winnicott, 1965).

During the phase of **absolute dependence**, which takes place until the infant is 3–6 months old, infants have no experience of an external object. They have no awareness of themselves as different from their environment, or awareness of me and not-me. When they look at their mothers, they see themselves; the mother provides a mirroring function through which infants see themselves. Since they lack a sense of time; they cannot link their experiences together in time. It is not until approximately 6 months of age that infants become aware that they do not control the sources of gratification. This awareness marks the beginning of the **self–object distinction**, at which point infants can see objects as existing outside of themselves.

Infants have no way of knowing about maternal care but depend on it for their survival. Their inherited potential cannot develop unless linked to maternal care. During this phase, caregivers express their maternal care for their infants through empathy rather than through words. Preverbal modes of expression predominate, as infants' mode of communication is through **gestures**.

Three major tasks confront infants during this phase: integration, personalization, and realization.

Integration. In his paper "Primitive Emotional Development" (1945), Winnicott proposes three developmental tasks that are characteristic of this phase. First is the task of **Integration**. He believed that the personality starts out in an unintegrated state. He stated, "To be known means to feel integrated. An infant who has had no one person to gather his bits together starts with a handicap in his own self-integrating task" (p. 140). The physical experiences of being kept warm, handled, and bathed, serve the process of integration.

Personalization. Second, the task of **personalization** follows. During this phase, infants are able to claim experiences as "my experiences." This term captures the feeling that the person has acquired a self that is located inside within its body. At this point, children can feel a lived psychic reality, an internal environment.

Realization. The final task is that of **realization,** when infants gradually develop a sense of reality. Infants realize that the environment is separate from the self and that they can communicate their intentions. They become aware that they can injure the object of their love (see Klein's "depressive position"). The fantasy of injuring the object is the first experience of agency. The experience of love and hate toward the same object makes a major contribution to the development of infants' sense of self.

Infants experience anxiety as a fear of annihilation, about which Winnicott said "The alternative to being is reacting, and reacting interrupts being and annihilates. Being and annihilation are the two alternatives" (Winnicott, 1960a, p. 47). Infants **come into being** depending on whether conditions are favorable or unfavorable.

They are only in a position to profit or suffer from disturbances. Too much doing or not enough responding on the part of the mother can result in an **impingement** to which the infant must react. Winnicott linked the concept of trauma to impingement. Traumas are impingements that occur before the individual has developed mechanisms that make the unpredictable predictable.

The Holding Environment

Satisfactory parental care involves a phase of *holding. Holding* is the activity through which mothers provide support to their infants' immature ego, thus strengthening it. It includes not just actual physical holding, but the creation of a total environment, which he called the **holding environment** that infants can experience as supportive. Good enough holding by the **good enough mother** promotes infants' development. Infants become persons by developing an "inside," that is, an inner psychic reality, and an "outside" that indicates a boundary between the self and the non-self.

Aggression

Winnicott agrees with Klein that **aggression** is inborn, but he disagrees with her belief that it is intentional. He sees aggression as playing two roles, first as "a source of energy," and second as "a reaction to frustration" (Winnicott, 1984, p. 92). As a source of energy, it is "almost synonymous with activity" (Winnicott, 1950, p. 204). Aggressive energy is a force through which infants can obtain a greater sense of being. As such, it a force that pushes for experiences that are necessary to come into being. Aggression, therefore, plays a role in the development of the self, the sense of reality, and the recognition of objects. Winnicott also sees aggression as a force that leads to creativity, which in turn children apply to the effort to experience life authentically. As a "reaction to frustration," aggression can become pathological or turn destructive against the self or others as a response to deprivation. This can occur when the true self is buried in a neglectful environment, forcing it into a position of having to act in order to feel real. As a result, the intention behind the aggression is not to be destructive, but rather to feel real. Winnicott (1958a/1965) stated, "the basis for the study of aggression must be a study of the roots of aggressive intention" (p. 204).

Hate

Winnicott expressed the view that mothers sometimes **hate** their children. In fact, he listed 18 reasons why a mother might hate her baby in "Hate in the Counter-Transference" (1949). He believed that the mother's hate of the baby preceded the baby's hate of the mother, and that these hateful feelings were not only natural but also healthy. Further, he believed that without hate there could be no love; that it is only through being hated that the infants can learn to trust and accept their own feelings of hate and love. As infants become aware of their mothers as whole persons, they are able to access their feelings of hatred toward her. Mothers must be able to tolerate the hateful feelings without acting upon or expressing those hateful feelings toward their infants.

Phase of Relative Dependence

The shift from Absolute to **Relative Dependence** occurs as the child becomes aware of its dependence on an outside object. In this phase, infants can differentiate between mother and others and can understand that they have "an inside, and that things come from outside" (Winnicott, 1945, p. 139). Infants develop the capacity to imitate their mothers. Characteristic of this phase is the capacity to comprehend the difference between what they can conceive subjectively and what they can perceive objectively. Infants demonstrate the beginnings of intelligence and of mind as distinct from the psyche. They are able to change from merging with their mothers to being separate from them, relating to their mothers as "not-me." The concepts of True Self and False Self are relevant to this phase. In addition, transitional phenomena occur and experiences of play begin.

True Self/False Self

When adequate holding takes place through development, the child acquires an authentic sense of being alive and feeling real, to which Winnicott referred as the **True Self.** Mothers give life to the true self through the strength they supply the during the infant's period of omnipotence (Davis & Wallbridge, 1981). Since infants experience anxiety as a fear of annihilation, the main function of the holding environment is the reduction of impingements on infants. If maternal care is not "good enough," infants do not come into being but instead develop a personality based on reactions to environmental impingements. These impingements prevent development of the True Self. The mother who is not "good enough" struggles to manage the child's omnipotence and instead substitutes her own, leading the infant to become compliant. This experience is a precursor to the emergence of the inauthentic and defensive **False Self**, which results from failures of the holding environment. The primary function of the False Self is to hide the True Self (Winnicott, 1960b). The True Self becomes buried underneath the False Self's deceptive mask that is presented to the outer world. Over time, with each "successful" deception, the person feels more as an imposter and more disconnected from his or her authentic True Self.

Winnicott (1960b) classifies the False Self organizations as a continuum ranging from less to more healthy (1) at one extreme the False Self presents itself to the world as real, and outside observers think this is the real person. At this extreme end of the spectrum, the True Self is hidden; (2) a less extreme manifestation occurs when the True Self is no longer hidden; it is acknowledged, but the False Self actively defends the True Self; (3) at a level closer to the healthy end of the spectrum, the False Self is actively searching for conditions which will make it possible for the True Self to come into its own; (4) still further toward health, the False Self is built on identifications; and (5) finally, in health, the False Self carries a polite and mannered social attitude that is used productively in social interactions (pp. 142–143).

Continuity of Being

In "Primary Maternal Preoccupation" (1956a/1958), Winnicott describes the infant's adaptation to the mother, and the preoccupation the infant has about the mother's ongoing "holding" activities. These activities include both physical holding and empathic responsiveness, both of which protect the infant from outside impingements. If the mother's attempts to provide "holding" responses are inadequate or unsuccessful, the infant's False Self will emerge and develop a pattern based on the failures in the environment. If this occurs, the True Self is not the one reacting to the failures, and a "**continuity of being**" (Winnicott, 1956b, p. 387) is preserved. If the ongoing holding activities of the mother are successful, the infant's "**going on being**" (Winnicott, 1956a/1958) is supported, which sets the stage for individuation. Winnicott used the term "going on being" to describe the natural and continuous growth and development of the authentic sense of self without interruption or impingement coming from the outside.

Transitional Phenomena

In this phase, children use **transitional phenomena** to mediate the worlds of omnipotence and reality. Winnicott (1953) proposes an "intermediate area of experiencing," an internal place where an individual is "engaged in the perpetual human task of keeping inner and outer reality separate yet inter-related" (p. 90). It is in this intermediate area that transitional phenomena take place. These phenomena assist infants with their separation and stranger anxieties.

Transitional objects are a type of transitional phenomena. They are objects that children endow with qualities or psychological functions that are associated with their mothers. By carrying these objects, they experience comfort and reassurance much as if they were close to their mothers. The most common type of transitional phenomenon is of objects that exist physically outside the self and to which an infant becomes attached. They constitute the first "not-me" possession (Winnicott, 1953, p. 89). For children, these objects lie between reality and fantasy. They help ease the anxiety of separation and stranger anxiety and permit the child to move from the intensity of annihilation anxiety to a somewhat less intense anxiety over potential loss of the object.

Play

Play is an extension of the use of transitional phenomena. Winnicott emphasized that the freedom to be creative, which playing permits, is essential in the development of a self. He believed that play takes place in what he called the "**potential space**" (Winnicott, 1971, p. 53), the intermediate area where transitional phenomena take place. He also believed that the emotional development of a child could not be seen simply in terms of the individual, but required consideration of the behavior of the environment as well. Winnicott believed that only through playing could a child (or adult) be creative, and this creativity was seen as an essential ingredient in the discovery, creation, and development of a self. This idea also influenced his thinking regarding how psychotherapy should be conducted, which he elaborates upon in the following passage from *Playing and Reality* (1971):

> Psychotherapy is done in the overlap of the two play areas, that of the patient and that of the therapist. If the therapist cannot play, then he is not suitable for the work. If the patient cannot play, then something needs to be done to enable the patient to become able to play, after which psychotherapy can begin. The reason why playing is essential is that it is in playing that the patient is being creative. (p. 54)

Toward Independence

Winnicott saw the phase of **Toward Independence** as synonymous with the oedipal phase of development. He did not elaborate his thoughts about this phase and believed his contribution to developmental ideas was in his insights about the earlier phases of development.

Case Illustration

The following case material is taken from *The Piggle: An Account of the Psychoanalytic Treatment of a Little Girl* (Winnicott, 1977, pp. 165–179). Winnicott saw this patient, named Gabrielle and nicknamed "The Piggle," over a period of 2½ years, starting when she was 2 years and 4 months old. Gabrielle's parents were required to seek Winnicott's assistance because she was experiencing worries and fantasies that kept her awake at night, sometimes leading to her scratching her own face. Her anxiety seemed to increase when her sister was born. This vignette occurs near the end of the treatment. It demonstrates Winnicott's treatment style, particularly his emphasis on play as a necessary component in the creation of conditions under which a patient can "come into being" and acquire a sense of self and ascribe meaning to life experiences. In this vignette, he accepts the roles the child assigns to him, and tries to use them to assist her in coming to terms with those aspects of her inner world that are most troubling to her. At the end of the vignette, Winnicott offers his comments on key aspects of the session (reprinted with permission from International Universities Press).

There was a rather special entry, characterized by shyness; Gabrielle was now 4 years and 3 months. When she came into the room she shut the door and went straight to the toys. I was sitting again on a chair, writing on the table.

Gabrielle: Come out [and she brought all the toys out on the floor, talking to herself a good deal]. The church goes there, doesn't it, Mr. Winnicott? [There were special arrangements of houses.] The little houses in a row and the big houses in another row.

We talked about these together as rows of children and grown-ups.

Gabrielle: Yes, these are the grown-ups, and these here are the children [and so on].

Then she apportioned the children to the grown-ups.

Gabrielle: Do you know when Susan [her sister, 2 years younger] was waiting for supper she fell out of the pram and cut her lip. She was eating her supper. Her lip was bitten. It was cured. Isn't that funny? Cured.

Me: Do you get cured?

Gabrielle: No. I had a cut which I scratched for a long long time.

She was indicating that she was the opposite of Susan, keeping her sores open. I could see that she was talking about me in my various roles.

Me: Susan hasn't been to see me.

(I knew that she had often felt like bringing Susan, but that it was very important to her that she not bring Susan and have me all to herself.) She went on playing, and said: "Now look, it came off the train; I can mend it myself." And she did.

Me: You can be a mender, so you don't need me as a mender now. So I am Mr. Winnicott.

Gabrielle: Some men were doing a mending job on the train. Do you know there was no seat and we had to stand and we walked and walked along and then we found a place and we sat somewhere where there was a bag; someone had left their bag there.

She was arranging two trucks, sometimes head to head and sometimes tail to tail. Then she said: "All the King's Horses could not put…."

Me: They could not mend Humpty Dumpty.

Gabrielle: No, because he was an egg.

Me: You feel you can't be mended.

Gabrielle: Every night Susan wants an egg, she is so fond of them; I am not very fond of eggs. Susan is so fond of eggs she eats nothing but eggs. Isn't that funny?

Here she was in trouble about actual mending.

Gabrielle: I have nowhere to fasten this. There is no hook. Can we find one?

There was a special arrangement of toys with various trains, trucks, and houses in parallel lines, orderly but not obsessionally accurate. Gabrielle commented, “Dr. Winnicott has got a lot of toys for me to play with,” and she continued manipulating the trains, sorting them out of the muddle they were in.

Gabrielle: The hook’s out of this one; isn’t that a silly-billy? I am mending it [and she did, very skillfully]. I really can put it in again.

Me: Gabrielle is a mender too.

Gabrielle: Daddy can mend things; we are both clever. Mother’s not clever at all.

Suddenly Gabrielle noticed the big bowl on the shelf above her head.

Gabrielle: I like that bowl with a Chinese picture on it.

And she worked out all the details of the children playing games. We had to turn it round and round. She said: “One of the children has fallen down.” She noticed everything and was pleased with it.

Gabrielle [singing]: I haven’t seen you for a long time so I was shy when I came to see you, and I shan’t see you tomorrow nor tomorrow nor tomorrow.

Me: Are you sad about this?

Gabrielle: Yes. I like to see you every day, but can’t because I have to go to school. I am supposed to go to school.

Me: You used to come here to be mended, but now you come because you like it.

Gabrielle: When I come to see you I am your visitor. You are my visitor when you come to Oxford. Isn’t that strange? Perhaps you will come after Christmas.

Me: Is there anything to be mended about you today?

Gabrielle: No, I don’t break any more. Now I break things up into pieces. This screw went in.

Me: Yes, you mended it yourself, and you can mend yourself.

Gabrielle: Today Susan got into the dog box. This is a new toy.

She was stepping on the elephant, and the elephant squeaked.

Here she asked me to help her mend the train that she was in difficulties with.

Gabrielle: You are a doctor, a real doctor, that is why you are called Dr. Winnicott.

Me: Do you like to be mended or do you like to come for pleasure?

Gabrielle: For pleasure, because then I can play more [she said this very definitely]. I can hear someone whistling outside.

I did not hear this and I said: “Or was it me writing?”

Gabrielle: No. Someone’s hooting now [true]. There are not enough hooks. When we were coming to you we were a bit early, so we walked around, so I must buy something for Susan and mummy. I like Susan and mummy.

Me: Here there is just Gabrielle and me. Is Susan cross when you come and see me?

Gabrielle: Do you know Susan…she likes to watch me dance. How old is she? She is two. I am four. Next birthday I will be five and Susan will be three.

By this time she had nearly all the toys arranged in parallel lines, about ten or a dozen of these lines, and one set of three houses set at an angle.

Gabrielle: Dr. Winnicott, I just go to the toilet. You look after the toys. Don’t let Daddy in.

She carefully shut the door as she went out, and was away 3 min.

Gabrielle: There. Mr. Winnicott I am going to stay a little bit longer than I usually do. I can play more if I have more time. I don't need to rush away.

Me: Sometimes you feel frightened about something, and then you feel you want to go suddenly.

Gabrielle: Because it gets late. I can't undo this [I undid it for her]. Did you think this could go up there? [i.e., on the shelf by the portrait of the 7-year-old girl]. This could go up there too. Don't take them down will you – leave them there.

Me: Till you come next time. You feel that this gives you some hope of coming to me again.

Gabrielle: For all the time.

Then she looked at the portrait, mounted as it is in an oval mount, and said: "Look, she's in an egg."

Me: If she hadn't got a place to be she would be like Humpty Dumpty and go to pieces; but you have a place here where you can be.

She then gave me a lecture on eggs.

Gabrielle: If one breaks an egg without boiling it, when it is soft, it runs all over and everything gets dirty, but if one boils it hard and opens it, it just crumbles.

Me: I put an egg round Gabrielle and she feels all right.

Gabrielle: Yes.

She then took all the blue houses and put them in a circle with the red one in the middle, saying: "I am going to make a row of houses like this," and she put all the houses up against each other in a close row.

Gabrielle: If I see any more, I will put them in the row.

She was now collecting little people and trees and animals: "A lot of things" (talking all the time). She stood them up on the carpet as far as possible. I could not hear what she was saying well because she was talking to herself, happy, easy, contented, creative, and imaginative. She had her back to me, and said something like: "I leave it like that. Mr. Winnicott can I take this one and this one and this one? I will bring them back. I will take two. I will leave three or four for you. I have got three." (In fact, at the end she had no need to take anything, and had apparently forgotten the matter.)

Gabrielle: Whose turn is it to clean the bath?

There seemed to be a complex answer to this. It had to do with rivalry with her sister over this privilege. I did not take it for granted that there is actually competition in this field at home, looking at it from the parents' point of view. She was making animal noises with some of the animals in her hand.

Gabrielle: I like to clean the bath. You stay there [she was talking to the animals]; not you, cow, you dog; you, cow, don't move at all; otherwise…you will be turned into witches.

Me: Are you telling me a dream?

Gabrielle: Yes. I don't like it. It's horrible. To be turned into a little person with

Me: Well? [I encouraged her to go on].

Gabrielle: Well they didn't build shops, and if they sold lavender they went around and sang: "Who'll buy my lavender?"…[singing]. A penny can spend. If

Susan doesn't let somebody go up the stairs they have to pay six pence; isn't that a lot?...I only make them pay one penny, not much is it?

I tried to get at what she was implying; it had to do with Susan being mean. Then she looked out of the window.

Gabrielle: Someone has a roof garden; that's funny; I can't get up there. I wonder how they water the flowers. They open the window with an iron stick and then put water up a chimney. They let it squirt all the flowers, and so everything gets watered. They put a spoon up the chimney and get all the water down, and then they do it again. [Then after a bit:] Is that your shed? Oh! You can't get to it, can you? Are those plastic flowers?

Me: No, they are real.

Gabrielle: I like plastic. Those are plastic [not really].

Me: Do you like real or plastic children and animals? [Here she opted for real].

Gabrielle: What is that wooden thing? [She had spotted the end of a wooden cylindrical ruler which another child had left and which was among the books.] Shall I bring it out?

Me: Rightho.

Gabrielle: What is it for?

Me: It's a ruler.

Gabrielle used the ruler as a rolling pin, as if it was exactly what she had been looking for. First of all it was to roll pastry. Here then was another role, that of cook, and I pointed this out to her. The rolling developed into a game which involved the whole room.

Gabrielle: When the woman comes to mend things, the cook pretends to go to sleep. You have to tell her to wake up, and then she cooks some more.

She was trying to express what happened to the other Winnicott roles when Winnicott is in one role. The Dr. Winnicott who mends has gone away for a holiday, so there is Mr. Winnicott who cooks. When she needs mending, then Dr. Winnicott comes back. She then went to the gas fire.

Gabrielle: How do you light the gas fire?

I went over and showed her.

Me: Now the mending Winnicott and the cooking Winnicott have gone away,

(For myself, in the setting, I was left with no doubt that the most valuable of the four roles is the play role, especially the one in which she is what I have called "alone in my presence.") There was another role that she reminded herself of, which had to do with the use of the wastepaper basket which could be said to be a Winnicott that helps her to get rid of what she has finished with (Dustbin Winnicott).

In the course of this, Gabrielle developed an organized game in which we rolled the ruler to and fro, and she came nearer and nearer, so that when she rolled the ruler it would bang against my knees. Here she was giving me a fifth way in which I had been important to her, someone that she bumped up against when she moved and who, in this way, could be used in her effort to distinguish what was not herself from what was truly herself. At one point when the ruler hit my knee, I turned over backward and played the game with gusto to give her the satisfaction she needed. (It is not possible for a child of this age to get the meaning out of a game unless first of all the game is played and enjoyed. As a matter of principle, the analyst always allows the enjoyment to become established before the content of the play is used for interpretation.) It seemed as if Gabrielle had finished making her list of the ways in which she had used me. There was a period at the end in which she got the feeling that she was staying a little longer than usual simply because she liked being with me when she was not feeling frightened, and when she was able to get pleasure and to express in a positive way her relationship to me as a person. At the very end she added one more to her list of roles and said: "I will leave you to pack up." And so she left, being very careful to shut the door completely. She collected her father from the waiting room. On this occasion, I did open the door and say goodbye to them both, because in a way this was a gesture due to the father, and I felt that Gabrielle had finished what she wanted to tell me.

Comments [By Winnicott]

1. Apportioning grown-ups to children – keeping me all to herself.
2. Development of the capacity to be her own "mender."
3. The train (analysis) had moved slowly, but went all the way to London – its destination.
4. Sadness over prospect of termination.
5. Secure about her place in my life.
6. Expression of having been solidly put together; she is now contented and creative.
7. Review of the various roles she used D.W.W. for.

Summary and Conclusions

Winnicott emerged as a major contributor to psychoanalysis during the time following Freud's death, when followers of Anna Freud were in conflict with followers of Melanie Klein regarding the future direction of psychoanalysis. Though he never formulated a systematic developmental theory, it is possible to infer his theory from his collected works. He came upon his ideas about development through his extensive clinical experiences. His ideas shifted away from Freud's classical drive theory to his own version of object relations theory. He added consideration of the contribution of the environment to development, and de-emphasized the importance of oedipal issues in the formation of the self.

Winnicott saw development in terms of phases of dependence between the mother and the child. In the earliest phase, *absolute dependence*, the mother and the infant are a unit. Infants have no experience of an external object and lack a sense of time. The mother's efforts to provide support to the infant's immature ego constitutes what he referred to as a *holding environment*. The mother's goal is to provide what Winnicott called *good enough* mothering to meet the child's developmental needs. The culmination of adequate *holding* is the sense of being alive and feeling real, which Winnicott referred to as the *true self*. On the other hand, failures in the *holding environment* will result in a defensive *false self*, which can lead to later psychopathology.

The phase of *relative dependence* begins when the child becomes aware of dependence on an outside object. During this phase, children try to manage their separation and stranger anxieties by endowing objects with psychological qualities that are associated with their mothers and carrying these *transitional objects* in order to experience comfort in the absence of their mothers. Winnicott's third phase of development, *toward independence*, is synonymous with the oedipal phase of development. He did not elaborate about this phase, believing that his contributions to developmental ideas lie in the earlier phases of development.

Keywords Absolute dependence • Aggression • Anxiety • Come into being • Continuity of being • Facilitating environment • False self • Gestures • Going on being • Good enough mother • Hate • Holding environment • Impingement • Integration • Maternal care • Maturational process • No such thing as an infant • Personalization • Potential space • Realization • Relative dependence • Self–object distinction • Toward independence • Transitional objects • Transitional phenomena • True self

References

Davis, M., & Wallbridge, D. (1981). The theory of emotional development. In *Boundary and space: An introduction to the work of Donald Winnicott* (pp. 29–85). London: H. Karnac Ltd.

Jacobs, M. (1995). *D.W. Winnicott*. London: Sage.

Kahr, B. (1996). *D.W. Winnicott: A biographical portrait*. London: Karnac Books.

Rodman, R. F. (2003). *Winnicott: Life and work*. New York, NY: Perseus Publishing.

Summers, F. (1994). *Object relations theories and psychopathology*. Hillsdale, NJ: The Analytic Press.

Winnicott, D. W. (1949). Hate in the counter-transference. *International Journal of Psychoanalysis*, 30, 69–74.

Winnicott, D. W. (1950). Aggression in relation to emotional development. In *Through paediatrics to psychoanalysis* (pp. 204–218). New York, NY: Basic Books.

Winnicott, D. W. (1953). Transitional objects and transitional phenomena. *International Journal of Psychoanalysis*, 34, 89–97.

Winnicott, D. W. (1956a/1958). Primary maternal preoccupation. In *Collected papers: Through paediatrics to psycho-analysis* (pp. 300–305). London: Tavistock.

Winnicott, D. W. (1956b). On transference. *International Journal of Psychoanalysis*, 37, 386–388.

Winnicott, D. W. (1958a/1965). Psycho-analysis and the sense of guilt. In M. Masud & R. Khan (Ed.), *The maturational processes and the facilitating environment: Studies in the theory of emotional development* (pp. 15–28). New York, NY: International Universities Press.

Winnicott, D. W. (1958b). *Collected papers: Through paediatrics to psycho-analysis*. London: Tavistock.

Winnicott, D. W. (1960a). The theory of the parent–infant relationship. *International Journal of Psychoanalysis*, 41, 585–595.

Winnicott, D. W. (1960b). Ego distortion in terms of true and false self (pp. 140–152). In *Maturational processes and the facilitating environment: Studies in the theory of emotional development*. London: Hogarth Press.

Winnicott, D. W. (1965). *Maturational processes and the facilitating environment: Studies in the theory of emotional development*. London: Hogarth Press.
Winnicott, D. W. (1971). *Playing and reality*. London: Tavistock.
Winnicott, D. W. (1975). *Through paediatrics to psycho-analysis*. London: Hogarth Press.
Winnicott, D. W. (1977). The piggle: An account of the psychoanalytic treatment of a little girl. New York: International Universities Press.
Winnicott, D. W. (1984). *Deprivation and delinquency*. London: Tavistock.
Winnicott, D. W. (1988). *Human nature*. New York, NY: Schocken Books.

Major Works

Winnicott, D. W. (1931). *Clinical notes on the disorders of childhood*. London: William Heinemann.
Winnicott, D. W. (1941). The observation of infants in a set situation. *International Journal of Psychoanalysis*, 22, 229–249.
Winnicott, D. W. (1945). *Primitive emotional development, International Journal of Psychoanalysis*, 26, 137–143.
Winnicott, D. W. (1949). Hate in the counter-transference. *International Journal of Psychoanalysis*, 30, 69–74.
Winnicott, D. W. (1950). Aggression in relation to emotional development. In *Through paediatrics to psychoanalysis* (pp. 204–218). New York, NY: Basic Books.
Winnicott, D. W. (1953). Transitional objects and transitional phenomena. *International Journal of Psychoanalysis*, 34, 89–97.
Winnicott, D. W. (1956a/1958). Primary maternal preoccupation. In *Collected papers: Through paediatrics to psycho-analysis* (pp. 300–305). London: Tavistock.
Winnicott, D. W. (1956b). On transference. *International Journal of Psychoanalysis*, 37, 386–388.
Winnicott, D. W. (1957). *Mother and child: A primer of first relationships*. New York, NY: Basic Books.
Winnicott, D. W. (1958b). *Collected papers: Through paediatrics to psycho-analysis*. London: Tavistock.
Winnicott, D. W. (1960a). The theory of the parent–infant relationship. *International Journal of Psychoanalysis*, 41, 585–595.
Winnicott, D. W. (1960b). Ego distortion in terms of true and false self (pp. 140–152). In *Maturational processes and the facilitating environment: Studies in the theory of emotional development*. London: Hogarth Press.
Winnicott, D. W. (1963). Dependence in infant care, child care, psychoanalytic setting. *International Journal of Psychoanalysis*, 44, 339–344.
Winnicott, D. W. (1965). *Maturational processes and the facilitating environment: Studies in the theory of emotional development*. London: Hogarth Press.
Winnicott, D. W. (1966). Correlation of a childhood and adult neurosis. *International Journal of Psychoanalysis*, 47, 143–144.
Winnicott, D. W. (1967). The location of the cultural experience. *International Journal of Psychoanalysis*, 48, 368–372.
Winnicott, D. W. (1968). Playing: Its theoretical status in the clinical situation. *International Journal of Psychoanalysis*, 49, 591–599.
Winnicott, D. W. (1969). The use of an object. *International Journal of Psychoanalysis*, 50, 711–716.
Winnicott, D. W. (1971). *Playing and reality*. London: Tavistock.
Winnicott, D. W. (1975). *Through paediatrics to psycho-analysis*. London: Hogarth Press.

Winnicott, D. W. (1977). *The piggle: An account of the psychoanalytic treatment of a little girl.* London: Hogarth Press.
Winnicott, D. W. (1984). *Deprivation and delinquency.* London: Tavistock.
Winnicott, D. W. (1987). *Babies and their mothers.* London: Free Association Books.
Winnicott, D. W. (1988). *Human nature.* New York, NY: Schocken Books.
Winnicott, D. W. (1992). *The family and individual development.* London: Routledge.
Winnicott, D. W. (1993). *Talking to parents.* Cambridge, MA: Addison-Wesley.
Winnicott, D. W. (1996). *Thinking about children.* London: Karnac Books.

Supplementary Readings

Davis, M., & Wallbridge, D. (1981). The theory of emotional development. In *Boundary and space: An introduction to the work of Donald Winnicott* (pp. 29–85). London: H. Karnac Ltd.
Jacobs, M. (1995). *D.W.* Winnicott. London: Sage.
Kahr, B. (1996). *D.W. Winnicott: A biographical portrait.* London: Karnac Books.
Rodman, R. F. (2003). *Winnicott: Life and work.* New York, NY: Perseus Publishing.
Summers, F. (1994). The work of D.W. Winnicott. In *Object relations theories and psychopathology* (pp. 137–190). Hillsdale, NJ: The Analytic Press.

Chapter 9
Margaret Mahler (1897–1985)

Publishing Era (1938–1980)

Biographical Information

Margaret Schonberger Mahler was born in Sopron, a Jewish village in western Hungary on May 10, 1897. Her father, Gusztav Schonberger, who had Hungarian roots, was a general practitioner who graduated from the University of Vienna and was the chief public health officer for the district. Her mother, Eugenia Weiner, who had Austrian roots, was a competent homemaker, but never mastered Hungarian. Completing the family was a sister, Suzanne, 4 years younger. In this upper middle class family, the sisters spoke Hungarian in the presence of their father and German with their mother. Mahler recalled a clear and painful conflict between her and her sister. Mahler's experience was that her mother was unavailable, hostile, and outright rejecting of her, while demonstrating consistent and flagrant favoritism toward Suzanne. Her mother was deeply unhappy and preoccupied with the household.

Mahler often turned to her father, who responded to her exceptional intellect and regarded her as his masculine extension. As a student, when Mahler periodically expressed love toward male teachers, her father gave the following pat reply, "You are man enough for yourself!" (Stepansky, 1988, p. 8). Looking at a childhood photograph, her mother stated that she looked homely, to which father replied, "But the photographer said that her beauty cannot be appreciated by ordinary people." Until she was 16, Mahler avoided mirrors and grew in the firm belief that she could be neither truly feminine nor attractive. She recalled that at age 13, Suzanne had swarms of boys hanging around the house, whereas she, at 17, was absorbed with Einstein's theory of relativity. She grew to believe that a man worth having could not love her. As an insecure provincial girl, she denied her femininity and learned to avoid defeat in an unkind world dominated by men. To compensate she developed a strong drive for independence, an attitude that her father encouraged.

At age 16, Mahler made a difficult decision and moved to Budapest to live with her aunt, her mother's favorite sister, in order to attend the Vaci Utcai Gimnazium. Her aunt, like her mother, made it known that she did not like Mahler, preferring her sister, and reluctantly allowed her to stay while attending a pre-med course of study. She was initially uncertain about the decision to pursue a "male" career and

J. Palombo et al., *Guide to Psychoanalytic Developmental Theories*,
DOI: 10.1007/978-0-387-88455-4_9, © Springer Science+Business Media, LLC 2009

study medicine, but her father encouraged her. She felt this was a turning point in accepting her lack of femininity and joining in direct competition with men. During her 2 years of study at the Gimnazium, she encountered a classmate who was to become her best friend, Alice Szekely-Kovacs, through whom she met Sandor Ferenczi, and other Hungarian intellectuals. Mahler's peer group included Alice and Emmy Balint, sisters of Michael Balint, who later became a prominent psychoanalyst. All three read and discussed Ferenczi's translation of Freud's, *Five Lectures on Psycho-Analysis* (Freud, 1910) delivered at Clark University in 1909. Mahler next read the *Three Essays on Infantile Sexuality* (Freud, 1905) and emerged with a strong appreciation for the unconscious and an intense curiosity about psychoanalysis. Ferenczi was fond of the young Mahler and encouraged her to come to Vienna and study psychoanalysis.

In September of 1916, Mahler entered the University of Budapest to begin premedical training. Ambivalent about her choice of careers, she eventually settled on pursuing a career in psychoanalysis through medicine while specializing in pediatrics. After the 1918–1919 school years, Mahler and several classmates decided to transfer to the University of Munich to begin formal medical training. There were two reasons for the relocation. First, as a Jewish woman, her chances of completing a university education were slim under the repressive Horthy political regime. Second, her parents decided Suzanne could only pursue harpsichord studies at the Odeon Conservatory in Munich under the wing of her older sister.

In her academic studies, she quickly stood out among her classmates, while the faculty regarded her highly. Her budding research interests took hold while assisting in measles research and developing a vaccine. The political environment grew hostile as the deepening anti-Semitic fog enveloped Germany. Hostility toward Jews became increasingly overt as non-German Jews became the first targets. The increasingly dangerous anti-Semitism coupled with the strangulating economic inflation led Mahler to transfer to the University of Jena to study with Professor Ibrahim, the leading German pediatric neurologist of the day.

Mahler found herself again the favorite of a teacher. She quickly joined Ibrahim's research efforts. She was able to appreciate the attendant emotional factors, as well as the psychosomatic nature of the disturbances they studied and used her psychoanalytic interests to demonstrate a psychological understanding that she found very compelling. Despite distinguishing herself academically, Mahler was in danger of expulsion, as the University of Jena was becoming a hotbed of pro-Nazi sympathizers. Among other measures, Mahler went to Karlsruhe to seek the help of Edwin Blos, Peter Blos' father, to ask his intervention with the General Student Board. Because of his considerable influence with the Board, Mahler was able to graduate. However, she spent her last semester at the University of Heidelberg, taking extension courses, where she completed her Jena degree. In 1922, she returned to Jena to take her written and oral examinations and passed magna cum laude, despite attempted obstruction from some faculty members. Because she was not a German citizen, she could not obtain a medical license. Consequently, she traveled to Austria, where she had citizenship, passed her qualifications and was able to begin the practice of medicine in 1923 at the age of 26.

Vienna

From 1922 until 1938, Mahler lived in Vienna, where she practiced medicine as a pediatrician, became a psychoanalyst, and married. After her arrival in Vienna in 1922, Mahler opened her private pediatric practice and began taking courses in psychoanalysis. Through the intercession of Ferenczi, she entered analysis with the imperious Helene Deutsch, after 4 years on her waiting list. While on the waiting list, Mahler became familiar with August Aichhorn who ran a series of child guidance clinics, which later provided her with valuable child analytic referrals. The analysis went badly due to Deutsch's critical attitude, thus repeating the rejecting maternal attitude, which Mahler knew so well. This analysis lasted about 14 months at which point Deutsch announced she was terminating their relationship because Mahler was not analyzable. Deutsch freely dispensed negative comments and her dislike for Mahler to her other patients and to colleagues.

Since a satisfactory training analysis was a requirement to becoming a psychoanalyst, Deutsch's notice to the institute caused Anna Freud to dismiss Mahler after she had been accepted as a candidate at the Vienna Psychoanalytic Institute. She went back to Ferenczi, who recommended that she begin another analysis, this time with a man. Mahler now turned to Aichhorn, her mentor and supporter. Aichhorn, as a core member of the establishment's inner sanctum, wielded considerable power. He was something of a rebel and expressed his dislike for hierarchy and bureaucracy. When Mahler presented herself and her plight to him, he assured her of her worth and proposed a secret analysis with himself. He proposed that after she had made sufficient progress, he would present the news of the analysis to members of the Institute's education committee. This most unorthodox arrangement met Aichhorn's need to upstage and upbraid his stiff collared colleagues and to fulfill Mahler's need for narcissistic repair. Mahler considered this analysis, which lasted almost three years, a most serious and worthwhile, if nonclassical undertaking, as they also became lovers. Six months later, she secured readmission to the Institute's training program and after 2½ years, she asked Willie Hoffer to accept her into analysis so as to successfully conclude her training analysis.

Mahler was well aware of the repetition of the Oedipus and her Cinderella complex with Aichhorn. Hoffer, who had supervised Mahler's first two control cases, was favorably disposed to his new analysand and introduced a much-needed objectivity. Mahler credits Aichhorn with a stream of well-paying referrals, which measurably improved her sometimes-desperate financial situation and introduced her to the Rorschach test, at which she became expert. Applying the Rorschach to organically brain damaged children inspired one of Mahler's first psychoanalytic papers, "Rorschach Interpretation as an Aid in Understanding the Psychology of the Brain-Damaged" (Mahler & Silberpfennig, 1938). Mahler received supervision from some of the most renowned names in early psychoanalytic history, among who are Anna Freud, Jenny Waelder, Marianne Kris, Jeanne Lampl-de Groot, and Willie Hoffer.

Mahler had set up the first psychoanalytically oriented well-baby clinic in Vienna, from which came the first child referrals for child psychoanalysis. Whereas

Mahler was highly respected for her skill as a pediatrician and regarded as a competent child psychoanalyst, she remained an outsider in the Viennese psychoanalytic establishment's "inner circle," even as those same psychoanalysts entrusted Mahler with the medical care of their children. She recalled Anna Freud and her inner circle treating her with contempt. Edith Sterba told Mahler that her certification by the education committee of the Vienna Psychoanalytic Institute in 1933 would have been unanimous except for the one dissenting vote cast by Helene Deutsch. She understood this exclusion from the "inner circle" primarily as a consequence of her rebelliousness in refusing to go along with the psychoanalytic attitude of neutrality, sterility, and detachment of emotion, which was a core part of adult and child analysis at the Vienna Institute in the 1920s and 1930s.

In 1936, at age 39, Mahler married Paul Mahler, having met him socially while she was in analysis with Hoffer. At the time, she was working on the issue of feeling attractive to men. Mahler considered the marriage a pseudosolution to unresolved psychological problems related to her need for intellectual superiority and her conflicted femininity. Paul was a cultured PhD chemist and prize winning bridge player from an overly protective Jewish family. She was already successful in her chosen field, while he was a struggling scientist/businessman. Even after resettlement to New York, Paul remained in low paying jobs as a chemist while her career prospered.

After the Nazi Anschluss of Austria in 1938, the persecution of Jews was soon in full swing. Aichhorn, who remained politically well connected, actively helped Mahler, protecting her and her husband from the Nazis. They were able to secure a temporary visa and made their way to asylum in Britain. There Mahler saw patients and administered the Rorschach to help pay the bills while Paul helped to facilitate the relocation of his family to London. They secured exit affidavits to immigrate to the United States. Now nearly penniless, she reluctantly accepted money from Ernst Jones, who insisted on helping her to pay for the trip to the States. A grateful Mahler was careful to repay every cent after her resettlement to New York in late 1938.

New York

Mahler found the nonpsychoanalytic community in New York far more accommodating than the medically controlled psychoanalytic establishment, which had a stranglehold on psychoanalysis, in complete disregard for Freud's insistence that lay analysts be allowed to practice. Officials in the Bureau of Child Guidance of the City Board of Education, Benjamin Spock and Bertram Lewis helped her establish a practice (see Freud, 1926). However, given the limited number of analysands in New York and the prospects of an avalanche of prestigious European analysts competing for business, the New York Psychoanalytic Society advised the recent arrivals to respect the sanctity of the American medical profession and not practice psychoanalysis until they got their medical licenses. Mahler passed her medical state boards on the first try.

The New York Psychoanalytic Society soon began to split into bitter rival factions. The Lawrence Kubie faction wanted the interpersonalists, David M. Levy, Rado, Clara Thompson, and Karen Horney out of the Society. Eventually the interpersonalists were expelled for holding politically incorrect views on theoretical orientation. They deviated too far into advocating the role of the social impact on intrapsychic processes (Richards, 2001). The dominance of ego psychology needed to be reasserted. Kubie asked Mahler, the newcomer, to chair the child analysis seminar, a prestigious position held by Levy, who was highly offended and thereafter resigned his membership in the Society. This assignment apparently paved the way for her formal acceptance into the Society following her presentation of the paper, "Pseudo Imbecility: A Magic Cap of Invisibility" in 1942.

After the glow of acclaim from the paper, she accepted a joint position as a consultant to the children's service of the New York State Psychiatric Institute and an appointment as an Associate in Psychiatry at Columbia University. These positions proved to be a good fit that provided many opportunities for professional growth. Despite this success, Mahler remained preoccupied with the Nazi persecution of Jews and with securing safe passage for her family members and friends. Sister Suzanne hid with Professor Tokas back in Budapest; her father died a month before the German invasion of Hungary in 1944; and her mother died in Auschwitz in 1945.

In 1950, Mahler had continued her psychoanalytic research activities focusing on both childhood tic syndromes and childhood psychoses. She accepted a teaching and supervisory position at the Philadelphia Psychoanalytic Institute, which itself had recently split, and commuted there every other weekend while continuing the bulk of her clinical activities in New York. Also in 1950, Mahler founded a therapeutic nursery at the Albert Einstein College of Medicine to continue work on childhood psychoses. During the next 5 years, Mahler's interest shifted to issues related to normal development. This interest led her to secure a research grant from NIMH (National Institutes of Mental Health) to fund a new study. A research project got underway at the therapeutic nursery, named the Masters Children's Center, which generated material for her two books. The first was *On Human Symbiosis and the Vicissitudes of Individuation: Infantile Psychosis* (1968) and the second, co-authored with Fred Pine and Annie Bergman, was *The Psychological Birth of the Human Infant* (Mahler, Pine, & Bergman, 1975).

In 1961, Mahler consulted over a 2-week period in Hampstead with Anna Freud who came to the position that the Separation–Individuation framework was too narrow a perspective to stand alone as a causal theory. However, she did build both Mahler as well as Spitz's (1965) work into her developmental lines and so ultimately found it useful (Young-Bruehl, 1988, p. 366). Mahler is remembered most for her pioneering work captured in the second book. In 1963, she split the research project on separation–individuation into two parts. Manual Furer headed the study of separation–individuation in psychotic patients, whereas Mahler led the research into normal developmental phases of separation–individuation. The team, which she assembled to study normal ego development and identity formation consisted of Anni Bergman, a therapist with experience in the treatment of psychotic children and Fred Pine, a settlement house psychologist.

Mahler spent her last years writing her memoirs and reflecting upon her own life-long separation–individuation developmental *Weltanschauung* ("an intellectual construction which solves all the problems of our existence uniformly on the basis of one overriding hypothesis, which, accordingly leaves no question unanswered and in which everything that interests us finds its fixed place" Rothgeb, 1973, p. 506). The attainment of personal autonomy and professional identity represented her heroic response to the traumatic challenges and dangers she faced repeatedly throughout her life. Upon her death in 1985 at age 88, Mahler left her estate to the Grey Panthers Project Fund for the specific purpose of assisting elderly, indigent academics and scholars in their work (Mahler in Stepansky, 1988).

Theory of Development

Mahler was among the first psychoanalytic writers to study childhood psychotic disorders from a developmental perspective in an attempt to shed light on their emergence in early childhood. She broke new ground by considering the effects of genetic and heritable factors as contributors to those disorders. As spelled out in the title of the book, *The Psychological Birth of the Human Infant* (Mahler et al., 1975), Mahler sought to give a description and explanation for the child's development as an individual who is separate and independent from the caregivers. Like others before her, she embraced libido theory and epigenesis. She maintained that the separation–individuation process should be seen in the context of libido theory and ego psychology. Using an organismic model that makes use of the metaphor of embryogenesis, she outlined the two overarching phases through which a child must progress to attain that goal. Mahler's model unfolds in the "Forerunners of the Separation–Individuation Process" (Mahler et al., pp. 41–51) as infants progress with caregivers from subphases of **normal autism** and then normal **symbiosis** prior to advancing to the complex second phase of **separation and individuation** with its four subphases. Mahler followed Freud's (1911, 1914), Ferenczi's (1913), and Spitz's (1965) tradition of considering the first 2 months of life as the infant being in an objectless, autistic shell (in the metaphor of an egg shell), a state of primary narcissism in which the infant is unresponsive to outside stimuli, where physiological processes consist of need satisfaction experiences and where psychological processes of primitive hallucinatory disorientation dominate. In recognition of the infant's obvious interactive capacities, she later renamed this period as the "pseudoautistic phase" and even later as "the awakening phase" (Mahler, 1983/1985). Mahler also followed Spitz and renamed Spitz's preobjectal stage (1965) as the normal symbiotic phase, which is also a metaphor representing the fusion of two organisms, mother and infant, with blurred boundaries. Beginning as an undifferentiated dual unity and gradually with the shadowy discrimination of outer from inner stimuli, the infant acquires the early beginnings of sensations of me and not me. The use of this term was also misleading in that, in so far as she borrowed it from biology, Mahler did not use it to refer to the interactive relationship two different individuals have in the mutually beneficial manner of a host and parasite, for example. With growing awareness of the outside world, the infant hatches out of the symbiotic phase and moves into the first of the four subphases consisting of **differentiation**, **practicing**, **rapprochement**, and **object constancy**. Mental health consists of the ability to be separate and autonomous while retaining one's individual identity. As she stated, "Separation and Individuation are conceived of as two complementary developments: separation consists of the child's emergence from a symbiotic fusion with the mother…and individuation consists of those achievements marking the child's assumption of his own individual characteristics" (Mahler et al., 1975, p. 4). Mahler traces the markers that characterize each of the two developmental tracks, those of separation and those of individuation. The separation track does not refer to physical separation, rather it leads children to become psychologically differentiated (self from other), to develop a set of internal boundaries, and to be capable of functioning autonomously. The individuation track leads children to develop their own intrapsychic structures that include cognition, perception, memory, and reality testing. These two tracks are intertwined and culminate in the development of separate self- and object-representations.

The Separation–Individuation model was deeply influenced by a preformed set of notions about normal development that determined the conclusions she drew from her observations; in other words, the researchers knew what they were looking for and they found it. Much as Freud before her had imposed on his theory of development the requirement that it conform with his observations of adult patient's psychopathology, Mahler posited, following psychoanalytic speculation, the phases of autism and symbiosis as pathological fixation points to explain childrens' earliest and most severe psychotic disturbances. She then extended those speculations to her naturalistic research setting and hypothesized the existence of the phases of nondifferentiation, normal autism followed by normal symbiosis (Mahler et al., 1975, pp. 3–51). Furthermore, Freud was influenced by the Victorian views on sexuality that pervaded nineteenth century Vienna, whereas Mahler appears to have been influenced by the individualism and frontier mentality of her adopted country so that independence became valued as a developmental norm.

Forerunners of the Separation–Individuation Process

This phase has two subphases: the normal autistic phase and the normal symbiotic phase.

Normal Autistic Phase: Birth to 2–3 Months

Mahler labeled this phase autistic because she believed it resembles the complete disconnection from the outside world of the autistic child. The major task of this phase is to gradually achieve homeostatic equilibrium with the environment. In other words, the infant's internal state is dynamic, is constantly changing, and is kept in balance and maintained by processing and responding to feedback from internal and external sources. This phase may be identified as an extension of infant's intrauterine experience. At first infants are unaware of the external world and are unresponsive to external stimuli. Only hunger or discomfort awakens infants from their half-waking, half-sleeping state. Physiological rather than psychological needs predominate.

The autistic phase has two subphases. The first subphase is a phase of absolute primary narcissism, in which infants are unaware of their caregivers, and the second subphase is a phase of conditional hallucinatory omnipotence, in which infants have a dim awareness of their caregiver, but only experiences her as she satisfies their physical needs. The sense of a **hallucinatory omnipotence** comes from the infant's inability to distinguish between whether internal or external forces are the agents that relieve their distress and whether they cause these to occur. Mahler, in 1983, changed the name of this phase from the pathological sounding "autism" to "awakening" (Austrian, 2002, p. 32; Kaplan, 1987, p. 39).

Normal Symbiotic Phase: 2–3 Months to 5 Months

During the normal **symbiotic** phase, infants struggle to maintain a harmonious sense of **homeostasis**. They begin to experience what is pleasurable as "good," and what is painful as "bad." Infants have a dim awareness of their caregivers, but function as if they are tied to the caregiver by a common boundary. Infant are in an undifferentiated state of fusion with their caregivers. As mentioned previously, this constitutes what Spitz called the "preobjectal stage." (Mahler et al., 1975, p. 48). As the infant slowly develops an awareness of the caregiver, the distinction between inner and outer world emerges gradually as "I" and "Not I." Islands of memory coalesce around pleasurable good, and unpleasurable bad experiences, marking the beginning of the **splitting** process and signaling the mother being experienced as a part object. The caregiver's "good enough holding behavior" and her "primary maternal preoccupation" (Winnicott, 1956) become the midwives of the separation/individuation process. The psychological birth of the infant occurs as it establishes and consolidates memory traces of pleasurable and unpleasurable experiences. These form the core of the child's self.

In her description of the infants' experience during this phase, Mahler's position was informed by Spitz' concept of the "dialogue" (Spitz, 1962), the total interaction between mother and infant and, specifically by Spitz's (1945) division of perception into coenesthetic and diacritic organizations, terms that we encountered previously in our discussion of Spitz. Coenesthetic receptivity refers to the activity of the pre-ego, that archaic state of being in which the mother is the infant's external ego (Spitz, 1965). In this pre-ego state, the infant familiarizes himself or herself with the caregiver's half of the symbiotic self, as evidenced in the social smile.

> "Here sensing is extensive, primarily visceral (added, viz, the gut), centered in the autonomic nervous system and manifests itself primarily in the form of emotions. Accordingly, I prefer to speak of this form of *perception*, which differs so fundamentally from sensory perception, as *reception*" (Spitz, 1962, p. 44).

Diacritic organization refers to perception, which takes place through peripheral sense organs. It is localized, circumscribed, and intensive with its centers in the cortex. Its manifestations are cognitive processes; among them are conscious thought processes (Spitz, 1962, p. 44). Mahler was attempting to describe through these constructs the nature of infants' experiences and their bond to their caregivers.

Separation–Individuation Proper: 5-36 Months and Beyond

The Separation-Individuation phase has four subphases: differentiation, practicing, rapprochement, and the beginning of self- and object-constancy.

Differentiation: 5–10 Month

The separation processes begin with the first major shift of libidinal investment (cathexis) that takes place during the differentiation phase when infants gradually leave behind the internal preoccupations of the symbiotic orbit, become more alert to outside stimuli, and enter into the external world. The development of **body ego** and eventually of the self begins with the shift from the investment of predominately **proprioceptive–enteroceptive** sensory modalities; that is the shift from the direct feedback from internal body sensations, such as those of awareness of body posture and movement along with pain and body organs, to the investment of **sensoriperceptive** modalities, that is the peripheral sensory modalities, such as vision, hearing, touch, and smell. These sensations contribute to the initial awareness of the infant's body image.

The individuation processes include a **hatching** dimension that begins when the infant develops a more permanently alert sensory system that reflects cognitive and neurological maturation. It is as though the infant wakes up to the world and discovers a sensory system, which includes the perceptual system and consciousness that connects him or her to what is on the outside. Infants appear more alert and their actions are intentional or goal-directed. During this individuation process, infants gradually begin to leave the physical orbit of their caregiver and by scanning the environment, begin to compare what is and is not mother, in particular scanning faces, and checking back with mother. A characteristic anxiety of this phase is stranger anxiety, which involves curiosity and fear of unfamiliar people. It is also called eighth-month anxiety, a concept borrowed from Spitz, his second ego organizer. This phenomenon is indicative of the early movement toward individuation with the infant's cognitive capacity to recognize mother's face (and voice, touch, and smell, etc.) from another face.

Practicing: 10–16 Months

The practicing subphase is ushered in by infants' earliest ability to move away from, not toward their mothers, by crawling, climbing, and other activities, with the caregivers functioning as a secure base toward whom children turn for emotional refueling. Children appear to be practicing the skills required to separate from and then reunite with their caregivers. Indications are that infants have established a specific bond to their caregivers. We see evidence of this bond in the use of a transitional object (Winnicott, 1953) as a means of carrying mother's qualities, which are transferred onto the inanimate object.

The characteristic anxiety of this period is the fear of losing the object or separation anxiety. Peek-a-boo games turn passive into active, that is, the child masters the fear of being engulfed by, or losing mother's love, by playing out those fears through the game. In one of his rare observations of a child, Freud noted that his 18-month-old grandson, who was lying in a crib, raised and lowered a ball on a string, having it disappear out of sight and return where he could see it. Freud suggested that this game represented the baby's attempts to master the comings and goings of his mother who the boy would watch entering and leaving the bedroom. Through this game, the boy transformed into pleasurable active mastery an unpleasurable state that he experienced passively (Freud, 1920, pp. 14–15). The child experiences periods of exhilaration and elation except when he realizes that the caregiver is absent, at which point a mood of **low-keyedness** or depressiveness overtakes the child. The child's emotional state is relieved once the caregiver returns.

The individuation processes begin with the second massive shift of emotional investment (libidinal cathexis) in the service of the infants' rapidly growing autonomous ego and their functions, which are exemplified by enhanced cognition and upright locomotion. Children develop a new perspective of the world and, by virtue of that, experience feelings of elation at the discoveries they are making. Children experience great narcissistic investment in body functions and the world of objects that surrounds them. Children can exercise their emerging cognitive functions and begin a period of exploration that Mahler calls a "love affair with the world" (Greenacre, 1957); the world becomes the child's oyster.

Rapprochement: 16–24 Months

Remembering that separation and individuation are proceeding along two separate, but intertwining tracks, with separation referring to an intrapsychic awareness of separateness from the caregiver and individuation referring to the acquisition of a distinct and unique individuality, the separation process in this phase heralds the final phase of the hatching process. Referring to the egg metaphor, hatching suggests a second birth, this one psychological. Mahler borrowed the work *rapprochement* from the French, which means to bring together. In this case, the reference is to infants' reunion with their mothers after the practicing period. The child no longer needs the caregiver to function as a home base from which to operate and the child's interest shifts to include social interaction with peers. The child begins to recognize that the caregiver is a separate person. At its peak, this subphase will lead to a rapprochement crisis, characterized by the child struggling with indecision as he or she tries to find the optimal distance to maintain from the caregiver. The child is acutely aware of physical separateness from the caregiver and separation anxiety increases. A pattern of shadowing and darting away from her appears. The wish for reunion with the caregiver is contaminated by the fear of re-engulfment accompanied by the consequence of loss of identity. The child will emerge from this crisis as an autonomous person with a distinct set of personality features. Mahler now introduces the concept of the self as an entity that is cohesive and has clear boundaries and agency. The crisis is precipitated by the realization that the world does not center on the child with an accompanying deflation in the sense of omnipotence. The loss of the caregiver's love (loss of the love of the love object), that is, the caregiver's disapproval is the major source of anxiety for the child during this phase.

In addition, the child develops an active social expansion of the mother–child world to include fathers as the child becomes aware of the father's special relationship to the mother. These experiences foreshadow the emergence of oedipal issues during the next phase.

As part of the individuation processes, the child develops the capacity for representational intelligence, which culminates in symbolic play and speech acquisition. Language development and vocal communication increases. The child is able to feel empathy for others and is capable of experiencing a wide range of affect states.

As infants become toddlers, the awareness of physical separateness from their caregiver dampens their mood of elation. They find active ways to cope with their mothers' absence, at times through symbolic play. The child achieves Piaget's (1936) capacity for object permanence, which means that the toddler has the cognitive capacity to understand that the caregiver continues to exist even if she can no longer see the caregiver.

During this subphase the child often will use the psychological mechanism of splitting to deal with ambivalent feelings toward the caregiver, that is, the caregiver will be endowed with positive attributes, as "good mother," and alternately, the caregiver will be endowed with negative ones, as "bad mothers." Substitute caregivers enable a magnification of this process. The emergence of this defense demonstrates the crisis nature of the rapprochement subphase in that it represents a challenge to stable functioning.

Internalization begins through the process of identification with mother and father; it starts to take place as evidenced by the compliance with rules and demands, which herald the beginnings of a superego. Accompanying these processes is the beginning development of gender identity. Girls develop penis envy, which raises their anxieties and anger at the caregivers, whereas boys delight in masturbation and clutch at their penises when anxious.

Mahler and colleagues state, "The clinical outcome of these rapprochement crises will be determined by (1) the development toward emotional (libidinal) object constancy; (2) the quantity and quality of later disappointments (stress traumata); (3) possible shock traumata; (4) the degree of castration anxiety; (5) the fate of the oedipus complex; and (6) the developmental crises of adolescence – all of which function within the context of the individual's endowment." (1975; p. 108).

Beginnings of Emotional Self- and Object-Constancy: 24–36 Months and Beyond

The major task of the separation component of this phase is the development of a sense of separateness from caregivers and the achievement of a sense of individuality. Children are better able to cope with their mothers' absence and engage with substitutes. They begin to feel comfortable with the absences by knowing mother will return. Body boundaries begin to be delineated.

Children have mastered stranger anxiety and can deal with the anxiety of the fear of losing the love of the caregiver and later in this subphase also castration anxiety, the fear of damage to the body. With the toilet training struggle of the anal phase, the child learns to deal with power and control issues and manifests the capacity to tolerate frustration, delay, and anxiety. An important indicator of children's mental health is their ability to maintain or restore self-esteem in the face of adverse conditions.

The major task of the individuation component of this phase is the attainment of emotional **object constancy**, a process through which the child internalizes a positively invested whole image of their caregiver. What gets internalized is a mental representation, which is hypothesized as a psychological structure inferred from the observation that the child can function more independently. The child's prior experience of trust and confidence in the caregiver, in conjunction with the acquisition of the capacity for object permanence, facilitate the development of emotional object constancy. The process of emotional object constancy formation is sufficiently organized and consolidated in the normal 3 year old to permit extended separations. This milestone is "represented socioculturally in the choice of age 3 as a common point of readiness for entry into nursery school" (cf. Freud, 1963; Mahler et al., 1975, p. 112).

With the cognitive maturation of the sense of time, the child can tolerate delays and endure separations. The process involves the gradual internalization of the caregiver as a stable, comforting, and reliable figure toward whom the child can tolerate ambivalent feelings, that is positive and negative feelings. Loving and hateful feelings (libidinal and aggressive drives) become joined permitting the child to dampen anger at the caregiver. These processes are assisted by the emerging cognitive functions of verbal communication, fantasy, and reality testing. Mahler and colleagues state that the "establishment of mental representations of the self as distinctly separate from representations of the object *paves the way* to self-identity formations" (1975, p. 117)

Several threats may defeat the child's efforts to attain a sense of separateness or of emotional object constancy. Among these threats are the child's awareness of sexual differences, which intensify castration anxieties; the struggles around toilet training that heighten these anxieties; the responses of fathers or other members of the community that may have adverse effects on the child's development; illnesses, accidents, or, finally, other untoward events that may derail the process (Mahler et al., 1975, pp. 118–119).

Case Illustration

This case is paraphrased from Mahler et al. (1975, Chapter 10, "Wendy," pp. 153–168). The case of Wendy illustrates the difficulty some infants and mothers have in the intrapsychic separation process with complications associated with moving out of the symbiotic orbit. Engaging the subsequent subphases of the separation–individuation process are adversely impacted. Also illustrated is the phenomenon of asymmetrical development. As certain aspects of development are engaged in conflict, others can move forward in smooth fashion.

Background

In the mid 1960s, a NIMH-funded long-term longitudinal study was launched to track the "variations of normalcy" in the separation–individuation process (Mahler et al., 1975, p. XI). The site was a nursery converted into an essentially naturalistic setting, where mother–child pairs could be observed in a playroom in spontaneous interaction and separations and reunions could be studied. The subject pairs were recruited by word of mouth and so were self-selected, having met certain general exclusionary criteria, such as gross psychopathology. Inferences from observations were consensually validated through repeated encounters in a somewhat standardized situation. The mothers were well educated and psychologically enlightened, with no need to work. Wendy's mother voluntarily agreed to participate in the research project. Very limited child guidance was offered in response to requests for consultations from mothers (Mahler et al., pp. 17–36).

Wendy appeared to be an attractive, cuddly, contented 3–4-month-old baby who displayed a selective smile response to her mother, Mrs. M, and who was deeply loved by her mother as "her symbiotic fulfillment" (Mahler et al., 1975, p. 153). Despite mother and infant being well attuned to each other, Wendy displayed signs of premature "quasi-differentiation" (Mahler et al., p. 153) by crying suddenly, apparently recognizing different people through intensive scanning and protesting when mother separated. Wendy's hyperalertness seemed to stem from an innate, precocious hypersensitivity, which required mother to envelope her in a firm protective mothering shield. Wendy seemed unable to take advantage of normal maturational growth opportunities within her own ego or to mobilize the environmental resources. Mother was unable to provide this shield, a task, which probably no mother could do. Wendy's early reactions to sudden changes in her environment characterized her entire separation–individuation process.

Mrs. M was unable to respond appropriately to Wendy's need for differentiation from the beginning. Even though Wendy was Mrs. M's third child, mother had developed a tendency to disengage herself abruptly when Wendy approached to explore her face visually or tactilely. When Wendy was denied access to mother's face, she became frustrated and protested angrily. Mrs. M was a beautiful, but insecure woman and mother who needed to prove herself constantly. She was self-disparaging, described herself as a bad mother, and emphasized that the children preferred the company of their father than the company of her. As the children displayed signs of differentiation and individuation, mother became discouraged and impatient. She was threatened by her children's growing up processes, which seemed related to her own ageing issues and to aspects of her personality, she regarded as negative. During the symbiotic phase mother was comfortable, but as the phase ended, mother was unable to enjoy the individuating child's playfulness and interactive mutuality was impossible.

Wendy was breastfed without complications and weaned in her fourth month. She was easy to feed, if unenthusiastic, molded well when mother was attentive to her every need. Her constitutional preference for visual experience probably diminished her interest in locomotion. She could communicate her discomfort and the wish for unsatisfied needs as longings. As an active agent, who made repeated efforts to engage her mother, Wendy's smile had an "irresistible" effect on her mother (Mahler et al., 1975, p. 155).

Wendy never adjusted well to the Center using splitting to cope with the attendant anxiety. She split the Center into everything "bad" (unfamiliar) and mother/siblings/home as "good" (familiar). This attitude was probably fueled by mother's ambivalent stance with respect to participation in the Project. While Wendy crawled at 6 months and walked at about 12 months, her reluctance to leave her mother minimized her separation loss. The Project team did not see in her the customary characteristics of the practicing phase. As long as the symbiotic closeness to mother was not threatened, Wendy was a delightful baby. However, there seemed to be a lack of internal motivation toward autonomous functioning. Even though Wendy "hatched," she seemed to sense mother's resistance to move beyond symbiosis and was never comfortable in the play setup being away from mother. Her older siblings facilitated her separation-individuation process at home when mother was absent. Wendy began the practicing phase at 18 months, a time when the child has normally entered the rapprochement period. Her mood remained dependent upon mother's mood and mother was unable to support Wendy's practicing and exploration. Consequently, the internal maturational pressure for separateness evoked in Wendy greater than average temper tantrums, negativeness, and passive-aggressive behaviors, as opposed to constructive aggression, symbolic play, and ability to handle frustrations. Wendy displayed a clear preference for experiences, which were autoerotic, kinesthetic, and tactile.

By 24 months, Wendy was finding it difficult to share her mother with other toddlers; she did not want to play with other toddlers and did not like the toddler room. She resisted communicating with words and entered her second year with the rapprochement crisis unresolved. As her second year unfolded, however, word usage improved and she was able to tolerate limited separations from mother, preferring the one-on-one company of male observers.

By 36 months, Wendy had become very feminine and appealing, but was still tied closely to her mother. She remained uninterested in other children, clearly preferring the company of adults, looked sad when attention was focused on another child, and when angry, would bite and hit her mother. Mother took to retreating from her maternal role leaving Wendy with babysitters, preferring to work at charitable functions outside the home. As Wendy moved into her third year, she remained a narcissistic child, preferring the autoerotic activity of solitary movement on the rocking horse, displaying a vigorous resistance to mother leaving her, resisting experiencing the joy of working on a puzzle, and using adults as substitute symbiotic mothers. It seemed as if Wendy was unable to hold an image of mother in her head in mother's absence, thus lacking emotional object constancy and its cognitive counterpart, object permanence. Into her third year, Wendy began to enjoy walking with her father, and found painting and coloring more interesting. Resistances to separation–individuation waxed and waned with Wendy developing at points a near phobic reaction to the playroom. Using play dough, she stuffed filler into all of a doll's orifices and between the doll's legs, and otherwise rendered the doll immobile, suggesting, not only anatomical gender concerns, but also a wish to close herself off from the world's expectations. While Wendy's play remained babyish, as her attachment to her father grew, early triangulation and spurious oedipal play became evident. Play also now involved throwing a doll away from her and retrieving it, suggesting attempts at mastering separation by being discarded and recovered by her mother. Play grew more sophisticated with the emergence of the doctor game involving a hurt doll, and then later a bear, which could not make wee-wee. Band-Aids were applied to the injuries in apparent attempts to undo castration anxiety. Play became more useful as a way to manage troubling dreams about threatening insects. Photographs were shown to Wendy to gauge identity formation. Wendy was unable to name the familiar and easily recognizable faces using "boy" or "girl" to refer to her peers and "baby" to refer to her. As the fourth year approached, growth spurts were apparent in language, identity, socialization, and ability to function outside of mother's presence.

In summary, the observers concluded that the eventual use of the pronoun "I" signaled major gains in the separation–individuation process for Wendy in her ability to manage anxieties over being left and being hurt.

Summary and Conclusions

In Mahler's model, the infant is born in a state of nondifferentiation, and progresses from a symbiotic state to a state of separateness and individuation. The separation-individuation hypothesis is an epigenetic model grounded in the ego psychological adaptive point of view and the object-relations perspective. In this organismic model, the child is biogenetically preprogrammed to move through the various phases of its organization, much like the processes that occur in cell division. The infant's psychological birth and the processes of separation and individuation are analogous to the division of a fertilized egg as embryologists describe it. The mother's psyche represents the initial fertilized egg. The infant's psyche is at first totally undifferentiated from that of the mother. As the nucleus of a self takes shape in the infant, a state of symbiosis occurs. Slowly a membrane begins to form around the nucleus. This process launches the process of separation. Ultimately, when infants have their own membrane, and their own well-formed nucleus, the process is completed. Cell division occurs at the end of the separation/individual phase with the establishment of object constancy. Emotional object constancy, which is the capacity to recall the whole object while dealing with loving and hateful feelings toward that object, is an indicator that the structures laid down are complete, as self-representations and object-representations are differentiated from one another.

For Mahler, growth reflects the formation of a self-representation and an object-representation. These representations result from the internalization of aspects of the person(s) with whom the child formed a relationship. Since this model also accepts the principles of ingestion as part of the developmental process, even the unconscious contents of the mother's psychic structure are transferable to the child. The characteristic patterns of mutual influence in the purely social exchanges between mother and infant provide an important basis for structuring the infant's experience. Representations of the self, the other, and the relationship all evolve simultaneously. They are inextricably linked together.

Here again, the child moves along the developmental progression unless interferences occur. These interferences may stem either from faulty biogenetic programming, as with autistic children, or from insufficient nourishment, as in borderline children, for whom the environment did not provide adequate responses during the rapprochement subphase of development.

Keywords Body ego • Differentiation • Hallucinatory omnipotence • Hatching • Homeostasis • Low–keyedness • Normal autism • Object constancy • Practicing • Proprioceptive-enteroceptive rapprochement • Sensoriperceptive • Separation and individuation • Splitting • Symbiosis

References

Austrian, S. G. (2002). *Developmental theories through the life cycle*. New York, NY: Columbia University Press.

Ferenczi, S. (1913). Stages in the development of the sense of reality. In *Sex in psychoanalysis: The selected papers of Sandor Ferenczi* (Vol. 1, pp. 213–239). New York, NY: Basic Books.

Freud, S. (1905). *Three essays on infantile sexuality* (SE, Vol. 7). London: The Hogart Press and the Institute of Psychoanalysis.

Freud, S. (1910). *Five lectures on psycho-analysis* (SE, Vol. 11, pp. 3–55). London: The Hogart Press and the Institute of Psychoanalysis.

Freud, S. (1911). *Formulations on the two principles of mental functioning* (SE, Vol. 12, pp. 213–226). London: The Hogart Press and the Institute of Psychoanalysis.

Freud, S. (1914). *On narcissism: An introduction* (SE, Vol. 14, pp. 73–102). London: The Hogart Press and the Institute of Psychoanalysis.
Freud, S. (1920). *Beyond the pleasure principle* (SE, Vol. 18, pp. 7-64). London: The Hogart Press and the Institute of Psychoanalysis.
Freud, S. (1926). The Question of Lay Analysis. Standard Edition, Vol. XX. London: The Hogarth Press and the Institute for Psychoanalysis.
Freud, A. (1963). The concept of developmental lines. *The Psychoanalytic Study of the Child, 18,* 245–266.
Greenacre, P. (1957). The childhood of the artist: Libidinal phase development and giftedness. *The Psychoanalytic Study of the Child, 12,* 47-72.
Kaplan, L. J. (1987). Discussion. Contemporary Psychoanalysis, 23: 27–44. (Personal communication from Mahler to John B. McDevitt on April 1986).
Mahler, M. S. (1942). Pseudoimbecility: A magic cap of invisibility. *Psychoanalytic Quarterly, 11,* 149–164.
Mahler, M. S. (1968). On human symbiosis and the vicissitudes of individuation. In M. Mahler (Ed.), The selected papers of Margaret S. Mahler (Vol. II, pp. 77–98). New York, NY: Jason Aronson.
Mahler, M. S. (1988). In P. E. Stepansky (Ed.), The memoirs of Margaret S. Mahler (179 pp.). New York, NY: Free Press
Mahler, M. S., Pine, F., & Bergman, A. (1975). *The psychological birth of the human infant: Symbiosis and individuation.* New York, NY: Basic Books.
Mahler, M. S., & Silberpfennig, J. (1938). Rorschach interpretation as an aid in understanding the psychology of the brain-damaged. *Schweizer Archiv fur Neurologie und Psychiatrie, 40,* 302–327.
Piaget, J. (1936). *The origins of intelligence in children.* Paris: Delachaux & Niestle.
Richards, A. D. (2001). Psychoanalytic discourse at the turn of the century: A plea for a measure of humility. *Journal of the American Psychoanalytic Association*, 51(Supplement), 73–89.
Rothgeb, C. (Ed.). (1973). *"The Question of a 'Weltanschauung.'"* In New Introductory Lectures on Psychoanalysis (1933). Lecture XXXV. Abstracts of the Standard Edition of the Complete Psychological Works of Sigmund Freud (237 pp.). New York, NY: International Universities Press.
Spitz, R. (1945). Diacritic and coenesthetic organizations. *Psychoanalytic Review, 32,* 146–162.
Spitz, R. (1962). *The first year of life: A psychoanalytic study of normal and deviant development of object relations.* Madison, CT: International Universities Press.
Spitz, R. A. (1965). The first year of life: A psychoanalytic study of normal and deviant development of object relations. Madison, CT: International Universities Press.
Stepansky, P. E. (Ed.). (1988). The Memoirs of Margaret S. Mahler (Recordings of Mahler's memoirs, compiled and edited by Stepansky). New York, NY: Free Press.
Winnicott, D. (1953). Transitional objects and transitional phenomena: A study of the first not-me possession. *International Journal of Psycho-Analysis, 34,* 89–97.
Winnicott, D. (1956). *Primary maternal preoccupation. In The maturational process and the facilitating environment.* New York, NY: International Universities Press.
Young-Bruehl, E. (1988). *Anna Freud: A biography.* New York, NY: Summit Books.

Major Works

Mahler, M. S. (1941). Schizophrenia in childhood. *Nervous Child, 1,* 137–150.
Mahler, M. S. (1944). Tics and impulsions in children: A study in motility. *Psychoanalytic Quarterly, 13,* 430–444.
Mahler, M. S. (1949a). A psychoanalytic evaluation of tic in psychopathology of children: Symptomatic tic and tic syndrome. *The Psychoanalytic Study of the Child*, 3–4, 279–340.
Mahler, M. S. (1949b). Remarks on psychoanalysis with psychotic children. *Quarterly Journal of Child Behavior, 1,* 18–21.

Mahler, M. S. (1952). On child psychosis and schizophrenia: Autistic and symbiotic infantile psychoses. *The Psychoanalytic Study of the Child, 7*, 286–305.

Mahler, M. S. (1958a). Autism and symbiosis: Two extreme disturbances of identity. *International Journal of Psychoanalysis, 39*, 77–83.

Mahler, M. S. (1958b). On two crucial phases of integration of the sense of identity: Separation–Individuation and bisexual identity. *Journal of the American Psychoanalytic Association, 6*, 136–139.

Mahler, M. S. (1961). On sadness and grief in infancy and childhood: Loss and restoration of the symbiotic love object. *The Psychoanalytic Study of the Child, 16*, 332–351.

Mahler, M. S. (1963). Thoughts about development and individuation. *The Psychoanalytic Study of the Child, 18*, 307–324.

Mahler, M. S. (1965a). On early infantile psychosis: The symbiotic and autistic syndromes. *Journal of the American Academy of Child Psychiatry, 4*, 554–568.

Mahler, M. S. (1965b). On the significance of the normal separation-individuation phase: With reference to research in symbiotic child psychosis. In M. Schur (Ed.), Drives, affects and behavior (Vol. 2, pp. 161–169). New York, NY: International Universities Press.

Mahler, M. S. (1974). Symbiosis and individuation: The psychological birth of the human infant. In The selected papers of Margaret S. Mahler (Vols. I and II). New York, NY: Jason Aronson.

Mahler, M. S. (1979). *The selected papers of Margaret S. Mahler* (Vols. I and II). New York, NY: Jason Aronson.

Mahler, M. S., & Elkish, P. (1953). Some observations on disturbances of the ego in a case of infantile psychosis. *The Psychoanalytic Study of the Child, 8*, 252–261.

Mahler, M. S., & Furer, M. (1960). Observations on research regarding the 'Symbiotic Syndrome' of infantile psychosis. *Psychoanalytic Quarterly, 29*, 317–327.

Mahler, M. S., & Gosliner, B. J. (1955). On symbiotic child psychosis: Genetics, dynamic and restitutive aspects. *The Psychoanalytic Study of the Child, 10*, 195–212.

Mahler, M. S., & Gross, I. H. (1945). Psychotherapeutic study of a typical case with tic syndrome. *Nervous Child, 4*, 359–373.

Mahler, M. S., & Luke, J. A. (1946). Outcome of the tic syndrome. *Journal of Nervous and Mental Disease, 103*, 433–445.

Mahler, M. S., & McDevitt, J. (1980). The separation–individuation process and identity formation. In S. I. Greenspan & G. S. Pollock (Eds.), The course of life: Psychoanalytic contributions toward understanding personality development, Vol. I: Infancy and Early Childhood (pp. 395–406). Bethesda, MD: National Institute of Mental Health.

Mahler, M. S., Pine, F., & Bergman, A. (1970). The mother's reaction to her toddler's drive for idividuation. In E. J. Anthony & T. Benedek (Eds.), Parenthood: Its pychology and pychopathology (pp. 257–274). Boston: Little, Brown.

Mahler, M. S., & Rangell, L. (1943). A psychosomatic study of maladie des tics (Gilles de la Tourette's Disease). *Psychiatric Quarterly, 17*, 579–603.

Mahler, M. S., Ross, J. R., & DeFries, Z. (1948). Clinical studies in benign and malignant cases of childhood psychosis (schizophrenia-like). *American Journal of Orthopsychiatry, 19*, 295–305.

Mahler, M. S., & Silberpfennig, J. (1941). Discussion of mother types encountered in child guidance clinics. *American Journal of Orthopsychiatry, 11*, 484.

McDevitt, J., & Mahler, M. S. (1980). Object constancy, individuality, and internalization. In S. I. Greenspan & G. S. Pollock (Eds.), The course of life: Psychoanalytic contributions toward understanding personality development, Vol. I: Infancy and Early Childhood (pp. 407–424). Bethesda, MD: National Institute of Mental Health.

Supplementary Readings

Galatzer-Levy, R. M., & Cohler, B. J. (1993). *The essential other: A developmental psychology of the self.* New York, NY: Basic Books.

Chapter 10
Otto F. Kernberg (1928–)

Publishing Era: 1963 to the present

Biographical Information

Otto Kernberg was born in Austria in 1928 and lived there until age ten, when his Jewish parents fled the Nazi regime and immigrated to Chile. In Santiago during the 1950s, he began his academic and professional career, earning his undergraduate, medical, and psychoanalytic degrees. He trained at the Chilean Psychoanalytic Society. Kernberg came to the United States for the first time in 1959 on a Rockefeller Foundation fellowship to study research in psychotherapy with Jerry Frank at Johns Hopkins. Eventually he moved to Topeka, Kansas. He is an alumnus of the Karl Menninger School of Psychiatry and a former director of the C. F. Menninger Memorial Hospital. At the Topeka Institute for Psychoanalysis, he was a Supervising and Training Analyst and Director of the Psychotherapy Research Project of the Menninger Foundation. After the Menninger Foundation experience, in 1973, he became Director of the General Clinical Service of the New York State Psychiatric Institute, and Professor of Clinical Psychiatry at the College of Physicians and Surgeons of Columbia University. In 1972, he was awarded the Heinz Hartmann Award of the New York Psychoanalytic Institute and Society and in 1975, he received the Edward A. Strecker Award from the Institute of the Pennsylvania Hospital. He married a fellow Chilean, Paulina Fischer (1935–2006) in 1954 (Coates, 2006; Pearce, 2006).

Kernberg's position on narcissism was informed by his work with patients hospitalized with borderline personality disorder, which was set in an ego psychology–object relations framework. These patients were closer to the psychotic end of the mental illness spectrum. For instance, Kernberg's patients with narcissistic disorders (1970a, 1970b, 1974a, 1974b, 1998), e.g., the "Oblivious type" operate as though they have no awareness of their impact on others. These patients match the Narcissistic Personality Disorder described in DSM-IV-TR (2000) (Gabbard, 2005, p. 487).

From 1976 to 1995, Kernberg was Associate Chairman and Medical Director of the New York Hospital-Cornell Medical Center, Westchester Division and Professor of Psychiatry. Kernberg is Executive Counselor at large of the American Psychoanalytic Association, former President of the International Psychoanalytic Association

J. Palombo et al., *Guide to Psychoanalytic Developmental Theories*,
DOI: 10.1007/978-0-387-88455-4_10,

(founded by Sigmund Freud in 1908) and Assistant Editor of the Journal of the American Psychoanalytic Association. In addition, he is a faculty member of the New York Psychoanalytic Institute. At present in 2007 Kernberg divides his time among three institutions: as a Training and Supervising Psychoanalyst at the Columbia Center for Psychoanalytic Training and Research, as a Professor of Psychiatry at Weill Medical Center of Cornell University, and as the Director of the Personality Disorders Institute of the New York-Presbyterian Hospital, Westchester Division. He lives in Scarsdale, New York.

Conceptual Framework

Kernberg achieved recognition as an extraordinary systematizer who, between 1975 and 1984, built a comprehensive psychoanalytic framework. His project integrated major aspects of Freud's drive theory with the structural model of ego psychology and its developmental perspective, particularly Jacobson's (1964) work on pathological forms of early identifications. To these viewpoints, he brought together the object relations theories of Klein (see Chap. 6) and Fairbairn (1952). Working with severely disturbed patients, Kernberg believed in the centrality of interpretative work leading to meaningful change. He also stressed the exploration of both the analyst's personality and the role of the analyst's passionate experiences in the process of change. Eventually, Kernberg's model consisted of a hierarchical integration of three different visions of normal and abnormal human development, those of S. Freud, of Klein, and of Jacobson and Mahler (Mitchell & Black, 1995, pp. 172–174).

Freud's vision of the human psyche was filled with sexual and aggressive instinctual impulses unfolding systematically and reaching their highest point of intensity during the Oedipus. During that phase, the child had to cope with his unconscious, dangerous, incestuous, and homicidal urges. To deal with these urges he was required to steer a complicated course between satisfying those desires while hiding and diverting their unacceptable intentions.

Klein's (1935/1964) vision of the essence of human experience was, as was Freud's, bifurcated. But whereas Freud envisioned a dual set of powerful instincts co-mingling and shaping human development, Klein envisioned two overarching powerful, primitive, intense modes of relating, first the paranoid–schizoid position and the infant's desperate need to defend against annihilation anxiety generated by the death instinct, followed by the depressive position and the toddler's terror-filled attempts to protect loved ones from damage done to them by her own destructiveness.

Klein extended and expanded the matrix of libidinal and aggressive instincts into the trajectory of the experience of the other person as sometimes good and sometimes bad leading toward the sense of the whole object. The child's loving mode (good breast) is driven by her passionate caring and deeply grateful orientation, whereas her hateful mode is shaped by a destructive, intensely jealous, and spitefully vindictive orientation. All human beings struggle throughout life to accept and to reconcile these two modes of experience. Their wish is to maintain a balance or an accommodation between the urge to love and the need to destroy (Mitchell & Black, 1995, pp. 88–98).

Jacobson's (1964) vision was influenced by Spitz (1957, 1965) and substantially reworked Freud's position by emphasizing the infant's subjectively experienced interaction with the maternal object and its shaping effects on the instincts. Intense good and bad feeling states with accompanying images of the ambivalently regarded mother eventually grew into varied and subtle feeling states in the context of superego development over a long period of time, not just coupled to the resolution of the oedipus. Instincts for Jacobson were seen as biological potentials, not givens unfolding according to an unwavering internal script (Mitchell & Black, 1995, pp. 48–53). Jacobson's vision was tied to that of Mahler (1968, Mahler et al., 1975), who conceived of children as embarking on a journey that began with their psychological birth, which was not coincident with their physical birth. Emerging from a diffuse symbiotic merger with their mother, infants traversed the first 6 months becoming increasingly differentiated and developing a distinct and reliable self-hood. Only gradually, during the next 30 months, did the separation–individuation process unfold, as the child's own ego capacities developed, forming a distinct, differentiated self with the capacity for object constancy.

Disregarding sharp theoretical boundaries, Kernberg sought to find the commonalities in the three visions focusing on the internalized object relations of severely disturbed individuals. By positing a hierarchical system that accounted for the three visions, he constructed a theoretical edifice that located psychopathology according to severity within the hierarchy. Kernberg maintained there was no need for a separate object relations school of thought as object relations was implicit in the existing psychoanalytic framework. He defined psychoanalytic object relations in the broadest terms as consisting of the study of both the nature and the origin of interpersonal relations and intrapsychic structures. These structures derive from fixated, modified, and reactivated past internalized relations with others in the context of present interpersonal relations. He encouraged the use of the term "human object-relations" to denote both intrapsychic and interpersonal (psychosocial) perspectives on human experience (Kernberg, 1976a, p. 58).

The developmental model that Kernberg constructed envisioned infants as organizing their experiences according to affective valence, moving back and forth between pleasurable and unpleasurable states, between soothing gratification and disturbing tension. Children face three major developmental tasks. The *first major developmental task* is to clarify what is self from what is other, a separation of self- from object-images. If this boundary is not established, no reliable distinction can be made between one's own experiences and one's own mind and the experiences and minds of others. Failure to accomplish this task is the precursor to **psychotic states** and results in Kernberg's *first level of psychopathological organization.*

The *second major developmental task* is to overcome **splitting**. Kernberg specifically refers to splitting as a representational process centered in Mahler's rapprochement subphase of the separation–individuation process (see Chap. 8).

The separated self- and object-images, while now differentiated, remain affectively segregated. Infants overcome this developmentally normal phenomenon as they experience whole-object relations in which good and bad, gratifying and frustrating representations can coexist. Because good and bad feelings are now blended, the singular intensity of loving or hating is tempered. A failure to accomplish this developmental task results in **borderline psychopathology**. The distinguishing feature between the psychotic and the borderline is that the patient with borderline personality knows or is aware of the images of self and other, but defensively retreat from combining good and bad self- and object-representations. This retreat characterizes Kernberg's *second level of psychopathological organization*.

The *third major developmental task* is to integrate good and bad self- and object-images into a fuller, more stable capacity to tolerate ambivalence in relationships with others. In situations where the child can maintain reliably ambivalent feelings, where self-object boundaries are intact and where self- and object-images are integrated, the child's psychopathology is now triangular in nature. The child needs to grow in the knowledge that two (mother and father) can have a relationship, which does not include him, and he can still survive, even thrive. In other words, psychopathology is located in the unresolved oedipal drama and, therefore, represents **neurotic psychopathology**, Kernberg's *third level of psychopathological organization*.

In Kernberg's developmental system, there are no drives at birth, but rather over the course of early development, the infant's diffuse good and bad affective states become consolidated and eventually channeled into sexual and aggressive drives. These libidinal and aggressive drives are conflictual in nature, just as in Freud's account. Whereas Freud saw drives as given and inborn, Kernberg acknowledged the existence of a constitutional predisposition, contending that drives are ultimately forged in interaction with others and are thus developmentally constructed. For Freud, the intrapsychic vicissitudes, that is, the predominant mode of sequential instinctual gratification was the central personality issue; for Kernberg, the basic issue in the developmental progression is the level of attained internal object relations. Kernberg used the nature of and the capacity for love and sexual expression as the key indicator in evaluating internal object relations. Psychotic patients do not understand love and sexuality as occurring on a continuum from privacy to intimacy. Either they have no relationships or they experience total confusion and feel terrified of merger with others. Borderline patients experience love and sexuality in highly idiosyncratic activities where perverse and often violent dimensions interfere with the integration of tenderness and mutuality. Neurotic patients are similar to those in the classical drive-defense category who relate to whole objects with an integrated self, but oedipal-phase conflicts and inhibitions compromise and beset their relationships with others. In Kernberg's synthesis, sexuality still plays a central role, but is no longer tied to the sequence of activation of erotogenic body zones. Rather, the meanings given to love and sexuality derive from the development of internalized object relations. Individuals express their sexuality along a continuum constituted of five levels. The first level, the most severe, is that of the narcissistic personality structure with a total incapacity to establish genital and tender relations with another human being. The second level is that of the typically moderately ill narcissistic personalities, who find expression through a mixture of promiscuity that ranges from heterosexual to polymorphous perverse sexual activities. The third level is found in individuals with borderline personality organization and is characterized by clinging infantile dependency upon the primitive idealized love object. The fourth level is seen in less severe types of personality organizations and neuroses and is characterized by stable and deep object relations without full sexual gratification. The fifth level, the highest, is represented in individuals who manifest a normal integration of genital sexuality with the capacity for tenderness in a committed, devoted object relation (Kernberg, 1976c, p. 186; Mitchell & Black, 1995, pp. 172–180).

Kernberg offers a concept of normality, which is an extension of the three-level model explained below. It involves a progression along a continuum with the goal being that of the attainment of a well-integrated, moderate, and realistic superego and an ego ideal in harmony with both the external world and instinctual needs. Primacy of genitality is predominant in the life of the person who can sublimate. A firm repression barrier provides a person with an effective restraint against instinctual impulses enabling a large conflict free-ego sphere (Kernberg, 1976b, p. 151).

Theory of Development

In this organismic framework, Kernberg proposed that development occurs in five stages during which individuals metabolized the nutriments that relationships provide. The products of this metabolization process become gradually differentiated into internal structure, through Kernberg's complex blending of Ego psychology, Jacobson and Kleinian concepts.

Normal Development

Stage 1. Normal Autism or Primary Undifferentiated Stage (Birth to 1 month):

The stage of **Normal Autism** or **Primary Undifferentiated Stage**, the earliest stage of development, precedes the consolidation of the "good" undifferentiated self-object constellation, which is built up under the pleasurable interactive experiences with the caregiver. Throughout this stage, the infants' normal, primary, undifferentiated self–object representation is gradually constructed from the experiences associated with the interaction with the caregiver (Kernberg, 1976a, pp. 59–60).

Stage 2. Normal Symbiosis or Stage of the Primary Undifferentiated Self–Object Representations (1 month to 6–8 months):

During the stage of **Normal Symbiosis** or **Primary Undifferentiated Self–Object Representation** infants' self- and object-images become differentiated within their emerging egos. In addition, infants consolidate "good" self- and object-representations in response to pleasurable, positive mother–infant interactions. Simultaneously, the infant organizes all negative experiences into "bad" self- and object-representations. These two separate object relations units constitute the first **introjections**, that is, the first psychological structures located in the infants' immature ego. Object relations units is the term that Kernberg uses to refer to the building blocks of psychological structures. Each unit consists of three elements, a self, an object, and an affect dimension. These elements combine in sequence and become the building blocks for a super ordinate system of internal structures. Kernberg specifically disclaims that this framework is a neurophysiological or mechanistic model of the functioning of the psyche (Kernberg, 1976a, pp. 60–64).

Children invest the good self- and object-representations with libido, whereas they invest the bad self- and object-representation with aggression. Initially, these two kinds of object relations units are separate because of the physiological inability of the infants' primitive ego structure to integrate them. Beginning at about the third to fourth month, the infants' ego actively splits the two kinds of self- and object-images apart in order to protect the good self- and object-images from the destructiveness of the bad images. At this point, splitting becomes the primary defense of the developing ego. This stage encompasses Mahler's symbiotic phase, in which self and object are not yet distinguished, and her differentiation subphase of the separation–individuation process. Kernberg collapsed the two phases into his developmental schema because he believed that in the differentiation subphase a fusion of self- and object-images could frequently reoccur.

Stage 3. Differentiation of Self- from Object-Representations (6–8 months to 18–36 months):

The stage of **Differentiation of Self- from Object-Representations** begins with the differentiation of self- and object-images, within the good and bad object relations units, and ends with the integration of both good and bad self-images and good and bad object images within the toddler's ego. At the beginning of this phase, re-fusion of self- and object-images can still happen under stress, but during this phase ego boundaries are sufficiently well established that they are maintained even under stressful conditions. By the end of this phase, a consolidation of the good and bad self-representations occurs that results in an integrated self-concept within which good and bad object images form total object representations, resulting in the capacity for object constancy (Kernberg, 1976a, pp. 64–67).

Stage 4. Integration of Self-Representations and Object-Representations and Development of Higher Level Intrapsychic Object Relations-Derived Structures (18–36 months throughout the Oedipus):

The stage of **Integration of Self-Representations and Object-Representations** involves the entire oedipal period during which the consolidation of libidinally and aggressively invested self-images occurs, resulting in a "definite self-system." Good and bad object images have coalesced into "total object representations." Differentiation of the ego, id, and superego into defined psychological structures becomes evident. Differing from Klein, Kernberg believed that repression developmentally replaces splitting as the primary defensive organization of infants during this phase, subsequently resulting in an integration of self- and object-representations and allowing for the formation of the tripartite psychic structure, that is, the ego, the superego, and the id.

Within the ego, negative introjects – that is, primitive self- and object-representations – are not split off into an immature ego organization, but rather are repressed within a unitary psychological system. With this reconfiguration, Kernberg is able to integrate Klein's object relations theory with ego psychology; and ego identity becomes established because of the integration of self- and object-representations. This integration gives rise to ideal self- and ideal object-representations. Following Jacobson, Kernberg believed that children must integrate ideal representations with earlier fantastical, sadistic superego forerunners, which under optimal circumstances combine with parental prohibitions to form the superego as an independent psychic agency (Kernberg, 1976a, pp. 67–72).

Stage 5. Consolidation of Superego and Ego Integration (The End of the Oedipus and Beyond):

In the stage of the **Consolidation of Superego and Ego Integration**, Kernberg postulates the consolidation of ego and superego. The superego's separateness from the ego decreases and the superego is gradually integrated into the personality. This integration fosters ego identity, which is enhanced through effective relationships with others. This is possible because of the processes that occur in the previous stage where self- and object-images were solidified (Kernberg, 1976a, pp. 72–75).

In summary, the two most important developmental steps that lead to the avoidance of severe psychopathology are (a) that self-object differentiation must take place and (b) that repression becomes the central organizing defense later in development displacing the immature ego's earlier reliance on positive and negative self- and object-splitting. Repression on a neurotic level is reinforced by mechanisms such as isolation and displacement, while splitting in the borderline is reinforced by projection and denial. Kernberg describes the ego leading to the consolidation of the self as a substructure within the ego identity. In severe character pathology, it is the self-structure that is characterized by the dominance of splitting (Kernberg, 1976a, pp. 55–83, especially pp. 44–45).

Abnormal Development

As we turn to the development of character pathology, it was Kernberg's intent that the normal and abnormal psychodynamics that we discussed above become articulated into a grand formulation describing both normal and pathological processes (Kernberg, 1976b, pp. 139–160; Summers, 1994, pp. 191–246).

Kernberg outlines three levels of character pathology that follow from his view of normal development and are central to his conceptual framework.

In the **higher level of organization of character pathology**, the neurotic patient has a relatively well-consolidated superego, which has a sadistic core with severe and punitive aspects. Also, the patient's ego is well integrated, ego identity contains harmonious components, the self-concept is stable, and the patient can maintain a consistent representation of the world. Basic defensive operations against unconscious conflicts are centered on repression. Allied defenses are inhibitory or phobic in nature or they are reaction formations against repressed instinctual needs. Overall, the patient's social adaptation is not seriously impaired, and he or she can experience guilt, mourning, and a range of affects. Although, the individual can partly inhibit drive expression, the oedipal nature of the individual's functioning clearly predominates. Representative types of pathology at this level of character organization include the hysteric, the obsessive-compulsive, and depressive-masochistic characters. The treatment of choice for maximum improvement in personality functioning for this level of character psychopathology is classical psychoanalysis. Analysts can expect a very good prognosis with the use of this modality with these patients. However, if this type of patient seeks relief for minor symptoms of recent origin, a course of brief psychotherapy may improve matters (Kernberg, 1976b, pp. 143–144).

In the **intermediate level of organization of character pathology**, the borderline patient's superego is more punitive and is less integrated. It tolerates the contradictory demands, which are sadistic and prohibitive and which fluctuate with the primitive, magical, overidealizing of the ego ideal. The patient's deficient superego cannot negotiate the struggle to reconcile demands for greatness and a physically attractive body against demands for moral perfection. Superego nuclei, that is, fragments of superego functions, are unanchored from the rest of the person's ego, thus interrupting ego regulation and exerting diminished capacity to experience guilt. This manifests, for example, in the unstable borderline whose behavior is impulsive and contradictory. In addition, the impoverished superego regulation fosters paranoid trends, antagonisms in the ego's value system, and severe mood swings. The patient's inadequate defensive reaction formations against instincts allow for a partial expression of instinctual behavior, which becomes evident through symptomatic behaviors. At this level, the patient has fewer inhibitory character defenses, which allow dissociated sexual and aggressive urges to manifest in the context of a consistent impulsivity in certain situations. Patients' core defenses fluctuate between higher and lower levels of organization. At the higher level are repression with intellectualization, rationalization, and undoing. This alternates at the lower level around dissociative trends with splitting, projection, and denial. Their object relations tend to be characterized as a regression from the oedipal phase with oral dimensions such as dependency and neediness.

Although patients have the capacity for stable object relations in the sense of deep and lasting commitments to others, the nature of these relations are markedly ambivalent and conflictual. Most patients with oral-type character pathology, especially those including the following dominant features: passive-aggressive, sadomasochistic, infantile, narcissistic, and/or borderline types and the sexual deviations operate at this level. The preferred treatment for this level of character psychopathology is a lengthier, perhaps somewhat modified, psychoanalysis and, at times, the goals must be less ambitious. Therapists can expect a less favorable prognosis with these patients (Kernberg, 1976b, pp. 144–145).

In the **lower level of organization of character pathology**, patients' early preoedipal superego integration is minimal and demonstrates a propensity for projection of superego nuclei. These nuclei manifest as primitive, sadistic fragments of interaction and are commonplace. Patients' core defenses are archaic forms of projection, projective identification, dissociation, splitting, denial, primitive idealization, devaluation, and omnipotence. Their fantasy life involves pregenital derivatives of aggression and libido that are sadistic, polymorphously perverse, and infantile, which contaminate all aspects of object relations. Their inner world includes exaggerated and chaotic self- and object-representations. An example of the manner in which this pathology finds expression at this level is patients' masturbatory activity that is accompanied by fantasies involving their parents. The patients' severe ego weakness at this level manifests by the inability to contain their anxiety, to control their impulses, or to sublimate their primitive drives. These individuals experience great difficulty in the worlds of work, love, and creativity.

Most patients at this archaic level include the infantile, narcissistic, inadequate, paranoid, schizoid, and antisocial personalities; the chaotic, impulse-ridden character disorders; the "as if" characters (those with pseudo presentations); most self-mutilators; and those with multiple sexual deviations and drug addictions. Psychoanalysis is usually contraindicated for patients with this lower level of character pathology. The treatment of choice is usually a substantially modified psychoanalytic procedure involving parameters of technique as outlined by Eissler (1953), who suggests modifications of the standard psychoanalytic technique such as decreased frequency of session, greater activity on the part of the therapist, more supportive interventions, and others. Therapists must expect that the prognosis in these cases is either pessimistic or guarded (Kernberg, 1976a, pp. 145–148).

Case Illustration

This case exemplifies the lower level of organization of character pathology and a fixation at Stage 3 (6–8 months to 18–36 months), Differentiation of Self- from Object-Representations. The patient is an example of a mixed personality organization of the paranoid and borderline types with a conversion symptom, chronic hand spasms. The case illustrated two technical principles in treating borderline patients: the management of silence and the use of interpretation. First, focusing on the immediate reality of the patient–therapist relation, combined with a gradual deepening of the interpretation of all elements of this relation, can be useful in interpreting the nature of and working through the silence. Second, a relatively rapid deepening of interpretation is required when comments on a surface level prove insufficient to modify and resolve transference acting out in the session, namely the patient's silence. The general implication is that acting out, whether expressed directly in the hours or in the patient's behavior outside the hours, requires an acceleration of the interpretative process in order to assure success in treatment.

This summary of the case is taken from Kernberg (1976c), pp. 168–173 (reprinted with permission from Jason Aronson an imprint of Rowman & Littlefield Publishers, Inc.).

The patient was a highly intelligent high school graduate in his early twenties who had come for treatment because of severe chronic and social isolation, inability to pursue advanced studies, and a chronic spasm of both hands, previously diagnosed by neurologists as a conversion symptom. Diagnosed with both paranoid and borderline personality organization and conversion symptoms, the treatment was psychoanalytic psychotherapy, three sessions a week. The patient's father was a businessman who traveled the Western United States frequently requiring the family to move to various cities. The patient was now living with a foster-care family in town. Every few days of the month, his parents, brothers, and sisters visited him. The patient's current functioning included taking courses at a local college in a rather disorganized fashion and working part time at a local store, where his geographical knowledge of the country was useful. His relationship with a girlfriend was distant and he spent many hours in isolation roaming about or watching TV in his room.

His father, who could be warm, was tyrannical, easy to anger, and occasionally physically violent, causing the patient to fear him throughout most of his life. The quiet mother kept in the background but exerted great influence on the father, of which the patient was vaguely aware. From early childhood, the patient's terror of his father had become obvious to all family members. Deliberate efforts on the father's part to establish a better relationship with his son were unsuccessful. In his adolescence, the patient became involved in an extreme right political group. This organization supported the revival of admiration for Nazi Germany, the persecution of Jews, and the destruction of American capitalism and imperialism, which the patient understood to be a conspiracy of international Jewry. By age 20, the patient had become disillusioned with this political group and ceased to engage in political activity.

Because of serious emotional difficulties at home and at school during his adolescence, he had seen various psychiatrists, one of whom had engaged him in intensive long-term psychotherapy. During the early sessions of the patient's treatment with Dr. Kernberg (Dr. K), he said he thought this psychiatrist was a homosexual who subtly tried to induce the patient to become a homosexual as well. The patient described over several sessions how on one occasion, the psychiatrist had touched his arm and he had felt that this was a direct homosexual approach. The psychiatrist had initially encouraged the patient to bring his own drawings to the hour or to draw them and, on one occasion, had smilingly asked the patient whether he had drawn a boy or a girl. When the psychiatrist touched the patient's arm, they had been talking about a confusion over whether another person mentioned by the patient was a man or a woman. The patient believed that this was proof that the psychiatrist was telling him (the patient) that he was a woman and not a man, and, furthermore, that the psychiatrist would seduce him. Shortly after this experience, the patient's spasm of his left hand started and later developed in the right hand as well.

The patient became rather tense when Dr. K attempted to clarify whether the patient was convinced his psychiatrist had tried to seduce him or whether he now thought this was a fantasy. While he said he realized it was a fantasy, his emotional tone seemed to betray a strong sense of conviction. When confronted with this inconsistency in his behavioral expression, he said he had struggled for many years to clarify whether this was a reality or a fantasy; his reasoning told him it was a fantasy, but his feelings made him wonder.

The patient had also tried to find out whether Dr. K was Jewish or German; he thought Dr. K's features were Jewish, but Dr. K's name was German. In addition, he thought he had heard that Dr. K trained in a German-speaking country. On various occasions, the patient attempted to speak German with Dr. K. Over the next 6 months in his treatment, the patient became more and more anxious. The patient came late, often remained silent for up to 20 min or occasionally missed sessions. It was apparent that the patient was extremely frightened of Dr. K and that a major transference resistance in the treatment had emerged due to his severe paranoid character constellation.

On one particular day, the patient came dressed in a black leather jacket and sat in a chair as far away from Dr. K as possible. The patient reflected on his studies, an outing with his girl friend, a forthcoming visit from his father, and then fell silent. Dr. K encouraged him to speak, but that effort led nowhere. Dr. K then mentioned that he looked anxious and fearful on coming into the office and wondered if his silence was an expression of fear of Dr K, the fear being so intense that he was unable to talk about it. The patient stared at Dr. K with a serious expression; Dr. K finally understood as a blend of suspiciousness and admiration.

After some further silence, Dr. K told the patient that he saw him looking at Dr. K with suspiciousness, but perhaps also with awe and admiration. In trying to combine this with his prolonged silence, Dr. K thought that what frightened the patient must have been something the patient saw that was so uncanny and strange in Dr. K that would he not dare express it. The patient produced a slight smile. Dr. K asked what his smile meant. The patient did not respond. Dr. K wondered if the smile was one of appreciation because Dr. K had correctly understood his expression or one of amusement because Dr. K was so far off the mark. In any case, Dr. K said he sensed that the patient now was less afraid of Dr. K. In addition, perhaps Dr. K had helped to reassure the patient that whatever it was he was seeing in Dr. K might be part of his fantasy rather than reality.

At this moment, the patient asked Dr. K whether he was aware that he looked like Eichmann. Dr. K reflected for a moment and then said that the patient's comment reminded him of the many times he had felt that Dr. K was a German Nazi and that this concern might have a double effect on him. On the other hand, Dr. K being a Nazi meant that Dr. K was associated with that part of him which felt like a Nazi attacking the Jews, and at that level, it might be reassuring to him that patient and Doctor, therefore, were allies. On the other hand, in so far as being a Nazi was something untoward and that, if Dr. K were a terrifying Eichmann, Dr. K would be too dangerous to provide him the understanding he needed for his serious psychological problems. In addition, Dr. K mentioned that, since he had come in wearing a black leather jacket, he might experience himself as being under the control of that Nazi part of himself. Furthermore, upon entering the office, he might have been fearful that Dr. K might not be a true Nazi, and seeing Dr. K as a Nazi was reassuring because Dr. K was not in danger from the patient. However, the patient's silence might mean that, although Dr. K was not in any danger from the Nazi part of him, it was also useless to expect any help from Dr. K as a Nazi.

In the long silence that followed the patient looked increasing sullen. Dr. K urged the patient to talk. The patient remained silent. Dr. K eventually pointed out to him that he looked sad. Dr. K told him that he looked as though he felt alone in the room. Then the patient said he knew perfectly well that Dr. K was neither Eichmann nor a Nazi. The patient also showed Dr. K his arms, saying that he had felt a strong spasm of his hands at the beginning of the hour but that now he could move them rather freely. Dr. K asked him how he understood that he was less nervous. The patient replied that he was no longer afraid of Dr. K. While Dr. K encouraged the patient to describe what he thought went on in the hour, he could not, falling silent again, but continuing to look quite relaxed.

After some time, Dr. K commented that he had the feeling that the patient was trying to make Dr. K explain what was going on inside of him, in effect, turning full responsibility for what was going on in the hour over to Dr. K. Dr. K said he understood that when treatment began the patient might have been too frightened to think, but did not feel that this was true any longer. There must be another explanation for his attempt to make Dr. K do all the work. The patient replied that he felt relaxed, felt understood by Dr. K, and that he was not fearful of Dr. K, as he was of his father. After a long silence, Dr. K thought the patient wanted to establish a dependent relation with Dr. K as a motherly father image, but the homosexual implications of such a longing frightened him. Instead, the patient tried to perceive Dr. K as a dangerous Nazi, which reassured him against the sexual temptations associated in his mind with any warm relationship between him and a fatherly figure. The spasm of his hands indicated the heightened homosexual fear in the early part of the hour with their later relaxation suggesting the capacity to tolerate intimacy.

Dr. K was about to communicate these thoughts to the patient, but was concerned that sharing this formulation might undermine the work the patient needed to do to achieve self-understanding. Dr. K's doing this work for him might gratify his acting out of these dependency wishes on Dr. K rather than help him become aware of them and accept them. Actually, confirmatory evidence of the use of the "Nazi relationship" as a defense against dependency longings became apparent in the next few sessions, as the patient was able to verbalize these homosexual fears in this context as treatment continued. Dr. K emphasized that the long silences and the difficulties struggling to understand what was going on in the hour made this a challenging treatment (Kernberg, 1976c, pp. 168–173).

Summary and Conclusions

Kernberg's developmental model is the first since Freud's psychosexual model to offer a unified integration of both normal and abnormal developmental trajectories maintaining an intrapsychic perspective. His scheme is an attempt at the integration of drive and object relations concepts from Freud, Klein, Jacobson, and Mahler. Greenberg and Mitchell (1983) argued that Kernberg, in attempting to stretch his theoretical tent, went too far and, in so doing, abandoned the essential core elements of both drive and object relations theories (pp. 327–333). Nevertheless, Kernberg constructed a novel framework, an intellectual *tour de force*, that remains the best effort at such an integration to date.

Kernberg proposed five stages of normal development. During Stage 1 (birth to 1 month), *Normal Autism or the Primary Undifferentiated Stage*, pleasurable interaction with the primary caregiver initiates the beginning of normal undifferentiated self–object representation that gradually builds up from these interactions. During Stage 2 (1 to 6/8 months), *Normal Symbiosis or Primary Undifferentiated Self–Object Representation*, the self- and object-images undergo differentiation within the child's ego. Pleasurable interactions with the primary caregiver are organized as "good" self–object representations while negative experiences get organized as "bad" self–object representations. During end of Stage 3 (6/8 months to 18/36 months), *Differentiation of Self- from Object-Representations*, the child arrives at an integration of both good and bad self-images and good and bad object images resulting in a state of object constancy. During Stage 4 (18/36 months throughout the Oedipus), *Integration of Self-Representations and Object-Representations and Development of Higher Level Intrapsychic Object Relations-Derived Structures*, repression replaces splitting as the primary defensive organization. With the differentiation of the id–ego–superego elements into a mature intrapsychic system the child experiences a totality of self- and object-representations resulting in a "definite self-system" that combine to form a unitary psychological suprasystem. Finally, during Stage 5 (The end of the Oedipus and beyond) *Consolidation of Superego and Ego Integration*, the end product of this stage is a stable, resilient ego identity.

The second part of Kernberg's framework is the three levels of abnormal development. In the higher level of character pathology, we find the neurotic individual with a severe and punitive superego. These patients can benefit from psychoanalysis and enjoy a very good prognosis. In the intermediate level of organization of character pathology, we find the preoedipal borderline patient. These patients can benefit from a modified psychoanalysis with a less favorable outcome. In the lower level of organization of character pathology, we find the early preoedipal disturbances involving severe personality-disordered individuals with archaic defenses and pessimistic, guarded outcomes.

Keywords Borderline psychopathology • Consolidation of superego and ego integration • Differentiation of self- from object-representations • Higher level of organization of character pathology • Integration of self-representations and object-representations • Intermediate level of organization of character pathology • Introjections • Lower level of organization of character pathology • Neurotic psychopathology • Normal autism • Normal symbiosis • Psychotic states • Splitting • Primary undifferentiated self–object representations • Primary undifferentiated stage

References

American Psychiatric Association. (1994). *Diagnostic and statistical manual of mental disorders* (4th ed., Text Revision). Washington, DC.

Coates, S. (2006). Obituary for Paulina Kernberg. *Kinderanalyse*

Eissler, K. R. (1953). The effect of the structure of the ego on psychoanalytic technique. *Journal of the American Psychoanalytic Association, 1*, 104–143.

Fairbairn, W. R. D. (1952). *Psychoanalytic studies of the personality.* Oxford: Routledge.

Gabbard, G. (2005). *Psychodynamic psychiatry in clinical practice* (4th ed.). Washington, DC: American Psychiatric Press.

Jacobson, E. (1964). *The self and the object world.* New York, NY: International Universities Press.

Kernberg, O. F. (1974a). Contrasting viewpoints regarding the nature and psychoanalytic treatment of narcissistic personalities: A preliminary communication. *Journal of the American Psychoanalytic Association, 22*, 255–267.

Kernberg, O. F. (1974b). Further contributions to the treatment of narcissistic personalities. *International Journal of Psycho-Analysis, 55*, 215–240. And in: *Borderline conditions and pathological narcissism* (pp. 263–314). New York, NY: Jason Aronson, 1975.

Kernberg, O. (1976a). Normal and pathological development. In *Object Relations Theory and Clinical Psychoanalysis* (pp. 55–80). New York, NY: Jason Aronson.

Kernberg, O. (1976b). A psychoanalytic classification of character pathology. In *Object Relations Theory and Clinical Psychoanalysis* (pp. 142–159). New York, NY: Jason Aronson.

Kernberg, O. (1976c). A transference and countertransference in the treatment of borderline patients. In *Object Relations Theory and Clinical Psychoanalysis* (pp. 161–184). New York, NY: Jason Aronson.

Kernberg, O. F. (1998). Pathological narcissism and narcissistic personality disorder: Theoretical background and diagnostic classification. In E. F. Ronningstam (Ed.), *Disorders of narcissism: Diagnostic, clinical and empirical implications* (pp. 29–51). Washington, DC: American Psychiatric Press.

Klein, M. (1935/1964). A contribution to the psychogenesis of manic-depressive states. In *Contributions to psychoanalysis, 1921–1945* (pp. 282–311). New York, NY: McGraw-Hill.

Mahler, M. (1968). *On human symbiosis and the vicissitudes of individuation, Vol. I: Infantile psychosis.* New York, NY: International Universities Press.

Mahler, M., Pine, F., & Bergman, A. (1975). *The psychological birth of the human infant.* New York, NY: Basic Books.

Mitchell, S. A., & Black, M. J. (1995). *Freud and beyond: A history of modern psychoanalytic thought.* New York, NY: Basic Books.

Pearce, J. (2006, April 15). Dr. Paulina F. Kernberg, Child Psychiatrist, Dies at 71. *New York Times.*

Spitz, R. (1957). *No and yes: On the genesis of human communication.* New York, NY: International Universities Press.

Spitz, R. (1965). *The first year of life.* New York, NY: International Universities Press.

Summers, F. (1994). *Object relations theories and psychopathology: A comprehensive text.* Hillsdale, NJ: The Analytic Press.

Major Works

Kernberg, O. (1963). “Discussion of the paper, Object relations theory and the conceptual model of psychoanalysis.” By John D. Sutherland, M. D. *British Journal of Medical Psychology, 36*, 121–124.

Kernberg, O. (1965). Notes on countertransference. *Journal of the American Psychoanalytic Association, 13*, 38–56. And in: *Borderline conditions and pathological narcissism* (pp. 49–67). New York, NY: Jason Aronson, 1975.

Kernberg, O. (1966). Structural derivatives of object relations. *International Journal of Psycho-Analysis, 47*, 236–252.

Kernberg, O. (1967). Borderline personality organization. *Journal of the American Psychoanalytic Association, 15*, 641–685. And in: *Borderline conditions and pathological narcissism* (pp. 3–47). New York, NY: Jason Aronson, 1975.

Kernberg, O. (1968). The treatment of patients with Borderline Personality Organization. *International Journal of Psycho-Analysis, 49*, 600–619. And in: *Borderline conditions and pathological narcissism* (pp. 69–109). New York, NY: Jason Aronson, 1975.

Kernberg, O. F. (1969). A contribution to the ego-psychological critique of the Kleinian School. *International Journal of Psycho-Analysis, 50*, 317–333.

Kernberg, O. F. (1970a). Factors in the psychoanalytic treatment of narcissistic personalities. *Journal of the American Psychoanalytic Association, 18*, 51–85. And in: *Borderline Conditions and Pathological Narcissism* (pp. 227–262). New York, NY: Jason Aronson, 1975.

Kernberg, O. F. (1970b). A psychoanalytic classification of character pathology. *Journal of The American Psychoanalytic Association, 18*, 800–822.

Kernberg, O. F. (1971a). Prognostic considerations regarding borderline personality organization. *Journal of the American Psychoanalytic Association, 19*, 595–635.

Kernberg, O. F. (1971b/1975). Differential diagnosis and treatment. In *Borderline conditions and pathological narcissism* (pp. 153–183). New York, NY: Jason Aronson.

Kernberg, O. F. (1972). Early ego integration and object relations. *Annals of the New York Academy of Sciences, 193*, 233–247.

Kernberg, O. F. (1973). Basic psychoanalytic concepts on the theory of instincts. In H. Nagera (Eds.), *The Hampstead Clinic psychoanalytic library* (Vol. III). New York, NY: Basic Books.

Kernberg, O. F. (1975a). Normal and pathological narcissism: Structural and clinical aspects. In: *Borderline conditions and pathological narcissism* (pp. 315–342). New York, NY: Jason Aronson.

Kernberg, O. F. (1975b). *Borderline conditions and pathological narcissism*. New York, NY: Jason Aronson.

Kernberg, O. F. (1976). Technical considerations in the treatment of borderline personality organization. *Journal of the American Psychoanalytic Association, 24*, 795–829.

Kernberg, O. F. (1979a). Some implications of object relations theory for psychoanalytic technique. *Journal of the American Psychoanalytic Association, 27*, 207–239.

Kernberg, O. F. (1979b). The contributions of Edith Jacobson: An overview. *Journal of the American Psychoanalytic Association, 27*, 793–819.

Kernberg, O. F. (1982). Self, ego, affects, and drives. *Journal of the American Psychoanalytic Association, 30*, 893–917.

Kernberg, O. F. (1984). *Severe personality disorders*. New Haven, CT: Yale University Press.

Kernberg, O. F. (1986). Identification and its vicissitudes as observed in psychosis. *International Journal of Psycho-Analysis, 67*, 147–158.

Kernberg, O. F. (1987a). An ego psychology–object relations theory approach to the transference. *Psychoanalytic Quarterly, 56*, 197–221.

Kernberg, O. F. (1987b). Projection and projective identification: Developmental and clinical aspects. *Journal of the American Psychoanalytic Association, 35*, 795–819.

Kernberg, O. F. (1988a). Clinical dimensions of Masochism. *Journal of the American Psychoanalytic Association, 36*, 1005–1029.

Kernberg, O. F. (1988b). Object relations theory in clinical practice. *Psychoanalytic Quarterly, 57*, 481–504.

Kernberg, O. F. (1988c). Psychic structure and structural change: An ego psychology–object relations theory viewpoint. *Journal of the American Psychoanalytic Association, 36S*, 315–337.

Kernberg, O. F. (1991). Transference regression and psychoanalytic technique with infantile personalities. *International Journal of Psycho-Analysis, 72*, 189–200.

Kernberg, O. F. (1992). Psychopathic, paranoid and depressive transferences. *International Journal of Psycho-Analysis, 73*, 13–28.

Kernberg, O. F. (2001). Object relations, affects, and drives: Toward a new synthesis. *Psychoanalytic Inquiry, 21*, 604–619.

Kernberg, O. F. (2003). The management of affect storms in the psychoanalytic psychotherapy of borderline patients. *Journal of the American Psychoanalytic Association*, *51*, 517–544.
Kernberg, O., Clarkin, J. F., & Yeomans, F. E. (2006). *Psychotherapy for borderline personality: Focusing on object relations*. Washington, DC: American Psychiatric Publishing.

Supplementary Readings

Bacal, H. A., & Newman, K. M. (1990). *Theories of object relations: Bridges to self psychology*. New York, NY: Columbia University Press.
Consolini, G. (Spring, 1999). Kernberg versus Kohut: A case study in contrasts. *Clinical Social Work Journal*, *27*(1), 71–86.
Greenberg, J. R., & Mitchell, S. A. (1983). *Object relations in psychoanalytic theory*. Cambridge, MA: Harvard University Press.
Mishne, J. M. (1993). *The evolution and application of clinical theory: Perspectives from four psychologies*. New York, NY: The Free Press.

Section IV
Life Cycle Theory

Freud's psychosexual model essentially stopped at the Oedipus phase of development; it remained for Erik **Erikson**, over 50 years later, to construct the first lifespan model of development that covers the entire life cycle in eight stages. For a period, that model became the gold standard against which all other adult models were compared.

Erikson was clear that he wanted to supplement, not supplant, Freud's model. His psychosocial model focused on ego development and an extension of the classical id psychosexual model, rooted in a positivist descriptive perspective. Erikson added a social and interpersonal dimension to what had been a theoretical structure with an exclusive focus on intrapsychic dynamics. When Erikson wrote the *Eight Ages of Man*, ego psychology had stressed the adaptive functions of the ego. This enabled Erikson to stay within the expanding psychoanalytic framework by proposing that human development is influenced both by social/cultural and biological factors, a focus that became known in psychoanalytic circles as the psychosocial approach.

Erikson based his model, as Freud had, on the organismic epigenetic principle that psychological development unfolds sequentially in stages from simple structures to more complex ones. This principle proposes that a genetic blueprint exists through which the parts give rise to the whole in building block fashion. Each succeeding part emerges, having its time of special ascendancy, until all parts have arisen to form a functioning whole, eventually creating a new entity. Therefore, the individual is a developing organism in which each stage is influenced by the preceding ones.

Chapter 11
Erik Erikson (1902–1994)

Publishing Era (1937–1980)

Biographical Information

Erik Salmonsen Hamburger Erikson was born on June 15, 1902 to Danish parents near Frankfurt. His biological mother, Karla Abrahamsen, came from a prominent cosmopolitan family of Jewish merchants in Copenhagen. The family's multicultural and mixed religious heritage is reflected in the fact that the family spoke no Yiddish. In 1898, when Karla was 21, she married a 27-year-old Jewish stockbroker, Valdemar Isidor Salmonsen. Little is known about Karla's husband except that his father was a lawyer on friendly terms with the Abrahamsen family and his mother was the daughter of the well-known portrait painter, David Monies. The marriage seems not to have lasted more than one night and in all probability was not consummated. Karla, in Rome for her honeymoon, wired her father to come escort her back home. According to family lore, by the time he arrived, Valdemar had fled to either Mexico or the United States, having told Karla that he had to leave precipitously because of his dealings in crime, fraud, and his involvement in financial irregularities. These circumstances gave rise to speculation as to the identity of Erikson's biological father. Karla's daughters, through a second marriage, indicated that their mother became pregnant under questionable circumstances. They suggested that either she was taken advantage of when in a drunken state at a party hosted by her brothers or she was not that sexually innocent and became pregnant while on a vacation on the Isle of Capri by a photographer whose identity she kept secret. Karla discovered she was pregnant two months before she was to deliver when on a vacation in Northern Germany. To avoid disgrace and scandal, the Abrahamsen family sent her to live with her aging aunts in Buehl, outside of Frankfurt. She gave birth in Frankfurt and named the baby Erik Salmonsen. The name Erik is believed to be that of the biological father. Erikson recalls his mother telling him how awkward she felt as a tall, swarthy, dark-haired mother walking a light skinned, blond haired, blue-eyed baby in a stroller in Buehl. He felt that she always spoke with sadness about those days, a sadness that contributed to his lifelong identity struggle.

When Erik was a toddler, Karla left for Germany to be near friends. On her journey, she stopped in Karlsruhe near the Black Forest to visit acquaintances. Erik,

J. Palombo et al., *Guide to Psychoanalytic Developmental Theories*,
DOI: 10.1007/978-0-387-88455-4_11,

who was now two, became ill and was treated by a prominent local Jewish pediatrician, Dr. Theodor Homburger. Karla and Homburger fell in love, married on Erikson's birthday when he was three, and took him on their honeymoon to Copenhagen. Theodor insisted that Erik be told that he was Erik's biological father and that Erik be given his stepfather's name. However, Theodor Homburger did not legally adopted him until 5 years after the marriage. The official name change was not made until later, between 1909 and 1911 (Friedman, 1999, p. 34).This "secret" was necessary to maintain middle class respectability, but it haunted Erikson throughout his life. An only child, he led an idyllic childhood until 1907, when at age 5, a half sister, Elna, was born. She died of diphtheria at age 2. A second half sister, Ruth, was born in 1909, when Erik was 7 and a third, Ellen, in 1912 when he was 10.

Erikson attended primary school (*Vorschule*) from six to nine and the *Karlsruhe Gymnasium* from 10 to 18. He graduated in 1920, this being his last exposure to formal education. The school had a classical curriculum exposing Erik to Greek, Latin, German literature, and ancient history and art. He excelled in the latter two. He did not take well to the strict and formal atmosphere associated with the classics, tested poorly, but did better in the informal atmosphere of *Bildung*, or general education. In all, he was a marginal student who chose not to continue his studies. Family tension grew as Theodor Homburger considered his adopted son a failure, who took little interest in Synagogue activities. During the last year of study, Erik became close friends with his classmate Peter Blos. Peter's father, Dr. Edwin Blos, was a Christian physician who had acquainted the boys with the great humanists of the day and with Eastern philosophy and religion. A popular book, which Erik read at the time, was Romain Rolland's *Mahatma Gandhi*. This work influenced his later psychobiography on Gandhi.

While Erik attended the *Gymnasium,* between 1914 and 1918, World War I consumed all of Europe in the dreadful slaughter of an entire generation of men. During this time, Erik's mother kept strict observance of Jewish and German customs, while occasionally continuing to speak Danish and to read Kierkegaard. Mother insisted on flying both the German and the Danish flags on the house. This served to magnify Erik's feelings of identity confusion both at school and in Synagogue, as he felt that he belonged fully to neither side (Friedman, 1999, pp. 35–37).

In 1921, Erikson, feeling alienated from society, joined the thousands of wandering youth, the *Kunstler* (Goethe, 1774/2004). He hiked around Europe for about a year, after which he decided to end his "escape" by enrolling in an art school, the *Badische Landeskunstschule* (Baden State Art School), back in Karlsruhe. Erik's decision to study art was a declaration to his stepfather that he was turning his back on the Jewish community and on the expectations that he would go on to study at a university and pursue a professional calling. A year later, in 1922, now age 20, he decided to enroll in a different art school, the *Kunst-Akademie* in Munich, where he exhibited large woodcuts, the highpoint of his artistic career. He spent 2 years in Munich before moving on to Florence where he met a community of wandering artists that included Peter Blos and other friends from their days at the *Gymnasium*. The period of 1920–1927, from age 19 to 27, represent Erikson's personal *Wanderschaft*, a time of meandering about Europe and reflecting on the spiritual aspects of the postponement of adulthood. Erikson struggled throughout his life to come to grips with and to define this 7-year-long troublesome period in his youth eventually settling on the term "identity crisis" to characterize it.

The Vienna Period (1927–1933): Erik Homburger

In 1927, at age 26, Erikson gave up wandering and returned to Karlsruhe to study and teach art. It was then that he received a letter from Peter Blos offering him a new beginning. Blos invited the depressed, unhappy, and sickly (prone to illnesses) Erikson to come to Vienna to help start a special school for children operating on psychoanalytic principles. With the Social Democrats in power, this liberal experiment in education, known as the "progressive movement," was sweeping across Vienna. This movement fit in with John Dewey's educational philosophy that children learn best when their interest is heightened and they are fully engaged in a project that unified diverse subjects. It promoted hands-on learning and interdisciplinary study and de-emphasized the prevalent method that valued rote memorization. This school was the Heitzing School, the brainchild of Anna Freud and Dorothy Tiffany Burlingham.

Erikson met the Freud family near Vienna, at a famous European spa, where the Freud and Burlingham families spent their summers. He started an analysis with Anna Freud, which was to last over 3½ years. He paid a token fee and, as was the custom, continued his analysis on a regular basis by frequently accompanying Anna Freud on family journeys. His days assumed a regularity he had not known for many years due to the strict schedule set by the school director, Peter Blos. In the mornings, he had his analytic sessions followed by teaching at the school for the balance of the day. Blos taught geography, the sciences, and life skills. Burlingham and other part-time teachers taught English, Latin, and Mathematics. Erikson taught art, history, and German literature. Instruction was cross-disciplinary. The school's milieu suffered from lax discipline due to the permissive style of the educational environment; as a result, tensions over how best to operate the school always existed between Anna Freud, Eva Rosenfeld, and Dorothy Burlingham, on the one hand, and Blos and Erikson, on the other. The Heitzing School closed in 1932, after a run of 5 years, when Rosenfeld moved to Berlin and many families of students returned to the United States (Friedman, 1999, pp. 61–67).

During this period, Erikson began clinical supervision under August Aichhorn. He also participated in child analysis seminars and workshops led by Anna Freud. Anna Freud felt that Erikson needed greater formal exposure to teaching methods; she encouraged him to enroll at the Montessori teachers' training school in Vienna, from which he graduated in 1932. This experience exposed him to children's use of objects and sensitized him to the purposefulness of children's play.

In addition, between 1929 and 1932, Erikson took many courses in the humanities at the University of Vienna, which Anna Freud discouraged because of the institution's anti-Semitism and its coolness toward psychoanalysis.

Another reason for his stay in Vienna, aside from studying to become a psychoanalyst and teach, was that he met Joan Serson, a young woman of mixed Canadian and American background and with whom he promptly fell in love. She was well educated, having earned a BA in education from Columbia University and a master's degree in sociology from the University of Pennsylvania. She was in Europe researching the origins of modern dance after World War I and exploring the possibility of a doctorate in education. They married 6 months later and by 1933, when he graduated from the Vienna Psychoanalytic Society, they had two sons, Kai and Jon. One of Freud's early followers, Ludwig Jekels, had already analyzed Joan Serson.

The American Period (1933–1994): Erik H. Erikson

Erikson finished his psychoanalytic training in 1933, at the age of 31. After the school closed, the Erikson family left for Denmark. A chance encounter with Hanns Sachs, a psychoanalyst, in a coffee shop in Copenhagen alerted Erikson to the possibilities of a warm reception and employment in Boston. Sachs was a Viennese psychoanalyst who had already established connections in Boston, having spent a year at Harvard Medical School, despite not being a physician. At this time, an exchange of letters between Erikson and Aichhorn revealed friction between the two over unfinished business, because Erikson had not selected Aichhorn as his analyst. Erikson always regretted this exchange and his high degree of candor in his response to Aichhorn. Having been met by Blos in New York, by Christmas 1933, the Erikson family relocated to Boston where it received a warm welcome. Despite having graduated only from *Gymnasium*, he secured positions at the Harvard Medical School and at Massachusetts General Hospital, where staff was eager for exposure to European psychoanalysts. In addition, he began consultation at the Judge Baker Guidance Center.

From 1933 to 1936, Erikson worked in Boston, learned English, initiated a research project and, with other staff members from the Harvard Psychological Clinic, began to study character formation in a group of college men. After the publication of this project, Erikson left Cambridge for New Haven, where he joined Yale University's Institute of Human Relations with considerable freedom to pursue whatever research he desired. As part of the Americanization process and cognizant of the growing anti-German sentiment, the Erikson family decided to change officially their name from Homburger to Erikson. He became a citizen in September 1939 (Friedman, 1999, pp. 143–147).

In 1938, Joan gave birth to a daughter named Sue, but just when she was about to deliver, she came down with mumps causing a crisis on the maternity unit of Grace-New Haven Hospital. At the time, it was the practice to separate mothers from their infants after birth, but with exposure to mumps, the baby could not be kept in the nursery. The problem was solved when mother asked that Sue be allowed to stay with her in the isolation unit. This event initiated the now common "rooming-in" practice, where babies stay in their mothers' room. In the same year, Erikson was offered a chance to observe the children of the Sioux Indians living on the Pine Ridge Reservation in South Dakota. He jumped at the opportunity and published a paper in 1939 titled "Observations on Sioux Education."

Immediately after the publication of this paper and with the encouragement of the anthropologist Scudder Mekeel, Erikson moved to California. At Berkeley, he accepted a position with the University of California's Institute of Child Welfare and joined a generational study on progress of normal children, headed by Jean Macfarlane. At San Francisco, he teamed up with Alfred Kroeber, the dean of American anthropologists, to study the Yurok Indians near Klamath, Oregon. During World War II, Erikson, eager to demonstrate his patriotism toward his newly adopted country, joined the Mt. Zion Veterans Rehabilitation Hospital in San Francisco under the direction of its founder, the psychoanalyst Jascha Kasanin. While there, Erikson wrote commentaries on Nazi culture, undertook submarine studies for the US Navy, and worked with returning traumatized veterans (Friedman, 1999, pp. 160–176).

Childhood and Society

In 1950, Erikson published *Childhood and Society* (Erikson, 1950), presenting his epigenetic life cycle, *The Eight Ages of Man*, a cultural supplement to the psychosexual developmental model. The publication brought Erikson immediate acclaim. His developmental scheme became immensely popular in professional circles that dealt with children, in particular early childhood educators, teachers, childcare workers, and others. Included in the volume are observations on the Sioux, on the Yurok, and on forms of children's play. Erikson deliberately avoided using psychoanalytic terminology to explain habits, customs, and the particular life cycle trajectories of various peoples. This volume, which was quickly recognized as a monumental achievement, for the first time integrated psychoanalysis with history and anthropology. In contrast to the praise he received from these circles, the psychoanalytic community was far less responsive to his proposal. It viewed his emphasis on the contribution of the environment as inconsistent with the emphasis on the inner forces that propel development. Mahler's theory of separation–individuation soon displaced his theory in those circles. Furthermore, the impact of his theory on psychoanalytic practice, whether with children or adults, was modest since no technical innovations resulted from his work. The full appreciation of the role of the environment on personality formation would come to fruition much later in the theories of attachment.

In 1949, the University of California Board of Regents decreed that all teachers must sign an expanded loyalty oath declaring that…"I am not a member of the

Communist Party..." Erikson refused to sign the new oath and submitted his resignation effective June 1, 1950. (Ironically, this same University offered him an honorary doctoral degree in 1968.) When it became clear that he would have to leave California, other institutions aggressively extended offers. Erikson, now 48, accepted an invitation from Robert Knight, formerly a psychiatrist at the Menninger Clinic, to move to the Berkshire Hills of New England and the Austin Riggs Center in Stockbridge, MA. Erikson was to work at Austin Riggs from 1950 to 1960 when he received an appointment as a professor at Harvard. During this decade, all three of the Erikson children, Kai, Jon, and Sue, moved away to college, earning degrees in economics, photography, and philosophy, respectively. Joan not only edited everything Erik wrote, she was involved in enhancing the quality of patients' lives at Riggs through the implementation of many domestic activities, which today would fall into the category of occupational therapy. Numerous speaking engagements followed, as well as writing projects that resulted in the publication of *Identity and the Life Cycle* (1959), later revised and published as *Identity: Youth and Crisis* (1968).

The friendship with David Rapaport that began in Berkeley continued when Rapaport moved to Austin Riggs. They had much in common. Both were from central Europe and both had earned Montessori degrees in kindergarten teaching. Rapaport read a draft of *Childhood and Society* and was deeply impressed by it. It was Rapaport who "tried to remedy perhaps Erikson's primary intellectual deficiency – a conceptual and theoretical vagueness and imprecision that was probably inherent in his artistic, nonlinear manner of expressing himself." (Friedman, 1999, p. 287). Rapaport's influence may be found in *Young Man Luther*, which was Erikson's most closely written, tightly organized, and thematically unified book. Rapaport was worried that Erikson's propensity toward incomplete research and incautious writing could provoke charges of psychoanalytic deviancy or neo-Freudianism. This issue bubbled over in the first attempt to publish the "Dream Specimen of Psychoanalysis," the commentary on the Irma Dream from Freud's *Interpretation of Dreams* (1900). Erikson aroused considerable controversy by suggesting that Freud lusted after Irma. The main point that Erikson was trying to make was that the manifest content of the dream should receive more attention than it was accorded in dream work. His first draft, with limited circulation, polarized the psychoanalytic community. Willie Hoffer, Ernest Jones, and Anna Freud were vigorously opposed to its publication, while Heinz Hartmann, Robert Knight, and David Rapaport were in favor. Erikson resisted any substantial changes in his argument and eventually the paper was published in 1954.

Young Man Luther

The historical Martin Luther had interested Erikson for some time because of the questions of identity, identity crisis, and moratorium that Erikson had repeatedly revisited. Martin Luther took on a special significance because Erikson was familiar with the towns in which Martin Luther had lived and roads which he had traveled. Erikson earlier had taken up the question of the transition into adulthood by studying the life of George Bernard Shaw and Shaw's lifelong quest to achieve ego identity, ego synthesis, continuity of personal character, and inner solidarity. Shaw had experienced what Erikson called a moratorium, defined as "an interval between youth and adulthood when someone tries to achieve an inner and outer sense of coherence, work that can be enjoyed, self-respect and the loyalty of others" (Coles, 1970, p. 170).

In *Young Man Luther* (1958), Erikson published both a biography and a psychological analysis, a study on neurosis and creativity. Erikson captured a young man and his family of origin struggling with the massive cultural changes associated with the waning of the Middle Ages. Martin removed himself from this struggle and took a "time out" at the Augustinian monastery in Erfurt at the age of 21. By the age of 23, Martin Luther was ordained a priest of the Roman Catholic Church and at age 33, his life became sharply focused as he nailed the 95 theses to the Castle Church door in Wittenberg. Erikson pointed out that millions of young people experience such a moratorium and many do not survive it in spirit and/or in body. "Now the concept of moratorium is not meant to unlock the secret of genius or creativity, but give a certain coherence to what does appear rather often and even somewhat predictably in a significant number of lives. The best that can be said is that a configuration of personal problems and social and political developments led a man like Luther to say and do things that even he would have found surprising, were he told about them in his youth." (Coles, 1970, p. 143).

Gandhi's Truth

Between 1957 and 1962, Erikson wrote a series of five essays that eventually became a book titled *Insight and Responsibility* (1964). These papers dealt with issues of clinical interest and ethics. One paper titled "The Golden Rule in the Light of New Insight," was first delivered at the Harvard Medical School and later in an expanded version in New Delhi in 1963. A year earlier, he led a seminar on the human life cycle attended by Hindus in Ahmedabad. The Eriksons stayed at the estate of a powerful mill owner, Ambalal Sarabhai. Gandhi and Sarabhai's sister, Anasuyaben, were worker advocates and fought for higher wages through Gandhi's first public fast for the mill workers in 1918 against Sarabhai. Now 14 years after Gandhi's assassination, Sarabhai had grown respectful of Gandhi's contribution, in spite of their decades-old political differences. In these contacts lay the seeds of Erikson's interest in his second psychobiography *Gandhi's Truth* (Erikson, 1969). The book, which focused on a middle-aged Gandhi, was thought, in part, to be a life cycle sequel to that of the youthful Luther.

Gathering data for a biography on Mahatma Gandhi proved more difficult than he had anticipated because the interviewees were old and aware of psychoanalytic terminology and fearful of being labeled "neurotic." Erikson carefully reconstructed Gandhi's childhood in India, his adolescence in England, his struggle to remain a vegetarian, his career as a barrister in South Africa, his initial exposure to societal prejudice, and finally, his decision to begin a grass roots movement on behalf of the poor and the disadvantaged. Gandhi's Hindu philosophy, called "Satyagraha" or life force, refers to the nature of the relationship between the oppressed and the oppressor within any sphere of life. He used it forcefully as a nonviolent but militant method against the moral arrogance of others. Erikson is careful to depict Gandhi as a "householder," one who invites others in, as if for care, and eventually taking all of India into his house. In his 15 years in South Africa, Gandhi learned the fundamentals of nonviolent protest, public boycotts, and confrontations. He returned to India from South Africa at age 45 in 1915 and proceeded to wander across India. Erikson drew the parallel between Luther's struggle and Gandhi's, whose identity became firm and had acquired a sense of inner cohesiveness and public purposefulness as a result of his experiences in South Africa. The publication of *Gandhi's Truth* earned Erikson the Pulitzer Prize and National Book Award.

World Acclaim

The mandatory retirement age at Harvard was 65, although some faculty stayed on until 70. President Nathan Pusey resisted Erikson's wish to teach longer and Erikson accepted retirement at the end of his 67th year. At the same time, Erikson's adolescent classmate, Peter Blos, retired from the New York Jewish Board of Guardians. This event rekindled memories of the competition between them from their days in Vienna.

As he found it more difficult to locate material to stimulate his writing, Erikson had a controversial set of meetings with Black Panther Huey Newton in 1971. In 1972, Erikson delivered the E. L. Godkin Lectures at Harvard's J.F. Kennedy School of Government, resulting in the volume *Toys and Reasons*. The Vietnam War was winding down and Watergate was heating up. In 1973, the Eriksons moved from Stockbridge to the Tibourn-Belvedere area over looking San Francisco Bay. That same year Erikson accepted an invitation to present the second annual Jefferson Lecture sponsored by the National Endowment for the Humanities. This proved a most stressful assignment because of a medical complication experienced by the Eriksons. The move to San Francisco and the short deadline for publication of the lectures heightened the sense of urgency. In addition, Erikson's fortunes were now shifting. Critics abounded due to the rise of the feminist perspective, the growth of self-psychology, and the criticisms from the Jewish left who felt that Erikson ignored Luther's virulent anti-Semitism and rejected his own Jewish roots. Erikson was devastated. Furthermore, the Eriksons were beset with financial problems at the same time that Erikson was diagnosed with prostate cancer in 1974.

Through the late 1970s and into the 1980s Erikson worked on papers concerning old age and the stage of Integrity vs. Despair, writing a celebrated article on Ingmar Bergman's film *Wild Strawberries*. Joan wanted Erikson to consider adding a ninth stage, but conceptually this did not get far. Erikson's intellectual capacities were lessening and his last writings were considered marginal. Joan made the decision to relocate both she and Erik back to Cambridge, this time to a nursing home where he died in 1994 at the age of 91.

Theory of Development

In his theory of development, Erikson combined his lifelong interests in psychoanalysis, children, normal human development, and the influence of society in the formation of an individual's psychology. His emphasis on the physical, the psychological, social, and cultural factors that are at play added balance to what had been an exclusive emphasis on drive theory and ego psychology. Erikson objected to what he called "originology." This is the tendency to reduce every human situation to an earlier one and to conclude that its origin lies in the most basic infantile precursor (Erikson, 1958, p. 18; Mitchell & Black, 1995, pp. 139–149). Erikson built upon the Freudian edifice, but in contrast to Freud, he emphasized strengths over weaknesses, health over neurosis, and the future over the past (Roazen, 1976, p. 195). In fact, this model of human development remains the most recognizable psychoanalytic contribution to developmental psychology.

Erikson proposed an organismic model, grounded in an epigenetic, psychosexual, and psychosocial matrix. As we have seen in our discussion of Spitz's work, epigenesis is a term borrowed from embryology that Erikson now made central to his framework. For Erikson, epigenesis refers to the process through which a succession of potentialities, each having its time of ascendancy in hierarchical fashion, builds upon prior ones to assemble the biological and psychological structures of the person. Three complementary systems organize development, "the biological process of the hierarchic organization of organ systems constituting a body (SOMA); there is the psychic process organizing individual experience by ego synthesis (PSYCHE); and there is the communal process of the cultural organization of the interdependence of person (ETHOS)" (Erikson, 1980, p. 17). In contrast to all prior psychoanalytic developmental theories, Erikson, in his scheme, gave as much weight to communal and cultural factors as to intrapsychic and biological factors. This emphasis on the broader environment's contribution to shaping the child's personality represents Erikson unique enhancement of our understanding of the forces at play during development.

Erikson's epigenetic eight-stage model extended Freud's psychosexual phases, with each stage corresponding to one of Freud's libidinal phases; thus the psychosocial phases build "a bridge of clinical experience to observations on society" (Erikson, 1950, p. 70). The stages, in sequential order are *Basic Trust vs. Basic Mistrust*, *Autonomy vs. Shame and Doubt*, *Initiative vs. Guilt*, *Industry vs. Inferiority*, *Identity vs. Role Confusion*, *Intimacy vs. Isolation*, *Generativity vs. Stagnation*, and *Integrity vs. Despair*.

Each stage of development is characterized by a dynamic polarity or normative psychosocial ego crisis, better understood as *dialectical tensions with states of disequilibria* rather than alternative positions in conflict. Erikson presented a framework with two centers that have a complex dialectical relation to one another, one process is located in the core of the individual and the other is located in the core of his communal culture (Erikson, 1968, pp. 22–23). The term "core crisis" denotes that at each stage a different dynamic tension occurs, an **ego syntonic** potential associated with a **sympathetic** strength that must outbalance its antithesis, and an **ego dystonic** potential that is counterbalanced by an **antipathetic** weakness (Erikson, 1980, pp. 39–48). In other words, Erikson tried to characterize healthy growth as a set of eight life cycle sequential engagements building on syntonic/sympathetic (compatible with ego strengths and capacities) potentials from basic trust through integrity. These positive potentials were in continual tension with the opposite position, dystonic/antipathetic (forces eroding ego strengths leading to ego weaknesses and pathologies) negative potentials from basic mistrust to disdain, which remain a constant threat to the individual and social order. For Erikson, this state of balance essentially constituted a definition of mental health. The polarities describe a spectrum ranging from the successful resolution of a crisis that leads to mental health, whereas the failure to resolve the crisis leads to psychopathology. Finally, the necessity to transcend and move on to the next stage requires the use of the strengths acquired by the favorable resolution of that stage, so that each stage builds on prior stages.

Each stage has six dimensions that when taken together, capture the essence of the stage (a) the **radius of significant relations** includes the primary caregiver; (b) a favorable outcome results from the resolution of the crisis and depends on the nature of the child's **basic ego strengths or virtues**; (c) an unfavorable outcome results from the failure to resolve the crisis and leads to **psychopathology**; (d) the **principle of social order** represents the guiding principle that dominates the person's worldview during this stage; (e) **ritualization**: The term "ritualization" comes from ethology, the study of animal behavior. It denotes phylogenetically preformed ceremonial acts, such as the flamboyant greeting ceremony of some birds. A typical human ritualization might be the customary greeting a mother extends to her infant upon awakening (Erikson, 1980, p. 28). It describes prototypical forms of interactions between people that are characteristic of the stage; and finally, (f) **ritualism**: In contrast to ritualization, "ritualism" is the stereotypic repetition of interactions that give the illusory appearance of an integration of the value of community, but in reality, the interactions are performed merely to simulate compliance with social expectations. An example would be a public official's attendance at church services to conform to the community's expectations of his religiosity, whereas in reality he holds no religious beliefs.

As stated in Rapaport's remark above, Erikson uses many terms and concepts in an idiosyncratic, poetic, and metaphoric way. Rather than defining these terms, he spends many pages in illustrating their meanings. This vagueness and imprecision best expresses the difficulties inherent in attempting to summarize his thoughts. Furthermore, Erikson recognized that others had carried out major conceptual work on the first six stages and that more work needed to be done on the last two life cycle stages.

In Table 11.1, Erikson provides a road map through which we can track each of the eight stages with the corresponding psychosexual stages and psychosocial crisis.

Table 11.1 Erikson's ages of man and dimension of each age

	A	B	C	D	E	F	G	H
Stages	Psychosexual stages and modes	Psychosocial crises	Radius of significant relations	Basic strengths	Core pathology basic antipathies	Related principles of social order	Binding ritualizations	Ritualisms
I Infancy	Oral-respiratory, sensory-kinesthetic (incorporative modes)	Basic trust vs. basic mistrust	Maternal person	Hope	Withdrawal	Cosmic order	Numinous	Idolism
II Early childhood	Anal–urethral, muscular (retentive–eliminative)	Autonomy vs. shame, doubt	Parental person	Will	Compulsion	"Law and order"	Judicious	Legalism
III Play age	Infantile-genital, locomotor (intrusive, inclusive)	Initiative vs. guilt	Basic family	Purpose	Inhibition	Ideal prototypes	Dramatic	Moralism
IV School age	"Latency"	Industry vs. inferiority	"Neighborhood," School	Competence	Inertia	Technological order	Formal (technical)	Formalism
V Adolescence	Puberty	Identity vs. identity confusion	Peer groups and outgroups; Models of leadership	Fidelity	Repudiation	Ideological worldview	Ideological	Totalism
VI Young adulthood	Genitality	Intimacy vs. isolation	Partners in friendship, sex, competition, cooperation	Love	Exclusivity	Patterns of cooperation and competition	Affiliative	Elitism
VII Adulthood	(Procreativity)	Generativity vs. stagnations	Divided labor and shared household	Care	Rejectivity	Currents of education and tradition	Generational	Authoritism
VIII Old age	(Generalization of sensual modes)	Integrity vs. despair	"Mankind" "My Kind"	Wisdom	Disdain	Wisdom	Philosophical	Dogmatism

Erikson (1980), Mental health study center, US Department of Health and Human Services DHHS Publication No. (ADM) 80–886, p. 21. Reprinted with permission from International Universities Press

In addition, he designates the primary concept that identifies the dimension of development involved in each stage.

The Eight Ages of Man

The First Stage: Basic Trust vs. Basic Mistrust (Birth to 18 Months)

The stage of **Basic trust vs. basic mistrust** corresponds to the oral respiratory (i.e., that relates to the process of breathing) and sensory stage of psychosexual development. This stage corresponds to the oral phase and the erogenous zone associated with that phase, i.e., the mouth. Children's conflicts center around issues of trust and mistrust. Borrowing from Anna Freud's definition of defenses, Erikson describes the characteristic defenses the child uses at this stage as including introjection, projection, projective identification, splitting, dissociation, regression, and fixation. Basic trust vs. basic mistrust reflects an inner division within the ego and a universal nostalgia for paradise lost. The individual maintains a sense of deprivation, of something lost that the child has had to abandon, and with which he or she must deal with throughout life. This division between inside and outside evolves from the process of the early ego's differentiation of the mechanisms of projection and introjection. "In introjection we feel as if an outer goodness had become an inner certainty. In projection, we experience an inner harm as an outer one: we endow significant people with the evil which actually is in us" (Erickon, 1950, pp. 248–249). The morphology, the fundamental psychological structure associated with the stage of Basic Trust, is **hope**, an expectation born of parental faith and care that has organized religion as one of its endpoints. All religions have in common a childlike surrender to and faith in a Provider, one who dispenses earthly fortune along with spiritual health, one who enables efforts at atonement which tries to make up for vague deeds against a maternal matrix, and one who restores faith in the goodness of one's strivings and in the kindness of the powers of the universe (Erikson, 1950, pp. 250–251).

The six dimensions of this stage are:

- *The radius of significant relations* includes the child's mother, the primary caretaker, and the original and basic libidinal object.
- *A favorable outcome* of this stage would lead to trust and optimism in fellow human beings. The outcome is due to the child's *basic ego strengths or virtues*, which includes a feeling of hope, the belief that fellow human beings are fundamentally reliable and sustaining, and the belief in the attainability of wishes.
- *An unfavorable outcome* or the core pathology of this stage manifests as a basic antipathy of others and withdrawal from them. Psychopathology at this stage includes schizoid and depressive states, suspicion and paranoia.
- *The related principle of social order* is cosmic order; that is, infants view their narrow perception of the world as encompassing the entire universe.

- *Ritualization.* The stage-specific interaction is based on the recognition of "I" and "Other" as basic to a human being's earliest ritual, which is *mutual recognition and affirmation of the mother–child bond.* It is the mutuality of recognition by both face and name. It evolves into the **numinous**, the aura of a hallowed presence or divinity. This mystical experience assures us of *separateness transcended* and of *distinctiveness confirmed* and, thus, of the very basis of "I." Religion and art are the institutions with the strongest traditional claim on the cultivation of numinosity (Erikson, 1980, p. 29). To every ritualization, there is an accompanying ritualism, to which it is related as if on a continuum. The former is repetitive, orienting, and playful. It is one of the number of socializing mechanisms prescribed by one's culture and represents healthy and functional dynamics.
- *Ritualism.* The stage-specific ritualism is **idolism**, "a visual addiction, which, indeed, can become a most dangerous collective delusional system" (Erikson, 1980, p. 30). An example of this form of idolism would be membership in a cult and/or "a distortion of the mother–infant bond where an illusion of the mother's perfection exists that can result in later pathological narcissistic idealization of the self with unrealistic expectations and overdependence" (Austrian, 2002, p. 47). An example of this is the child who is egocentric and impatient, and who has poor frustration tolerance.

The Second Stage: Autonomy vs. Shame and Doubt (18 Months to 3/4 Year)

The stage of **Autonomy vs. Shame and Doubt** corresponds to the anal phase and the erogenous zone associated with that phase, i.e., the anus. Children's conflicts center around their desire to be autonomous and feelings of shame that they may have to submit to others' expectations. The characteristic defenses that children use at this stage include the earlier ones and, in addition, denial and reversal. Muscular maturation sets the stage for experimentation with two simultaneous sets of social modalities: holding on and letting go. The basic conflicts can ultimately lead to hostile or to benign attitudes and expectations. To hold on can become a destructive and cruel form of retaining or restraining, and it can become a pattern of care: to have and to hold. To let go can turn into an inimical letting loose of destructive force, or it can become a relaxed "to let pass" and "to let be." (Erikson, 1950, pp. 251–254)

Feelings of shame constrain a child to feel exposed and conscious that others are watching, in a word, to feel self-conscious. The child is completely exposed, visible and not ready to be visible. Children express their shame by their impulse to bury their faces or to wish to sink into the ground. This response represents rage turned against the self. Children who feel shame would like to force the world not to look at them and would like to destroy the eyes of those that turn them. For Erikson, visual shame precedes auditory guilt. Too much shaming does not lead to propriety; rather it results in a secret determination to get away with things, unseen (pp. 252–253).

Doubt is the brother of shame. Whereas shame is dependent on the consciousness of being upright and exposed, doubt is the consciousness of having a front and a back, a "behind." This area of the body, the sphincters and buttocks, is invested with libidinal and aggressively charged energies. The child cannot see this Dark Continent, yet can feel that it is magically dominated by others, who would invade and attack its power and autonomy, and who designate as evil those bowel products that were acceptable when passed and left behind. These experiences can lead to compulsive doubting and, in adults, to paranoia, fears of hidden persecutors, and secret persecutory threats from behind and from within the behind (pp. 253–254).

The morphology, the fundamental psychological structure associated with the stage of Autonomy, is **will** that is fostered in the child and modified as life progresses and that serves to preserve a sense of justice (Erikson, 1950, p. 254).

The six dimensions are:

- *The radius of significant relations* widens from the circle of the mother to those of other caregivers.
- *A favorable outcome* leads children to view themselves as both apart from and dependent on their parents. A *basic ego strength or virtue* is the child's ability to exercise its will, which eventually leads to autonomy, enabling the child to exercise free choice, self-restraint, and self-control.
- *An unfavorable outcome* or the core pathology of this stage is the interpersonal difficulty developing a balance of loving and hating, cooperation and willfulness and freedom of self-expression or its suppression, and a defiant shamelessness or compulsive doubting.
- *The related principle of social order* is that of "Law and Order"; that is, that rigid rules should guide all conduct and should be enforced unquestioningly.
- *Ritualization.* This stage-specific ritualization is what Erikson calls **judicious**. The child develops the capacity to differentiate, within its culture, good from bad conduct and acquires the ability playfully to test limits with adults and to some extent with peers. If others view testing negatively, the outcome may be a negative identity in adolescence, a self-fulfilling prophecy (Erikson, 1980, p. 254).
- *Ritualism.* The stage-specific ritual is **legalism**. In the adult, we would see self-righteousness or a lack of impulse control resulting in a tendency toward exploitation of the law for one's own gain (Austrian, 2002, p. 48).

The Third Stage: Initiative vs. Guilt (3/4 to 5/6Years)

The stage of **Initiative vs. guilt** corresponds to the infantile-genital (phallic/oedipal) phase and the erogenous zone associated with that phase, i.e., the phallus. Children are involved in a conflict around their desire to be assertive or proactive and their fear of possible retaliation for their competitiveness and guilt associated with the Oedipus. The infant's capacity to move around lends support for the basic social modality of "making" and "being on the make." For the boy making suggests his use of the phallic-intrusive mode of relating. The boy's assertiveness is on the ascendency. For the girl being on the make suggests the inclusive, enveloping mode of relating. The girl's affiliative tendencies begin to emerge. Characteristic defenses against the guilt generated by unacceptable wishes include sublimation, repression, reaction formation, undoing, isolation, internalization, and displacement. Whereas children's desire for autonomy leads them to concentrate on keeping potential rivals out, the desire to take the initiative brings with it the anticipation of rivalry with others. This stage, in which erotic feelings are stirred and are accompanied by castration fear, finds the child having grandiose fantasies of being a giant or a tiger, but these fantasies evoke terror of the possible repercussions.

The morphology, the fundamental psychological structure associated with the stage of Initiative, is **purposefulness** guided by a sense of persistent moralistic vigilance. This structure is forged within the social modalities of intrusion and inclusion that suggests a bisexual orientation in both sexes. For the girl, penis envy transforms her view of herself from feeling a sense of loss to a budding appreciation of the potential vitality of her inner space. This view is consistent with the passive renunciation of male activity and the playful pursuit of activities associated with the expression of birth giving and motherhood. For the boy, the castration complex resolves itself through identification with the father's achievements and capacity for assertiveness.

The six dimensions are:

- *The radius of significant relations* widens from the narrow focus on the parents to include the basic family.
- *A favorable outcome* brings with it the development of the capacity for initiative, a period of vigorous reality testing, an enhancement of the child's imagination, and the imitation of the behavior of others. The ethos (the cultural mores) of social institutions offers children idealizable adults who are recognizable by the uniforms they wear and functions they perform. These heroic figures become sufficiently fascinating to replace those of picture books and fairy tale (Erikson, 1950, p. 258). The *basic ego strengths or virtues* identified in this period are the capacity for purposeful action and direction. Children experience an urge to imagine and pursue their own goals based on internalized standards.
- *An unfavorable outcome* or the core pathology that characterizes this stage is a basic self-righteousness intolerance, hysteria-denial (leading to conversion reactions), overcompensation, psychosomatic symptoms, and inhibition.
- *The related principle of social order* is found in the search for ideal prototypes the child can imitate.
- *Ritualization.* The stage-specific ritualization is **authenticity** in play. Children are able to relive old experiences and anticipate new ones. They are able to experiment with different roles and identifications. The result is a consolidation of "I" influenced by a growing awareness of what the child wants vs. what they can be.
- *Ritualism.* The rituals specific to this stage are the **impersonation** of others by moving among roles, while making no commitment to any role. The danger children face is that of assuming a negative role vs. taking no role at all. The other ritual characteristic of this stage is **inhibition** of actions, feelings, or thoughts, which may lead to psychological constraints that prevent freedom of thought, expression, and activity.

The Fourth Stage: Industry vs. Inferiority (5/6 to 11/12 Years)

The stage of **Industry vs. Inferiority** corresponds to the latency phase of development, a phase during which the sexual drives are more or less quiescent, children struggle with the wish for competence in the tasks they undertake and the fear of failure and personal deficiency. The characteristic defenses a child uses at this stage include the earlier defenses with particular emphasis on reaction formation, sublimation, rationalization, somatization, disavowal, inhibition of affect, and identification with the aggressor. This period sets the stage for entrance into life, which begins in all cultures with going off to elementary school. The logical extension of formal learning includes the development of an understanding of the roles of parenthood and of the world of work, which defines the potential to become a family provider. A distinction is drawn between play and work, as the child learns the fundamentals of the use of technology, and the make-believe world. The child may develop the capacity for initiative and the skills required through work to become a valuable member of society. The child must face the inner upheavals associated with the violent drives that should be dormant during this stage but are not extinguished, as well as the outer frustrations that accompany the development of new collaborative and competitive activities.

The morphology, the fundamental psychological structure associated with the stage of Industry, is the development of **competencies** that permit the child to survive in world. The child must master the task he or she confronts rather than retreat to or externalize the oedipal dynamics, becoming marginalized in the world of work struggling with tendencies toward conformity and mediocrity (Erikson, 1950, pp. 258–161).

The six dimensions are:

- *The radius of significant relations* widens from that of the basic family to that of others in the neighborhood and at school.
- *A favorable outcome* brings with it experiences through which children view themselves as useful, contributing members of society. The *basic ego strength or virtue* is that of competence.
- *An unfavorable outcome* or the core pathology that characterizes this stage is inertia and a sense of inadequacy and inferiority. Children may withdraw from the world that expects proficiency in tasks and may become content with mediocrity.
- *The related principle of social order* is the mastery of the technological tools the community provides.
- *Ritualization*. The stage-specific ritualization is the achievement of a capacity to fit into the **technological ethos** of the culture. Working with and besides others is the child's first exposure to the division of labor and of differential opportunity within society.
- *Ritualism*. The stage-specific ritual is **formalism**. A person can display this dimension as an attitude in which work becomes an obligation and success is the only criterion of feeling valued. The individual becomes a conformist and a thoughtless slave to technology and those who exploit it.

The Fifth Stage: Identity vs. Identity Confusion (Pubescence to the End of Adolescence, 9/12 to 25 Years of Age)

The stage of **Identity vs. Identity Confusion** corresponds to the phase of adolescent development and the phase of puberty, a phase during which hormonal changes become dominant, adolescents struggle searching for a set of roles that are concordant with their social context, and their need to find an adequate place for themselves in society. Characteristic defenses the adolescent uses at this stage include the use of earlier defenses with the emergence of asceticism, estheticism, altruistic surrender, uniformism (see Chap. 5), and intellectualization. The maturational disturbance that pubescence creates produces a massive upheaval in the latency child's relatively smooth, calm life. With rapid body changes, young adolescents become more interested in how they look to others than with who they are. They are also preoccupied with how to connect the roles and skills cultivated earlier with current interests. Their attempts to maintain continuity and sameness challenges adolescents as they artificially appoint well-meaning people to adversarial roles and install idols and ideals as guardians of their newfound identity. The shaping of ego identity in this stage is an ambitious task of integration, as past identifications with the vicissitudes of the libido, the aptitudes of endowment, and the social role opportunities require coherent alignment. Ego identity results when the accrued confidence that the sameness and continuity of the past matches the present, as evidenced in the tangible promise of a work trajectory or "career."

The morphology, the fundamental psychological structure associated with the stage of Identity, is **fidelity** that evolves into a resilient ego integrity in which others validate the adolescent's perception of self-sameness and self-continuity. The adolescent's mind is an ideological mind that requires and involves passage through an idiosyncratic moratorium in which decision making is suspended on one's work trajectory in order to consolidate past identifications and develop a sense of coherent ego identity (Erikson, 1950, pp. 261–263).

The six dimensions are:

- *The radius of significant relations* widens from the neighborhood and school to peers, other groups, and into models of leadership.
- *A favorable outcome* brings with it a coherent sense of identity that includes the capacity to form an intimate relationship with another within the context of the community in which the adolescent lives. In addition to these, this stage includes the achievement of self-confidence, the consolidation of a sexual identity, and the formulation of career goals. *Basic ego strength or virtue* involve the synthesis and integration of the tasks of prior stages, and the fidelity to significant others and loyalty to an ideology.
- *An unfavorable outcome* or core pathology consists in role confusion manifesting in doubt as to one's sexual identity, delinquency, or outright psychosis. Adolescents can keep themselves together by overidentifying with heroes of cliques and crowds to the point of an apparent complete loss of identity. Falling in love is only partly a matter of sexual expression. For adolescents love is an attempt at

arriving at a definition of an identity by projecting their diffuse ego image on to another and by seeing that image reflected back and thus clarified. That is why so much of adolescent love is conversational.
- *The related principle of social order* is an ideological worldview in which a set of values and ideals that are concordant with the adolescent's community establish themselves as guides to future conduct.
- *Ritualization.* The stage-specific ritualization is **ideological** as adolescents are powerfully motivated to seek affirmation from peers and confirmation by rituals, creeds, and programs that define what is evil, uncanny, and inimical.
- *Ritualism.* The stage-specific ritual is "**totalism**," in which adolescents test fidelity by forming cliques and by stereotyping themselves, their ideals, and their enemies. The readiness for this global life style of categorization of others explains the appeal of cruel totalitarian doctrines.

The Sixth Stage: Intimacy vs. Isolation (25–40 Years)

The stage of **Intimacy vs. Isolation** corresponds to the young adult phase of development and with genitality in young adulthood, which is a phase during which young adults attempt to find expression in mature sexuality within the context of a relationship, but face the prospect of having to withdrawn from social contacts should they fail in that effort.

The characteristic defenses individuals use at this stage include all defenses used in prior phases as well as altruism, humor, suppression, anticipation, and sublimation. Under stress, the person may use such neurotic mechanisms as intellectualization, repression, displacement, and reaction formation and dissociation (Vaillant, 1977, pp. 384–386). Intimacy refers to the capacity to commit oneself to concrete affiliations and partnerships and to develop the ethical strength to abide by such commitments, even though they may call for significant sacrifices and compromises.

The morphology, the fundamental psychological structure associated with the stage of Intimacy, is **love**, which signifies that the adult has reached the capacity for mutually gratifying genital orgasm or "genitality." For this condition to be of lasting social significance, the relationship should include mutuality of orgasm with a love partner of the other sex, with whom one is able and willing to regulate the cycles of work, procreation, and recreation. Such conditions go far beyond mere sexuality and require the support of the large community for their attainment (Erikson, 1950, pp. 263–266).

The six dimensions are:

- *The radius of significant relations* widens from that of peers, and other groups to include partners in friendship, sex, competition, and cooperation.
- *A favorable outcome* brings with it the capacity to engage enthusiastically in the worlds of work and love, within a cooperative and collaborative spirit. The *basic ego strength or virtue* resides in the capacity for love within the context of "genitality"; that is, of the capacity for sexual intimacy.

- *An unfavorable outcome* or core pathology that characterizes this stage is the avoidance of close friendships. This avoidance can lead to exclusivity, isolation, self-absorption, and the failure to develop intimacy with another.
- *The related principle of social order* is the development of patterns of cooperation and competition with others.
- *Ritualization.* The stage-specific ritualization is **affiliation**, that is, individuals find expression of their need for others through different living styles, which permit intimacy while preserving personal identity.
- *Ritualism.* The stage-specific ritual is **elitism**, which finds expression in snobbery and clannishness.

The Seventh Stage: Generativity vs. Stagnation (40–65 Years)

The stage of **Generativity vs. Stagnation** corresponds to the phase of adult development. During this phase, adults can find expression of their potential through procreativity and achievement, but face disillusionment should they find themselves unable to fulfill their ambitions. The defenses characteristic of this stage are the same as those individuals use during Stage Six. The primary concern of Generativity is the establishment and guidance of the next generation. Generativity includes productivity and creativity. Merely wanting children is insufficient to achieve true Generativity. Some parents have not developed the capacity to parent due to early negative childhood experiences, excess self-love, and a lack of faith, known as basic mistrust. Even in communities where a philosophical or spiritual tradition against procreation exists, such institutions value relationships, caring for others, and charity towards others.

The morphology, the fundamental psychological structure associated with the stage of Generativity, is the capacity to demonstrate **care** in any variety of modalities (Erikson, 1950, pp. 266–268).

The six dimensions include:

- *The radius of significant relations* widens from partners in friendship, sex, competition, and cooperation to include divided labor and a shared household.
- *A favorable outcome* brings with it feelings of responsibility for the world's children. *The basic ego strength or virtue* is caring for others.
- *An unfavorable outcome or core pathology* that characterizes this stage is the rejection of others reflected in the lack of caring for others, and a regression to pseudointimacy, in which individuals believe they are the child in need of care or they retreat to early psychological or physical invalidism.
- *The related principles of social order* are the currents of education and tradition that are dominant in the community.
- *Ritualization.* The stage-specific ritualization is the generational **transmission of values and ideals**. This occurs through ceremonies and rituals favored by communities. The purpose of the rituals is to express care for others and to teach others.
- *Ritualism.* The stage-specific ritual is **authoritarianism**, which promotes regimentation and depersonalization of the family and community.

The Eighth Stage: Ego Integrity vs. Despair (65 Years to Death)

The stage of **Ego Integrity vs. Despair** corresponds to the phase of development of maturity or old age and the processes associated with aging. Individuals can attain the serenity found in wisdom and communal respect or face the prospect of embitterment at a life that was wasted. The defense characteristics of this stage are the same as those used during Stage Six. Ego integrity relies on the ripening of the ego strengths of the earlier seven stages. Whereas it is difficult to define ego integrity, it is an experience of the spiritual world order. Some constituents of this state of mind include the ego's proclivity for order and meaning and the postnarcissistic love of humanity over that of the self. Individuals accept the certitude of their finality and arrive at a new and different form of love for their parents. They become reconciled with the occurrences of the distant times, their past pursuits, and past generations. With the experience of integrity comes a readiness to defend the values associated with their life style against all physical and economic threats. The particular style of integrity the individual develops thus becomes the "patrimony of his soul," (Erikson, 1950, p. 268) the seal of his moral paternity, his legacy. With such a consolidation of the ego, death loses its sting. The fear of death characterizes the lack of integrity.

The morphology, the fundamental psychological structure associated with the stage of ego-integrity, is **wisdom** that evolves directly from basic trust; it is the individual's ability to face his or her finitude. The outcome will be that healthy children will not fear life if their elders have enough integrity not to fear death (Erikson, 1950, pp. 268–269).

The six dimensions include:

- The *radius of significant relations* widens from that of divided labor and shared household to all of mankind, which Erikson termed "my kind." (1980, p. 21).
- *A favorable outcome* is an acceptance of one's life trajectory and that one's one and only life cycle is the ultimate expression of life. The *basic ego strength or virtue* characteristic of this stage is wisdom. Wisdom represents a detached concern with life in the face of death itself, as it is expressed both in the sayings of the ages. It is expressed through those personal experiences that convey the probability that ultimately life's meaning can be uncovered.
- *An unfavorable outcome* or core pathology that characterizes this stage is disdain of others, disgust with one's self, and despair at one's fate. Despair expresses the feeling that time is now short, too short to attempt to start life anew or try out other roads to integrity. Disgust hides despair, if only in the form of a "thousand little disgusts," which do not add up to one large feeling of remorse.
- *The related principle of social* order is wisdom, which is the ability to face adversity with equanimity and contemplate the possibility of life's end without bitterness or disappointment.
- *Ritualization*. The stage-specific ritualization is "**philosophical**" (Erikson, 1980, p. 21); that is contemplative. Ego integrity implies an emotional sense of wholeness that permits participation in communal activities, as well as an acceptance

of the responsibility of leadership. Maintaining a sense of integrity in the face of disintegration of body and mind provides the sustenance for durable hope in wisdom.
- *Ritualism.* The stage-specific ritual is **dogmatism**, which is the antithesis of openness and flexibility to adapt to changing circumstances (Erikson, 1980, p. 21). When linked with undue power, dogmatism can become coercive orthodoxy.

Case Illustration

Since we could find no published clinical material by Erikson, we substituted an examination of his first psychobiography of Martin Luther. What follow this introduction is a summary of some major themes contained in Erikson (1958).

Martin Luther is remembered as a compelling, historical giant who launched the Reformation, a religious rebellion against the Roman Catholic Church, and changed the course of history. Erik Erikson chose Martin Luther to be the subject of his first significant psychoanalytic-historical study, *Young Man Luther* (1958), reframing the details of Luther's youth into an example illustrating the interpretation of Erikson's life cycle model (1950). Regrettably, there are so few details about Luther's early life that it had to be reconstructed largely from inference stretched around the few known facts. This summary focuses on Luther's young adult identity crisis, the psychosocial moratorium, and Erikson's controversial interpretation of Luther's psychological dynamics. The biographical parallels between Erikson's youth and that of Luther's are well known, in particular the ambivalent relationship each had to their fathers and the need to postpone entry into adulthood and its identification with work. Because Erikson apparently wrote such limited therapy case write-ups, we turn to the examination of his first psychobiography subject, Martin Luther, with its unavoidable immersion in history as context.

Luther's time was a world of cataclysmic, violent cultural, political, and religious change. It was a world Luther understood as a combat zone where the forces of good and evil contested in a palpable way for supremacy. Martin Luther was born on November 10, 1483 in Eisleben, a small Saxon town in east-central Germany and died there during a chance visit on February 18, 1546 at the age of 63. His father, Hans Luder, was a copper and silver miner who demonstrated early potential for improving his family's prospects. Having high aspirations for his son, he wanted Martin to marry early and become a lawyer, then an emerging profession with some measure of status and security. Mother, Margerethe Lindemann, came from an old family and the marriage seemed a good one. Her family helped Hans eventually prosper through the smelting business. Four boys were born to this union, two died of the plague; Martin the second son, and Martin's younger brother, James, survived. The question of the nature of the relationship between Luther and his father has long preoccupied scholars. It is true that children were considered the property of the father and were regarded as little beasts that needed domestication.

In such an authoritarian world, fathers ruled at home and as teachers in the classroom. Cruel punishment could be easily administered at the whim of the authority figure. Luther's few recorded reflections about his mother speak to her whippings as needing to be restrained lest they break a child's spirit. It is generally thought that father was a harsh, dictatorial disciplinarian who had a life plan that Martin was to fulfill. Martin had a promising student career at the University of Erfurt where he earned a baccalaureate degree in 1502, received a master's degree in January 1505 and in the spring began the study of law. Martin's abrupt decision to reverse course to not become a lawyer, to not marry and, instead, enter the monastery at age 21, left his father angry and resentful, reflecting a lifelong ambivalent relationship toward his father (Marius, 1999, pp. 19–42).

Erikson emphasized the many variations of son–father relationships in Luther's life including, son Martin and father Hans; monk Martin and consoling superior Dr. Staupitz; subject Martin and prince and protector Frederick the Wise; sinner Martin and the merciful Christ; son Hans and father Martin; rebellious priest and punishing Father, His Holiness the Pope; and later when the religious schism was irreconcilably clarified, the Pope called Martin "the child of Satan" and Martin called the Pope the "Antichrist." The theme of obedience or defiance by the son toward the father (or father symbol) was a powerful organizer throughout Martin's life.

Our interest lies is in the 12-year period between 1505, the year Luther entered the monastery at age 21, and 1517, the year he protested the Papal indulgences (payments now for salvation later) and nailed his 95 theses on the Church door in Wittenberg at the age of 32. At the time Luther decided to enter the monastery, he was a promising law student who, as Luther described the episode decades later, became terrified during a terrible thunderstorm. Luther understood the storm as a supernatural event with a divine message. Believing he was about to die he cried out "Help, St. Anne (the patron Saint of Miners). I will become a monk." Luther's sensitive, superstitious temperament was given to bouts of severe sadness and agonizing self-doubt and an all-consuming fear of death. Because of the prevailing opinion that monks were considered fundamentally lazy people who lived lives as hermits at the church's expense, they were resented. So to give up a law career to become a monk, even a monk-theologian, was to become a nonentity.

Luther entered the Augustinian monastery rather than the neighboring Carthusian (both were situated in Erfurt), probably because the Augustinians were better known as having an academic orientation, while the Carthusian order was more revered in monastic life and embraced a stricter set of ascetic practices. The Augustinian monastery was founded and supported by Elector Frederick the Wise of Saxony (1463–1525), who was to become Luther's prince and protector. Frederick the Wise was a good friend of Johannes Staupitz, the man who was to become a father figure to Luther providing him with reassurance and comfort as Luther struggled with his decision and his inner demons of torment and unworthiness.

Monastic life was rigid and systematically regimented; every hour of every day was occupied in a planned schedule, including seven of prayer. After a year as a novice, Luther made his final vow renouncing the outside world and accepting a life of poverty, obedience, and chastity. In 1507 at age 23, he was ordained in the priesthood.

At his first mass he was speaking haltingly, terrified he would make a mistake. His father was in the congregation and, according to Luther, angrily said after mass, "Don't you know that it is written 'Honor thy father and mother?' Luther explained that the decision to defy his father and become a monk was based on Martin's understanding of a divine message conveyed in a storm to which Hans replied," Take care that it was not an evil spirit."

On the occasion of his son's ordination, Martin's father challenged his son's capacity to remain celibate, taunted Martin's sincere attempt to repress sexuality, and refused to "give him away" in marriage to the church. This spiritually unsuccessful ordination ended Martin's honeymoon with monasticism and led to an eventual divorce when Martin suddenly married at age 41. This pleased his father whose now only son could extend the Luther name into the next generation. Later Luther was to declare that no young man under 30 should enter monastic life due in large part to the unnatural pressure to restrain sexual impulses, which compromised the vows of purity and chastity so necessary to succeed as a monk. Considering the positive side of father's ambivalence toward his son, it needs to be mentioned that his father on some level also was proud of his son's accomplishment in that he invited many friends to observe the ordination mass and made a substantial monetary gift to the monastery (Erikson, 1958, pp. 144–147, 237; Marius, 1999, pp. 43–54).

Legend has it that after becoming a priest Luther experienced an unusual episode in the monastery choir and "suddenly fell to the ground, raving like one possessed and roared with the voice of a bull: "It isn't me!" (Erikson, 1958, p. 23). Erikson understood this "… fit to be part of a most severe identity crisis – a crisis in which the young monk felt obliged to protest what he was *not* (possessed, sick, sinful) perhaps in order to break through to what he was or was to be" (Erikson, p. 36). Erikson believes the episode to be plausible given Luther's undisputed series of extreme mental states involving weeping, sweating, and fainting coupled with a manic attitude toward work, industry, and productivity throughout his life.

In later life, during one of these affective storms or "spells," Luther remembered Dr. Staupitz saying, "It couldn't have been Christ who terrified you, for Christ consoles." Understood as a manifestation of intense neurotic ambivalence toward the father, "The fit [in the choir], then, is both unconscious obedience to the father and implied rebellion against the monastery; the words uttered both deny the father's assertion (that his son was possessed rather than holy) and, confirm the vow which Martin had made in that first known anxiety attack during the thunderstorm when he had exclaimed, 'I want to be a monk'" (Erikson, 1958, pp. 37–38). Erikson explained Luther's intense absorption in scatology and accompanying struggle toward rebellion as an overarching displacement: "a central theme in this [ambivalent paternal] transference was anal defiance" (Erikson, p. 147). Luther's struggle to attain a cohesive self-identity was to continue for another 10 years.

Erikson regarded Luther's depression a natural mood, both an adaptation to the human condition of a young man and a dimension of existence common to monastic life called *tristitia*, the melancholic world mood of the religious man. Luther seems to have "later abandoned the melancholic mood altogether for occasional violent mood swings between depression and elation, between self-accusation and the abuse of others. Sadness, then, was primarily the over-all symptom of his youth, and was a symptom couched in a traditional attitude provided by his time" (Erikson, 1958, p. 40).

Religious scholars refer to this period from 1507 to 1517 as the "years of silence," ironically, because, while Luther certainly was noisy, he had not yet become notorious (Marius, 1999, pp. 54–78). During this time at the monastery, Luther left the cloister in 1511 and journeyed to Rome with another Augustinian monk as part of a larger delegation to represent his monastery in a reorganizational dispute with the Vatican over who should control the Augustinian monasteries in Saxony. As he toured Rome, his disillusionment with the state of affairs in the Roman Catholic Church took hold, in particular the marketing of religious relics and the practice of selling indulgences.

Luther reluctantly earned his doctorate in theology at the age of 28 in 1512 and later was reassigned outside to an Augustinian branch, the church in Wittenberg, as its resident priest to preach to its monks and parishioners. As Luther prepared and delivered his sermons on Psalms, Romans, Galatians, and Hebrews, he had a revelation that led him to interpret the scriptures in a different way that challenged traditional Roman Catholic teachings to Papal authority. Controversy and dangerous times followed for Luther. However, he had found his voice and it was loud and steady. The spark that ignited the rebellion and eventually led to the Protestant Reformation was the arrival of Johann Tetzel. By 1517, the unscrupulous and highly successful indulgence seller, Tetzel, was approaching Wittenburg to exploit money from superstitious, vulnerable townsfolk. Luther had had enough; he became mobilized and nailed his 95 theses to its church door. This signaled the sharpening of Luther's direction; at age 32 his resolve and his life's purpose became clear. With this event, Erikson closed Luther's 12-year psychosocial moratorium.

Erikson applied the term "psychosocial moratorium" to designate a "span of time after childhood, but before their deeds and work count toward a future identity" (Erikson, 1958, p. 43). It was a means of marking time, not infrequently by continuing one's education, often before arriving at a crossroads during the late twenties, at which time a commitment to a direction in life may emerge, with a sense of purposefulness, in what can be called a second birth, or rebirth, the forming of a resilient sense of ego identity (Erickson, 1950b, 1958; Marius, 1999).

Summary and Conclusions

Erikson's model uses a mixed metaphor, combining the epigenetic and contextual metaphors to describe his version of development. A child's early development follows the same course as that articulated by Freud in his description of the unfolding libidinal phases: oral, anal, and phallic/oedipal. Erikson complements these phases by extending libidinal development into adolescence, young adulthood, and onto senescence. What is novel about Erikson's approach is that he views all development to occur not only in interaction with the maternal responses to the child, but also within the broader social context in which the child is situated.

The outcome of each developmental stage is a mental attitude toward life tasks that may be positive if the child is successful in negotiating that stage, or negative if the child fails to negotiate it successfully. The polarities that characterize these outcomes are the ones made famous by his "Eight Ages," i.e., Basic Trust vs. Basic Distrust, Autonomy vs. Shame and Doubt, Initiative vs. Guilt, Industry vs. Inferiority, Identity vs. Identity Confusion, Intimacy vs. Isolation, Generativity vs. Stagnation, and Ego Integrity vs. Despair.

The reason we view this model as making use of a mixed metaphor is that, unlike other organismic theories that deal with the way in which a child metabolizes nurturance, Erikson proposed that the outcome of a stage leads to the expression of a psychological attitude in relation to others and to life tasks. These psychological attitudes appear to be the products of the meanings drawn by the person from his or her life experiences. Erikson fails to explain how it is that good nurture leads to trust, that is, how a set of physical/biological interactions with the environment leads to a psychic structure that translates those interactions into experiences that have meanings; meanings that reflect a person's interactions with others. This developmental model highlights the incoherences that result from the uses of a mixed metaphor. There is something poetical rather than literal in this theory. Erikson's background as an artist obviously contributed to a humanistic perspective that helped this theory to achieve a high level of popularity in its time.

Keywords Affiliation • Antipathetic • Authenticity • Authoritarianism • Autonomy vs. shame and doubt • Basic ego strength or virtue • Basic trust vs. basic mistrust • Care • Competencies • Dogmatism • Ego dystonic • Ego syntonic • Elitism • Fidelity • Formalism • Generativity vs. stagnation • Hope • Identity vs. Identity confusion • Ideology • Idolism • Impersonation • Industry vs. inferiority • Inhibition • Initiative vs. guilt • Integrity vs. despair • Intimacy vs. isolation • Judicious • Legalism • Love • Numinous • Philosophical • Principle of social order • Psychopathology • Purposefulness • Radius of significant relations • Ritualism • Ritualization • Sympathetic • Technological ethos • Totalism • Transmission of values and ideals • Will • Wisdom

References

Austrian, S. G. (Ed.). (2002). *Developmental theories through the life cycle*. New York, NY: Columbia University Press.

Coles, R. (1970). *Erik H. Erikson: The growth of his work*. Boston: Little, Brown.

Erikson, E. H. (1950). *Childhood and Society*. New York: W.W. Norton.

Erikson, E. H. (1958). *Young man Luther: A study in psychoanalysis and history*. New York, NY: W.W. Norton.

Erikson, E. H. (1968). *Identity, youth and crisis*. New York, NY: W.W. Norton.

Erikson, E. H. (1969). *Gandhi's truth*. New York, NY: W.W. Norton.

Erikson, E. H. (1980). Elements of a psychoanalytic theory of psychosexual development. In S. I. Greenspan & G. H. Pollack (Eds.), *The course of life: Psychoanalytic contributions toward understanding personality development, Vol. I: Infancy and early childhood*, National Institute of Mental Health. Washington, DC: US Government Printing Office. pp. 11–61.

Friedman, L. J. (1999). *Identity's architect: A biography of Erik Erikson.* New York, NY: Scribner.

Goethe, J. W. (1774/2004). *The sorrows of young Werther* (B. Pike, Trans.). New York, NY: Modern Library, Random House.

Marius, R. (1999). *Martin Luther: The Christian between god and death.* Cambridge, MA: Belknap Press of Harvard University.

Mitchell, S. A., & Black, M. (1995). *Freud and beyond: A history of modern psychoanalytic thought.* New York, NY: Basic Books.

Roazen, P. (1976). *Erik H. Erikson: The power and limits of a vision.* New York, NY: Free Press.

Vaillant, G. F. (1977). *Aadaptation to life.* Boston: Little, Brown and Company.

Major Works

Erikson, E. H. (1937). Configuration in play – Clinical notes. *Psychoanalytic Quarterly*, *6*, 139–214.

Erikson, E. H. (1940). On submarine psychology. Written for the Committee on National Morale for the Coordinator of Information. Unpublished manuscript.

Erikson, E. H. (1942). Hitler's imagery and German youth. *Psychiatry*, 5, 475–493.

Erikson, E. H. (1945). Childhood and tradition in two American Indian tribes. *The Psychoanalytic Study of the Child*, *1*, 319–350.

Erikson, E. H. (1946). Ego development and historical change – Clinical notes. *The Psychoanalytic Study of the Child*, *2*, 359–396.

Erikson, E. H. (1950). Growth and crises of the 'Healthy Personality.' In C. Kluckhohn and H. Murray (Eds.). *Personality in nature, society, and culture* (2nd ed., pp. 185–223). New York, NY: Knopf.

Erikson, E. H. (1951). Sex differences in the play configurations of preadolescents. *American Journal of Orthopsychiatry*, *21*, 667–692.

Erikson, E. H. (1953). Wholeness and totality. In C. J. Friedrich (Ed.). *Totalitarianism.* Cambridge, MA: Harvard University Press.

Erikson, E. H. (1956). Ego identity and the psychosocial moratorium. In H. L. Witmer and R. Kosinsky (Eds.). *New perspectives for research in juvenile delinquency, U.S. Children's Bureau Publication #356* (pp. 1–23).

Erikson, E. H. (1958). The nature of clinical evidence. *Daedalus*, 87, 65–87.

Homburger, E. (1937). Configurations in Play. The Psychoanalytic Quarterly, 6, 139–212.

Supplementary Readings

Berzoff, J. (1989). Fusion and heterosexual women's friendships: Implications for expanding adult developmental theories. *Women and Therapy*, *8*(4), 93–107.

Gergen, K. J. (1991). *The saturated self: Dilemmas of identity in contemporary life.* New York, NY: Basic Books.

Levinson, D., & Levinson, J. (1996). *The seasons of a woman's life.* New York, NY: Knopf.

Mitchell, S. J. (1993). *Hope and dread in psychoanalysis.* New York, NY: Basic Books.

Section V
Interpersonal Theory

Interpersonal theory places primary emphasis on social relationships, rather than on individual intrapsychic dynamic, as the source of the experiences that are responsible for the formation of the self and its development. In contrast to object relations theories, interpersonal theory places less emphasis on the children's fantasies, wishes, as critical to the formation of intrapsychic structures. Its focus is on individuals' needs for relationships and the anxieties generated when those needs are threatened.

Harry Stack Sullivan, the founder of the interpersonal school, first used the term "interpersonal theory" to describe his approach to psychiatry because he believed that it is an "illusion" to consider that personal individuality can exist or develop independently from relationships (Sullivan, 1950). The interpersonal perspective is in contrast to Freud's drive model, which places primary emphasis on the development of internal processes, and is closer to the object relations viewpoint. However, it differs from object relations theories in that it does not focus on the internalization of relationships or of others as central to personality formation. From the perspective of interpersonal theory, it is possible to understand people only by observing their interpersonal interactions, and a personality can develop only through interpersonal interactions. Healthy development is dependent on relationships.

This theory also sees anxiety as resulting from interpersonal events. As such, it suggests that the focus of treatment should be on the social or the interpersonal situation within which people live, rather than on their internal individual dynamics disconnected from their interpersonal context. Psychotherapeutic treatment must include that the therapist not only observes the patient, but also participates in the interaction with the patient through the establishment and maintenance of a relationship. Just as a therapist operating from a cognitive perspective is primarily interested in patients' dysfunctional thinking, an interpersonal therapist is primarily interested in helping patients become more aware of their dysfunctional relationship patterns, as well as how patients perceive themselves in the psychotherapeutic relationship. Interpersonal theory, therefore, puts the therapist in a more active role than classical psychoanalysis proposes.

With its stress on the importance of the social context as critical to personality development, interpersonal theory represents a sharp break from prior theories as it embraces the contextual root metaphor rather than an organismic metaphor. This shift places the theory within the social constructivist philosophical tradition. The theory has influenced other theoretical perspectives that have incorporated the importance of interpersonal dynamics into their approach. For example, relational theories have drawn from the interpersonal perspective. Interpersonal theories share an awareness of the importance of both patients' and therapists' contribution to the intersubjective field within which psychotherapeutic gain can occur.

Some confusion surrounds the differences between "interpersonal" and "relational" theories. As mentioned previously, Sullivan called his theory "interpersonal." Since then, many other theories have emerged that have at their core an emphasis on the dynamics of human relations. Thus, the umbrella term "relational" has been loosely applied to any theory with an emphasis on human relations and the significance of the social context. Mitchell (1991) states that "all of the major currents within postclassical psychoanalytic thought have grappled, to different degrees, and each in its own fashion, with the replacement of Freud's drive metapsychology with a theoretical framework based most fundamentally on relations between self and others." (p. 5). Mitchell chooses to give priority to the interpersonal world over the biological realm. According to Berzoff, Flanagan, and Hertz (1996), this position now dominates all of the postclassical trends of psychoanalytic thought.

A shortcoming of current relational theories is their avoidance of devising a developmental theory. In part, this is due to methodological considerations, as the focus of those theories is on the clinical setting and the here-and-now interactions between therapists and patients rather than on factors located in the patients' past that led to the current dilemmas. In part, it is also because its constructivist approach requires that a developmental theory reflect the social and cultural values and outlook of the setting in which it is formulated. In this view, developmental theories are ethnocentrically derived narratives whose validity is difficult to establish. Consequently, we are unable to include any relational theory, other than that of Sullivan, in this work.

References

Berzoff, J., Flanagan, L. M., & Hertz, P. (1996). Inside out and outside in: Psychodynamic clinical theory and practice in contemporary multicultural contexts. Northvale, NJ: Jason Aronson.

Mitchell, S. A. (1991). Editorial philosophy. *Psychoanalytic Dialogues*, 1, 1–7.

Sullivan, H. S. (1950). The illusion of personal individuality, *Psychiatry*, 13, 317–332.

Chapter 12
Harry Stack Sullivan (1892–1949)

Publishing Era (1925–1947)

Biographical Information

Harry Stack Sullivan was born on February 21, 1892 in Norwich, New York, the only child of Timothy Sullivan and Ella Stack Sullivan. Timothy was a laborer working on Ella's father's farm when they married in 1885. Her family felt that she was marrying beneath her status. Timothy and Ella had previously lost two boys, both born in the month of February, one in 1888 and the other in 1890. The first baby died in convulsions due to cholera infantum. The second baby also died in convulsions due to entero colitis (Perry, 1982). Given these circumstances, it is likely that Harry's mother felt a special sense of protectiveness over him.

His background was Irish-American and Catholic. His mother and her family were the most important figures in his upbringing, while knowledge of his father and his father's family is scant. He eventually came to believe that his mother actively kept him apart from his father, and it was only after her death, when Sullivan was in his thirties, that he was able to come to know his father. The one way that Sullivan's father remained involved and influential was in his insistence on regular church attendance. Exposure to the sexual asceticism taught by the church later impressed Sullivan as posing problems for young adolescents. Being an only child and growing up without a connection to his father, Sullivan was led to theorize that all boys who are only children had problems with their fathers (Perry, 1982).

From ages 2½-4, his mother was absent and his grandmother raised him. The reasons for this absence are unknown, but some speculate that it may have been due to a hospitalization for depression. At this time the family moved to a farm in the village of Smyrna in rural Chenango County in south central New York State, where only a few hundred people lived. Until his schooling began at age 5½, he had no access to other children. His relationships were with adults, mainly women, and with farm animals. His father was rarely available as he worked all day on the farm. His interpersonal theory was undoubtedly influenced heavily by the loneliness he felt in his early years.

Through the years, Sullivan referred to himself by several different names. He used the name Harry Stack Francis Sullivan, adding the name "Francis" when he was confirmed at age 13. He later used the name H.F. Sullivan, removing the name

J. Palombo et al., *Guide to Psychoanalytic Developmental Theories*,
DOI: 10.1007/978-0-387-88455-4_12, © Springer Science+Business Media, LLC 2009

"Stack" because he felt he had not lived up to the high hopes his mother had for the Stack name. Still later, as a surgeon in Chicago, he went by the name H. Stack Sullivan. He eventually settled on the name Harry Stack Sullivan (Perry, 1982).

In the early grades at school, he was a loner until he found his first "chum" at age 8½, an event that he later identified as vital to his psychological survival. His chum's name, Clarence Bellinger, was 5 years older than Harry. Clarence lived on a nearby farm, though they did not meet until they encountered each other through school. Their relationship grew progressively more intimate over a period of 6 years until Clarence left to study medicine. Indications are that this intimacy was not sexual (Perry, 1982). Clarence's departure left Harry feeling alone once again until he graduated from high school 2 years later. He was valedictorian of his high school class, graduating in 1908 at age 16.

The high rate of suicide for Chenango County at this time caught Harry's attention. This led him to an awareness of the impact of mental illness and served as an early impetus to a career in psychiatry. He won a scholarship to Cornell University and finally left Smyrna for Ithaca, New York. He started his higher education in the College of Arts and Sciences, planning originally to become a physicist. During his second semester at Cornell, at age 17, he struggled to come to terms with his sexuality. Sullivan considered the next 2 years to be a period during which he experienced a schizophrenic break. Though no hospital record exists to confirm it, it is likely that he spent at least some of the time between 1909 and 1911 in psychiatric hospitalization. He later theorized that the "lust dynamism" appeared at age 17 and that it had the potential to lead to a psychotic episode (Perry, 1982).

From 1911 to 1915, Sullivan attended the Chicago College of Medicine and Surgery. The period from 1915 to 1921 was difficult for Sullivan, as he struggled to find consistent and secure employment and to come to terms with the psychiatric issues that debilitated him while at Cornell. In his book *Conceptions of Modern Psychiatry* (1947) he states that he had his "first personal experience with psychoanalysis" (p. 178) in 1915. He continued to live in Chicago until 1921 when he left to begin working at St. Elizabeth's Hospital in Washington, DC. It was there that he started his formal study of schizophrenia. In 1926, he stated in a professional meeting that "interpersonal factors seem to be effective elements in the psychiatry of schizophrenia" (Sullivan, 1962, p. 104). This was his first formal use of the term "interpersonal" (Perry, 1982).

From 1925 to 1929, Sullivan ran an experimental treatment ward for schizophrenic patients at the Sheppard-Pratt Hospital in Baltimore. He selected employees who were very much like himself, eventually proposing the theory that "like cures like" (Sullivan, 1962, p. 223). He was among the first to use paraprofessionals to treat hospitalized patients with schizophrenia. Sullivan was given a great deal of freedom to set up the ward in whatever way he thought was most productive. He chose a ward of all male patients, and he selected and trained all the male attendants. No female staff was permitted on the ward. It was not widely known that, during those 5 years, almost all the men on the ward – both the attendants and the patients – were gay (Allen, 1995). He also held classes for the attendants and socialized with them at his home. Rumors of Sullivan's homosexuality persisted throughout his life. In 1927, at age 35, he began living with a 15-year-old boy named James

(Jimmie) Inscoe, to whom he referred as his foster son. It is unclear how they came to meet. They lived together for 20 years.

Starting in 1926, Sullivan began the effort to find a place for psychiatric research in the scientific community. He organized the First Colloquium on Personality Investigation in 1928. He also campaigned for the improvement of psychiatric education for medical students (Perry, 1982).

Sullivan left Sheppard-Pratt Hospital and moved with Jimmie Inscoe to New York City in 1930. His father died in 1931. In that same year, Sullivan started a private practice, but he did not get as many patients as he had hoped. He applied for bankruptcy a year later and continued to have great financial difficulties for the rest of his life.

Sullivan founded the journal *Psychiatry* in 1938 and served as one of the three coeditors, along with Ernest Hadley and Thomas Harvey Gill. He left New York City in 1939 when he was offered the post of professor and chair of a new Department of Psychiatry at Georgetown University Medical School. He lived in Bethesda, Maryland for the rest of his life. He was a consultant for the Selective Service during World War II. The dropping of the atomic bomb on Hiroshima in 1945 affected him profoundly, confirming for him the fragility of the human condition. This event propelled him to use the last 3 years of his life to engage in efforts to help others acquire knowledge about raising children to become productive, creative, and happy people.

Sullivan went to Europe in 1949 for a meeting of a new organization, the World Federation for Mental Health. On his way home from the trip he passed through Paris, France. He died in Paris from a meningeal hemorrhage on January 14, 1949 at age 57. During his life time, Sullivan published a single book, *Conceptions of Modern Psychiatry* (1947), all the other works were published posthumously by his students, who collected and edited his lecture notes (Mullahy, 1952; Sullivan, 1954, 1956, 1964, 1972).

Theory of Development

Freud had differentiated neurotic transferences from psychotic transferences. He believed that patients with psychotic transferences were not amenable to treatment through psychoanalysis because they could not form analyzable transferences. Sullivan took the revolutionary step of extending Freud's psychoanalytic theory to the treatment of severe mental disorders, especially schizophrenia. At the time, most psychoanalysts agreed with Freud that those conditions were incurable. In contrast to Freud, Sullivan insisted that social and cultural factors accounted in large part for the conditions (Sullivan, 1962).

The Self-System

Sullivan proposed that the **self-system** was central to each person's personality organization. It begins in infancy and is reinforced by other's responses. Eventually, a set of personality traits emerge that coalesce around the person's self-esteem. Sullivan differed with Freud in several ways. First, he viewed anxiety as resulting primarily from social interactions. Second, for Sullivan, the unconscious depended upon the individual social context. He used the term "covert processes" (Sullivan, 1953, p. 177) to refer to private experiences that are not susceptible to social influence. He believed, however, that these processes, though private, were derived from experiences that were essentially interpersonal. Third, Sullivan saw psychiatry as "an expanding science concerned with the kinds of events or processes in which the psychiatrist participates while being an observant psychiatrist" (Sullivan, p. 13). This notion of the psychiatrist as "participant observer" is in contrast to Freud's view of the analyst, whose stance should be detached, surgeon like, and antiseptic.

To a large degree, Sullivan based his theories on his personal experiences, in particular those of his grammar school and preadolescent years (ages 8–12). He proposed an interpersonal theory in which social and cultural factors interact with psychic forces to form the essence of personality. He believed that reciprocal relationships were essential to development, stating that all people need a "communal existence with a necessary environing medium" (Sullivan, 1953, p. 98). From this interpersonal perspective, he articulated a treatment approach that held that a human relationship could reach even the most disturbed patients. He found strong support in Sandor Ferenczi's work, as Ferenczi also had an interest in the treatment of cases with serious disorders and had wanted to extend psychiatry to include people of all diagnostic categories. Both Sullivan and Ferenczi disagreed with the view that analysts should take a detached stance, believing they should actively intervene on behalf of patients.

Sullivan emphasized the process through which human beings perceive their experiences and the outer world. Perception is located between the outer world and the person's mind or inner world. What ultimately resides in a person's mind is the result of interpersonal experiences. These experiences occur in three modes as follows:

1. The **prototaxic mode of experience** is the simplest and earliest mode of experience. The term "sentience" captures the essential quality of this mode of experience. It consists of a "discrete series of momentary states of the sensitive organism, with special reference to the zones of interaction with the environment" (Sullivan, 1953, p. 29). In the prototaxic mode, there is no logical sequence to events.
2. In the **parataxic mode of experience,** an individual experiences self as a separate unit. Characteristic of this mode is magical thinking. The person interprets events that occur in time as causally related; the first event causes the second event. When operating in this mode, a person interprets everything in terms of how it relates to self.
3. In the **syntaxic mode of experience**, children are capable of relying on consensual validation of their perceptions. In other words, instead of relying on their evaluation of causes for events, they are able to check out those evaluations with other people. This mode appears during the period of language development and involves developing a code that is based on past experience, which the person

can use in anticipation of future experiences. A characteristic of this mode of experience is the achievement of realistic appraisals of the world.

Dynamisms

Sullivan replaces Freud's idea of mechanisms of the human mind with the idea of **dynamism**. He defines dynamism as "the relatively enduring pattern of energy transformations which recurrently characterize the organism in its duration as a living organism" (Sullivan, 1953, p. 103). He sees personality as a dynamic living organism made up of interacting dynamisms, which are recognizable as a recurring pattern of identity. Personality is an ongoing dynamic relationship made up of dynamisms in a continuous state of flux. Sullivan identified two dynamisms that he saw as most relevant to psychiatry – the **fear dynamism**, which involves the maintenance of feelings of insecurities related to interpersonal situations, and the **lust dynamism**, which involves tensions pertaining to the genitals. He also identified another class of dynamism, those related to the zonal needs. He used the term "zonal needs" to account for "factors of biological organization which provide energy for transformation in several zones of interaction", such as the oral, anal and urethral zones (Sullivan, 1953, p. 124). Two dynamisms in this class are particularly relevant to the developmental epoch of infancy (1) the infant's need for food and water, which Sullivan states "is satisfied in the nursing situation as a dynamism, an integrating tendency," (Sullivan, pp. 124–125) and (2) the infant's need to be rid of solid and liquid waste products, which Sullivan sees as "concerned with the communal existence and functional activity of the organism" (Sullivan, p. 127).

Personifications

According to Sullivan, personality develops as a result of an enduring pattern of recurrent interpersonal situations. Through these interpersonal situations, infants develop **personifications** of themselves and of others; that is, inner representations that allow infants to make sense of themselves and of the world. The infant's personification of good/satisfying mother is the result of the patterns of behavior she exhibits in recurrent situations, which are elicited by the infant's needs. A personification is not the real mother; it is an inner representation based on the infant's experience. Infants differentiate their experience of their mothers into two personifications: good mother and bad mother. The self-system begins when the infant develops three personifications that organize experience. During **good me** experiences, the mother is pleased with the infant and supplies rewards of tenderness. These experiences refer to aspects of the self that the infant experiences as positive. **Bad me** experiences result from increases in the mother's anxiety. These experiences refer to aspects of the self that the infant experiences as negative. With **Not me** experiences there is intense anxiety. These experiences refer to aspects of the self that are so anxiety inducing that they are kept out of consciousness, cannot be communicated, and persist throughout life as symbols.

Developmental Epochs

Sullivan believed that the self is resistant to change. Further, he believed that the self is actively engaged in the effort to escape the influences of experience and that understanding this theorem was critical to undertaking psychiatric work. He refers to this as the **theorem of escape**. Sullivan applied a second theorem to interpersonal relations, which he called the **theorem of reciprocal emotion**. This theorem states that "integration in an interpersonal situation is a reciprocal process in which (1) complementary needs are resolved, or aggravated; (2) reciprocal patterns of activity are developed or disintegrated; and (3) foresight of satisfaction, or rebuff, of similar needs is facilitated" (Sullivan, 1953, p. 198).

Sullivan referred to the developmental stages in his theory as **developmental epochs**. He did not assign particular age ranges to his developmental theory, but believed that people move in an orderly progression from one stage to another. In his view, the person's social environment largely influences the timing of the movement from one stage to the next (Sullivan, 1947). These epochs include *infancy*, *childhood*, the *juvenile era*, *preadolescence*, *early adolescence*, and *late adolescence*.

Infancy

In the **infancy** epoch, which covers the first year of life, infants operate through the prototaxic mode of experience. They know only momentary states and have no sense of before or after, making no sequential connection between the two. Experience occurs in undifferentiated episodes. According to Sullivan, experience is an enduring record of the total state of the organism, which includes all the events impinging on it. Infants experience two types of tensions, tensions of need and tensions of anxiety.

Tensions of need. **Tensions of need** have their origin in the body. They are tensions that can be satisfied. Examples of this type of tension include oxygen starvation, food and water starvation, and injury to the body. Sullivan referred to these needs as "physicochemically conditioned recurrent needs," (Sullivan, 1953, p. 59) which require interpersonal cooperation, specifically tenderness, to satisfy. In Sullivan's view, satisfaction of a need resolves the tension in the related interpersonal situation.

Tensions of anxiety. Interpersonal situations bring about **tensions of anxiety**. These include anxiety induced in the infant from the mother's anxiety. Sullivan pointed out that mother's anxiety about *anything* induces anxiety in the infant, and the only way to reduce this tension is for the mother to stop being anxious. Sullivan sees anxiety as a source of disruption in interpersonal relations; it is "almost always an ingredient in breaking up interpersonal situations, which otherwise would be useful in the satisfaction of needs" (Sullivan, 1953, p. 95). Anxiety plays an important role in the infant's capacity to begin differentiating between experiences. To the infant, the mother sounds and looks different when she is anxious than she sounds and looks when she is not anxious. Infants at first anticipate and then later perceive a good, satisfying, mother or a bad, anxious, mother. Infants initially apply the discrimination of good/bad, satisfying/anxious to their mother and later apply it throughout life to all their interpersonal relationships.

In the latter half of the first year, infants develop the capacity to identify and differentiate experiences. Eventually they progress to a point of being able to generalize on these experiences. They are then able to organize what is primarily a prototaxic experience into more complex experiences, namely signs and symbols. This signals the transition from the prototaxic to the parataxic mode of experience. In the parataxic mode of experience, infants develop a connection to time, as they acquire the capacity to experience one event as immediately preceding or following another. They associate events that occur closely together as being causally related; although they can discriminate between similar and different occurrences.

At this point, infants begin learning about their bodies and can differentiate it from everything else. This differentiation, or pattern of experience, is important because with further experience it eventually evolves into a symbol that includes all that the infant could consider as "my," starting with "my body". This capacity also leads the infant to a beginning conception of external reality, that is, that which is *not* part of my body.

By the end of the ninth month, infants begin to organize experience into patterns. They experience anxiety when they perceive a threat to their fragile self-system. Learning occurs through the following processes, based on the **anxiety gradient**, that is the level and intensity of their discomfort, they recognize when anxiety is increasing and can alter their behavior to reduce their anxiety. Through trial and error, when infants experience success it is likely that they will repeat this behavior, even continuing to repeat it into adulthood. Infants can also differentiate between being rewarded and being punished. Typically, this occurs through their experiences of pain, the refusal of contact or attention from others, or the stimulation of anxiety. Through trial and error learning by human example, infants learn to identify facial expressions, such as smiling, frowning, crying, and also learn to distinguish "sounds *made by him* and sounds *heard by him*," (Sullivan, 1953, p. 149). The coordination of ear-receptors and the voice-producing apparatus leads to the development of speech.

Childhood

After 12 months, the developmental epoch of infancy ends and **childhood** begins. This epoch lasts until approximately the point at which formal education begins. The development of language marks the transition from infancy to childhood. Children thus enter the syntaxic mode of experience, which includes the acquisition of two key parts of interpersonal communication, gesture and speech. Children develop a baby talk and use words as one might use pictures in a book to illustrate communications that are not verbal. At this point, the child has learned the right word for a situation, a word upon which both child and mother agree. During this epoch, personifications of good mother and bad mother are fused into one real person.

Three important experiences occur in the socialization of the child: Interpersonal experiences are more frequent; they are more consistent, in that there are more repetitions of a particular pattern of events; and they involve the parents' expectations for the child. Sullivan referred to this final group of socialization experiences as "the *sanity* of the educational efforts" (Sullivan, 1953, p. 173). By this he meant that the parents' expectations of the child can affect the child's socialization based on whether the expectations match or do not match the child's capacities.

At this point in development, when children encounter a need that meets social disapproval, they feel compelled to struggle against that need due to the anxiety it generates. The child discovers at this time a new pattern of behavior, **sublimation**. Through this process, children are able to substitute a more socially acceptable behavior for a behavior that produces anxiety. This process occurs unconsciously. Learning involves refinements in behavior, which occurs through sublimation.

Throughout childhood, there are increasing demands from authorities for the child's cooperation, which creates a new tool through which to educate the child, fear. Punishment used to educate creates a new type of learning. The child sees connections between violations of authority and pain. Parents' efforts to teach, along with the peculiarities of their own personalities, produces a child who is either obedient, often associated with "good me," or a child who is rebellious, often associated with "bad me." Children are often unable to understand what authorities are demanding of them. In order to cope with these demands, the child begins to develop an ability to conceal and deceive, patterns often taught or modeled by authority figures.

Two patterns of behavior emerge, **rationalizations**, or words used to avoid anxiety or punishment; and **"as if" performances**, comprising dramatizations and preoccupations. During dramatizations, the child tries to act or sound like the adults that are serving as models. Preoccupations, by contrast allow the child to stay preoccupied with something so as to be left alone; if successful in avoiding anxiety, this pattern can lead ultimately to an obsessional style of behavior.

Sullivan believed that **malevolence** is perhaps the greatest disaster that occurs in childhood development. He described children who were in need of tenderness and who behaved in ways they thought would be successful in bringing it about. However, instead of being rewarded with tenderness they not only were denied that satisfaction, but also were treated in a manner that produced added anxiety. In these situations, children learned that showing a need for tenderness led to great injury, as a consequence, the direction of development changed because the children perceived the responses as stemming from a malevolent being and end up acquiring that personality trait.

Juvenile Era

The **juvenile era** begins with the entrance into school and ends with what Sullivan referred to as the finding of a "chum." The need for peer connections characterizes this epoch. It is a time when juveniles have their first experiences with socialization. The presence of other people complicates their world and modifies the limitations and idiosyncratic socializing influences of their homes. The school society begins to rectify or modify the personality traits the child acquired at the home.

Two contributions to growth occur in this era. First is the experience of social subordination, during which juveniles encounter a change in the type of authority they confront, such as those of schoolteachers, and others, who formally enforce limits. They have to respond to those demands and be able to see how their peers deal with these authorities. Second is the experience of social accommodation, during which juveniles realize the many differences that exist among people. They understand the necessity to accommodate to people of the same age, in all their differences.

During this epoch, juveniles are capable of seeing authority figures as people. As a result, they tend to verify with peers their perceptions of the relative strengths and weaknesses of parents. In addition, in this peer environment, two types of learning take place: competition and compromise, both of which can eventually develop into troublesome personality traits. The effect of this learning is to make it hard for juveniles to remember what went on in their childhoods, unless those experiences had been appropriate. Eventually, with the increasing power of the self-system to control awareness, juveniles can give up their childhood viewpoints.

At this time, juveniles also begin to perceive the existence of social in-groups and out-groups. According to Sullivan, in juvenile society, there are three areas into which one can fit - popular, average, and unpopular; to be considered part of the out-group leads to feelings ostracized. By the end of this era, juveniles will ideally achieve the following abilities (a) the ability to recognize the needs that arise in interpersonal relations, (b) the ability to recognize the circumstances that lead to the satisfaction of those needs, and (c) the ability to recognize when to stop taking chances to enhance their prestige.

Preadolescence

Preadolescence begins with finding a chum of the same sex. Sullivan specifies that this happens somewhere between 8½ and 10 years of age. Characteristic of this epoch is the first experience of love of another person and the beginning of the need for interpersonal intimacy. The preadolescent becomes sensitive to the needs, wishes, and priorities of another person. In the company of a chum, preadolescents feel freer to talk about matters that earlier they had learned not to talk about. Sullivan saw the acquisition of a chum as a protection against mental illness. He also saw the absence of a chum as an area of developmental concern.

This era presents great possibilities for psychotherapeutic change because preadolescents are now capable of seeing themselves through the eyes of another. This capacity makes it possible for them to correct ideas they have about themselves. An important part of this era is the developing patterns of leadership relationships. Male adolescents tend to form gangs, made up of interlocking groups of two persons who are chums, which Sullivan refers to as "two-groups." For the first time, consensual validation of the preadolescent's personal worth is possible. Sullivan speaks exclusively of males in this regard "because by this time the deviations prescribed by the culture make it pretty hard to make a long series of statements which are equally obviously valid for the two sexes" (Sullivan, 1953, p. 249).

The intimacy that comes from preadolescent socialization can correct a variety of what Sullivan referred to as **warps** developed earlier in development. For example, egocentric people often form a chumship with another who is also on the fringe of ostracism, thus becoming capable of feeling less ostracized. Whereas juveniles who come to preadolescence having taken on a malevolent personality are still driven in this phase to seek a chum, an entry into a group can open the preadolescent's mind to the possibility that he or she can be treated tenderly or be accepted. Those who learned in the juvenile era to pull people down in order to feel better about themselves often find themselves not needing to exploit this tendency in preadolescence. Isolated juveniles often become part of a group in preadolescence. Those who were irresponsible in the juvenile era often feel a greater need for intimacy and are able to become more mature in this phase. Sullivan proposes the following definition of love in this phase: "When the satisfaction or the security of another person becomes as significant to one as is one's own satisfaction or security, then the state of love exists" (Sullivan, 1947, pp. 42–43).

Preadolescents begin to develop the capacity to use judgment in the assessment and organization of social groups. Two-groups of chums interact with larger social groups, which in turn assess them for their status in the hierarchy of groups. Some preadolescents experience delays and do not feel the same compelling need for intimacy. These delays can increase the risk to the individual's personality, particularly if the preadolescent forms a relationship with an adolescent; the risk being the establishment of a homosexual way of life. Finally, preadolescents experience loneliness in its full impact in this phase. Lonely preadolescents will seek companionship even if this effort makes them feel intensely anxious. This effort to relieve loneliness despite intense anxiety often results in what Sullivan called "evidences of serious defect of personal orientation" (Sullivan, 1953, p. 262), a defect in orientation in living (as opposed to orientation in time and space) which may be due to a lack of experience needed to make correct appraisals of situations.

Early Adolescence

Early adolescence starts with the beginnings of genital interest, to which Sullivan refers as "the lust dynamism." As patterns of sexual behavior emerge, early adolescents find it necessary to make sense of life in this epoch. Their responses depend on how they handle three needs. These are (a) the need for personal security, that is, the freedom from anxiety; (b) the need for intimacy, that is, the need to collaborate with at least one other person; and (c) the need for lust satisfaction.

A change in the object that is to satisfy the need for intimacy surfaces; as shift occurs from seeking someone like themselves to seeking someone of the opposite sex. Lust collides with other dynamisms in the personality. Lust may collide with the need for security, as anxiety is associated with the motivation toward genital activity. The need for intimacy may collide with the need for security, as when adults are uncomfortable with the adolescent engaging in intimacy and when adolescents are vulnerable to ridicule from elders. The need for intimacy may collide with lust, which manifest as awkwardness in many situations. These collisions may lead preadolescents or early adolescents to get into homosexual or autosexual activity in order to satisfy lust. Adolescents often have difficult experiences with their first attempts at heterosexual activity. Examples of these difficulties include (a) precocious orgasm, which damages self-esteem and gives the appearance of impotence; (b) feelings of guilt, shame, aversion, or revulsion with anything associated with sexuality; and (c) preoccupation with the experience if it had not gone well, which can lead to a deterioration of self-respect.

Early adolescents are challenged to separate interpersonal relations that are based on intimacy from those that are based on lust. They must find a balance between their needs for intimacy and their wishes to satisfy their lust. When the lust dynamism matures prematurely, as with the early onset of puberty, it can result in immature responses such as Don Juanism. This response can manifest in overly lustful juveniles. Alternatively, it can result in what Sullivan refers to as women who are "teasers" and men who are "hymen hunters." These preadolescents have an overly strong need to be envied. The lust dynamism is a system of integrating tendencies or motives that leads people to desire to be involved with, or to avoid others. Sullivan believed that in the practice of psychiatry, it is essential to pay attention to the role that lust plays in a person's problems.

Late Adolescence

Late adolescence starts when youths discover that they enjoy genital behavior and develop an appreciation of how to fit that enjoyment into the rest of their lives. Great growth occurs during this era as late adolescents refine their limited experiences into expansive endeavors, such as the pursuit of higher education. At times, they may combine their need for friendship and for the expression of the lust dynamism into an interest in one person. Conflicts between what they have internalized through the earlier phases and the emerging wish for self-expression are common. When late adolescents have endured a great deal of anxiety in earlier epochs, this anxiety can affect their self-system, which could lead to inappropriate personifications of self and others, or distortions of how they see themselves and the world.

Limitations that arise internally because of handicaps from an individual's past may prevent favorable change from taking place. Sullivan called these limitations "restrictions on freedom of living" (Sullivan, 1953, p. 305). Examples include restricted contact with others that results from adopting an isolated way of living in order to minimize anxiety; or restricted interests that lead the late adolescent to avoid life challenges in order to minimize anxiety. Other examples include engaging in pseudosocial rituals that result from superficial ways of relating to people; ritual avoidances that close the person off from others through rationalizations; and ritual preoccupations in which intense interests serve to remove the late adolescents from contact with others.

Case Illustration

The following case material is taken from Kvarnes & Parloff (1976, pp. 12–13), in which Sullivan is acting in the role of consultant. The case is a 25-year-old male who is being treated in 1946 by Dr. Robert Kvarnes at Sheppard-Pratt Hospital in Maryland. In this vignette, Sullivan is responding to beginning case material presented to him by Dr. Kvarnes. The vignette serves as an illustration of the approach Sullivan takes to treatment, including his emphasis on the role played by lust in a person's problems, and the importance of the role played by a "chum" in a person's development (reprinted with permission from W.W. Norton & Company).

What I would like to know about anybody is largely missing. Some of it can be inferred, but none of it can be inferred very reliably. Starting from the present backward, which is certainly not the way I like to proceed, but it is sometimes necessary, we do gather that he has had some genital contact with women. That he came near, I gather, to marrying one. If he had any genital contact with her it was mutual manipulation, but anyway during his Navy career he did have some contact with loose women. He thought it was all unsatisfactory to them, I gather. He had some instances of precocious ejaculation, which would make him a member of the human race, male type. That he had an idea that his genitals were small and he has seen somebody else's. I suppose one's experience can be that private that one can have seen only one other penis in growing to this age. The next step - has he been able to establish any intimate relations with one of his own sex, and by intimate I mean the thing suggested on the auto trip, namely a great deal of free and revealing talk of himself and the other fellow. Then I have only to guess. I hear he made the trip with a chum. If he had a chum, that is jolly, but I would certainly be most enthusiastic to know about this phase that precedes his interest in women, when he would be either a success or a failure in establishing free and easy relations with another man. Even if I had no particular faith in developmental history (and I have very great faith in it), I could not overlook the fact that he was male, his friend was male, and therefore just to give an idea of what might be a wise basis for progress, I would like to know what experience he had in being frank, free, and easy with members of his own sex. It is inferable that he had a chum, but those inferences are risky. The whole history of his relationship with this man with whom he took the auto trip stands out as an exceedingly important field on which I have little data. Still, he did make the trip and they got as far as Kansas and they had an accident. I hope you know a lot about that accident. The shock of an accident to an unstable person would vary a good deal depending on whether the accident involved people other than the driving party and whether it seriously imperiled the life of his companion and finally himself, and the same with the accident on the return trip. These two people who had at least a speaking acquaintance were together 3 weeks or so, far, indeed, from home, and because it was a human contact not long before the appearance of a severe mental disorder, it would interest me deeply.

I hope you see why the interest in this. I am attempting to explore what I can expect to do as a man with a man, quite aside from the developmental importance of such events (Kvarnes & Parloff, 1976, pp. 12–13).

Summary and Conclusions

Sullivan extended Freud's psychoanalytic theory to the treatment of severe mental disorders. In contrast to Freud, however, he insisted that social and cultural factors played a significant role in these conditions. In Sullivan's view, the primary source of anxiety is social interactions. He emphasized three modes through which people perceive their experiences. Within the *prototaxic mode*, which is the earliest, there is no logical sequence to events. In the *parataxic mode*, the individual begins to experience a separate sense of self. The *syntaxic mode* is the period of language development, during which a person is able to evaluate causes to events and check them out with others.

Sullivan divides his developmental theory into *epochs*. During the epoch of *infancy*, the child experiences *tensions of need*, which originate in the body, and *tensions of anxiety*, which are brought about by interpersonal situations. Sullivan deliberately avoided using Freudian language, feeling that it was too distancing. For example, he replaces Freud's idea of mechanisms of the human mind with the idea of *dynamism*. He sees personality as made up of interacting interpersonal *dynamisms*, which occur as patterns that shape one's identity. Through these interpersonal situations, infants develop three *personifications* of themselves and others, which serve to organize their experiences: *good me*, aspects of self-experienced as positive; *bad me*, aspects of self-experienced as negative; and *not me*, aspects of self that are kept out of consciousness.

Language marks the transition from infancy to *childhood*. During this epoch, children interact more frequently interpersonally; as a result patterns of behavior emerge. The *juvenile era* begins with the acquisition of a "chum" and includes first experiences of socialization. The epoch of *preadolescence* includes the first experiences of love of another person. Challenges of this epoch include making sense of the need for personal security, the need for intimacy, and the need to satisfy lust. Finally, the challenge of Sullivan's final developmental epoch, *late adolescence*, is for each person to come to terms with genital behavior and to develop the means to fit that enjoyment into the rest of their lives.

Keywords Anxiety gradient • "As if" performances • Bad me • Childhood • Developmental epochs • Dynamism • Fear dynamism • Early adolescence • Good me • Infancy • Juvenile era • Late adolescence • Lust dynamism • Malevolence • Not me • Parataxic mode of experience • Personifications • Preadolescence • Prototaxic mode of experience • Rationalizations • Selective attention • Self-system • Sublimation • Syntaxic mode of experience • Tensions of need • Tensions of anxiety • Theorem of escape • Theorem of reciprocal emotion • Warps

References

Allen, M. S. (1995). Sullivan's closet: A reappraisal of Harry Stack Sullivan's life and his pioneering role in American psychiatry. *Journal of Homosexuality*, 29(1), 1–18.

Kvarnes, R. G., & Parloff, G. H. (1976). *A Harry Stack Sullivan case seminar: Treatment of a male schizophrenic*. New York, NY: W.W. Norton.

Mullahy, P. (Ed.) (1952). The Contributions of Harry Stack Sullivan: A symposium on interpersonal theory in psychiatry and social science. New York: Hermitage House.

Perry, H. S. (1982). *Psychiatrist of America: The life of Harry Stack Sullivan*. Cambridge, MA: Harvard University Press.

Sullivan, H. S. (1947). *Conceptions of modern psychiatry*. New York, NY: W.W. Norton.

Sullivan, H. S. (1953). *The interpersonal theory of psychiatry*. New York, NY: W.W. Norton.

Sullivan, H. S. (1962). *Schizophrenia as a human process*. New York, NY: W.W. Norton.

Major Works

Sullivan, H. S. (1924). Schizophrenia: Its conservative and malignant features. *American Journal of Psychiatry*, 81, 77–91.

Sullivan, H. S. (1927). Affective experience in early schizophrenia. *American Journal of Psychiatry*, 83, 467–483.

Sullivan, H. S. (1931). The training of the psychiatrist, IV: Training of the general medical student in psychiatry. *American Journal of Orthopsychiatry*, 1, 371–379.

Sullivan, H. S. (1936). A note on the implications of psychiatry: The study of interpersonal relations for investigation in the social sciences. *American Journal of Sociology*, 42, 848–861.

Sullivan, H. S. (1938). Anti-semitism. *Psychiatry,* 1, 593–598.

Sullivan, H. S. (1947). *Conceptions of modern psychiatry*. New York, NY: W.W. Norton.

Sullivan, H. S. (1950). The illusion of personal individuality. *Psychiatry*, 13, 317–322.

Sullivan, H. S. (1953). *The interpersonal theory of psychiatry*. New York, NY: W.W. Norton.

Sullivan, H. S. (1954). *The psychiatric interview*. New York, NY: W.W. Norton.

Sullivan, H. S. (1956). *Clinical studies in psychiatry*. New York, NY: W.W. Norton.

Sullivan, H. S. (1964). *The fusion of psychiatry and social science*. New York, NY: W.W. Norton.

Sullivan, H. S. (1972). *Personal psychopathology*. New York, NY: W.W. Norton.

Supplementary Readings

Allen, M. S. (1995). Sullivan's closet: A reappraisal of Harry Stack Sullivan's life and his pioneering role in American psychiatry. *Journal of Homosexuality*, 29(1), 1–18.

Kvarnes, R. G., & Parloff, G. H. (1976). *A Harry Stack Sullivan case seminar: Treatment of a male schizophrenic*. New York, NY: W.W. Norton.

Perry, H. S. (1982). *Psychiatrist of America: The life of Harry Stack Sullivan*. Cambridge, MA: Harvard University Press.

Section VI
Theories of the Self

Daniel Stern and **Heinz Kohut** represent contributors who departed significantly from the psychoanalytic theories in existence at the time. Although they do not share a common theoretical frame of reference, we group them together in this section because of their rejection of drive theory and their substitution of the concept of self for the tripartite model of the mind, the ego, the id, and the superego. However, each defines the concept "self" differently, although they appear to have in common the view that in speaking of the "sense of self" they refer to the person's subjective experience of being a self. For Stern, the self is a psychological structure with definable attributes, although the characterization of these attributes does not exhaust what constitutes a self. Kohut provides two definitions, the first, which is a narrow definition, the "sub-ordinate" view of the self, refers to "a specific structure in the mental apparatus (Kohut, 1991, p. 449). In the second definition, the "super ordinate" view of the self, the self is the "core of the personality" (p. 454), and is equivalent to the "person."

Stern, who came from a strong background in infant research, challenged the view that development can be reconstructed from adult psychopathology and that infants are not born with a sense of self. He proposed that development unfolds along the lines of a set of domains of the *self*, each domain beginning at a different point during development and each enduring throughout the rest of the life span. These domains rested on the empirical findings of infant research.

Kohut challenged a different aspect of psychoanalytic metapsychology. His dissent was much more inclusive than that of Stern; and his work incorporated findings from the clinical work with his patients. The implications of his contributions were far-reaching and the impact of that work contributed to the overthrow of the hegemony of ego psychology. Kohut made no claim of proposing a developmental theory, because of that what we present material taken from scattered references in his work and elaborated on by Palombo (see Palombo, 2008).

Kohut proposed that the concept of selfobject functions is central to our in-depth understanding of psychic processes that occur in the *self*, by which he referred to the person, rather than to the ego. For Kohut, the unique sources from which people draw in order to develop are the specific psychological functions that others perform, i.e., selfobject functions. These functions help the person maintain a sense of self-cohesion and well-being. Caregivers' empathy is instrumental in addressing children's needs. During our entire life span, we remain interrelated to others and dependent on others to provide us with the ambient needs that we require to survive.

Both Stern and Kohut began from a positivist perspective that privileged data collection that would confirm or falsify hypotheses, Kohut initially being an unwavering ego psychologist and Stern an infant researcher. However, in their later work, both drifted into a hermeneutic perspective that made the construction of a data-based developmental theory problematic. In this respect, both theories incorporate mixed metaphors and each model adheres to both organismic and contextual perspectives. Stern favored a narrative viewpoint, whereas Kohut's contributions led to a hermeneutic, interpretive viewpoint.

References

Kohut, H. (1991). Four basic concepts in self psychology (1979). In P. H. Ornstein (Ed.), *The search for the self: Selected writings of Heinz Kohut: 1978-1981* (Vol. 4, pp. 447–470). Madison, CT: International Universities Press.

Palombo, J. (2008). Self psychology theory. In B. A. Thyer (Ed.), *Comprehensive handbook of social work and social welfare: Human behavior in the social environment* (Vol. 2, pp. 163–205). New Jersey: Wiley.

Chapter 13
Daniel Stern (1934–)

Publishing Era: 1963 to the Present

Biographical Information

Daniel Stern was born on August 16, 1934 in New York City. His wife, Nadia Bruschweiler-Stern, is a pediatrician and child psychiatrist, and the Director of the Brazelton Centre of Switzerland. He and Nadia coauthored *The Birth of the Mother: How the Motherhood Experience Changes You Forever* (1998). His extensive use of empirical observation of the interactions between infants and their mothers formed the basis of his developmental theory. His ideas have served to challenge many long-held beliefs within the field of psychoanalytic developmental psychology.

Academic Training

After graduating from high school in 1952, Stern began a rigorous course of academic training that lasted until 1971, after which he began his teaching career. He also started at this time to study and write about mother–child interactions. Stern earned his B.A. in Biochemistry and Art History in 1956 from Harvard University in Cambridge, MA. He then went on to medical school at the Albert Einstein College of Medicine of Yeshiva University in Bronx, New York from 1956 to 1960, receiving his New York State Medical License in 1960 at the age of 26. His postgraduate training included a medical internship and residency at Bellevue Hospital in New York from 1960 to 1962, followed by research that he conducted as part of his military service at the National Heart Institute of the National Institute of Health in Bethesda, MD from 1962 to 1964. From 1964 to 1967, he completed his psychiatry residency with Columbia University Presbyterian Hospital and the New York State Psychiatric Institute, becoming Board Eligible in psychiatry in 1967. He earned a certificate in psychoanalytic medicine in 1971 after spending the years 1965–1971 working with the Psychoanalytic Clinic of Columbia University.

J. Palombo et al., *Guide to Psychoanalytic Developmental Theories*,
DOI: 10.1007/978-0-387-88455-4_13,

Teaching

Starting in 1972, Stern began working as a Lecturer for the Center for Psychoanalytic Training and Research at Columbia University in New York, a role in which he continues today. In 1985, he accepted positions as Invited Professor in both the Department of Child Psychiatry at the University of Geneva, Switzerland and the Department of Psychiatry and Pediatrics at the University of Padua, Italy. That same year he also became a nonresident member of the Centre for Advanced Studies in Behavioral Science in Stanford, CA. From 1986 to 1999 he served as Professor in the Department of Psychology at the University of Geneva. Starting in 1990 he also taught as an Adjunct Professor of Psychiatry at Cornell University Medical School. In 1994–1995, he was a Visiting Scholar in the Department of Pediatrics and Education at Harvard University. In 1995, he was the Julian and Jesse Harrison Distinguished Visiting Professor at the University of Tennessee in Memphis. He also served as an Invited Professor in the Department of Psychology at the University of Paris in 1996 and at the University of Rome in 1998 and 1999.

Publications

Stern's first publication was "Studies on starvation-induced hyper-mobilization of free fatty acids," published in the journal *Life Sciences* in 1963. He published three more articles that pertained to biological processes in 1964, 1965, and 1969. His first publication that explored the bond between mothers and infants was in 1971, "A micro-analysis of mother-infant interaction: Behavior regulating social contact between a mother and her three and one-half month old twins," for the *Journal of the American Academy of Child Psychiatry*. From here, he went on to publish more than 20 articles between the years 1971 and 1985 investigating the subtleties of the relationship between mothers and their children.

In 1985, he published the classic *The Interpersonal World of the Infant: A View from Psychoanalysis and Developmental Psychology*, which contains the heart of his developmental framework. He has since published five more books, including *Diary of a Baby* (1990), *The Motherhood Constellation: A Unified View of Parent-Infant Psychotherapy* (1995), *The Birth of the Mother: How the Motherhood Experience Changes You Forever* (1998), which he coauthored with his wife Nadia Bruschweiler-Stern, The *First Relationship: Infant and Mother* (2002), and *The Present Moment in Psychotherapy and Everyday Life* (2004). Between the years 1985 and 2000 he also published more than 40 additional articles and 65 book chapters, while also conducting hundreds of academic presentations.

The Boston Change Process Study Group

Formed in 1995, this group included psychoanalysts, developmentalists, and analytic theorists who came together with the mission of integrating knowledge of developmental studies with psychodynamic therapeutic considerations. The agenda of this group was to study the process of change as it occurs both in normal development and in psychoanalytic therapies (Boston Study Group, 2008). In addition to Daniel Stern, this group included his wife Nadia Bruschweiler-Stern, Karlen Lyons-Ruth, Ph.D., Alexander Morgan, M.D., Jeremy Nahum, M.D., Alexandra Harrison, M.D., Edward Tronick, Ph.D., and Louis Sander, M.D.

Stern published the article "The Process of Therapeutic Change Involving Implicit Knowledge: Some Implications of Developmental Observations for Adult Psychotherapy" (1998) in the *Infant Mental Health Journal* as a member of this group. This issue of the *Journal* contains several papers describing the work of the group and their proposed model of therapeutic change. This model offers the idea of "moments of meeting," in which "participants interact in a way that creates a new implicit, intersubjective understanding of their relationship and permits a new 'way-of-being-with-the-other'" (p. 300). In the same issue, Peter Fonagy attempted to place this model in the context of attachment theory. Fonagy highlights Stern's concept of "open space," in which there is "disengagement born of confidence of the availability of the other, presumably affirmed by the marked presence of the other at the 'moment of meeting'" (1998, p. 349). Fonagy cites this idea as being "at the heart of the change process" (p. 349) and further states that the group's assumptions lead to an interpersonalist psychology.

In 2004, Stern published, *The Present Moment in Psychotherapy and Everyday Life*, a work that summarizes his reflection on the discussions held with the members of the Boston Change Process study group. Seeming to move away from his early Piagetian constructivist position as seen in his work with infant observation, he appears to be steering in a more radical constructivist direction. In a section of the book titled "*The Nonexistent Past*," he states:

> There are past events that radically influence the present, not by actively shaping it in an ongoing fashion, but rather by imposing initial constraints and degrees of freedom on what are possible experiences. These constraints include neurophysiological alterations that are irreversibly fixed early in development. Due to sensitive/critical periods, trauma, conflict... *his past is no longer active. It is a past only in the historical sense or the narrative sense, when viewed from the outside. Phenomenologically it does not exist and never will exist* (our italics, p. 206).

His emphasis in this work is on the significance of implicit relational knowing and the effects of the mutual interaction between patient and therapist that can remain uninterpreted. Patients change in the therapeutic context because of the effects of their experience and not necessarily because of the revelations they encounter of unconscious dimensions of their conflicts.

The Web site for the Boston Change Process Study Group includes the following description of Stern's work:

> For more than thirty years he has worked at the interface between research and practice; between developmental psychology and psychodynamic psychotherapy; between infant observation/experimentation and the clinical reconstruction of early experience; between the interpersonal and intrapsychic perspectives. This work has served a bridging and integrating function in furthering our understanding of clinical theory, practice, and development.
>
> Boston Change Process Study Group (2008)

Stern currently lives in Geneva, Switzerland where he is an honorary professor of Psychology at the University of Geneva. He is also an Adjunct Professor of Psychiatry at Cornell University Medical School in Ithaca, NY and Lecturer for the Center for Psychoanalytic Training and Research at Columbia University in New York.

Theory of Development

Daniel Stern was among the first psychoanalysts to bring into developmental theory the emerging research on infants (see Lichtenberg, 1983). This research challenged many of ego psychology's preconceptions about early development. Stern's framework is built upon data gathered from infants observed in laboratory settings. He blended the observations derived from experimental work into a subjective/intersubjective framework, which he adapted into the interpersonal structural model of Sullivan (1953). As we have seen, whereas Mahler reformulated her observations to make her data conform to the drive/defense and ego psychological models, Stern rejected this retrospective and pathomorphic approach based on psychopathology. He offered instead a scheme that is not epigenetic but rather is based on a normative and prospective approach; that is, it uses principles of normal child development that are forward looking.

Stern began by challenging Mahler's claim that infants are born into an undifferentiated state from which they emerge through the process of separation-individuation. Infant research led him to conclude that human relatedness begins at birth. For Stern, the infant's sense of self is present at birth as a single, distinct, integrated unit, permitting the infant to be an agent of action, capable of experiencing feelings. Infant competencies include seeking stimuli, having innate preferences, and being capable of ordering their experiences and of maintaining self-regulation. This view departed from Freud's idea of a "stimulus barrier" protecting the infant from external stimulation (Freud, 1920), and from Mahler's idea of infants being born in a state of normal autism, unrelated to others (Mahler, Pine, & Bergman, 1975). Stern recognized that "The clinical infant breathes subjective life into the observed infant" (1985, p. 14), by which he meant that the clinical perspective can assist observers in understanding infants' experiences. He offered an organismic model of development that integrated biological, social, and subjective factors into a coherent theory.

In preference to the terms "stage" or "phase," which denote a specific epoch that reaches ascendancy and then recedes into the history of the life span, Stern chose the term "domain" to describe developmental eras. Each domain emerges during a specific period of the child's life; it continues and remains fully functional throughout the life span. The domains represent the adaptive tasks the infant must negotiate at a given time. They appear in an orderly temporal succession and are elaborated as the child matures. Basic clinical issues are issues for the life span, rather than issues of a particular developmental phase.

In *The Interpersonal World of the Infant* (1985), Stern proposed four domains: Domain I: *The Emergent Self*, Domain II: *The Core Self*, Domain III: *The Subjective Self*, and Domain IV: *The Verbal Self*. Later on, he added a fifth domain, Domain V: *The Narrative Self* (Stern, 1990).

Domain I: The Domain of the Emergent Self: 0–2 Months

Stern contends that from birth infants occupy a state of "alert inactivity" (Stern, 1985, p. 39), during which they are capable of taking in external events. During the first 2 months of life, infants are actively forming an **emergent sense of self**. Infants, therefore, "begin to experience a sense of an emergent self from birth" (Stern, 1985, p. 10). A total sense of self has not yet solidified; it is instead in a state that Stern referred to as **"coming into being."** Stern believes that the infant is already differentiated and is able to engage with others while in this state of emergence. Infants can thus distinguish accurately among a variety of people and stimuli, they are predesigned to be aware of self-organizing processes. They never experience periods of total self/other undifferentiation and are selectively responsive to external social events and never experience an autistic-like phase. There is no confusion between self and other in the beginning or at any point during infancy.

Stern proposed the following general principles with regard to the infant's capacities in this domain. Infants seek sensory stimulation and have distinct biases or preferences. From birth on, infants test hypotheses about what is occurring in the world. Furthermore, affect and cognition cannot be separated.

Four key processes are involved in the formation of a sense of an emergent self.

Amodal perception. This term refers to the infant's innate capacity to take information received in one sensory modality and translate it into another. In order to accomplish this subtle task, the infant is able to encode inputs from different modalities into representations. Infants are able to perceive qualities from any human behavior, represent them abstractly, and then translate them into other modalities.

Physiognomic perception. Infants live in the world of feelings; they translate all stimulation into affects.

Vitality affects. Infants experience feelings of vitality that do not fit into our existing vocabulary of feelings. Since the concept that Stern was trying to communicate did not fit well into any of the theories of affects that were current at the time, he identified feelings that were part of the domain of affect but not included in the original categorical affects. Consequently, he created the term *vitality affects* to capture the uniqueness of those affects. He used this term to distinguish vitality affects from the traditional or Darwinian *categorical affects* of anger, joy, and sadness. These affective qualities are difficult to detect, grasp, or quantify. They emerge when motivations, especially those related to appetites or tensions, change. "The infant experiences these qualities from within, as well as in the behavior of others" (Stern, 1985, p. 54). Dance and music are examples of vitality affects because they express affects without drawing from the signals that are part of typical categories of affect. The concept of vitality affects may offer clues to how an infant organizes experience.

Constructionist approaches *to relating social experiences.* At first, infants perceive the human form as disparate physical stimuli that require assembling. They are first able to delineate physical aspects of a person such as size, motion, and other attributes, which they then gradually integrate into a whole, such as a face, or later, a whole human body. The processes through which this occurs are assimilation, accommodation, identifying invariants, and associative learning.

Domain II: The Core Sense of Self: 2–7 Months

According to Stern, "the age of two months is almost as clear a boundary as birth itself" (Stern, 1985, p. 37). As the domain of the **core sense of self** gains ascendency, the period of roughly 2–6 months is perhaps the most exclusively social period of life. The social smile is in place, vocalizations directed at others come into play, mutual gaze is sought, predesigned preferences for the human face and voice are operating fully, and the infant undergoes that biobehavioral transformation that results in a highly social partner (p. 72). In addition, numerous changes occur in infants. They begin to make direct eye contact. Learning takes place more quickly than previously, motor patterns mature, and sensorimotor intelligence reaches a higher level. Infants approach interpersonal experiences with an organizing perspective that they chose for themselves. They have control over their own actions and are able to own their affects. They are aware that their bodies are distinct from those of others.

Two aspects of development organize the sense of a core self. First, there are the **self-invariant experiences**; second are the concerns with the social world or the **self with the other**.

Self-Invariants

Stern identifies four types of self-experiences that are necessary in the construction of a core self. The infant also needs experiences with others in order to organize a core sense of self. These self-experiences are considered to be fixed and as such are referred to as **islands of consistency** or as self-invariants; they are self-agency, self-coherence, self-affectivity, and self-history (pp. 72–82).

Self-agency. **Self-agency** refers to the infants' ability to be the author of their own actions. This type of self-experience includes making choices that precede an action, taking into account the feedback that does or does not occur during the action, and understanding the predictability of consequences that follow the action. Without self-agency, there can be paralysis, the sense of nonownership of self-action, and/or the experience of loss of control to external agents. Infants recognize these capacities as invariant experiences that they can express voluntarily and that can affirm their sense of agency.

Self-coherence. **Self-coherence** refers to the invariants in interpersonal experience that lend unity to the child's experiences. Several elements contribute to self-coherence. They include the **unity of locus**, the **coherence of motion**, the **coherence of the temporal structures**, the **coherence of intensity structures**, and the **coherence of form**. Without self-coherence, there would be fragmentation of bodily experience, depersonalization, and/or out-of-body experiences; that is, derealization. (a) The unity of locus subsumes the type of self-experience in which the child is aware that an entity can only be at one place at a time or that some events are contingent upon each other. For example, infants are preprogrammed to associate a mother's voice with the movement of her lips. They realize that an object they perceived visually is the same as the one they manipulate with their hands. (b) Under coherence of motion, Stern subsumes the infant's awareness that objects that are in motion retain their identity as objects, that is, an object that is displaced from one location to another remains the same object. (c) Coherence of temporal structures relates to the experience that time provides as an organizing structure within which different entities exist. Infants are aware that their hands move in synchronous fashion with other limbs. They understand that sensory experiences that occur simultaneously belong together. (d) Coherence of intensity structures reflects infants' awareness that the intensity levels of one set of behaviors match that of another set of stimuli. For example, infants are aware that the more intensely they cry, the greater the propioceptive feedback they get from bodily sensations. (e) Coherence of form refers to infants' experience of the invariance and continuity of physical objects in spite of the changes they may undergo. For example, infants continue to recognize that the same mother belongs to the same face even when she changes expressions from one moment to another.

Self-affectivity. **Self-affectivity** refers to infants' ability to recognize and come to expect that certain affects, such as joy, interest, anger, or distress, are associated with certain invariant events. These events include propioceptive feedback, internal patterns of arousal, and emotion-specific qualities of feelings. Propioceptive feedback comes from the affect states that co-occur with particular bodily states. The invariant patterns of arousal represent the autonomic nervous system's particular response to specific affect states; that is, the bodily sensations that accompany specific feelings. Each emotion is associated with a specific qualitative bodily response that accompanies each event. For example, infants experience invariant patterns of feeling response in conjunction with their mothers' smile, frown, or expression of joy. Without the sense of self-affectivity, there can be anhedonia, that is, the inability to experience pleasure or withdrawal into dissociative states, or both.

Self-history (memory). **Self-history** refers to the sense of continuity that is a critical ingredient of relationships with others. It is related to the capacity to form memories and to recall them in contexts with others. Infants' memories are nondeclarative, nonverbal, and nonconscious. For the most part, they are procedural. For example, infants can recognize the smell of mother's milk and her voice. This refers to recollections of episodes of real-life experiences that become averaged and generalized. If several episodes that are alike accumulate, they may soon lead the infant to form a generalized episode. Stern coined the term **RIGs (representations of interactions that have**

been generalized) to capture the basic unit for the representation of the core self: "A RIG is something that has never happened before exactly that way, yet it takes into account nothing that did not actually happen once" (Stern, 1985, p. 110). Without self-history, there can be temporal dissociation, fugue states, and amnesias.

The Self with the Other

During experience of the **self with the other**, infants can experience themselves as being with another person without merging or being in symbiotic states. They can experience security with another with whom they are in physical proximity. As they engage in games such as "peek-a-boo," they experience others as regulating the level of their arousal. During such period, through the mutual exchanges, caregivers regulate their infants' affect states and infants experience their caregivers as essential self-regulating others.

Infants' subjective experience of being with another is that the caregivers have their own organization, cohesion, and agency. Infants experience *lived episodes* or have experiences that connect a set of related events within a specific context, which if repeated become RIGs. The experience of being with the other gradually forms RIGs, which endows the infant with the capacity to create what Stern referred to as an **evoked companion**, that is, another who is present within oneself. Self-regulating experiences with inanimate things are the familiar experiences that children have with what Winnicott calls transitional objects.

Domain III: The Subjective Sense of Self: 7–15 Months

Between the seventh and ninth months infants enter the domain of the subjective sense of self, discovering that they have minds, and that other people have minds that are different from theirs. Infants become aware that they have an inner subjective experience and that these can be shared with someone else who also has inner subjective experiences. The infant has now developed the capacity for intimacy at the mental level.

In this domain, infants are still preverbal, so subjective experiences can only be shared with others through nonverbal means. The types of subjective sharing experiences that are possible include (1) Sharing the focus of attention – As someone points to an object, the infant, by following that person's line of vision, becomes aware of the person's intention. This process is called **joint attention**. (2) Sharing of intentions – Beginning at 9 months the infant intends to communicate, using signaling behavior such as pointing to objects, to do so. (3) Sharing of affective states – Infants at 9 months notice a connection between their own feelings and the feelings that they evoke in another person.

Stern used the term **interaffectivity** to capture the state that is created when parents use mirroring responses or respond to their infant with empathy. He describes three things that are necessary in order to achieve this state. The parent must be able to read the infant's feelings. The parent's behavior must be responsive to the infant's behavior. The infant must be able to feel the connection of this parental response to the original feeling experience.

Stern uses the term **affect attunement** to describe parental use of behaviors that induce a shared affective state. Affect attunement and amodal perception make intersubjective experiences possible. Without the sense of subjective self there can be cosmic loneliness or, at the other extreme, psychic transparency.

Domain IV: The Verbal Sense of Self: 15–30 Months

The domain of the **verbal sense of self** is the child's *world of words*. During the second year, the infant acquires language. Language creates two lines of development. The first line includes language as a new way to relate; the possible ways of being with another increase enormously. The second line acknowledges the potential problems that can arise as a result of this newfound capacity. For example, language causes a split in the experience of the self by "driving a wedge between two simultaneous forms of personal experience: as it is lived and as it is verbally represented" (Stern, 1985, p. 162).

At around 15 months, symbolic play and language are possible. The acquisition of language is a major influence in the achievement of separation and individuation, but it is also a powerful force in terms of its ability to bring about togetherness. At around 18 months, children are capable of delayed imitation of others' behaviors. This signals an end to Piaget's sensorimotor phase. "Deferred imitation" (Piaget, 1954) is now possible in which a child may observe behavior and later imitate it. This demonstrates several acquired capacities that include (a) The capacity to represent accurately events and other's actions, (b) the capacity to physically perform similar actions as others perform, (c) the capacity to represent in long-term memory and retrieve encoded representations, (d) the capacity to hold two versions of the same reality simultaneously, the representation of the act and their own execution of the act, and (e) the capacity to see the relationship between themselves and the person who performs the act.

Children now begin to see themselves objectively and to reflect on themselves. They begin to use pronouns "I," "me," and "mine" to refer to themselves. Empathic acts are now possible because the child is able to imagine the self as an object who can be experienced by the other as well as the other's subjective state.

Language leads to the ability to narrate one's own life story. Language also permits the infant to participate in the wider culture. Without language, with its ability to communicate meaning, the infant would be excluded from the culture, would learn little socialization, and would receive no validation of personal knowledge.

Stern also sees another side to language acquisition that it has an alienating effect between self-experience and togetherness. Language leads children to reinterpret self-experiences and intersubjective experiences so that they may no longer match their core preverbal experiences. The socializing effect of language leads to a slippage between the personal world and the external social world, so that, for example, the verbal account of an internal state is not entirely concordant with what the child experienced because words cannot exactly replicate the internal experience.

Domain V: The Narrative Sense of Self: 30–48 Months

The domain of the **narrative sense of self** can be described as the world of stories. Narrative-making may prove to be a universal human phenomenon reflecting the design of the brain. Other such phenomena are the need to categorize and the need to attach. Human activity is now understood in terms of psychological story plots involving the following: (1) actors have drives and motives directed toward goals, (2) stories take place in a historical context and physical setting that help to interpret the plot, and (3) each story has a dramatic line with a beginning, middle, and ending with multiple high and low points of dramatic tension (Stern, 1989, 1993).

The mind tends to integrate separate, unrelated actions into a single story plot. All people in all cultures from 2½ to 4 years through old age express their history, beliefs, values, and practices in the form of stories as psychological narratives. The human mind seems naturally to seek explanations for what happens to us and around us. Stories transcend the actual and create a new reality. When there are discrepancies and contradictions between the lived past and the narrated past, the official stories are often coconstructions organized around various motives. For example, a physically abused child may narrate a story excusing and protecting her parents, saying to herself, "They beat me because they care so much about me and what I do." In normal development, ordinary story making has the important role of facilitating self-definition or understanding one's autobiography where children simultaneously discover and create themselves.

Case Illustration

The following excerpt details many of the changes that represent to Stern a period of "dramatic leap in development," which occurs during the first two weeks of life [From Stern (1977) (reprinted with permission from Harvard University Press)].

The smile. During the first 2 weeks of life smiles are seen during dreaming sleep (also called irregular or rapid eye movement – REM sleep) and during drowsiness. They are rarely seen when the infant is awake and alert with his eyes open. Some of these smiles are fleeting; some are prolonged; some are asymmetrical and quite wry-looking, where only one corner of the mouth goes up, and others are beatific. They appear to bear no relationship to anything going on in the external world and are solely the reflection of cycles of neurophysiological excitation and discharges within the brain, unrelated to gas bubbles or any other part of the body except the brain's intrinsic activity. It has been called endogenous smiling because of its internal origin and its unrelatedness to anything external. They have also been called reflexive.

At sometime between 6 weeks and 3 months, depending on the study, the smile becomes exogenous, elicited by external events. Different sights and sounds will now reliably elicit a smile. However, among all the external stimuli once again it is the stimuli of a human face, the human gaze, a high-pitched voice, and tickling that are now the most predictable elicitors of the smile. Thus, in becoming exogenous, the smile becomes predominantly a social smile. Still the morphology of the smile does not change, although what triggers it does.

Beginning around the third month, the smile takes another developmental leap and becomes an instrumental behavior. By instrumental we mean simply that the infant will now produce the smile in order to get a response from someone, such as a return smile from mother or a word from her. The smile itself, however, still looks the same.

The last developmental advance is that around the fourth month the smile comes under sufficiently smooth and coordinated performance that it can begin to be performed simultaneously along with a part or parts of other facial expressions; more complex expressions emerge, such as a smile performed with a slight frown. More study is needed here to determine when expressions from different motivational patterns begin to integrate to form more complex and often ambivalent expressions.

These stages in the development in the smile would be impossible without the parallel advances in the infant's perceptual and cognitive abilities that permit the same old smile to appear under different conditions, in response to different stimuli, and in the service of different functions.

Why do we believe these transformations to be largely the unfolding of innate tendencies? The remarkable similarity in course and timetable for infants raised in very different environmental and social conditions lends some weight to the argument. Even more convincing are the studies of blind children who have had no visual opportunity to see or imitate smiles or receive visual reinforcement or feedback for their smiles. Until 4–6 months their smiles are relatively normal compared with sighted children and follow the same developmental stages and timetable. However, beginning around the fourth to sixth month the blind children begin to show a dampening or muting of facial expressiveness in general, so that the display of their smiles is less dazzling and captivating. This suggests that after an initial epoch of the unfolding of innate tendencies (under the impact of average experiences), some visual feedback or reinforcement appears to be necessary to maintain the fullest range of display of the smile behavior.

To summarize this developmental history: the smile moves from a reflexive activity (internally triggered) to a social response (externally elicited by human and other stimulation) to an instrumental behavior (produced to elicit social responses from others) to a sufficiently coordinated behavior to combine with other facial expressions. This general course, though probably the most common for facial expressions, is certainly not the same for all expressive behaviors. Unlike the smile, the laugh is not present at birth and does not appear to go through an endogenous phase. It appears first as a response to external stimuli somewhere between the fourth and eighth month. At first, from 4–6 months it is most easily elicited by tactile stimulation, such as tickling. From 7 to 9 months auditory events become more effective, and from 10 to 12 months it is most readily triggered by visual events. Still like the smile, its form changes little from its first appearance throughout the rest of life. It is present in the blind and has been reported in feral children brought up by animals. Early on, it too becomes an instrumental behavior.

Summary and Conclusions

Stern was among the first psychoanalysts to incorporate infant research into his developmental theory, which he built on empirical evidence gathered by infant observers, rather than on reconstructions based on data collected from the regressed states of adults. He challenged Mahler's idea that infants are born into an undifferentiated state or symbiotically attached to their caregivers. Instead, he proposed that infants have the ability to relate and can have emerging sense of self from birth on.

We consider Stern's model to be organismic because he proposes that infants are born as stimulus seekers requiring sensory stimulation in order to mature. This view is in contrast to the traditional view that held that the psychic apparatus was designed to rid itself of stimulation in order to reestablish a homoeostatic state. Stimuli become a form of nourishment without which psychological growth cannot occur.

Stern uses the term *domains* to describe his developmental eras. Initially, Stern proposed four domains of the sense of self that emerge at different periods and endure throughout a person's life: the Emergent Self, the Core Self, the Subjective Self, and the Verbal Self. Later on, he added a fifth domain, that of the Narrative Self. As with any organism, Stern proposed that as each domain emerged, a variety of processes take place in interaction with the environment that defined the infant's maturational capabilities.

Within each domain, the infant must work through adaptive tasks. Within the first domain, roughly ages 0–2 months, the infant is actively forming an *emergent sense of self*. Infants test hypotheses about what is occurring in the world. Within the second domain, roughly ages 2–7 months, the *core sense of self* is developing. This period includes four types of self-experiences, which are necessary in order for the core sense of self to come together: *self-agency*, the infant's ability to author his or her own experiences; *self-coherence*, interpersonal experiences that help unify the child's experiences; *self-affectivity*, the ability to recognize and come to expect affects such as joy, anger, etc.; and *self-history*, a sense of continuity that is critical for the formation of relationships with others. Stern identified RIGs as the basic unit for the representation of the core self. Within the third domain, roughly ages 7–15 months, a *subjective sense of self* emerges. During the consolidation of the Core Sense of Self, which occurs between 2 and 7 months, the infant begins to store in its episodic memory mental representations of events that occurred in interactions with caregivers. He specifies that these mental representations become transformed into RIGs. These processes are reminiscent of the translocation of experiences mentioned earlier. Psychic structure is built up as a result of such internalization of experiences, without which psychopathology ensues. Other examples are found during other phases where he discusses the role of attunement and deferred imitation. Infants discover that they have a mind and that other people have different minds. Stern uses the term *affect attunement* to describe the parent's use of behaviors that induce a shared affective state. Within the fourth domain, roughly ages 15–30 months, the *verbal sense of self* emerges. Children can now use words. They see themselves objectively and reflect on themselves. Empathy is now possible. Within the final domain, roughly ages 30–48 months, a *narrative sense of self* emerges, during which human activity is now understood in terms of psychological story plots.

Keywords Affect attunement • Amodal perception • Coherence of form • Coherence of intensity structures • Coherence of the temporal structures • Coherence of motion • Coming into being • Constructionist approaches • Core sense of self • Emergent sense of self • Evoked companion • Interaffectivity • Islands of consistency • Joint attention • Narrative sense of self • Physiognomic perception • Representations of interactions that have been generalized (RIGs) • Self-affectivity • Self-agency • Self-coherence • Self-history • Self-invariant experiences • Self with others • Subjective sense of self • Unity of locus • Verbal sense of self • Vitality affects

References

Boston Change Process Study Group. (2008). *About the members*. Retrieved January 28, 2008, from http://www.changeprocess.org/members.html

Fonagy, P. (1998). Moments of change in psychoanalytic theory: Discussion of a new theory of pychic change. *Infant Mental Health Journal*, *19*(3), 346–353.

Freud, S. (1920). Beyond the pleasure principle. *Standard Edition*, 18, 7–64.

Lichtenberg, J. D. (1983). *Psychoanalysis and infant research*. New Jersey: The Analytic Press.

Mahler, M., Pine, F., & Bergman, A. (1975). *The psychological birth of the human infant: Symbiosis and individuation*. New York: Basic Books.

Piaget, J. (1954). *The construction of reality in the child*. Translation by M. Cook. First published in 1937. New York: Basic Books.

Stern, D. N. (1985). *The interpersonal world of the infant: A view from psychoanalysis and developmental psychology*. New York: Basic Books.

Stern, D. N. (1989). Developmental prerequisites for the sense of narrated self. In A. M. Cooper, O. F. Kernberg, & E. S. Person (Eds.), *Psychoanalysis: Toward the second century* (pp. 168–178). New Haven: Yale University Press.

Stern, D. N. (1990). *Diary of a baby*. New York: Basic Books.

Stern, D. N. (1993). Why study children's narratives? *The Signal: Newletter of the World Association for Infant Mental Health*, *1*(3), 1–3.

Stern, D. N. (1998). The process of therapeutic change involving implicit knowledge: Some implications of developmental observations for adult psychotherapy. *Infant Mental Health Journal, 19*(3), 300–308.
Sullivan, H. S. (1953). *The interpersonal theory of psychiatry*. New York: W.W. Norton.

Major Works

Stern, D. N. (1985). *The interpersonal world of the infant*. New York: Basic Books.
Stern, D. N. (1990). *Diary of a baby*. New York: Basic Books.
Stern, D. N. (1995). *The motherhood constellation: A unified view of parent–infant psychotherapy*. New York: Basic Books.
Stern, D. N. (1998). *The birth of the mother: How the motherhood experience changes you forever*. New York: Basic Books.
Stern, D. N. (2002). *The first relationship: Infant and mother*. Cambridge, MA: Harvard University Press.
Stern, D. N. (2004). *The present moment in psychotherapy and everyday life*. New York: W.W.Norton.

Supplementary Readings

Applegate, J. (Fall, 1989). Mahler and Stern: Irreconcilable differences? *Child and Adolescent Social Work*, 6(3), 163–173.
Freud, S. (1920). *Beyond the pleasure principle* (SE, Vol. 18, pp. 7–64). London: The Hogarth Press and the Institute of Psychoanalysis.
Inhelder, B. & Piaget, J. (1966). Cognitive development and its contribution to the diagnosis of some phenomenon of mental deficiency. *Merrill-Palmer Quarterly*, 12, 299–319.
Mahler, M., Pine, F., & Bergman, A. (1975). *The psychological birth of the human infant: Symbiosis and individuation*. New York: Basic Books.
Piaget, J. (1954). *The construction of reality in the child*. Translation by M. Cook. First published in 1937. New York: Basic Books.
Vygotsky, L. S. (1962). *Thought and language*. Translated by E. Haufmann and G. Vakar. Cambridge, MA: M.I.T. Press.
Winnicott, D. W. (1963). From dependence towards independence in the development of the individual. *The maturational process and the facilitating environment*. New York: International Universities Press.

Chapter 14
Heinz Kohut (1913–1981)

Publishing Era (1950–1984)

Biographical Information

Heinz Kohut was born in Vienna on May 3, 1913 to Felix and Else Kohut, who were of Jewish decent. His father had prepared himself for a career as a concert pianist but was forced to go into business by World War I. Some details of Kohut's childhood are clouded by controversy because of the uncertainty about their origin. In 1977, at the age of 64, he wrote the *Two analyses of Mr. Z.* to fulfill an obligation to a publisher. Kohut published it 2 years later (Kohut, 1979/1991). The paper purports to deal with a patient whom Kohut analyzed at two different points in his professional career. At the first point, Kohut was a committed classical analyst who applied principles of drive theory to the treatment of the man. Five years later, Kohut reported that the man returned for a second analysis, during which Kohut applied his newly formulated theory of self-psychology. The first analysis left major elements in the man's psychopathology unresolved, whereas the second analysis was concluded successfully having dealt with the man's narcissistic character traits that were incompletely understood through drive theory.

After Kohut's death, colleagues who knew him intimately revealed an interesting set of facts. They noted the existence of remarkable parallels between the history of the patient and Kohut's own history. Strozier (2001), a historian who wrote Kohut's definitive biography, undertook a detailed examination of those parallels and concluded that Mr. Z. was none other than Kohut himself. All attempts to identify the existence of the patient that Kohut had described led to dead ends. A consensus emerged within Kohut's circle of colleagues and friends that he had disguised his own experiences in Mr. Z., presenting the contrast between his own analysis with Ruth Eisler and his own self-analysis after he had arrived at his insights regarding narcissistic disorders. He had thus replicated, in part, the feat of Freud's self-analysis, reinterpreting the occurrences in his life through the lens of his own discoveries. In writing Kohut's biography, Strozier extrapolated many details of Kohut's early life from the account that Kohut gave of Mr. Z. Several elements of Kohut's early history, his relationship with his father and mother, and other formative experiences were exposed in that paper.

J. Palombo et al., *Guide to Psychoanalytic Developmental Theories*,
DOI: 10.1007/978-0-387-88455-4_14, © Springer Science+Business Media, LLC 2009

A further confounding factor in reconstructing Kohut's biography is his failure, as an adult, to acknowledge his Jewish origins. After his arrival in the USA in 1940, he seemed to have reinvented his background to exclude any association with his Jewish heritage. In fact, during his entire tenure at the Chicago Institute for Psychoanalysis, he never publicly acknowledged his Jewish origins to anyone, going so far as to mislead his colleagues into believing that his name was of Czech Protestant origins and that he was the product of a mixed marriage, his mother being Catholic and his father Protestant. In fact, his mother did convert to Catholicism after her arrival in Chicago, and he, with his wife Betty, attended a Unitarian Church. Strozier subsequently obtained extensive documentation of his family's Jewish origins, many of whom died in the Holocaust. He also obtained evidence of Kohut's circumcision and the Jewish name given on that occasion, which was Wolf Hersch (Strozier, 2001, p. 11).

Kohut was separated from his father at the age of 1½, when his father enlisted in the army during World War I. There was little contact between them until his father's return at the age of 5. Their relationship remained distant until Felix died of leukemia in 1937 at the age of 49, when Kohut was 24. Whereas he longed for a close relationship with his idealized, distant father, he experienced his relationship with his mother as oppressively close, constantly wishing to free himself from the gravitational pull she exerted on him.

From the ages of 6–10, he was home schooled, primarily because Else could not bear to part from him and wished to control her brilliant and adored child's education. She provided him with tutors who not only instructed him in formal subjects but also provided the foundations for a broad cultural education. Once he entered the Gymnasium at the age of 11, Else turned away from him, took a lover, and left him with "the *emptiness* of *my* birthday parties as a child" (Strozier, 2001, p. 23). Felix remained in the background, presumably preoccupied with his business. At around that time, Else hired a young university student, whose job was to provide Heinz with as broad an exposure as possible to cultural events. He would take Heinz to museums, art galleries, concerts, the opera, or read with him great works of literature. Kohut indicated that he greatly valued that relationship and minimized the significance of some homosexual overtones that colored the closeness to this man. At the Gymnasium, he became friends with Siegmund Levarie, whom he was to join when he immigrated to Chicago, and with whom he shared his lifelong interest in music.

Upon graduation from high school, at the age of 19, Kohut entered the University of Vienna. He registered in the medical faculty, which required 6 years to complete. He lived at home during those years, except for a 6-month internship in Paris at the *Hopital St. Louis*, next to the Cathedral of Notre Dame, where he specialized in treating patients with syphilis. It was during this period, in 1937, that Kohut's father died. In spite of the distance between them, Kohut was devastated by the loss and entered psychotherapy with a psychologist named Walter Marseilles. Meantime, Anti-Semitism was rearing its ugly head in Vienna, presaging the annexation of Austria by the Nazis in 1938. Early in 1938, Kohut entered analysis with the prominent analyst August Aichhorn, whom we encountered previously. By happenstance,

Elizabeth Meyer, who was later to become Kohut's wife, had come to Vienna to study psychoanalysis at that time and took courses taught by Aichhorn.

In March 1938, Germany invaded Austria. That turn of events profoundly affected Kohut. He told Strozier, "It was the end of a world, it was the end of an era." "I had the feeling it was the end of my life," meaning that it was the end of his cultural existence (Strozier, 2001, p. 55). Although he had finished all of his course work at the medical faculty, he could not graduate because he was Jewish. Meantime, Freud was preparing to depart Vienna. Kohut never tired of retelling the story of how Aichhorn alerted him to the exact time of Freud's departure, permitting Kohut to go to the train station to see him leave. He recalled that as the train pulled away, Kohut tipped his hat to Freud, and Freud waved back at him. This was the only contact Kohut ever had with Freud. In a fortunate twist of fate, Kohut was allowed to take his final exams, for which he had to prepare hastily, and received his M.D.

Chicago

Kohut was permitted to leave Vienna in March 1939 with the help of Rabbi Murmerstein, who was instrumental in helping many others leave also. After a tumultuous year in a relocation camp in England, he immigrated to the USA with the help and support of his friend Levarie, who welcomed him in Chicago. Levarie introduced him to Robert Wadsworth, a librarian and musicologist who became Kohut's best friend. Soon after his arrival, Else joined him, and immediately established herself by opening a small shop of women's clothing and accessories.

In pursuit of his medical career, Kohut completed an internship and went on to a residency in the prestigious neurology department of the University of Chicago's Billings Hospital. He managed to avoid being drafted when the war with Japan broke out and spent his time immersed in his work. His mastery of neurology led the chair of the department to anticipate a brilliant career for Kohut in that specialty. However, Kohut decided on a different path and in 1942 applied for admission to the Chicago Institute for Psychoanalysis, which at the time was under the direction of its founder Franz Alexander, a charismatic energetic advocate for psychoanalysis who managed to attract many of the leading immigrant psychoanalysts to teach at the institution. As a freestanding institute with no ties to any academic university, its structure and curriculum were modeled on the Berlin institute, where Alexander had collaborated with Karl Abraham. Remarkably, the Institute rejected Kohut's application and he was encouraged to undertake a "therapeutic analysis" to resolve his problems prior to reapplying. The details of this unusual rejection remain undiscovered. Undeterred by this setback, Kohut sought out as his analyst Ruth Eissler, a well-established orthodox analyst who was well connected with other members of the Chicago Institute. In tandem with the analysis with Eissler, Kohut took the boards in neurology and psychiatry, making explicit his determination to follow a career in psychoanalysis.

His personal life remained enigmatic to his friends and colleagues. He developed an intense relationship with Barbara Bryant, whom he saw daily for about a year-and-a-half, and suddenly broke off the relationship with no explanation. Although they had socialized extensively among his circle of friends, he refrained from any mention of his mother to her or to others. She knew that his mother lived in Hyde Park, but no more. All the while, Kohut made regular visits to his mother every Sunday and was supported by an allowance she gave him. He kept even his closest friends in the dark about her. During this period Else converted to Catholicism. Later on, he would speak of her as suffering from a "hidden psychosis." During the last years of her life, she did become overtly paranoid, confirming what Kohut had long suspected and which explained to him much of his mother's idiosyncratic behaviors. She died in a nursing home in 1972 at the age of 82.

In 1946, Kohut reapplied for admission to the Chicago Institute; however, this acceptance was provisional and did not give him permission to begin treatment of a patient. During Alexander's tenure, the Chicago Institute had created a stir by recommending deviations in the standard conduct of analysis, such as reducing the frequency of analytic sessions, scheduling appointments irregularly, and refraining from interpreting symptoms. Kohut remained in close correspondence with Aichhorn, who advised him to remain true to Freud's teaching and not get embroiled in that controversy. Kohut followed his advice and immersed himself in Freud's work. Meanwhile, he was now permitted to begin analyzing patients to fulfill the requirements for graduation as an analyst. By the fall of 1950, he had fulfilled all the requirements, taken the exam, and graduated.

Prior to his graduation, he had met Elizabeth Meyer, a social worker who worked at the Institute. She was a non-Jew of German-American origins. As mentioned earlier, she had gone to Vienna to study with Aichhorn and had been analyzed by Jenny Waelder. They fell in love and married within 6 months in October 1948. A son, Thomas, was born in March 1950.

Mr. Psychoanalysis

Kohut was a consummate clinician who was steeped in Freud and classical metapsychology. He saw his patients four or five times a week for prolonged periods, in some cases as long as 10 years. His patients felt deeply attached to him, almost always felt he understood them, and experienced his involvement with them as truly genuine. A response he gave to an analyst who was in analysis with him summarizes his attitude regarding his use of psychoanalytic technique. Strozier reports him to have said "when he [Kohut] had to make a choice between doing what he felt was right as a matter of principle and what he thought would be a more human response, making the more human response would rarely be an error" (p. 122).

Professionally, he took an active role in the affairs of the Institute, revamping its curriculum by adding a 2-year course on Freud's major contributions. He became active in the American Psychoanalytic Association; he served on the editorial board of its journal, chaired some of its committees, and in 1964 was elected its President. These activities gave him access to many of the leading lights in psychoanalysis at the time and permitted him to develop close relationships with Heinz Hartmann and Anna Freud. He received recognition for his adherence to psychoanalytic orthodoxy and spoke with pride when he joked that others referred to him as "Mr. Psychoanalysis."

Until the publication of his paper on empathy in 1959, Kohut had published few papers, mostly on music and literature. In this paper, he broke new ground by insisting that the essence of the psychoanalytic method is to understand the meaning of patients' experiences rather than on providing drive-based explanations for their roots. He wished to "de-biologize" psychoanalysis by cutting its moorings from the metapsychology of the drives. The paper was recognized as controversial because it undercut the positivist direction of Hartmann and others. However, its larger impact was not felt until years later with the publication of the *Analysis of the Self* in 1971. Few realized at the time that the paper had launched what was to become self-psychology as a new paradigm. In fact, all of the ideas that were to emerge later were summarized in his presidential address given on completion of his term at the American Psychoanalytic Association in 1965 (Kohut, 1966/1978) under the title "Forms and transformations of narcissism." Whereas the explicit focus of that address was on understanding narcissism in its healthy and unhealthy manifestations, implicitly, Kohut had uncovered an *anomaly* in drive theory that would ultimately lead to its overthrow by self-psychology (Kuhn, 1970). The core of Kohut's critique lay in his view that not all narcissism is pathological; in fact, aspects of narcissism such as self-esteem are essential components of mental health. Drive theory had been trapped in the cultural view that self-regard was pathological and reflected an unhealthy preoccupation with oneself.

The New Paradigm

In April 1969, Kohut brought together a group of younger colleagues to present to them some of the work encompassed in the manuscript of the *Analysis of the Self.* Included in the group, which was to constitute a set of disciples who would disseminate his work, were Arnold Goldberg, Michael Basch, Ernest Wolf, Paul and Anna Ornstein, and Paul and Marian Tolpin (two others members, John Gedo and David Marcus, dropped out). In regular meetings, Kohut solicited from them feedback on the ideas he was formulating and assigned them the task of representing him at events where his contributions were to be discussed.

Kohut sent copies of his manuscript to Anna Freud and Hartman, both of whom spoke approvingly of its contents, little realizing the dimensions of the revolution it was to bring about. Few people appreciated the radical shift in direction that was to follow its publication in 1971. At first sight, the work seemed to represent no more than an emendation of psychoanalytic metapsychology. The publication of the *Restoration of the Self,* which followed in 1977, left little doubt that a major reassessment of classical psychoanalytic theory was about to take place. Along with this recognition came an acrimonious debate and accusations that Kohut had regressed back to the heretical position that Alexander had occupied at the Chicago Institute for Psychoanalysis. In subsequent years, self-psychology as a movement grew substantially, gaining supporters in the USA and abroad. In particular, the significance of empathy in the clinical setting received the broadest acceptance of any of Kohut's contributions.

Kohut's satisfaction in seeing his ideas triumph was alloyed with serious concerns about his health. Soon after the publication of the *Analysis of the Self*, he was diagnosed with lymphoma. He made the decision not to share that information with anyone but his family. For years, until he was close to his death, none of his close colleagues or patients knew about that diagnosis. In 1977, he had coronary bypass surgery to correct an arterial blockage. Tragically, whereas the surgery was successful, he developed a serious infection and complications that incapacitated him for months. By October 1981, when he gave his farewell address to the self-psychology conference in Berkeley, he knew he was dying of the lymphoma that had ravaged his system. He chose to speak about empathy as one of his most lasting contributions. He died 4 days later on October 8, 1981 at the age of 69. His last work *How Does Analysis Cure?* was published posthumously in 1984.

Theory of Development[1]

Kohut never directly observed infants to draw inferences about their development from those observations. Following Freud, he justified his inferences regarding the development of the self based on the consistency of his reconstructions during treatment with his theoretical concepts, and the assumption that regressed states of adults reflect earlier developmental periods. He proposed that empathy is the central tool for the observation of psychological states. Without empathy, there can be no understanding of a patient's subjective experiences (Kohut, 1959, 1982). Although his clinical theory is consistent with a hermeneutic approach, the developmental model we infer from his formulation is a hybrid nonepigenetic organismic model that incorporates a narrative perspective. Since this developmental model does not lend itself to segmentation along phases or stages, we will use the neutral term *period* to characterize the events of specific chronological ages. We will refer to the period of the development of the *Virtual self* (0–2 months), the *Cohesive self* (2–30 months), *Oedipal Period* (30–48 months), *Latency* (4–13 years), *Adolescence* (14–18 years), and *Entry into Adulthood* (19–25 years).

[1]Since Kohut never proposed a systematic developmental theory, the model we offer is one that Palombo (2008) has inferred and reconstructed from Kohut's entire work (excerpts are reprinted with permission from John Wiley & Sons).

The Concept of Self

Kohut conceptualizes the development of the **self** as the result of the empathic milieu that parents create to sustain the child during development. Kohut calls this milieu a "**matrix of empathy**" (see Kohut, 1978b, p. 752 footnote). Kohut speaks of parents as providers of **selfobject functions**; these are the caregivers that traditional psychoanalytic theory identifies as "objects." Caregivers provide selfobject functions to the child through their responses to the child's psychological needs, such as the need for affirmation and protection. In contrast to traditional theory, Kohut viewed the child as proactive and stimulus seeking, rather than seeking the discharge of accumulated drive energies.

In his early writings, Kohut used the concepts of self and self-representation interchangeably. In time, he came to believe that the use of the term *self* was a more "**experience near**" concept that conveyed to the analyst the immediacy of the patient's experience, a concept that facilitated the process of empathic observation. By experience near, he sought to convey the need to avoid theoretical jargon both in speaking to patients and in the early stages of the formulation of a theory.

Kohut made clear the distinction between the concept of the self, and the concepts of ego, id, and superego. The latter three were *agencies* of the mind that were at different levels of abstraction from the former. The self was a structure within the mind that reflects the content of one's experiences and encompasses the agencies of the mind. Kohut distinguished between the self in the narrower sense, or the ***subordinate view of the self***, and the self in the broader sense, the ***superordinate view of the self***. The subordinate view of the self has a developmental line that paralleled Mahler's (1975) separation-individuation line of object cathexis. That line describes the attachment to, or the cathexis of, others. The superordinate view of the self, representing the more mature expression of Kohut's thinking, describes the psychological development of the person.

The Development of the Bipolar Self

To describe the development of the self is to give an account of the natural history of the self in interaction with its selfobjects, which is what Kohut called the "**bipolar self**." The bipolar self includes the two major selfobject functions, those of the **Grandiose Self**, and the **Idealized Parent Imago**. Included within the bipolar self is an intermediate area of talents and skills. In his posthumously published work, *How does analysis cure?* (1984), Kohut added a third selfobject function that of the **Twinship or Alter-Ego** functions.

Selfobject Functions

The concept "selfobject," one of his most seminal concepts, was introduced by Kohut to describe an aspect of the relationship between self and others (Kohut, 1971). Selfobject functions are psychological functions with which people are not born. Initially, they are mental states that have not acquired the stability, autonomy, and continuity to be considered psychic structures within the self that permit the person to function effectively. Children experience them as part of or within their sense of self, even though others provide those functions. Eventually children internalize these experiences into the matrix of their sense of self as psychological structures, at which point they represent enduring functions that accrue to the self. The awareness of these functions is generally absent, much as one is not aware of one's heartbeat except when it skips a beat or stops functioning, at which point the experience of the absence of the selfobject function is experienced as an injury to the self. Selfobjects may be defined as the set of experiences that, when present, lead to feelings of cohesion and stability; but which, when absent, lead to feelings of disruption and fragmentation (see Table 14.1).

Table 14.1 Selfobject functions and self-experience when responses are adequate or inadequate

Psychological functions essential for self-cohesion	Self-experience if response is adequate	Self-experience if response is inadequate
The grandiose self: mirroring selfobject functions		
Affirmation Admiration Approval Acknowledgment	Sense of worth and positive self regard	Sense of inadequacy and worthlessness Person will feel depreciated, blamed, criticized, or dismissed Anger toward oneself or significant other
The idealized parent imago: idealizing selfobject functions		
Safety that results from faith in the strength and omnipotence of another who is seen as a protector	Feeling powerful and effective as a human being	Insecurity; vulnerability; uncertainty; feeling unsafe
Regulation of excitement and overstimulation	Self-control; self-discipline; self-regulation	Sense of feeling out of control
Being soothed, comforted, and calmed by another who provides solace and vitality	Capacity for enthusiasm and equanimity	Feeling ignored, neglected, or undermined
Learning rules of conduct that represent the culture's values and ideals	Person develops a value system, a set of ideals that serve as a guide through life; sense of purpose	Disappointment toward significant other General disillusionment
The alter-ego: twinship selfobject functions		
Experience of a common bond with others	Feeling of kinship with others so that nothing human feels alien	Sense of incompatibility and alienation
Experience of intactness of one's inborn givens and natural endowments	Sense of well-being and wholesomeness	Major differences in values, interests, activities Confusion and alienation from significant other

Kohut identified the specific selfobjects within the context of the transferences patients formed during analysis, which are associated with specific psychological structures. The structures are the **grandiose self**, the **idealized parent imago**, and the **alter ego**. The selfobject functions associated with each of these are (a) the **mirroring selfobject functions**, (b) the **idealizing selfobject functions**, and (c) the **twinship selfobjects functions**.

The grandiose self: The functions associated with the grandiose self are the mirroring functions that include the experiences of being affirmed and acknowledged by another who mirrors ones internal state. The result is a sense of worth, positive self-regard. The experiences of gaining respect from others and feeling approved of by others who praise and compliment us in an authentic way are associated with this selfobject function. These experiences add to a sense of dignity and self-respect that people enjoy. Experiences of admiration and of feeling lovable result in the sense of poise, self-confidence, and self-assurance. Those of being cheered on in the pursuit of novel experiences and encouraged in the mastery of challenges that stretch one's reach lead to a sense of firmness in the sense of self, and enhance the assertive pursuit of activities (Kohut, 1968/1978, p. 489; 1971, pp. 26–28).

The idealized parent imago: The functions associated with the idealized parent imago are the idealizing functions that include the experiences of safety that result from the faith in the strength and omnipotence of someone who acts as a protector. Sharing in the strength of that person and feeling protected results in the function of feeling empowered and effective as a human being. The experience of having ones' excitement or overstimulating affects modulated by another can result in the functions of self-control, self-discipline, and self-regulation. The experiences of being soothed, comforted, and calmed by another, who provides solace and support as well as joyous vitality, can result in the capacity for enthusiasm and equanimity. Finally, the experience of learning rules of conduct that represent the content of the culture's values and ideals becomes consolidated into a value system, and a set of ideals that serve as guides in the person's life. These give a sense of purpose in the pursuit of life's goals (Kohut, 1968/1978, pp. 479–481; 1971, pp. 37–49).

Alter-ego: The functions associated with the alter-ego are the twinship selfobject functions. These functions were initially associated with the mirror transferences, being considered an archaic form of those transferences but were later given a separate status (Kohut, 1984, p. 193). The functions associated with the alter-ego include the experience of a common bond with others that unite human beings together and that lead to the feeling of kinship with others so that nothing human feels alien. The experience of the intactness of oneself provides the sense of well-being and wholesomeness without which we feel dehumanized.

The Virtual Self (0–2 Months)

The self develops as a result of the empathic interchanges between child and caregiver. From a developmental perspective, the self emerges from the "**virtual self**." The virtual self may be thought of evocatively, rather than literally as having its genesis in the minds of the caregivers who anticipate the arrival of the infant. Caregivers' fantasies about their offspring represent significant aspects of the context into which a child is born. These fantasies, expectations, hopes, and fears all provide a milieu into which the newborn will reside. They will be imprinted upon the child. They will shape the responses of the caregivers and, in interaction with the child's temperament, they will form the nucleus of experiences that will determine the direction of the child's development (See Kohut, 1978; Kohut, 1977, pp. 100–101).

The Cohesive Self (2–30 Months)

At birth, most infants have a cohesive self upon which experiences, both internal and external, register and upon which is laid the interactive patterns that subsequently become part of the organization of the self. The **cohesive self** includes the innate givens the child brings through heredity to the world, which Kohut called talents and skills. Some children with severe neurological problems may not have such a cohesive self at birth.

The cohesive self also includes those aspects of the virtual self that the milieu superimposes on the child. It is a prestructural self in the sense that enduring patterns of functioning are not yet embedded into the core of the self, but rather are performed by the caregivers. The selfobject providers make themselves available to the infant to ensure that its welfare complements this matrix.

The self unfolds ontogenetically from infancy to a mature cohesive self. It is initially composed of two poles, which, like a double helix, remain in a tension state with one another throughout one's lifetime (Kohut, 1977, pp. 171–191). The poles are composed of experiences related to the grandiose self and those of the idealized parent imago. As these poles interact with a person's inborn gifts, talents, limitations, and deficits, an enduring set of psychic structures develop that, in part, define the content of the self. The other part of the self is composed of the totality of the subjective experiences: past, present, conscious, and unconscious.

Through the first pole of the self, that of the grandiose self, the child experiences a sense of pride by virtue of the parents' admiration, which the child experiences as being special. Eventually, these experiences are transformed into a sense of self-assurance, self-confidence, and positive self-esteem that the child carries into adulthood. This line of development leads to the laying down of psychic structures eventually to be identified as a set of ambitions that act as powerful motives for admiration and recognition. A person may then be about to channel these ambitions into career paths that lead to significant accomplishments.

Along the second pole, that of the idealized parent imago, are those experiences a young child has of feeling protected by powerful parents who are endowed with magical capacities. The wish to partake from, and to share in, this sense of power leads the child to become attached to what the child perceives as its source. Children eventually internalize those experiences, which become the source of the capacity for self-soothing and self-regulation. As enduring functions, these structures lead to the capacity for self-discipline and self-idealization. They form the core of a set of ideals that the person will endeavor to reach.

As the infant develops and the sense of self matures, these two poles come to a nodal point in development around the ages of 3 and 4. At that time, the **nuclear self** emerges, which is the core of the self that is shaped by the infant's experiences. It manifests through the stable and consistent use by the child of the first personal pronoun "I" to refer to him or herself. Positive self-esteem reflects the harmonious tension between ambitions and ideals within the context of the uses of one's talents. The capacities for joy, pride, and enthusiasm reflect the cohesiveness, firmness, and harmony of the sense of self.

The self is susceptible to regression, disruptions, and temporary or permanent **fragmentation** under stress. The functional state of the structures of the self need not be ever constant as an indication of health. Rather, the stability and the tension gradient between the poles of the self are the indicators for health. When an individual's ambitions and ideals are realized, the resultant experience is joy and triumph. For the same reason, the failure to achieve these goals produces despair.

For Kohut, the central dynamic involved in anxiety was the threat to the integrity of the sense of self; undefended, the sense of self would fragment under its impact. The circumstances that might produce such a threat may range from the fear of isolation and the loss of a connection with those who perform selfobject functions to the fear of narcissistic injury, such as that which results from experiences of shame. The most common defense against such fears is disavowal by which the person remains aware of the reality he or she confronts, but denies its meaning. The denial leads to actions that are obviously symptomatic, such as behaviors that indicate an inordinate need for attention or that are manifestly grandiose.

Optimal Frustration

Optimal frustration is essential to the **transmuting internalization** of selfobject functions. Transmuting internalization, the process through which self-structure is formed, consists in taking in a function that a parent performs and integrating it into one's sense of self. Kohut postulates two major components to optimal frustration (Kohut, 1984, p. 70). The first presumes the presence of an empathic caregiver capable of monitoring the child's capacity to live up to the caregivers' expectations. This presumes a caregivers' readiness to perform the selfobject functions the child requires when the child urgently needs those functions and when the limits of the child's capacity to tolerate the frustration is reached. The second component of optimal frustration is conceived as one in which caregivers delay intervening to allow the child to experiment and to practice without interference. The use of optimal frustration also entails that the caregiver endures the pain of watching the seeming ineptitude of an unskilled novice at the task of life. The child engages in a process in which the pain of trial and error, of success or failure, becomes tolerable and need not be avoided at all costs. To delay is to endure, and to endure makes it possible for creativity and inventiveness to come forth. The children's assertiveness is challenged as they attempt to solve the problem under the benign oversight of the caregiver. If the caregiver cannot endure the child's playful attempts at mastery and cannot permit the creativity that comes from such play, the child's efforts are thwarted. On the other hand, if the playfulness is accompanied by unresponsiveness, the urgent need for the function becomes dominant, and the child faces the threat of fragmentation in the absence of the function.

Through optimal frustration, children have an opportunity to exercise the functions they already possess and are not co-opted into having others perform them. Children are also challenged to perform functions that they did not possess, while not being set up to fail at impossible tasks. While the child is challenged to meet the demands of the task, the child is assured that he or she will not fail. Psychological structure is a residue of the process of delay and tolerable frustration that accompanies the loss of selfobject functions and the reintegration that occurs following the breach in the relation and the reinstitution of selfobject functions. Experiences of disruption or fragmentation that are caused by intolerable frustration will interfere with, undermine, or, at times, actually break down structural organization. No structure can result from a self-state in which an infant is so overwhelmed by external or internal stimuli as to feel intense discomfort or pain. Optimal frustration is, therefore, critical to the process of structuralization. Kohut characterized the process as one of rupture and repair.

Aggression and Sexuality

For Kohut, healthy **assertiveness** is not the expression of an instinctual drive, but rather the manifestation of a sense of cohesion (Kohut, 1984, p. 24). It denotes children's anticipation of the challenges they will encounter. An observer may characterize the child's enjoyment of novel experiences as satisfying aggressive or assertive efforts and may appear to have a "driven" quality, but for the child they are the natural accompaniment of an evolving sense of self.

Raw **aggression** or **sexuality** represents "**disintegration products**" of a fragmenting self (Kohut, 1972/1978b; 1978/1990, p. 389). The loss of self-cohesion, at times, may be accompanied either by vengeful rage at the frustrating object or by sexualized responses. Rage responses may occur because the frustration is intolerable. Rage will also be the child's response to the caregiver's failure to recognize that he or she has been injured. The caregiver's nonresponsiveness is experienced as a negation of the child's very existence, a negation that may be experienced as annihilative in its impact. For the child not to have an injury acknowledged is to be dehumanized. If the child's plea and cry for comfort and for healthy responses are left unanswered, despair ensues. On the other hand, the empathic responsiveness of the caregiver can lead to an attenuation of the injury and may initiate the healing process.

Aggression can then manifest itself in the form of protest or in the diffuse expression of anger. Rage may have no ideational content in the form of a target toward whom it is directed (See also Kohut, 1972/1978b, pp. 111–131; 1977). The aggressive and sexual drives, therefore, are constituents of the self. They are components present from birth that are not separately identifiable except at times when disruptions of the self bring on fragmentation. They then emerge as disintegration products, rather than as healthy expressions of the self. Healthy sexual expression emerges in an age-appropriate way as the child matures. A child's solitary masturbation is not the reflection of a healthy activity that is appropriate for a child that age; rather, it is indicative of the experience of loneliness in the absence of the needed selfobject function (Kohut, 1984, pp. 157–158). Psychosexual development, therefore, is not characterized by phase-specific preoccupation with individual body parts that are reflective of growth. To the contrary, children will use body parts, of which they slowly become aware, as sources of comfort when the caregivers are unavailable to provide the necessary selfobject functions.

Oedipal Period (30–48 Months)

The **oedipal period** may be understood as the period during which the child, having achieved a stable sense of continuity and cohesion, attempts to further integrate the differential selfobject functions provided by the caregivers that would lead to gender identity. These include the functions connected with the internalizations of social norms and expectations, the development of healthy assertiveness, and the clarification of gender associated with sexual role functions. Thus, the selfobject experiences associated with this period continue to be those of the grandiose self, of the idealized parent imago, and of the alter-ego functions although enlarged and modified by the child's emerging maturational needs (Kohut, 1977, pp. 230–239).

Kohut believed the myth of Oedipus might very well have been appropriate to understand some of the phenomena that Freud observed in the Viennese society of his day, where sexuality was suppressed. It remains an open question whether the child-rearing patterns and the family structure of those days played a central role in normal development and in the development of neurotic disturbances. Specifically, what remains to be explained are the phenomena observed in children of today between the ages of 3 and 6, hence the term *oedipal period* rather than *oedipal phase.*

According to Kohut, the oedipal period is the descriptive term for a developmental period rather than an explanation for what is to be expected to occur during that period. The healthy thrust of oedipal children's development is the coalescing within them of the set of feelings and experiences that lead to self-assurance, self-confidence, and feelings of strength derived from the support the child receives from caregivers. The combination of feelings of having been chosen for a mission in life and having a set of guardian angels who are watchfully keeping an eye over them gives assurance of the presence of the functions necessary to progress through this period. The feelings of specialness may derive from the child's experience of being mother's favorite or father's special child. The feelings of protective watchfulness may also come from either caregiver. The child enters this period with a heightened sense of grandiosity, feeling stimulated to greater exhibitionistic feats.

For the boy, **exhibitionism** may assume a "phallic" quality, not so much because he is endowed with a penis, but rather because as a boy, he has experienced a subtle responsiveness to and approval for the expression of aggression, intrusiveness, and assertiveness. The caregivers may have joyfully resonated with the child's courageous forays into the world and may even have subtly suggested that there are worlds to be conquered and worlds from which he is excluded. The experience of exclusion from the caregiver's intimate closeness may stir the child's curiosity and perhaps abet his wish to enter into that world. His unmodified grandiosity may have led him to experience the exclusion as an injury to his feeling significant. He may respond with rage at the injury and regressively seek to merge once more with either caregiver as a way of healing the wound. This byplay, while appearing to have a configuration similar to that of a young Oedipus, is perhaps no more than the expression of a child's offended grandiosity. The child at some point may sexualize the injury or the deficit that results from the unempathic responses given by the caregivers, by becoming seductive toward mother, much as the classical view of the oedipal struggle dictates. However, this sexualization represents the child's attempt at healing the injury and at avoiding the fragmenting effect that it may have had. It does not represent the expression of the normal sexual drive, as Freud believed.

For the girl, the caregiver's **omnipotence** is experienced as a benign environment in which she can thrive. The magical qualities, associated with fathers who disappear in the mornings to "go to work" and reemerge in the evenings, are heightened by the exclusiveness of the joyous closeness that their reunion brings. A mother who wants to share in the husband's return may interfere with the child's wish to prolong this intimacy and to continue to benefit from it. If the girl is rebuffed and experiences the mother's intrusion as injurious to her, the untoward effects of the injury may result in a regressive merger with mother or in rage at her. Here again, the rage is not necessarily the expression of envy of mother and rivalry for her position and for what she possesses; rather, it is the rage of a wounded child whose caregiver was insufficiently responsive to her needs.

During this period, for both boys' and girls' sexual and aggressive issues do not come to the forefront until a disruption occurs between the child and the caregiver. If children's vulnerabilities are touched, their sense of self is injured; and themes of sexualization and aggression emerge, representing the disintegration products of the self rather than its cohesive expression. The reasons for this disintegration may be due not only to the injuries suffered at the hands of the caregiver, but also at times, it may result from the overstimulation produced by the interaction with the caregiver. Thus, whereas for the boy the issue is the intensification of his grandiosity, for the girl the grandiosity and wish for mirroring find a similar content but somewhat different expression; here the issues revolve around the qualities that the social context defines as feminine. That she might seek admiration from her father is socially determined; hence, the specialness of the little girl for the father is bound up with the selfobject function of total admiration, acceptance, and loving enjoyment of the little child. Here, too, the child may experience the mother's interference in this joyous union as an injury that also may lead the child to regress, fragment, or become seductive toward father. The motive behind the behavior, however, is not the drive that seeks expression, but rather the child's injury at not having an empathic response from the caregiver.

For children, therefore, the central issue of this period is not the sexual possession of the mother or father, but, rather, the establishment or reestablishment of the lost merger with the caregiver as selfobjects. Healthy competitiveness, rivalry, and the wish to excel are attributes of a child's wish to be exclusively the center of the caregivers' admiration. These are not the expressions of some innate aggression or hostility, but rather will become transformed into the healthy assertiveness of a self-confident growing child.

In different areas, both boys and girls are exposed to the increasing demands for socialization that caregivers make of them as they mature. The caregivers hand out prohibitions and approbations rather freely; the child is expected to conform to the social injunctions that are embodied in them. Caregivers transmit a moral code to the child, less by precept and more by example. The child and the caregivers are united in their agreement of what constitutes right and wrong. Certain consequences follow from certain actions. This becomes understandable to the child who now cognitively begins to move to a developmental period in which causal relationships can be constructed around specific experiences. Internalization of these standards and rules of conduct comes about through the progressive deidealization of the caregiver and the internalization of the regulatory function embodied in the relationship. The functions become detached from the caregivers themselves and are slowly integrated into the self of the child.

The injunctions and prohibitions constitute what may now be called the superego of the child. Superego is redefined as that component of the child's sense of self that embodies the prohibitions and the approbations formerly located within the caregiver but now smoothly internalized and constituting part of what becomes a code of conduct. Superego, therefore, is not a separate structure within the self but a component of the self, a component that embodies the self-critical and self-approving functions. What was the ego-ideal and was associated by Freud with the transformation of primitive grandiosity and sense of omnipotence is now attributable to the transformations related to the idealized parent imago. The result of the oedipal period is that the child transmutingly internalizes further selfobject functions, specifically, those associated with the transformation of grandiosity and those connected with the transformations of the idealization of caregivers. Through this process, children acquire a value system to which they adhere with little protest. The internalized code represents the capacity for self-regulation, which is enacted through behaviors that are indicative of conformity to that code of conduct. Furthermore, the consolidation of gender differentiation occurs with the increased reality perception by the child of societal demands and expectations.

Latency (4–13 Years)

Through the utilization of their potential and its expression in purposeful goal-directed activity, latency-aged children experience a further consolidation of the cohesive self. Physical, social, and psychological manifestations of this growth become evident in each child's effort at mastering his or her environment. The caregivers' selfobject functions become a background for the child's creative development. The freedom to stretch into new and unexplored areas is now open. The silence with which children accept their caregivers' limits and expectations reflects the smooth merger with those functions and the continuing exploration of their own capacities.

The capacity for **self-regulation** is perhaps most clearly exemplified in the latency-aged child's acceptance of rules and regulations in the playing of games. However, the remnants of grandiosity are not completely eradicated. They may manifest in the form of competitiveness with adults and peers. Competitiveness in latency-aged children is perhaps better understood as the wish to ward off the blows to their grandiosity. In this respect, one might best think of the child not so much as bent on winning but rather bent on not losing. To lose to another person is equivalent to being deflated and to experiencing a sense of worthlessness. Children may then redouble their efforts to win because of the threat that losing represents to them. Therefore, when a child is capable of accepting defeat by being "a good sport" and not "being a sore loser," by not feeling personally injured, and not reacting with rage or feeling that the rules of fair play have been violated, these expressions may be considered indications of the stability of the cohesive self and of the transformation of the grandiosity into the more modulated self-assurance that society expects (See Freedman, 1996).

Adolescence (14–17 Years)

The relatively stable sense of self-cohesion that is evident during latency may be temporarily disrupted by the upheavals brought on by puberty. Adolescents arrive at this period with specific developmental needs for responses from their caregivers. The nature of the self-object functions required at this stage is different from those of prior periods. The caregivers, who are the vehicles through whom these selfobject functions are performed, are required to play a different role from that played in former periods. Their ability to be responsive to the adolescent's needs is determined not only by the relationship that they have had to their child prior to that period but also by the issues that are activated within them by the adolescent. The issues of their own adolescence may become entwined with their responses to the adolescent (see Kohut, 1978a; Palombo, 1988, 1990).

When adolescents bring with them unresolved issues or selfobject deficits from prior developmental periods, the task of traversing this period is rendered more complex. These deficits, or regressions to prior modes of functioning, do not constitute the essence of the age-appropriate struggle. Rather, a modification of the caregivers' responses in providing selfobject functions is central to the negotiation of this period.

There is also no single path that all adolescents must travel. There is no set script, narrative, or myth that guides their development; that is, there is no model adolescent phase for all adolescents. Rather, individual differences exist in the way each adolescent will address and resolve issues. Their endowments, the availability of selfobjects to complement them or to compensate for possible deficits will determine that path taken. Each adolescent must construct a unique personal narrative out of past and present experiences.

It is important to note that an age-appropriate loosening of the sense of cohesion may result in experiences of temporary fragmentation. These adolescent processes may lead to a diffuseness in the cohesiveness of the self that challenges the adolescent's level of integration to reach a sense of equilibrium. The restoration of a balance would represent the reassessment of the meanings of prior experiences and their integration into a new set of meanings. The capacity for formal operational thought may facilitate the process. Thus, although temporary regressions to older modes of behaving and relating in responses to stress or conflict may become manifest, these are in sharp contrast to the highly mature symbolic forms of thinking that may also be present.

From adolescents' perspective, the caregivers can no longer perform the selfobject functions that were once associated with them. Thoughts and reminders of their recent helplessness and of their childhood offend adolescents' grandiosity. They turn to a peer group for the performance of those functions and for the gratification of their exhibitionistic needs. Adolescents attempt to recapture the center of the arena, making the broader world of the community their stage through athletic activities, academic achievement, or by attempting challenging feats and dangerous actions. They thus leave behind the narrow world of their household. Realistic achievement enhances their self-confidence and provides an impetus for further feats of greatness. They measure their accomplishments against what is now judged to be the biased opinions of their caregivers. Success and recognition must come not from the caregivers but from those who are now deemed truly capable of making an objective judgment.

It is difficult to overstate the extent to which adolescents' reassessment of their caregivers is due to their growing creative cognitive capacities and broadened perspective. As providers of selfobject functions, adolescents perceived their caregivers through the veil of their own needs; this perspective was clouded by the narrowness of their cognitive capacities. Now, the disparity between previous and current perceptions of caregivers jars them into reassessing their relationship to those caregivers. Massive **deidealization** of caregivers may have devastating results for adolescents. A less dramatic deidealization may lay the groundwork for the internalization and consolidation of the functions caregivers once provided. Those functions may also be acquired from others, such as teachers, athletic stars, or even peers. Adolescents lodge their admiration in others, or may place their faith in value systems that seem totally opposed to the caregivers' values. Adolescents seem to wish to injure their caregivers and, by consciously rebelling against them, to avenge themselves on them. This may be the case since the injury to the adolescent of a traumatic deidealization leads to such rage that only vengeful injury wreaked upon the caregivers brings satisfaction. On the other hand, some adolescents, in their hostile rebelliousness against the caregivers, may attempt to force caregivers to provide those selfobject functions, thus setting up irresolvable conflicts between caregivers and themselves (See Goldman & Gelso, 1997).

It would be incorrect to think that adolescents mourn their detachment from caregivers. If adolescents can smoothly internalize the selfobject functions performed for them, they may walk away from the caregivers feeling a sense of wholesome independence, or comfortable dependence on them manifesting no sign of mourning. On the other hand, if the selfobject functions are not internalized, then one might indeed see the adolescents' depressiveness, moodiness, and mournfulness as indicative of the difficulties dealing with the longing to separate. These states are the manifestation of the emptiness that adolescents feel and the painful experience of the absence of functions that were not internalized, which they now sorely need.

Adolescence, then, is not a recapitulation of prior phases (Palombo, 1988). It is a new period in its own right in which further internalizations of selfobject functions occur and become consolidated into a more cohesive sense of self. For the healthy adolescent, grandiosity takes the form of an ambition to achieve, feelings of self-confidence and self-assurance accompany this ambition, and the beginning exploration of life goals. The caregivers' values are reassessed and revised. The re-internalization of those values makes adolescents truly feel that the values are their own, that those values are there to please them rather than to please caregivers. Ideals may begin to take shape as they explore the direction that their life is to take; and with the simultaneous assessment of their capacities, a career goal may finally seem to loom on the horizon as a desirable goal to achieve.

Late Adolescence (18–20)

During late adolescence, clinical observation reveals a number of shifts in the adolescent's sense of self. The painful self-consciousness that was previously noticeable begins to dissipate. The egocentrism and sense of uniqueness give way to more empathic attitudes toward others. Self-regulation becomes possible and is less dependent on others for reinforcement. Affect states are less labile, mood swings decrease; a greater modulation of these states is evident. Greater self-confidence and self-assurance are manifested. The capacity to be assertive without having to be hostile is also observable. Regressions are less frequent and less severe when they do occur. There is less need to experiment with fringe activities, such as substance abuse or delinquency, because of peer pressures. Fantasy appears more in the service of creativity or for trial action than for defensive purposes.

A number of factors appear to contribute to the processes underlying these changes. First, adolescents reassess their past in light of present experiences. In some measure, they reinterpret and reintegrate past events ascribing to them a different set of meanings than previously existed. As a result, adolescents will view their childhoods differently than they previous had and, depending on their introspective capacities, place themselves at a distance from past events and the present. A new perspective will result from this process. Second, the increased capacity for selfobject experiences at a symbolic rather than a concrete level leads to a shift in the meanings that others have, or have had, for the adolescent. The adolescent begins to look beyond the narrow circle of family and peers for selfobject experiences. While seeking avenues for self-actualization, adolescents search for values and ideals that are consonant with the rest of their experiences. Third, the integration of gender role and sexuality into the rest of self-experience acquires an urgency that was not present before. The meanings of gender and of sexual expression or of its inhibition become focal preoccupations. Fourth, the advent of formal operational thought at the onset of adolescence plays an important role in the transformation in the adolescent's experience.

Because of these processes, a unification and consolidation in the sense of cohesion emerges that represents a different configuration of the self than previously existed. This new configuration represents a restructuring of the nuclear self that had emerged in early childhood (Kohut, 1971, p. 43; 1972/1978; Palombo, 1990). The adolescent is then able to select an avenue through which to express values previously acquired, as well as ambitions and ideals. The adolescent's inner resources may be mobilized to move in the direction of the attainment of a life goal (Kohut, 1978). At this point, it may make sense to speak of an *inner program* that the person is propelled to actualize. The nuclear self is not only formed in response to the need for adaptation; at times, it occurs irrespective of the adaptive consequences of the adolescent's behavior. Thus, the "unrealistic" aspirations of some youths, which to some adults appear foolish and impractical, represent the perennial generational struggles. These result from the tension between the older generations' exhortations to adolescents to adapt and the adolescents' rebelliousness. Adolescents may insist on the modification of reality to suit their internal needs – needs that are embodied within the nuclear self. Through this process, adolescents creatively leap forward to undertake new challenges, which when successful serve to amaze the on looking older generation.

The restructuring of a nuclear self does not foreclose the possibility of continual growth in the course of the life cycle. Neither does it guarantee that destabilizations will not occur. The achievement of the consolidation of the nuclear self may also be culture bound. In cultures in which the opportunities for the exercise of formal operational thought are neither valued nor made possible, a nuclear self may still evolve, although the timing of its emergence and the form it would take may be quite different from that of the middle-class Western culture.

Entry into Adulthood (21–26 Years)

As the late adolescent enters into adulthood, this period begins to represent the attainment of functioning as an independent center of initiative (Kohut, 1977, p. 94). During this period a consonance between ambitions, ideals, and native endowments form a coherent whole. The tension arc between life goals, innate capacities, and the motivation to strive toward those goals is in sufficient balance to provide a sense of well-being and a secure sense of positive self-regard. The hallmark of maturity is the positive self-esteem individuals feel because they are secure in the knowledge of who they are, of what they want from life, and what they feel capable of achieving.

Such maturity does not use as its exclusive criterion for health either adaptation or adjustment to the environment. Adaptation represents the biological counterpart of attempts at survival, yet there are higher values in this hierarchy than survival. These are the values derived from ideals whose worth is deemed higher than life itself. In a sense we speak here of going "beyond adaptation," beyond the short-term or long-term perpetuation of existence, to the perpetuation of those values that transcend life itself and without which human existence has little meaning. The meaning of life to the person determines that person's sense of well-being, the connectedness with his or her heritage and history, and the continuity with subsequent generations may matter more than life itself (Kohut, 1966/1978).

Yet, life without selfobjects to provide the ongoing supports that are so necessary for any existence is meaningless. Although the quality of selfobject relations shifts with the onset of maturity, their necessity is unquestioned. Reliance upon others' selfobject functions runs as a thread throughout existence. The ideal is not to be freed of reliance on selfobjects but rather to accept our need for others as integral to our sense of humanity. The sustaining effects of religion or an ideology as a source of comfort in a lonely existence represent a higher form of selfobject functions for people. Relationships with spouses provide sources of admiration or strength and are further examples of such functions. Children may become partial selfobjects by representing to parents the hope bequeathed to the world of some aspect of one's self that is valued, idealized, and internalized by the child.

The fulfillment of a life purpose is an integral part to the achievement of a sense of cohesion. Joy, pride, and enthusiasm for a cause accompany such a happy outcome. When these are absent, disappointment and despair may prevail and a depressive anxiety may set in that denotes tragedy in that person's life. Tragic Man, as Kohut calls the unfulfilled life, is a person for whom the tensions between ambitions and ideals cannot be reconciled, and disappointment in one's self is overwhelming, leading to a sense of futility and meaninglessness. The result is self-contempt and despair.

For those who can maintain a sense of self-cohesion and a consolidation of their nuclear sense of self, the avenues are open for the appreciation of humor, for the possibility of creativity, for the expression of wisdom, and for the capacity for empathy for others. For them also is the gift of the capacity to confront old age and death with a degree of acceptance of its inevitability, not embittered by the thought that life did not give them what they sought from it.

Based on Kohut's work we are led to the following definition of mental health and of normality: Mental health is the achievement of self-esteem that comes from a stable balance between one's goals and ambitions that permits the actualization of one's potential, one's skills, and one's talents (Kohut, 1977, p. 284; see also Kohut, 1984, p. 7). The balanced tension between ideals and ambitions leads to feelings of joy, enthusiasm, and pride, whereas an imbalance between these leads to the symptoms characteristic of many of the disturbances of the self. In the course of maintaining this balance, a person may relate to others as selfobjects or as mature and differentiated objects. Health is equivalent to a sustained sense of self-cohesion that reflects the person's sense of well-being.

Case Illustration

Kohut often cited the case of Miss F. as one of the first in which he found clear evidence of the need for mirroring within the transference. His classical interpretations of oedipal conflicts having fallen on deaf ears, he shifted his stance to empathically listening to the patient and realized that what she needed harkened back to a function she had failed to internalize during her developmental years. He went on to conceptualize the "need" as related to her narcissistic vulnerability and to the absence of a selfobject function [From Kohut (1971, pp. 283–284) (reprinted with permission from International Universities Press)].

Miss F., age twenty-five, had sought analysis because of a number of diffuse dissatisfactions. Despite the fact that she was active in her profession, and had numerous social contacts and a series of love relationships, she felt that she was different from other people and isolated from them. Although she had many friends, she thought that she was not intimate with anyone; and, despite the fact that she had had several love relationships and some serious suitors, she had rejected marriage because she knew that such a step would be a sham. In the course of the analysis it gradually became evident that she suffered from sudden changes in her mood which were associated with a pervasive uncertainty about the reality of her feelings and thoughts. In metapsychological terms, her disturbance was due to a faulty integration of the grandiose self into the total psychic apparatus, with the resulting tendency toward swings between (1) states of anxious excitement and elation over a secret "preciousness" which made her vastly better than anyone else (during times when the ego came close to giving way to the grandiose substructure, i.e., the strongly cathected grandiose self); and (2) states of emotional depletion, blandness, and immobility (which reflected the ego's periodic enfeeblement when it used all its strength to wall itself off from its unrealistic, grandiose substructure). The patient established object relations not primarily because she was attracted to people but rather as an attempt to escape from the painful narcissistic tensions. Yet, while in later childhood as well as in adult life her social relations were, on the surface, comparatively undisturbed, they did little to mitigate the pain caused by the underlying narcissistic disturbance.

Genetically, as we could reconstruct with great certainty, the fact that the mother had been depressed during severe periods early in the child's life had prevented the gradual integration of the narcissistic-exhibitionistic cathexes of the grandiose self. During decisive periods of her childhood, the girl's presence and activities had not called forth maternal pleasure and approval. On the contrary, whenever she tried to speak about herself, the mother deflected, imperceptibly the focus of attention to her own depressive self-preoccupations, and thus the child was deprived of that optimal maternal acceptance which transforms crude exhibitionism and grandiosity into adaptably useful self-esteem and self-enjoyment. Although the traumatic fixation on the infantile form of the grandiose self was not complete since the mother's depressive state had not been unmitigated, the pathological condition had later become reinforced by Miss F. 's relationship with her only sibling, a brother three years older than she, who (himself lacking in reliable parental approval) treated the sister sadistically, pushed himself into the limelight on all possible occasions, and used his superior intelligence to deflect parental attention from what the sister proudly said or did, thus interfering again with the realistic gratification of her narcissistic needs.

Summary and Conclusions

Kohut arrived at his psychoanalytic insights through his experience with patients with narcissistic personality disorders. Central to his approach was the use of empathy as a tool with which to "vicariously introspect" (Kohut, 1958) about patients' self-experiences. At first, he attempted to extend the ego psychological framework to explain his findings. However, it became evident that his formulations regarding the self required that he take a completely new direction, which led to a paradigm shift in psychoanalysis and to the overthrow of the hegemony of ego psychology.

The thrust of self psychology at its inception was to reformulate the theory of narcissism. Freud had considered narcissism as the pathological investment of the ego by the libidinal drive. Developmentally drive investment moved from the ego to the cathexis of others, which represented a more mature expression of libidinal cathexis. Kohut, having rejected the existence of drive theory, stood that formulation on its head by maintaining that the view that self-investment is pathological reflected Viennese morality and the condemnation of activities considered selfish, egotistic, and conceited. That view diminished the significance of such experiences as pride in oneself, self-esteem, and self-confidence. He concluded that there are healthy as well as unhealthy forms of narcissism. Contrasting his view with those of Freud's, Kohut held that the central concern of present-day generation is self-cohesion; Tragic Man represents the human failure to attain self-cohesion because of a serious personality flaw. For Kohut, Freud's central concern for those of his generation was dealing with the guilt engendered by the oedipal struggle; Guilty Man represented the embodiment of the conflict related to incestuous wishes.

Kohut went far beyond this emendation of ego psychology and proposed an alternative theory that came to be known as self psychology. His rejection of the drives as central motivators in development led him to substitute the need for self-cohesion as the determining factor in feelings of well-being. Being a clinician, Kohut did not formulate a comprehensive theory that encompassed a developmental theory, a theory of the causes of certain types of psychopathology, and a theory of what is curative about analysts' interventions. Rather, he presented a framework from which these may be inferred.

In this chapter, we presented Palombo's version of a self psychological theory of development inferred from Kohut's writings. A central construct of this developmental theory is that of selfobject functions. Based on an organismic model, the construct proposes that children experience others as providing three types of psychological responses necessary for the maintenance of self-cohesion; these are the mirroring, the idealizing, and the alter-ego selfobject functions. Through the process of transmuting internalization, these functions are "translocated" (Atwood & Stolorow, 1984, p. 39) from caregivers as the providers of the functions to the child, which leads to the formation of psychological structures. Since people have a lifelong need for these functions, the course of development leads from the concrete expression of these selfobject functions by caregivers to more abstract and less tangible forms. Rather than direct admirations and affirmation, which a child requires, an adult can be satisfied with the knowledge of his or her accomplishments without explicit recognition from others.

The result of these reformulations of the developmental progression led Kohut to reinterpret the central issues that were proposed by Freud's phases. Children do not grow because of their cathexis of others rather their experience of others' responses lead to the maintenance of self-cohesion. The Oedipus period is not one in which children seek to compete with parents of the same sex for affection rather it is a stage during which children require the ongoing affirmation and admiration as well as the idealization of their caregivers.

With the emergence of self psychology, criticisms and controversies have abounded. Some claim that Kohut borrowed from others or at least was informed by the concepts of earlier object relations theorists without acknowledging his indebtedness. Others claim that self psychology does not offer a new paradigm but rather should be categorized as a variant of object relations theory. During his lifetime, Kohut disavowed having been influenced by any of his contemporaries, claiming that his formulations emerged from his own creative efforts. He rejected the characterization of his theories as fitting in with object relations theories as he felt that those theories continued to maintain an allegiance to the existence of drives.

Keywords Adolescence • Aggression • Assertiveness • Bipolar self • Cohesive self • Deidealization • Disintegration products • Entry into adulthood • Exhibitionism • Experience near • Fragmentation • Grandiose self • Horizontal split • Idealized parent imago • Idealized parent imago • Latency • Matrix of empathy • Mirroring selfobject • Nuclear self • Oedipal period • Omnipotence • Optimal frustration • Self • Selfobject functions • Self-regulation • Sexuality, Subordinate view of the self • Superordinate view of the self • Transmuting internalization • Twinship or alter-ego • Vertical split • Virtual self

References

Atwood, G. E., & Stolorow, R. D. 1984. *Structures of subjectivity: Explorations in psychoanalytic phenomenology*. New York: The Analytic Press.

Freedman, S. 1996. Role of self-object experiences in affective development during latency. *Psychoanalytic Psychology*, 13(1), 101–128.

Goldman, G. F., & Gelso, C. J. 1997. Kohut's theory of narcissism and adolescent drug abuse treatment. *Psychoanalytic Psychology*, 14(1), 81–95.

Kohut, H. 1959. Introspection, empathy and psychoanalysis. *Journal of the American Psychoanalytic Association*, 7, 459–483.

Kohut, H. 1966/1978. Forms and transformations of narcissism. In P. H. Ornstein (Ed.), *The Search for the self: Selected writings of Heinz Kohut: 1950–1978* (Vol. 1, pp. 427–460). New York: International Universities Press.

Kohut, H. 1968/1978. The psychoanalytic treatment of narcissistic personality disorders. In P. H. Ornstein (Ed.), *The Search for the Self: Selected writing of Heinz Kohut: 1950–1978* (Vol. 1, 477–509). New York: International Universities Press.

Kohut, H. 1971. The Analysis of the sel*f*. New York: International Universities Press.

Kohut, H. 1972/1978b. Thoughts on narcissism and narcissistic rage. In P. H. Ornstein (Ed.), *The Search for the self: Selected writings of Heinz Kohut: 1950–1978* (Vol. 2, 615–658). New York: International Universities Press.

Kohut, H. 1977. *The restoration of the self.* New York: International Universities Press.

Kohut, H. 1978a. Discussion of "on the adolescent process as a transformation of the self" by Ernest S. Wolf, John E. Gedo, and David Terman. In P. H. Ornstein (Ed.), *The Search for the self: Selected writings of Heinz Kohut 1950–1978* (pp. 659–662). New York, International Universities Press.

Kohut, H. 1978b. Remarks about the formation of the self: Letter to a student regarding some principles of psychoanalytic research. In P. H. Ornstein (Ed.), *The search for the self: Selected writings of Heinz Kohut 1950–1978* (Vol. 2, pp. 737–770). New York: International Universities Press.

Kohut, H. 1978/1990. Introductory remarks to the panel on "Self Psychology and the Sciences of Man." In P. H. Ornstein, *The search for the self: Selected writings of Heinz Kohut: 1978–1981* (Vol. 3, pp. 387–393). Madison, CT: International Universities Press.

Kohut, H. 1979/1991. Four basic concepts in self psychology (1979). In P. H. Ornstein (Ed.), *The search for the self: Selected writings of Heing Kohut: 1978–1981* (Vol. 4, pp. 447–470). Madison, CT: International Universities Press.

Kohut, H. 1982. Introspection, empathy, and the semi-circle of mental health. *International Journal of Psycho-Analysis*, 63, 395–407.

Kohut, H. 1984. *How does analysis cure?* Chicago: The University of Chicago Press.

Khun, T. S. 1970. *The structure of scientific revolutions* (2nd ed). Chicago: University of Chicago Press.

Mahler, M. S. 1975. *The psychological birth of the human infant.* New York: Basic Books.

Palombo, J. 1988. Adolescent development: A view from self psychology. *Child & Adolescent Social Work Journal*, 5(3), 171–186.

Palombo, J. 1990. The cohesive self, the nuclear self, and development in late adolescence. In S. C. Feinstein (Ed.), *Adolescent psychiatry* (Vol. 17, pp. 338–359). Chicago: University of Chicago Press.

Palombo, J. 2008. Self psychology theory. In B. A. Thyer (Ed.), *Comprehensive handbook of social work and social welfare: Human behavior in the social environment* (Vol. 2, pp. 163–205). New Jersey: Wiley.

Strozier, C. B. 2001. *Heinz Kohut: The making of a psychoanalyst.* New York: Farrar, Straus, Giroux.

Major Works

Cocks, G. (Ed.). 1994. *The curve of life: Correspondence of Heinz Kohut 1923–1981.* Chicago: The University of Chicago Press.

Elson, M. (Ed.). 1987. *The Kohut seminars on self psychology and psychotherapy with adolescents and young adults.* New York: W. W. Norton.

Goldberg, A. (Ed.) 1978. In collaboration with H. Kohut. *The psychology of the self: A casebook.* New York: International Universities Press.

Kohut, H. 1971. *The analysis of the self.* New York: International Universities Press.

Kohut, H. 1977. *The restoration of the self.* New York: International Universities Press.

Kohut, H. 1984. *How does analysis cure?* Chicago: The University of Chicago Press.

Kohut, H. 1985. *Self psychology and the humanities: Reflections on a new psychoanalytic approach.* New York: W. W. Norton.

Ornstein, P. H. (Ed.). 1978. *The search for the self: Selected writings of Heinz Kohut 1950–78* (Vols. 1 & 2 New York: International Universities Press.

Ornstein, P. H. (Ed.). 1991. *The Search for the self: Selected writings of Heinz Kohut 1978–1981* (Vols. 3 & 4 New York: International Universities Press.

Tolpin, P., & Tolpin, M., (Eds.) 1996. *Heinz Kohut: The Chicago Institute lectures.* Hillsdale, NJ: The Analytic Press.

Supplementary Readings

Goldberg, A. (Ed.). 1978. *The psychology of the self: A casebook.* New York: International Universities Press.

Shapiro, S. 1995. *Talking with patients: A self psychological view of creative intuition and analytic discipline.* Northvale, NJ: Jason Aronson.

Strozier, C. B. 2001. *Heinz Kohut: The making of a psychoanalyst.* NY: Farrar, Straus, Giroux.

Wolf, E. S. 1988. *Treating the self: Elements of clinical self psychology.* New York: The Guilford Press.

Section VII
Attachment Theories

Fonagy (2001) stated, "Attachment theory is almost unique among psychoanalytic theories in bridging the gap between general psychology and clinical psychodynamic theory." (p. 5). Attachment theories are firmly embedded in a positivist perspective and are paradigmatic of developmental theories that utilize the organismic metaphor. They are rooted in the work of ethologists who studied animals' attachment patterns. As with all evolutionary theories, the fundamental assumption is that human beings, like every other organism, have evolved and survived because of their abilities to adapt to their environments.

Attachment theory has brought to focus the significance of biological, neuropsychological, cognitive, and social factors in children's development. In so doing, it advanced our understanding of development in major ways. Unfortunately, prominent psychoanalysts of his day accused Bowlby of having weakened the intrapsychic perspective that is central to psychoanalytic theory, a shift that led to his banishment from the psychoanalytic community and to the dismissal of his contributions for most of his life. Some critics considered attachment theory to be a theory of the pathological effects of separation, rather than a theory of normal development. Others saw the problem as residing in what they interpreted as his behavioral perspective. In spite of this opposition, a large psychoanalytic literature emerged around the topics of loss, bereavement, and death (Kubler-Ross, 1969; Palombo, 1981).

In time, psychoanalytic theorists could no longer ignore the significance of the data collected by researchers and began to integrate those finding into their theories. In particular, they sought to explore the implications for children's development, for some of the disorders children display, and for their value to clinical practice. However, so far, these integrative efforts may best be described as attempts to graft a robust set of data onto an existing mature theoretical framework. The success of the incorporation of attachment theory into the broader psychoanalytic paradigm has varied depending on clinicians' applications of the theory to their settings. Those who work with mother/infant dyads report major breakthroughs, as do those who work with patients who have suffered significant deprivations and abuse early in their lives. The reports from clinicians who see adults who are less disturbed indicate that the straightforward application of attachment theory takes too simplistic a view of those patients' complex dynamics.

We consider two variants of attachment theory. In Part 1, we present the first variant, which we call *traditional attachment theories*. Here we summarize **Bowlby's**, **Ainsworth's**, and **Main's** contributions. Bowlby's evolutionary perspective took the form of finding a linkage between the psychoanalytic construct of mental representation and the concept of Internal Working Model. Ainsworth enlarged the theory by identifying three major patterns of attachment, the securely attached, the anxious/avoidant, and the anxious/resistant. Her work laid the groundwork for follow up research by developmental psychologists, who found ample confirmation of her findings. Main contributed further to the classification of patterns of attachment with the identification of a fourth category, disorganized/disoriented. She also developed an instrument that identified the intergenerational transmission of attachment patterns.

In Part 2, we discuss the second variant as elaborated by Allen Schore and Peter Fonagy, which we call *neurodevelopmental attachment theories: the return to psychoanalysis*. Each of those two contributors took a different path to integrate attachment theory with psychoanalysis. Schore chose the path he calls a psychoneurobiological point of view. He presents a hybrid that grafts not only attachment theory but also the findings of the neurosciences onto a coalesced version of psychoanalytic metapsychology that includes elements of drive theory, ego psychology, object relations theory, and self psychology. He makes a signal contribution in the application of this model to our understanding of the effects of child maltreatment on the type of attachment these children develop. On the other hand, Fonagy's unique contribution was to introduce the concept of "mentalization" to bridge attachment theory, the construct of Theory of Mind, and psychoanalytic theory. He also brought a rapprochement between psychoanalytic theory and the neuroscience with his concept of Interpersonal Interpretive Mechanism.

Other psychoanalysts have contributed significantly to attachment theory; however, their contributions did not add to the expansion of a developmental theory as such but extended the concepts of mental representation and proposed psychotherapeutic approaches to the treatment of attachment disorders (Lyons-Ruth, 1998; Zeanah & Anders, 1987). Some of these psychoanalytic investigators attempted to address the relationship between the Internal Working Models construct and those of self-representations and object-representations. These efforts were directed at bridging the gap between attachment theory and psychoanalytic object relations theory.

References

Fonagy P. (2001). *Attachment theory and psychoanalysis*. Other Press. New York.

Kubler-Ross E. (1969). *On death and dying: What t he dying have to teach doctors, nurses, clergy, and their own families*. Touchstone. New York.

Lyons-Ruth K. (1998). Implicit relational knowing: Its role in development and psychoanalytic treatment. *Infant Mental Health Journal, 19*(**3**)**,** 282–289.

Palombo J. (1981). Parent loss and childhood bereavement: Some theoretical considerations. *Clinical Social Work Journal* **9**, 1333.

Zeanah C. H., & Anders T. F. (1987). Subjectivity in parent-infant relationships: A discussion of internal working models. *Infant Mental Health Journal*, **83,** 237–250.

Part 1
Traditional Attachment Theories

Chapter 15
John Bowlby (1907–1990)

Publishing Era (1952–1990)

Biographical Information

John Bowlby was born in 1907. His father, a surgeon, encouraged him to pursue a medical career, but Bowlby initially decided to follow his interest in psychology by volunteering in an institution for delinquent children. He found these children to display little affect. His experience there fueled his interest in the effects of early deprivation on children's development. Observing the pathologic effects of early maternal separation from or loss on these adolescents left an indelible impression on him, convincing him that some of the psychopathology he observed resulted either from those early losses or from disturbed relationships between the children and their mothers. He reluctantly decided to enter medical school and completed his training in psychiatry. Concurrently, he became a candidate in the British Psychoanalytic Society. Joan Riviere, a colleague of Melanie Klein psychoanalyzed him. Klein supervised him during his training. He subsequently graduated as a psychoanalyst and in 1938 married Ursula Longstaff, with whom he had four children.

Following his service in the army in 1945, he became the head of the children's department at the Tavistock Clinic, which he promptly renamed the "Department of Children and Parents" to reflect the importance he placed on the family environment on children's development. In 1951, the World Health Organization commissioned him to write a report on the state of children's health worldwide. The publication of his book *Maternal Care and Mental Health* (1952) received international acclaim and established his reputation as an advocate for children. In this publication, following in the footsteps of his predecessors, Anna Freud and Rene Spitz, Bowlby proposed that it is "essential for mental health... that the infant and young child should experience a warm, intimate and continuous relationship with his mother (or permanent mother – substitute) in which both will find satisfaction and enjoyment" (1952, p. 11). Furthermore, he concluded that evidence existed that many forms of psychoneurosis and character disorders were attributable either to deprivation of maternal care or to discontinuities in the children's relationship with their mother figure. Subsequently, in his work at Tavistock, he undertook the task of accounting for the processes through which the many and varied effects that maternal deprivation and the discontinuities in the children's bond to their caregivers produce.

J. Palombo et al., *Guide to Psychoanalytic Developmental Theories*,
DOI: 10.1007/978-0-387-88455-4_15, © Springer Science+Business Media, LLC 2009

During the early years of his career as a psychoanalyst, Melanie Klein's object relations perspective influenced Bowlby, but he soon diverged from her position. Psychoanalysts were highly critical of the alternative theory that he proposed because of its emphasis on environmental factors and its seeming negation of the significance of the unconscious. He was never welcomed back among the circle of his former colleagues, although he remained in Tavistock until his retirement.

The Tavistock Years

At the Tavistock Clinic, Bowlby continued a psychoanalytic tradition begun by Anna Freud's work with the children displaced by war and by Rene Spitz who, as we have seen as early as 1936, was using film to record the effects on children of their separations from their mothers. Bowlby began collaborating with James Robertson, who filmed children who had been separated from their parents. Two deeply moving films, *John* and *A Two-Year-Old Goes to Hospital*, left a haunting impression on clinicians who saw them. Those films left little doubt of the devastating effects of children's separation from their caregivers. A major practical consequence of Bowlby's contribution was to modify the practice of separating children from their parents when in hospital or placed in institutions. Professionals charged with the care of children took notice and made sure that when it became necessary to separate children from their parents a substitute caregiver would attend specifically to them so that they could form a bond between them. This practice was later modified to having the children's parents or primary caregivers be present in the child's immediate environment whenever a separation needed to occur.

At around 1950, Bowlby began collaborating with Mary Salter Ainsworth, who was trained as a research psychologist. Working independently, she had written a dissertation on *An Evaluation of Adjustment Based upon the Concept of Security* (see Chap. 16). Bowlby later credited Ainsworth with the introduction of the concept of the "secure base" to describe the children's responses to the bond with their caregivers by dedicating a book to her (Bowlby, 1988).

Exclusion from the Psychoanalytic Community

Beginning in 1958, Bowlby (1958,1960a,1960c) published a set of controversial papers on the subject of the child's tie to the primary caregiver and the response to the loss of that caregiver. One paper, "Grief and Mourning in Infancy and Early Childhood" (1960c), was followed by discussions by Freud (1960), Schur (1960), and Spitz (1960). In that paper, Bowlby advanced his fundamental proposition that grief and mourning occur in infancy whenever the responses regulating attachment behavior are activated and the caregiver remains unavailable. If the loss occurs between about 6 months and 3–4 years, the effects can be highly unfavorable on personality development. The loss responses the child experiences are essentially the same as those observed in adults. Bowlby used the term mourning to denote the overall psychological processes set in motion by loss. Grief, on the other hand, is referred to the sequence of subjective states following loss in the mourning process. He regarded depression as a normal part of mourning that lies outside of the dynamic seen in guilty depression caused by an attack on the ego by the superego, as ego psychologists claimed. The emphasis on data collection through inference from reconstruction had delayed recognition of his fundamental proposition.

In her response, Anna Freud pointed out the differences in theoretical orientations (1960). She claimed that Bowlby was concerned with the biology of attachment behavior while psychoanalysis does not deal with drive activity, but rather with the mental representations of the drives. She highlighted Bowlby's theoretical misconceptions. He had maintained that psychoanalysis placed need satisfaction through the Pleasure Principle as primary and attachment to the mother as secondary in importance. Anna Freud clarified that setting up a struggle for priority between the two does not make sense because the Pleasure Principle governs all mental processes of the immature and insufficiently structured personality, including attachment. The second theoretical disagreement centered on Bowlby's misuse of the term Infantile Narcissism. He used it in its descriptive, behavioral sense as the subject being withdrawn and self-sufficient, whereas in the metapsychological sense, it refers to the early phase of libido distribution and organization. She next turned to disagreements on clinical points and took up the three phases of behavior after separation from the mother. She agreed with the description of what occurs in the first two phases, but not the third. Bowlby first used the term denial to characterize the third phase. She suggested withdrawal, but Bowlby had already changed it to detachment. She disputed the duration of bereavement, expressing reluctance to use the term mourning to describe parental loss in infants because their personalities were insufficiently structured and the times for bereavement (the preferred term) were so variable. Adult mourning fundamentally was different from infant bereavement. On the last point, the aftereffects of separation, there was harmony between Bowlby's position and that of psychoanalysis.

Schur (1960) was more forceful in his response than Anna Freud. Whereas he was in complete agreement with Bowlby's description of the infant's attachment to the mother, he considered Bowlby's attempts at psychoanalytic theorizing so incorrect and at variance with basic psychoanalytic concepts that it resulted in the reshuffling of psychoanalytic terminology. Focusing on the oral phase and orality, Schur launched a detailed critique of Bowlby's position. He maintained that Bowlby wanted to dethrone the centrality of orality and was otherwise preoccupied with a denial of the significance of this phase. Bowlby, Schur maintained, was incorrect that psychoanalysis had concentrated exclusively on the issue of satisfaction of the infant's oral hunger. Psychoanalysis recognized the first phase of psychosexual development to be a prototypical situation during which the first structures and their relationship to tension and tension relief originated. The pleasure–unpleasure principle was a regulating principle of the mental apparatus that paved the way for secondary process. Other aspects of the oral phase that Bowlby had either neglected or misrepresented were the use of the oral mode for incorporation, introjection leading to the first identifications, and the value psychoanalysis places on perceptual stimulation during feeding, and the promotion of the hungry infant as the prototype of the first in the hierarchy of danger situations, the fear of annihilation.

Spitz (1960) agreed with most of Bowlby's descriptions of loss and separation save one. Bowlby had rejected Spitz's proposition that the damage to object-deprived infants was due to the turning of aggression upon the self in children because of their inability to focus aggression outside. Spitz noted that his own subjects were under 12 months of age while Bowlby's were 18 months of age and older. Spitz charged that Bowlby seemed not to have understood early development or disregarded it as well as the role played by aggression.

In his response to Schur's criticism, Bowlby (1961b) stated that in "Separation Anxiety" (1960a), he had "sketched briefly the sequence of responses to be observed when young children are removed from their mothers and placed with strangers" (p. 9). The responses were protest, despair, and detachment. He pointed out the connection between protest and separation anxiety, despair and grief and mourning, and detachment and defense. Furthermore, all these three phases are part of a single process which, when treated, clarifies the nature of all the phases. Bowlby insisted that the child's tie to the mother is best thought of "as the outcome of a number of instinctual response systems, mostly normal in character" (p. 9). He felt that the data fully substantiated the intimate relationship between grief and separation anxiety and ended with a reaffirmation of the correctness of his views as buttressed by the findings from the observations of ethologists.

The breach created by these fundamental differences regarding psychoanalytic explanations of attachment and loss initially led his colleagues to regard him as a nonconformist. They shunned him at professional meetings and some colleagues even viewed him as a heretic who was betraying his allegiance to psychoanalysis. Eventually, his response was to exclude himself from the psychoanalytic community, in spite of his deep involvement at Tavistock. The effect was that his work was excluded from the mainstream of psychoanalysis for decades only to gain grudging recognition toward the end of his life.

Darwin Biography

In 1990, just prior to his death, Bowlby published a lengthy biography on Charles Darwin. He became intrigued with Darwin because of the debilitating illness from which he had suffered following his return from his travels on the *Beagle*, from 1832 to 1836. As described in his extensive correspondence, Darwin complained of suffering intermittently from "palpitation, flatulence and nausea, trembling or shivering, blurred vision, paraesthesias (tingling sensations), faintness, becoming easily and chronically tired, and fear of dying. Other common symptoms include dizziness, headaches, emotional sweating, and chest pains on activity or from emotion" (Bowlby, 1990, p. 458). These symptoms would leave him bedridden for days at a time, with little relief from the medical interventions prescribed by eminent doctors of the day. What is curious about Darwin's descriptions of his illness is that in spite of the acuteness of his capacity as an observer, he left no precise description of his illness. Physicians have speculated as to the causes of the Darwin's illness, although controversy continues to this day as to its precise diagnosis.

Bowlby attempted to make the case that Darwin's illness was caused by "hyperventilation syndrome" (p. 10). Hyperventilation syndrome is a condition that results from overbreathing, that is, rapid shallow or deep breathing. The effect of overbreathing at first results in lower blood levels of carbon dioxide, which in turn reduces the amount of oxygen that the body requires. A physiological alarm system sets off a stress response that at times will produce a panic attack. Many of the symptoms that Darwin described are common to this condition. Whereas the causes for the syndrome are unclear, modern day medicine often attributes the condition to a combination of physiological and psychological causes.

Bowlby expressed the belief that Darwin suffered from that condition that waxed and waned from the age of 30 until he was 60 and went on to live symptom-free for the next 13 years (p. 6). The condition was particularly severe during three periods of his life. The first occurred before the birth of his first child, the second during his father's terminal illness and death, and the third when he experienced a deep disappointment in a senior admired colleague who did not support the theory proposed in the *Origin of Species.* According to Bowlby, these events reactivated a set of psychological trauma from which Darwin had suffered. Central to an understanding of the dynamics was Darwin's loss of his mother when he was 8½ years old and equally important was his older sister's insistence that no mention be made of the mother thereafter. In the ensuing years, his relationship with his father remained uncomfortably tense and strained. Bowlby states

> Principal features of my thesis are that his mother's early death, and especially the way in which members of the family responded to it by sealing it in silence, made him intensely sensitive to any illness or possible death in the family, while his father's disparaging criticisms of him made him especially vulnerable to any criticism from emotionally significant senior colleagues (1990, p. 13).

Bowlby was convinced that Darwin's life history confirmed his theory that disruptions in early attachments to mothers can produce serious psychological difficulties. It is interesting to note that he took great pains, in an appendix to the book, to rebut other explanations for the symptoms given by tropical disease experts. One alternative explanation is that Darwin suffered from Chagas's disease. This disease, which is common in South America, results from the bite of an insect and manifests many of the symptoms from which Darwin suffered. In fact, Darwin reports that an insect had bitten him during his stay in Argentina. We are left to speculate as to which of the two accounts is true.

Bowlby died on September 2, 1990, at his summer home in Isle of Skye, Scotland. He was 83 years old.

Theory of Development

Bowlby originated attachment theory because of the shortcomings he found in psychoanalytic theory. As we saw in earlier chapters, psychoanalytic theory (drive theory and ego psychology) proposed that the process through which infants' earliest investment of their mothers occurs is the discharge of the built-up tension created in the infant by the oral component of the libidinal drive. Klein proposed that infants nursing at their mothers' breast led to their "cathexis" of the breast, i.e., for the infant the breast represented the mother. Bowlby designated this theory the ***Secondary Drive theory***. He states, "I propose to call this the theory of Secondary Drive, terminology which is derived from Learning Theory. It has also been called the cupboard love theory of object relations" (1958, p. 351). Presumably, the primary drive represents the need for attachment. According to Bowlby, Freud did not appreciate the significance of infants' attachment to their mothers.[1] Furthermore, he maintained that psychoanalytic theory, in particular, Melanie Klein's emphasis on the child's fantasy life, paid insufficient attention to the role of environmental factors on children's development. Consequently, it failed to account for the significance of the role of the mother in the child's development. Bowlby also criticized psychoanalytic theories for not relying sufficiently on direct observations of infants and children to support their hypotheses.

Ethological/Evolutionary Approach

Finding Freud's adherence to Lamarckian evolutionary theory rather than to Darwinian Theory unsatisfactory, Bowlby, influenced by the ethologist Robert Hinde, turned to the ethological literature for answers. **Ethology**, consistent with modern evolutionary theory, proposed that instinctive behavior reflects the principles of survival of the species. He felt that it is possible to understand the workings of this instinctive behavior through the contributions made by ethology, information theory (cybernetics), and the evolutionary concept of adaptation. Attachment behaviors are "**species-specific behavior patterns**" that are instinctive and are activated in the service of survival. By instinctive responses, he refers to behaviors such as sucking, clinging, following, crying, and smiling. Beginning in 1958, Bowlby published a series of papers (Bowlby, 1958, 1960a, 1960b, 1960c, 1961a, 1963) that outlined his thoughts and provided the foundation for his three-volume work on attachment (Bowlby, 1969, 1973, 1980).

Based on empirical data obtained by ethologists such as Konrad Lorenz and the psychologist Harry Harlow, Bowlby determined that attachment was driven less by the need for nourishments and more by behaviors that led to proximity of infants to caregivers. He posited that infants seek shelter and safety from predators in the service of survival by forming a **secure bond** with their caregivers. Separation from the haven that caregivers provide leads to the expression of distress signals, such as clinging, crying, and calling the caregivers, called **attachment behaviors**. The adult counterpart of these behaviors in children is the **caretaking behaviors**.

[1] Bowlby consistently refers to the caregivers as "mother." However, he makes it clear that what he means is any person with whom the child has formed a special affectional bond. This may include fathers, nursery school caregivers, or others.

The infants' responses do not imply that the behaviors are "motivated" as the term "instinctual" implies when used in psychoanalytic theory. A complex mechanism that controls their activation and their termination governs instinctive. The responses are activated by a disruption of infants' bond to their mothers and are terminated by the reunion of the two. Each set of responses is accompanied by emotional experiences that are comforting when children are in contact with their mothers, and produce anxious responses when separated from her. These responses are not limited to the early years but endure throughout the life cycle.

Bowlby makes a clear distinction between the *causal factors* of behaviors and the *functions* the behaviors serve. Causal factors may include hormonal levels, actions of the central nervous system, and environmental stimuli. By contrast, the functions that behaviors serve constitute the *special consequences* that arise when a system is active in the organism's environment of evolutionary adaptedness and that result from the way the system is constructed. This model of motivation distinguishes causation from function within an evolutionary framework.

Since the unit of biological adaptation is the population and the survival of populations is dependent on the cooperation of individuals, much of one individual's endowment is complementary to that of another of different age or sex in the same population. Behavior patterns mediating attachment of youth to adults are complementary to those mediating care of youth by adults; in the same way, systems mediating adult masculine behavior in one individual are complementary to those mediating adult feminine behavior in another. This observation emphasizes the fact that instinctive behavior is never intelligible merely in terms of a single individual but rather must be understood in terms of a group of individuals collaborating with each other (Bowlby, 1969, Vol. I, p. 141).

Attachment and Internal Working Models

Attachment, therefore, consists of a behavioral system that is activated by the interaction between infants and their mothers, who constitute the environment of behavioral adaptedness. The set goal, which is the end result, of the behaviors is **proximity to the mother** who provides a shelter that safeguards the infant from predators. Infants' ties to their mothers are related to this behavioral system. The behavioral systems mediate the instructions given by the physiological processes, which are causal factors, and the set goal that is to be attained, which are factors related to the functions the system performs. If the infant maintains proximity to the **sensitive caregiver**, the infant monitors the environment through visual and auditory channels to be reassured of the continuity of the presence of the caregiver. When infants are separated from their mothers a set of behaviors are activated to bring about a reunion. When these are insufficient, the child will follow the mother. The attachment system may be activated by other conditions such as fatigue, the presence of strangers, anything frightening, or the physical or emotional unavailability of the caregiver.

An **exploratory behavioral system** is present side-by-side with the attachment system. Bowlby states that this system "evolved for the special function of extracting information from the environment" (1969, Vol. I, p. 238). It is activated by the curiosity that novel stimuli arouse in the child and it is terminated when familiarity with the stimuli is established. Children are preprogrammed to explore their environment from within the secure base of the relationship with their mothers. Closely tied to this system is the alarm or fear system that the perception of danger evokes if children stray too far from their caregivers. The latter system produces anxiety, leading them to withdraw and reunite with the secure base.

Emotions, which at times are intense, accompany all these activities, whether they involve attachment, separation, loss, exploration, or fear. Those emotions are positive if the affectional bond with the caregiver predominates; they are negative if the caregivers are unavailable or if the child confronts danger. The result is that proximity positively reinforces attachment behaviors, whereas separations painfully reprimand loss of proximity.

Internal Working Models

In an effort to link his concepts with those of object relations theory, Bowlby proposed the construct of "internal working models." In healthy development, infants develop **Internal Working Models (IWM)** of the external world and of their internal milieu, as well as the interaction between the two. These models are cognitive maps that resemble the psychoanalytic concept of representations and that stand for selected aspects of the environment. Language permits the building of hierarchically organized models that guide the behavioral systems. This construct, which echoes the concept of self-representation and object representations from object relations theory, is broader than those concepts because its general functions are to construct maps or models of all aspects of the external world rather than focusing exclusively on the intrapsychic dynamics of the child. IWM are not simple replicas of the self and of others in interaction with each other but complex structures that are affected and modifiable by experience.

Bowlby did not believe that development occurs in phases, rather that patterns of attachment are formed that may be modified by experience or persist throughout the life span. Early attachment behaviors and experiences with caregivers determine the patterns that organize the attachment behaviors for the rest of the person's life span. Each child may follow one of a set of developmental pathways that is open and that results from interactions with the environment. Attachment behaviors, such as attachment to parents, spouses, and one's children, endure throughout the life span, and when found in adults these are not necessarily pathological. Psychopathology occurs not because of fixations or regressions, but because disturbances in attachment behaviors have taken place. Such disturbances may result from caregivers' threats to terminate the bond to the child, actual physical or emotional disruptions of the bond, or circumstances that thwart efforts at reunion. Such is the case when an unresolved grief response following the loss of a loved one endures far beyond the time such grief ought to last.

Attachment, Separation, and Loss

Distinctive behaviors emerge following a separation from or the loss of a significant other. A characteristic sequential pattern manifests as external behaviors and accompanies internal experiences. In the initial phase, the child's overt behavioral displays are of **protest**, which reflect *separation anxiety*. Next are behaviors that demonstrate the child's **despair** that reflect the processes of *grief and mourning*. Finally, the child manifests **detachment** from the external world as a *defense* against the intolerable psychic pain to which he or she undergoes.

Protest: separation anxiety: Psychoanalytic theory distinguished between fear as arising from an actual external threat and anxiety as arising without the presence of any external threat. Bowlby finds it hard to sustain this distinction. Whenever separations activate instinctive responses with no possibility of reaching termination, he maintains that **separation anxiety** will arise in the infant. Infants then are pushed toward their mothers by escape responses, and pulled toward her by clinging and following. Escape responses are behaviors that increase the distance from mother and produce alarm in the child. He proposed the concept of **primary anxiety** to describe infants' response to a rupture in the attachment to their mothers, distinguishing between *conditioned anxiety* and *expectant anxiety*. *Conditioned anxiety* is based on a primitive form of learning such as conditioning; it occurs before the child can process cognitively what is occurring. *Expectant anxiety* is a more advanced form of cognitive processing based on memory organized by means of symbols. The child has internal representations of caregivers and can now react not only to actual but also to imagined dangers.

If separated from mother, otherwise healthy children between the ages of 15 and 30 months behaviorally will manifest severe distress. They will scan the environment for signs of mother's return and reject all attempts at engagement by substitutes. If they are exposed to repeated loss, they will at first experience conditioned anxiety; if the separations occur repeatedly then expectant anxiety will take place, that is, they will anticipate a repetition of past losses.

Despair: grief and mourning: During this phase, which follows the period of protest, the children will withdraw and become increasingly hopeless that a reunion with their mothers will occur. The child will demonstrate signs of loss and, eventually, show signs that indicate deep **grief and mourning** for her.

Detachment: defense: In this final phase, children appear indifferent to their surroundings. If their mothers reappear for a brief period, the children will seem indifferent, lacking the ability to discriminate among caregivers and appearing to relate to them superficially. If this phase becomes prolonged, they will potentially lose the ability to become attached to any single person and to manifest signs of being affected by the loss should a loss occur. These responses on the part of children are characteristic of a defense against the feelings engendered by the loss of their mothers.

Attachment

Bowlby hypothesizes that attachment behavior is made up of a number of component instinctive responses, which are at first relatively independent of each other. These instinctive responses mature at different times during the first year of life and develop at different rates; they serve the function of binding the child to mother and contribute to the reciprocal dynamic of binding the mother to child. The following provides approximate periods for the appearances of these responses:

Soon after birth, separation from the caregiver activates crying as well as clinging and smiling. Subjective feelings associated with these experiences are ones of "primary anxiety." When infants are reunited with their mothers, the anxiety ceases and it is replaced by the experience of comfort.

Prior to 6 months, we observe fear and avoidance of strangers and a turning to mother for comfort. There is evidence that the human face and voice are of special interest to infants in their earliest weeks of life; however, during that period children have no concept of another human being. During those early weeks, infants manifest an interest in their caregiver's moist, warm nipple to which they respond by sucking, and to her sparkling eyes to which they respond by smiling. As the weeks go by, these fragmentary, perceptual experiences become coalesced and infants will attribute them to the same source.

By the age of 9 weeks, infants will stop crying when held by their caregivers. Infants respond differentially to their caregivers in comparison to others in their environment. When separated from their mothers, the infants cry.

By 15 weeks, infants will cry when they observe their mother leaving them.

By 20 weeks, they will vocalize, attempting to call their mother.

By 24 weeks, they will follow their mothers.

By 30 weeks, they will greet her differentially from others.

By 8 months, they will use mother as a base from which to explore their environment. They will also run to mother when frightened.

From 9 to 18 months the five patterns of attachment behaviors, such as sucking, clinging, crying, following, and smiling, become organized into more sophisticated goal-corrected systems that serve to maintain proximity to the mother.

Beginning in the first year and with language acquisition, children begin to construct working models of themselves, their mothers, and the world around them. These working models include blueprints of how others will respond and interact with the children, as well as how they will respond to those responses. The children will consider these expectations when they anticipate changes in their ties to others.

By the time that the child enters the second year and acquires mobility, typical attachment behaviors become evident. The attachment system continues to be regularly activated until the third year. The attachment behaviors manifest as intensely and as frequently as during the first year. Although the child's greater understanding of his surroundings may change, the circumstances that elicit the behavior remain the same.

During the third year, proximity to mother becomes less urgent. Infants become aware of the mother's impending departure. They are better able to accept temporary separations.

After their third birthday, children become more secure with familiar substitute attachment figures even in other than familiar places. This is true as long as the children are confident that their mothers will return and a reunion will take place.

At the age of 4, a greater attenuation of the attachment response occurs as the child becomes ready to enter preschool.

By the ages of 5 and 6 into latency, children will comfortably play with others in the absence of their mothers, although they will return to her for comfort should something go wrong.

During adolescence and into adulthood changes occur in the mode of expression and the persons toward whom the attachment behavior becomes activated. The process of adolescence further attenuates attachment to parents. Great individual variations of expression exist. Some adolescents cut themselves off from their parents, whereas others remain intimately tied. Most continue their bond throughout their adult lives.

As individuals get older and they cannot continue to direct their attachment behaviors toward their peers because of the potential for their loss, those behaviors become redirected toward members of the younger generations.

In His Own Words

The excerpt that follows illustrates, among other factors, Bowlby's insistence on an empirical base of observation for his theory. The care with which he formulates his findings indicates that he approached the data much as a researcher approaches the investigation of new phenomena. What is impressive, however, is that he pays particular attention to the emotions that accompany the children's behaviors and his empathy for their distress [Excerpted from Bowlby (1960) (reprinted with permission from Blackwell Publishing)].

First let us consider the data.

Our observations concern healthy children of 15–30 months admitted to a hospital, perhaps for investigation or elective surgery, or to some other residential institution and there cared for in traditional ways. By traditional ways we mean that the child is handled by a succession of strange nurses, mainly students, who will variously bathe, feed, and change him. The nurses will be on shift duty, and often within a few weeks most will have moved to other departments. No matter how kind each may be in her fragment of care, there will be no nurse whom he can come to know or with whom he can enter into a stable relationship. He may see his mother for a short time each day, but it may be less often. In this context a child of 15–30 months who has had a normal relationship to his mother and has not previously been parted from her will commonly show a predictable sequence of behavior. This sequence can usefully be broken into three phases according to what attitude to his mother is dominant; we describe these phases as those of protest, despair, and detachment. Though in presenting them it is convenient to differentiate them sharply, it is to be understood that in reality each merges into the next, so that the child may be for days or weeks in a state of transition from, or alternation between, one phase and another.

The initial phase, that of Protest, may last from a few hours to a week or more. During it the young child appears acutely distressed at having lost his mother and seeks to recapture her by the full exercise of his limited resources. He will often cry loudly, shake his cot, throw himself about, and look eagerly toward any sight or sound that might prove to be his missing mother. All his behavior suggests strong expectation that she will return. Meantime he is apt to reject all alternative figures who offer to do things for him, though some children will cling desperately to a nurse.

During the phase of Despair, which succeeds protest, his preoccupation with his missing mother is still evident, though his behavior suggests increasing hopelessness. The active physical movements diminish or come to an end, and he may cry monotonously or intermittently. He is withdrawn and inactive, makes no demands on the environment, and appears to be in a state of deep mourning. This is a quiet phase, and sometimes, clearly erroneously, is presumed to indicate a diminution of distress.

Because the child shows more interest in his surroundings, the phase of Detachment, which sooner or later succeeds protest and despair, is often welcomed as a sign of recovery. He no longer rejects the nurses, accepts their care and the food and toys they bring, and may even smile and be sociable. This seems satisfactory. When his mother visits, however, it can be seen that all is not well, for there is a striking absence of the behavior characteristic of the strong attachment normal at this age. So far from greeting his mother he may seem hardly to know her; so far from clinging to her he may remain remote and apathetic; instead of tears there is a listless turning away. He seems to have lost all interest in her.

Should his stay in hospital or residential nursery be prolonged and should he, as is usual, have the experience of becoming transiently attached to a series of nurses each of whom leaves and so repeats for him the experience of the original loss of his mother, he will in time act as if neither mothering nor contact with humans had much significance for him. After a series of upsets at losing several mother figures to whom in turn he has given some trust and affection, he will gradually commit himself less and less to succeeding figures and in time will stop altogether taking the risk of attaching himself to anyone. Instead he will become increasingly self-centered and, instead of directing his desires and feelings toward people, becomes preoccupied with material things such as sweets, toys, and food. A child living in an institution or hospital who has reached this state will no longer be upset when nurses change or leave. He will cease to show feelings when his parents come and go on visiting day, and it may cause them pain when they realize that; although he has an avid interest in the presents they bring, he has little interest in them as special people. He will appear cheerful and adapted to his unusual situation and apparently easy and unafraid of anyone. But this sociability is superficial: he appears no longer to care for anyone.

We have had some difficulty in finding the best term to denote this phase. In previous papers and in the early drafts of this one the term "denial" was used. It gave rise to many difficulties, however, and is now abandoned in favor of the more purely descriptive term "detachment." An alternative is "withdrawal" but this has two disadvantages for my purpose. In the first place there is a danger that it might convey the picture of an inactive child withdrawn from the world, a picture that is the opposite of what often obtains. In the second, in psychoanalytic writing it is commonly associated with libido theory and the idea of instinct as a quantity of energy that can be withdrawn, a model I am not using. Not only does the term "detachment" have neither of these disadvantages, but it is a natural counterpart of "attachment." The nature of the defense process or processes that give rise to it is, of course, a matter for detailed study.

Returning now to the empirical data, I wish to emphasize that the behavior seen in the phases of Protest and Despair is not, as is sometimes alleged, confined to children whose relations to their mothers are already impaired. Though we have no large series of well-observed cases to quote, we are satisfied that there is clear evidence that it occurs in children whose previous relationships would be judged to have been anything between excellent and fairly unfavorable. It appears to be only in children whose relationships are already severely impaired, and who may therefore already be in a phase of Detachment that such behavior is absent.

In examining the theoretical problems raised by these observations it is convenient to consider them with reference to these three phases of behavior. The phase of Protest raises the problem especially of separation anxiety, Despair that of grief and mourning, and Detachment that of defence. Each of them is central to psychoanalytic theory and will therefore need detailed discussion. The thesis to be advanced is that the three types of response – separation anxiety, grief and mourning, and defence – are phases of a single process and that when treated as such each illumines the other two.

Summary and Conclusions

Impressed by his observation of the effects of early separation of children from their mothers, Bowlby found that ego psychological explanations for symptoms the children manifest were unsatisfactory. He argued that the theory was based on a premise that what sustains the relationship between mothers and their infants is the nurture they provide. He identified that theory as the secondary drive theory, the theory that attachment to the caregiver is due to the nourishment she or he provides, referring to it derogatorily as "the cupboard love theory of object relations" (1958, p. 351). That theory insufficiently appreciated the role of the environment on children's development. Consequently, he turned to alternative explanations. He found answers, in particular, in the work of contemporary ethologists, who embraced modern evolutionary theory as critical to understand all behavior.

Bowlby formulated his theory of attachment on ethological and evolutionary premises, a position that led to his exclusion from the psychoanalytic circle of his peers. Infants, he proposed, are innately driven to seek proximity to their mothers, who provide a secure base that protects them from predators. Attachment behaviors, such as sucking, clinging, following, crying, and smiling, are behaviors that separations activate and that serve to restore the infants' proximity to their mothers.

If the infants are not reunited with their mothers, a sequence of responses is activated by the separation. Infants will go through a phase of *protest*, displaying severe emotional distress. If the separation is prolonged, they enter into a period of *despair*, which is characterized by feelings of helplessness and hopelessness resembling adult's grief and mourning. The child appearing withdrawn and detached from the surroundings characterizes the final phase of prolonged separation. *Detachment* is a defense that serves children to deal with the powerful feelings that buffet them.

Children develop IWM of themselves, their caregivers, and the interactions among the two. The concept of IWM represents Bowlby's effort to bridge attachment theory and object relations theory, an effort that drew skeptical responses from his psychoanalytic peers.

A further elaboration of attachment theory led Bowlby to propose an *exploratory behavioral system* through which children gain information about the world around them as they are drawn to novel stimuli. If, in the course of their explorations, the children perceive what they interpret to be dangerous, an alarm system is triggered that produces anxiety. This fear system alerts the children of the need to return to the secure base from which they had strayed. Furthermore, an affectional bond develops between children and their caregivers that becomes a powerful force in maintaining attachment patterns. These patterns carry over to other relationships and last throughout the life span.

Keywords Attachment behaviors • Attachment • Caretaking behaviors • Ethology • Grief and mourning • Exploratory behavioral system • Internal Working Models • Primary anxiety • Protest, despai, and detachment • Proximity to the mother • Secondary drive theory • Secure bond • Sensitive caregiver • Separation anxiety • Species-specific behavior patterns

References

Bowlby, J. (1952). *Maternal care and mental health: A report on behalf of the World Health Organization as a contribution to the United Nations programme for the welfare of homeless children*. Geneva: World Health Organization.

Bowlby, J. (1958). The nature of the child's tie to his mother. *International Journal of Psycho-Analysis, 39*, 350–374.

Bowlby, J. (1960a). Grief and mourning in infancy and early childhood. *The Psychoanalytic Study of the Child, 15*, 9–53.

Bowlby, J. (1960b). Separation anxiety. *International Journal of Psycho-Analysis, 41*: 89–114.
Bowlby, J. (1960c). Symposium on 'psycho-analysis and ethology': Ethology and the development of object relations. *International Journal of Psycho-Analysis, 41*, 313–318.
Bowlby, J. (1961a). Processes of mourning. *International Journal of Psycho-Analysis, 42*, 317–341.
Bowlby, J. (1961b). Note on Dr. Max Schur's comments on grief and mourning in infancy and early childhood. *The Psychoanalytic Study of the Child, 16*, 206–208.
Bowlby, J. (1963). Pathological mourning and childhood mourning. *Journal of the American Psychoanalytic Association, 11*, 500–542.
Bowlby, J. (1969). *Attachment and loss, Vol. I: Attachment*. New York: Basic Books.
Bowlby, J. (1973). *Attachment and loss, Vol. II: Separation, anxiety and danger*. New York: Basic Books.
Bowlby, J. (1980). *Attachment and loss, Vol. III: Loss: Sadness and depression* . New York: Basic Books.
Bowlby, J. (1988). *A secure base: Parent–child attachment and healthy human development*. New York: Basic Books.
Bowlby, J. (1990). *Charles Darwin: A new life*. New York: W. W. Norton.
Freud, A. (1960). Discussion of Dr. John Bowlby's paper. *The Psychoanalytic Study of the Child, 15*, 53–62.
Schur, M. (1960). Discussion of Dr. John Bowlby's paper. *The Psychoanalytic Study of the Child, 15*, 63–84.
Spitz, R. (1960). Discussion of Dr. John Bowlby's paper. *The Psychoanalytic Study of the Child, 15*, 85–208.

Major Works

Bowlby, J. (1969). *Attachment and loss, Vol. I: Attachment*. New York: Basic Books.
Bowlby, J. (1973). *Attachment and loss, Vol. II: Separation, anxiety and danger*. New York: Basic books.
Bowlby, J. (1980). *Attachment and loss, Vol. III: Loss: Sadness and depression* . New York: Basic books.

Supplementary Readings

Cassidy, J., & Shaver, P. R. (Eds.). (1999). *Handbook of attachment: Theory, research, and clinical applications*. New York: Guilford Press.

Chapter 16
Mary Salter Ainsworth (1913–1999)

Publishing Era (1951–1999)

Biographical Information

Mary Salter Ainsworth began her career as a psychologist, earning her Ph.D. from the University of Toronto. Her dissertation titled *An Evaluation of Adjustment Based upon the Concept of Security* was completed in 1940. It focused on the issue of the child's need for security, a topic closely related to attachment to which she was to make a major contribution later on. During the war, she served in the Canadian Army Corp. Upon her discharge, she returned to the University of Toronto to conduct research in personality development. Following her husband's move to London in 1950, she became involved in Tavistock Clinic's research projects and began a lifelong working relationship with Bowlby. At first, she joined others in the psychoanalytic community who expressed skepticism of his views on attachment. Her attitude changed following her studies of children and families in Uganda (see Bretherton, 1992; Main, 1999).

In 1954, she took an opportunity offered at the East African Institute of Social Research in Uganda to study Ganda families and children. As an acute observer, she collected data on the interactions between children and their mothers. Two years later, she accepted a teaching position at Johns Hopkins University in Baltimore, where she continued to collect data on these types of interactions, observing children in their homes and using the developmental framework she and Bowlby constructed jointly.

The analysis of her voluminous narrative accounts of observations from both the Ganda study and her work with the families she observed at Johns Hopkins led her to formulate the Strange-Situation procedure, a standardized protocol for the study of young children's reactions to separations from their mothers at ages 12–13 months (Ainsorth, Blehar, Waters, & Wall, 1978). She postulated three types of attachments that now provide the foundation of all empirical research on attachment; these are the "anxious/avoidant," the "securely attached," and the "anxious/resistant." Bowlby refers to this work in his first volume, acknowledging Ainsworth's contribution to attachment theory. Main (Main & Solomon, 1986) added a fourth category, the disorganized/disoriented.

J. Palombo et al., *Guide to Psychoanalytic Developmental Theories*,
DOI: 10.1007/978-0-387-88455-4_16,

While at Johns Hopkins, Ainsworth was successfully analyzed following her divorce and retained a sympathetic attitude to psychoanalysis for the rest of her life; however, she never formally attempted to integrate psychoanalytic theory into her work.

Theoretical Contributions

Ainsworth's Strange-Situation procedure provided attachment theory with an empirical tool with which to categorize patterns of mother/infant attachment. It made possible the use of a standardized approach that all investigators could use (Ainsworth et al., 1978, pp. 31–44). This protocol gained international acceptance and became integral to attachment theory. Developmental psychologists in particular have used it extensively; their published findings constitute a vast literature. Investigators from diverse fields have applied the categories to their research to uncover the neurobiological underpinnings of attachment and to explore the continuity or discontinuity of those categories in latency, adolescence, and adulthood. Others have extended the categories to the clinical setting, applying them to the diagnosis of psychopathology and to the treatment of mother/infant dyads (see Cassidy & Shaver, 1999).

A critical factor that Ainsworth uncovered in her observations of the families she studied was the relationship between the mothers' sensitivity to their infants and the type of attachment that the infants formed to their mothers. The concept of **maternal sensitivity** acquired special meaning in her and all subsequent studies. She uncovered four subgroups of maternal sensitivity that became parameters in measurement of the interactions between mothers and their infants. These are sensitivity–insensitivity, acceptance–rejection, cooperation–interference, and accessibility–ignoring. (Each of these is described in the excerpt from Ainsworth printed later.)

The Strange-Situation procedure involves eight "episodes" of brief duration, lasting from 30 s to 3 min, in which the mother is first left alone with the baby. After 3 min, a stranger enters the room, converses with the mother, and approaches the baby, at which point the mother leaves the room while the stranger stays alone with the baby. The stranger leaves the room upon the mother's return. The mother greets the baby and deals with any reactions he or she may have had to the separation. She then leaves the room once more while the baby is now left alone for 3 min. The stranger then reenters the room and attempts to interact with the baby. Finally, the stranger leaves and the mother is reunited with the baby (see Table 16.1).

Attachment Classification

Ainsworth found confirmation of her observations in the Strange Situation from the narratives of her observations gathered in the homes of Ganda and Baltimore children. The following is the classification of attachments in accordance with the

Table 16.1 Summary of episodes of the strange situation

Number of episodes	Persons present	Duration	Brief description of action
1	Mother, baby, and observer	30 s	Observer introduces mother and baby to experimental room, then leaves.
2	Mother and baby	3 min	Mother is nonparticipant while baby explores; if necessary, play is stimulated after 2 min.
3	Stranger, mother, and baby	3 min	Stranger enters. First minute: Stranger silent. Second minute: Stranger converses with mother. Third minute: Stranger approaches baby. After 3 min mother leaves unobtrusively.
4	Stranger and baby	3 min or less[a]	First separation episode; Stranger's behavior is geared to that of the baby.
5	Mother and baby	3 min or more[b]	First reunion episode. Mother greets and/or comforts baby, then tries to settle him again in play. Mother then leaves, saying "bye-bye."
6	Baby alone	3 min or less[a]	Second separation episode.
7	Stranger and baby	3 min or less[a]	Continuation of second separation. Stranger enters and gears her behavior to that of baby.
8	Mother and baby	3 min	Second reunion episode. Mother enters, greets baby, then picks him up. Meanwhile stranger leaves unobtrusively.

From Ainsworth et al. (1978, p. 37) (reprinted with permission from Lawrence Erlbaum an imprint of Taylor & Francis Group, LLC)
[a]Episode is curtailed if the baby is unduly distressed
[b]Episode is prolonged if more time is required for the baby to become reinvolved in play

patterns that infants exhibited in the Strange-Situation procedure (Ainsworth et al., 1978, pp. 55–64):

Group A: *anxious/avoidant* (Ainsworth et al., 1978, pp. 59–60): The **anxious/avoidant** child avoids interacting with mother during the reunion episodes, may avert his or her gaze, and is not distressed by the separation. He or she does not resist contact with mother and treats the stranger in the same way.

Subgroup A_1. The child forcefully avoids mother during the reunion episodes, at times, even turning away from her. If mother picks the child up, he or she shows little interest in maintaining the contact and may squirm away.

Subgroup A_2. The child exhibits a mixed response in reunion episodes with mother. He or she may seek proximity while at the same time giving indications of avoiding contact. The child may cling if picked up but soon squirms indicating he or she wishes to be put down.

Group B: *securely attached* (Ainsworth et al., 1978, pp. 60–62): The **securely attached** child will greet mother with a smile on reunion, seeming to welcome her return. Whereas the child may or may not interact with the stranger, the child actively seeks interaction with mother, seeking proximity and contact with her. He or she will wish for the contact to be maintained and protests if put down after being picked up. The child is distressed during the separation from mother and clearly wants to be reunited with her.

Subgroup B_1. The child appears not to be distressed by the separations from mother, but greets her warmly when she returns following the separation episode. He or she may manifest some avoidance behavior but does not resist being picked up.
Subgroup B_2. The child seeks proximity with mother more actively than B_1 children do. He or she greets her, approaches her, and wishes to have contact with her. However, he or she does not manifest mixed feeling toward her.
Subgroup B_3. The child seeks physical contact with mother, showing little sign of avoidance of proximity; in fact, he or she insists on maintaining the contact. The child is increasingly distressed by the separations, manifesting the greatest distress in the second separation episode.
Subgroup B_4. The child is completely preoccupied with his or her mother when in the presence of the stranger. There is much anxiety, crying, and inappropriate gestures or motions. He or she exhibits some ambivalence, although not as much as Group C children.

Group C: anxious/*resistant* (Ainsworth et al., 1978, pp. 62–63): The **anxious/resistant** child exhibits clear-cut ambivalence toward mother during the reunion episodes, seeking proximity while at the same time resisting the contact that is made. With the stranger, he or she will exhibit more anger or passivity than children in the other groups.

Subgroup C_1 The child exhibits anger both pripor to separations and following reunion. He or she is extremely distressed during the separation episodes and is particularly angry while with the stranger.
Subgroup C_2 The child generally exhibits open passivity, but little anger. They are limited in their exploration of the environment, and tend to use passive modes of communication with their mothers.

Of her sample of 106 infants, 59 or 56% were male and 47 or 44% were female. Seventy infants or 66% fell into Group B, the Securely Attached category, whereas 23 or 22% were classified as falling into Group A, the Anxious/Avoidant, and 13 or 12% fell into Group C, the Anxious/Resistant category. The distribution of boys and girls in each category did not differ significantly. Nineteen percent of the boys and 25% of the girls fell into Group A; 69% of the boys and 62% of the girls fell into Group B, and 12% of the boys and 13% of the girls fell into Group C (Ainsworth et al., 1978, p. 98) (Table 16.2).

It is noteworthy that Ainsworth considered these categories to constitute phenomenological descriptions of children's behaviors that were not necessarily

Table 16.2 Distribution of Ainsworth's sample by attachment classification and gender

			Boys		Girls	
Attachment classification	Number	Percentage	Number	Percentage	Number	Percentage
Group A: Anxious/avoidant	23	22	11	19	12	25
Group B: Securely attached	70	66	41	69	29	62
Group C: Anxious/resistant	13	12	7	12	6	13
Total	106	100	59	100	47	100

indicative of the mental health or ill health of the children. A common confusion among those uninitiated into the attachment literature is that the children in the secure category are free of emotional problems whereas those in the insecure categories are not. Ainsworth's work indicates that secure children may be at a lesser risk to developing such problems than insecurely attached children, but no correlations exist between the type of category under which a child is classified and the existence of emotional problems. As we will see later, this is not the case with Main's insecure disorganized/disoriented attachment, which is indicative of a disrupted relationship with the caregiver and a pathological outcome for the child.

Main's Contributions to Attachment Theory

Mary Main was fascinated with Noam Chomsky's work in linguistics, which led her to apply to Johns Hopkins University in Baltimore in 1968. At Johns Hopkins, she was required to complete an apprenticeship and was assigned to work under Mary Ainsworth on infant–mother attachment in spite of her hesitation to enter that field because the research was unrelated to the field of linguistics. While spending the required 2 years acquiring a broad knowledge base in psychology and psychophysiology, she became acquainted with Hinde's work on ethnology that had been so influential in Bowlby's work. Under Ainsworth's guidance, she eventually found the work with infants and their mothers sufficiently gratifying that she completed a dissertation titled *Exploration, Play, and Cognitive Functioning as Related to Child–Mother Attachment* (Main, 1974).

Main's contributions to attachment theory are sufficiently significant to require their inclusion in this chapter. She identified a fourth category, the disorganized/disoriented attachment, a form of childhood psychopathology. She also devised the Adult Attachment Interview through which she established the existence of a continuity in attachment patterns from caregivers to their children.

Disorganized/Disoriented Attachments

Main observed that a minority of children classified as insecure/avoidant or insecure/resistant in the Ainsworth studies did not quite fit either of these two categories, because they exhibited behaviors that differed from those of children in those two categories. They had been initially classified by Main as uncategorizable. These children exhibited behaviors that appeared disorganized as they alternated between crying loudly for their parent and moving away from that parent when picked up. Alternatively, they exhibited behaviors that were indicative of being disoriented to their environment or being in a trance-like state. Main and her collaborators designated these children as belonging to a fourth category of insecure children, which they called **disorganized/disoriented attachment** (Main & Solomon, 1986).

Main and her collaborators hypothesized that instead of being a haven of safety, the mothers of these infants were frightening to them, suggesting that the children had been either maltreated or neglected. The maltreating caregivers had the following behavioral characteristics: They had difficulty in controlling their aggression; they were unsympathetic to the distress of their children, and they tended to isolate themselves from others. These maternal characteristics were found to coexist with those children categorized as having this type of insecure attachment. Later studies confirmed this hypothesis. These children appear to be at risk for the development of dissociative disorder, phobias, anxiety, and heightened aggressiveness (Main & Morgan, 1996).

The Adult Attachment Interview

Main then attempted to obtain data on the types of internal working models that guide caregivers' responses to attachment by eliciting their accounts – usually the mothers' histories – of their own attachment experiences. In the early 1980s, Main and her collaborators developed the **Adult Attachment Interview** protocol (see Hesse, 1999) in which subjects are asked detailed questions about their histories in an effort to determine their "states of mind with respect to attachment" (Hesse, 1999, p. 395). The protocol consists of 18 questions with a set of probes that elicit information from and recollections of the subjects' attachment histories. The responses of the subjects were then transcribed and a coding system applied to categorize those responses. The coding of the transcript focused less on the content of the subjects' histories and more on the coherence or incoherence of the story they tell about those experiences. Main and her colleagues used four "conversational maxims for cooperative, rational discourse" that the linguistic philosopher Grice (1989) proposed to define a narrative's "coherence." The four maxims are "quality," that is, that the responses are truthful; "quantity," that is, that they are of appropriate length; "manner," that is, they are clear and sequential, and "relevance," that is, they have a bearing on the topic being discussed. In other words, to be coherent the account had to be consistent and collaborative.

A detailed examination of the transcripts found a correlation to exist between the attachment pattern revealed by the adult's internal working model and the type of attachment that adult's child developed. After studies replicated and established the validity of the findings, the following four categories of adult attachment states of mind and the corresponding categories derived from the Strange-Situation test were uncovered: (1) the **adult secure-autonomous attachment** (F) corresponds to children's secure attachment (B), (2) the **dismissing attachment** (Ds) corresponds to children's anxious/avoidant attachment (A), (3) the **preoccupied attachment** (E) corresponds to children's anxious/resistant attachment (C), and the **unresolved/ disorganized attachment** (U/D) corresponds to children's disorganized/disoriented attachment (D) (see Table 16.3).

These findings established the existence of an **intergenerational transmission of attachment** patterns. An exception to the correlation between the mother's recollections of her attachment experience and that of her child was demonstrated in cases where a modification occurred between the adult's recollected experiences and a subsequent relationship with someone who produced a change in the adult's internal working model.

Table 16.3 AA I classification and corresponding patterns of infant strange situation behavior

Adult state of mind with respect to attachment	Infant strange-situation behavior
Secure/autonomous (F)	*Secure (B)*
Coherent, collaborative discourse. Valuing of attachment, but seems objective regarding any particular event/relationship. Description and evaluation of attachment-related experiences is consistent, whether experiences are favorable or unfavorable. Discourse does not notably violate any of Grice's maxims.	Explores room and toys with interest in preseparation episodes. Shows signs of missing parent during separation, often crying by the second separation. Obvious preference for parent over stranger. Greets parent actively, usually initiating physical contact. Usually some contact maintaining by second reunion, but then settles and returns to play.
Dismissing (Ds)	*Avoidant (A)*
Not coherent. Dismissing of attachment-related experiences and relationships. Normalizing ("excellent, very normal mother"), with generalized representations of history unsupported or actively contradicted by episodes recounted, thus violating Grice's maxim of quality. Transcripts also tend to be excessively brief, violating the maxim of quantity.	Fails to cry on separation from parent. Actively avoids and ignores parent on reunion (i.e., by moving away, turning away, or leaning out of arms when picked up). Little or no proximity or contact seeking, no distress, and no anger. Response to parent appears unemotional. Focuses on toys or environment throughout procedure.
Preoccupied (E)	*Resistant or ambivalent (C)*
Not coherent. Preoccupied with or by past attachment relationships/experiences, speaker appears angry, passive, or fearful. Sentences often long, grammatically entangled, or filled with vague usages ("dadadada," "and that"), thus violating Grice's maxims of manner and relevance. Transcripts often excessively long, violating the maxim of quantity.	May be wary or distressed even prior to separation, with little exploration. Preoccupied with parent throughout procedure, may seem angry or passive. Fails to settle and take comfort in parent on reunion, and usually continues to focus on parent and cry. Fails to return to exploration after reunion.
Unresolved/disorganized (U/d)	*Disorganized/disoriented (D)*

(continued)

Table 16.3 (continued)

Adult state of mind with respect to attachment	Infant strange-situation behavior
During discussions of loss or abuse, individual shows striking lapse in the monitoring of reasoning or discourse. For example, individual may briefly indicate a belief that a dead person is still alive in the physical sense, or that this person was killed by a childhood thought. Individual may lapse into prolonged silence or eulogistic speech. The speaker will ordinarily otherwise fit Ds, E, or F categories.	The infant displays disorganized and/or disoriented behaviors in the parent's presence, suggesting a temporary collapse of behavioral strategies. For example, the infant may freeze with a trance-like expression, hands in air; may rise at parent's entrance, then fall prone and huddled on the floor; or may cling while crying hard and leaning away with gaze averted. Infant will ordinarily otherwise fit A, B, or C categories.

From Hesse, 1999, p. 399. Reprinted with permission from Guilford Press
Note: Description of the adult attachment classification system is summarized from Main, Kaplan, and Cassidy (1985) and from Main and Goldwyn (1984, 1998). Descriptions of infant A, B, and C categories are summarized from Ainsworth et al. (1978), and the description of the infant D category is summarized from Main and Solomon (1990)

Ainsworth's Theory of Development

Ainsworth's developmental framework borrows heavily from that of Bowlby but includes her own contributions. Establishing that the critical factor that differentiates the children's responses to separation *is maternal sensitivity* to the child's emotional state, she distinguished four phases in the development of children's attachment to their mothers. The first three of these occur during the first year of life. The phases are (1) the initial preattachment phase, (2) the phase of attachment-in-the-making, (3) the phase of clear-cut attachment, and finally (4) the phase of goal-corrected partnership that does not begin until the end of the third year (see Ainsworth et al., 1978, pp. 23–28).

Initial preattachment. The **initial preattachment phase** begins at birth and extends into the 8th–12th week. While not being able to discriminate one person from another, the baby is responsive to stimuli, especially those that come from people. The infant uses a variety of signaling behaviors, such as crying and vocalizing that have the effect of promoting proximity with others who respond to those signals. Some of the infant's behaviors become organized as action patterns that Piaget identified as sensorimotor schemas. These schemas permit infants to anticipate how the environment would respond to their activities.

Attachment-in-the-making. The **attachment-in-the-making phase** extends roughly between the first and tenth month. Infants are able to discriminate familiar from unfamiliar people and direct their proximity-promoting behaviors to those persons who can respond to their cries. The infant, while still incapable of forming an attachment, is able to display a preference for one person over another.

Clear-cut attachment. The **clear-cut attachment phase** begins toward the second half of the first year and continues through the second and third year. This phase has been studied extensively. With the newly acquired ability to walk, the infant can now maintain proximity by going to the caregiver as well as by signaling her. An extensive repertoire of behaviors becomes available to the infant, whose goal is to maintain proximity to the caregiver. The fact that infants achieve the capacity for **object permanence** during this phase, that is, the understanding that *physical objects* have a separate and independent existence, does not mean that they have developed the capacity for **object constancy**, that is, the understanding that *people* about whom they have strong feelings continue to exist even when not within their sight. Consequently, they become distressed when mother leaves their visual field, attempting to follow her, call out to her, or protest her departure. From the secure base that the caregiver provides, the infant begins to explore the environment.

Goal-corrected partnership: The **goal-corrected partnership phase** does not begin until the end of the third year. At this point, infants develop the capacity for object representation. Infants have formed then an internal working model that permits them to sustain a separation. The toddler also can now begin to understand that mother's availability may be restricted by tasks in which she is involved and that she may not be able to respond as quickly as he or she would like her to. A "partnership" has taken place in which the toddler's attachment behaviors are modified to take into account mother's ability to respond.

In Her Own Words

Relationship Between Strange-Situation Behavior and Maternal Behavior

We excerpt here Ainsworth's summary descriptions of maternal sensitivity to illustrate some of the parameters she used in her research to assess that parameter. Excerpted from Ainsworth et al. (1978, pp. 299–301) (reprinted with permission from Lawrence Erlbaum, an imprint of Taylor & Francis Group, LLC).

Because our hypothesis is that different experiences in interaction with the mother are largely responsible for qualitative differences in infant–mother attachment, the relationship between maternal behavior and patterns of Strange-Situation behavior is of particular interest. Of most relevance to our hypothesis are studies of maternal behavior prior to or at least contemporaneous with the Strange-Situation assessments of patterns of infant behavior. Here we are concerned solely with maternal behavior at home or in other "uncontrolled" situations, for the behavior of the mother in the strange situation was at least partially controlled by instructions and by the structure of the situation, so that there was relatively little scope for individual differences to be manifested.

The findings reported are of particular importance because they are based on extensive observations of mother–infant interaction at home throughout the first year of life. In comparison with the mothers of A and C babies, the mothers of Group-B infants were found to be more sensitively responsive to infant signals and communications, including crying signals. In the first quarter of the baby's first year, their sensitivity to signals was specifically shown in their behavior relevant to feeding, in their contingent responsiveness in face-to-face situations, and in their "tender, careful holding" when in close bodily contact with the baby. They were relatively mobile in emotional expression and tended to lack rigidity and compulsiveness in dealing with the baby throughout the first year. When rated in regard to fourth-quarter behavior, they were also found to be psychologically accessible to their infants, accepting rather than rejecting, and cooperative rather than interfering. They continued to be responsive to infant crying signals, and showed more affectionate behavior when in contact with their babies than did the mothers of non-B babies.

Group-A mothers were clearly more rejecting than non-A mothers; they more frequently had their positive feelings toward the infant overwhelmed by anger and irritation. They also expressed their rejection in terms of aversion to close bodily contact with their infants. They gave them more unpleasant experiences in the context of bodily contact. They showed a relative lack of emotional expression, which was interpreted as reflecting a way of controlling the expression of anger. They were rigid and compulsive in dealing with their babies. Their insensitivity to infant signals, as well as their rigidity, seems to have fed their frequent tendencies to interfere with the baby's activity in progress.

Group-C mothers, like Group-A mothers, were relatively insensitive to infant signals, but they were clearly less rejecting. They showed no aversion to close bodily contact; yet they were inept in holding their babies and manifested little affectionate behavior when in contact with them, but rather used holding time largely for routines, even in the fourth quarter.

In summary, we may conclude that different patterns of infant Strange-Situation behavior are associated with different constellations of maternal behavior both before the strange situation and subsequent to it. During the strange situation, however, maternal behavior was controlled both through instructions and through the structure of the episodes themselves. Therefore, in that situation infant behavior was largely freed from its usual contingencies with maternal behavior. Nevertheless, individual differences in infant behavior emerged under these circumstances that, although consistent with individual behavioral differences shown in previous interaction with their mothers, could not be attributed to individual differences in the contingencies provided by maternal behavior in the strange situation. This kind of continuity in patterns of infant behavior, despite control of maternal behavior, suggests that the determinants of infant behavior toward an attachment figure include an inner organizational component, as well as situational determinants. We have no doubt that the long experience an infant has in interaction with his mother in the course of his first year of life is chiefly responsible for the way in which he organizes his behavior toward her, but the resulting organization becomes to some extent independent of the particulars of his interaction with her in any given situation.

Summary and Conclusions

Ainsworth began working with Bowlby in 1950. She collected data on the interactions between mothers and their children. Using the developmental framework she and Bowlby constructed jointly; she developed the *Strange-Situation* procedure, a standardized protocol for the study of children's reactions to separations from their mother.

Through this procedure, she delineated three types of attachment. In *anxious/avoidant* attachment, the child avoids interacting with the mother during reunion episodes. The child may do so forcefully or as a mixed response. *Securely attached* children welcome the mother back and will greet her with a smile. One subgroup of these children appears to not become distressed by separation from the mother. Another subgroup in this category seeks proximity to the mother more actively. A third subgroup may seek physical contact with the mother. Finally, a fourth subgroup seems to be completely preoccupied with the mother when in the presence of a stranger. In *anxious/resistant* attachment, the child is clearly ambivalent toward the mother upon her return. Some of these children express anger both prior to and following separation. Others express their discontent more passively.

Main noticed that some children classified as insecure/avoidant or insecure/resistant did not seem to fit those categories well, and therefore identified a fourth category of attachment, which she called disorganized/disoriented attachment. She hypothesized that children in this group may have been maltreated or neglected.

Main's second contribution to attachment theory was the creation of the Adult Attachment Interview. She developed this instrument in order to obtain data on the types of internal working models that guide people's attachment to their children. She asked adults detailed questions about their own attachment experiences. She discovered a correlation between the attachment pattern revealed by the adult's internal working model and the type of attachment that the adult's child developed, thus establishing the existence of an intergenerational transmission of attachment pattern.

Ainsworth conceptualized four phases in the development of children's attachment to their mothers. During the *initial preattachment phase*, the infant uses a variety of signaling behaviors in an effort to gain proximity to others. During the phase of *attachment-in-the-making*, the infant directs his or her proximity-promoting behaviors to those persons who can respond. The phase of *clear-cut attachment* is the period during which infants acquire the ability to walk, and thus are able to maintain proximity by going to the caregiver. Finally, during the phase of *goal-corrected partnership* the infant has acquired the capacity for object representation and has formed an internal working model that sustains during separation.

Keywords Adult secure-autonomous attachment • Adult Attachment Interview • Anxious/avoidant attachment • Anxious/resistant attachment • Attachment-in-the-making phase • Clear-cut attachment phase • Dismissing attachment • Disorganized/disoriented attachment • Goal-corrected partnership phase • Intergenerational transmission of attachment • Maternal sensitivity • Object constancy • Object permanence • Preattachment phase • Preoccupied attachment • Secure attachment • Strange-Situation procedure • Unresolved/disorganized

References

Ainsworth, M. D. S., Blehar, M., Waters, E., & Wall, S. (1978). *Patterns of attachment: A psychological study of the strange situation* (p. 37). New Jersey: Lawrence Erlbaum.

Bretherton, I. (1992). The origins of attachment theory: John Bowlby and Mary Ainsworth. *Developmental Psychology, 28*, 759–775.

Cassidy, J., & Shaver, P. R. (Eds.). (1999). *Handbook of attachment: Theory, research, and clinical applications*. New York: Guilford Press.

Grice, P. (1989). *Studies in the way of words*. Cambridge, MA: Harvard University Press.

Hesse, E. (1999). The adult attachment interview: Historical and current perspectives. In J. Cassidy & P. Shaver (Eds.), *Handbook of attachment: Theory, research, and clinical applications* (pp. 395–433). New York: Guilford Press.

Main, M. (1999). Mary D. Salter Ainsworth: Tribute and portrait. *Psychoanalytic Inquiry, 19*(5), 882–937.

Main, M., Hesse, E., & Goldwyn, R. (2008). Studying differences in language usage in recounting attachment history: An introduction to the AAI. In H. Steele & M. Steele (Eds.), *Clinical applications of the Adult Attachment Interview* (pp. 31–68). New York: Guilford Press.

Main, M., & Morgan, H. (1996). Disorganization and disorientation in infant strange situation behavior: Phenotypic resemblance to dissociative states. In L. K. Michelson & W. J. Ray (Eds.), *Handbook of dissociation: Theoretical, empirical, and clinical perspectives* (pp. 107–138). New York: Plenum.

Main, M., & Solomon, J. (1986). Discovery of an insecure-disorganized/disoriented attachment patter: Procedures, finding, and implications for the clarification of behavior. In T. B. Brazelton & M. W. Yogman (Eds.), *Affective development in infancy* (pp. 95–124). Westport, CT: Ablex Publishing Corp.

Siegel, D. J. (1999). *The developing mind: Toward a neurobiology of interpersonal experience*. New York: Guilford Press.

Major Works

Ainsworth, M. D. S., Blehar, M., Waters, E., & Wall, S. (1978). *Patterns of attachment: A psychological study of the strange situation* (p. 37). New Jersey: Lawrence Erlbaum.

Main, M., & Solomon, J. (1986). Discovery of an insecure-disorganized/disoriented attachment pattern: Procedures, finding, and implications for the clarification of behavior. In T. B. Brazelton & M. W. Yogman (Eds.), *Affective development in infancy* (pp. 95–124). Westport, CT: Ablex Publishing Corp.

Supplementary Reading

Grossmann, K. E., Grossmann, K., & Waters, E. (Eds.). (2005). *Attachment from infancy to adulthood: The major longitudinal studies*. New York: Guilford Press.

Hesse, E., & Main, M. (1999). Second-generation effects of unresolved trauma in nonmal treating parents: Dissociated, frightened, and threatening parental behavior. *Psychoanalytic Inquiry, 19*(4), 481–540.

Main, M. (1974). Exploration, play, and cognitive functioning as related to child–mother attachment. *Dissertation Abstracts International, 34*(11-B), 5718–5719.

Main, M. (1995a). Discourse, prediction, and recent studies in attachment: Implications for psychoanalsysis. In T. Shapiro & R. N. Emde (Eds.), *Research in psychoanalysis: Process, development, outcome* (pp. 209–244). Madison, CT: International Universities Press.

Main, M. (1995b). Recent studies in attachment: Overview, with selected implications for clinical work. In S. Goldberg, R. Muir, & J. Kerr (Eds.), *Attachment theory: Social, developmental, and clinical perspectives* (pp. 407–474). Hillsdale, NJ: Analytic Press.

Main, M. (2000). The organized categories of infant, child, and adult attachment: Flexible vs. inflexible attention under attachment-related stress. *Journal of the American Psychoanalytic Association, 48*(2), 1055–1096.

Main, M., Hesse, E., & Kaplan, N. (2005). Predictability of attachment behavior and representational processes at 1, 6, and 19 years of age: The Berkeley Longitudinal Study. In K. E. Grossmann, K. Grossmann, & E. Waters (Eds.), *Attachment from infancy to adulthood: The major longitudinal studies* (pp. 245–304). New York: Guilford Press.

Main, M., Kaplan, N., & Cassidy, J. (1985). Security in infancy, childhood and adulthood: A move to the level of representation. *Monograph of the Society for Research in Child Development, 50*(1–2), 66–104.

Part 2
Neurodevelopmental Attachment Theories: The Return to Psychoanalysis

Attachment theory came full circle to Freud's early neurological interests in the works of Schore and Fonagy. Schore became interested in neurobiological factors that undergird attachments. He redefined attachment theory as a *regulatory theory*, in which caregivers through the regulation of the infant's affective states induce in the child responses that may result in the internalization of those regulatory patterns. According to Schore, the brain's right hemisphere, especially the orbitofrontal region of the cortex, is involved in the maturation that occurs as a result of these interactions. Schore extended this organismic metaphor to state that brain development is contingent on specific responses from infants' caregivers. He went on to specify the mechanisms through which this occurs and the maladaptation that result when the processes fail.

Schore formulated his views on the development of the self after his extensive reading of the neurological and neuropsychological literature. In 1994, he published a monumental work titled *Affect Regulation and the Origin of the Self: The Neurobiology of Emotional Development.* In this work, he achieved his goal of articulating a coherent developmental framework that integrates the disciplines of the neurosciences and psychoanalysis. In it, he brought together aspects of Mahler's (Mahler, Pine, &Bergman, 1975) psychoanalytic development theory and the information on brain function that he extracted from his scholarly reading of the neuroscience literature.

By the time Schore published his work, Stern's (1985) developmental theory had superseded Mahler's framework. Schore shifted his focus to attachment theory, with its substantial empirical support, because it lent itself to integration with the neuroscience findings. Schore did not conduct direct observations or carry out research on children or adults. Although he attempted the more ambitious task of uncovering the neurobiological substrates of the development of the self and subjectivity, in this section, we focus exclusively on his contribution to attachment theory. Schore maintained that attachment is a regulatory theory that conforms to an evolutionary perspective. Linking and extending Bowlby's theory, as did Sroufe and others, he emphasized that the mother's responsivity to her infant determines whether a secure or an insecure attachment will ensue.

Fonagy contributed significantly to efforts to bring about a rapprochement between psychoanalysis and attachment theory. Through constructive criticism of the contributions of developmental psychologists, he has built upon their findings and succeeded in incorporating these into his framework. As a bridge between the two theories, he used the concept of mentalization, which he operationalized as the *reflective function.* He then took a major step forward by including the findings from neurobiology and extending the definition of mentalization. The concept of Interpersonal Interpretive Mechanism (Fonagy, 2003) goes beyond attachment as a simple need for proximity to a caregiver; it provides a description of the neurobiological substrates that undergird the construal of meaning from experiences. This construct suggests that a specific set of brain functions require stimulation by caregivers for attachment to be possible and for children to ascribe meanings to their experiences.

References

Fonagy, P. (2003). The development of psychopathology from infancy to adulthood: The mysterious unfolding of disturbance in time. *Infant Mental Health Journal,24*(3), 212–239.

Mahler, M. S., Pine, F., Bergman, A. (1975). *The psychological birth of the human infant: Symbiosis and individuation.* New York: Basic Books, Inc.

Schore, A. N. (1994). *Affect regulation and the origin of the self: The neurobiology of emotional development.* Hillsdale, NJ: Lawrence Erlbaum.

Stern, D. N. (1985). *The interpersonal world of the infant.* New York: Basic Books.

Chapter 17
Allen N. Schore (1943–)

Publishing Era: 1991 to the Present

Biographical Information[1]

Allan N. Schore was born in Manhattan, New York, on February 20, 1943. His father was a chemical engineer and his mother was described as a gifted stay-at-home mom. A sister was born 4 years later. Schore's earliest recollections were of his intense curiosity about scientific matters. He recalls that his curiosity led him to write on the subject even in English classes in elementary school. His father's interests and career inspired him and continued to influence him throughout his life. In his account of his early experiences, he emphasized that complementary to that thread was his parents' capacity for empathy and the overt expression of feelings. These two parallel influences brought together the realms of science and emotion and left deep imprints on him.

Graduating from high school in 1960, Schore chose to attend the University of Rochester as a college primarily because he wanted the ambience of a small university. While at Rochester, he met his wife Judy, who became a lifelong companion and stalwart supporter of his work through the years. He became interested in psychology late during his studies at Rochester and eventually majored in psychology, with minors in English and Chemistry. For his graduate studies, which began in 1965, he chose the University of Pittsburgh. The program there was dominated by courses in cognitive psychology, in contrast to most other psychology programs that embraced behaviorism as the dominant paradigm. Even then, his broad interests in psychological matters led him to take courses on physiological psychology and other related topics. This interest represented an early effort at integrating the psychological and biological domains. He obtained his Ph.D. in 1970, having written his dissertation on the topic of *The Effect of Various Cognitive Sets on Cognitive Tasks*.

While working on his dissertation, he became a trainee at the Pittsburgh Child Guidance Clinic, where he assessed children and families by administering projective

[1] In a phone interview, on December 4, 2007, Allan Schore, giving generously of his time, provided Joseph Palombo with much of the information contained in the biographical section.

J. Palombo et al., *Guide to Psychoanalytic Developmental Theories*,
DOI: 10.1007/978-0-387-88455-4_17, © Springer Science+Business Media, LLC 2009

and other test batteries. There, he was also exposed to psychoanalytic concepts, although he obtained much greater exposure later during his internship at the Lafayette Clinic in Detroit, MI. In the latter setting, he attended lectures by Umberto Nagera, who had been a leading light at the Hampstead Clinic and a protégé of Anna Freud. His work in clinical psychology was complemented by training in neuropsychological testing, which gave him an opportunity to study the neurobiological basis for such mental disorders as schizophrenia.

Following the completion of his internship, he toyed briefly with the idea of going to medical school. Nevertheless, he decided against medicine as a career and instead took off for a few months prior to seeking employment. He went to work in his father's lab, accompanying him in many of his professional activities within a large corporation that provided automation equipment to industry. Schore, impressed by the diversity of markets for the equipment, learned the importance of cross-disciplinary cooperation in responding to industrial needs.

During the late 1960s and early 1970s, California was a Mecca for mental health practitioners. It provided generously for the needs of the mentally ill and allocated significant funds for those employed in providing services. For Schore and Judy California offered an open space in which to practice, think, and create. From 1970 through 1980, he was chief psychologist at the Southern California Kaiser Permanente Medical Group, where he served as Senior Neuropsychologist in the Department of Psychiatry, conducting assessments on children, adolescents, and adults, and lecturing in the departments of pediatrics, neuropsychology, and psychiatry. While in that position, he became interested in the relationship between certain DSM III disorders and the possible organicity that undergirds them.

Soon after their arrival in California, a daughter and, subsequently, a son were born to the Schores. He and Judy decided on a pattern of child rearing that shaped much of their lives for the next 20 years. He started out taking 1 day off from work during the week to acquaint himself with developments in a broad array of related disciplines, while attending to the children's needs. In 1980, he left his position at Kaiser Permanente and entered full-time private practice. Having just completed a twice-a-week analysis, which he felt was highly beneficial, he felt prepared to undertake the serious study of subjects in which he had become increasingly interested.

The next 10 years represent a period of intellectual incubation for Schore, who was fortunate in having the resources of an extensive medical library at a neighboring university. Led only by his curiosity, he began to read broadly at first in psychology, soon finding himself immersed in exploring other domains ranging from cell biology to biochemistry. He took copious notes and broke off from reading only every few weeks to synthesize and integrate what he had read. During this period of self-imposed isolation, he remained connected to developments in psychoanalysis through Judy, who was deeply involved in the California Institute for Clinical Social Work, from which she graduated with a Ph.D. in Clinical Social Work and later became its dean of students. Schore did continue to see patients in long-term psychotherapy, which provided him with a different data set to integrate into his intellectual pursuits. Since they knew little about the content of his intellectual pursuits, some of his colleagues and friends expressed concern about his well-being during this period, fearing that he had isolated himself from the entire world. They had little understanding of the motives for this self-imposed reclusiveness. From his perspective, he felt the need to create a private space within which he could make room for his creativity.

Finally, toward the end of this 10-year period, he felt ready to share his work and the product of his endeavors. He was convinced that he had arrived at an important juncture in the history of psychoanalysis. His insights had led him to find the road to the integration of psychoanalysis and the neurosciences, which had eluded many before him. It was as though he had returned to Freud's *Project* armed with updated neurobiological findings that made possible the resolution of some of the intractable problems Freud had confronted.

An early paper titled "Early superego development: The emergence of shame and narcissistic affect regulation in the practicing period" was rejected by the *Journal of the American Psychoanalytic Association*. However, in 1991, this same paper was accepted by the journal *Psychoanalysis and Contemporary Thought*. The themes in this paper were continuous with those that Mahler, Winnicott, and Stern had addressed. With this acceptance, Schore felt that he had succeeded in reintroducing developmental neuroscience to psychoanalysis. With the publication of this paper, he felt vindicated that he was pursuing the right path. However, he believed that more was needed to accomplish his mission, that of awakening the profession to the vast domain that remained to be explored. He consequently sent copies of the paper to a large group of psychoanalysts to inform them of his effort. To his delight, he received numerous responses, all of them positive. He now felt that the psychoanalytic community was ready to give him the recognition he deserved.

In 1994, the monumental work titled *Affect Regulation and the Origin of the Self: The Neurobiology of Emotional Development* was accepted for publication. The publisher, Erlbaum, was initially skeptical that a readership of this work would be found. To make sure that others in the profession would take notice, Schore sent copies to approximately 40 prominent professionals around the world. He included with each copy a letter pointing out the relevance of his work to theirs. The recognition he received from the psychoanalytic community was insufficient for him, as he was leery of simply getting self-confirming feedback from fellow professionals. Consequently, he submitted a paper to the journal *Behavior and Brain Science* to assure himself that he was operating on sound ground. The paper was rejected. Fortunately, Carroll Izard, a prominent researcher in the field of affect who was one of the peer reviewers, responded personally, advising Schore to explore attachment theory. Izard suggested that the literature on attachment had a much more robust empirical base than that of psychoanalysis. At that point, Schore shifted his focus to study Bowlby and to integrate attachment theory into his theory of affect.

From then on, recognition came on many fronts. He was asked to contribute chapters to numerous volumes; he received many invitations to speak around the world, and he has been rewarded with great acclaim. Schore's work represents a paradigm shift from earlier contributions to psychoanalytic developmental theories. He was the first, in modern times, to return successfully to Freud's attempt to integrate psychoanalysis and the neurosciences. His hypothesis that attachment is a regulatory theory and that the right hemisphere mediates affect regulation represents a creative leap that promises to advance all developmental theories.

Theory of Development

Schore attempted to update psychoanalytic theory by presenting a **psychoneurobiological view** of the origins of the self. In his first book, *Affect Regulation and the Origin of the Self: The Neurobiology of Emotional Development* (1994), he specified the structure of the developing unconscious in terms of recent brain research. *Psychic structures* refer to those specific brain systems, particularly **right-brain systems** that underlie the various mental functions that process affect states. He delineated the origins of the self by describing the ontogenetic evolution of the **neurobiology of subjectivity** and intersubjectivity. Whereas other psychoanalytic developmental theories, such as those that propose an epigenetic model, drew analogies between biological and psychological processes, Schore wished to describe the neurobiological processes themselves. His theoretical program was that of elucidating the neurobiological underpinnings of the emotional interchanges between infant and caregiver and of delineating the manner in which the infant's brain processes and regulates emotional information. He posited that the specific functions of the right hemisphere, the frontal and prefrontal cortex, and the associated subcortical systems are the critical structures associated with these processes.

The sense of self, he suggested, is derived from the *experience-dependent self-organization* of the early developing right hemisphere. Brain development is contingent upon certain types of stimulations that result from exposure to the environment. Neurobiologists distinguish between sensitive periods and critical periods. **Sensitive periods** are phases during which some brain systems/functions are **experience-expectant**; that is, these brain systems are dependent on certain types of stimuli in order to develop. Experience-expectant systems have more plasticity than other systems, and developmental failures are more reversible in those systems than in systems that are subject to critical periods. For example, a child who has not been exposed to strangers during his or her first year of life may experience anxiety when first encountering a stranger, but soon will become habituated and not feel anxious. **Critical periods**, by contrast, are phases during which some brain systems or functions are **experience-dependent**; that is, these brain systems must have certain types of stimuli in order to develop. For example, if an infant hears only the sound of his native language, his auditory cortex will not develop the capacity to hear or reproduce some sounds used by other languages. That child will grow up to speak with an accent if he or she attempts to learn that "foreign language." Experience-dependent systems have less plasticity and their developmental failures are less reversible than systems that are subject to sensitive periods. The description of the emergence of the sense of self is best approached through an understanding of the process of attachment, which is experience-dependent. The absence of stimulation of experience-dependent right brain systems, during critical periods of development, will cause some forms of insecure attachments, the effects of which are irreversible.

The Neurobiology of Secure Attachments

Schore began with the assumption that the social environment affects brain development, especially during the critical periods of infant development. It also affects gene expression. During critical or sensitive periods of early brain development, certain conditions or stimuli are essential and necessary for brain growth. The regulation of emotions is a critical part of this process. Following Winnicott, he proposed that an efficient self-system develops within a context of a "good enough mother" (Shore, 2002, p. 448). When the interactions between infants and caregivers are synchronous and well modulated the infant can develop a secure attachment; her responses maximize positive affect states and minimize negative states. Such synchronized responses help to regulate the infant's state, a process that enhances neural growth in the frontal cortex. The psychological outcome is the internalization of regulatory function and the capacity for autoregulation. Schore notes, however, that affect regulation does not imply that the caregiver merely reduces the negative affects so as to reestablish homeostasis; it may also involve the amplification of positive affects through playfulness that leads to outbursts of joyful laughter, and those emotions that Stern called "vitality affects" (Stern, 1985, pp. 53–61).

The Rupture and Repair Sequence

Failures in attunement that produce hyperarousal in the infant threaten to rupture the communicative bond between the members of dyad. Such ruptures, if followed by reattunement, may lead to a repair of that bond, setting a pattern that is essential for the building of psychological structure, that is, regulatory functions. Through the repeated sequence of rupture and repair, infants develop regulatory functions that allow them to modulate and regulate affect states resulting in secure attachment. Such are the beneficial effects of the **rupture and repair sequence**. On the other hand, if the ruptures are prolonged and unresolved, the effect is traumatic to the infant, who has to resort to nonadaptive means of coping in order to survive. The result is a failure to develop critical regulatory functions; the consequence is an insecurely attached infant. The failure to develop such regulatory functions and a secure attachment places these infants at risk for later psychopathology. For Schore, a direct link exists between a secure attachment and the successful establishment of regulatory functions, and an insecure attachment and the unsuccessful establishment of regulatory functions (see also Beebe, 1986; Beebe, Knoblauch, Rustin, & Sorter, 2005). Schore suggests that we can define adaptive infant mental health as the earliest expression of efficient and resilient strategies for coping with novelty and stress, and maladaptive infant mental health as a deficit in the same coping mechanisms. Both are outcomes of attachment (Schore, 2001a, p. 17).

Internal Working Models

The patterns that the synchronic emotional interchanges between infant and caregiver produce constitute the core of the self. They embody the processes through which children are able to regulate themselves and lead to the establishment of Internal Working Models, that is, of representations of the child, the caregivers, and the interactions among them. The infant's early internal working models of the attachment relationship are processed and stored in the nondeclarative memory systems in the right cortex, the hemisphere dominant for implicit learning. Information processed implicitly, that is nonconsciously and nonverbally, is stored in nondeclarative memory.[2]

According to Schore, because of its central role in unconscious functions, the right hemisphere is the repository of unconscious internal working models of attachment relationships. Schore offered data showing that the right hemisphere contains an **affective–configurational representational system** that encodes self-and-object images, while the left hemisphere utilizes a lexical–semantic mode. These data could link together the concept of mental representation with the neurobiological functions that undergird them.

Schore on Attachment Theory

According to Schore, Bowlby had attempted to address the question of how and why certain early ontogenetic events, such as early separations from or the loss of caregivers, had such an inordinate negative effect on the lives of children. Schore's answer to that question focused on the context in which the mother and her infant experience connections to one another that are vital to the emotional communications among the members of the dyad. In brief, whereas Bowlby focused on the functions that attachment serves, Schore focused on the neurobiological structures that undergird those functions.

[2]Nondeclarative memory consists of procedural memory, priming, associative, and nonassociative learning. *Procedural memory* is the storage area of nonconscious memories such as motor skills and associations. Memories are inflexibly stored in a manner related to the context in which the person first acquired them. *Priming* assists retrieval when a partial stimulus serves to elicit the entire memory of an event. *Associative learning* is conditioned or operant learning. *Nonassociative learning* manifests itself primarily in reflexes, such as knee jerk reaction. *Declarative memory* consists of episodic memory and semantic memory. For the most part, declarative memory is conscious memory, that is, experiences and the information it acquires are processed explicitly. Episodic memory is tied to specific moments in one's life. It refers to the memory of things personally experienced, as opposed to the knowledge of facts one has learned. Semantic memory is memory for facts; it is our dictionary memory. Since at birth, the infant hippocampus, the organ responsible for the formation of declarative memories is underdeveloped, the infant's experiences are initially stored in nondeclarative memory. *Working memory* is a short-term memory buffer that retains auditory inputs and/or visual images. A "central executive" organizes the contents of working memory. The central executive is the mechanism that directs attention toward one stimulus or another and determines which items are stored in working memory.

Finding that recent contributions from neuroscience offer support for Bowlby's assertion that attachment is an instinctive behavior with a biological function, Schore extended Bowlby's theoretical formulation. He stressed that in addition to the infant's search for a *secure base* and the *affectional bond* that underlies the evolutionary function of attachment are the *regulatory functions* that caregivers provide to their infants. *Schore, therefore, extended Bowlby's biological control systems to include the brain systems that regulate the affectively driven instinctive behavior.*

The affectional bond forms the cornerstone of the emotional communication among the members of the dyad and is the means through which the caregiver enhances the infant's regulatory processes.

Schore states:

> Attachment is instinctive behavior with a biological function... emotional processes lie at the foundation of a model of instinctive behavior, and... a biological control system in the brain regulates affectively driven instinctive behavior. This control system can now be identified as the orbitofrontal system and its cortical and subcortical connections. This 'senior executive of the emotional brain' acts as a regulatory system, and is expanded in the right hemisphere, which is dominant in human infancy and centrally involved in inhibitory control (2000, p. 23).

Attachment results from the emotional interchanges between the infant and its caregiver and from processes that mediate the construction of the *social brain*, that is, the brain systems specifically dedicated to processing social interactions and communication.

Attachment Redefined as a Regulatory System

Schore proposed that attachment transactions mediate the ***social construction of the human brain***, specifically the social emotional brain that the unique operations of the right brain support. Schore argued that ***attachment theory is fundamentally a regulatory theory***; that is, *the primary function of attachment is that of regulating the child's affect states*. The brain systems involved are found in the brain's orbitofrontal region and its subcortical connections. They constitute a senior executive of the emotional brain that acts as a regulatory system.[3] The processes through which the regulatory systems function are the: "[R]esonant emotional transactions [that] involve synchronized and ordered directed flow of energy in the infant's and mother's brains" (2002, p. 444). There are psychoneurobiological regulatory events that mediate the attachment process, and these regulatory mechanisms are essential to the organization of the infant's "right mind," that is, right brain. He concluded that since psychological functions are the product of the brain structures that undergird them, *regulation is a central organizing principle of human development and motivation*, and that *the self-system is located in the early maturing right brain.*

[3]The idea that attachment functions primarily as a regulatory process was first introduced by Sroufe (1995).

Psychoneurobiological Development

During development, nonverbal and emotional modes of communication play a critical role in the dialogue between mother and infant during the *first 9–12 months* after birth. The right hemisphere, which is dominant for the first 18 months of the infant's life and which processes the information at a nonconscious level, mediates these communications. Infants use smell, taste, and touch to interact with the caregiver. The use of the visual channel becomes central to the affective exchanges as the infant gazes at the caregiver and the caregiver gazes at the infant in return. Since some right brain functions are experience dependent, the quality of the experience between infant and caregiver is critical to the processing of social-emotional information and to facilitating attachment functions. Positive experiences will ensure adaptive growth, whereas negative experience, if sustained, may impair such growth.

By *15–30 months* of age, with the development of verbal language, sustained interactions between the left and right hemisphere take place. The child arrives at the developmental stage that Stern calls "the verbal self" (1985). By the second year, the child becomes capable of self-awareness and self-recognition. He or she can maintain a cohesive sense of self, can distinguish self from others, can appraise reality, and can emotionally understand and react to bodily and environmental stimuli. Eventually, the child develops the capacity for **autoregulation**, that is, self-regulation, and shifts from reliance on the caregiver for regulatory functions to self-reliance, as conditions require.

As stated earlier, the internal working models of the securely attached child lead to the expectation that experiences of repair follow ruptures and that positive emotions will prevail once more. Through the continued presence and modifications by experience, the types of attachment a child forms influence development at later stages of life. During *latency*, children use their ability to read the faces of their peers to empathically synchronize their responses and maintain the flow of affective communication with others.

In *adolescence*, the brain undergoes a significant reorganization, a process that contributes to the multiple psychological changes seen at this time. Overproduction and pruning of synapses is the hallmark of adolescence. The data suggest that the right brain circuits that support self-regulation and stress coping mechanisms are significantly reorganized. This allows for early internal working models of attachment to become more complex over the course of the life cycle. When events emotionally overwhelm and disorganize securely attached adolescents, it is possible for them to access emotionally available parents for interactive regulation.

The Neurobiology of Attachment

Based on extensive data from research in neurobiology, Schore maintained that the right brain is dominant at birth. It mediates all emotional communications between infant and caregiver and is involved in the regulation of the synchronic exchanges of emotions between the dyad. Since, according to Schore, most mothers cradle their infants on the left side, the right hemisphere decodes the flow of visual and auditory information from infant to mother and from mother to infant, thus facilitating the flow of emotional information. The right hemisphere contains a vocabulary of nonverbal emotional signals (facial expressions, prosody, and gestures). We refer to this vocabulary as the *nonverbal affective lexicon* (Bowers, Bauer, & Heilman, 1993). The capacity for empathy reflects the activities of the receptive component of emotional communication. These processes occur at a nonconscious level and provide the building blocks for the experience-dependent growth of the structure in the right brain.

Schore goes to great length to detail the infant's specific brain mechanisms that subserve emotional communication and the processing and regulation of emotional information. He discusses the processes implicated in secure attachments separately from those of insecure attachments. Two major brain systems contribute to the processes of attachment: the right hemisphere and the ***orbito frontal region*** *within the right hemisphere*, as well as the associated subcortical regions, in particular the ***limbic system,*** which is a subcortical region that specializes in the processing of certain affects, such as fear. In this chapter, it is only possible to summarize his position without citing the extensive neurological and neuropsychological literature that he has reviewed. In what follows, we discuss the impact of the type of affectional bond between infant and caregiver on each of these brain systems. When predominantly positive, the affectional bond gives rise to a child with a secure attachment to its caregiver; when predominantly negative or fear provoking, that bond gives rise to a child with an insecure attachment.

The Orbital Frontal Region

By the end of the first year, the orbital frontal areas enter into a period of growth. The prefrontal region performs an executive control function for the entire right cortex; this center regulates emotions. The orbital frontal area processes information from the external environment and integrates it with subcortically processed information it receives from the person's internal visceral environment. This incoming information is integrated with the child's emotional states, leading to actions such as approach or withdrawal and fight or flight.

The orbital frontal system plays a major role in the internal state of the organism, the temporal organization of behavior, and the appraisal and adjustment or correction of emotional responses – that is, affect regulation. This system monitors and autoregulates the duration, frequency, and intensity of both positive and negative affect states. This allows both for the ability to use affects as signals and for a self-comforting capacity that can modulate distressing psychobiological states and reestablish positively toned ones. It enables the person to cope actively and passively with stress and external challenges (Schore, 1997, p. 834).

Finally, through its connections to the memory systems, the orbital frontal areas allow the person to recall the internal working models and their associated feelings. In essence, these capacities represent not only the type of attachment people form but also the kind of object relationships or internalized object representation that characterize their personalities.

The Limbic System

The limbic system consists of a hierarchically organized set of interconnected areas that include the amygdala, the basal ganglia, and the anterior cingulate. These structures are closely connected to the insula, and orbital frontal cortex, which are regions implicated in the regulation of emotions, the organization of new learning, and the capacity to adapt to a changing environment. Various components of this system are responsible for appraising the salience of a stressor, and then initiating and organizing a psychobiological response.

In addition, the limbic system, through its extensive connection with the autonomic nervous system, is specialized for the reception of information from the child's own body. The autonomic nervous system has two components, the **sympathetic nervous system**, an energy-expending system, and the **parasympathetic nervous system**, an energy-conserving system. Both these subsystems are implicated in the somatic expression of emotional states. What this means is that a co-occurring **somatic emotional marker** (Damasio, 1994) that colors the infant's subjective experience accompanies every experience. The synchronized emotional communication between infant and caregiver includes not only the infant's reading of the messages sent by the caregiver but also those that come from the infant's own viscera. The autonomic nervous system consequently monitors the infants' emotional states as well as their responses to stress integrating them to attain a homeostatic balance.

The amygdala, present at birth, responds to external stimuli and modulates autonomic and arousal systems. The right amygdala processes olfactory stimuli, permitting the infant to recognize mother's scent. At 8 weeks, the anterior cingulate begins to regulate separation behaviors and modulates autonomic activity. Soon after, the insula, which is involved in the subjective awareness of inner body feelings and emotionality, and the right parietal cortical area, which is involved in the physical representation of the self, come on line. The development of these areas is experience dependent, that is, they rely on appropriate stimulation for their growth.

The Neurobiology of Insecure Attachments

As Main discovered, children with disorganized/disoriented type D attachments have low stress tolerance and instead of finding a haven of safety in the relationship they are alarmed by the parent (Main & Morgan, 1996). According to Schore, when caregivers either neglect or maltreat a child, the child's response to such a trauma comprises two separate response patterns, ***hyperarousal*** and ***dissociation.*** In the initial stage, an alarm reaction is initiated in which the sympathetic component of the autonomic nervous system, the fight/flight response, is suddenly and significantly activated, resulting in increased heart rate, blood pressure, and respiration. Distress is expressed in crying and screaming. *This state of fear – terror is mediated by sympathetic hyperarousal and reflects increased levels of the major stress hormone corticotropin releasing factor, which in turn regulates noradrenalin and adrenaline activity*. The result is hyperarousal.

In the second stage, the child disengages from stimuli in the external world and attends to an internal world. *The parasympathetic state of conservation – withdrawal becomes dominant and the child lapses into feelings of helplessness and hopelessness*. The child then withdraws and strives to be invisible in order to avoid being the focus of attention. The child uses dissociation as a defense to deal with the trauma. Numbing, avoidance, compliance, and restricted affects are evident. In this state, the pain-numbing and blunting endogenous opiates and behavior inhibiting stress hormones, such as cortisol, are elevated. This intensified parasympathetic arousal allows the infant to maintain homeostasis in the face of the internal state of sympathetic hyperarousal.

According to Schore, hyperarousal occurs in infants' responses to their caregivers' facial expression, which conveys fear and terror. The infant is overwhelmed by the implied aggression, which he or she imagines the caregiver to convey, and is traumatized by the experience. He or she may in turn attempt to defend against the overwhelming feelings that are aroused by dissociating from its surroundings. The entire event becomes encoded in the infant's right brain implicit memory system, which sets the stage for the reenactment of the experience when exposed to events that evoke the memory.

Resulting from the trauma is an interference in the capacity to perceive others' emotional states as well as an impaired capacity to regulate and modulate their own internal emotional states. The accompanying developmental failures produce severe difficulties in forming attachments to others as well as serious psychopathology. A type D disorganized/dissociated form attachment ensues.

In His Own Words

Excerpt from Schore (2005, pp. 204–217) (reprinted with permission from Pediatrics in Review).

Interactive Affect Regulation: A Fundamental Mechanism of Attachment Dynamics

The primary goals for the infant during the first postnatal year are the creation of an attachment bond of emotional communication with the primary caregiver and the development of self-regulation. From birth onward, infants use their expanding coping capacities to interact with the social environment. In the earliest proto-attachment experiences, infants use their maturing motor and developing sensory capacities, especially smell, taste, and touch, to interact with the social environment (Van Toiler & Kendal-Aced, 1995; Weller & Feldman, 2003). At around 8 weeks of age, there is a dramatic progression of social and emotional capacities. Within episodes of mutual gaze, the caretaker (usually the mother) and infant engage in nonconscious and spontaneous facial, vocal, and gestural communications. Such highly arousing, affect-laden, face-to-face interactions allow the infant to be exposed to high levels of social and cognitive information.

In face-to-face emotional transactions, the mother makes herself contingent, easily predictable, and manipulatable by the infant. To regulate the high positive arousal, the dyad synchronizes the intensity of their affective behavior within split seconds. These episodes of "affect synchrony" occur in the first expression of social play and generate increasing levels of joy and excitement. In these interactions, both partners match states and simultaneously adjust their social attention, stimulation, and accelerating arousal to each other's responses. According to Lester, Hoffinan, and Brazelton, "synchrony develops as a consequence of each partner's learning the rhythmic structure of the other and modifying his or her behavior to fit that structure." (Lester, Hoffman, & Brazelton, 1985). In such moments, the empathic caregiver's sensory stimulation coincides with the infant's endogenous rhythms, allowing the mother to appraise the nonverbal expressions of her infant's internal arousal and psychobiological states, regulate them, and communicate them back to the infant.

In this process of "contingent responsivity," the tempo of their engagement, disengagement, and reengagement is coordinated. The more the empathic mother tunes her activity level to the infant during periods of social engagement, the more she allows him or her to recover quietly in periods of disengagement. The more she attends to the child's reinitiating cues for reengagement, the more synchronized becomes their interaction. Thus, the caregiver facilitates the infant's information processing by adjusting the amount, variability, and timing of the onset and offset of stimulation to the infant's unique, temperamentally determined integrative capacities. These interactively regulated, synchronized interactions promote the infant's regulatory capacities and are fundamental to his or her healthy affective development.

In such interactions the mother must be attuned not so much to the child's overt behavior as to the reflections of the rhythms of his or her internal state, enabling the dyad to create "mutual regulatory systems of arousal." To regulate the infant's arousal, she must be able to regulate her own arousal state. The capacity of the infant to experience increasing levels of positive arousal states is amplified and externally regulated by the primary caregiver and depends on her capacity to engage in an interactive communication of emotions that generates feelings in herself and her child. Maternal sensitivity, therefore, acts as an external organizer of the infant's biobehavioral regulation.

Research also shows frequent moments of misattunement in the dyad or ruptures of the attachment bond. In early development, an adult provides much of the modulation of infant states, especially after a state of disruption or a transition between states, and this intervention allows for the development of self-regulation. The key to this beneficial interaction is the caregiver's capacity to monitor and regulate her own (especially negative) affect. In this essential regulatory pattern of "rupture and repair," the attuned "good-enough" caregiver who induces a stress response in her infant through a misattunement remedies the situation and helps her infant regulate his or her negative affect via her participation in "interactive repair." The process of reexperiencing positive affect following negative experience allows the child to learn that negative affect can be tolerated and that relational stress can be regulated. Infant resilience emerges from an interactive context in which the child and parent together make the transition from positive to negative and back to positive affect. The adaptive regulatory capacity of resilience in the face of stress is an ultimate indicator of secure attachment and optimal mental health.

Affect synchrony that creates states of positive arousal and interactive repair that modulates states of negative arousal are the fundamental building blocks of attachment and its associated emotions. These arousal-regulating transactions, which continue throughout the first year, underlie the formation of an attachment bond of emotion regulation between the infant and primary caregiver. Indeed, psychobiological attunement and the interactive mutual entrainment of physiologic rhythms are fundamental processes that mediate attachment. Thus, throughout the life span, attachment is a primary mechanism for the regulation of biologic synchronicity within and between organisms.

These data clearly suggest that affect regulation is not just the reduction of affective intensity or the dampening of negative emotion. Affect regulation involves an intensification of positive emotion, a condition necessary for more complex self-organization. The attuned mother of the securely attached child not only minimizes the infant's negative states through comforting transactions but also maximizes his positive affective states in interactive play. Regulated affective interactions with a familiar, predictable primary caregiver create a sense of safety and a curiosity that fuels the child's exploration of novel socioemotional and physical environments. This ability is a marker of adaptive infant mental health.

Summary and Conclusions

Schore is the first to return successfully to Freud's attempt to integrate psychoanalysis with the neurosciences. He hypothesized that attachment theory is a regulatory theory. Its primary function is that of regulating the child's affect states, self-regulation being a central organizing principle of human development. He drew from recent brain research to propose a psychoneurobiological view of the origins of the self, proposing that psychological functions are the product of the brain structures that undergird them. For example, he suggested a biological location for the internal working models, the right hemisphere of the brain.

Schore believed that recent contributions from neuroscience support Bowlby's assertion that attachment is instinctive behavior, but he replaced Bowlby's biological control system with the brain systems that regulate instinctive behavior.

According to Schore, the social environment affects brain development, and the regulation of emotions is a critical part of this process. Attachment occurs as a result of the emotional interchanges between the infant and caregiver. If there are failures in attunement, the bond between infant and caregiver may be threatened. It is important that reattunement follows ruptures in this bond. The result of this *rupture and repair sequence* is the building of psychological structure. The failure to develop regulatory functions and a secure attachment leaves the infant vulnerable to psychopathology later in life.

Schore detailed the specific brain mechanisms that are involved in emotional communication and the processing and regulation of emotional information. He also traced psychoneurobiological development through specific age ranges by citing specific psychological functions appropriate to each age range, and then linking the function to its brain counterpart.

Keywords Affective–configurational representational system • Attachment theory is a regulatory theory • Autonomic nervous system • Autoregulation • Critical period • Dissociation • Experience-dependent • Experience-expectant • Hyperarousal • Limbic system • Neurobiology of subjectivity • Nondeclarative memory systems • Orbitofrontal region • Parasympathetic nervous system • Psychoneurobiological point of view • Right brain systems • Rupture and repair pattern • Sensitive period • Social construction of the human brain • Somatic emotional marker • Sympathetic nervous system

References

Beebe, B. (1986). Mother–infant mutual influence and precursors of self- and object representation. In J. Masling (Ed.), *Empirical studies of psychoanalytic theories* (Vol. 2, pp. 27–48). Hillsdale, NJ: The Analytic Press.

Beebe, B., Knoblauch, S., Rustin, J., & Sorter, D. (2005). Forms of intersubjectivity in infancy research and adult treatment: A systems view. In B. Beebe, K. S., J. Rustin, & D. Sorter (Eds.), *Forms of intersubjectivity in infant research and adult treatment* (pp. 1–28). New York: Other Press.

Bowers, D., Bauer, R. M., & Heilman, K. M. (1993). The nonverbal affect lexicon: Theoretical perspectives from neuropsychological studies of affect perception. *Neurology*, *7*(4), 433–444.

Damasio, A. R. (1994). *Descartes' error: Emotion, reason, and the human brain*. New York: G.P. Putnam's Sons.

Lester, E. M., Hoffman, J., & Brazelton, T. B. (1985). The rhythmic structure of mother–infant interaction in term and preterm infants. *Child Development* 56:15–27.

Main, M., & Morgan, H. (1996). Disorganization and disorientation in infant strange situation behavior: Phenotypic resemblance to dissociative states. In L. K. Michelson & W. J. Ray (Eds.), *Handbook of dissociation: Theoretical, empirical, and clinical perspectives* (pp. 107–138). New York: Plenum.

Schore, A. N. (1991). Early superego development: The emergence of shame and narcissistic affect regulation in the practicing period. *Psychoanalysis and Contemporary Thought*, *14*(2), 187–250.

Schore, A. N. (1994). *Affect regulation and the origin of the self: The neurobiology of emotional development*. Hillsdale, NJ: Lawrence Earlbaum.
Schore, A. N. (1997). A century after Freud's project: Is a rapprochement between psychoanalysis and neurobiology a hand? *Journal of the American Psychoanalytic Association*, *45*(3), 807–840.
Schore, A. N. (2000). Attachment and the regulation of the right brain. *Attachment and human Development*, *2*(1), 23–47.
Schore, A. N. (2001a). Effects of a secure attachment relationship on right brain development, affect regulation, and infant mental health. *Infant Mental Health Journal*, *22*(1–2), 7–66.
Schore, A. N. (2002). Advances in neuropsychoanalysis, attachment theory, and trauma research: Implications for self-psychology. *Psychoanalytic Inquiry*, *22*(3), 433–484.
Schore, A. N. (2005). Attachment, affect regulation, and the developing right brain: Linking developmental neuroscience to pediatric. *Pediatrics in Review*, *26*(6), 204–217.
Sroufe, L. A. (1995). *Emotional development: The organization of emotional life in the early years*. Cambridge: Cambridge University Press.
Stern, D. N. (1985). *The interpersonal world of the infant*. New York: Basic Books.
Van Toiler, S., & Kendal-Aced, M. (1995). A possible protocognitivc role for odor in human infant development. *Brain Cognition*, *29*, 275–293.
Weller, A., & Feldman, R. (2003). Emotion regulation and touch in infants: The role of cholecystokinin and opioids. *Peptides*, *24*, 779–788.

Major Works

Schore, A. N. (1994). *Affect regulation and the origin of the self: The neurobiology of emotional development*. Hillsdale, NJ: Lawrence Earlbaum.
Schore, A. N. (2001a). Effects of a secure attachment relationship on right brain development, affect regulation, and infant mental health. *Infant Mental Health Journal*, *22*(1–2), 7–66.
Schore, A. N. (2001b). The effects of early relational trauma on right brain development, affect regulation, and infant mental health. *Infant Mental Health Journal*, *22*(1–2), 201–269.
Schore, A. N. (2001c). Minds in the making: Attachment, the self-organizing brain, and developmentally-oriented psychoanalytic psychotherapy. *British Journal of Psychotherapy*, *17*(3), 299–328.
Schore, A. N. (2003). *Affect regulations and the repair of the self*. New York: W. W. Norton.
Schore, A. N. (2005). A neuropsychoanalytic viewpoint: Commentary on paper by Steven H. Knoblauch. *Psychoanalytic Dialogues*, *15*(6), 829–854. Supplementary Readings.
Bradley, S. J. (2000). *Affect regulation and the development of psychopathology*. New York: Guilford Press.
Cozolino, L. (2002). *The neuroscience of psychotherapy: Building and rebuilding the brain*. New York: W. W. Norton.
Siegel, D. J. (1999). *The developing mind: Toward a neurobiology of interpersonal experience*. New York: Guilford Press.

Chapter 18
Peter Fonagy (1952–)

Publishing Era: 1984 to the Present

Biographical Information[1]

Peter Fonagy was born in Budapest, Hungary in 1952. His family moved from Hungary to Paris. When Peter was 14, he left Paris and arrived in Britain alone, knowing no English. Peter was self-described as a troubled youth seriously failing in school, as well as in life. At age 17, he contacted the Anna Freud Center in London and began an analysis with Anne Hurry, now a senior member of the Center. The successful analysis was life changing and left Fonagy feeling very grateful both to Ms. Hurry and to the Center. The analysis enabled Fonagy to pass entrance exams to gain access to the University College London (UCL), to graduate in 1974 with a B.Sc. degree in Psychology, to begin a career, and to gain a British passport. In 1980, he earned a Ph.D. in neuropsychology, also from UCL, and trained in clinical psychology. He applied to the Institute of Psycho-Analysis where he was in a training analysis with Clifford York and had supervision from Drs. Ilse Hellman and Dinora Pines.

Throughout Fonagy's university education and professional training, he remained in close contact with the Centre. Friendships made there endured and Fonagy saw many students become leaders in the field. A very special friendship at this time developed with George Moran, who became the Center's Director until his untimely death in 1991. Fonagy admired Moran's clinical work and supervised his research on the psychoanalytic treatment of brittle diabetes. Fonagy became a consultant to research at the Center. In addition, Moran requested that Fonagy "build bridges to the University" and help him fundraise for the Centre's work. Both Moran and Fonagy owed their inspiration to Al Solnit of the Yale Child Study Center who guided and protected them throughout a troubled period. Fonagy became Research Director at the Centre in 1989 and has remained in that role since. At the same time, Fonagy was trained in child and adolescent psychoanalysis at the Centre, supervised by three outstanding Centre clinicians: Rose Edgcumbe, Anne-Marie Sandler, and Marion Burgner.

[1] Adapted from Peter Fonagy: Curriculum; www.annafreudcentre.org (November, 1996).

J. Palombo et al., *Guide to Psychoanalytic Developmental Theories*,
DOI: 10.1007/978-0-387-88455-4_18,

As Research Director, Fonagy followed his psychoanalytic mentor, the distinguished Joseph Sandler. Fonagy encouraged a diversity of research questions and methodological approaches, led by talented and independent researchers who are credited for the Center retaining its distinguished research reputation through three projects. First, Fonagy began a collaboration with Dr. Miriam Steele, who was also at the time in analytic training at the Centre, and her husband Howard. The London Parent–Child Project, which she began, continued to produce unique follow-up data, testifying to the ability, energy, creativity, and quality of the Steeles' personal contact with the participants. Dr. Miriam Steele, with Dr. Jill Hodges, at the same time developed a major new attachment project with children entering adoptive placements. Second, the very different work of Professor Mark Solms in the fields of Freud scholarship and neuropsychoanalysis also had a great impact within and outside the analytic world. Recognized worldwide for his brilliant, tireless, and highly creative contributions Solms began bridging the disciplines of psychoanalysis and neuroscience. The third project at the Center has been outcome research, which is where Fonagy started with George Moran. Fonagy's main collaborator in this area has been Mary Target, whom many consider an extraordinary intellectual and gifted clinician.

Fonagy's other responsibilities have included active participation in the International Psychoanalytic Association and the British Psychoanalytic Society, operating as Sub-Department head of Clinical Health Psychology and managing the Freud Chair at UCL, and filling the Directorship of the Child and Family Center at the Menninger Clinic in the US, a Center, which Fonagy established with his close friend, Efrain Bleiberg.

Fonagy is a distinguished lecturer, teacher. He has received numerous awards, honors, and accolades. He has reinforced his commitment to the leadership responsible for directing the Center, giving up other cherished roles, to help the Centre to adapt child psychoanalysis to thrive in the twenty-first century. He has strengthened and maintained linkages with UCL and the Yale Child Study Center. At present Fonagy is Adjunct Professor of Psychiatry at Baylor College of Medicine, Chief Executive Officer at Anna Freud Center, London, and Clinical Professor of Psychiatry at Yale University School of Medicine.

Conceptual Framework[2]

Fonagy has been a major proponent of a rapprochement between psychoanalytic theory and attachment theory. Although he by no means offers a comprehensive developmental theory, we summarize that segment of his work that is relevant to our focus in this volume.

[2]Over the years, Fonagy has had many collaborators with whom he has published his work. Prominent among these is Mary Target. Since he usually appears as the senior author, in this chapter, we attribute these theories to him, although he might also wish to credit others for their contributions.

Attachment Theory and Psychoanalytic Theory

Fonagy began his project of bringing a rapprochement between attachment theory and psychoanalytic theory by delineating the points of contact and the divergences between them. First in a long paper (1999) and later in a monograph titled *Attachment Theory and Psychoanalysis* (2001), he discussed systematically each of the major psychoanalytic theories, delineating differences and points of agreement. We review and summarize his major points as they highlight both the strengths and weaknesses of attachment theory.

Among points of contact between the two theories are the following. First, both theories agree that anxiety occurs in response to loss, whether external or internal. Second, both theories try to account for the fact that children interpret the events to which they are exposed and that the representations of these events do not necessarily reflect external reality but rather the psychic reality that they construe from their interpretations. Third, both agree that personality development occurs in the early social context when the impact of the events of the early years is critical to the children's development. Fourth, both focus on the significance of maternal sensitivity, even though they define what constitutes such sensitivity differently. Fifth, Fonagy indicated that both theories rely on the premise that an autonomous need for relationships exists in all human beings. By autonomous, he seemed to mean that the need was basic and primary to all human beings. However, Fonagy believed that Bowlby misrepresented psychoanalytic theory when he accused it of relying on the notion that children's attachment to their mothers occurs solely through the feeding experience. In addition, both theories are committed to the view that understanding the process through which children form self and object representations and the functions these serve in furthering children's development is critical to understanding the continuities in children's thoughts, feelings, and behaviors. Finally, mentalization, which includes the capacity to understand that others have beliefs, desires, and intentions of their own, is central to both theories. As we will see, Fonagy goes on to make that construct a cornerstone of his revisions of attachment theory.

The divergences between attachment theorists and the proponents of psychoanalytic theory highlight some of the criticisms that the latter directed to the former. For psychoanalytic theorists, attachment theory took a naive, simplistic view of the parenting process. It failed to appreciate the contributions made to the maturational process by the child's unique interpretation of events and experiences to which the child is exposed. It paid insufficient attention to the elaboration of the personality as the child matures. Furthermore, it did not explain the discontinuities in attachment patterns over the life span. It underrated the importance of psychological development beyond the early years. It failed to appreciate that early relationship does not necessarily set the template for future growth. Finally, since no consistent personality types were linked to secure attachments, the early mother/infant relationship could not be the prototype for later relationships (Fonagy, 1999, 2001).

More importantly, according to Fonagy, attachment theory did not account for the existence of unconscious motivation, which is central to all psychoanalytic theories. It also did not consider the significance of affects in the socialization process.

By making attachment the central construct, it minimized the role of other motivational systems, such as sexuality and aggression, in the development of the personality. Finally, it ignored biological vulnerabilities of the infant other than those caused by neglect or separation.

Concerning the outcomes of secure or insecure attachments, attachment theory's predictive value resided in its linkage of early traumatic experiences in insecurely attached children with later psychopathology. Secure attachment, on the other hand, appeared to act as a protective factor against later psychopathology (Fonagy, 1998).

Internal Working Models

As we have seen, part of Bowlby's legacy to psychoanalysis had been the uncertain status of his ***Internal Working Models* (IWM)** within a broad object relations theory. Whereas the construct provided a potential link between attachment theory and psychoanalytic theory, most psychoanalysts were skeptical of the possibility of a successful integration between the two theories. Fonagy took up the challenge of specifying the precise way in which this link may operate. In part, he found the link in a reinterpretation of the psychoanalytic concept of mental representation. He drew a distinction between IWM and mental representations as formulated in psychoanalytic theories by pointing to the underlying processes that undergird their formation. IWM are processed implicitly and stored in nondeclarative, procedural memory, whereas mental representations are processed explicitly and stored in episodic memory (Fonagy, 2001, p. 263).

According to Fonagy, the shift between attachment theory's concept of IWM and psychoanalytic theory's mental representation had to include a shift from a *behavioral perspective* to an understanding of *the role that internal representations* play in social relations. The issue revolved around the conceptualization of **maternal sensitivity** and the means through which infants internalize their caregivers' responses. Attachment theory assumed that sensitive responsiveness to the child by the mother occurred through her *behavior and personality*, whereas psychoanalytic theory assumed that the "good enough mother's" responsiveness involved much more, including *her own psychic organization and the manner in which the child internalized those experiences*. For Fonagy, the transmission of patterns of attachment was related to the internalization by the infant of the caregivers' psychodynamics. He reinterpreted Bowlby's account of the role of maternal sensitivity as a causal factor in determining the quality of object relations and psychic development. The child develops the capacity for self-reflection through the internalization of the caregiver's mirroring responses and self-reflection is equivalent to the capacity for mentalization. Secure attachment is, therefore, the product of the successful acquisition of the capacity for mentalization, whereas insecure attachment occurred when the infants identified with the caregiver's defensive behavior. In the latter case, the infant acquired internal experiences that poorly represented reality and the interactions with the caregiver. Personality distortions eventually ensue (Fonagy, 2001, p. 173). Maternal sensitivity and the capacity for mentalization became necessary conditions for the development of secure attachment. In contrast to the IWMs of attachment theory, children form internal representations through their reflection upon the mothers' mirroring of their internal state.

Theory of Development

As we have seen, Fonagy took as his starting point the distinction between the concepts of IWM and mental representations. Mental representations refer to the child's experience of both external world and internal processes. They do not necessarily reflect reality but are subject to distortion and modification by the child's psychodynamics. He then proposed the concept of **mentalization** as central to the integration of attachment theory and psychoanalysis. The concept of mentalization is closely related to the construct of **Theory of Mind**.

> The term theory of mind refers to the ability of typically developing children to attribute mental states such as desires, beliefs, and intentions, to themselves and others, as a way of making sense of and predicting the behavior of others (Tager-Flusberg & Baron-Cohen, 1993). The ability entails understanding that other people's behaviors are intentional or purposive, that a desire either to express their state of mind or to communicate with others motivates them. A pathological deficit in theory of mind abilities is believed to underlie autism. Palombo (2006, p. 74).

The **False Belief Task** has been used as a test to determine the presence or absence of Theory of Mind in children. In this task, the examiner sits at a table across from the child being tested. On the table are two identical boxes (box a and box b) with lids on them. The examiner invites a visitor, Sally, to come into the room and to place an object, such as a candy bar, into one of the boxes (box a) and to then leave the room. The examiner asks the child to remove the candy bar from the box a placing it in box b and then invites the guest back into the room. The examiner then asks the child where the child believes Sally would think the candy bar to be. If the child responds that she would think it to be in the original box, Box a, then the child has Theory of Mind, because the child knows that Sally cannot know of the switch. If the child's response is that Sally would think it to be in Box b, then the child does not have Theory of Mind since the child believes that Sally somehow knows of the switch. Generally, typically developing children acquire the capacity for Theory of Mind between the ages of 3½–4. Children with autism generally do not acquire that capacity (see Baron-Cohen, 1993, p. 60; Palombo, 2008).

Theory of Mind describes how it is possible to *attribute false beliefs to others*, whereas mentalization or reflective function denotes the understanding of *one's own as well as others behavior in mental state terms*.

> Mentalization or reflective function is the developmental acquisition that permits children to respond not only to another person's behavior, but to the child's conception of others' attitudes, intentions, or plans. Mentalization enables children to "read" other people's minds. By attributing mental states to others, children make people's behavior meaningful and predictable. As children learn to understand other people's behavior, they can flexibly activate, from

> the multiple sets of self-object representations they have organized on the basis of prior experience, the one(s) best suited to respond adaptively to particular relationships.

Fonagy and Target (1998, p. 92).

Mentalization includes these abilities but also comprises affect states and children's ability to reflect on their own intentions. The **reflective function** enables children to conceive that others have beliefs, feelings, attitudes, desires, hopes, knowledge, imagination, pretends, plans, and so on. The process involved in the development of mentalization led Fonagy to an appreciation of the role of reflective awareness of others' mental states to the development of mental representations of others. Fonagy expressed the belief that the parents' capacity to adopt the **intentional stand** toward an infant, that is, the ability to exercise the function of mentalization, is central to the transmission of attachment patterns between caregivers and their infants. This ability accounts for the observations made of the influence of the caregiver's sensitivity on attachment. It enables children to make others' behavior meaningful and predictable. It also enables them to activate the appropriate self-representations and representations of others in a particular interpersonal context. When that occurs, the child has acquired the capacity for mentalization.

In this reformulation, Fonagy is suggesting that the child's acquisition of IWM is directly related to the development of the reflective function, that is, mentalization. Affects are critical in this process as infants attach meanings to their internal experiences through their relationship with the caregiver within the context of a secure relationship. "My caregiver thinks of me as thinking and therefore I exist as a thinker" (Fonagy, 2000, p. 129); he also states, "Thus a theory of mind is first of all a theory of self" (Fonagy, 2000, p. 132).

Development of the Self

Central to Fonagy's theory of development is that infants' attachment behaviors, such as crying, vocalizing, and smiling, stimulate the caregivers to respond not only by restoring proximity to the infant, as Bowlby had claimed, but also, through their capacity to mentalize, to reflect the infants' affective state. Infants experience their mother's accurate mirroring of their state as indicative of her empathy for their self-state. Infants' anxieties are contained and they gradually realize that they have thoughts and feelings and that these are different from those of the caregiver. This gives infants the opportunity to create representations of their anxieties, which Fonagy calls a second order or **symbolic representation**; that is, the child develops the capacity to represent a representation or to reflect about an inner state.

Fonagy appears to be using an object relations model in the description of this process. Infants internalize their caregivers' state, which they then incorporate into their self and object representations. He states, "The self exists only in the context of the other; the development of the self is tantamount to the aggregation of experiences of self in relationships" (Fonagy, Gergely, Jurist, & Target, 2002, p. 40). "The self is not innately given it is constructed out of early relationships" (p. 126). "*At the core the mature child's self is the other at the moment of reflection*" (Fonagy, 2000, p. 173, italic in original).

An example of maternal sensitivity occurs when a mother reflects or mirrors the child's anxiety, and this perception organizes the child's experience, who now knows what he or she is feeling. Mothers' sensitivity to the child's state is an essential ingredient to the outcome of development. Parents with high reflective capacities are more likely to promote secure attachments in their children. From the point of view of cognitive development, secure attachment enhances the development of symbolic cognitive capacities. It is predictive of the capacity for memory, comprehension, and communication.

Mentalization also facilitates the development of the capacity for self-regulation, which consists in the acquisition of a procedure for the regulation of aversive states of arousal. In fact, secure attachment results from the capacity for self-regulation, which is itself dependent on the mother's capacity for mentalization. Early relationships equip individuals with an information processing control system. This regulatory system is the most important evolutionary function of attachment.

As his thinking evolved, Fonagy elaborated on his views regarding the development of the self. He enlarged the concept of mentalization to include the fact that children are not simply the recipients of others' empathic responses, but they interpret and ascribe meanings to the events to which they are exposed. This required Fonagy to posit a neurobiological mechanism though which this occurs. He suggested the Interpersonal Interpretive Mechanism to solve this problem. The **Interpersonal Interpretive Mechanism (IIM)** is a brain function that requires specific activation by environmental stimuli. It is an overarching neural structure – a neural mechanism with a key evolutionary function. This brain function is not innate, in the sense that it can develop on its own; rather, it requires a specific stimulus to activate it. The environmental stimulus is mother's sensitive responsiveness to the child. Such responsiveness enhances the capacity for mentalization and the reflective function, which in turn triggers processes that lead to the development of the capacity for self-regulation. When that occurs, the child develops a secure attachment to the caregiver that is based on a representational model that includes the IIM. Conversely, when the process fails to develop, that child ends up insecurely attached (Fonagy, 2003).

The manner in which the child experiences the environment acts as a filter in the expression of genotype to phenotype. The genotype is the set of inherited characteristics with which the child is born, whereas the phenotype is the product of the interaction between the genotype and the environment in which the child matures. The specific genes that are expressed during development shape the particular genotype that emerges (Fonagy, 2003). The expression of the genotype is related not to the child's objective environment, but to the IIM, that is, to how the child interprets the events to which he or she has been exposed. The IIM is genetically defined and localized in the medial prefrontal cortex. Damage to these areas is consistently associated with social and personality deficits that can be thought of as loss of interpersonal interpretive capacity, namely, impaired social judgments, impaired pragmatics, deficient self-regulation, and an impoverished dissociation of social situations with personal affect as the markers. The difference in this formulation from that of traditional attachment theory is that "*what is lost in a separation is not the bond but the opportunity to generate a higher order regulatory mechanism: the mechanism for the appraisal and reorganization of mental contents*" (Fonagy & Target, 2002, p. 325, our italtics).

This formulation of the dynamics of attachment permitted Fonagy to specify what goes wrong when a child develops an insecure attachment. Trauma, in the form of maltreatment or neglect, disrupts the neurobiological functions that involve the representation of feelings, thoughts, beliefs, and desires, and results in dissociation, much as Schore had maintained. Children do not experience their mothers as accurately reflecting their affective state and develop an insecure attachment. The child's internal world becomes incomprehensible, terrifying, or painful. In some instances, borderline psychopathology may arise as children struggle to adapt to their inability to mentalize their own or their caregivers' states. The absence of mentalization leads to an unstable sense of self. What is critical is not the loss of the early relationship but the child's failure to develop a mental processing system that generates mental representations.

Case Illustration

Gyorgy Gergley was the therapist in this case, which illustrates a child with an arrest in the capacity to understand and produce symbolic and pretend play. Excerpted from Fonagy et al. (2002, pp. 301–306) (reprinted with permission from Other Press).

Mat was brought to psychotherapy by his mother at 4.1 years of age with a series of behavioral and impulse-control problems. In his mother's view the most serious of these was failure to achieve toilet training by 4 years of age and the child's strong tendency to withhold his feces. Mat would obstipate for several days, would refuse to pass stool sitting on the toilet, and would oblige only if given a diaper. His mother also complained bitterly about Mat's uncontrollable emotional outbursts, frequent tantrums, and externalizing violent behavior, both at the day-care center and at home. He often attacked smaller children at the day-care center, and he tortured his dog at home. He was also described as being obstinate, oppositional, and controlling ("giving orders") in his relationship with his mother. Mat's mother complained that he was always asking "silly questions," which indicated serious castration anxiety, fantasies of physical intrusion, a phobic fear of babies, and an anxious interest in Cesarean births.

Mat was a sickly child, with a history of illnesses (croup, a form of acute respiratory distress in children, pneumonia, allergies) and hospitalizations. Following the pediatrician's advice, his mother stayed at home with him for the first 3 years of his life. He started to go to day care only shortly before starting therapy and only for the morning hours. Mat showed an anxious, ambivalent attachment attitude to his mother, clinging to her yet avoiding her gaze at the same time. He exhibited strong separation anxiety when left in day care or when entering my room for therapy.

Mat's mother was a stiff, poker-faced woman with flat emotionality who, nevertheless, did not hesitate to convey to me her exasperation, dissatisfaction, and often openly hostile feelings (including anger and disgust) toward her son. She was rather dismissive of her child, whom she described as hopelessly spoiled and worthless. She was cold, intrusive, and overcontrolling in her interactions with Mat. She told me that she often "lost her head," shouting at him and beating him up. They lived in a closely symbiotic relationship that was dominated by aggression, rage, and often escalating negative affects. She struck me as being remarkably incapable of feeling empathy or attunement to her child's mental states, and as being in general quite unable to cope with her son's negative emotions. When faced with Mat's negative affective displays, she often reacted with complementary and realistic negative emotions herself, which typically led to an escalation of the child's negative state.

A good example of this is her description of the recurring pattern of interaction in relation to Mat's willful refusal to open his bowels. When left in the nursery by his mother, Mat would refuse to pass stool, but when he was picked up by her in the afternoon, he could hardly withhold it on the way home. At home she would make him sit on the toilet and would sit down next to him herself. He would, however, refuse to pass stool (even though often in pain), and they would be sitting there like this for hours. She would get more and more angry with him and would plead with him to do it, reinforcing her pleas by threatening him with punishments and by making promises. Eventually, she would become deeply resentful, put diapers on Mat, place him in his crib, and attempt to leave the room. Facing the prospect of separation, however, Mat would then promptly soil his diapers. This would outrage his mother, because she would need to come back and change him. At this point she would often shout at him and hit him in her rage.

I had the strong impression that Mat's mother was quite incapable of attending to and reading the dispositional displays that would allow her to identify her child's mental states. This was corroborated by the almost incredible story about Mat's older sister that Mat's mother shared with me in a rather casual tone of voice. Mat's sister was born practically blind, but this fact went unnoticed by her parents for several years. They found out about her condition only when at around the age of 3 or 4 years she was taken to a routine medical checkup in her nursery school. Both parents had apparently missed the girl's almost total inability to see them clearly unless very close and directly facing them. This made me wonder about the seriousness of this dismissive mother's insensitivity to and lack of monitoring of the dispositional facial cues of her children.

For a long time Mat showed seriously regressive functioning during therapy sessions. When he arrived, he would be extremely frightened, crying and clinging to his mother and trying to stop her from going out to the waiting room. Mat was clumsy and somewhat dirty and smelly; he breathed heavily, continually salivated slightly, and was easily frightened of small sounds. He would disregard my presence and avoid eye contact with me, and he would not react verbally or otherwise to my attempts at making contact with him. He only spoke to me when giving orders.

Here, we will concentrate on two pathological features of Mat's behavior that became increasingly apparent during the early phases of the therapy.

One was Mat's inadequate and sometimes bizarre use of language. He did not obey the implicit pragmatic rules (Grice, 1975) underlying normal communicative exchanges: he would very often not respond to verbal inquiries but would sometimes repeat the question in a monotonous, echolalic fashion. When speaking, he would sometimes mix up the first-, second-, and third-person pronouns in his sentences. His interpretations were concretistic and literal, and he often used words with obscure, idiosyncratic meanings and interpreted expressions independently of their context of use.

The second strikingly dysfunctional feature was the fact that Mat seemed *incapable of either producing or understanding symbolic play and pretense.* His play activities consisted solely of repetitive, stereotypic actions using mainly wooden building blocks to make towers and roads. He was fascinated with toy cars, which he pushed back and forth between the wooden structures. However, for the most part he avoided using figurative toys such as dolls, and he did not engage in any pretend activities. My efforts at engaging him in symbolic play were generally futile. In fact, Mat showed a clear aversion to human or animal toy figures and would turn away from them or throw them away when they were offered to him. According to his mother, he never played with figurative toys at home either: he was only interested in computer games and in building blocks. He never had a transitional object. His paintings were composed of diffuse lines and smeared paint, without any discernible figurative content.

It also soon became clear that Mat had serious difficulties with interpreting pretend activities and communications and had trouble understanding the marked, exaggerated pretend mode of expressions. For example, while he was painting, I pointed at the orange-colored water in his cup and said: "Look, it's just like orange juice!" He looked up with fright and said: "But you cannot drink that!" "Of course I can," I replied jokingly, with a marked pretend intonation and raising the cup to my mouth, obviously pretending to drink the "orange juice." Mat became even more frightened (apparently believing that I was actually drinking the painting water) and shouted: "Don't do that, it cannot be drunk!" On another occasion I took out a puppet figure of a fox and asked Mat if he wanted to play with the puppet. He said immediately that he didn't. But I proceeded to animate the puppet, making it walk around while speaking with a "foxy" marked intonation. Mat looked at the fox with intense fear, as if it had really come alive. Then, nearly crying, he begged me to stop, almost shouting that he didn't like puppets. A final example: in one session, Mat and I played a board game in which one could win small treasure chests when arriving at certain positions. Without following the rules of the game, Mat always put his pieces on the winning positions and collected all the treasure chests, while I received nothing. I pretended to cry (in a clearly marked manner), complaining that I didn't get any treasure. Mat looked at me with fright, shouting: "Don't do that! Only babies cry! You are not a baby!"

Both Mat's inability to understand or produce pretend play and his dysfunctions of language use described above are core features of the symptomatology of childhood autism. Other features of Mat's pathology, such as his difficulties with impulse control, his tendency for tantrums, his perseverative, repetitive, and stereotypic object-manipulative activities with nonfigurative objects, his lack of eye contact, and his obsessive interest in vehicles, were also suggestive of a possible autistic disorder. Children with autism seem to lack the metarepresentational ability for "decoupling" (Baron-Cohen et al., 1985; Leslie, 1994) that is argued to be a representational prerequisite both for understanding intentional mental states in others such as false beliefs and for understanding pretense (Leslie, 1987). In normal development, children start to understand and produce pretend play by the end of the second year (Harris and Kavanaugh, 1993), and they pass the so-called false-belief theory-of-mind tasks (Wimmer & Perner, 1983) by 4 years of age (see Chap. 5). Children with autism, however, tend to fail on these tasks even at a significantly higher mental age than 4 years. The related ability to distinguish appearance from reality (understanding that something looks like X, but is really Y) also emerges at around 4 years of age (Flavell, Flavell, and Green, 1987). I tested Mat on two versions of the standard false-belief tasks as well as on a standard appearance-reality task at 4.6 and at 5.0 years (an age at which normal children already pass these tasks). He failed each time, showing a clear lack of understanding of false beliefs as well as of the appearance-reality distinction.

While this provided potentially supporting evidence for the possibility that Mat was, in fact, autistic, this early suspicion was clearly refuted by later developments in the therapy, when his previously dormant ability to understand and use pretend play started to emerge. In the light of these developments, it became clear that his pervasive difficulties with understanding and producing symbolic play and pretense were not due to a genetically based lack of metarepresentational competence, but had a psychosocial origin. We believe that Mat was arrested in his development functioning at the level of "psychic equivalence" (cf. Fonagy & Target, 1996 and Chap. 6) because of the deviant and traumatizing affect-mirroring environment that his mother provided him with.

Summary and Conclusions

Fonagy did not offer a comprehensive developmental theory. He attempted to reconcile differences between attachment theory and psychoanalytic theory, analyzing ways in which they are similar and different. One similarity he noted was the fact that both theories sought to understand the process through which children form self and object representations, and the functions these served in furthering development. Through this effort, he created the concept of *mentalization* to capture the capacity to understand that others have beliefs, desires, and intentions of their own, a concept that he believed served as a bridge between the two theories.

Fonagy attempted to show how Bowlby's concept of *IWM* could serve a link between attachment theory and psychoanalytic theory. He hypothesized that secure attachment was the product of the successful acquisition of the capacity for mentalization. He proposed that the ability to exercise the function of mentalization was central to the transmission of attachment patterns. To Fonagy, the function of attachment behaviors was not only to stimulate the caregiver to provide proximity, but also to stimulate the caregiver to reflect the infant's affect states through mentalization. Mentalization assists in the development of the capacity for self-regulation, which in turn leads to secure attachment.

Regarding self-development, Fonagy proposed the concept of IIM, the psychic structure involved in a child's effort to interpret experiences. This brain function served as a higher order regulatory function. He believed that the loss involved in separation from the caregiver was not the loss of the early relationship, but the loss of the opportunity to develop a "mental processing system" that generates mental representations, which in turn led to an unstable sense of self.

Keywords False Belief task • Intentional stance • Internal Working Models • Interpersonal Interpretive Mechanism • Maternal sensitivity • Mentalization • Reflective function • Theory of Mind • Symbolic representation

References

Baron-Cohen, S. (1993). From attention-goal psychology to belief-desire psychology: The development of a theory of mind, and its dysfunction. In S. Baron-Cohen, H. Tager-Flusberg, & D. J. Cohen (Eds.), *Understanding other minds* (pp. 59–82). Oxford: Oxford University Press.

Flavell, J., Flavell, E. R., & Green, F. L. (1987). Young children's knowledge about the apparent–real and pretend–real distinction. *Developmental Psychology, 23*, 816–822.

Fonagy, P. (1998). Moments of change in psychoanalytic theory: Discussion of a new theory of psychic change. *Infant Mental Health Journal, 19*(3), 346–353.

Fonagy, P. (1999). Points of contact and divergence between psychoanalysis and attachent theories: Is psychoanalytic theory truly different. *Psychoanalytic Inquiry, 19*(4), 448–481.

Fonagy, P. (2000). Attachment and borderline personality disorder. *Journal of the American Psychoanalytic Association, 48*(4), 129–146.

Fonagy, P. (2001). *Attachment theory and psychoanalysis*. New York: Other Press.

Fonagy, P. (2003). The development of psychopathology from infancy to adulthood: The mysterious unfolding of disturbance in time. *Infant Mental Health Journal, 24*(3), 212–239.

Fonagy, P., Gergely, G., Jurist, E. L., & Target, M. (2002). *Affect regulation, mentalization, and the development of the self*. NY: Other Press.

Fonagy, P., & Target, M. (1996). Playing with reality. I. Theory of mind and the normal development of psychic reality. *International Journal of Psycho-Analysis*, 77, 217–233.

Fonagy, P., & Target, M. (1998). Mentalization: A protective factor and a focus of psychotherapy. *Psychoanalytic Dialogues, 8*(1), 28–95.

Fonagy, P., & Target, M. (2002). Early intevention and the development of self-regulation. *Psychoanalytic Inquiry, 22*(3), 307–335.

Grice, H. P. (1975). Logic and conversation. In R. Cole and J. Morgan (Eds.), *Syntax and semantics: Speech acts* (pp. 41–58). New York: Academic Press.

Harris, P. L., & Kavanaugh, R. D. (1993). Young children's understanding of pretence. *Monograph of the Society for Research in Child Development, 58* (1, Serial No. 237).

Palombo, J. (2006). *Nonverbal learning disabilities: A clinical perspective*. NY: W. W. Norton.

Palombo, J. (2008). Mindsharing: Transitional objects and selfobjects as complementary functions. *Clinical Social Work Journal, 36*, 143–154.

Wimmer, H., & Perner, J. (1983). Beliefs about beliefs: Representation and constraining function of wrong beliefs in young children's understanding of deception. *Cognition, 13*, 103–128.

Major Works

Fonagy, P. (2001). *Attachment theory and psychoanalysis*. New York: Other Press.

Fonagy, P. (2005). *Attachment, trauma and psychoanalysis: When psychoanalysis meets neuroscience.* IPA 44th Conference on Trauma: New developments in psychoanalysis, Rio de Janeiro.

Fonagy, P., Gergely, G., Jurist, E. L., & Target, M. (2002). *Affect regulation, mentalization, and the development of the self.* NY: Other Press.

Fonagy, P., & Target, M. (2003). *Psychoanalytic theories: Perspectives from developmental psychopathology*. Philadelphia: Whurr. Supplementary Readings.

Fonagy, P., Steele, M., Moran, G., Steele, H., & Higgitt, A. (1993). Measuring the ghost in the nursery: An empirical study of the relation between parents' mental representations of childhood experiences and their infants' security of attachment. *Journal of the American Psychoanalytic Association*, *41*(4), 957–990.

Chapter 19
Conclusion

We have come to the end of our journey. Through the previous 18 chapters, we studied the historical panorama of the most prominent psychoanalytic developmental theories and their authors whose personal stories influenced the unfolding of their respective models.

In our Introduction, we outlined three sets of issues that are central to the construction of a developmental theory. Regarding the methodological problems, we specified three perspectives from which observers may describe psychological phenomena, the *descriptive*, the *interpersonal*, and the *intrapersonal*, i.e., the intrapsychic. We also proposed that it is possible to conceptualize the central organizing feature of a theory as the root metaphor to which the theory adheres, the three primary root metaphors being, the *mechanistic*, the *organismic*, and the *contextual*. Finally, we raised the controversy as to whether we may view developmental theories as paradigms based on *positivist* perspectives or on *social constructivist* and *hermeneutic* perspectives.

In our section openers to each trend, we referred to these issues and attempted to indicate the positions held by the various authors. We now return full-circle to the beginning, to retrace our steps and set our discussion into the broader intellectual context in which the dialogue between psychoanalytic theorists is taking place. We begin with a brief historical review of the major intellectual traditions that influenced psychoanalytic theories and discuss how they found expression in the differing trends into which we divided those theories. We offer a chart that locates each theory discussed in this work within the intellectual tradition to which it belongs (see Chart 19.1). Finally, we address the issue of what the future holds for psychoanalytic developmental theories.

Intellectual Underpinning of Psychoanalytic Developmental Theories

Embedded within every psychological theory is a set of assumptions that shape the perspective from which investigators view the phenomena they are studying. Often, these assumptions are not stated explicitly, with the result that, at times, readers are

J. Palombo et al., *Guide to Psychoanalytic Developmental Theories*, DOI: 10.1007/978-0-387-88455-4_19, © Springer Science+Business Media, LLC 2009

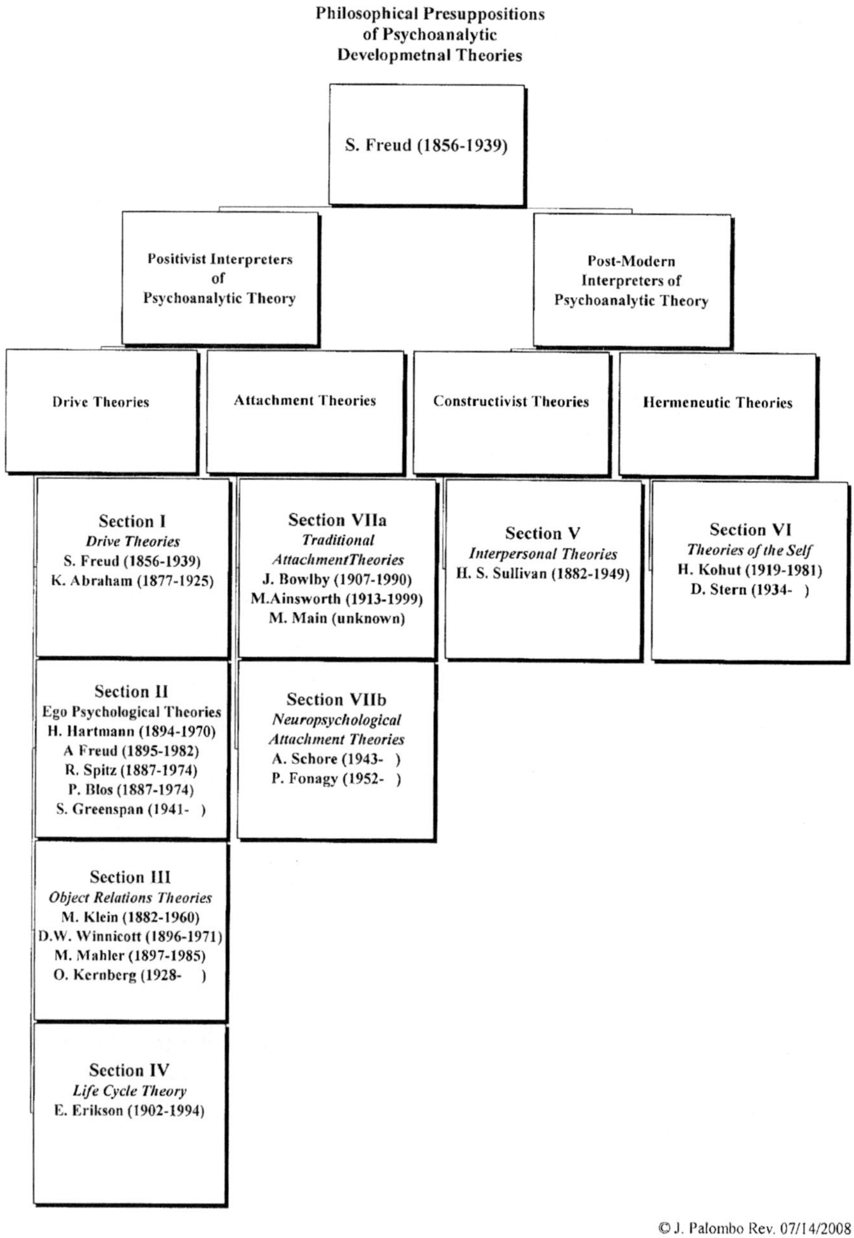
Philosophical Presuppositions
of Psychoanalytic
Developmetnal Theories
S. Freud (1856-1939)
Positivist Interpreters of Psychoanalytic Theory
Post-Modern Interpreters of Psychoanalytic Theory
Drive Theories
Attachment Theories
Constructivist Theories
Hermeneutic Theories
Section I
Drive Theories
S. Freud (1856-1939)
K. Abraham (1877-1925)
Section VIIa
Traditional AttachmentTheories
J. Bowlby (1907-1990)
M.Ainsworth (1913-1999)
M. Main (unknown)
Section V
Interpersonal Theories
H. S. Sullivan (1882-1949)
Section VI
Theories of the Self
H. Kohut (1919-1981)
D. Stern (1934-)
Section II
Ego Psychological Theories
H. Hartmann (1894-1970)
A Freud (1895-1982)
R. Spitz (1887-1974)
P. Blos (1887-1974)
S. Greenspan (1941-)
Section VIIb
Neuropsychological Attachment Theories
A. Schore (1943-)
P. Fonagy (1952-)
Section III
Object Relations Theories
M. Klein (1882-1960)
D.W. Winnicott (1896-1971)
M. Mahler (1897-1985)
O. Kernberg (1928-)
Section IV
Life Cycle Theory
E. Erikson (1902-1994)
© J. Palombo Rev. 07/14/2008

Chart 19.1

left to guess at the presuppositions from which the writer interprets the world. When these are revealed, clarity emerges that permits the reader to know precisely the perspective from which the theory is derived. It also permits practitioners to function more effectively in their clinical encounters with patients as they can maintain a consistent interpretive perspective.

Historically, two major intellectual streams influenced psychoanalytic theories, the **positivist perspective** and the **postmodern worldview** (Blight, 1981; Gergen, 1998; Palombo, 2000; Phillips, 1990; Searle, 1995; Shevrin, 1995; Toulmin, 1986). We use these two labels with a great deal of caution because they mean different things to different people. In this context, we use them to identify two trends that we believe have exerted major influences on psychoanalytic theorizing. The dialogue and controversies engendered between these positions led to two distinctive interpretations of Freud since the early sixties. The first, the positivist perspective, insisted that psychoanalysis belongs among the sciences and must adhere to positivist, empirical principles. This interpretation maintained that Freud attempted to emulate the physical sciences by suggesting a metapsychology modeled on the physics of his day (Hartmann, 1959; Rapaport, 1951). The second interpretation of Freud, which we include under the postmodern movement, is that of **social constructivism** and **hermeneutics**. Social constructivists maintain that the social and cultural milieu in which people develop determines their worldview (Berger & Luckmann, 1966; Gergen, 1985, 1998; Gill, 1988; Hoffman, 1989; Schwandt, 1995). Whereas those who subscribe to the hermeneutic perspective believe that it is important to make a distinction between the natural sciences and the human sciences. The methods of the natural sciences are not concordant with psychoanalysis, which must find its place among the human sciences that has its own methodology. The human sciences address subjectivity and the *meaning* of human experience rather than the causal relationships that may exist between phenomena (Bleicher, 1980; Dilthey, 1962; Palmer, 1969; Phillips, 1991; Sass, 1989; Strenger, 1991).

The Positivist Perspective

The positivist perspective had its origins in the British Empiricist philosophy of John Locke (1632–1704) and David Hume (1711–1776), as well as that of the "scientific method" of the French sociologist August Comte's (1798–1857) (Aarsleff, 1982; Ayer, 1973, 1982; Bernstein, 1983; Passmore, 1985; Poincare, 1952a, 1952b; Popper, 1980; Quine, 1951; Russell, 1912; Toulmin, 1953). This perspective maintained that an external reality existed independently of us. It was fixed and unchanging; we observed it through our senses. Data collected through sense perception was the source of all knowledge. We derived our understanding of the universe through the establishment of causal relationships between phenomena. It was possible to propose hypotheses and collect data through which we could confirm or falsify them. From these hypotheses, we derived *Laws of Nature* that have universal applicability and were context independent. These were then set within a larger framework called theories or paradigms.

Freud's Science Perspective

The first interpreters of Freud insisted that he embraced the prevalent view of science and its methodology. They maintained that Freud saw his work in historical continuity to that of Galileo's experiments with free-falling bodies and inclined planes that eventually led to Newton's formulations of the three laws of motion. In the same vein, Freud in the late 1800s having been trained and steeped in the tradition of nineteenth century scientific methods sought to explain the disorders of the mind by finding order in the workings of the mind and by establishing causal relationships among mental phenomena. His tools were honed in the laboratories of his medical and neurological training. For Freud, science was a systematic public enterprise controlled by logic and by empirical fact, whose purpose was to formulate the truth about the natural world. Self-reports from patients, their introspections, and associations were the source of data for psychological events and were equivalent to sensory observation in the physical realm (Arlow, 1959; Basch, 1978; Buie, 1981; Guttman, 1973; Hartmann, 1959). Freud stated:

> … a speculative theory…would begin by seeking to obtain a sharply defined concept as its basis. But I am of opinion that is just the difference between a speculative theory and a science erected on empirical interpretation. The latter will not envy speculation its privilege of having a smooth, logically unassailable foundation but will gladly content itself with nebulous, scarcely imaginable basic concepts, which it hopes to apprehend more clearly in the course of its development, or which it is even prepared to replace by others. For these ideas are not the foundation of science, upon which everything rests: That foundation is observation alone. They are not the bottom but the top of the whole structure, and they can be replaced and discarded without damaging it.
>
> Freud (1914, p. 77)

Developmental Theories

As we indicated in this work, all drive theorists as well as attachment theorists subscribed to the proposition that psychoanalysis belongs within the sciences and either implicitly or explicitly adhere to a positivist perspective. The differences in the expression of their views originate in the methodologies they applied to support their hypotheses and the root metaphors they use to organize their data. For the most part, they used descriptive and interpersonal methodologies to report on the phenomena they observed and to explain the dynamics of the workings of the mind.

From a methodological perspective, some ego psychologists, including Hartmann, Anna Freud, and Blos, as well as some object relations theorists, such as Klein, Winnicott, and Mahler, accepted Freud's principle that it is possible to reconstruct normal development from the data that patients present during analysis.

Exceptions to these are the theories of Spitz, Greenspan, Kernberg, and those of attachment theorists.

Spitz was an innovator who relied on direct observation of infants to obtain data for his theory. He formulated the construct of ego organizers from his experimental studies of infants rather than from preconceptions of how infants ought to respond during periods of their development (Spitz, 1965). Greenspan's interest in psychological theories other than psychoanalysis led him to attempt to integrate a different set of data than that available to analysts into a more complex developmental theory. He brought to his formulation of a developmental theory not only the dimension of the contribution of neurological differences in children but also the neglected domain of cognition. His six developmental stages represent a major modification of traditional ego psychology (Greenspan, 1989). Kernberg modified drive theory by providing it with a more substantial empirical base (Kernberg, 1976). He returned to Freud and Abraham's original intentions by proposing a framework that integrated normal and pathological development and drew parallels between them. Finally, attachment theorists, from Bowlby on, were deeply committed to an evolutionary perspective, which is entirely science based (Bowlby, 1981, 1984).

As to the root metaphor that each author embraced, all adhered to a variant of the organismic metaphor in their developmental theories. Although when we view their theories in their totality, that is, when we include their clinical theories, all use hybrids that include more than one root metaphor. For example, Freud uses two metaphors the mechanistic and organismic, whereas Kohut uses the organismic and contextual. For some, such as Sigmund Freud, Spitz, Blos, and Greenspan, the ontogenetic perspective is dominant, whereas others, such as Mahler and Erikson, prefer the embryological/epigenetic perspective. Attachment theorists overtly embrace the evolutionary perspective, which views all organisms as struggling to adapt to their environment, some being more successful than others in their efforts at survival.

The Postmodern Worldview

What unifies the postmodern movement is not a single set of beliefs or ideas but the rejection of positivism and of any grand theory that purports to explain phenomena from an objective perspective (Docherty, 1993; Teicholz, 1999, 2009; Thompson, 2004). Furthermore, we can only understand human experience within the social and cultural context in which the person is situated. That context determines the person's view of the world. These interpreters of Freud maintained that whereas his intent might have been to create a scientific psychology, in his clinical practice he developed a theory through which to interpret the psychological meanings of events to his patients and the motives that prompted their symptoms (Frie & Orange, 2009; Gill, 1977, 1988; Holt, 1977, 1981; Klein, 1973, 1976).

Two intellectual strains that preceded the postmodern movement have relevance to psychoanalytic theories: the social constructivist and the hermeneutic. These emerged separately, but we integrate them into the postmodern movement because both embrace the rejection of a single unified worldview. Before we turn to discuss these schools of thought, we review some of the criticism directed at Freud's metapsychology that led some critics to embrace these positions.

Critique of Freud's Metapsychology

Within psychoanalysis, the shortcomings of the positivist position led some to subscribe to the elements of the postmodern trend identified with social constructivism and hermeneutics. These interpreters of Freud were critical of his positivist position. For example, George Klein (Klein, 1973, 1976), among others (Gill, 1977; Holt, 1966), articulated a major criticism when he stated that there were no grounds for considering Freud's metapsychology to be a pure psychology because he framed its propositions in the natural science language of force, energy, and structure. A pure psychology dealt with meanings, motives, and intentions, not with energy. Klein maintained that it was necessary to make a distinction between Freud's metapsychology and his clinical theory. Freud's metapsychology was a *mythology* that had little connection to facts or the functions of the mind. Concepts, such as Eros, the Life Instinct, and Thanatos, the Death Instinct, have no connection with any known scientific findings. Others were critical of Freud's views of the psychology of women because these reflected his immersion in Viennese culture rather than scientific fact. The proposition that penis envy was central to women's development, the view that for women biology was destiny, and that they were by virtue of that *narcissistic, masochistic, and passive* (see Deutsch, 1944), clearly reflected the cultural beliefs of his day.

However, these critics maintained that his clinical theory was of unquestionable value, having benefited countless patients. In contrast to metapsychological concepts, which dealt with entities, clinical constructs address the meanings that patients ascribe to their experiences. These critics pointed to Freud's capacity for empathy and to his nonjudgmental dispassionate approach to clinical phenomena, which he considered as the ideal for the physician of his day, as evidence for the legitimacy of retaining his clinical theory. They insisted that whereas at one level he functioned as a dedicated scientist collecting data, forming hypotheses, verifying them, and creating theories to order his hypotheses, at a different level, he functioned as the humane physician who was interested in curing his patients from the illnesses that afflicted them. His concern led to an understanding of the motives behind their actions and their symptoms.

Having rejected the science perspective and the mythology associated with the metapsychology, these psychoanalytic theorists searched for a different intellectual framework on which to erect psychoanalytic clinical theory. They turned for answers to one of two alternative intellectual visions of reality: the social constructivist or the hermeneutic. As we will see, these solutions created a different set of problems, among them the problem of the justification for a developmental theory, which once revealed led to beneficial insight into what they had repressed.

Social Constructivism

Historically, social constructivism, in the psychological domain, grew out of the work of Jean Piaget (1896–1980) and Lev Vygotsky (1896–1934). Piaget founded his Genetic Epistemology (Piaget, 1972) on the principle that sense perception alone is insufficient to provide knowledge; reason is also a major source of all knowledge. We come to know the world not only through observation and experience, but also through the contributions that our minds make to our understanding of phenomena. He saw the need to posit **schemas** (categories), which our minds contribute, to organize our perceptions. Without them, we can have no knowledge of the world. For Piaget, the concept of schemas became central to understanding the child's construction of the world (Gruber & Voneche, 1977; Phillips, 1981; Piaget, 1970). Vygotsky's intellectual roots were in the Soviet belief that the social, economic, and cultural context determined the child's worldview. Through the acquisition of language, these contexts funneled to children the concepts and thoughts of their environment. Language itself colored the worldview of each person and provided a unique interpretation of the universe to which he or she is exposed (Vygotsky, 1978, 1986; Wertsch, 1985).

For the social constructivist, reality is, in part, a construction of our minds, which imposes its organization on the data derived from our senses. The vision of social constructivists is that there are multiple realities. There are no "naked facts" that a person can observe unalloyed by the very structure of the schemas that thought contributes. The social context provides the categories through which we organize our thoughts (Guba, 1990; Lincoln, 1990).

Social constructivism considers it impossible to arrive at **universal laws of human nature**. The aim of constructivist science is to create **idiographic knowledge** rather than **nomothetic knowledge**. Idiographic knowledge consists of finding patterns within the data that are applicable only to specific settings. We perceive patterns in our surroundings. These patterns are not inherent in the surround itself. They are creations of our own. Nomothetic knowledge, on the other hand, consists in finding "laws of nature" applicable universally. The nomothetic approach does not take into account the interaction between observers and observed and consequently ignores the contribution of the observer to what he or she is observing. Paradigms, therefore, are culture-bound *worldviews* embedded in the socialization of adherents that have no validity beyond that context. Accommodation between paradigms is impossible since every perspective has equal validity to the inquirer, hence inquiry can never be value free (Berger & Luckmann, 1966; Gergen, 1985; Schwandt, 2000).

A consistent psychoanalytic social constructivist developmental theory would use the interpersonal perspective for data collection. Its major root metaphor would be contextual since its commitment would be to emphasize the contribution to the child's developmental progression of the interaction among people within the social and cultural context. Sullivan's developmental theory, which represents an early expression of this position, belongs to this tradition (Sullivan, 1947, 1953). However, as we noted earlier, there are inherent problems to the construction of a developmental theory as evidenced by the fact that relational theorists have not proposed such a theory so far (Teicholz, 1999, p. 252). First, for social constructivists, the "self" is a social artifact that is shaped by the context in which the person is raised (Cushman, 1991). The self is a historical phenomenon; it is not as an entity that has an essence and properties that endure through cross-cultural contexts. It is impossible to generalize about the self. There are no nomothetic propositions that have validity for the self. The concept of a developmental basis for psychopathology becomes difficult to retain.

Hermeneutics

Historically, as a discipline, hermeneutics began in the Middle Ages with the study and interpretation of Biblical text. The goals that scholars sought to attain were to develop a science for the accurate interpretation of the text that provided clues to the authors' intentions as well as establishing the historical accuracy of the events the text described. In time, these goals proved to be elusive in part because it became impossible to dissociate the contribution of the readers' interpretation of the text from its content. The worldview the readers brought to the text colored what they imagined the authors' intentions to be (Bleicher, 1980; Clarke, 1997; Dilthey, 1962; Madison, 1988; Mueller-Vollmer, 1986).

Hermeneutics distinguished between the natural sciences, which use positivist methods to study phenomena, and the human sciences, for which positivist approaches were inappropriate. Instead, they proposed the use of empathy as a "scientific tool" for the collection of data about human beings (Dilthey, 1962; Kohut, 1959; Titchener, 1912). **Empathy** is the tool through which we acquire an understanding of others' feelings, thoughts, and intentions. It requires the projection of the self into others' subjective state and entering into their experiences. We apprehend the meanings of our subjective experiences and that of others through introspection and empathy. The object that we wish to understand is what the other person had in mind. Psychological propositions deal with **intentions and meanings**; they deal with self-experience and subjectivity (Stolorow, 1992; Stolorow, Atwood, & Brandchaft, 1994). Understanding others' motives is central to gaining insight into the reasons for their thoughts and actions. Life itself may be read as the text of a narrative, which we study and interpret. Each person approaches the reading of this life text with his or her own presuppositions, biases, and unique insights.

Given that empathy is the primary tool for data collection, the construction of a developmental theory is contingent upon our ability to enter into the subjective states of the developing child and interpreting the meanings that those states may have to the child. Using the contextual metaphor, the object is to construct a **coherent narrative** that provides a historical account of the child's experiences. Stern's narrative self (Stern, 1989, 1993) and Palombo's interpolation of Kohut's theory of development (in Chap. 14) are examples of such an approach. Among the problems with this approach is that it becomes difficult to distinguish the theory's author contribution and interpretations of the child's experience from the child's own experience. The implicit assumption is that our common human experience allows us to conjecture, through empathy, what another human being experiences.

What the Future Holds

Having reviewed the past, in what follows, we would like to conclude with a glimpse of what the future may hold for psychoanalytic developmental theories. In proposing a model of development, we ask what issues might future contributors consider central to such a theory? How would they address the methodological issues that confront scientific approaches to psychological phenomena, such as the emergence of nonlinear dynamic theories (at times referred to as complexity theory or chaos theory) as a substitute for linear causal relationships? Will it be possible for them to integrate the emerging knowledge from the neurosciences into a coherent view of the development of the self and of subjectivity? How will they explain what propels development forward? Will they substitute evolutionary theory for the drives or the human need for objects? How will they explain children's capacity for resilience and the protective factors that prevent the emergence of psychopathology? Will they undertake to extend the studies of women's issues into a theory of the development of young girls? How will they conceive of the gay and lesbian issues within such a theory? Will they integrate the findings of cultural anthropologists regarding child-rearing practices that appear to conflict with Western notions of optimal caregiving? The answers given by investigators to these questions will depend, in part, on developments in psychoanalytic metapsychology. Those answers may also be affected by trends beyond psychoanalysis, such as the shifting intellectual currents that pull psychoanalytic practice in two different directions, the positivist and the postmodern.

In the dialogue between these two positions, the proponents of the positivist perspective appear to have the upper hand with regard to the necessity for a developmental theory. The emphasis on clinical theory by social constructivists and hermeneuticists leaves little room for data collection outside the clinical setting. Furthermore, the relativism implied by their position leads to a rejection of any theory that claims that its findings have universal applicability.

The positivist perspective, however, has continued to evolve; it attempts to find continuity with Freud's *Project*, to which the dialogue reverts (Schore, 1997). This perspective takes into account the new trends in the sciences, which enlarge and modify its purview. These developments support the positivist position and strengthen the belief that the road to a new psychoanalytic development theory may be found within an evolutionary perspective that attempts to integrate the findings of the neurosciences with psychoanalytic theory. Although we are aware of the hazards involved in plotting a path in uncharted territory, in what follows, we lay out a possible agenda to arrive at a new framework for a developmental theory.

Neuroscience and Psychoanalysis

In his unfinished work *Project for a Scientific Psychology* (1895/1950a), Freud intended to use the state of the neurology and psychiatry of the day to reframe a "psychology of the brain" (Gay, 1988, pp. 78–87). In letters to Fleiss in mid-1895, Freud articulated his reasons for undertaking the *Project.* They were (1) "to bridge the existing conceptual gap between normal and pathological functioning" (2) "to reduce the general laws of the mind to purely mechanical-physiological considerations" (Sulloway, 1979, p. 123), and (3) to come to neurophysiological terms with the core issue in Freud's "increasingly psychodynamic approach to the neuroses" – that of repression (Sulloway, pp. 112–113). Freud confronted two problems, first, to explain the sources of anxiety, which he attributed to energy buildup in the psyche, and second, to account for the repression of sexual energies by brain mechanism, without positing an "observing ego" that told the brain what it should repress. With regard to the first problem, although his proposal in *Aphasia* (Freud, 1891/1953) was far in advance of the localization thinking of his day, his assumption that the primary function of brain processes was to discharge the built-up energy was erroneous. Energy that built up, he believed, produced unpleasure and only its discharge could bring relief. The contemporary view is that the brain seeks and requires stimulation for it to develop (Gazzaniga, Ivry, & Mangun, 2002, p. 611).

As to the second problem, he confronted the question of "How would the brain know that sexual energies were unacceptable?" In other words, how could purely neurophysiological processes recognize that an idea was socially reprehensible? Freud had progressed in his understanding of the mechanism of repression at the clinical level; however, he wanted to go further and explain the precise neurophysiological mechanisms involved. Since sexuality was central to his theorizing, not having an explanation for that mechanism defeated his effort at establishing a neurological explanation for his theory of neurosis. Unable to explain the dynamics of repression (Sulloway, 1979, pp. 163–231) in the newly emerging neurobiological framework of his day, a frustrated Freud gave up on the *Project* (Freud, 1895). He went on to translate the neurological explanations into psychological dynamics, setting aside their neurological roots and moved on to collecting case material and dream data for what he was to consider his crowning achievement, *The Interpretation of Dreams* (Freud, 1900).

Neuropsychoanalysis: A New Paradigm

The movement, now called ***neuropsychoanalysis***, returns the agenda to the exploration of the domains that Freud was unable to chart (see Nersessian & Solms, 1999). A major driving force behind the efforts to integrate **neuroscience** and psychoanalysis has been the emergence of clinical data that presented psychoanalytic theory with anomalies, which it could not explain. Such are the discovery of medications that eliminated symptoms without the necessity for prolonged analytic treatment and the emergence of new knowledge about brain function that challenged old clinical practices that appeared no longer effective. Furthermore, the foundational concept of developmental psychopathology, which mandates that unresolved psychological conflicts or deficits in the sense of self are responsible for patients' symptoms, requires revision. Such a revision can only occur in the context of a reformulated developmental theory. A **new paradigm** has to emerge that is coherent and that has applicability to clinical practice. Two issues that require serious attention in the construction of a new developmental theory are those of a new methodology to replace the old Newtonian explanatory system and the strategies for the integration of the disciplines of neurobiology and psychoanalysis.

Methodological Issues

The emergence of **nonlinear dynamic theory** is a field systems perspective that has led to an appreciation that a small change in the initial conditions that exist in a system can produce large changes in that system at a later point in time. Known as the butterfly effect, it suggests that the flutter of a butterfly's wings in Brazil can lead to a hurricane in Florida (Casti, 2000, p. 239). This perspective provides a powerful methodology to explain the complexity of the interaction among the factors at play during development (Barton, 1994; Gleick, 1987; Goerner, 1993). When applied to psychoanalytic theory, nonlinear dynamic systems can unify the diverse components of developmental theory, theory of pathology, and theory of cure (Miller, 2004; Palombo, 1999; Piers, 2000; Spruiell, 1993). By focusing on the interactions between mothers and infants, patients and therapists, it can take into an account the interpersonal as well as the intersubjective (Beebe & Lachmann, 1988, 1997; Beebe, Rustin, Sorter, & Knoblauch, 2005; Tronick, 2002, 2007). The application of this methodology to the study of human development can locate and trace orderly distributions, progressions and patterns in seemingly random and unpredictable systems (see Thelen & Smith, 1994). Clinicians have long known that growth is discontinuous, unpredictable, and ever changing with seemingly randomized bursts of development, but were at a loss to explain these phenomena (see also Palombo, 2006, pp. 6–7; Panksepp, 1998, pp. 93–94). Palombo states:

> In simple terms non-linear equations present an alternative to the view that events are related to one another in simple linear cause and effect relationships. Instead of seeing causal relationships as "A" leading to "B", non-linear equations explore what happens when the cause "A" gets reinserted each time into the series of the effects "B." We then get an effect "AB" which itself is again affected by the initial cause "A" to become "AAB" and so on. What emerges is *chaos*. However, chaos is a misleading term to describe the sequence of events, for chaos is not the same as randomness. Chaos is highly structured. It produces a set of events that retain a constant orderly pattern. What is distinctive of that pattern is that it reproduces itself at the macro level as well as at the micro leading to the familiar images that are called fractals. These patterns are the product of an inherent order that is guided by an operator that is called an "attractor". These attractors shape the sequence giving them their orderly appearance.
>
> Palombo (2000, pp. 5–6)

The authors of *Intimate Attachments* (Shane, Shane, & Gales, 1997) provide an example of the application of nonlinear dynamic systems theory to a proposed metapsychology. They attempt to integrate three theories: (a) *a theory of development* grounded in Bowlby's theory of attachment and current research in brain function, (b) *a theory of psychopathology* based on trauma as the primary factor in the disruption of the developmental process, and (c) *a theory of the clinical process* that conceives of the provision of a positive new experience to the traumatized patient as central to the therapeutic process into a unified "new self psychology." They state:

> We are convinced that it is only through the application of a nonlinear dynamic systems perspective that one can at least approach this immense complexity in the effort to conceptualize and integrate these findings from related disciplines into a single model of psychoanalysis, still leaving room for further expansion as scientific, clinical, and theoretical advances occur in the contemporary biopsychosocial field.
>
> Shane et al. (1997, p. 30)

A psychoanalytic developmental theory that relies on this methodology would be capable of taking into account the interplay among neurobiological, social/cultural, and intrapsychic factors (see Palombo, 2006). It would appreciate the contribution that observers make on the subjects they observe. It would provide robust data on which to construct a theory that transcends the narrow confines of any single cultural perspective. Finally, by being entwined with other disciplines on whose findings it would rely, such a theory would find its place within what Kuhn called an interdisciplinary matrix (Kuhn, 1970). Such a matrix provides reinforcement to any individual theory through its linkages with other disciplines. Psychodynamic hypotheses would rely on not only data from the clinical setting but also from neurobiological findings, social contextual observations, and introspective data.

Strategies for the Integration of Neurobiology and Psychoanalysis

In an article that was a landmark in advancing the agenda of the integration of psychoanalysis and the neuroscience, the Nobel Prize-winning psychoanalyst, Eric Kandel points a possible way for the achievement of such an integration. He proposed the following five principles that he considered foundational for the future advancement of our understanding of human development. They are:

> Principle 1. All mental processes, even the most complex psychological processes, derived from operations of the brain..... As a corollary, behavioral disorders that characterize psychiatric illness are disturbances of brain function, even in those cases where the causes of the disturbances are clearly environmental in origin. Principle 2. Genes and their protein products are important determinants of the pattern of interconnections between neurons in the brain and the details of functioning.... As a corollary, one component contributing to the development of mental illnesses is genetic. Principle 3. Altered genes do not, by themselves, explain all of the variances of a given major mental illness. Social or mental

> factors also contribute to poor outcome. Just as combinations of genes contribute to behavior, including social behavior, so can behavior and social factors exert actions on the brain by feeding back upon it to modify the expression of genes and the function of nerve cells. Principle 4. Alterations in gene expression induced by learning give rise to changes in patterns of neural connections. These changes not only contribute to the biological bases of individuality but presumably are responsible for initiating and maintaining abnormalities of behavior that are induced by social contingencies. Principle 5. Insofar as psychic therapy or counseling is effective and produces a long-term change in behavior, it presumably does so through learning, producing changes in gene expression that alter the strength of semantic connections and structural changes that alter the anatomical interconnections between nerve cells and the brain.
>
> Kandel (1998, p. 460)

Two strategies have emerged for bridging neuroscience and psychoanalysis. (1) We call the first, *The Rosetta Stone* strategy, and (2) the second *The Psychoanalytic Neurodevelopmental Model* strategy. The **Rosetta Stone strategy**, much like an enhanced dictionary, draws parallels between the two conceptual systems, the neurobiological and the psychoanalytic. It takes metapsychological constructs and attempts to find corresponding neurobiological constructs that are equivalent. It then attempts to find commonalities among the phenomena that make plausible their interrelationships. Such are the strategies that Solms and Turnbull (Solms & Turnbull, 2002) use in their work, as does Schore in his work (Schore, 2001a, 2001b). For example, Schore takes the term *affect regulation* and correlates it with the functions of the orbital frontal region of the brain. Both strategies accept nonlinear dynamic systems theory as the preferred model through which to explain the interrelationship between brain function and psychodynamics (Applegate & Shapiro, 2005; Siegel, 1999).

There are several problems with the strategy of mapping psychoanalytic constructs onto specific brain systems. First, neurological research is often based on lesion studies. It often uses localizationist approaches, that is, methods that identify specific brain functions with specific brain regions. Lesions studies have been criticized as looking at the "hole and not the rest of the doughnut." They ignore the fact that the brain functions are a set of interrelated systems that are closely meshed together and that brain functions are widely distributed (cf. the work of Luria, 1973, 1979, who conceptualized the major brain systems and their interactions with one another). To attribute to one system an equivalence with a psychoanalytic construct such as "repression" or "unconscious" leads to reductionism. Second, the comparison made between the constructs of one discipline with those of the other derived from different observational methods with different methodologies. The construct validity of each is not comparable. Finally, some critics claim that the effort is bound to fail because each paradigm uses its own language system and the two languages are impossible to translate into one another (Goldberg, 2004). Attempt to do so leads to incoherence.

The **Psychoanalytic Neurodevelopmental Model** begins with known psychiatric diagnostic entities, such as anxiety disorder, PTSD, learning disabilities, OCD, or depression, and identified neuropsychological deficits. It examines the research conducted by neurobiologists on the brain mechanisms involved in such disorders (Cozolino, 2002, 2006). It then uses the findings of that research to determine their applicability to clinical practice. Neuroscientists recognize that the brain is an open adaptive system, whose interactions with the environment of attuned caregivers literally promote the development of neural circuits in the infant's brain. Furthermore, this model focuses on the effects of specific constraints that endowment or brain dysfunctions impose on each person's development. It offers hypotheses to explain the impact of these constraints on personality formation. The major problem with this model is that it remains insufficiently developed and continues to be a work in progress.

The View Beyond the Horizon

If we examine the trends we discussed from a historical perspective, we can conceive of a progression in theories of development that resembles that of developmental lines evolving with each new proposal. Some of the constructs within those lines, such as those of the drives, withered and were left behind, whereas others survived to be incorporated into later theories. For example, if we take one of the central questions that preoccupied investigators as focusing on the issue of "What drives development?" the history of developmental theories appears to have evolved since Freud's first formulations. The first proposal embraced by ego psychologists placed emphasis on drives as representing sexual and aggressive instincts that propel the trajectory to maturation. Object relations theorists added the dimension of the ego as object seeking. This perspective was followed by the emphasis on the social and cultural context as significant contributors to development, as represented by both Erikson's life cycle *Ages of Man* and Sullivan's interpersonal theory; Erikson retains aspects of drive theory whereas Sullivan found no use for it. The next formulations suggested that the search for cohesion and meaning are constitutive of the human condition. Stern's narrative self and Kohut's cohesive sense of self held to this view. This proposal was followed by the view that instinctual factors involved in survival are primary to attachment. Finally, explanations that implicate brain function supplemented the evolutionary perspective of attachment theorists.

The paths these theories followed proceeded from implicating inner psychological forces as primary in development to viewing biological factors in interaction with the environment as the predominant features that propelled it. All of these views accepted the proposition that as human beings we seek contact with others, who help sustain us and give meaning to our existence. We can only conjecture as to the form that the next mutation in its evolution the next developmental theory will take.

If we permit our imagination to soar, our vision would be as follows: First, we remind our readers that Freud had undertaken two monumental syntheses of European intellectual trends. The first model of the synthesis of mind, which culminated with the publication of *The Interpretation of Dreams* in 1900, brought together the speculations of French psychiatrists regarding the *origins of mental illness*, the theories of German scientists regarding *biological and physical phenomena*, and existing theories regarding *sexuality*. Each field attempted to clarify the bewildering array of forces that were the cause of mental illness. The second synthesis, the psychosexual phases synthesis, culminated with the publication of the *Three Essays on Sexuality* (1905d). This theory was absorbed into the first synthesis, creating a commanding explanatory framework that includes mental health, mental illness, and human sexuality. By proposing a universal biological life force he called libido, Freud bridged the biological and psychological worlds with a theory of the interaction of drives linked to mental processes. After 100 years we are now awaiting a third grand synthesis, a synthesis that will reconcile the two major intellectual trends that have divided the house of psychoanalysis (Palombo, 2000) for the past half century, the positivist and the postmodern. The former views mental health and illness and the product of biological factors in interaction with the environment, whereas the latter sees them as part of the human condition, which responds to social forces or to the general malaise and existential angst to which humanity is prone.

Keywords Coherent narrative • Empathy • Hermeneutic perspective • Idiographic knowledge • Intentions and meanings • Neuropsychoanalysis • Neuroscience • New paradigm • Nomothetic knowledge • Nonlinear dynamic theory • Positivist perspective • Postmodern worldview • Psychoanalytic neurodevelopmental model • Rosetta Stone strategy • Schema • Social constructivist perspective • Universal Laws of Human Nature

References

Aarsleff, H. (1982). *From Locke to Saussure: Essays on the study of language and intellectual history*. Minnesota: University of Minnesota Press.

Applegate, J. S., & Shapiro, J. R. (2005). *Neurobiology for clinical social work: Theory and practice*. New York: W.W. Norton.

Arlow, J. A. (1959). Psychoanalysis as scientific method. In H. S. (Ed.), *Psychoanalysis scientific method and philosophy* (pp. 201–211). New York: New York University Press.

Ayer, A. J. (1973). *The central questions of philosophy*. New York: Penguin Books.

Ayer, A. J. (1982). *Philosophy in the twentieth century*. New York: Vintage Books.

Barton, S. (1994). Chaos, self-organization, and psychology. *American Psychologist*, *49*(1), 5–14.

Basch, M. F. (1978). Psychic determinism and freedom of will. *International Review of Psycho-Analysis*, *5*, 257–264.

Beebe, B., & Lachmann, F. M. (1988). Mother–infant mutual influence and precursors of psychic structure. In A. Goldberg (Ed.), *Progress in self-psychology* (Vol. 3, pp. 3–25). New Jersey: The Analytic Press.

Beebe, B., & Lachmann, F. M. (1997). Mother–infant structures and presymbolic self and object representations. *Psychoanalytic Dialogues*, *7*, 30–182.

Beebe, B., Rustin, J., Sorter, D., & Knoblauch, S. (2005). An expanded view of forms of intersubjectivity in infancy and their application to psychoanalysis. In B. Beebe, S. Knoblauch, J. Rustin, & D. Sorter (Eds.), *Forms of intersubjectivity in infant research and adult treatment* (pp. 55–88). New York: Other Press.

Berger, P. L., & Luckmann, T. (1966). *The social construction of reality: A treatise in the sociology of knowledge*. New York: Doubleday Anchor Books.

Bernstein, R. J. (1983). *Beyond objectivism and relativism: Science hermeneutics and praxis*. Philadelphia: University of Pennsylvania Press.

Bleicher, J. (1980). *Contemporary hermeneutics: Hermeneutics as method philosophy and critique*. London: Routledge & Kegan Paul.

Blight, J. G. (1981). Must psychoanalysis retreat to hermeneutics? Psychoanalytic theory in light of Popper's evolutionary epistemology. *Psychoanalysis and Contemporary Thought, 4*, 147–205.

Bowlby, J. (1981). Psychoanalysis as a natural science. *International Review of Psycho-Analysis, 8*, 243–257.

Bowlby, J. (1984). Psychoanalysis as a natural science. *Psychoanalytic Psychology, 1*(1), 7–22.

Buie, D. H. (1981). Empathy: Its nature and limitations. *Journal of the American Psychoanalytic Association, 29*, 281–308.

Casti, J. L. (2000). *Paradigms regained: A further exploration of the mysteries of modern science*. New York: Harper Collins.

Clarke, B. H. (1997). Hermeneutics and the "relational" turn: Schafer, Ricoeur, Gadmaer, and the nature of psychoanalytic subjectivity. *Psychoanalysis and Contemporary Thought, 20*(1), 3–68.

Cozolino, L. (2002). *The neuroscience of psychotherapy: Building and rebuilding the brain*. New York: W. W. Norton.

Cozolino, L. (2006). *The neuroscience of human relationships: Attachment in the developing social brain*. New York: W. W. Norton.

Cushman, P. (1991). Ideology obscured: Political uses of the self in Daniel Stern's infant. *American Psychologist, 46*(3), 206–219.

Deutsch, H. (1944). *The Psychology of women*. New York: Grune & Stratton.

Dilthey, W. (1962). *Pattern and meaning in history: Thoughts on history and society*. New York: Harper Torch Books, The Academy Library.

Docherty, T. (Ed.). (1993). *Postmodernism: A reader*. New York: Columbia University Press.

Freud, S. (1891/1953). *On aphasia: A critial study* (E. Stengle, Trans.). New York: International Universities Press.

Freud, S. (1895/1950a). Project for a scientic psychology. In J. Strashey (Ed.), *The Standard edition* (Vol. I, pp. 283–386). London: Hogarth Press.

Freud, S. (1900). The interpretation of dreams. In J. Strashey (Ed.), *Standard edition* (Vol. 5). London: Hogarth Press.

Freud, S. (1914). On narcissism. In J. Strashey (Ed.), *Standard edition* (Vol. 14, pp. 67–104). London: Hogarth Press.

Frie, R., & Orange, D. M. (Eds.). (2009). Beyond Postmodernism: New dimensions in clinical theory and practice. New York: Routledge.

Gay, P. (1988). *Freud: A life for our time*. New York: W.W. Norton.

Gazzaniga, M. S., Ivry, R. B., & Mangun, G. R. (2002). *Cognitive neuroscience: The biology of the mind* (2nd ed.). New York: W.W. Norton.

Gergen, K. J. (1985). The social constructionist movement in modern psychology. *American Psychologist, 40*(3), 266–275.

Gergen, K. J. (1998). Social construction and psychoanalytic promise: Commentary on paper by Michael J. Bader. *Psychoanalytic Dialogues, 8*(1), 45–53.

Gill, M. G. (Ed.). (1977). *Metapsychology is not psychology.* In Gill, M. M., & Holzman, P. S. (Eds.) Psychology versus Metapsychology, Psychological Issues IX (4). New York: International Universities Press. pp. 71–105.

Gill, M. G. (1988). Metapsychology revisited. In *The annual of psychoanalysis* (Vol. 16, pp. 35–48). New York: International Universities Press.

Gleick, J. (1987). *Chaos: Making a new science*. New York: Viking.

Goerner, S. J. (1993). What is chaos? Or, can science's sense of the world really change? *The General Psychologist, 29*(3), 87–93.

Goldberg, A. (2004). David Milrod's "The Concept of the Self and the Self Representation." *Neuro-Psychoanalysis, 6*(1), 91–92.

Greenspan, S. I. (1989). The development of the ego: Biological and environmental specificity in the psychopathological developmental process and the selection and construction of ego defenses. *Journal of the American Psychoanalytic Association, 37*(3), 639–686.
Gruber, H. E., & Voneche, J. J. (Eds.). (1977). *The essential Piaget*. New York: Basic Books.
Guba, E. G. (Ed.). (1990). *The paradigm dialogue*. Newbury Park: Sage.
Guttman, S. A. (1973). Psychonalysis and science: The concept of structure. In The Chicago Institute of Psychoanalysis (Ed.), *The Annual of Psychoanalysis* (Vol. 1, pp. 73–81). New York: Quadrangle Press.
Hartmann, H. (1959). Psychoanalysis as a scientific theory. In S. Hook (Ed.), *Psychoanalysis, scientific method and philosophy* (pp. 3–37). New York: New York University Press.
Hoffman, E. (1989). *Lost in translation: A life in a new language*. New York: E.P. Dutton.
Holt, R. R. (1966). A review of some of Freud's biological assumptions and their influence on his theories. In L. Greenfield (Ed.), *Psychoanalysis and current biological thought* (pp. 93–124). Madison: University of Wisconsin Press.
Holt, R. R. (1977). Drive or wish? A reconsideration of the psychoanalytic theory of motivation. In M. M. Gill & P. S. Holzman (Eds.), *Psychology versus metapsychology* (Vol. 9, pp. 158–197). New York: International Universities Press.
Holt, R. R. (1981). The death and transfiguration of metapsychology. *International Review of Psycho-Analysis, 8*, 129–143.
Kandel, E. R. (1998). A new intellectual framework for psychiatry. *American Journal of Psychiatry, 155*(4), 457–469.
Kernberg, O. F. (1976). *Object relations theory and clinical psychoanalysis*. New York: Jason Aronson.
Klein, G. (1976). *Psychoanalytic theory: An exploration of essentials*. New York: International Universities Press.
Klein, G. S. (1973). Two theories or one? *Bulletin of the Menninger Clinic, 37*, 99–132.
Kohut, H. (1959). Introspection, empathy and psychoanalysis. *Journal of the American Psychoanalytic Association, 7*, 459–483.
Kuhn, T. S. (1970). Reflections on my critics. In I. Lakatos & Musgrave, A. (Eds.), *Criticism and the growth of knowledge* (pp. 231–278). Cambridge: Cambridge University Press.
Lincoln, Y. S. (1990). The Making of a constructivist: A Remembrance of transformations past. In E. G. Guba (Ed.), *The paradigm dialogue* (pp. 67–87). Newbury Park: Sage.
Luria, A. R. (1973). *The working brain: An introduction to neuropsychology*. New York: Basic Books.
Luria, A. R. (1979). *The making of mind: A personal account of Soviet psychology*. Cambridge: Harvard University Press.
Madison, G. B. (1988). The hermeneutics of (inter)subjectivity, or: The mind/body problem deconstructed. *Man and World, 21*, 3–33.
Miller, M. L. (2004). Dynamic systems and the therapeutic action of the analyst. In J. Reppen, J. Tucker, & M. A. Schulman (Eds.), *Way beyond Freud: Postmodern psychoanalysis observed*. London: Open Gate Press.
Mueller-Vollmer, K. (Ed.). (1986). *The hermeneutics reader: Texts of the German tradition from the enlightenment to the present*. Oxford: Basil Blackwell.
Nersessian, E., & Solms, M. (Eds.). (1999). *Neuro-psychoanalysis: An interdisciplinary journal for psychoanalysis and neuroscience* (Vol. I–VIII). Madison, CT: International Universities Press.
Palmer, R. E. (1969). *Hermeneutics: Interpretation theory in Schleiermacher, Dilthey, Heidegger, and Gadamer*. Evanston: Northwestern University Press.
Palombo, J. (2000). Psychoanalysis: A house divided. *Psychoanalytic Social Work, 7*(1), 7–26.
Palombo, J. (2006). *Nonverbal learning disabilities: A clinical perspective*. New York: W. W. Norton.
Palombo, S. R. (1999). *The emergent ego: Complexity and coevolution in the psychoanalytic process*. Madison, CT: International Universities Press.
Panksepp, J. (1998). *Affective neuroscience: The foundation of human and animal emotions*. New York: Oxford University Press.
Passmore, J. (1985). *Recent philosophers*. La Salle, IL: Open Court Publishing.

Phillips, D. C. (1990). Postpositivistic science: Myths and realities. In E. G. Guba (Ed.), *The paradigm dialogue* (pp. 31–45). Newbury Park: Sage.

Phillips, J. (1991). Hermeneutics in psychoanalysis: Review and reconsideration. *Psychoanalysis and Contemporary Thought, 14*(2), 371–424.

Phillips, J. L. (1981). *Piaget's theory: A primer*. San Francisco: W. H. Freeman.

Piaget, J. (1970). *The place of the sciences of man in the system of sciences*. Paris: Mouton/UNESCO.

Piaget, J. (1972). *The principles of genetic epistemology*. New York: Basic Books.

Piers, C. (2000). Character as self-organizing complexity. *Psychoanalysis and Contemporary Thought, 23*(1), 3–34.

Poincare, H. (1952a). *Science and hypothesis*. New York: Dover.

Poincare, H. (1952b). *Science and method*. New York: Dover.

Popper, K. (1980). Science: Conjectures and refutations. In E. D. Klemke, R. Hollinger, & A. D. Kline (Eds.), *Introductory readings in the philosophy of science* (pp. 19–34). New York: Prometheus Books.

Quine, W. V. (1951). Two dogmas of empiricism. *The Philosophical Review, 60*(1), 20–43.

Rapaport, D. (1951). The conceptual model of psychoanalysis. In M. Gill (Ed.), *The collected papers of David Rapaport* (pp. 405–431). New York: Basic Books.

Russell, B. (1912). *The Problems of philosophy*. Oxford: Oxford University Press.

Sass, L. A. (1989). Humanism, hermeneutics, and humanistic psychoanalysis: Differing conceptions of subjectivity. *Psychoanalysis and Contemporary Thought, 12*(3), 433–504.

Schore, A. N. (1997). A century after Freud's project: Is a rapprochement between psychoanalysis and neurobiology a hand? *Journal of the American Psychoanalytic Association, 45*(3), 807–840.

Schore, A. N. (2001a). Effects of a secure attachment relationship on right brain development, affect regulation, and infant mental health. *Infant Mental Health Journal, 22*(1–2), 7–66.

Schore, A. N. (2001b). The effects of early relational trauma on right brain development, affect regulation, and infant mental health. *Infant Mental Health Journal, 22*(1–2), 201–269.

Schwandt, T. A. (1995). Constructivist, interpretivist approaches to human inquiry. In N. K. Denzin & Y. S. Lincoln (Eds.), *Handbook of qualitative research* (pp. 118–137). Thousand Oaks, CA: Sage.

Schwandt, T. A. (2000). Three epistemological stances for qualitative inquiry: Interpretivism, hermeneutics, and social constructivism. In N. K. Denzin & Y. S. Lincoln (Eds.), *Handbook of qualitative research* (2nd ed., pp. 189–213). Thousand Oaks, CA: Sage.

Searle, J. R. (1995). *The construction of social reality*. New York: The Free Press.

Shane, M., Shane, E., & Gales, M. (1997). *Intimate attachments: Toward a new self psychology*. New York: Guilford Press.

Shevrin, H. (1995). Is psychoanalysis one science, two sciences, or no science at all? A discourse among friendly antagonists. *Journal of the American Psychoanalytic Association, 43*(4), 963–986.

Siegel, D. J. (1999). *The developing mind: Toward a neurobiology of interpersonal experience*. New York: Guilford Press.

Solms, M., & Turnbull, O. (2002). *The brain and the inner world: An introduction to the neuroscience of subjective experience*. New York: Other Press.

Spitz, R. A. (1965). *The first year of life: A psychoanalytic study of normal and deviant development of object relations*. New York: International Universities Press.

Spruiell, V. (1993). Deterministic chaos and the sciences of complexity: Psychoanalysis in the midst of a general scientific revolution. *Journal of the American Psychoanalytic Association, 41*(1), 3–44.

Stern, D. N. (1989). Developmental prerequisites for the sense of narrated self. In A. M. Cooper, O. F. Kernberg, & E. S. Person (Eds.), *Psychoanalysis: Toward the second century* (pp. 168–178). New Haven: Yale University Press.

Stern, D. N. (1993). Why study children's narratives? *The Signal: Newletter of the World Association for Infant Mental Health, 1*(3), 1–3.

Stolorow, R. D. (1992). *Contexts of being: The intersubjective foundations of psychological life*. Hillsdale, NJ: The Analytic Press.

Stolorow, R. D., Atwood, G. E., & Brandchaft, B. (Eds.). (1994). *The intersubjective perspective*. Northvale, NJ: Jason Aronson.

Strenger, C. (1991). Between hermeneutics and science: An essay on the epistemology of psychoanalysis. In *Psychological issues* (Vol. 59). Madison, CT: International Universities Press.

Sullivan, H. S. (1947). *Conceptions of modern psychiatry*. New York: W. W. Norton.

Sullivan, H. S. (1953). *The interpersonal theory of psychiatry*. New York: W. W. Norton.

Sulloway, F. J. (1979). *Freud, biologist of the mind: Beyond the psychoanalytic legend*. New York: Basic Books.

Thelen, E., & Smith, L. (1994). *A dynamic systems approach to the development of cognition and action*. Cambridge, MA: MIT Press.

Thompson, M. G. (2004). Postmodernism and psychoanalysis: A Heideggerian critique of postmodernist malaise and the question of authenticity. In J. Reppen, J. Tucker, & M. A. Schulman (Eds.), *Way beyond Freud: Postmodern psychoanalysis observed* (pp. 173–202). London: Open Gate Press.

Teicholz, J. G. (1999). Kohut, Loewald, and the Postmoderns: A comparative study of self and relationship. Hillsdale, NJ: The Analytic Press.

Teicholz, J. G. (2009). A strange convergence: postmodern theory, infant research, and psychoanalysis. In R. Frie & D. Orange (Eds.), Beyond Postmodernism: New dimensions in clinical theory and practice (pp. 69–90). New York: Routledge.

Titchener, E. (1912). The schema of introspection, American Journal of Psychology, *23*, 485–508.

Toulmin, S. (1953). *The philosophy of science*. London: Hutchinson's University Library.

Toulmin, S. (1986). Self psychology as a "postmodern" science. *Psychoanalytic Inquiry*, *6*(3), 459–478.

Tronick, E. Z. (2002). A model of infant mood states and Sandarian affective waves. *Psychoanalytic Dialogues*, *12*, 73–99.

Tronick, E. Z. (2007). *The neurobehavioral and social-emotional development of infants and children*. New York: W.W. Norton.

Vygotsky, L. (1986). *Thought and language (translated by Alex Kozulin)*. Cambridge, MA: The MIT Press.

Vygotsky, L. S. (1978). *Mind in society: The development of higher psychological processes*. Cambridge, MA: Harvard University Press.

Wertsch, J. V. (1985). *Vygotsky and the social formation of mind*. Cambridge, MA: Harvard University Press.

Appendix A

Stages or Phases of Development

A nettlesome issue we encountered that requires special attention is the confusion surrounding the concept of "stages" and "phases" to describe periods of development. Freud used these terms loosely and at times interchangeably, although he was inclined to use the term phase more consistently to refer to the different libidinal periods. Abraham clearly refers to stages of development. Most ego psychologists, with the exception of Spitz, refer to phases of development without defining the distinction between a phase and a stage. Most object relations theorists tend to follow that convention, except that Klein uses the concept of "positions," whereas Kernberg divides development into stages. Erikson in his description of the "Eight Ages of Man," actually refers to the eight periods as stages. Sullivan avoids the use of the terms, preferring to refer to "epochs" instead. Stern clearly defines the concept of "domains" as his preferred term. Kohut avoids both terms and is inclined to use the term "periods." Greenspan reverts to the use of the concept of stages.

Attachment theorists present a mixed picture. Bowlby specifically avoids the terms stages or phases in his description of the developmental process and patterns of attachment. However, he speaks of the *phases* of the process that children go through following a loss. Ainsworth refers to phases of development during the process of attachment. Schore and Fonagy do not refer to phases or stages of development. In this work, we have followed the convention of using the terms that each author has used to characterize developmental periods (see Table A.1).

To clarify the distinction between the terms stages and phases, we cite the following discussion found in the Appendix to Spitz's (1965) book, *The first year of life: A psychoanalytic study of normal and deviant development of object relations*. In this appendix, Cobliner reviews some of the criteria that Piaget used to determine what constitutes a stage of development. He gives the following:

a) A stage is marked by dominant characteristics which are interdependent and form a *totality*, a structural whole.
b) Stages are set off by breaks in the unfolding psyche. There is a *sudden* acquisition at its beginning; this gain is consolidated, integrated with previous acquisitions.

Table A.1 Authors' use of the concepts "stages," "phases," or alternative terms

Author	Uses concept of developmental stages	Uses concept of developmental phases	Does not use either concept of stage or phase	Use a different concept
Sigmund Freud		X		
Karl Abraham	X			
Heinz Hartmann		X		
Anna Freud		X		
Rene Spitz	X			
Peter Blos		X		
Melanie Klein			X	Positions
Donald Winnicott		X		
Margaret Mahler		X		
Otto Kernberg	X			Levels
H. H. Sullivan			X	Epochs
Erik Erikson	X			Modes
Daniel Stern			X	Domains
Heinz Kohut			X	Periods
Stanley Greenspan	X			
John Bowlby			X	
Mary Ainsworth			X	
Allan Schore			X	
Peter Fonagy			X	

Later on a new acquisition is being prepared. Psychic growth is both continuous and discontinuous.

c) The date of an acquisition of psychic faculties, skills, or mechanisms characteristic for the particular stage varies considerably from population to population and within that population, from individual to individual.

d) [T]he serial order of the acquisition remains *constant*; it is the same for all populations, it is universal.

Piaget stresses that the elements of a given stage are *invariably integrated into the next higher ones*; this is indeed the hub of his concept of stages (italics in original, pp. 314–315).

Cobliner goes on to state "Piaget's concept of stages, his sharp division of psychic unfolding into distinct episodes, finds no corresponding parallel in classical psychoanalytic theory." (p. 315). However, he maintains that Spitz, whose scheme utilizes the concept of stages, accounts "for a wider spectrum of phenomena than Piaget's" (p. 316).

Part of the problem of making the distinction between stages and phases may reside in the fact that Piaget's theory narrowly addresses cognitive development, whereas psychoanalytic theories deal with the emotional dimensions of relationships. Psychometric tools are available to test for levels of cognitive development, whereas no such tools exist for libidinal investment in others, which complicates the issue of either determining the onset of a stage/phase or determining the component elements that constitute a stage/phase. Furthermore, in contrast to Piaget's clear-cut criteria for what constitutes a developmental stage, psychoanalytic developmental theorists do not provide a consensus definition either for the concept of stage or for the concept of phase.

One feature of psychoanalytic theories that further complicates the issues of definition is the use of the organismic metaphor, in particular the analogy drawn between psychological development and ontogeny or epigenesis. As we have seen, Freud popularized a version of the principle that ontogeny recapitulates phylogeny that was erroneous. Those developmental theorists who continued to use the term ontogeny did not revise its definition to place it in line with modern evolutionary biology. Others, who chose to use the epigenetic model, drew the analogy with embryology as a more accurate metaphor for psychological development. However, the embryological model alone could not provide parallels to stages or phases. Other principles had to be imposed on the model in order to make it psychologically meaningful. For example, Mahler's epigenetic model ascribed a value to separation and individuation, rather than to interdependence, which would be equality consistent with the model. In any case, the distinction between stages and phases was lost in the process.

We may infer the following tentative definition for the concept of phase from the usage that ego psychologists and object relations theorists have made of the term. A developmental phase is a period that emerges ontogenetically or epigenetically, during which a new set of psychological phenomena emerge irrespective of whether a consolidation of the elements of the prior phase has occurred. The new phenomena achieve dominance and become focal issues for the individual. Phases are discontinuous in the sense that they have an approximate chronological beginning and end, although elements of each phase may be carried over to subsequent phases if an adaptive resolution has taken place, such as when sublimation occurs. They are also hierarchical in that the chronologically earlier phases represent less mature forms of differentiation than later phases. Fixations can occur at specific phases, in which case these would impede the progression to the next phases; furthermore, individuals can regress from a higher phase of development to a lower one when confronted by trauma or other obstacles.

Given these considerations, we can conclude that, whereas a theory that makes use of the epigenetic metaphor to describe the developmental sequence is on more solid ground that one that makes use of the model of ontogeny, the rationale for a differentiation between stages or phases of development remains difficult. We are left with historical convention for the use of the term phase with no firm theoretical ground for it. It is not surprising that some chose to avoid the terms and substituted their own concepts instead.

References

Spitz, R. A. (1965). *The first year of life: A psychoanalytic study of normal and deviant development of object relations* (pp. 301–356). New York, NY: International Universities Press (Appendix by W. G. Cobliner, titled "The Geneva School of Genetic Psychology and Psychoanalytic: Parallels and Counterparts").

Appendix B

Comparative chart of psychoanalytic developmental theories

Theorist/school/ publishing era	Major works	Concepts/terms	Main contributions/ideas
Sigmund Freud 1856-1939 *School* Classical Psychoanalysis Drive Theory *Publishing era* 1888-1950	• 1894 - The neuro-psychoses of defence • 1895 - Studies on hysteria (case of Anna O) • 1895/1950 - *Project for a scientific psychology* • 1900 - *The interpretation of dreams* • 1901 - *The psychopathology of everyday life* • 1905 - Three essays on the theory of sexuality • 1905 - Fragment of an ana-lysis of a case of hysteria (case of Dora) • 1909 - Notes upon a case of obsessional neurosis (case of The Rat Man) • 1910 - Five lectures on psycho-analysis • 1912 - Dynamics of trans-ference • 1912 - Totem and taboo • 1914 - On the history of the psychoanalytic movement • 1914 - On narcissism • 1915 - Instincts and their vicissitudes • 1915 - Papers on meta psychology • 1917 - Mourning and melan-cholia	• Anal phase • Castration anxiety • Cathexis • Conscious • Constancy principle • Defense mechanisms (Isolation; Identification; Introjection; Projection; Reaction formation; Repression; Reversal; Turning against the self; Undoing) • Drive/drive theory • Narcissism • Phallic/urethral/narcissistic phase • Pleasure-unpleasure principle • Polymorphous perverse sexuality • Preconscious • Primary and secondary • process • Psychic determinism • Psychosexual stages • Reality principle • Regression • Resistance • Structural hypothesis • Superego • Topographic hypothesis • Transference • Tripartite model • Unconscious	• Father of psychoanalysis • Discovered the existence of a dynamic unconscious • The unconscious is the source of our motivations • Fundamental human motivation is drive discharge • Outlined the "psychical apparatus" of mental processes in his topographical hypothesis (pcs,cs,unc); later proposed the tripartite structural hypothesis (id, ego, superego) • Cs: what one is aware of at a given moment; Pcs: available memory; Ucs: all things that are not available to awareness, including things that have their origins there (such as drives or instincts) and things we put there because we cannot bear them (such as memories and emotions associated with trauma) • Id: instincts or drives (movement from need to wish is "primary process"); Ego: relates to reality to get needs met ("reality principle") and searches for objects to fulfill drives ("secondary process"); Superego: conscience and ego ideal • Outlined psychosexual stages of development. Oral (0-18 months): focus of pleasure is the mouth - task is weaning; Anal (18 months-3 years): focus of pleasure is the anus - task is potty training; Phallic (3-7 years): focus of pleasure is the genitals - task is Oedipal crisis; Oedipal crisis (3-5 years): major point at which psychopathology is centered.; Latency (7 years to puberty): sexual impulse suppressed in the service of learning; Genital (puberty-adult): resurgence of sex drive in adolescence

	• 1917 - On transformation of instinct as exemplified in anal erotism • 1918 - From the history of an infan tile neurosis (case of The Wolf Man) • 1919 - A child is being beaten • 1920 - Beyond the pleasure principle • 1921 - Group psychology and the analysis of the ego • 1923 - The ego and the id • 1923 - The infantile genital organization of the libido • 1924 - The dissolution of the Oedipus complex • 1926 - The question of lay analysis • 1927 - The future of an illusion • 1926 - Inhibitions, symptoms and anxiety • 1930 - Civilization and its discontents • 1939 - Moses and monotheism		• Discovered phenomenon of transference. Analysis of transference is most important part of treatment because original conflicts will be reenacted in relationship with therapist. • Neurotic symptoms are attempts to defend against unconscious wishes that are unacceptable. They are developmental obstacles • Resistance is used to defend against awareness of unacceptable wishes • Treatment includes free association, analysis of resistance and transference, and dream analysis
Heinz Hartmann 1894-1970 *School* Ego Psychology *Publishing era* 1917-1966	• 1927 - *The fundamentals* of psychoanalysis • 1939 - Ego psychology and the problem of adaptation • 1939 - Psychoanalysis and the concept of mental health • 1948 - Comments on the psychoanalytic theory of instinctual drives • 1945 - The genetic approach in psychoanalysis	• Adaptive point of view • Alloplastic change • Autoplastic change • Average expectable environment • Change in function • Conflict-free ego • Ego-dystonic	• Emphasized greater appreciation of environmental influences on intrapsychic world • Shifted emphasis from chaotic id motivating all thoughts and actions, to emphasis on a resilient ego capable of coping with drives, superego, and the environment • Emphasized the primacy of the ego in development • Introduced the idea of ego as independent of id and having autonomy and intentionality • Adaptive point of view: infants are born with the equipment they need to adapt to their environment

(continued)

Comparative chart of psychoanalytic developmental theories (continued)

Theorist/school/ publishing era	Major works	Concepts/terms	Main contributions/ideas
	• 1946 - Comments on the formation of psychic structure • 1949 - Notes on the theory of aggression • 1950 - Psychoanalysis and developmental psychology • 1950 - Comments on the psychoanalytic theory of the ego • 1952 - The mutual influences in the development of the ego and the id • 1955 - Notes on the theory of sublimation • 1956 - Notes on the reality principle • 1956 - The development of the ego concept in Freud's work • 1958 - Comments on the scientific aspects of psychoanalysis • 1960 - *Psychoanalysis and moral values* • 1962 - Notes on the superego • 1964 - Concept formation in psychoanalysis • 1964 - *Essays on ego psychology* • 1964 - *Papers on psychoanalytic psychology* • 1966 - *Psychoanalysis: A general psychology*	• Ego-syntonic • Neutralization • Primary autonomous ego functions • Secondary autonomous ego functions • Structural theory • Sublimation • Synthetic function of the ego	• A child will flourish if provided an environment that is reasonably responsive to his or her needs (average expectable environment) • The ego's cognitive functions are important for learning about reality for the purposes of adaptation. • Synthetic function of the ego is important because it involves the ability to synthesize experiences and thus adapt to reality • Modifications of ego occur through two processes (1) alloplastic change - people attempting to change their environment to cope with challenges, (2) autoplastic change - people attempting to change themselves to accommodate their environment

Anna Freud 1895-1982 *School* Ego Psychology *Publishing era* 1922-1982	• *The writings of Anna Freud* are published in 8 volumes • Vol. 1: Introduction to psychoanalysis: Lectures for child analysts and teachers (1922-1935) • Vol. 2: The ego and the mechanisms of defense (1936) • Vol. 3: Infants without families: Reports on the Hampstead nurseries (1939-1945) • Vol. 4: Indications for child analysis and other papers (1945) • Vol. 5: Research at the Hampstead Child Therapy Clinic and other papers (1956-1965) • Vol. 6: Normality and pathology in childhood: Assessment of development (1965) • Vol. 7: Problems of psychoanalytic training, diagnosis, and the technique of therapy (1966-1970) • Vol. 8: Psychoanalytic psychology of normal development • 1962 - Assessment of childhood disturbances • 1963 - The concept of developmental lines	• Adolescent phase • Anaclitic phase • Avoidance • Defense mechanisms (Altruism; Asceticism; Avoidance; Denial; Displacement; Identification with the Aggressor; Intellectualization; Sublimation) • Developmental lines • Egocentricity • Instinctual anxiety • Latency phase • Object constancy • Objective anxiety • Phallic-oedipal phase • Superego anxiety	• One of the first to practice child psychoanalysis • Enlarged the structural point of view • Her work, along with Hartmann's, defines the ego psychology perspective • Added eight more defense mechanisms to her father's original list of nine defenses • Looking at a patient's defenses will reveal their history of ego development • Development moves back and forth along multiple lines of development; a child can develop in one area, but not in another • The level a child reaches on a developmental line is the result of the interaction of drives, ego development, and its relation to the nurturing environment • Made a distinction between normal and pathological development
Rene Spitz 1887-1974 School	• 1945 - Diacritic and Coenesthetic Organization	• Anaclitic depression • Autoerotism • Body ego	• Did not believe that drives determine the direction of a child's development; documented the effects of environmental deprivation on a child's development

(continued)

Comparative chart of psychoanalytic developmental theories (continued)

Theorist/school/ publishing era	Major works	Concepts/terms	Main contributions/ideas
Ego Psycholog *Publishing era* 1945-1965	• 1945 - Hospitalism: An inquiry into the genesis of psychiatric conditions in early childhood • 1946 - Anaclitic depression • 1946 - The smiling response: A contribution to the ontogenesis of social relations • 1951 - The psychogenetic diseases in infancy • 1955 - The primal cavity: A contribution to the genesis of perception and its role for psychoanalytic theory • 1957 - *No and yes: On the genesis of human communication* • 1958 - On the genesis of superego components • 1959 - *A genetic field theory of ego formation: Its implication for pathology* • 1961 - Early prototypes of ego defenses • 1965 - *The first year of life: A psychoanalytic study of normal and deviant development of object relations* • 1962 - Autoerotism re-examined • 1964 - The derailment of dialogue	• Coenesthetic mode of functioning • Critical periods • Diacritic mode of functioning • Eight-month anxiety • Ego organizers • Failure to thrive syndrome • Fixation points • Hospitalism • Marasmus • Maturation • Negation • Preobjectal • Primary narcissism • Semantic no • Smiling response	• His ideas came from direct observation of infants • An infant deprived of adequate mothering is prone to developmental deficits, which can lead to "failure to thrive syndrome" • Proposed that development occurs unevenly with periods of stability followed by periods of transformation, and that certain times represent "critical periods" of development • "Hospitalism" describes maternal deficits due to long-term institutionalization; "anaclitic depression" refers to children who became depressed after separation form their mothers • An infant's early psychological development occurs within three stages; each stage includes specific affective behaviors, or "ego organizers": First ego organizer is the "smiling response" - signals the beginning of object relations; Second ego organizer is "eight-month anxiety" - infant can now distinguish between familiar and unfamiliar persons, which can lead to stranger anxiety; Third ego organizer is capacity for "negation" - acquisition of "semantic no" and shift from passive to active

Peter Blos 1887-1974 *School* Ego Psychology *Publishing era* 1941-1998	• 1954 - Prolonged male adolescence: The formulation of a syndrome and its therapeutic implications • 1958 - Preadolescent Drive Organization • 1962 - *On adolescence: A psychoanalytic interpretation* • 1965 - The initial stage of male adolescence • 1967 - The second individuation process of adolescence • 1968 - Character formation in adolescence • 1970 - *The young adolescent: Clinical studies* • 1972 - The function of the ego ideal in adolescence • 1974 - Twelve to sixteen: Early adolescence • 1976 - When and how does adolescence end? • 1979 - *The adolescent passage: Developmental issues* • 1980 - Modifications in the traditional psychoanalytic theory of female adolescent development • 1981 - Psychoanalytic perspectives on the "more disturbed" adolescent • 1985 - *Son and father: Before and beyond the Oedipus complex*	• Adolescence proper • Asceticism • Drive organization • Homosexual defense • Incomplete adolescence • Miscarried adolescence • Pregenitality • Preoedipal mother • Second separation individuation process • Uniformism	• Focused his developmental theory entirely on adolescence • *Phases of development* • Latency (7-11): sets foundation for passage into adolescence • Preadolescence (11-13): increase in libidinal and aggressive drives • Early adolescence (13-15): adolescent is heavily influenced by peer pressure and faces the challenges of separation from early object ties • Adolescence proper (15-18): appropriate sexual drives and higher levels of thought emerge • Late adolescence (18-20): psychic structure solidifies and stability finds expression in work, love, and ideology • Postadolescence: the harmonizing of the component parts of the personality; transition from adolescence to adulthood • Conceptualized the entire phase of adolescence as the "second separation-individuation process", emphasizing the developmental necessity of shedding family dependencies

(continued)

Comparative chart of psychoanalytic developmental theories (continued)

Theorist/school/ publishing era	Major works	Concepts/terms	Main contributions/ideas
Stanley Greenspan 1941- *School* Theories of the Self *Publishing era* 1972 to the present	• 1979 - *Intelligence and adaptation: An integration of psychoanalytic and Piagetian developmental psychology* • 1981 - *Psychopathology and adaptation in infancy and early childhood* • 1989 - *The development of the ego: Implications for personality theory, psychopathology, and the psychotherapeutic process* • 1997 - *The growth of mind and the endangered origins of intelligence* • 2003 - *The clinical interview with the child (third edition)* • 2004 - *The first idea: How symbols, language, and intelligence evolved from our primate ancestors to modern humans*	• Engaging • Neuronal connections • Preverbal self • Regulation • Sensation • Shared attention • Symbolic self • Synchronic interchanges • Thinking self • Willful self	• Charted critical stages in the development of mind • Proposed that emotions, not cognitive stimulation, serve as the mind's primary architect • *Six stages of functional/emotional development are*: 1. From birth on - no differentiation between self and environment; task is to make sense of sensation and develop capacity for regulation 2. 2-4 months on - Engaging and relating to others; "synchronic interchanges" occur between infant and caregiver • 4-8 months on - intentionality; infant uses feelings to express intentions; boundary between "me" and "you" develops 4. 9-18 months on - "preverbal self" emerges within caregivers' context; child can deal with ambivalent feelings; emerging capacity to communicate verbally widens possibilities 5. 18 months on - "symbolic self"; feelings are put into words; child creates internal world using images, ideas, and symbols 6. 30 months on - "thinking self"; emotional thinking, logic, and a sense of reality develop
Melanie Klein 1882-1960 *School* Object Relations *Publishing era* 1923-1960	• 1923 - The development of the child • 1924 - The role of school in the libidinal development of the child • 1926 - Infant analysis • 1926 - Infant analysis • 1927 - Symposium on child-analysis • 1927 - The psychological principles of infant analysis	• Bad breast • Death instincts • Denial • Depressive position • Depressive anxiety • Envy	• One of the first to practice child psychoanalysis • Disagreed with Anna Freud in two ways (1) Believed children could be analyzed using essentially the same techniques as those used with adults and (2) Believed that children are capable of establishing transferences • Challenged the timing of the Oedipus complex, proposing that it takes place at the end of the first year, rather than the fourth or fifth year

• 1928 - Early stages of the Oedipus conflict • 1929 - Infantile anxiety situations reflected in art, creative impulse • 1929 - Personification in the play of children • 1930 - The importance of symbol formation in the development of the ego • 1931 - A contribution to the theory of intellectual inhibition • 1932 - *The psycho-analysis of children* • 1935 - A contribution to the psychogenesis of manic depressive states • 1940 - Mourning and its relation t o manic-depressive states • 1945 - The Oedipus Complex in the light of early anxieties • 1946 - Notes on some schizoid mechanisms • 1948 - A contribution to the theory of anxiety and guilt • 1952 -Some theoretical conclusions regarding the emotional life of the infant • 1952 - The mutual influences in the development of ego and id • 1952 - The origins of transference • 1955 - On identification • 1958 - On the development of mental functioning • 1960 - A note on depression in the schizophrenic • 1961 - *Narrative of a child analysis*	• Fantasies • Femininity complex • Femininity phase • Good breast • Idealization • Internal representations • Introjection • Life instincts • Manic defense • Object relations • Omnipotence • Paranoid-schizoid position • Part object • Phantasies • Positions • Projection • Projective identification • Schizoid • Splitting • Symbol formation • Whole object	• Speaks of "positions" rather than phases of development, to emphasize speaking of a whole way of organizing one's internal world • Paranoid-schizoid position: infants phantasize danger coming from the outside; Depressive position: Child recognizes his mother as a "whole object," a real and separate person (crucial step in development) • Early object relations is first a "part-object" relationship, specifically to the mother's breast • Introduced concept of "good breast" (gratifying) and "bad breast" (ungratifying), with "good breast" serving as prototype for all gratifying objects and "bad breast" serving as prototype for all persecutory objects • Development is organized around phantasies infants have of relationships to the object • Ego/superego develop from internalization of object relations • Introduced idea of projective identification: fantasy of projecting oneself into another object, taking possession of it, and attributing to it one's own characteristics • 1930 paper opened the area of symbol formation and of the relation between inner processes and cognitive development • Attempted to relieve guilt in children by having them direct toward the therapist aggressive and Oedipal feelings they could not express to their parents

(continued)

Comparative chart of psychoanalytic developmental theories (continued)

Theorist/school/ publishing era	Major works	Concepts/terms	Main contributions/ideas
Donald Winnicott 1896-1971 *School* Object Relations *Publishing era* 1931-1971	1931 - *Clinical notes on the disorders of childhood* • 1941 - The observation of infants in a set situation • 1945 - Primitive emotional development • 1949 - Hate in the counter-transference • 1950 - Aggression in relation to emotional development • 1953 - Transitional objects and transitional phenomena • 1956 - Primary maternal preoccupation • 1956 - On transference • 1957 - *Mother and child: A primer of first relationships* • 1958 - Psycho-analysis and the sense of guilt • 1958 - *Collected papers: Through paediatrics to psycho-analysis* • 1960 - The theory of the parent-infant relationship • 1960 - Ego distortion in terms of true and false self • 1965 - *Maturational processes and the facilitating environment: Studies in the theory of emotional development*	• Absolute dependence • Come into being • Continuity of being • Facilitating environment • False self • Going on being • Good enough mother • Holding environment • Impingement • Integration • Maternal care • Maturational process • No such thing as an infant • Personalization • Potential space • Realization • Relative dependence • Self-object distinction • Toward independence • Transitional object • Transitional phenomena • True self	• Believed the environment played a critical role in development • Saw development in terms of three phases of dependence between the mother and child (1) Phase of "Absolute dependence": earliest; mother and child are a unit; infant has no experience of an external object; (2) "Phase of relative dependence": begins when the child becomes aware of dependence on an outside object; (3) "Toward independence": synonymous with the oedipal phase of development • Proposed three developmental tasks (1) Integration - personality starts out in an unintegrated state; (2) Personalization - infants are able to claim experiences as "my experiences"; (3) Realization - infant develops a sense of reality • A child develops in relation to an object, an essential other (usually the mother). A child "comes into being" based on whether environmental conditions are favorable or unfavorable. Too much doing, or not enough responding results in "impingement," to which the child must react • The mother must supply a "holding environment" for the child, which allows for the child's transition to being more autonomous. Good enough holding by the "good enough mother" promotes a child's development

	• 1968 - Playing: Its theoretical status in the clinical situation • 1969 - The use of an object • 1971 - *Playing and reality* • 1975 - *Through paediatrics to psycho-analysis* • 1977 - *The piggle: An account of the psychoanalytic treatment of a little girl* • 1984 - *Deprivation and delinquency* • 1987 - *Babies and their mothers* • 1988 - *Human nature* • 1992 - *The family and individual development* • 1993 - *Talking to parents* • 1996 - *Thinking about children*		• When adequate holding takes place, the child acquires an authentic "true self"; if adequate holding does not take place, an inauthentic "false self" will develop, the primary function of which is to act as a mask that hides the "true self" • "Transitional objects" are objects that a child endows with qualities that are associated with their mother; these objects help the child bridge the gap between internal and external
Margaret Mahler 1897-1985 *School* Object Relations *Publishing era* 1938-1980	• 1958 - On two crucial phases of integration of the sense of identity: Separation-Individuation and bisexual identity • 1960 - Observations on research regarding the "Symbiotic Syndrome" of infantile psychosis • 1963 - Thoughts about development and individuation • 1965 - On early infantile psychosis: The symbiotic and autistic syndromes • 1965 - On the significance of the normal separation-individuation phase: With reference to research in symbiotic child psychosis	• Autistic phase • Body ego • Coenesthetic receptivity • Diacritic organization • Differentiation subphase • Hallucinatory omnipotence • Hatching • Low keyedness • Normal autism • Object constancy • Practicing subphase • Rapprochment subphase • Representations • Sensoriperceptive • Separation-individuation phase	• Proposed a theory of psychological birth and development of a child from ages 0-3 • An infant's psychological birth and the processes of separation and individuation are analogous to the division of a fertilized egg • Failure to proceed successfully through the developmental phases will result in psychopathology • *Phases of development* • Autistic phase (0-1 month): undifferentiated • Symbiotic phase (1-5 months): child sees self and object as the same • Differentiation subphase of separation-individuation (5-10 months): beginning differentiation of self and object

(continued)

Comparative chart of psychoanalytic developmental theories (continued)

Theorist/school/ publishing era	Major works	Concepts/terms	Main contributions/ideas
	• 1970 - The mother's reaction to her toddler's drive for individuation • 1974 - Symbiosis and individuation: The psychological birth of the human infant • 1975 - *The psychological birth of the human infant* • 1979 - *The selected papers of Margaret S. Mahler* • 1980 - Object constancy, individuality, and internalization • 1980 - The separation-individuation process and identity formation	• Splitting • Symbiotic phase	• Practicing subphase of S-I (10-16 months): child can leave the object through crawling, but is pulled by object and outside world • Rapprochement Subphase of S-I (16-24 months): child needs object's presence, wants to share everything with the object • Object constancy (24-36 months): child can maintain a stable mental representation of the object whether it is there or not
Otto Kernberg 1928- *School* Object Relations *Publishing era* 1963 to the present	• 1966 - Structural derivatives of object relations • 1967 - Borderline personality organization • 1968 - The treatment of patients with borderline personality organization • 1970 - A psychoanalytic classification of character pathology • 1971 - Prognostic considerations regarding borderline personality organization • 1972 - Early ego integration and object relations • 1973 - Basic psychoanalytic concepts on the theory of instincts	• Borderline psychopathology • Consolidation of superego and ego integration • Differentiation of self from object • Higher level of organization of character pathology • Integration of self-representations and object-representations • Intermediate level of organization of character pathology • Introjection • Lower level of organization of character pathology • Neurotic psychopathology • Normal autism	• Integrated major aspects of drive theory with the structural model of ego psychology and its developmental perspective • Three tasks of development (1) clarify what is self and what is other; (2) overcome "splitting"; and (3) integrate good and bad self- and object-images • *Five stages of normal development are*: 1. Normal autism or Primary undifferentiated (0-1 month) - the infant's normal primary undifferentiated self-object representations are gradually constructed through interactions with the primary caregiver 2. Normal symbiosis or primary undifferentiated self-object representations (1-6/8 months) - self and object become differentiated

• 1975 - Normal and pathological narcissism: Structural and clinical aspects • 1975 - *Borderline conditions and pathological narcissism* • 1976 - Technical considerations in the treatment of borderline personality organization • 1979 - Some implications of object relations theory for psychoanalytic technique • 1982 - Self, ego, affects, and drives • 1984 - *Severe Personality Disorders* • 1986 - Identification and its vicissitudes as observed in psychosis • 1987 - An ego psychology-object relations theory approach to the transference • 1987 - Projection and projective identification: Developmental and clinical aspects • 1988 - Object relations theory in clinical practice • 1988 - Psychic structure and structural change: An ego psychology-object relations theory viewpoint • 1991 - Transference regression and psychoanalytic technique with infantile personalities • 1992 - Psychopathic, paranoid and depressive transferences • 2001 - Object relations, affects, and drives: Toward a new synthesis	• Normal symbiosis • Primary undifferentiated self-object representations • Primary undifferentiated stage • Psychotic states • Splitting	3. Differentiation of self- from object-representations (6/8-18/36 months) - integration of both good and bad self-images and good and bad object-images; object constancy 4. Integration of self-representations and object-representations and development of higher level intrapsychic object relations-derived structures - libidinal and aggressive self-images solidify into a "definite self-system" (occurs through Oedipal period) 5. Consolidation of superego and ego integration (end of Oedipus and beyond) - integration of superego fosters ego identity • *Three levels of character pathology are*: 1. Higher level of organization - ego and superego are relatively well integrated; ego identity is harmonious; self-concept is stable 2. Intermediate level of organization - superego is punitive, less integrated, and unanchored to the rest of the person's ego, thus interrupting ego regulation; fewer character defenses; more unstable and impulsive behavior 3. Lower level of organization - superego integration is minimal; severe ego weakness; inner world includes chaotic and exaggerated self- and object-representations; inability to contain anxiety or control impulses

(continued)

Comparative chart of psychoanalytic developmental theories (continued)

Theorist/school/ publishing era	Major works	Concepts/terms	Main contributions/ideas
	• 2003 - The management of affect storms in the psychoanalytic psychotherapy of borderline patients • 2006 - *Psychotherapy for borderline personality: Focusing on object relations*		
Erik Erikson 1902-1994 *School* Life Cycle Theory Psychosocial *Publishing era* 1937-1980	• 1937 - Configuration in play - Clinical notes • 1940 - On submarine psychology • 1942 - Hitler's imagery and German youth • 1945 - Childhood and tradition in two American Indian tribes • 1946 - Ego development and historical change - Clinical notes • 1950 - Growth and crises of the "Healthy Personality" • 1951 - Sex differences in the play configurations of preadolescents • 1953 - Wholeness and totality • 1956 - Ego identity and the psychosocial moratorium • 1958 - The nature of clinical evidence	• Affiliation • Antipathetic • Authenticity • Authoritarianism • Basic ego, strength, and virtues • Competencies • Dogmatism • Ego-dystonic • Ego-syntonic • Elitism • Formalism • Ideology • Idolism • Impersonation • Legalism • Principle of social order • Radius of significant relations • Ritualism • Ritualization • Technological ethos • Totalism • Transmission of values and ideals	• Views development as occurring not only in interaction with the maternal responses to the child, but also within the broader social context in which the child is situated • Believed development continues throughout the life cycle • Ego is developed through a series of psychosocial crises. At each stage the ego has a task to master, a crisis to overcome, that includes not only aspects of instinctual drives, but also social and personal skills • Eight stages of development (1) Trust vs. mistrust (0-18 months); (2) Autonomy vs. shame and doubt (18 months to 3 years); (3) Initiative vs. guilt (3-5 years); (4) Industry vs. inferiority (5-13 years); (5) Identity vs. role confusion (13-21 years); (6) Intimacy vs. isolation (21-40 years); (7) Generativity vs. stagnation (40-60 years); (8) Integrity vs. despair (60 years to death) • Progress through each stage is determined by the degree of success at the preceding stages

Harry Stack Sullivan 1892-1949 *School* Interpersonal *Publishing era* 1924-1947	• 1924 - Schizophrenia: Its conservative and malignant features • 1927 - Affective experience in early schizophrenia • 1931 - The training of the psychiatrist, IV: Training of the general medical student in psychiatry • 1936 - A note on the implications of psychiatry: The study of interpersonal relations for investigation in the social sciences • 1938 - Anti-Semitism • 1950 - The illusion of personal individuality • 1947 - *Conceptions of modern psychiatry* • 1953 - *The interpersonal theory of psychiatry* • 1954 - *The psychiatric interview* • 1956 - *Clinical studies in psychiatry* • 1964 - *The fusion of psychiatry and social science* • 1972 - *Personal psychopathology*	• Anxiety gradient • "As if" performances • Bad me • Developmental epochs • Dynamism • Fear dynamism • Good me • Lust dynamism • Malevolence • Not me • Parataxic mode of experience • Personifications • Prototaxic mode of experience • Rationalizations • Selective attention • Sublimation • Syntaxic mode of experience • Tensions of need • Tensions of anxiety • Theorem of escape • Theorem of reciprocal emotion • Warps	• Extended Freud's theory to the treatment of severe mental disorders; in contrast to Freud, he believed that social and cultural factors played a role in these disorders • It is only possible to understand people by observing their interpersonal interactions, and personality develops through these interpersonal interactions • The primary source of anxiety is interpersonal interactions • All experience occurs in three modes (1) prototaxic - undifferentiated; no awareness of self as a separate entity, (2) parataxic - momentary, unconnected ways of being, and (3) syntaxic - language, meaning, symbol activity • Divides his developmental theory into six "epochs" (1) infancy; (2) childhood; (3) juvenile era; (4) preadolescence; (5) early adolescence; and (6) late adolescence • Replaced Freud's idea of mechanisms of the mind with the idea of "dynamism" - personality is made up of interacting interpersonal dynamisms, which occur as patterns that shape one's identity • Defenses are against other people, not against one's own unconscious • Through interpersonal situations, people develop "personifications" of themselves, images of themselves that are important parts of the structure of their personality (1) Good me - come from experiences which are rewarding in character, (2) Bad me - come from experiences that arouse anxiety, and (3) Not me - keeps a person from noticing things they do not want to see about themselves
Daniel Stern 1934- *School*	• 1985 - *The interpersonal world of the infant* • 1990 - *Diary of a baby*	• Affect attunement • Affiliation • Antipathetic	• Responsible for revolution in infant research. Challenged Mahler's idea that infants are born into undifferentiated state; showed that human social relatedness is present from birth

(continued)

Comparative chart of psychoanalytic developmental theories (continued)

Theorist/school/ publishing era	Major works	Concepts/terms	Main contributions/ideas
Theories of the Self Infant Research *Publishing era* 1963-present	• 1995 - *The motherhood constellation: A unified view of parent-infant psychotherapy* • 1998 - *The birth of the mother: How the motherhood experience changes you forever* • 2002 - *The first relationship: Infant and mother* • 2004 - *The present moment in psychotherapy and everyday life*	• Amodal perception • Coherence of form, intensity structures, and temporal structures • Coming into being • Core sense of self • Emergent sense of self • Evoked companion • Interaffectivity • Islands of consistency • Joint attention • Narrative sense of self • Physiognomic perception • RIGS • Self-affectivity • Self-agency • Self-coherence • Self-history • Subjective sense of self • Verbal sense of self • Vitality affects	• Affect attunement" is the way to indicate a sharing of internal states • Used the term "domains" to describe his developmental eras • *Five domains of the sense of self are*: 1. Emergent self (0-2 months) - infant is actively forming emergent sense of self, testing hypotheses about the world 2. Core self (2-7 months) - self experiences necessary for a self to come together include self-agency, self-coherence, self-affectivity, self-history; introduced concept of RIGs (Representation of Interactions that have been Generalized) - these come from lived experiences; several lived episodes lead to a sense of a generalized episode; the basic unit for representation of the "core self" 3. Subjective self (7-12 months) - quantum leap in development; infant discovers he/she has a mind and so do other people; enters the domain of intersubjective relatedness 4. Verbal self (15-30 months) - language; symbolic play 5. Narrative self - (30-48 months) - human activity is understood in terms of psychological story plots
Heinz Kohut 1913-1981 *School* Theories of the Self Self Psychology *Publishing era* 1957-1984	• 1959 - Introspection, empathy and psychoanalysis • 1966/1978 - Forms and transformations of narcissism • 1968/1978 - The psychoanalytic treatment of narcissistic personality disorders	• Bipolar self • Cohesive self • Compensatory structures • Deidealization • Disintegration products • Empathy • Entry into adulthood	• Breaks from drive theory. Places development of "self" as the central organizing principle instead of drives. Sex and aggression are secondary phenomena, expressions of the needs of a fragmenting self. Founder of Self Psychology • Empathy defines the psychological field. It is the method used to gather data about a person's inner world

	• 1971 - *The analysis of the self* • 1972/1978 - Thoughts on narcissism and narcissistic rage • 1977 - *The restoration of the self* • 1978 - Discussion of "On the adolescent process as a transformation of the self" • 1978 - Remarks about the formation of the self - Letter to a student regarding some principles of psychoanalytic research • 1978/1990 - Introductory remarks to the Panel on "Self Psychology and the Sciences of Man" • 1979 - Four basic concepts in self-psychology • 1982 - Introspection, empathy, and the semi-circle of mental health • 1984 - *How does analysis cure?* • 1985 - *Self Psychology and the humanities: Reflections on a new psychoanalytic approach*	• Exhibitionism • Experience near • Fragmentation • Grandiose self • Horizontal split • Idealized parental imago • Mirroring • Nuclear self • Omnipotence • Optimal frustration • Self • Selfobject • Self-regulation • Subordinate view of the self • Superordinate view of the self • Transmuting internalization • Twinship or alter-ego • Vertical split • Virtual self	• Introduced concept of "selfobject": experienced as part of the self; fulfills functions the self cannot perform for itself • A self needs three things from a selfobject (1) "mirroring" - need for admiration and approval; (2) "idealizing" - need for acceptance and support from an idealized other; and (3) "twinship" - need for the presence of a like other • Crucial factor in development of pathology is the self-selfobject relationship. Failures in selfobject responses result in fear of loss of self (since selfobject is part of the self) • Grandiose self" - Infant will try to regain the lost state of narcissism by creating inside a state of perfection. Parent needs to mirror the developing grandiose self at this time • Idealized parental imago" - A child spends energies in the idealization of the parent. The parent needs to supply self needs at this time, such as safety, regulation of excitement, soothing, teaching rules of behavior, and conveying values • If parents are unable to mirror their child's grandiosity, the narcissistic needs will become frustrated and will either be repressed ("horizontal split") or disavowed ("vertical split") • "Transmuting internalization" is the process which results in new psychological structure
John Bowlby 1907-1990 *School* Traditional Attachment Theory	• 1952 - *Maternal Care and Mental health: A report on behalf of the World Health Organization as a contribution to the United Nations program for the welfare of homeless children*	• Attachment behaviors • Caretaking behaviors • Despair • Ethology • Grief and mourning	• Founded attachment theory, and based it on ethological premises, which led to exclusion from psychoanalytic circles • Development does not occur in phases. Patterns of attachment are formed that may be modified by experience or may persist throughout the lifespan

(continued)

Comparative chart of psychoanalytic developmental theories (continued)

Theorist/school/ publishing era	Major works	Concepts/terms	Main contributions/ideas
Publishing era 1938-1988	• 1958 - The nature of the child's tie to his mother • 1960 - Grief and mourning in infancy and early childhood • 1960 - Separation anxiety • 1960 - Symposium on 'Psycho-Analysis and Ethology': Ethology and the development of object relations • 1961 - Processes of mourning • 1961 - Note on Dr. Max Schur's comments on grief and mourning in infancy and early childhood • 1963 - Pathological mourning and childhood mourning • 1969 - *Attachment and loss: Vol. I: Attachment* • 1973 - *Attachment and loss: Volume II: Separation, anxiety and danger* • 1980 - *Attachment and loss: Volume III: Loss: Sadness and depression*	• Exploratory behavioral system • Internal working models • Primary anxiety • Protest, despair, and detachment • Proximity to the mother • Secondary drive theory • Secure base • Sensitive caregiver • Separation anxiety • Species-specific behavior patterns	• Early attachment behaviors and experiences with caregivers determine the patterns of attachment • Psychopathology is due to disturbances in attachment behaviors, not fixations or regressions • Infants are innately driven to seek proximity to their mothers, who provide a "secure base" that protects from predators • Attachment behaviors" (sucking, clinging, following, crying, and smiling) are "species-specific" behaviors activated by separations and designed to restore proximity to the mother • If infants are not reunited with their mothers, infants will go through a period of "protest," followed by a period of "despair," followed by a period of "detachment" • If children are not exposed to traumatic separations, they are able to develop "internal working models" of themselves and caregivers (similar to the psychoanalytic concept of "representations")
Mary Ainsworth 1913-1999 *School* Traditional Attachment Theory *Publishing era* 1955-1983	• 1978 - *Patterns of attachment: A psychological study of the strange situation*	• Anxious-avoidant attachment • Anxious-resistant attachment • Attachment-in-the-making phase • Clear-cut attachment phase	• Developed the "strange situation" lab procedure to assess infant attachment styles. It consisted of eight episodes, including two episodes of separation and reunion. The infant's behavior after the parents return forms the basis for classifying the infant in one of the three attachment categories (1) secure attachment, (2) anxious-avoidant attachment, or (3) anxious-resistant attachment

		• Maternal sensitivity • Object constancy • Object permanence • Patterns of attachment • Preattachment phase • Secure attachment • Strange situation procedure	
Mary Main Birth date unknown *School* Traditional Attachment Theory *Publishing era* 1974 to the present	• 1974 - Exploration, play, and cognitive functioning as related to child-mother attachment • 1985 - Discovery of an insecure-disorganized/disoriented attachment pattern: Procedures, finding, and implications for the clarification of behavior • 1988 - *Interview-based adult attachment classifications: Related to infant-mother and infant-father attachment.* (Unpublished manuscript) • 1996 - Disorganization and disorientation in infant strange situation behavior: Phenotypic resemblance to dissociative states • 2000 - The organized categories of infant, child, and adult attachment: Flexible vs. inflexible attention under attachment-related stress • 2005 - Predictability of attachment behavior and representational processes at 1, 6, and 19 years of age: the Berkeley Longitudinal Study	• Adult attachment interview • Adult secure-autonomous attachment • Dismissing attachment • Disorganized/disoriented attachment • Intergenerational transmission of attachment • Preoccupied attachment • Unresolved/disorganized	• Identified a fourth pattern of attachment • Disorganized/disoriented attachment" - some children exhibited behaviors that appeared disorganized as they alternated between crying loudly for the parent to moving away from the parent when picked up; behaviors indicated being disoriented to their environment, or being trance-like • Hypothesized that instead of being a haven of safety, the mothers of these infants were actually frightening to them, suggesting that the children had either been maltreated or neglected • Devised the adult attachment interview - elicited caregiver's histories of their own attachment experiences; found a correlation between attachment pattern revealed by the adult's Internal Working Model and the type of attachment that adult's child developed, thus establishing the existence of an "intergenerational transmission of attachment" patterns

(continued)

Comparative chart of psychoanalytic developmental theories (continued)

Theorist/school/ publishing era	Major works	Concepts/terms	Main contributions/ideas
Allan Schore 1943- *School* Neurodevelopmental Attachment Theory *Publishing era* 1991 to the present	• 1991 - Early superego development: The emergence of shame and narcissistic affect regulation in the practicing period • 1994 - *Affect regulation and the origin of the self: The neurobiology of emotional development* • 1997 - A century after Freud's Project: Is a rapprochement between psychoanalysis and neurobiology a hand? • 2000 - Attachment and the regulation of the right brain • 2001 - Effects of a secure attachment relationship on right brain development, affect regulation, and infant mental health • 2002 - Advances in neuropsychoanalysis, attachment theory, and trauma research: Implications for self-psychology • 2005 - Attachment, affect regulation, and the developing right brain: Linking developmental neuroscience to pediatrics	• Affective-configurational representational system • Attachment is a regulatory theory • Autonomic nervous system • Autoregulation • Critical period • Dissociation • Experience dependent • Hyperarousal • Limbic system • Neurobiology of subjectivity • Nondeclarative memory systems • Orbitofrontal region • Parasympathetic nervous system • Psychoneurobiological point of view • Right brain systems • Rupture and repair sequence • Sensitive period • Social construction of the human brain • Somatic emotional marker • Sympathetic nervous system	• The first to successfully return to Freud's attempt to integrate psychoanalysis with the neurosciences • Hypothesizes that attachment is a regulatory theory and its primary function is to regulate the child's affect states; regulation is a central organizing principle of human development • Draws from brain research to propose a psychoneurobiological view of the origins of the self • Psychological functions are the products of the brain structures that undergird them • Internal Working Models are located in the right hemisphere of the brain • Replaced Bowlby's biological control system with the brain systems that regulate instinctive behavior • The social environment affects brain development, and regulation of emotions is a critical part of this process • Attachment occurs as a result of emotional interchanges between infant and caregiver • If there are failures in attunement, the bond between infant and caregiver may be threatened; if the bond is ruptured, it is important that reattunement take place; this "rupture and repair sequence" builds psychological structure
Peter Fonagy 1952- *School*	• 1993 - Measuring the ghost in the nursery: An empirical study of the relation between parents' mental representations of childhood experiences and their infants' security of attachment	• False Belief task • Intentional stance • Internal Working Models (IWM)	• Attempts to reconcile differences between attachment theory and psychoanalytic theory, analyzing ways they are similar and different

Neurodevelopmental Attachment Theory *Publishing era* 1998 to the present	• 1998 - Mentalization: A protective factor and a focus of psychotherapy • 1998 - Moments of change in psychoanalytic theory: Discussion of a new theory of psychic change • 1999 - Points of contact and divergence between psychoanalysis and attachment theories: Is psychoanalytic theory truly different • 2000 - Attachment and borderline personality disorder • 2001 - *Attachment theory and psychoanalysis* • 2002 - *Affect regulation, mentalization, and the development of the self* • 2002 - Early intervention and the development of self-regulation • 2003 - The development of psychopathology from infancy to adulthood: The mysterious unfolding of disturbance in time • 2003 - *Psychoanalytic theories: Perspectives from developmental psychopathology* • 2005 - Attachment, trauma and psychoanalysis: When psychoanalysis meets neuroscience	• Interpersonal Interpretive mechanism (IIM) • Maternal sensitivity • Mentalization • Mental processing system • Reflective function • Theory of Mind • Symbolic representation	• Both theories seek to understand the process through which children form self- and object-representations, and the functions these serve in furthering development • Created the concept of "mentalization" - the capacity to understand that others have beliefs, desires, and intentions of their own; he sees this concept as a bridge connecting the two theories • Believed that Bowlby's concept of Internal Working Models connects attachment theory to psychoanalytic theory • Secure attachment is the product of successful acquisition of the capacity for mentalization • The ability to exercise the function of mentalization is central to the transmission of attachment patterns • The function of attachment patterns is to not only to stimulate proximity to the caregiver, but also to stimulate the caregiver to reflect the infant's affect state through mentalization • Proposed the concept of Interpersonal Interpretive Mechanism (IIM); this is the psychic structure involved in a child's effort to interpret experiences; damage to the IIM results in loss of interpretive capacity or poor judgments • The most critical loss involved in separation from a caregiver is the loss of the opportunity to develop a "mental processing system" that generates mental representations, which in turn leads to an unstable sense of self

Appendix C

Who Analyzed Who

The custom of associating a "personal" or "didactic" psychoanalysis as a fixed requirement to practice psychoanalysis can be traced to Freud's self-analysis in 1897–1898. It was not until Freud found it necessary to standardize the teaching of psychoanalysis that it became one of the three pillars of preparation for psychoanalytic practice. Freud had been engaged in spreading psychoanalysis to his new adherents in the Zurich psychiatric community when he confronted the question of the training requirements to practice psychoanalysis. It was readily apparent that there was no formal training. Freud felt that was a major weakness in dispersing his ideas of what constituted correct interpretations of his theories and their application to the practice of psychoanalysis. It also represented an impediment to the forward momentum for the psychoanalytic movement. This unresolved issue became central in the eventual schism with the Zurich group that included Carl Jung.

In the 1918 Congress in Budapest, Hermann Nunberg proposed the need for a training analysis as a requirement to practice. His proposal met with intense resistance from those who felt it was too authoritarian an expectation. In 1923, Karl Abraham and the Berlin Psychoanalytic Institute implemented Max Eitingon's three-dimensional plan as the recommended training standard. It included formal coursework (theoretical training), supervised clinical practice (practical training), and a minimum of 1 year in a training analysis (didactic analysis). In the 1925 Congress at Bad Homburg, the Berlin model was formalized; psychoanalysis was transforming itself into a guild and the days of unregulated, free-for-all (wild) analysis were numbered (Gay, 1988, p. 463; Makari, 2008, pp. 372–373) Gay, P (1988). Freud: A life for our time. New York: W. W. Norton & Company Makari, G. J. (2008). Revolution of mind: The creation of psychoanalysis. New York: Harper Collins.

Training institutions now consider undergoing psychoanalysis an absolute requirement for preparation to practice psychoanalysis. The distinction between what constitutes a "personal" rather than "didactic" psychoanalysis is blurred. The presumption is that one undertakes a personal psychoanalysis to work through unresolved conflicts, whereas a didactic analysis has as its goal removing personal impediments that might interfere with the treatment of patients. Currently, institutes that train psychoanalysts bypass this distinction by insisting that candidates who wish to enroll in their program undergo an analysis by a "training analyst," that is a psychoanalyst who is either on the faculty of the institute or qualified to undertake such analyses.

We include this appendix because we consider this part of the history of psychoanalysis not only to be significant, but also likely that the developmental theorists we include in this work may have been significantly influenced by the analyses they had undertaken. Table C.1 lists the theorists, whether or not each had undergone an analysis and if so, with whom.

We were able to confirm that 16 of the 20 theorists completed an analysis. Of those 16 theorists, we were able to confirm who the analyst was in 13 cases, whereas in the other three cases (Greenspan, Ainsworth, and Schore) we were able to confirm only that the theorist had undergone an analysis, but with whom remains unknown. In the final four cases (Abraham, Kernberg, Stern, and Main) we were unable to confirm any information at all regarding whether they ever participated in a personal or didactic psychoanalysis.

Table C.1 Who analyzed who, by theorist

Theorist	Did this theorist undergo a personal psychoanalysis?	Who was this theorist's analyst?
Sigmund Freud	Yes	Self
Karl Abraham	Unknown; probably not	Unknown
Heinz Hartmann	Yes	Sigmund Freud Sandor Rado
Anna Freud	Yes	Sigmund Freud
Rene Spitz	Yes	Sigmund Freud (didactic analysis)
Peter Blos	Yes	Salomea Isakower
Melanie Klein	Yes	Sandor Ferenczi Karl Abraham
Donald Winnicott	Yes	James Strachey Joan Riviere
Margaret Mahler	Yes	Helene Deutsch, August Aichhorn, Wille Hoffer, and Edith Jacobson
Otto Kernberg	Unknown	Unknown
Harry Stack Sullivan	Yes	Clara Thompson
Erik Erikson	Yes	Anna Freud
Daniel Stern	Unknown	Unknown
Heinz Kohut	Yes	August Aichhorn Ruth Eisler
Stanley Greenspan	Yes	Unknown
John Bowlby	Yes	Joan Riviere
Mary Ainsworth	Yes	Unknown
Mary Main	Unknown	Unknown
Allen Schore	Yes	Unknown
Peter Fonagy	Yes	Anne Hurry Clifford York (training analysis)

References

Gay, P. (1988). Freud: A life for our time. New York: W. W. Norton & Company.
Makari, G. J. (2008). Revolution of mind: The creation of psychoanalysis. New York: Harper Collins.

Author Index

Subject Index

R

Breinigsville, PA USA
20 July 2010
241981BV00004B/9/P

9 780387 884547